Winner of the Koret Jewish Book Award in Biography,
Autobiography, and Literary Studies

A *Washington Post Book World* Best Book of the Year

An *Economist* Best Book of the Year

A *Philadelphia Inquirer* Best Book of the Year

A *New York Sun* Book of the Year

⟫•⟪

PRAISE FOR *A Tale of Love and Darkness*

"What made *A Tale of Love and Darkness* an event is the power with which it entwines the history of an immigrant family—a lonely, depressed mother, a distant father, and their son—with the larger historical story; Europe's rejection, the frantic search for refuge among the Arabs in Palestine, the idealism and the disappointments, the establishment of Israel and the war that followed . . . The book is a digressive ingenious work that circles around the rise of a state, the tragic destiny of a mother, a boy's creation of a new self."   —*The New Yorker*

"It appears to merely chronicle Oz's life from childhood in British-ruled Jerusalem to literary fame, but every event, every factual detail, every discovery opens myriad doors to unexpected revelations . . . It is impossible to give a full account of this book's riches."
                                                    —*The Washington Post Book World*

"Remarkable . . . in many ways the best book that [Oz] has ever written . . . Oz's narrative of his Jerusalem childhood in the 1940s . . . calls on all his resources as a novelist for an extraordinary evocation of place, person, and period . . . Touching, haunting, wrenching, amusing, and sometimes downright hilarious . . . this book is both richly panoramic and intensely personal . . . Consistently absorbing . . . One of the most enchanting and deeply satisfying books that I have read in many years."
                                                    —*The New Republic*

"Chekhov is all over *A Tale of Love and Darkness* . . . waiting for Kafka to mug him. And mug him Kafka will, even in this glorious, masterly lamentation, these 'Speak, Memory!' Dead Sea Scrolls."
—*The New York Times Book Review*

"[*A Tale of Love and Darkness* is] fascinating, beautifully written and closer to a great 19th-century novel than to the ironic minimalism of our time. No serious reader should miss this testimony from an extraordinary writer."
—*The Forward*

"Moving and frank . . . partly family saga, partly *Bildungsroman*, partly self-portrait."
—*The New York Review of Books*

"A memoir that, as the title suggests, embodies Oz's sense of internal rift. Some of that sense is devoted to public matters . . . It is a painful story, yet transformed, even lightened, by a novelist's ability to get closer while standing back."
—*The Boston Globe*

"Detailed and beautiful . . . As he writes about himself and his family, Oz is also writing part of the history of the Jews . . . We are in the hands here of a capable, practiced seducer. It is also as if the reader had the most wonderful grandfather who is willing to tell everything about his life and make it all interesting, even funny, even meaningful, even moving."
—*Los Angeles Times*

"A deeply sensitive memoir of the Israeli novelist's childhood and adolescence, from Lithuania to Jerusalem. At times funny, at times tragic, Amos Oz weaves his family's history into the broader story of the birth of Israel, attended by blood."
—*The Economist*

"Besides an evocative, intensely gripping tale of self-discovery and, ultimately, self-actualization, Oz's delicious, often heartrending prose offers a rare account of Jerusalem transforming from post-war British control into a vital city within the independent state of Israel. Once the eye falls upon Amos Oz's rich prose, the other senses quickly succumb, because, like everything Oz, all things are plural, even the telling of a single man's story."
—*The Seattle Times*

"At this particular moment in the Middle East, Oz is a powerful figure, and his suddenly available personal story exposes the roots of his political convictions . . . Because of his memoir—its human core, its love of details of character, its author's decent, even modest, assertion that all relations should be tempered with understanding and mercy, from the closest to the most distant, from the familial to the international—Oz has recently been compared to Chekhov." —*The Nation*

"Autobiography in the key of compelling fiction."
—*The Philadelphia Inquirer*

"In his new memoir, which is easily the finest book he has ever written, the Israeli novelist Amos Oz unfolds *A Tale of Love and Darkness*, as if to demonstrate how intertwined love in all its manifestations is with darkness; how, indeed, love rests on a darkness that is at once terrifying and sustaining." —*The New York Sun*

"*A Tale of Love and Darkness* is Amos Oz's beautiful, compelling memoir about his life and the life of his ancestors, from Odessa to Palestine to Israel." —*New York Post*

"The story of how the author became a writer, how Klausner was transformed into Oz. But it's also a journey in reverse, a reclaiming of his past and present history." —*Seattle Weekly*

"[Oz's] memoir, in a translation that preserves the author's gorgeous, discursive style and his love of wordplay, is a social history embedded within an autobiography . . . sophisticated and searing."
—*New York Magazine*

"The glory and the dream may be tattered, the visionary gleam elusive these days, but not in the heart and soul of Amos Oz as he revisits his childhood—and the glory days of Zionism—in *A Tale of Love and Darkness*, surely one of this year's best books." —*The Washington Times*

"This long-anticipated memoir by acclaimed Israeli writer Amos Oz, one of the most widely read Hebrew novelists of our time, is an especially rewarding encounter. Anyone intrigued by the tumultuous Middle East will find much of interest in this lyrical saga, which succeeds both as a revelatory tale of the artist as young man and a gripping portrait of the young Jewish state itself." —*The Miami Herald*

"A marvel for its writing, for its humor and its sadness, for its combination of autobiography, family history for several generations and the history of modern Israel." —*The American Jewish World*

"Brims over with riches . . . epic in scope." —*The Sunday Denver Post*

"A remarkable story of survival and courage." —*The Charlotte Observer*

A Tale of Love
and Darkness

AMOS OZ

———➤◦◄———

A TALE OF LOVE
AND DARKNESS

TRANSLATED FROM THE HEBREW BY
Nicholas de Lange

A Harvest Book · Harcourt, Inc.
ORLANDO   AUSTIN   NEW YORK   SAN DIEGO   TORONTO   LONDON

www.HarcourtBooks.com

This is a translation of *Sipour Al Ahava Vehoshekh*.

First published in the UK by Chatto & Windus.

The Library of Congress has cataloged the hardcover edition as follows:
Oz, Amos.
[Sipur 'al ahavah ve-hoshekh. English]
A tale of love and darkness/Amos Oz;
translated from the Hebrew by Nicholas de Lange.
p. cm.
1. Oz, Amos—Childhood and youth. 2. Authors, Israeli—Biography. I. Title.
PJ5054.O9Z47313 2004
892.4'36—dc22 2004007302
ISBN-13: 978-0151-00878-0 ISBN-10: 0-15-100878-7
ISBN-13: 978-0156-03252-0 (pbk.) ISBN-10: 0-15-603252-x (pbk.)

Text set in Minion
Designed by Cathy Riggs

Printed in the United States of America

First Harvest edition 2005
A C E G I K J H F D B

A Tale of Love
and Darkness

I

I WAS BORN and bred in a tiny, low-ceilinged ground-floor apartment. My parents slept on a sofa bed that filled their room almost from wall to wall when it was opened up each evening. Early every morning they used to shut away this bed deep into itself, hide the bedclothes in the chest underneath, turn the mattress over, press it all tight shut, and conceal the whole under a light gray cover, then scatter a few embroidered oriental cushions on top, so that all evidence of their night's sleep disappeared. In this way their bedroom also served as study, library, dining room, and living room.

Opposite this room was my little green room, half taken up with a big-bellied wardrobe. A narrow, low passage, dark and slightly curved, like an escape tunnel from a prison, linked the little kitchenette and toilet to these two small rooms. A lightbulb imprisoned in an iron cage cast a gloomy half-light on this passage even during the daytime. At the front both rooms had just a single window, guarded by metal blinds, squinting to catch a glimpse of the view to the east but seeing only a dusty cypress tree and a low wall of roughly dressed stones. Through a tiny opening high up in their back walls the kitchenette and toilet peered out into a little prison yard surrounded by high walls and paved with concrete, where a pale geranium planted in a rusty olive can was gradually dying for want of a single ray of sunlight. On the sills of these tiny openings we always kept jars of pickles and a stubborn cactus in a cracked vase that served as a flowerpot.

It was actually a basement apartment, as the ground floor of the building had been hollowed out of the rocky hillside. This hill was our next-door neighbor, a heavy, introverted, silent neighbor, an old, sad hill with the regular habits of a bachelor, a drowsy, still wintry hill, which never scraped the furniture or entertained guests, never made a noise or disturbed us, but through the walls there seeped constantly toward us, like a faint yet persistent musty smell, the cold, dark silence and dampness of this melancholy neighbor.

Consequently through the summer there was always a hint of winter in our home.

Visitors would say: It's always so pleasant here in a heat wave, so cool and fresh, really chilly, but how do you manage in the winter? Don't the walls let in the damp? Don't you find it depressing?

Books filled our home. My father could read sixteen or seventeen languages and could speak eleven (all with a Russian accent). My mother spoke four or five languages and read seven or eight. They conversed in Russian or Polish when they did not want me to understand. (Which was most of the time. When my mother referred to a stallion in Hebrew in my hearing, my father rebuked her furiously in Russian: *Shto s toboi?! Vidish malchik ryadom s nami!*—What's the matter with you? You can see the boy's right here!) Out of cultural considerations they mostly read books in German or English, and presumably they dreamed in Yiddish. But the only language they taught me was Hebrew. Maybe they feared that a knowledge of languages would expose me too to the blandishments of Europe, that wonderful, murderous continent.

On my parents' scale of values, the more Western something was, the more cultured it was considered. For all that Tolstoy and Dostoevsky were dear to their Russian souls, I suspect that Germany—despite Hitler—seemed to them more cultured than Russia or Poland, and France more so than Germany. England stood even higher on their scale than France. As for America, there they were not so sure: after all, it was a country where people shot at Indians, held up mail trains, chased gold, and hunted girls.

Europe for them was a forbidden promised land, a yearned-for landscape of belfries and squares paved with ancient flagstones, of trams and bridges and church spires, remote villages, spa towns, forests, and snow-covered meadows.

Words like "cottage," "meadow," or "goose girl" excited and seduced me all through my childhood. They had the sensual aroma of a genuine, cozy world, far from the dusty tin roofs, the urban wasteland of scrap iron and thistles, the parched hillsides of our Jerusalem suffocating under the weight of white-hot summer. It was enough for me to whisper to myself "meadow," and at once I could hear the lowing of cows with little bells tied around their necks, and the burbling of brooks. Closing my eyes, I could see the barefoot goose girl, whose sexiness brought me to tears before I knew about anything.

As the years passed I became aware that Jerusalem, under British rule in the 1920s, 1930s, and 1940s, must be a fascinatingly cultured city. It had big businessmen, musicians, scholars, and writers: Martin Buber, Gershom Scholem, S. Y. Agnon, and a host of other eminent academics and artists. Sometimes as we walked down Ben Yehuda Street or Ben Maimon Avenue, my father would whisper to me: "Look, there is a scholar with a worldwide reputation." I did not know what he meant. I thought that having a worldwide reputation was somehow connected with having weak legs, because the person in question was often an elderly man who felt his way with a stick and stumbled as he walked along, and wore a heavy woolen suit even in summer.

The Jerusalem my parents looked up to lay far from the area where we lived: it was in leafy Rehavia with its gardens and its strains of piano music, it was in three or four cafés with gilded chandeliers on the Jaffa Road or Ben Yehuda Street, in the halls of the YMCA or the King David Hotel, where culture-seeking Jews and Arabs mixed with cultivated Englishmen with perfect manners, where dreamy, long-necked ladies floated in evening dresses, on the arms of gentlemen in dark suits, where broad-minded Britons dined with cultured Jews or educated Arabs, where there were recitals, balls, literary evenings, *thés dansants,* and exquisite, artistic conversations. Or perhaps such a Jerusalem, with its chandeliers and *thés dansants,* existed only in the dreams of the librarians, schoolteachers, clerks, and bookbinders who lived in Kerem Avraham. At any rate, it didn't exist where we were. Kerem Avraham, the area where we lived, belonged to Chekhov.

Years later, when I read Chekhov (in Hebrew translation), I was convinced he was one of us: Uncle Vanya lived right upstairs from us,

Doctor Samoylenko bent over me and examined me with his broad, strong hands when I had a fever and once diphtheria, Laevsky with his perpetual migraine was my mother's second cousin, and we used to go and listen to Trigorin at Saturday matinees in the Beit Ha'am Auditorium.

We were surrounded by Russians of every sort. There were many Tolstoyans. Some of them even looked like Tolstoy. When I came across a brown photograph of Tolstoy on the back of a book, I was certain that I had seen him often in our neighborhood, strolling along Malachi Street or down Obadiah Street, bareheaded, his white beard ruffled by the breeze, as awesome as the Patriarch Abraham, his eyes flashing, using a branch as a walking stick, a Russian shirt worn outside the baggy trousers tied around his waist with a length of string.

Our neighborhood Tolstoyans (whom my parents referred to as Tolstoyshchiks) were without exception devout vegetarians, world reformers with strong feelings for nature, seekers after the moral life, lovers of humankind, lovers of every single living creature, with a perpetual yearning for the rural life, for simple agricultural labor among fields and orchards. But they were not successful even in cultivating their own potted plants: perhaps they killed them by overwatering, or perhaps they forgot to water them, or else it was the fault of the nasty British administration that put chlorine in our water.

Some of them were Tolstoyans who might have stepped straight out of the pages of a novel by Dostoevsky: tormented, talkative, suppressing their desires, consumed by ideas. But all of them, Tolstoyans and Dostoevskians alike, in our neighborhood of Kerem Avraham, worked for Chekhov.

The rest of the world was generally known as "the worldatlarge," but it had other epithets too: enlightened, outside, free, hypocritical. I knew it almost exclusively from my stamp collection: Danzig, Bohemia, and Moravia, Bosnia and Herzegovina, Ubangi-Shari, Trinidad and Tobago, Kenya, Uganda, and Tanganyika. That worldatlarge was far away, attractive, marvelous, but to us it was dangerous and threatening. It didn't like the Jews because they were clever, quick-witted, successful, but also because they were noisy and pushy. It didn't like what we were doing here in the Land of Israel either, because it begrudged us even this meager strip of marshland, boulders, and desert. Out there, in the world, all the walls were covered with graffiti: "Yids, go back to Palestine," so we came back to Palestine, and now the worldatlarge shouts at us: "Yids, get out of Palestine."

It was not only the worldatlarge that was a long way away: even the Land of Israel was pretty far off. Somewhere, over the hills and far away, a new breed of heroic Jews was springing up, a tanned, tough, silent, practical breed of men, totally unlike the Jews of the Diaspora, totally unlike the residents of Kerem Avraham. Courageous, rugged pioneers, who had succeeded in making friends with the darkness of night, and had overstepped every limit, too, as regards relations between a boy and a girl and vice versa. They were not ashamed of anything. Grandpa Alexander once said: "They think in the future it's going to be so simple, a boy will be able to go up to a girl and just ask for it, or maybe the girls won't even wait to be approached, but will go and ask the boys for it, like asking for a glass of water." Shortsighted Uncle Betsalel said with polite anger: "Isn't this sheer Bolshevism, to trample on every secret, every mystery?! To abolish all emotions?! To turn our whole life into a glass of lukewarm water?!" Uncle Nehemia, from his corner, let fly a couple of lines of a song that sounded to me like the growling of a cornered beast: "Oh, long is the journey and winding the road, I travel o'er mountain and plain, Oh Mamma, I seek you through heat and through snow, I miss you but you're far away! . . ." Then Aunt Zippora said, in Russian: "That'll do, now. Have you all gone out of your minds? The boy can hear you!" And so they all changed to Russian.

The pioneers lived beyond our horizon, in Galilee, Sharon, and the Valleys. Tough, warmhearted, though of course silent and thoughtful, young men, and strapping, straightforward, self-disciplined young women, who seemed to know and understand everything; they knew you and your shy confusion, yet they would treat you with affection, seriousness, and respect, treat you not like a child but like a man, albeit an undersized one.

I pictured these pioneers as strong, serious, self-contained people, capable of sitting around in a circle and singing songs of heartrending longing, or songs of mockery, or outrageous songs of lust; or of dancing so wildly that they seemed to transcend the physical. They were capable of loneliness and introspection, of living outdoors, sleeping in tents, doing hard labor, singing, "We are always at the ready," "Your boys brought you peace with a plowshare, today they bring peace with a gun," "Wherever we're sent to, we go-o-o"; they could ride wild horses or wide-tracked tractors; they spoke Arabic, knew every cave and wadi, had a way with pistols and hand grenades, yet read poetry and philosophy; they were large men with inquiring minds and hidden feelings, who could converse in a near whisper by candlelight in their tents in the small hours of the morning about the meaning of our lives and the grim choices between love and duty, between patriotism and universal justice.

Sometimes my friends and I went to the Tnuva delivery yard to watch them arriving from over the hills and far away on a truck laden with agricultural produce, "clad in dust, burdened with arms, and with such heavy boots," and I used to go up to them to inhale the smell of hay, the intoxicating odors of faraway places: it's where they come from, I thought, that great things are happening. That's where the land is being built and the world is being reformed, where a new society is being forged. They are stamping their mark on the landscape and on history, they are plowing fields and planting vineyards, they are writing a new song, they pick up their guns, mount their horses, and shoot back at the Arab marauders: they take our miserable human clay and mold it into a fighting nation.

I secretly dreamed that one day they would take me with them. And make me into a fighting nation too. That my life too would become a new song, a life as pure and straightforward and simple as a glass of water on a hot day.

Over the hills and far away, the city of Tel Aviv was also an exciting place, from which came the newspapers, rumors of theater, opera, ballet, and cabaret, as well as modern art, party politics, echoes of stormy debates, and indistinct snatches of gossip. There were great sportsmen in Tel Aviv. And there was the sea, full of bronzed Jews who could swim. Who in Jerusalem could swim? Who had ever heard of swimming Jews? These were different genes. A mutation. "Like the wondrous birth of a butterfly out of a worm."

There was a special magic in the very name of Tel Aviv. As soon as I heard the word "Telaviv," I conjured up in my mind's eye a picture of a tough guy in a dark blue T-shirt, bronzed and broad-shouldered, a poet-worker-revolutionary, a man made without fear, the type they called a *Hevreman*, with a cap worn at a careless yet provocative angle on his curly hair, smoking Matusians, someone who was at home in the world: all day long he worked hard on the land, or with sand and mortar, in the evening he played the violin, at night he danced with girls or sang them soulful songs amid the sand dunes by the light of the full moon, and in the early hours he took a handgun or a sten out of its hiding place and stole away into the darkness to guard the houses and fields.

How far away Tel Aviv was! In the whole of my childhood I visited it five or six times at most: we used to go occasionally to spend festivals with the aunts, my mother's sisters. It's not just that the light in Tel Aviv was different from the light in Jerusalem, more than it is today, even the laws of gravity were different. People didn't walk in Tel Aviv: they leaped and floated, like Neil Armstrong on the moon.

In Jerusalem people always walked rather like mourners at a funeral, or latecomers at a concert. First they put down the tip of their shoe and tested the ground. Then, once they had lowered their foot, they were in no hurry to move it: we had waited two thousand years to gain a foothold in Jerusalem and were unwilling to give it up. If we picked up our foot, someone else might come along and snatch our little strip of land. On the other hand, once you have lifted your foot, do not be in a hurry to put it down again: who can tell what coil of vipers you might step on. For thousands of years we have paid with our blood for our impetuousness, time and time again we have fallen into the hands of our enemies because we put our feet down without looking where we were putting them. That, more or less, was the way people walked in Jerusalem. But Tel Aviv! The whole city was one big grasshopper. The people leaped by, and so did the houses, the streets, the squares, the sea breeze, the sand, the avenues, and even the clouds in the sky.

Once we went to Tel Aviv for Passover, and the morning after we arrived I got up early, while everyone was still asleep, got dressed, went out, and played on my own in a little square with a bench or two, a swing, a sandpit, and three or four young trees where the birds were already singing. A few months later, at New Year, we went back to Tel Aviv, and the square wasn't there anymore. It had been moved, complete with its little trees, benches, sandpit, birds, and swing, to the other end of the road. I was astonished: I couldn't understand how Ben Gurion and the duly constituted authorities could allow such a thing. How could somebody suddenly pick up a square and move it? What next—would they move the Mount of Olives, or the Tower of David? Would they shift the Wailing Wall?

People in Jerusalem talked about Tel Aviv with envy and pride, with admiration, but almost confidentially: as though the city were some kind of crucial secret project of the Jewish people that it was best not to discuss too much—after all, walls have ears, and spies and enemy agents could be lurking around every corner.

Telaviv. Sea. Light. Sand, scaffolding, kiosks on the avenues, a brand-new white Hebrew city, with simple lines, growing up among the citrus groves and the dunes. Not just a place that you buy a ticket for and travel to on an Egged bus, but a different continent altogether.

For years we had a regular arrangement for a telephone link with the family in Tel Aviv. We used to phone them every three or four months, even though we didn't have a phone and neither did they. First we would write to Auntie Hayya and Uncle Tsvi to let them know that on, say, the nineteenth of the month—which was a Wednesday, and on Wednesdays Tsvi left his work at the Health Clinic at three—we would phone from our pharmacy to their pharmacy at five. The letter was sent well in advance, and then we waited for a reply. In their letter, Auntie Hayya and Uncle Tsvi assured us that Wednesday the nineteenth suited them perfectly, and they would be waiting at the pharmacy a little before five, and not to worry if we didn't manage to phone at five on the dot, they wouldn't run away.

I don't remember whether we put on our best clothes for the expedition to the pharmacy, for the phone call to Tel Aviv, but it wouldn't surprise me if we did. It was a solemn undertaking. As early as the Sunday before, my father would say to my mother, Fania, you haven't forgotten that this is the week that we're phoning Tel Aviv? On Monday my mother would say, Arieh, don't be late home the day after tomorrow, don't mess things up. And on Tuesday they would both say to me, Amos, just don't make any surprises for us, you hear, just don't be ill, you hear, don't catch cold or fall over until after tomorrow afternoon. And that evening they would say to me, Go to sleep early, so you'll be in good shape for the phone call, we don't want you to sound as though you haven't been eating properly.

So they would build up the excitement. We lived in Amos Street, and the pharmacy was a five-minute walk away, in Zephaniah Street, but by three o'clock my father would say to my mother:

"Don't start anything new now, so you won't be in a rush."

"I'm perfectly OK, but what about you with your books, you might forget all about it."

"Me? Forget? I'm looking at the clock every few minutes. And Amos will remind me."

Here I am, just five or six years old, and already I have to assume a historic responsibility. I didn't have a watch—how could I?—and so every few moments I ran to the kitchen to see what the clock said, and then I would announce, like the countdown to a spaceship launch: twenty-five minutes to go, twenty minutes to go, fifteen to go, ten and a half to go—and at that point we would get up, lock the front door carefully, and set off, the three of us, turn left as far as Mr. Auster's grocery shop, then right into Zechariah Street, left into Malachi Street, right into Zephaniah Street, and straight into the pharmacy to announce:

"Good afternoon to you, Mr. Heinemann, how are you? We've come to phone."

He knew perfectly well, of course, that on Wednesday we would be coming to phone our relatives in Tel Aviv, and he knew that Tsvi worked at the Health Clinic, and that Hayya had an important job in the Working Women's League, and that Yigal was going to grow up to be a sportsman, and that they were good friends of Golda Meyerson (who later became Golda Meir) and of Misha Kolodny, who was known as Moshe Kol over here, but still we reminded him: "We've come to phone our relatives in Tel Aviv." Mr. Heinemann would say: "Yes, of course, please take a seat." Then he would tell us his usual telephone joke. "Once, at the Zionist Congress in Zurich, terrible roaring sounds were suddenly heard from a side room. Berl Locker asked Harzfeld what was going on, and Harzfeld explained that it was Comrade Rubashov speaking to Ben Gurion in Jerusalem. 'Speaking to Jerusalem,' exclaimed Berl Locker, 'so why doesn't he use the telephone?'"

Father would say: "I'll dial now." And Mother said: "It's too soon, Arieh. There's still a few minutes to go." He would reply: "Yes, but they have to be put through" (there was no direct dialing at that time).

Mother: "Yes, but what if for once we are put through right away, and they're not there yet?" Father replied: "In that case we shall simply try again later." Mother: "No, they'll worry, they'll think they've missed us."

While they were still arguing, suddenly it was almost five o'clock. Father picked up the receiver, standing up to do so, and said to the operator: "Good afternoon, Madam. Would you please give me Tel Aviv 648." (Or something like that: we were still living in a three-digit world). Sometimes the operator would answer: "Would you please wait a few minutes, Sir, the Postmaster is on the line." Or Mr. Sitton. Or Mr. Nashashibi. And we felt quite nervous: whatever would they think of us?

I could visualize this single line that connected Jerusalem and Tel Aviv, and via Tel Aviv the rest of the world. If this one line was engaged, we were cut off from the world. The line wound its way over wastelands and rocks, over hills and valleys, and I thought it was a great miracle. I trembled: what if wild animals came in the night and bit through the line? Or if wicked Arabs cut it? Or if the rain got into it? Or if there was a fire? Who could tell? There was this line winding along, so vulnerable, unguarded, baking in the sun, who could tell? I felt full of gratitude to the men who had put up this line, so brave-hearted, so dexterous, it's not easy to put up a line from Jerusalem to Tel Aviv. I knew from experience: once we ran a wire from my room to Eliyahu Friedmann's room, only two houses and a garden away, and what a business it was, with the trees in the way, the neighbors, the shed, the wall, the steps, the bushes.

After waiting a while, Father decided that the Postmaster or Mr. Nashashibi must have finished talking, and so he picked up the receiver again and said to the operator: "Excuse me, Madam, I believe I asked to be put through to Tel Aviv 648." She would say: "I've got it written down, Sir. Please wait" (or "Please be patient"). Father would say: "I am waiting, Madam, naturally I am waiting, but there are people waiting at the other end too." This was his way of hinting to her politely that although we were indeed cultured people, there was a limit to our endurance. We were well brought up, but we weren't suckers. We were not to be led like sheep to the slaughter. That idea—that you could treat Jews any way you felt like—was over, once and for all.

Then all of a sudden the phone would ring in the pharmacy, and it was always such an exciting sound, such a magical moment, and the conversation went something like this:

"Hallo, Tsvi?"

"Speaking."

"It's Arieh here, in Jerusalem."

"Yes, Arieh, hallo, it's Tsvi here, how are you?"

"Everything is fine here. We're speaking from the pharmacy."

"So are we. What's new?"

"Nothing new here. How about at your end, Tsvi? Tell us how it's going."

"Everything is OK. Nothing special to report. We're all well."

"No news is good news. There's no news here either. We're all fine. How about you?"

"We're fine too."

"That's good. Now Fania wants to speak to you."

And then the same thing all over again. How are you? What's new? And then: "Now Amos wants to say a few words."

And that was the whole conversation. What's new? Good. Well, so let's speak again soon. It's good to hear from you. It's good to hear from you too. We'll write and set a time for the next call. We'll talk. Yes. Definitely. Soon. See you soon. Look after yourselves. All the best. You too.

But it was no joke: our lives hung by a thread. I realize now that they were not at all sure they would really talk again, this might be the last time, who knew what would happen, there could be riots, a pogrom, a blood bath, the Arabs might rise up and slaughter the lot of us, there might be a war, a terrible disaster, after all Hitler's tanks had almost reached our doorstep from two directions, North Africa and the Caucasus, who knew what else awaited us? This empty conversation was not really empty, it was just awkward.

What those telephone conversations reveal to me now is how hard it was for them—for everyone, not just my parents—to express private feelings. They had no difficulty at all expressing communal feelings—they were emotional people, and they knew how to talk. Oh, how they could talk! They were capable of conversing for hours on end in excited tones about Nietzsche, Stalin, Freud, Jabotinsky, giving it everything they had, shedding tears of pathos, arguing in a singsong, about colonialism, anti-Semitism, justice, the "agrarian question," the "woman question," "art versus life," but the moment they tried to give voice to a private feeling, what came out was something tense, dry, even frightened, the result of generation upon generation of repression and negation. A double negation in fact, two sets of brakes, as bourgeois European manners reinforced the constraints of the religious Jewish community. Virtually everything was "forbidden" or "not done" or "not very nice."

Apart from which, there was a great lack of words: Hebrew was still not a natural enough language, it was certainly not an intimate language, and it was hard to know what would actually come out when you spoke it. They could never be certain that they would not utter something ridiculous, and ridicule was something they lived in fear of. They were scared to death of it. Even people like my parents who knew Hebrew well were not entirely its masters. They spoke it with a kind of obsession for accuracy. They frequently changed their minds, and reformulated something they had just said. Perhaps that is how a shortsighted driver feels, trying to find his way at night through a warren of side streets in a strange city in an unfamiliar car.

One Saturday a friend of my mother's came to visit us, a teacher by the name of Lilia Bar-Samkha. Whenever the visitor said in the course of the conversation that she had had a fright or that someone was in a frightful state, I burst out laughing. In everyday slang her word for "fright" meant "fart." No one else seemed to find it funny, or perhaps they were pretending not to. It was the same when my father spoke about the arms race, or raged against the decision of the NATO countries to rearm Germany as a deterrent to Stalin. He had no idea that his bookish word for "arm" meant "fuck" in current Hebrew slang.

As for my father, he glowered whenever I used the word "fix": an innocent enough word, I could never understand why it got on his nerves. He never explained of course, and it was impossible for me to ask. Years later I learned that before I was born, in the 1930s, if a woman got herself in a fix, it meant she was pregnant. "That night in the packing room he got her in a fix, and in the morning the so-and-so made out he didn't know her." So if I said that "Uri's sister was in a fix" about something, Father used to purse his lips and clench the base of his nose. Naturally he never explained—how could he?

In their private moments they never spoke Hebrew to each other. Perhaps in their most private moments they did not speak at all. They said nothing. Everything was overshadowed by the fear of appearing or sounding ridiculous.

2

OSTENSIBLY, IN those days it was the pioneers who occupied the highest rung on the ladder of prestige. But the pioneers lived far from Jerusalem, in the Valleys, in Galilee, and in the wilderness on the shores of the Dead Sea. We admired their rugged, pensive silhouettes, poised between tractor and plowed earth, that were displayed on the posters of the Jewish National Fund.

On the next rung below the pioneers stood the "affiliated community," reading the socialist newspaper *Davar* in their T-shirts on summer verandas, members of the Histadrut, the Hagganah, and the Health Fund, men of khaki and contributors to the voluntary Community Chest fund, eaters of salad with an omelette and yogurt, devotees of self-restraint, responsibility, a solid way of life, homegrown produce, the working class, party discipline, and mild olives from the distinctive Tnuva jar, *Blue beneath and blue above, we'll build our land with love, with love!*

Over against this established community stood the "unaffiliated," aka the terrorists, as well as the pious Jews of Meah Shearim, and the "Zion-hating," ultra-orthodox communists, together with a mixed rabble of eccentric intellectuals, careerists, and egocentric artists of the decadent-cosmopolitan type, along with all sorts of outcasts and individualists and dubious nihilists, German Jews who had not managed to recover from their Germanic ways, Anglophile snobs, wealthy Frenchified Levantines with what we considered the exaggerated manners of uppity butlers, and then the Yemenites, Georgians, North Africans, Kurds, and Salonicans, all of them definitely our brothers, all of them undoubtedly promising human material, but what could you do, they would need a huge amount of patience and effort.

Apart from all these, there were the refugees, the survivors, whom we generally treated with compassion and a certain revulsion: miserable wretches, was it our fault that they chose to sit and wait for Hitler instead of coming here while there was still time? Why did they allow themselves to be led like sheep to the slaughter instead of organizing and fighting back? And if only they'd stop nattering on in Yiddish, and stop telling us about all the things that were done to them over there, because that didn't reflect too well on them, or on us for that matter. Anyway, our faces here are turned toward the future, not the past, and if we do have to rake up the past, surely we have more than enough uplifting Hebrew history, from biblical times, and the Hasmoneans, there's no need to foul it up with this depressing Jewish history that's nothing but a bundle of troubles (they always used the Yiddish word *tsores,* with an expression of disgust on their faces, so the boy realizes that these *tsores* are a kind of sickness that belonged to them, not to us). Survivors like Mr. Licht, whom the local kids called Million *Kinder.* He rented a little hole-in-the-wall in Malachi Street where he slept on a mattress at night, and during the day he rolled up his bedding and ran a small business called Dry Cleaning and Steam Pressing. The corners of his mouth were always turned down in an expression of scorn or disgust. He used to sit in the doorway of his shop waiting for a customer, and whenever one of the neighborhood children went past, he would always spit to one side and hiss through his pursed lips: "A million *Kinder* they killed! Kiddies like you! Slaughtered them!" He did not say this sadly, but with hatred, with loathing, as though he were cursing us.

My parents did not have a clearly defined place on this scale between the pioneers and the *tsores*-mongers. They had one foot in the affiliated community (they belonged to the Health Fund and paid their dues to the Community Chest) and the other in the air. My father was close in his heart to the ideology of the unaffiliated, the breakaway New Zionist of Jabotinsky, although he was very far from their bombs and rifles. The most he did was put his knowledge of English at the service of the underground and contribute an occasional illegal and inflammatory leaflet about "perfidious Albion." My parents were attracted to the intelligentsia of Rehavia, but the pacifist ideals of Martin Buber's Brit Shalom—sentimental kinship between Jews and Arabs, total abandonment of the dream of a Hebrew state so that the Arabs would take pity on us and kindly allow us to live here at their feet—such ideals appeared to my parents as spineless appeasement, craven defeatism of the type that had characterized the centuries of Jewish Diaspora life.

My mother, who had studied at Prague University and graduated from the university in Jerusalem, gave private lessons to students who were preparing for the examinations in history or occasionally in literature. My father had a degree in literature from the University of Vilna (now Vilnius), and a second degree from the university at Mount Scopus, but he had no prospect of securing a teaching position in the Hebrew University at a time when the number of qualified experts in literature in Jerusalem far exceeded that of the students. To make matters worse, many of the lecturers had real degrees, gleaming diplomas from famous German universities, not like my father's shabby Polish-Jerusalemite qualification. He therefore settled for the post of librarian in the National Library on Mount Scopus, and sat up late at night writing his books about the Hebrew novella or the concise history of world literature. My father was a cultivated, well-mannered librarian, severe yet also rather shy, who wore a tie, round glasses, and a somewhat threadbare jacket. He bowed before his superiors, leaped to open doors for ladies, insisted firmly on his few rights, enthusiastically cited lines of poetry in ten languages, endeavored always to be pleasant and amusing, and endlessly repeated the same repertoire of jokes (which he referred to as "anecdotes" or "pleasantries"). These jokes generally came out rather labored: they were not so much specimens of living humor as a positive declaration of intent as regards our obligation to be entertaining in times of adversity.

Whenever my father found himself facing a pioneer in khaki, a revolutionary, an intellectual turned worker, he was thoroughly confused. Out in the world, in Vilna or Warsaw, it was perfectly clear how you addressed a proletarian. Everyone knew his place, although it was up to you to demonstrate clearly to this worker how democratic and uncondescending you were. But here, in Jerusalem, everything was ambiguous. Not topsy-turvy, as in communist Russia, but simply ambiguous. On the one hand, my father definitely belonged to the middle class, albeit the slightly lower middle class; he was an educated man, the author of articles and books, the holder of a modest position in the National Library, while his interlocutor was a sweaty construction worker in overalls and heavy boots. On the other hand, this same worker was said to have some sort of degree in chemistry, and he was also a committed pioneer, the salt of the earth, a hero of the Hebrew Revolution, a manual laborer, while Father considered himself—at least in his heart of hearts—to be a sort of rootless, shortsighted intellectual with two left hands. Something of a deserter from the battlefront where the homeland was being built.

Most of our neighbors were petty clerks, small retailers, bank tellers, cinema ticket sellers, schoolteachers, dispensers of private lessons, or dentists. They were not religious Jews; they went to synagogue only for Yom Kippur and occasionally for the procession at Simhat Torah, yet they lit candles on Friday night, to maintain some vestige of Jewishness and perhaps also as a precaution, to be on the safe side, you never know. They were all more or less well educated, but they were not entirely comfortable about it. They all had very definite views about the British Mandate, the future of Zionism, the working class, the cultural life of the land, Dühring's attack on Marx, the novels of Knut Hamsun, the Arab question, and women's rights. There were all sorts of thinkers and preachers, who called for the Orthodox Jewish ban on Spinoza to be lifted, for instance, or for a campaign to explain to the Palestinian Arabs that they were not really Arabs but the descendants of the ancient Hebrews, or for a conclusive synthesis between the ideas of Kant and Hegel, the teachings of Tolstoy and Zionism, a synthesis that would give birth here in the Land of Israel to a wonderfully pure and healthy way of life, or for the promotion of goat's milk, or for an alliance with America and even with Stalin with the object of driving out the British, or for everyone to do some simple exercises every morning that would keep gloom at bay and purify the soul.

These neighbors, who would congregate in our little yard on Saturday afternoons to sip Russian tea, were almost all dislocated people. Whenever anyone needed to mend a fuse or change a washer or drill a hole in the wall, they would send for Baruch, the only man in the neighborhood who could work such magic, which was why he was dubbed Baruch Goldfingers. All the rest knew how to analyze, with fierce rhetoric, the importance for the Jewish people to return to a life of agriculture and manual labor: we have more intellectuals here than we need, they declared, but what we are short of is plain manual laborers. But in our neighborhood, apart from Baruch Goldfingers, there was hardly a laborer to be seen. We didn't have any heavyweight intellectuals either. Everyone read a lot of newspapers, and everyone loved talking. Some may have been proficient at all sorts of things, others may have been sharp-witted, but most of them simply declaimed more or less what they had read in the papers or in myriad pamphlets and party manifestos.

As a child I could only dimly sense the gulf between their enthusiastic desire to reform the world and the way they fidgeted with the brims of their hats when they were offered a glass of tea, or the terrible embarrassment that reddened their cheeks when my mother bent over (just a little) to sugar their tea and her decorous neckline revealed a tiny bit more flesh than usual: the confusion of their fingers, which tried to curl into themselves and stop being fingers.

All this was straight out of Chekhov—and also gave me a feeling of provinciality: that there are places in the world where real life is still happening, far away from here, in a pre-Hitler Europe, where hundreds of lights are lit every evening, ladies and gentlemen gather to drink coffee with cream in oak-paneled rooms, or sit comfortably in splendid coffeehouses under gilt chandeliers, stroll arm in arm to the opera or the ballet, observe from close up the lives of great artists, passionate love affairs, broken hearts, the painter's girlfriend falling in love with his best friend the composer, and going out at midnight bareheaded in the rain to stand alone on the ancient bridge whose reflection trembles in the river.

Nothing like this ever happened in our neighborhood. Things like this happened only over the hills and far away, in places where people live recklessly. In America, for instance, where people dig for gold, hold up mail trains, stampede herds of cattle across endless plains, and whoever kills the most Indians ends up getting the girl. That was the America we saw at the Edison Cinema: the pretty girl was the prize for the best shooter. What one did with such a prize I had not the faintest idea. If they had shown us in those films an America where the man who shot the most girls was rewarded with a good-looking Indian, I would simply have believed that that was the way it was. At any rate—in those far-off worlds. In America, and in other wonderful places in my stamp album, in Paris, Alexandria, Rotterdam, Lugano, Biarritz, St. Moritz, places where godlike men fell in love, fought each other politely, lost, gave up the struggle, wandered off, sat drinking alone late at night at dimly lit bars in hotels on boulevards in rain-swept cities. And lived recklessly.

Even in those novels by Tolstoy and Dostoevsky that they were always arguing over, the heroes lived recklessly and died for love. Or for some exalted ideal. Or of consumption and a broken heart. Those suntanned pioneers too, on some hilltop in Galilee, lived recklessly. Nobody in our neighborhood ever died from consumption or unrequited love or idealism. They were anything but reckless. Not just my parents. Everyone.

We had an iron rule that one should never buy anything imported, anything foreign, if it was possible to buy a locally made equivalent. Still, when we went to Mr. Auster's grocery shop on the corner of Obadiah and Amos streets, we had to choose between kibbutz cheese, made by the Jewish cooperative Tnuva, and Arab cheese: did Arab cheese from the nearby village, Lifta, count as homemade or imported produce? Tricky. True, the Arab cheese was just a little cheaper. But if you bought Arab cheese, weren't you being a traitor to Zionism? Somewhere, in some kibbutz or moshav, in the Jezreel Valley or the hills of Galilee, an overworked pioneer girl was sitting, with tears in her eyes perhaps, packing this Hebrew cheese for us—how could we turn our backs on her and buy alien cheese? Did we have the heart? On the other hand, if we boycotted the produce of our Arab neighbors, we would be deepening and perpetuating the hatred between our two peoples. And we would be partly responsible for any blood that was shed, heaven forbid. Surely the humble Arab fellah, a simple, honest tiller of the soil, whose soul was still undefiled by the miasma of town life, was nothing more or less than the dusky brother of the simple, noble-hearted muzhik in the stories of Tolstoy! Could we be so heartless as to turn our backs on his rustic cheese? Could we be so cruel as to punish him? What for? Because the deceitful British and the corrupt effendis had set him against us? No. this time we would definitely buy the cheese from the Arab village, which incidentally really did taste better than the Tnuva cheese, and cost a little less in the bargain. But still, on the third hand, what if the Arab cheese wasn't clean? Who knew what the dairies were like there? What if it turned out, too late, that their cheese was full of germs?

Germs were one of our worst nightmares. They were like anti-Semitism: you never actually managed to set eyes on an anti-Semite or a germ, but you knew very well that they were lying in wait for you on every side, out of sight. Actually, it was not true that none of us had ever set eyes on a germ: I had. I used to stare for a long time very intently at a piece of old cheese, until I suddenly began to see thousands of tiny squirming things. Like gravity in Jerusalem, which was much stronger then than now, the germs too were much bigger and stronger. I saw them.

A little argument used to break out among the customers in Mr. Auster's grocery shop: to buy or not to buy Arab cheese? On the one hand, "charity begins at home," so it was our duty to buy Tnuva cheese only; on the other hand, "one law shall there be for you and for the stranger in your midst," so we should sometimes buy the cheese of our Arab neighbors, "for you were strangers in the land of Egypt." And anyway, imagine the contempt with which Tolstoy would regard anyone who would buy one kind of cheese and not another simply because of a difference of religion, nationality, or race! What of universal values? Humanism? The brotherhood of man? And yet, how pathetic, how weak, how petty-minded, to buy Arab cheese simply because it cost a couple of mils less, instead of cheese made by the pioneers, who worked their backs off for our benefit!

Shame! Shame and disgrace! Either way, shame and disgrace!

The whole of life was full of such shame and disgrace.

Here was another typical dilemma: should one or should one not send flowers for a birthday? And if so, what flowers? Gladioli were very expensive, but they were cultured, aristocratic, sensitive flowers, not some sort of half-wild Asiatic weed. We could pick as many anemones and cyclamen as we liked, but they were not considered suitable for sending to someone for a birthday, or for the publication of a book. Gladioli conjured up recitals, grand parties, the theater, the ballet, culture—deep, fine feelings.

So we'd send gladioli. And hang the expense. But then the question was, wasn't seven overdoing it? And wasn't five too few? Perhaps six then? Or should we send seven after all? Hang the expense. We could surround the gladioli with a forest of asparagus fern, and get by with six. On the other hand, wasn't the whole thing outdated? Gladioli? Who on earth sends gladioli nowadays? In Galilee, do the pioneers send one another gladioli? In Tel Aviv, do people still bother with gladioli? And what are they good for anyway? They cost a fortune, and four or five days later they end up in the trash. So what shall we give instead? How about a box of chocolates? A box of chocolates? That's even more ridiculous than gladioli. Maybe the best idea would be simply to take some serviettes, or one of those sets of glass holders, curly ones made of silvery metal, with cute handles, for serving hot tea, an unostentatious gift that is both aesthetic and very practical and that won't get thrown away but will be used for many years, and each time they use them, they'll think, just for an instant, of us.

3

EVERYWHERE YOU could discern all kinds of little emissaries of Europe, the promised land. For example, the manikins, I mean the little men who held the shutters open during the day, those little metal figures: when you wanted to close the shutters, you swiveled them around so that all night long they hung head down. The way they hung Mussolini and his mistress Clara Petacci at the end of the World War. It was terrible, it was scary, not the fact that they were hanged, they deserved that, but that they were hanged head down. I felt almost sorry for them, although I shouldn't: are you crazy or something? Feeling sorry for Mussolini? It's almost like feeling sorry for Hitler! But I tried an experiment, I hung upside down by my legs from a pipe attached to the wall, and after a couple of minutes all the blood rushed to my head and I felt I was going to faint. And Mussolini and his mistress were hung like that not for a couple of minutes but for three days and nights, and that was after they were killed! I thought that was an excessively cruel punishment. Even for a murderer. Even for a mistress.

Not that I had the faintest idea what a mistress was. In those days there wasn't a single mistress in all of Jerusalem. There were "companions," "partners," "lady friends, in both senses of the word," there may even have been the odd affair. It was said, very cautiously, for instance, that Mr. Tchernianski had something going on with Mr. Lupatin's girlfriend, and I sensed with a pounding in my heart that "something going on with" was a mysterious, fateful expression that concealed something sweet and terrible and shameful. But a mistress?! That was something altogether biblical. Something larger than life. It was unimaginable. Maybe in Tel Aviv things like that existed, I thought, they always have all sorts of things that don't exist or aren't allowed here.

I started to read almost on my own, when I was very young. What else did we have to do? The evenings were much longer then, because the earth revolved more slowly, because the galaxy was much more relaxed than it is today. The electric light was a pale yellow, and it was interrupted by the many power cuts. To this day the smell of smoky candles or a sooty paraffin lamp makes me want to read a book. By seven o'clock we were confined to our homes because of the curfew that the British imposed on Jerusalem. And even if there wasn't a curfew, who wanted to be out of doors in the dark at that time in Jerusalem? Everything was shut and shuttered, the cobblestone streets were deserted, every passing shadow in those narrow streets was trailed by three or four other shadows.

Even when there was no power cut, we always lived in dim light because it was important to economize: my parents replaced the forty-watt bulbs with twenty-five-watt ones, not just for economy but on principle, because a bright light is wasteful, and waste is immoral. Our tiny apartment was always crammed full with the sufferings of the whole human race. The starving children in India, for whose sake I had to finish everything that was put on my plate. The survivors of Hitler's hell whom the British had deported to detention camps in Cyprus. The ragged orphan children still wandering around the snowbound forests of devastated Europe. My father used to sit working at his desk till two in the morning by the light of an anemic twenty-five-watt bulb, straining his eyes because he didn't think it was right to use a stronger light: the pioneers in the kibbutzim in Galilee sit up in their tents night after night writing books of verse or philosophical treatises by the light of guttering candles, and how can you forget about them and sit there like

Rothschild with a blazing forty-watt bulb? And what will the neighbors say if they see us suddenly lit up like a ballroom? He preferred to ruin his eyesight rather than draw the glances of others.

We were not among the poorest. Father's job at the National Library brought him a modest but regular salary. My mother gave some private lessons. I watered Mr. Cohen's garden in Tel Arza every Friday for a shilling, and on Wednesdays I earned another four piasters by putting empty bottles in crates behind Mr. Auster's grocery, and I also taught Mrs. Finster's son to read a map for two piasters a lesson (but this was on credit and to this day the Finsters have not paid me).

Despite all these sources of income, we never stopped economizing. Life in our little apartment resembled life in a submarine, as they showed it in a film I saw once at the Edison Cinema, where the sailors had to close a hatch behind them every time they went from one compartment to another. At the very moment I switched on the light in the toilet with one hand I switched off the light in the passage with the other, so as not to waste electricity. I pulled the chain gently, because it was wrong to empty the whole Niagara cistern for a pee. There were other functions (that we never named) that could occasionally justify a full flush. But for a pee? A whole Niagara? While pioneers in the Negev were saving the water they had brushed their teeth with to water the plants? While in the detention camps in Cyprus a whole family had to make a single bucket of water last for three days? When I left the toilet, I switched off the light with my left hand and simultaneously switched on the light in the passage with my right hand, because the Shoah was only yesterday, because there were still homeless Jews roaming the Carpathians and the Dolomites, languishing in the deportation camps and on board unseaworthy hulks, as thin as skeletons, dressed in rags, and because there was hardship and deprivation in other parts of the world too, the coolies in China, the cotton pickers in Mississippi, children in Africa, fishermen in Sicily. It was our duty not to be wasteful.

Apart from which, who could say what each day would bring? Our troubles were not yet over, and it was as good as certain that the worst was still to come. The Nazis might have been vanquished, but there were more pogroms in Poland, Hebrew speakers were being persecuted in Russia, and here the British had not yet said their last word, the Grand Mufti was talking about butchering the Jews, and who knew what the

Arab states were planning for us, while the cynical world supported the Arabs from considerations of oil, markets, and other interests. It was not going to be easy for us, even I could see that.

The one thing we had plenty of was books. They were everywhere: from wall to laden wall, in the passage and the kitchen and the entrance and on every windowsill. Thousands of books, in every corner of the apartment. I had the feeling that people might come and go, be born and die, but books went on for ever. When I was little, my ambition was to grow up to be a book. Not a writer. People can be killed like ants. Writers are not hard to kill either. But not books: however systematically you try to destroy them, there is always a chance that a copy will survive and continue to enjoy a shelf life in some corner of an out-of-the-way library somewhere, in Reykjavik, Valladolid, or Vancouver.

If once or twice it happened that there was not enough money to buy food for Shabbat, my mother would look at Father, and Father would understand that the moment had come to make a sacrifice, and turn to the bookcase. He was an ethical man, and he knew that bread takes precedence over books and that the good of the child takes precedence over everything. I remember his hunched back as he walked through the doorway, on his way to Mr. Meyer's secondhand bookshop with two or three beloved tomes under his arm, looking as though it cut him to the quick. So must Abraham's back have been bowed as he set off early in the morning from his tent with Isaac on his shoulder, on their way to Mount Moriah.

I could imagine his sorrow. My father had a sensual relationship with his books. He loved feeling them, stroking them, sniffing them. He took a physical pleasure in books: he could not stop himself, he had to reach out and touch them, even other people's books. And books then really were sexier than books today: they were good to sniff and stroke and fondle. There were books with gold writing on fragrant, slightly rough leather bindings, that gave you gooseflesh when you touched them, as though you were groping something private and inaccessible, something that seemed to tremble at your touch. And there were other books that were bound in cloth-covered cardboard, stuck with a glue that had a wonderful smell. Every book had its own private, provocative scent. Sometimes the cloth came away from the cardboard, like a saucy skirt, and it was hard to resist the temptation to peep into the dark space between body and clothing and sniff those dizzying smells.

Father would generally return an hour or two later, without the books, laden with brown paper bags containing bread, eggs, cheese, occasionally even a can of corned beef. But sometimes he would come back from the sacrifice with a broad smile on his face, without his beloved books but also without anything to eat: he had indeed sold his books, but had immediately bought other books to take their place, because he had found such wonderful treasures in the secondhand bookshop, the kind of opportunity you encounter only once in a lifetime, and he had been unable to control himself. My mother forgave him, and so did I, because I hardly ever felt like eating anything except sweet corn and ice cream. I loathed omelettes and corned beef. To be honest, I was sometimes even jealous of those starving children in India, because nobody ever told them to finish up everything on their plate.

When I was about six, there was a great day in my life: Father cleared a small space for me in one of his bookcases and let me put my own books there. To be precise, he granted me about a quarter of the length of the bottom shelf. I hugged all my books, which up till then had lain on a stool by the side of my bed, carried them in my arms to Father's bookcase, and stood them up in the proper way, with their backs turned to the world outside and their faces to the wall.

It was an initiation rite, a coming of age: anyone whose books are standing upright is no longer a child, he is a man. I was like my father now. My books were standing to attention.

I had made one terrible mistake. When Father went off to work, I was free to do whatever I wanted with my corner of the bookcase, but I had a wholly childish view about how these things were done. So it was that I arranged my books in order of height. The tallest books were the ones that by now were beneath my dignity, children's books, in rhyme, with pictures, the books that had been read to me when I was a toddler. I did it because I wanted to fill the whole length of shelf that had been allotted to me. I wanted my section to be packed full, crowded, overflowing, like my father's shelves. I was still in a state of euphoria when

Father came home from work, cast a shocked glance toward my bookshelf, and then, in total silence, gave me a long hard look that I shall never forget: it was a look of contempt, of bitter disappointment beyond anything that could be expressed in words, almost a look of utter genetic despair. Finally he hissed at me with pursed lips: "Have you gone completely crazy? Arranging them by height? Have you mistaken your books for soldiers? Do you think they are some kind of honor guard? The firemen's band on parade?"

Then he stopped talking. There came a long, awesome silence from my father, a sort of Gregor Samsa silence, as though I had turned into a cockroach before his eyes. From my side too there was a guilty silence, as though I really had been some kind of wretched insect all along, and now my secret was out and everything was lost.

At the end of the silence Father began talking, and in the space of twenty minutes he revealed to me the facts of life. He held nothing back. He initiated me into the deepest secrets of the librarian's lore: he laid bare the main highway as well as the forest tracks, dizzying prospects of variations, nuances, fantasies, exotic avenues, daring schemes, and even eccentric whims. Books can be arranged by subject, by alphabetical order of authors' names, by series or publishers, in chronological order, by languages, by topics, by areas and fields, or even by place of publication. There are so many different ways.

And so I learned the secret of diversity. Life is made up of different avenues. Everything can happen in one of several ways, according to different musical scores and parallel logics. Each of these parallel logics is consistent and coherent on its own terms, perfect in itself, indifferent to all the others.

In the days that followed I spent hours on end arranging my little library, twenty or thirty books that I dealt and shuffled like a pack of cards, rearranging them in all sorts of different ways.

So I learned from books the art of composition, not from what was in them but from the books themselves, from their physical being. They taught me about that dizzying no-man's-land or twilight zone between the permitted and the forbidden, between the legitimate and the eccentric, between the normative and the bizarre. This lesson has remained with me ever since. By the time I discovered love, I was no greenhorn. I knew that there were different menus. I knew that there was a motorway and a scenic route, and also unfrequented byways where the foot of man had barely trodden. There were permitted things that were almost forbidden and forbidden things that were almost permitted. There were so many different ways.

Occasionally my parents allowed me to take books from my father's shelves outside into the yard to shake off the dust. No more than three books at a time, so as not to get them out of order, so that each one would get back to its proper place. It was a heavy but delicious responsibility, because I found the smell of book dust so intoxicating that I sometimes forgot my task, my duty, my responsibilities, and stayed outside until my mother became anxious and dispatched my father on a rescue mission to make sure I was not suffering from heatstroke, that I had not been bitten by a dog, and he always discovered me curled up in a corner of the yard, deep in a book, with my knees tucked under me, my head on one side, my mouth half open. When Father asked me, half angrily, half affectionately, what was the matter with me this time, it took a while for me to come back to this world, like someone who has drowned or fainted, and returns slowly, reluctantly, from unimaginable distant parts to this vale of tears of everyday chores.

All through my childhood I loved to arrange and rearrange things, each time slightly differently. Three or four empty egg cups could become a series of fortifications, or a group of submarines, or a meeting of the leaders of the great powers at Yalta. I made occasional brief sorties into the realm of unbridled disorder. There was something very bold and exciting about this: I loved emptying a box of matches on the floor and trying to find all the infinite possible combinations.

Throughout the years of the World War there hung on the wall in the passage a large map of the theaters of war in Europe, with pins and different-colored flags. Every day or two Father moved them in accordance with the news on the wireless. And I constructed a private, parallel reality: I spread out on the rush mat my own theater of war, my virtual reality, and I moved armies around, executed pincer movements and distractions, captured bridgeheads, outflanked the enemy, resigned myself to tactical withdrawals that I later turned into strategic breakthroughs.

I was a child fascinated by history. I attempted to rectify the errors of the commanders of the past. I refought the great Jewish revolt against the Romans, rescued Jerusalem from destruction at the hands of Titus's army, pushed the campaign onto the enemy's ground, brought Bar Kochba's troops to the walls of Rome, took the Coliseum by storm, and planted the Hebrew flag on top of the Capitol. To this end I transported the British army's Jewish Brigade to the first century AD and the days of the Second Temple, and reveled in the devastation that a couple of machine guns could inflict on the splendid legions of the accursed Hadrian and Titus. A light aircraft, a single Piper, brought the proud Roman Empire to its knees. I turned the doomed struggle of the defenders of Masada into a decisive Jewish victory with the aid of a single mortar and a few hand grenades.

And in fact that selfsame strange urge I had when I was small—the desire to grant a second chance to something that could never have one—is still one of the urges that set me going today whenever I sit down to write a story.

Many things have happened in Jerusalem. The city has been destroyed, rebuilt, destroyed, and rebuilt again. Conqueror after conqueror has come, ruled for a while, left behind a few walls and towers, some cracks in the stone, a handful of potsherds and documents, and disappeared. Vanished like the morning mist down the hilly slopes. Jerusalem is an old nymphomaniac who squeezes lover after lover to death before shrugging him off her with a yawn, a black widow who devours her mates while they are still in her.

Meanwhile, far away on the other side of the world, new continents and islands were being discovered. My mother used to say, You're too late, child, forget it, Magellan and Columbus have already discovered even the most far-flung islands. I argued with her. I said, How can you be so sure? After all, before Columbus came along, people thought all the world was known and there was nothing left to discover.

Between the rush mat, the legs of the furniture, and the space under my bed I sometimes discovered not only unknown islands but new stars, solar systems, entire galaxies. If I'm ever put in prison, no doubt I'll miss my freedom and one or two other things, but I'll never suffer from boredom so long as I'm allowed to have a box of dominoes, a pack of cards, a couple of boxes of matches or a handful of buttons. I'll spend my days arranging and rearranging them, moving them apart and together, forming little compositions. It may be because I was an only child: I had no brothers and sisters, and very few friends, who soon tired of me because they wanted action and couldn't adjust to the epic pace of my games.

Sometimes I would start a new game on Monday, then spend the whole of Tuesday morning at school thinking out the next move, make one or two moves that afternoon, and leave the rest for Wednesday or Thursday. My friends hated it, they went outside and played at chasing one another around the backyards, while I went on pursuing my own game of history on the floor day after day, moving troops, besieging a castle or a city, routing, taking by storm, starting a resistance movement in the mountains, attacking fortresses and defense works, liberating and then reconquering, extending or contracting frontiers marked out by matchsticks. If a grown-up accidentally trod on my little world, I would declare a hunger strike or a moratorium on teeth brushing. But eventually doomsday would come, and my mother, unable to stand the accumulation of dust, would sweep everything away, ships, armies, cities, mountains, coasts, entire continents, like a nuclear holocaust.

Once, when I was about nine, an elderly uncle by the name of Nehemiah taught me a French proverb: "In love as in war." I knew nothing at that time about love, except for the obscure connection in the Edison Cinema between love and dead Indians. But from what Uncle Nehemiah had said I drew the inference that it was best not to hurry. In later years I realized that I had been totally mistaken, at least so far as warfare was concerned: on the battlefield, speed is of the essence. Perhaps my mistake came from the fact that Uncle Nehemiah himself was a slow-moving man who hated change. When he was standing up, it was almost impossible to make him sit down, and once he was seated, he could not be induced to stand up. Get up, Nehemiah, they would say to him, for goodness sake, make a move, what's the matter with you, it's very late, how long are you going to go on sitting there, till tomorrow morning, till next year, till kingdom come?

And he would answer: At least.

Then he would reflect, scratch himself, smile slyly to himself as though he had fathomed our ruse, and add: Where's the fire?

His body, like all bodies, had a natural disposition to remain where it was.

I am not like him. I'm very fond of change, encounters, travel. But I was fond of Uncle Nehemiah too. Not long ago I looked for him, without success, in Givat Shaul Cemetery. The cemetery has grown; soon it'll reach the edge of Lake Beit Neqofa or the outskirts of Motsa. I sat on a bench for half an hour or so; in the cypress trees a stubborn wasp hummed and a bird repeated the same phrase five or six times, but all I could see were gravestones, trees, hills, and clouds.

A thin woman dressed in black with a black headscarf walked past me, with a five- or six-year-old child holding on to her. The child's little fingers were gripping the side of her dress, and both of them were crying.

4

ALONE AT home one late winter afternoon. It was five or half past, and outside it was cold and dark, windswept rain lashed the closed iron shutters, my parents had gone to have tea with Mala and Staszek Rudnicki in Chancellor Street, on the corner of the Street of the Prophets, and would be back, they had promised me, just before eight, or at a quarter past or twenty past eight at the latest. And even if they were late, there was nothing to worry about, after all they were only at the Rudnickis', it wasn't more than a quarter of an hour away.

Instead of children Mala and Staszek Rudnicki had two Persian cats, Chopin and Schopenhauer. There was also a cage in a corner of the salon containing an old, half-blind bird. So the bird wouldn't feel lonely they had put another bird into its cage, made by Mala Rudnicki from a painted pinecone on stick legs, with multicolored paper wings embellished with a few real feathers. Loneliness, Mother said, is like a hammer blow that shatters glass but hardens steel. Father treated us to a learned discourse on the etymology of the word "hammer," with all its ramifications in various languages.

My father was fond of explaining to me all sorts of connections between words. Origins, relationships, as though words were yet another complicated family from Eastern Europe, with a multitude of second and third cousins, aunts by marriage, great-nieces, in-laws, grandchildren and great-grandchildren. Even words like "aunt" or "cousin" had their own family history, their own network of relationships. Did we know, for example, that "aunt" came from the Latin *amita*, which properly denotes a father's sister, while "uncle" came from the Latin *avunculus*, which means specifically a mother's brother? The Hebrew word for uncle, *dod,* also means a lover, although I am not convinced that it was really the same word originally. You must remind me some time, Father said, to have a look in the big dictionary and check precisely where these words came from and how their use has changed over the generations. Or rather, don't remind me, go and fetch the dictionary right away and let's educate ourselves here and now, you and I, and while you're at it, take your dirty cup to the kitchen.

In the yards and in the street the silence is so black and wide that you can hear the sound of the clouds flying low among the roofs, stroking the tops of the cypresses. A dripping faucet in the bath and a rustling or scratching sound so faint that it is barely audible, you sense it at the tips of the hairs on the back of your neck, coming from the space between the wardrobe and the wall.

I switch on the light in my parents' room, and from my father's desk I take eight or nine paper clips, a pencil sharpener, a couple of small notebooks, a long-necked inkwell full of black ink, an eraser, and a packet of thumbtacks, and use all these to construct a new frontier kibbutz. A wall and a tower in the depth of the desert on the rug; arrange the paper clips in a semicircle, stand the pencil sharpener and eraser on either side of the tall inkwell that is my water tower, and surround the whole with a fence made of pencils and pens and fortified with thumbtacks.

Soon there will be a raid: a gang of bloodthirsty marauders (a couple of dozen buttons) will attack the settlement from the east and south, but we will play a trick on them. We'll open the gate, let them advance into the farmyard where the blood bath will take place, the gate will be barred behind them so that they cannot escape, then I shall give the order to fire, and at that instant, from every rooftop and the top of the inkwell that serves as the water tower, the pioneers, represented by my white chessmen, will open fire, and with a few furious salvos they will wipe out the trapped enemy force, "chanting hymns of glory, singing loud the story of the slaughter gory, then I'll raise a song of praise" and promote the rush mat to serve as the Mediterranean Sea, with the bookcase standing for the coast of Europe, the sofa as Africa, the Straits of Gibraltar passing between the legs of the chair, a scattering of playing cards representing Cyprus, Sicily, and Malta, the notebooks can be aircraft carriers, the eraser and pencil sharpeners destroyers, the thumb-tacks mines, and the paper clips will be submarines.

It was cold in the apartment. Instead of putting on another pullover, as I was told to do, to save electricity, I would put on the electric heater, just for ten minutes or so. The heater had two elements, but there was an economy switch that was always set to light only one of them. The lower one. I stared at it and watched the coil begin to glow. It lit up gradually: at first you couldn't see anything, you just heard a series of crackling sounds, as when you walk on grains of sugar, and after that a pale purplish gleam appeared at either end of the element and a hint of pink began to spread toward the center, like a faint blush on a shy cheek, which turned into a deep blush, which soon ran riot in a shameless display of naked yellow and lecherous lime green, until the glow reached the middle of the coil and glowed unstoppably, a red-hot fire like a savage sun in the shiny metal dish of the reflector that you couldn't look at without squinting, and the element now was incandescent, dazzling, unable to contain itself; any moment now it would melt and pour down on my Mediterranean Sea like an erupting volcano raining cascades of molten lava to destroy my flotilla of destroyers and submarines.

All this time its partner, the upper element, slumbered cold and indifferent. The brighter the other one glowed, the more indifferent this one appeared. Shrugging its shoulders, watching everything from a ringside seat but totally unmoved. I suddenly shuddered, as though I could sense on my skin all the pent-up tension between the two coils, and realized that I had a simple, quick way to ensure that the indifferent coil too would have no choice but to glow, so that it too would quiver fit to burst with overflowing fire—but that was forbidden. It was forbidden not only because of the crying waste but also because of the danger of overloading the circuit, of blowing a fuse and plunging the house in darkness, and who would go out in the middle of the night to fetch Baruch Goldfingers for me?

The second coil was only if I was crazy, completely crazy, and to hell with the consequences. But what if my parents came back before I had managed to switch it off? Or if I managed to switch it off in time but the coil didn't have time to cool down and play possum, then what could

I say in my defense? So I must resist the temptation. Hold myself back. And I might as well start clearing up the mess I made and put everything away in its place.

5

SOMETIMES THE facts threaten the truth. I once wrote about the real reason for my grandmother's death. My grandmother Shlomit arrived in Jerusalem straight from Vilna one hot summer's day in 1933, took one startled look at the sweaty markets, the colorful stalls, the swarming side streets full of the cries of hawkers, the braying of donkeys, the bleating of goats, the squawks of pullets hung up with their legs tied together, and blood dripping from the necks of slaughtered chickens, she saw the shoulders and arms of Middle Eastern men and the strident colors of the fruit and vegetables, she saw the hills all around and the rocky slopes, and immediately pronounced her final verdict: "The Levant is full of germs."

My grandmother lived in Jerusalem for some twenty-five years, she knew hard times and a few good ones, but to her last day she found no reason to modify her verdict. They say that the day after they arrived, she ordered my grandfather, as she would every single day they lived in Jerusalem, winter and summer alike, to get up at six or six thirty every morning and to spray Flit in every corner of the apartment to drive away the germs, to spray under the bed, behind the wardrobe, and even into the storage space and between the legs of the sideboard, and then to beat all the mattresses and the bedclothes and eiderdowns. From my childhood I remember Grandpa Alexander standing on the balcony in the early morning in his vest and bedroom slippers, beating the pillows like Don Quixote attacking the wineskins, bringing the carpet beater down on them repeatedly with all the force of his wretchedness or despair. Grandma Shlomit would stand a few steps behind him, taller than he, dressed in a flowery silk dressing gown buttoned all the way up, her hair tied with a green butterfly-like bow, as stiff and upright as the headmistress of a boarding school for young ladies, commanding the field of battle until the daily victory was won.

In the context of her constant war against germs Grandma used to boil fruit and vegetables uncompromisingly. She would wipe the bread twice over with a cloth soaked in a pinkish disinfectant solution called Cali. After each meal she did not wash the dishes but gave them the treatment normally reserved for Passover Eve, boiling them for a long time. Grandma Shlomit boiled her own person, too, three times a day: summer and winter alike she took three baths in nearly boiling water, to eradicate the germs. She lived to a ripe old age, the bugs and viruses crossing to the other side of the street when they saw her approaching in the distance, and when she was over eighty, after a couple of heart attacks, Dr. Kromholtz warned her: Dear lady, unless you desist from these fervid ablutions of yours, I am unable to take responsibility for any possible untoward and regrettable consequences.

But Grandma could not give up her baths. Her fear of germs was too strong for her. She died in the bath.

Her heart attack is a fact, but the truth is that she died from an excess of hygiene. Facts have a tendency to obscure the truth. It was cleanliness that killed her. Although the motto of her life in Jerusalem, "The Levant is full of germs," may testify to an earlier, deeper truth than the demon of hygiene, a truth that was repressed and invisible. After all, Grandma Shlomit came from northeastern Europe, where there were just as many germs as there were in Jerusalem, not to mention all sorts of other noxious things.

Here then is a peephole that may afford us a glimpse of the effect of the sights of the Orient, its colors and smells, on my grandmother and perhaps on other immigrants and refugees who like her came from gloomy shtetls in Eastern Europe and were so disturbed by the pervasive sensuality of the Levant that they resolved to defend themselves from its menace by constructing their own ghetto.

Menace? Or perhaps the truth is that it was not the menace of the Levant that made my grandmother mortify and purify her body with those boiling-hot ablutions morning, noon, and night every day that she lived in Jerusalem but rather its seductive sensual charms, and her own body, and the powerful attraction of those teeming markets that made her breathing tight and her knees weak with that abundance of unfamiliar vegetables, fruit, spicy cheeses, pungent odors, and guttural foods that so tormented and excited her, and those lustful hands that groped and burrowed into the most intimate recesses of fruit and vegetables, the chilis and spicy olives and the nudity of all that ripe, bare red meat, dripping blood, hanging shamelessly naked from the butchers' hooks, and the dizzying array of spices, herbs, and powders, all the multi-colored lascivious lures of that pungent, highly seasoned world, not to mention the penetrating aromas of freshly roasted, cardamom-flavored coffee, and the glass containers full of colorful drinks with lumps of ice or slices of lemon in them, and those powerfully built, deeply tanned, hirsute market porters, naked to the waist, the muscles of their backs rippling with effort under their hot skin that gleamed as rivulets of perspiration ran down it in the sun. Perhaps Grandma's cult of cleanliness was nothing more or less than a hermetic, sterile spacesuit. An antiseptic chastity belt that she had voluntarily buckled on, since her first day here, and secured with seven locks, destroying all the keys?

Or maybe it was neither the hygiene nor her desires nor the fear of her desires that killed her but her constant secret anger at this fear, a suppressed, malignant anger, like an unlanced boil, anger at her own body, at her own longings, and also a deeper anger, at the very revulsion these longings gave rise to, a murky, poisonous anger directed both at the prisoner and at her jailer, years and years of secret mourning for the ceaseless passage of desolate time and the shriveling of her body and the desires of that body, the desires, laundered and cleansed and scraped and disinfected and boiled a thousand times, for that Levant, filthy, sweaty, bestial, exciting to the point of swooning, but swarming with germs.

6

ALMOST SIXTY years have gone by, yet I can still remember his smell. I summon it, and it returns to me, a slightly coarse, dusty, but strong and pleasant smell, reminiscent of touching rough sackcloth, and it borders on the memory of the feel of his skin, his flowing locks, his thick mustache that rubbed against the skin of my cheek and gave me a pleasant feeling, like being in a warm, dark old kitchen on a winter day. The poet Saul Tchernikhowsky died in the autumn of 1943, when I was little more than four years old, so that this sensual recollection can only have survived by passing through several stages of transmission and amplification. My mother and father often reminded me of those moments, because they enjoyed boasting to acquaintances that their child sat on Tchernikhowsky's lap and played with his mustache. They always turned to me for confirmation of their story: "Isn't it true that you can still remember that Saturday afternoon when Uncle Saul sat you on his lap and called you 'little devil'? It's true, isn't it?"

My task was to recite for them the refrain: "Yes, it's true. I remember it very well."

I never told them that the picture I remembered was a little different from their version. I did not want to spoil it for them.

My parents' habit of repeating this story and turning to me for confirmation did indeed strengthen and preserve the memory of those moments for me, which had it not been for their pride might well have faded and vanished. But the difference between their story and the picture in my memory, the fact that the memory I retained was not merely a reflection of my parents' story but had a life of its own, that the image of the great poet and the little child according to my parents' staging was somewhat different from my own, is proof that my story is not merely inherited from theirs. In my parents' version the curtain opens on a blond child in shorts sitting on the lap of the giant of Hebrew poetry, stroking and tugging at his mustache, while the poet bestows on the youngster the accolade of "little devil" and the child—oh, sweet innocence!—repays him with his own coin by saying, "No, you're a devil!" to which, in my father's version, the author of "Facing the Statue of Apollo" replied with the words "Maybe we're both right" and even kissed me on my head, which my parents interpreted as a sign of things to come, a sort of anointing, as if, let us say, it had been Pushkin bending over and kissing the head of the little Tolstoy.

But in the picture in my mind, which my parents' recurrent searchlight beams may have helped me preserve but definitely did not imprint in me, in my scenario, which is less sweet than theirs, I never sat on the poet's lap, nor did I tug at his famous mustache, but I tripped and fell over at Uncle Joseph's home, and as I fell, I bit my tongue, and it bled a little, and I cried, and the poet, being also a doctor, a pediatrician, reached me before my parents, helped me up with his big hands, I even remember now that he picked me up with my back to him and my shouting face to the room, then he swung me around in his arms and said something, and then something else, certainly not about handing on the crown of Pushkin to Tolstoy, and while I was still struggling in his arms, he forced my mouth open and called for someone to fetch some ice, then inspected my injury and declared:

"It's nothing, just a scratch, and as we are now weeping, so we shall soon be laughing."

Whether because the poet's words included both of us, or because of the rough touch of his cheek on mine, like the roughness of a thick warm towel, or whether indeed because of his strong, homely smell, which to this day I can conjure up (not a smell of shaving lotion or soap, nor a smell of tobacco, but a full, dense body smell, like the taste of chicken soup on a winter day), I soon calmed down, and it transpired that, as so often happens, I was more in shock than in pain. And the bushy Nietzsche mustache scratched and tickled me a little, and then, as far as I can remember, Dr. Saul Tchernikhowsky laid me down carefully but without any fuss on my back on Uncle Joseph's couch (that is Professor Joseph Klausner), and the poet-doctor or my mother put on my tongue some ice that Auntie Zippora had hurriedly brought.

So far as I can remember, no witty aphorism worthy of immortalization was exchanged on that occasion between the giant among the poets of the formative Generation of National Revival and the sobbing little representative of the later so-called Generation of the State of Israel.

It was only two or three years after this incident that I managed to pronounce the name Tchernikhowsky. I was not surprised when I was told that he was a poet: almost everyone in Jerusalem in those days was either a poet or a writer or a researcher or a thinker or a scholar or a world reformer. Nor was I impressed by the title Doctor: in Uncle Joseph and Auntie Zippora's home, all the male guests were called Professor or Doctor.

But he was not just any old doctor or poet. He was a pediatrician, a man with a disheveled mop of hair, with laughing eyes, big warm hands, a thicket of a mustache, a felt cheek, and a unique, strong, soft smell.

To this day, whenever I see a photograph or drawing of the poet Saul or his carved head that stands in the entrance of the Tchernikhowsky Writers' House, I am immediately enveloped, like the embrace of a winter blanket, by his comforting smell.

Like so many Zionist Jews of our time, my father was a bit of a closet Canaanite. He was embarrassed by the shtetl and everything in it, and by its representatives in modern writing, Bialik and Agnon. He wanted us all to be born anew, as blond-haired, muscular, suntanned Hebrew Europeans instead of Jewish Eastern Europeans. He always loathed the Yiddish language, which he termed "jargon." He saw Bialik as the poet of victimhood, of "eternal death pangs," while Tchernikhowsky was the harbinger of the new dawn that was about to break, the dawn of "The Conquerors of Canaan by Storm." He would reel off "Facing the Statue of Apollo" by heart, with tremendous gusto, without even noticing that the poet, while still bowing down to Apollo, unwittingly bursts into a hymn to Dionysus.

He knew more of Tchernikhowsky's poems by heart than anyone else I have met, probably more than Tchernikhowsky himself did, and he recited them with pathos and gusto, such a muse-inspired, and therefore musical, poet, without the complexes and complexities so typical of the shtetl, writing shamelessly about love and even about sensual pleasures. Father said: Tchernikhowsky never wallows in all sorts of *tsores* or *krechtzen*.

At such moments my mother would look at him skeptically, as though surprised by the crude nature of his pleasures but refraining from comment.

He had a distinctly "Lithuanian" temperament, my father, and he was very fond of using the word "distinctly" (the Klausners came from Odessa, but before that they came from Lithuania, and before that apparently from Mattersdorf, now Mattersburg in eastern Austria, near the Hungarian border). He was a sentimental, enthusiastic man, but for most of his life he loathed all forms of mysticism and magic. He considered the supernatural to be the domain of charlatans and tricksters. He thought the tales of the Hasidim to be mere folklore, a word that he always pronounced with the same grimace of loathing that accompanied his use of such words as "jargon," "ecstasy," "hashish," and "intuition."

My mother used to listen to him speak, and instead of replying she would offer us her sad smile, and sometimes she said to me: "Your father is a wise and rational man; he is even rational in his sleep."

Years later, after her death, when his optimistic cheerfulness had faded somewhat, along with his volubility, his taste also changed and may have moved closer to that of my mother. In a basement in the National Library he discovered a previously unknown manuscript of I. L. Peretz, an exercise book from the writer's youth, which contained, in addition to all sorts of sketches and scribbles and attempts at poetry, an unknown story titled "Revenge." My father went off for several years to London, where he wrote a doctoral dissertation on this discovery, and with this encounter with the mystically inclined Peretz he moved away from his earlier penchant for the Sturm und Drang of early Tchernikhowsky. He began to study the myths and sagas of faraway peoples, glanced at Yiddish literature, and gradually succumbed, like someone finally relaxing his grip on a handrail, to the mysterious charm of Peretz's stories in particular and Hasidic tales in general.

However, in the years when we used to walk to his Uncle Joseph's in Talpiot on Saturday afternoons, my father was still trying to educate us all to be as enlightened as he was. My parents often used to argue about literature. My father liked Shakespeare, Balzac, Tolstoy, Ibsen, and Tchernikhowsky. My mother preferred Schiller, Turgenev, Chekhov, Strindberg, Gnessin, Bialik, and also Mr. Agnon, who lived across the road from Uncle Joseph in Talpiot, although I have the impression there was not much love lost between the two men.

A polite but arctic chill fell momentarily on the little road if the two of them ever happened to meet, Professor Joseph Klausner and Mr. S. Y. Agnon; they would raise their hats an inch or so, give a slight bow, and probably each wished the other from the depth of his heart to be consigned for all eternity to the deepest hell of oblivion.

Uncle Joseph did not think much of Agnon, whose writing he considered prolix, provincial, and adorned with all sorts of over-clever cantorial grace notes. As for Mr. Agnon, he nursed his grudge and had his revenge eventually when he speared Uncle Joseph on one of his spits of irony, in the ludicrous figure of Professor Bachlam in his novel *Shirah*. Fortunately for Uncle Joseph, he died before *Shirah* was published, thus sparing himself considerable distress. Mr. Agnon, on the other hand, lived on for many a year, won the Nobel Prize for Literature, and earned a worldwide reputation for himself, although he was condemned to the bitter tribulation of seeing the little cul-de-sac in Talpiot in which they had both lived renamed Klausner Street. From that day until the day he died, he had to suffer the indignity of being the famous writer S. Y. Agnon of Klausner Street.

And so to this day a perverse fate has willed that Agnon's house should stand in Klausner Street, while a no less perverse fate has willed that Klausner's house should be demolished and replaced by a very ordinary square building that houses very average apartments, overlooking the hordes of visitors who pass through Agnon's house.

7

EVERY SECOND or third Saturday we would make the pilgrimage to Talpiot, to Uncle Joseph and Auntie Zippora's little villa. Our house in Kerem Avraham was some six or seven kilometers distant from Talpiot, a remote and somewhat dangerous Hebrew suburb. South of Rehavia and Kiriat Shmuel, south of Montefiore's Windmill, stretched an expanse of alien Jerusalem: the suburbs of Talbiyeh, Abu Tor, and Katamon, the German Colony, the Greek Colony, and Bakaa. (Abu Tor, our teacher Mr. Avisar once explained to us, was named after an old warrior whose name meant "father of the bull," Talbiyeh was once the estate of a man named Taleb, Bakaa means a "plain or valley, the biblical Valley of the Giants," while the name Katamon is an Arabic corruption of the Greek *kata monēs,* meaning "beside the monastery.") Farther still to the south, beyond all these foreign worlds, over the hills and far away, at the end of the world, glimmered isolated Jewish dots, Mekor Hayyim, Talpiot, Arnona, and Kibbutz Ramat Rahel, which almost abutted on the extremities of Bethlehem. From our Jerusalem, Talpiot could be seen only as a tiny gray mass of dusty trees on a distant hilltop. From the roof of our house one night our neighbor Mr. Friedmann, an engineer, pointed out a cluster of shimmering pale lights on the far horizon, suspended between heaven and earth, and said: "That's Allenby Barracks, and over there you may be able to see the lights of Talpiot or Arnona. If there is more violence," he said, "I wouldn't like to be them. Not to mention if there's all-out war."

We would set out after lunch, when the city had shut itself off behind barred shutters and sunk into a Sabbath afternoon slumber. Total silence ruled in the streets and yards among the stone-built houses with their corrugated iron lean-tos. As though the whole of Jerusalem had been enclosed in a transparent glass ball.

We crossed Geulah Street, entered the warren-like alleys of the shabby ultra-Orthodox quarter at the top of Ahva, passed underneath washing lines heavy with black, yellow, and white clothes, among rusty iron railings of neglected verandas and outside staircases, climbed up through Zikhron Moshe, which was always swathed in poor Ashkenazi cooking smells, of *chollent,* borscht, garlic and onion and sauerkraut, and continued across the Street of the Prophets. There was not a living soul to be seen in the streets of Jerusalem at two o'clock on a Saturday afternoon. From the Street of the Prophets we walked down Strauss Street, which was perpetually bathed in shadow from the ancient pine trees in the shade of two walls, on the one side the moss-grown gray wall of the Protestant Hospital run by the Deaconesses, and on the other the grim wall of the Jewish hospital, Bikkur Holim, with the symbols of the twelve tribes of Israel embossed on its splendid bronze gates. A pungent odor of medicines, old age, and Lysol escaped from these two hospitals. Then we crossed Jaffa Road by the famous clothes shop, Maayan Shtub, and lingered for a moment in front of Ahiasaf Brothers bookshop, to allow my father to feast his hungry eyes on the abundance of new Hebrew books in the window. From there we walked the whole length of King George V Avenue, past splendid shops, cafés with high chandeliers, and rich stores, all empty and locked for the Sabbath, but with their windows beckoning to us through barred iron grilles, winking with the seductive charm of other worlds, whiffs of wealth from distant continents, scents of brightly lit, bustling cities dwelling securely on the banks of wide rivers, where there were elegant ladies and prosperous gentlemen who did not live their lives between one attack or government decree and the next, knowing no hardship, relieved of the need to count every penny, free from the oppressive rules of pioneering and self-sacrifice, exempt from the burdens of Community Chest and Medical Fund contributions and rationing coupons, comfortably installed in beautiful houses with chimney stacks rising from their roofs or in spacious apartments in modern blocks, with carpets on the floor, with a doorman in a blue uniform guarding the entrance and a boy in a red uniform manning the elevator, and servants and cooks and butlers and factotums at their beck and call. Ladies and gentlemen who enjoyed a comfortable life, unlike ours.

Here, in King George V Avenue, as well as in German-Jewish Rehavia and rich Greek and Arab Talbieh, another stillness reigned now, unlike the devout stillness of those indigent, neglected Eastern European alleys: a different, exciting, secretive stillness held sway in King George V Avenue, empty now at half past two on a Saturday afternoon, a foreign, in fact specifically British, stillness, since King George V Avenue (not only because of its name) always seemed to me as a child to be an extension of that wonderful London Town I knew from films: King George V Avenue with its rows of grand, official-looking buildings extending on both sides of the road in a continuous, uniform façade, without those gaps of sad, neglected yards defaced by rubbish and rusting metal that separated the houses in our own areas. Here on King George V Avenue there were no dilapidated verandas, no broken shutters at windows that gaped like a toothless old mouth, paupers' windows revealing to passersby the wretched innards of the home, patched cushions, gaudy rags, cramped piles of furniture, blackened frying pans, moldy pots, misshapen enamel saucepans, and a motley array of rusty tin cans. Here on either side of the street was an uninterrupted, proud facade whose doors and lace-curtained windows all spoke discreetly of wealth, respectability, soft voices, choice fabrics, soft carpets, cut glass, and fine manners. Here the doorways of the buildings were adorned with the black glass plates of lawyers, brokers, doctors, notaries, and accredited agents of well-known foreign firms.

As we walked past Talitha Kumi Buildings, my father would explain the origin of the name, as though he had not done so a fortnight before and a month before that, and my mother protested that he would put us all to sleep with his explanations. We passed Schiber's Pit, the gaping foundations of a building that was never built, and the Frumin Building, where the Knesset would later have its temporary home, and the semicircular Bauhaus façade of Beit Hama'alot, which promised all who entered the severe delights of pedantic German-Jewish aesthetics, and we paused for a moment to look out over the walls of the Old City across the Mamillah Muslim Cemetery, hurrying each other along (It's a quarter to three already, and there's still a long way to go!), walking on past the Yeshurun Synagogue and the bulky semicircle of the Jewish Agency building. (Father would half-whisper, as though disclosing state secrets: "That's where our cabinet sits, Doctor Weizmann, Kaplan, Shertok, sometimes even David Ben-Gurion himself. This is the throbbing heart of the Hebrew government. What a pity it's not a more impressive national cabinet!" And he would go on to explain to me what a "shadow cabinet" was and what would happen in the country when the British finally left, as one way or another they surely would.)

From there we walked downhill toward the Terra Sancta College (where my father was to work for ten years, after the War of Independence and the siege of Jerusalem, when the university buildings on Mount Scopus were cut off and the Periodicals Department of the National Library, among others, found a temporary refuge here, in a corner of the third floor).

From Terra Sancta a twenty-minute walk brought us to the curved David Building, where the city suddenly stopped and you were confronted by open fields on your way to the railway station in Emek Refaim. To our left we could see the sails of the windmill at Yemin Moshe, and up the slope to our right the last houses in Talbiyeh. We felt a wordless tension as we left the confines of the Hebrew city, as though we were crossing an invisible border and entering a foreign country.

Soon after three o'clock we would walk along the road that divided the ruins of the Ottoman pilgrims' hostel, above which stood the Scottish church, and the locked railway station. There was a different light here, a cloudier, old, mossy light. This place reminded my mother of a little Muslim street on the outskirts of her hometown in western Ukraine. At this point Father would inevitably start to talk about Jerusalem in the days of the Turks, about the decrees of Jemal Pasha, about decapitations and floggings that took place before a crowd gathered right here on the paved square in front of this very railway station, which was, as we knew, built at the end of the nineteenth century by a Jerusalem Jew named Joseph Bey Navon, who had obtained a concession from the Ottomans.

From the square in front of the railway station we walked down Hebron Road, passing in front of the fortified British military installations and a fenced-off cluster of massive fuel containers over which a sign in three languages proclaimed VACUUM OIL. There was something strange and comical about the Hebrew sign, lacking as it did any vowels. Father laughed and said this was yet more proof that it was high time to modernize Hebrew writing by introducing separate letters for vowels, which, he said, are the traffic police of reading.

To our left a series of roads led downhill toward the Arab quarter of Abu Tor, while to our right were the charming lanes of the German Colony, a tranquil Bavarian village full of singing birds, barking dogs, and crowing cocks, with dovecotes and red-tiled roofs dotted here and there among cypresses and pine trees, and little stone-walled gardens shaded by leafy trees. Every house here was built with a cellar and an attic, words the very sound of which afforded sentimental pangs to a child like me, born in a place where no one had a dark cellar under his feet or a dimly lit attic above his head, or a larder or a hamper or a chest of drawers or a grandfather clock or a well in his garden fitted with a hoist.

As we continued down Hebron Road, we passed the pink stone mansions of wealthy effendis and Christian Arab professionals and senior civil servants in the British mandatory administration and members of the Arab Higher Committee, Mardam Bey al-Matnawi, Haj Rashed al-Afifi, Dr. Emile Adwan al-Boustani, the lawyer Henry Tawil Tutakh, and the other wealthy residents of the suburb of Bakaa. All the shops here were open, and sounds of laughter and music came from the coffeehouses, as if we had left the Sabbath itself behind us, held back behind an imaginary wall that blocked its way somewhere between Yemin Moshe and the Scottish Hospice.

On the wide pavement, in the shade of two ancient pine trees in front of a coffeehouse, three or four gentlemen of mature years sat on wicker stools around a low wooden table, all wearing brown suits and each sporting a gold chain that emerged from his buttonhole, looped across his belly, and disappeared into a pocket. They drank tea from glasses or sipped coffee from little decorated cups, and rolled dice onto the backgammon boards in front of them. Father greeted them cheerily in Arabic that came out of his mouth sounding more like Russian. The gentlemen stopped talking for a moment, eyed him with mild surprise, and one of them muttered something indistinct, perhaps a single word, or perhaps a reply to our greeting.

At half past three we passed the barbed wire fence around Allenby Barracks, the British military base in south Jerusalem. I had often stormed into this camp, conquered, subdued, and purged it, and raised the

Hebrew flag over it in my games on the rush mat. From here I would press on toward the heart of the foreign occupier, sending groups of commandos to the walls of the High Commissioner's residence on the Hill of Evil Counsel, which was captured again and again by my Hebrew troops in a spectacular pincer movement, one armored column breaking into the residence from the west from the barracks, while the other arm of the pincers closed in with complete surprise from the east, from the barren eastern slopes that descended toward the Judaean desert.

When I was a little more than eight, in the last year of the British Mandate, a couple of fellow conspirators and I built an awesome rocket in the backyard of our house. Our plan was to aim it at Buckingham Palace (I had discovered a large-scale map of central London in my father's collection).

I typed out on my father's typewriter a polite letter of ultimatum addressed to His Majesty King George VI of England of the House of Windsor (I wrote in Hebrew—he must have someone there who can translate for him): If you do not get out of our country in six months at the latest, our Day of Atonement will be Great Britain's Day of Reckoning. But our project never came to fruition, because we were unable to develop the sophisticated guiding device (we planned to hit Buckingham Palace but not innocent English passersby) and because we had some problems devising a fuel that would take our rocket from the corner of Amos and Obadiah Streets in Kerem Avraham to a target in the middle of London. While we were still tied up in technological research and development, the English changed their minds and hurriedly left the country, and that is how London survived my national zeal and my deadly rocket, which was made up of bits of an abandoned refrigerator and the remains of an old bicycle.

Shortly before four we would finally turn left off Hebron Road and enter the suburb of Talpiot, along an avenue of dark cypresses on which a westerly breeze played a rustling tune that aroused in me wonder, humility, and respect in equal measure. Talpiot in those days was a tranquil garden suburb on the edge of the desert, far removed from the city center and its commercial bustle. It was planned on the model of well-cared-for Central European housing schemes constructed for the peace and quiet of scholars, doctors, writers, and thinkers. On either side of the road stood pleasant little single-story houses set in pretty gardens, in each of which, as we imagined, dwelt some prominent scholar or well-known professor like our Uncle Joseph, who although he was childless was famous throughout the land and even in faraway countries through the translations of his books.

We turned right into Kore Hadorot Street as far as the pine wood, then left, and there we were outside Uncle's house. Mother would say: It's only ten to four, they may still be resting. Why don't we sit down quietly on the bench in the garden and wait for a few minutes? Or else: We're a little late today, it's a quarter past four, the samovar must be bubbling away and Aunt Zippora will have put the fruit out.

Two Washingtonias stood like sentries on either side of the gate, and beyond them was a paved path flanked on either side by a thuja hedge that led from the gate to the wide steps, up which we went to the front porch and the door, above which was engraved on a fine brass plate Uncle Joseph's motto:

JUDAISM AND HUMANISM

On the door itself was a smaller, shinier copper plate on which was engraved both in Hebrew and Roman letters:

PROFESSOR DR. JOSEPH KLAUSNER

And underneath, in Aunt Zippora's rounded handwriting, on a small card fixed with a thumbtack, was written:

Please refrain from calling between two and four o'clock.
Thank you.

8

ALREADY IN the entrance hall I was seized by respectful awe, as though even my heart had been asked to remove its shoes and walk in stockinged feet, on tiptoe, breathing politely with mouth closed, as was fitting.

In this entrance hall, apart from a brown wooden hat tree with curling branches that stood near the front door, a small wall mirror, and a dark woven rug, there was not an inch of space that was not covered with rows of books: shelves upon shelves rose from the floor to the high ceiling, full of books in languages whose alphabets I could not identify, books standing up and other books lying down on top of them; plump, resplendent foreign books stretching themselves comfortably, and other wretched books that peered at you from cramped and crowded conditions, lying like illegal immigrants crowded on bunks aboard ship. Heavy, respectable books in gold-tooled leather bindings, and thin books bound in flimsy paper, splendid portly gentlemen and ragged, shabby beggars, and all around and among and behind them was a sweaty mass of booklets, leaflets, pamphlets, offprints, periodicals, journals, and magazines, that noisy crowd that always congregates around any public square or marketplace.

A single window in this entrance hall looked out, through iron bars reminiscent of a hermit's cell, at the melancholy foliage of the garden. Aunt Zippora received us here, as she received all her guests. She was a pleasant elderly woman, bright of face and broad of beam, in a gray dress with a black shawl around her shoulders, very Russian, with her white hair pulled back and arranged in a small, neat bun, her two cheeks proffered in turn for a kiss, her kindly round face smiling at you in welcome. She was always the first to ask how you were, and usually didn't wait for your answer but launched straight into news of our dear Joseph, who hadn't slept a wink again all night, or whose stomach was back to normal again after protracted problems, or who had just had a wonderful letter from a very famous professor in Pennsylvania, or whose gallstones were tormenting him again, or who had to finish an important long article by tomorrow for Ravidovitch's *Metsuda,* or who had decided to ignore yet another insult from Eisig Silberschlag, or who had finally decided to deliver a crushing response to the abuse issuing from one of those leaders of the Brit Shalom gang.

After this news bulletin Aunt Zippora would smile sweetly and lead us into the presence of the uncle himself.

"Joseph is waiting for you in his drawing room," she would announce with a peal of laughter, or "Joseph is in the living room already, with Mr. Krupnik and the Netanyahus and Mr. Jonitchman and the Schochtmans, and there are some more honored guests on their way." And sometimes she said: "He's been cooped up in his study since six o'clock this morning, I've even had to take him his meals there, but no matter, no matter, just you come straight through, do come along, he'll be glad, he's always so glad to see you, and I'll be glad too, it's better for him to stop working for a while, to take a little break, he is ruining his health! He doesn't spare himself at all!"

Two doors opened off the entrance hall: one, a glass door whose panes were decorated with flowers and festoons, led to the living room, which also served as a dining room; the other, a heavy, somber door, led us into the professor's study, sometimes known as the "library."

Uncle Joseph's study seemed to me the antechamber to some palace of wisdom. There are more than twenty-five thousand volumes, Father once whispered to me, in your uncle's private library, among them priceless old tomes, manuscripts of our greatest writers and poets, first editions inscribed to him personally, volumes that were smuggled out of Soviet Odessa by all sorts of devious subterfuges, valuable collectors' items, sacred and secular works, virtually the whole of Jewish literature and a good deal of world literature as well, books that Uncle bought in Odessa or acquired in Heidelberg, books that he discovered in Lausanne or found in Berlin or Warsaw, books he ordered from America and books the like of which exist nowhere but in the Vatican Library, in Hebrew, Aramaic, Syriac, classical and modern Greek, Sanskrit, Latin, medieval Arabic, Russian, English, German, Spanish, Polish, French, Italian, and languages and dialects I had never even heard of, like Ugaritic and Slovene, Maltese and Old Church Slavonic.

There was something severe and ascetic about the library, about the straight black lines of the dozens of bookshelves extending from the floor to the high ceiling and even over the doorways and windows, a sort of silent, stern grandeur that brooked no levity or frivolity and compelled all of us, even Uncle Joseph himself, always to speak in a whisper here.

The smell of my uncle's enormous library would accompany me all the days of my life: the dusty, enticing odor of seven hidden wisdoms, the smell of a silent, secluded life devoted to scholarship, the life of a secretive hermit, the severe silence of ghosts billowing up from the deepest wells of knowledge, the whisper of dead sages, outpourings of secret thoughts of long-buried authors, the cold caress of the desires of preceding generations.

From the study too, through three tall, narrow windows, could be seen the gloomy, rather overgrown garden, immediately beyond whose wall began the desolation of the Judaean desert and the rocky slopes that cascaded down toward the Dead Sea. The garden was hemmed in by tall cypresses and whispering pines, among which stood occasional oleanders, weeds, unpruned rose bushes, dusty thujas, darkened gravel paths, a wooden garden table that had rotted under the rain of many winters, and an old, stooped, and half-withered pride of India. Even on the hottest days of summer there was something wintry, Russian, and downcast about this garden, whose cats were fed by Uncle Joseph and Aunt Zippora, childless as they were, on kitchen scraps, but where I never saw either of them stroll or sit in the evening breeze on one of the two discolored benches.

I was the only one who wandered in this garden, always alone, on those Sabbath afternoons, escaping from the tedious conversation of the scholars in the sitting room, hunting leopards in its undergrowth, digging under its stones for a hoard of ancient parchments, dreaming of conquering the arid hills beyond its wall with a wild charge of my troops.

All four high, wide walls of the library were covered with crowded but well-ordered books, rank upon rank of precious blue-, green-, and black-bound volumes embossed in gold or silver. In places they were so cramped that two rows of books were forced to stand one behind the other on a single shelf. There were sections with florid Gothic lettering that made me think of spires and turrets, and zones of Jewish holy books, Talmuds and prayer books and law codes and Midrashic compilations, a shelf of Hebrew works from Spain and another with books from Italy, and a section with the writings of the Hebrew Enlightenment, from Berlin and elsewhere, and an endless expanse of Jewish thought and Jewish history and early Near Eastern history, Greek and Roman history, Church history both ancient and modern, and the various pagan cultures, Islamic thought, eastern religions, medieval history, and there were wide Slavic regions that left me mystified, Greek territories, and gray-brown areas of ring binders and cardboard folders stuffed with off-prints and manuscripts. Even the floor was covered with dozens of piled-up books, some of them laid open facedown, some full of little markers, while others huddled like frightened sheep on the high-backed chairs that were intended for visitors, or even on the windowsills; while a black ladder that could be moved all around the library on a metal track gave access to the upper shelves that clung on under the high ceiling. Occasionally, I was permitted to move it from bookcase to bookcase very carefully on its rubber wheels. There were no pictures, plants, or ornaments. Only books, more books, and silence filled the room, and a wonderful rich smell of leather bindings, yellowing paper, mold, a strange hint of seaweed and old glue, of wisdom, secrets, and dust.

In the center of his library, like a large dark destroyer that had dropped anchor in the waters of a mountain-girt bay, stood Professor Klausner's desk, entirely covered with piles and piles of reference works, notebooks, an assortment of different pens, blue, black, green, and red, pencils, erasers, inkwells, containers full of paper clips, rubber bands, and staples, manila envelopes, white envelopes, and envelopes with attractive colorful stamps on them, sheets of paper, leaflets, notes, and index cards, foreign volumes piled open on top of open Hebrew volumes, interleaved here and there with sheets torn from a spiral-bound pad, inscribed with the cobwebs of my uncle's spidery handwriting, full of crossings out and corrections, like corpses of bloated flies, full of little slips of paper, and Uncle Joseph's gold-rimmed spectacles lay on top of the pile as though hovering over the void, while a second, black-framed, pair lay on top of another pile of books, on a little trolley beside his chair, and a third pair peered out from among the pages of an open booklet on a small chest that stood beside the dark sofa.

On this sofa, curled up in the fetal position, covered to his shoulders in a green and red tartan rug, like a Scottish soldier's kilt, his face bare and childlike without his glasses, lay Uncle Joseph himself, thin and small, his elongated brown eyes looking both happy and a little lost. He gave us a feeble wave of his translucent white hand, smiled a pink smile between his white mustache and his goatee, and said something like this:

"Come in, my dears, come in, come in" (even though we were already in the room, standing right in front of him, though still close to the door, huddled together—my mother, my father, and myself—like a tiny flock that had strayed into a strange pasture) "and please forgive me for not standing up to greet you, do not judge me too harshly, for two nights and three days now I have not stirred from my desk or closed my eyes, ask Mrs. Klausner and she will testify on my behalf, I am neither eating nor sleeping, I do not even glance at the newspaper while I finish this article, which, when it is published, will cause a great stir in this land of ours, and not only here, the whole cultural world is following this debate with bated breath, and this time I believe I have succeeded in silencing the obscurantists once and for all! This time they will be forced to concur and say Amen, or at least to admit that they have nothing more to say, they have lost their case, their game is up. And how about you? Fania my dear? My dear Lonia? And dear little Amos? How are you? What is new in your world? Have you read a few pages from my *When a Nation Fights for Its Freedom* to dear little Amos yet? I believe, my dears, that of all that I have written there is nothing that is more suitable than *When a Nation Fights for Its Freedom* to serve as spiritual sustenance to dear Amos in particular and the whole of our wonderful Hebrew youth in general, apart perhaps from the descriptions of heroism and rebellion that are scattered through the pages of my *History of the Second Temple.*

"And how about you, my dears? You must have walked here. And such a long way. From your home in Kerem Avraham? I recall how, when we were still young, thirty years ago, when we still lived in the picturesque and so authentic Bukharian Quarter, we used to set out on Saturdays and walk from Jerusalem to Bethel or Anatot and sometimes as far as the tomb of the Prophet Samuel. Dear Mrs. Klausner will give you something to eat and drink now if you will kindly follow her to her realm, and I shall join you as soon as I have finished this difficult paragraph. We are expecting the Voyslavskys today, and the poet Uri Zvi, and Even-Zahav. And dear Netanyahu and his charming wife visit us almost every Sabbath. Now come closer, my dears, come closer and see with your own eyes, you too my dear little Amos, take a look at the draft on my desk: after my death they should bring groups of students here, generation after generation, so that they may see with their own eyes the torments that writers endure in the service of their art, the struggles I have had and the lengths I have gone to to ensure that my style is simple and fluent and crystal clear, see how many words I have crossed out in each line, how many drafts I have torn up, sometimes more than half a dozen different drafts, before I was happy with what I had written. Success flows from perspiration, and inspiration from diligence and effort. As the good book saith, blessings of heaven up above, and blessings of the deep on the bottom. Only my little joke, naturally, please forgive me, ladies. Now, my dears, follow in Mrs. Klausner's footsteps and slake your thirst, and I shall not tarry."

From the far side of the library you could go out into a long narrow corridor that was the bowels of the house, and from this corridor the bathroom and a storeroom led off to the right, while straight ahead was the kitchen and pantry and the maid's room, which opened off the kitchen (although there was never any maid), or you could turn left right away into the living room or keep going toward the end of the corridor to the door of my uncle and aunt's white, flowery bedroom, which contained a large mirror in a bronze frame on either side of which was an ornamental candle sconce.

So you could reach the living room by any one of three routes: you could turn left from the entrance hall as you came into the house, or go straight ahead into the study, leave it by the corridor, turn left at once, as Uncle Joseph used to do on Sabbaths, and find yourself directly at the seat of honor at the head of the long black dining table that extended for almost the entire length of the living room. In addition, there was a low, arched doorway in a corner of the living room that led into a drawing room that was rounded on one side like a turret, with windows that looked out on the front garden, the Washingtonias, the quiet little street, and Mr. Agnon's house, which stood directly opposite, on the other side of the road.

This drawing room was also known as the smoking room. (Smoking was forbidden in Professor Klausner's house during the Sabbath, although the Sabbath did not always prevent Uncle Joseph from working at his articles.) There were several heavy, soft armchairs, sofas covered with cushions embroidered in oriental style, a wide, soft rug and a big oil painting (by Maurycy Gottlieb?) of an old Jew wearing phylacteries and a prayer shawl, holding a prayer book, which he was not reading because his eyes were closed, his mouth open, and his face expressed tortured religiosity and spiritual exaltation. I always had the feeling that this pious Jew knew all my shameful secrets, but instead of reproving me, he silently pleaded with me to mend my ways.

At that time, when the whole of Jerusalem was cramped into one-and-a-half- or two-bedroom apartments partitioned between two rival families, Professor Klausner's mansion seemed to me like a model for a sultan's palace or that of the Roman emperors, and often before I went to sleep, I would lie in bed imagining the restoration of the Davidic kingdom, with Hebrew troops standing guard over the palace in Talpiot. In 1949, when Menahem Begin, the leader of the opposition in the Knesset, put Uncle Joseph's name forward in the name of the Herut movement as a rival candidate to Chaim Weizmann for the presidency of Israel, I conjured up an image of my uncle's presidential residence in Talpiot surrounded on every side by Hebrew troops with two gleaming sentries standing on either side of the entrance under the brass plate promising all those who approached that Jewish and humanist values would be united and never come into conflict with each other.

"That crazy child is running around the house again," they said; "just look at him, running to and fro, all out of breath, flushed and perspiring, as though he's swallowed quicksilver." And they scolded me: "What's the matter? Have you been eating hot peppers? Or are you simply chasing your own tail? Do you think you are a dreidel? Or a moth? Or a fan? Have you lost your beautiful bride? Have your ships sunk at sea? You're giving us all a headache. And you're getting in Aunt Zippora's way. Why don't you sit down calmly for a change? Why don't you find a nice book and read it? Or shall we find you some pencils and paper so you can sit quietly and draw us a pretty picture? Well?"

But I was already on my way, galloping excitedly from the hall to the corridor and the maid's room, out into the garden, and back, full of fantasies, feeling the walls and knocking on them to discover hidden chambers, invisible spaces, secret passages, catacombs, tunnels, burrows, secret compartments, or camouflaged doors. I haven't given up to this day.

9

IN THE DARK glass-fronted sideboard in the living room were displayed a floral dinner service, long-necked glass jugs, prized items of china and crystal, a collection of old Hanukkah menorahs, and special dishes for Passover. On top of a display cabinet stood two bronze busts: a sullen

Beethoven facing a calm, pinch-lipped Vladimir Jabotinsky, who stood carefully polished, resplendent in uniform, with an officer's peaked cap and an authoritative leather strap across his chest.

Uncle Joseph sat at the head of the table talking in his reedy, feminine voice, pleading, wheedling, at times almost sobbing. He would speak about the state of the nation, the status of writers and scholars, the responsibilities of cultural figures, or about his colleagues and their lack of respect for his research, his discoveries, his international standing, while he himself was none too impressed with them, in fact he despised their provincial pettiness and their pedestrian, self-serving ideas.

Sometimes he would turn to the wider world of international politics, expressing anxiety at the subversiveness of Stalin's agents everywhere, contempt for the hypocrisy of the sanctimonious British, fear of the intrigues of the Vatican, who had never accepted, and never would accept, Jewish control of Jerusalem in particular and the Land of Israel in general, cautious optimism about the scruples of the enlightened democracies, and admiration, not without reservations, for America, which stood in our times at the head of all democracies even though it was infected by vulgarity and materialism and lacked cultural and spiritual depth. In general, the heroic figures of the nineteenth century, men like Giuseppe Garibaldi, Abraham Lincoln, William Gladstone, were great national liberators and outstanding exponents of civilized and enlightened values, whereas this new century was under the jackboot of those two butchers, the Georgian shoemaker's son in the Kremlin and the crazed ragamuffin who had seized control of the land of Goethe, Schiller, and Kant . . .

His guests listened in respectful silence or expressed agreement in a few quiet words so as not to interrupt the flow of his lecture. Uncle Joseph's table talk consisted of emotive monologues: from his seat at the head of the table, Professor Klausner would censure and denounce, reminisce or share his opinions, ideas, and feelings about such matters as the plebeian wretchedness of the leadership of the Jewish Agency, forever fawning on the Gentiles, the status of the Hebrew language, under constant threat from the Scylla and Charybdis of Yiddish on the one hand and the European languages on the other, the petty jealousy of some of his professorial colleagues, the shallowness of the younger writers and poets, particularly those born in the land, who not only failed to master a single language of European culture but limped even in Hebrew, or the Jews of Europe who had failed to understand Jabotinsky's prophetic warnings, and the American Jews, who even now, after Hitler, still clung to their fleshpots instead of settling in the Homeland.

Occasionally one of the male guests would venture a question or comment, like someone throwing a twig on a bonfire. But very rarely would one of them dare to take issue with some detail or other in their host's discourse; most of the time they all sat respectfully, uttering polite cries of agreement and contentment, or laughed when Uncle Joseph adopted a sarcastic or humorous tone, in which case he invariably explained: I was only joking when I said what I said a moment ago.

As for the ladies, their role in the conversation was limited to that of nodding listeners, who were expected to smile in the appropriate places and convey by their facial expressions delight at the pearls of wisdom that Uncle Joseph scattered before them so generously. I do not recall Aunt Zippora herself ever sitting at the table: she was forever scurrying back and forth between the kitchen or the larder and the living room, topping up the biscuit dish or the fruit bowl, adding hot water to the tea from the large silver-plated samovar, always hurrying, with a little apron around her waist, and when she had no tea to pour and there was no need for fresh supplies of cakes, biscuits, fruit, or the sweet concoction known as *varinye*, she would stand near the door between the living room and the corridor, to Uncle Joseph's right and a couple of paces behind him, with her hands joined on her stomach, waiting to see if anything was needed or if any of the guests wanted something, from a damp napkin to a toothpick, or if Uncle Joseph indicated to her politely that she should fetch from the far right-hand corner of the desk in his library the latest number of the periodical *Leshonenu* or the new volume of poems by Yitzhak Lamdan from which he wanted to quote a passage to support his argument.

Such was the invariable order of things in those days: Uncle Joseph sitting at the head of the table, pouring forth words of wisdom, polemic, and wit, and Aunt Zippora standing in her white apron, serving or waiting till she was needed. And yet, my uncle and aunt were utterly devoted to each other and lavished signs of affection on each other, an elderly, chronically ill, childless couple, he treating his wife like a baby and behaving toward her with extreme sweetness and affection, she treating her husband like a pampered only child, swaddling him in scarves and coats in case he caught cold and beating an egg in milk and honey to soothe his throat.

Once I happened to catch sight of them sitting side by side on their bed, his translucent hand in hers, while she carefully trimmed his fingernails, whispering all sorts of endearments to him in Russian.

Uncle Joseph had a penchant for putting emotional inscriptions in books: each year, from the time I was nine or ten, he gave me a volume of the *Children's Encyclopedia,* in one of which he wrote, in letters that slanted slightly backward, as though recoiling:

To my clever and hard-working
 little Amos
  with heartfelt hopes
   that he will grow up to be a credit to his people
    from
     Uncle Joseph
     Jerusalem-Talpiot, Lag Ba-Omer, 5710

As I stare at this inscription now, more than fifty years later, I wonder what he really knew about me, my Uncle Joseph, who used to lay his cold little hand on my cheek and question me, with a gentle smile beneath his white mustache, about what I had been reading lately, and which of his books I had read, and what Jewish children were being taught at school these days, which poems by Bialik and Tchernikhowsky I had learned by heart, and who was my favorite biblical hero, and without listening to my answers he told me that I ought to familiarize myself with what he had written about the Maccabees in his *History of the Second Temple,* while on the future of the state I should read his strongly worded article in yesterday's *Hamashkif,* or in the interview he gave to *Haboker* this week. In the inscription itself he had taken care to add the vowel points where there was any risk of ambiguity, while the last letter of his name fluttered like a flag in the wind.

In another inscription, on the title page of a volume of David Frischmann's translations, he wished me, in the third person:

May he succeed in the path of life
and learn from the words of the great translated in this book
that one must follow one's conscience
and not the human herd—the mass that rule at this time,
from his affectionate
Uncle Joseph
Jerusalem-Talpiot, Lag Ba-Omer, 5714

On one of those occasions Uncle Joseph said something like this:

"I am a childless man, after all, ladies and gentlemen, and my books are my children, I have invested the blood of my soul in them, and after my death it is they and they alone that will carry my spirit and my dreams to future generations."

To which Aunt Zippora responded:

"*Nu*, Osia, that's enough now. *Sha*. Osinka. That's quite enough of that. You know the doctors have told you not to get excited. And now you've let your tea get cold. It's stone cold. No, no, my dear, don't drink it, I'll go and get you a fresh glass."

Uncle Joseph's anger at the hypocrisy and baseness of his rivals sometimes led him to raise his voice, but his voice was never a roar, rather a high-pitched bleat, more like a sobbing woman than a scoffing, denouncing prophet. Sometimes he struck the top of the table with his frail hand, but when he did so, it seemed less like a blow than a caress. Once, while he was in the midst of a tirade against *Bolschewismus* or the Bund or the proponents of Judeo-German "jargon" (as he termed Yiddish), he knocked over a jug of lemonade, which spilled into his lap, and Aunt Zippora, who was standing in her apron by the door just behind him, hurried over and mopped at his trousers with her apron, apologized, helped him to his feet, and led him off to the bedroom. Ten minutes later she brought him back, changed and dry and gleaming, to his friends who had been waiting politely around the table, talking quietly about their hosts, who lived just like a pair of doves: he treated her like a daughter of his old age, and he was her darling baby and the apple of her eye. Sometimes she would lace her plump fingers in his translucent ones and for a moment the two of them would exchange a look, and then lower their eyes and smile at each other coyly.

And sometimes she gently undid his tie, helped him to take off his shoes, laid him down to rest for a while, his sad head resting on her bosom and his slight form clinging to the fullness of her body. Or else she would be standing in the kitchen washing up and weeping soundlessly, and he would come up behind her, place his pink hands on her shoulders, and utter a string of chirrups, chuckles, and twitters, as though he were trying to soothe a baby, or perhaps volunteering to be her baby.

10

AS A CHILD the thing I most admired Uncle Joseph for was that, as I had been told, he had invented and given us several simple, everyday Hebrew words, words that seemed to have been known and used forever, including "pencil," "iceberg," "shirt," "greenhouse," "toast," "cargo," "monotonous," "multicolored," "sensual," "crane," and "rhinoceros." (Come to think of it, what would I have put on each morning if Uncle Joseph had not given us the word "shirt"? A "coat of many colors"? And what would I have written with without his pencil? A "lead stylus"? Not to mention "sensual," a rather surprising gift from this puritanical uncle.)

Joseph Klausner was born in 1874 in Olkieniki, Lithuania, and died in Jerusalem in 1958. When he was ten, the Klausners moved from Lithuania to Odessa, where he progressed through the traditional Jewish educational system from the cheder to the modern-style yeshiva, and thence to the Hibbat Zion movement and the circles of Ahad Ha'am. At the age of nineteen he published his first article, titled "New Words and Fine Writing," in which he argued for the bounds of the Hebrew language to be extended, even by the incorporation of foreign words, so as to enable it to function as a living language. In the summer of 1897 he went to study in Heidelberg in south Germany, because in Tsarist Russia the universities were closed to Jews. During his five years in Heidelberg he studied philosophy with Professor Kuno Fischer, became deeply attracted to Eastern history à la Renan, and was profoundly influenced by Carlyle. His studies led from philosophy and history to literature, Semitic languages, and oriental studies (he mastered some fifteen languages, including Greek and Latin, Sanskrit and Arabic, Aramaic, Persian, and Amharic).

Tchernikhowsky, his friend from the Odessa days, was studying medicine at Heidelberg at the same time, and their friendship deepened into a warm, fruitful affinity. "A passionate poet!" Uncle Joseph would say about him, "an eagle of a Hebrew poet, with one wing touching the Bible and the landscape of Canaan while the other spreads over the whole of modern Europe!" And he sometimes said of Tchernikhowsky: "The soul of a simple, pure child in the sturdy body of a Cossack!"

Uncle Joseph was selected to be a delegate representing Jewish students at the First Zionist Congress in Basel, and at the following one, and he once even exchanged a few words with the father of Zionism, Theodor Herzl himself. ("He was a handsome man! Like an angel of God! His face had an inner glow! He looked to us like an Assyrian king with his black beard and his inspired, dreamy expression! And his eyes, I'll remember his eyes to my dying day, Herzl had the eyes of a young poet in love, blazing, lugubrious eyes that bewitched everyone who looked into them. And his high forehead also endowed him with majestic splendor!")

On his return to Odessa, Klausner wrote, taught, and engaged in Zionist activity until, at the tender age of twenty-nine, he inherited from Ahad Ha'am the editorship of *Hashiloah*, the main monthly of modern Hebrew culture. To be more precise, Uncle Joseph inherited from Ahad Ha'am a "periodical letter," and he turned it into a monthly immediately by inventing the Hebrew word for "monthly."

A man who has the ability to generate a new word and to inject it into the bloodstream of the language seems to me only a little lower than the Creator of light and darkness. If you write a book, you may be fortunate enough to be read for a while, until other, better books come along and take its place; but to produce a new word is to approach immortality. To this day I sometimes close my eyes and visualize this frail old man, with his pointed white goatee, his soft mustache, his delicate hands, his Russian glasses, shuffling along absentmindedly with his eggshell footsteps like a tiny Gulliver in a Brobdingnag peopled by a multicolored throng of mighty icebergs, tall cranes, and massive rhinoceroses, all bowing politely to him in gratitude.

He and his wife, Fanni Wernick (who from the day of their marriage was invariably known as "my dear Zippora," or, in the presence of guests, "Mrs. Klausner"), made their home in Rimislinaya Street, Odessa, into a kind of social club and meeting place for Zionists and literary figures.

Uncle Joseph always radiated an almost childlike cheerfulness. Even when he spoke of his sadness, his deep loneliness, his enemies, his aches and illnesses, the tragic destiny of the nonconformist, the injustices and humiliations he had had to suffer all through his life, there was always a restrained joy lurking behind his round spectacles. His movements, his bright eyes, his pink baby cheeks projected a cheery, optimistic vivaciousness that was life-affirming and almost hedonistic: "I didn't sleep a wink again all night," he would always say to his visitors, "the anxieties of our nation, fears for our future, the narrow vision of our dwarf-like leaders, weighed more heavily on me in the dark than my own considerable problems, not to mention my pain, my shortness of breath, and the terrible migraines I suffer night and day." (If you could believe what he said, he never closed his eyes for a moment between at least the early 1920s and his death in 1958.)

Between 1917 and 1919 Klausner was a lecturer, and eventually professor, at the University of Odessa, which was already changing hands with bloody fighting between Whites and Reds in the civil war that followed Lenin's revolution. In 1919 Uncle Joseph and Aunt Zippora and my uncle's elderly mother, my great-grandmother Rasha-Keila née Braz, set sail from Odessa to Jaffa on board the *Ruslan*, which was the Zionist *Mayflower* of the Third Aliyah, the postwar wave of immigration. By Hanukkah of that year they were living in the Bukharian Quarter of Jerusalem.

My grandfather Alexander and my grandmother Shlomit, with my father and his elder brother David, on the other hand, did not go to Palestine even though they were also ardent Zionists: the conditions of life there seemed too Asiatic to them, so they went to Vilna, the capital of Lithuania, and arrived there only in 1933, by which time, as it turned out, anti-Semitism in Vilna had grown to the point of violence against Jewish students. My Uncle David especially was a confirmed European, at a time when, it seems, no one else in Europe was, apart from the members of my family and other Jews like them. Everyone else turns out to have been Pan-Slavic, Pan-Germanic, or simply Latvian, Bulgarian, Irish, or Slovak patriots. The only Europeans in the whole of Europe in the 1920s and 1930s were the Jews. My father always used to say: In Czechoslovakia there are three nations, the Czechs, the Slovaks, and the Czecho-Slovaks, i.e., the Jews; in Yugoslavia there are Serbs, Croats, Slovenes, and Montenegrines, but, even there, there lives a group of unmistakable Yugoslavs; and even in Stalin's empire there are Russians, there are Ukrainians, and there are Uzbeks and Chukchis and Tatars, and among them are our brethren, the only real members of a *Soviet* nation.

Europe has now changed completely, and is full of Europeans from wall to wall. Incidentally, the graffiti in Europe have also changed from wall to wall. When my father was a young man in Vilna, every wall in Europe said, "Jews go home to Palestine." Fifty years later, when he went back to Europe on a visit, the walls all screamed, "Jews get out of Palestine."

Uncle Joseph spent many years writing his magnum opus on Jesus of Nazareth, in which he maintained—to the amazement of Christians and Jews alike—that Jesus was born and died a Jew and never intended to found a new religion. Moreover, he considered him to be "*the* Jewish moralist *par excellence.*" Ahad Ha'am pleaded with Klausner to delete this and other sentences, to avoid unleashing a colossal scandal in the Jewish world, as indeed happened both among Jews and among Christians when the book was published in Jerusalem in 1921: the ultras accused him of having "accepted bribes from the missionaries to sing the praises of That Man," while the Anglican missionaries in Jerusalem demanded that the archbishop dismiss Dr. Danby, the missionary who had translated *Jesus of Nazareth* into English, as it was a book that was "tainted with heresy, in that it portrays our Saviour as a kind of Reform rabbi, as a mortal, and as a Jew who has nothing at all to do with the Church." Uncle Joseph's international reputation was acquired mainly from this book and from the sequel that followed some years later, *From Jesus to Paul.*

Once Uncle Joseph said to me: "At your school, my dear, I imagine they teach you to loathe that tragic and wonderful Jew, and I only hope that they do not teach you to spit every time you go past his image or his cross. When you are older, my dear, read the New Testament, despite your teachers, and you will discover that this man was flesh of our flesh and bone of our bone, he was a kind of wonder-working Jewish pietist, and although he was indeed a dreamer, lacking any political understanding whatever, yet he has his place in the pantheon of great Jews, beside Baruch Spinoza, who was also excommunicated. Know this: those who condemn me are yesterday's Jews, narrow-minded, ineffectual worms. And you, my dear, to avoid ending up like them, must read good books—read, reread, and read again! And now, would you be kind enough to ask Mrs. Klausner, dear Aunt Zippora, where the skin cream is? The cream for my face? Please tell her, the old cream, because the new cream is not fit to feed to a dog. Do you know, my dear, the huge difference between the 'redeemer' in Gentile languages and our messiah? The messiah is simply someone who has been anointed with oil: every priest or king in the Bible is a messiah, and the Hebrew word 'messiah' is a thoroughly prosaic and everyday word, closely related to the word for face cream—unlike in the Gentile languages, where the messiah is called Redeemer and Savior. Or are you still too young to understand this lesson? If so, run along now and ask your aunt what I asked you to ask her. What was it? I've forgotten. Can you remember? If so, ask her to be kind enough to make me a glass of tea, for, as Rav Huna says in *Tractate Pesahim* of the Babylonian Talmud, 'Whatever the master of the house tells you to do, do, except leave,' which I interpret as referring to tea leaves. I am only joking, of course. Now run along, my dear, and do not steal any more of my time, as all the world does, having no thought for the minutes and hours that are my only treasure, and that are seeping away."

When he arrived in Jerusalem, Uncle Joseph served as secretary to the Hebrew Language Committee, before he was nominated to a chair of Hebrew literature in the Hebrew University of Jerusalem, which was opened in 1925. He had hoped and expected to be put in charge of the department of Jewish history, or at least of the teaching of the Second Temple period, but, as he said, "the grandees of the university, from the exalted heights of their Germanness, looked down on me." In the department of Hebrew literature Uncle Joseph felt, in his own words, like Napoleon on Elba: since he was prevented from moving the whole European continent forward, he shouldered the task of imposing some progressive and well-organized order on his little island of exile. Only after some twenty years was the chair of history for the Second Temple era (536 BCE to 70 AD) established, and Uncle Joseph was finally put in charge of this subject, without relinquishing his position as the head of the Hebrew literature department. "To absorb alien culture and to turn it into our own national and human flesh and blood," he wrote, "that is the ideal I have fought for most of my life, and I shall not abandon it to my dying day."

And elsewhere he wrote, with Napoleonic fervor, "If we aspire to be a people ruling over our own land, then our children must be made of *iron!*" He used to point to the two bronze busts on the sideboard in his living room, the raging, passionate Beethoven and Jabotinsky in his splendid uniform and his resolutely pursed lips, and say to his guests: "The spirit of the individual is just like that of the nation—both reach upward and both become unruly in the absence of a vision." He was fond of Churchillian expressions like "our flesh and blood," "human and national," "ideals," "I have battled for the best part of my life," "we shall not budge," "the few against the many," "alien to his contemporaries," "generations yet to come," and "to my dying breath."

In 1929 he was forced to flee when Talpiot was attacked by Arabs. His house, like Agnon's, was looted and burned, and his library, like Agnon's again, was badly damaged. "We must re-educate the younger generation," he had written in his book *When a Nation Fights for Its Freedom,* "we must clothe it in a spirit of heroism, a spirit of steadfast opposition. . . . Most of our teachers have still not overcome the submissive defeatist Diaspora spirit, whether of the European or the Arab Diaspora, that lurks within them."

Under Uncle Joseph's influence my grandfather and grandmother also became New Zionist Jabotinskyites, and my father actually grew close to the ideas of the Irgun—the paramilitary underground—and its political wing, and Menahem Begin's Herut Party, even though Begin actually aroused in such broad-minded, secular Odessan Jabotinskyites rather mixed feelings, mingled with a certain restrained condescension: his Polish shtetl origins and his excessive emotionalism may have made him appear somewhat plebeian or provincial, and however indisputably dedicated and stalwart a nationalist, he may have appeared not quite enough of a man of the world, not quite *charmant* enough, too lacking in poetry, in the ability to radiate the charisma, the grandeur of spirit, that touch of tragic loneliness, that they felt became a leader possessed of the qualities of a lion or an eagle. What was it Jabotinsky wrote about the relationship between Israel and the nations after the national revival: "Like a lion confronting other lions." Begin did not look much like a lion. Even my father, despite his name, was not a lion. He was a short-sighted, clumsy Jerusalem academic. He was not capable of becoming an underground fighter, but made his contribution to the struggle by composing occasional manifestos in English for the underground in which he denounced the hypocrisy of "perfidious Albion." These manifestos were printed on a clandestine printing press, and lithe young men used to go around the neighborhood at night posting them on every wall and even on the telegraph poles.

I, too, was a child of the underground; more than once I drove out the British with a flanking movement of my troops, sank His Majesty's fleet after a daring ambush at sea, kidnapped and court-martialed the High Commissioner and even the King of England himself, and with my own hands I raised the Hebrew flag (like those soldiers raising the Stars and Stripes at Iwo Jima on an American stamp) on the flagpole at Government House on the Hill of Evil Counsel. After driving them out, I would sign an agreement with the conquered, perfidious British to set up a front of the so-called civilized, enlightened nations against the waves of savage orientals with their ancient curly writing and their curved scimitars that threatened to burst out of the desert to kill, loot, and burn us with bloodcurdling guttural shrieks. I wanted to grow up to be like the good-looking, curly-haired, tight-lipped statue of David by Bernini, reproduced on the title page of Uncle Joseph's *When a Nation Fights for Its Freedom*. I wanted to be a strong, silent man with a slow, deep voice. Not like Uncle Joseph's reedy, slightly querulous voice. I didn't want my hands to be like his soft, old lady's hands.

He was a wonderfully frank man, my great-uncle Joseph, full of self-love and self-pity, vulnerable and craving recognition, brimming with child-like merriment, a happy man who always pretended to be miserable. With a kind of cheery contentment he loved to talk endlessly about his achievements, his discoveries, his insomnia, his detractors, his experiences, his books, articles, and lectures, all of which without exception had caused a "great stir in the world," his encounters, his work plans, his greatness, his importance, and his magnanimity.

He was at once a kind man and a selfish, spoiled one, with the sweetness of a baby and the arrogance of a wunderkind.

There, in Talpiot, which was intended to be a Jerusalemite replica of a Berlin suburb, a peaceful wooded hill where, in the fullness of time, red-tiled roofs would gleam among the foliage and villas would each provide a calm and comfortable home for a famous writer or renowned scholar, Uncle Joseph would go for a stroll sometimes in the evening breeze along the little street that was later to become Klausner Street, his thin arm entwined with the plump arm of Aunt Zippora, his mother, his wife, the child of his old age, and his right-hand person. They walked with tiny, delicate steps just past the house of the architect Kornberg, who occasionally took in paying guests of a polite and cultured kind, at the end of the cul-de-sac that was also the end of Talpiot, the end of Jerusalem, and the end of the settled land: beyond stretched the grim, barren hills of the Judaean desert. The Dead Sea sparkled in the distance like a platter of molten steel.

I can see them standing there, at the end of the world, on the edge of the wilderness, both very tender, like a pair of teddy bears, arm in arm, with the evening breeze of Jerusalem blowing above their heads, the rustle of pine trees, and a bitter smell of geraniums floating on the clear dry air, Uncle Joseph in a jacket (which he suggested should be called in Hebrew "jacobite") and tie, wearing slippers on his feet, his white hair bare to the breeze, and Auntie in a flowery, dark silk dress with a gray woolen wrap around her shoulders. The whole width of the horizon is occupied by the blue bulk of the hills of Moab beyond the Dead Sea; beneath them passes the old Roman Road that continues to the walls of the Old City, where before their eyes the domes of the mosques are turning gold, the crosses on the church towers and the crescents atop the minarets gleam in the glow of the setting sun. The walls themselves are turning gray and heavy, and beyond the Old City one can see Mount Scopus, crowned by the buildings of the university that is so dear to Uncle Joseph, and the Mount of Olives, on whose slopes Aunt Zippora will be buried, though his own wish to be buried there will not be granted because at the time of his death East Jerusalem will be under Jordanian rule.

The evening light intensifies the pink color of his babylike cheeks and his high brow. On his lips floats a distracted, slightly bewildered smile, as when a man knocks on the door of a house where he is a regular visitor and where he is used to being very warmly received, but when the door opens, a stranger suddenly looks out at him and recoils in surprise, as though asking, Who are you, sir, and why exactly are you here?

My father, my mother, and I would leave him and Aunt Zippora to stand there for a while longer; we quietly took our leave and made for the stop of the No. 7 bus, which would surely arrive in a few minutes from Ramat Rahel and Arnona, because the Sabbath was over. The No. 7 took us to the Jaffa Road, where we caught the 3B to Zephaniah Street, a five-minute walk from our home. Mother would say:

"He doesn't change. Always the same sermons, the same stories and anecdotes. He has repeated himself every Sabbath as long as I've known him."

Father would reply:

"Sometimes you are a little too critical. He's not a young man, and we all repeat ourselves sometimes. Even you."

Mischievously, I would add my parody of a line from Jabotinsky's "Beitar Hymn":

"With blood and *zhelezo* we'll raise a *gezho*." (Uncle Joseph could hold forth at length about how Jabotinsky chose his words. Apparently, Jabotinsky could not find a suitable rhyme in Hebrew for the word *geza*, "race," so he provisionally wrote the Russian word *zhelezo*, "iron." And so it came out: "With blood and *zhelezo* / We'll raise a race / Proud, generous, and tough," until his friend Baruch Krupnik came along and changed *zhelezo* to the Hebrew word *yeza*, "sweat": "With blood and sweat / We'll raise a race / Proud, generous, and tough."

My father would say:

"Really. There are some things one doesn't joke about."

And Mother said:

"Actually, I don't think there are. There shouldn't be."

At this Father would interpose:

"That's quite enough for one day. As for you, Amos, remember you're having a bath tonight. And washing your hair. No, I'm certainly not letting you off. Why should I? Can you give me one good reason to put off washing your hair? No? In that case you should never even try to start an argument, if you haven't got the slightest shadow of a reason. Remember this well from now on: 'I want' and 'I don't want' aren't reasons, they can only be defined as self-indulgence. And, incidentally, the word 'define' comes from a Latin word meaning 'end' or 'limit,' and every act of definition denotes tracing a limit or border dividing what is inside it from what is outside, in fact it may well be related to the word 'defense,' and the same image is mirrored in the Hebrew word from definition, derived as it is from the word for 'fence.' Now, cut your fingernails, please, and throw all the dirty clothes in the laundry basket. Your underwear, your shirt, your socks, the lot. Then into your pajamas, a cup of cocoa, and bed. And that's enough of you for today."

II

AND SOMETIMES, after we had taken our leave of Uncle Joseph and Aunt Zippora, if it wasn't too late, we would linger for twenty minutes or half an hour to call on the neighbors across the road. We would sneak, as it were, to the Agnons' house, without telling Uncle and Auntie where we were going, so as not to upset them. Sometimes we bumped into Mr. Agnon as he came out of the synagogue while we were on our way to the No. 7 bus stop, and he tugged at my father's arm and warned him that if he, that is to say my father, declined to visit the Agnon home and treat it to the radiance of the lady's face, it, that is to say the Agnon home, would be deprived of her radiance. In this way Agnon brought a smile to my mother's lips, and my father would accede to his invitation, saying: "Very well, but only for a few minutes, if Mr. Agnon will forgive us, we shall not stay long, we have to get back to Kerem Avraham, as the child is tired and has to get up for school in the morning."

"The child is not tired at all," I said.

And Mr. Agnon said:

"Hearken, pray, good Doctor: out of the mouths of babes and sucklings thou hast established strength."

The Agnons' house was set in a garden surrounded by cypresses, but to be on the safe side it was built with its back to the street, as though hiding its face in the garden. All you could see from the street were four or five slit windows. You entered through a gate concealed among the cypresses, walked along a paved path by the side of the house, climbed four or five steps, rang the bell at the white door, and waited for the door to be opened and for you to be invited to turn to your right and to climb the half-dark steps to Mr. Agnon's study, from which you reached a large paved rooftop terrace that looked out onto the Judaean desert and the hills of Moab, or else to turn left, to the small, rather cramped living room whose windows looked into the empty garden.

There was never full daylight in the Agnons' house, it was always in a kind of twilight with a faint smell of coffee and pastries, perhaps because we visited just before the end of the Sabbath, toward evening, and they would not switch on the electric light until three stars at least had appeared at the window. Or perhaps the electric light was on, but it was that yellow, miserly Jerusalem electricity, or Mr. Agnon was trying to economize, or there was a power failure and the only light came from a paraffin lamp. I can still remember the half darkness, in fact I can almost touch it; the grilles on the windows seemed to imprison and accentuate it. The reason for it is hard to tell now, and it may have been hard to tell even then. Whatever the reason, whenever Mr. Agnon stood up to pull out a book from the shelves that looked like a crowded congregation of worshippers dressed in shabby dark clothes, his form did not cast one shadow but two or three or even more. That is the way his image was engraved on my childhood memory and that is the way I remember him today: a man swaying in the half-light, with three or four separate shadows around him as he walked, in front of him, to his right, behind him, above him, or beneath his feet.

Occasionally Mrs. Agnon would make some remark in a sharp, commanding voice, and once Mr. Agnon said to her, with his head a little to one side and with a hint of a sarcastic smile: "Kindly permit me to be master in my own house so long as our guests are with us. Once they have left, you shall be the mistress." I remember this sentence clearly, not only because of the unexpected mischievousness it contained (which nowadays we would term subversive), but principally because of his use of the word "mistress," which is rare in Hebrew. I came across it again many years later when I read his story "The Mistress and the Pedlar." I have never come across anyone else apart from Mr. Agnon who used the word "mistress" to mean the lady of the house. Although perhaps in saying "mistress" he meant something slightly different.

It is hard to tell: after all, he was a man with three or more shadows.

My mother behaved toward Mr. Agnon, how should I say, as though she were on tiptoe all the time. Even when she was sitting down, she seemed to be sitting on tiptoe. Mr. Agnon himself hardly spoke to her, he spoke almost exclusively to my father, but as he spoke to my father, his glance seemed to rest for a moment on my mother's face. Strangely, on the rare occasions when he addressed a remark to my mother, his eyes seemed to avoid her and turn to me. Or to the window. Or maybe this is not how it was, but simply the way it is etched in my imagination: living memory, like ripples in water or the nervous quivering of a gazelle's skin in the moment before it takes flight, comes suddenly and trembles in a single instant in several rhythms or various focuses, before being frozen and immobilized into the memory of a memory.

In the spring of 1965, when my first book, *Where the Jackals Howl*, was published, I sent a copy with some trepidation to Agnon, with an inscription on the flyleaf. Agnon sent me a nice letter in reply, said some things about my book, and concluded as follows:

"What you wrote to me about your book conjured up the image of your late mother. I recall her once some fifteen or sixteen years ago bringing me a book from your father. You may have been with her. She stood upon the doorstep, and her words were few. But her face remained with me in all its grace and innocence/honesty for many days. Yours sincerely, S.Y. Agnon."

My father, who at Agnon's request translated the article "Buczacz" for him from a Polish encyclopedia when Agnon was writing *A City and the Fullness Thereof,* would twist his lips as he defined him as a "Diaspora writer": his stories lack wings, he said, they have no tragic depth, there is not even any healthy laughter but only wisecracks and sarcasm. And if he does have some beautiful descriptions here and there, he does not rest or put down his pen until he has drowned them in pools of verbose buffoonery and Galician cleverness. I have the impression my father saw Agnon's stories as an extension of Yiddish literature, and he was not fond of Yiddish literature. In keeping with his temperament of a rationalistic Lithuanian *Misnaged,* he loathed magic, the supernatural, and excessive emotionalism, anything clad in foggy romanticism or mystery, anything intended to make the senses whirl or to blinker reason—until the last years of his life, when his taste changed. Admittedly, just as on the death certificate of my grandmother Shlomit, the one who died of an excess of cleanliness, it is recorded simply that she died of a heart attack, so my father's curriculum vitae states merely that his last research was on an unknown manuscript of Y. L. Peretz. These are the facts. What the truth is I do not know, because I hardly ever spoke to my father about the truth. He hardly ever talked to me about his childhood, his loves, love in general, his parents, his brother's death, his own illness, his suffering, or suffering in general. We never even talked about my mother's death. Not a word. I did not make it easy for him either, and I never wanted to start a conversation that might lead to who knew what revelations. If I started to write down here all the things we did not talk about, my father and I, I could fill two books. My father left me a great deal of work to do, and I'm still working.

My mother used to say about Agnon:

"That man sees and understands a lot."

And once she said:

"He may not be such a good man, but at least he knows bad from good, and he also knows we don't have much choice."

She used to read and reread the stories in the collection *At the Handles of the Lock* almost every winter. Perhaps she found an echo there of her own sadness and loneliness. I too sometimes reread the words of Tirzah Mazal, née Minz, at the beginning of "In the Prime of Her Life":

In the prime of her life my mother died. Some one and thirty years of age my mother was at her death. Few and evil were the days of the years of her life. All the day she sat at home, and she never went out of the house. . . . Silent stood our house in its sorrow; its doors opened not to a stranger. Upon her bed my mother lay, and her words were few.

The words are almost the same as those that Agnon wrote to me about my mother: "She stood upon the doorstep, and her words were few."

As for me, when many years later I wrote an essay called "Who Has Come?" about the opening of Agnon's "In the Prime of Her Life," I dwelled on the apparently tautological sentence "All the day she sat at home, and she never went out of the house."

My mother did not sit at home all the day. She went out of the house a fair amount. But the days of the years of her life, too, were few and evil.

"The years of her life?" Sometimes I hear in these words the duality of my mother's life, and that of Lea, the mother of Tirzah, and that of Tirzah Mazal, née Minz. As if they too cast more than one shadow on the wall.

Some years later, when the General Assembly of Kibbutz Hulda sent me to the university to study literature, because the kibbutz school needed a literature teacher, I summoned up my courage and rang Mr. Agnon's doorbell one day (or in Agnon's language: "I took my heart and went to him").

"But Agnon is not at home," Mrs. Agnon said politely but angrily, the way she answered the throngs of brigands and highwaymen who came to rob her husband of his precious time. Mistress Agnon was not exactly lying to me: Mr. Agnon was indeed not at home, he was out at the back of the house, in the garden, whence he suddenly emerged, wearing slippers and a sleeveless pullover, greeted me, and then asked suspiciously, But who are you, sir? I gave my name and those of my parents, at which, as we stood in the doorway of his house (Mrs. Agnon having disappeared indoors without a word), Mr. Agnon remembered what wagging tongues had said in Jerusalem some years before, and placing his hand on my shoulder he said to me, "Aren't you the child who, having been left an orphan by his poor mother and distanced himself from his father, went off to live the life of the kibbutz? Are you not he who in his youth was reprimanded by his parents in this very house, because he used to pick the raisins off the cake?" (I did not remember this, nor did I believe him about the raisin picking, but I chose not to contradict him.) Mr. Agnon invited me in and questioned me for a while about my doings in the kibbutz, my studies (And what are they reading of mine in the university these days? And which of my books do you prefer?), and also inquired whom I had married and where my wife's family came from, and when I told him that on her father's side she was descended from the seventeenth-century Talmudist and kabbalist Isaiah Horowitz, his eyes lit up and he told me two or three tales, by which time his patience was exhausted and it was evident that he was looking for a way of getting rid of me, but I summoned up my courage, even though I was sitting there on tiptoe, precisely as my mother had done before me, and told him what my problem was.

I had come because Professor Gershom Shaked had given his first-year students in Hebrew literature the task of comparing the stories set in Jaffa by Brenner and by Agnon, and I had read the stories and also everything I could find in the library about their friendship in Jaffa in the days of the Second Aliyah, and I was amazed that two such different men could have become friends. Yosef Hayyim Brenner was a bitter, moody, thickset, sloppy, irascible Russian Jew, a Dostoevskian soul constantly oscillating between enthusiasm and depression, between compassion and rage, a figure who at that time was already installed at the center of modern Hebrew literature and at the heart of the pioneering movement, while Agnon was then (only) a shy young Galician, several years Brenner's junior and still almost a literary virgin, a pioneer turned clerk, a refined, discriminating Talmud student, a natty dresser and a careful, precise writer, a thin, dreamy, yet sarcastic young man: what on earth could have drawn them so close to each other in the Jaffa of the days of the Second Aliyah, before the outbreak of the First World War, that they were almost like a pair of lovers? Today I think that I can guess something of the answer, but that day in Agnon's house, innocent as I was, I explained to my host the task I had been set, and innocently inquired if he would tell me the secret of his closeness to Brenner.

Mr. Agnon screwed up his eyes and looked at me, or rather scrutinized me, for a while with a sidelong glance, with pleasure, and a slight smile, the sort of smile—I later understood—that a butterfly catcher might smile on spotting a cute little butterfly. When he had finished eyeing me, he said:

"Between Yosef Hayyim, may God avenge his death, and me in those days there was a closeness founded on a shared love."

I pricked up my ears, in the belief that I was about to be told a secret to end all secrets, that I was about to learn of some spicy, concealed love story on which I could publish a sensational article and make myself a household name overnight in the world of Hebrew literary research.

"And who was that shared love?" I asked with youthful innocence and a pounding heart.

"That is a strict secret," Mr. Agnon smiled, not to me but to himself, and almost winked to himself as he smiled, "yes, a strict secret, that I shall reveal to you only if you give me your word never to tell another living soul."

I was so excited that I lost my voice, fool that I was, and could only mouth a promise.

"Well then, strictly between ourselves I can tell you that when we were living in Jaffa in those days, Yosef Hayyim and I were both madly in love with Samuel Yosef Agnon."

Yes, indeed: Agnonic irony, a self-mocking irony that bit its owner at the same time as it bit his simple visitor, who had come to tug at his host's sleeve. And yet there was also a grain of truth hidden here, a vague hint of the secret of the attraction of a very physical, passionate man to a thin, spoiled youth, and also of the refined Galician youth to the venerated, fiery man who might take him under his fatherly wing, or offer him an elder brother's shoulder.

Yet it was actually not a shared love but a shared hatred that unites Agnon's stories to Brenner's. Everything that was false, rhetorical, or swollen by self-importance in the world of the Second Aliyah (the wave of immigration that ended with World War I), everything mendacious or self-glorifying in the Zionist reality, all the cozy, sanctimonious, bourgeois self-indulgence in Jewish life at that time, was loathed in equal measure by Agnon as by Brenner. Brenner in his writing smashed them with the hammer of his wrath, while Agnon pricked the lies and pretenses with his sharp irony and released the fetid hot air that inflated them.

Nonetheless, in Brenner's Jaffa as in Agnon's, among the throngs of shams and prattlers there shine dimly the occasional figures of a few simple men of truth.

Agnon himself was an observant Jew who kept the Sabbath and wore a skullcap; he was, literally, a God-fearing man: in Hebrew, "fear" and "faith" are synonyms. There are corners in Agnon's stories where, in an indirect, cleverly camouflaged way, the fear of God is portrayed as a terrible dread of God: Agnon believes in God and fears him, but he does not love him. "I am an easygoing sort of a man," says Daniel Bach in *A Guest for the Night*, "and I do not believe that the Almighty desires the good of his creatures." This is a paradoxical, tragic, and even desperate theological position that Agnon never expressed discursively but allowed to be voiced by secondary characters in his works and to be implied by what befalls his heroes. When I wrote a book on Agnon, *The Silence of Heaven: Agnon's Fear of God*, exploring this theme, dozens of religious Jews, most of them from the ultra-Orthodox sector, including youngsters and women and even religious teachers and functionaries, wrote personal letters to me. Some of these letters were veritable confessions. They told me, in their various ways, that they could see in their own souls what I had seen in Agnon. But what I had seen in Agnon's writings I had also glimpsed, for a moment or two, in Mr. Agnon himself, in that sardonic cynicism of his that verged almost on desperate, jesting nihilism. "The Lord will no doubt have mercy on me," he said once, with reference to one of his constant complaints about the bus service, "and if the Lord does not have mercy on me, maybe the Neighborhood Council will, but I fear that the bus cooperative is stronger than both."

I made the pilgrimage to Talpiot two or three more times during the two years I studied at the university in Jerusalem. My first stories were being published then in the weekend supplement of *Davar* and in the quarterly *Keshet*, and I planned to leave them with Mr. Agnon to hear what he thought of them; but Mr. Agnon apologized, saying "I regret that I do not feel up to reading these days," and asked me to bring them back another day. Another day, then, I returned, empty-handed but carrying on my belly, like an embarrassing pregnancy, the number of *Keshet* containing my story. In the end I lacked the courage to give birth there, I was afraid of making a nuisance of myself, and I left his house as I had arrived, with a big belly. Or a bulging sweater. It was only some years later, when the stories were collected in a book (*Where the Jackals Howl* in 1965), that I summoned up the courage to send it to him. For three days and three nights I danced around the kibbutz, drunk with joy, silently singing and roaring aloud with happiness, inwardly roaring and weeping, after receiving Mr. Agnon's nice letter, in which he wrote, *inter alia*, ". . . and when we meet, I shall tell you *viva voce* more than I have written here. During Passover I shall read the rest of the stories, God willing, because I enjoy stories like yours where the heroes appear in the full reality of their being."

Once, when I was at the university, an article appeared in a foreign journal by one of the leading lights in comparative literature (perhaps it was by the Swiss Emil Steiger?), who gave it as his opinion that the three most important Central European writers of the first half of the twentieth century were Thomas Mann, Robert Musil, and S. Y. Agnon. The article was written several years before Agnon won the Nobel Prize, and I was so excited that I stole the journal from the reading room (there were no photocopiers at the university in those days) and hurried with it to Talpiot to give Agnon the pleasure of reading it. And he was indeed pleased, so much so that he wolfed down the whole article as he stood on the doorstep of his house, in a single breath, before so much as asking me in; after reading it, rereading it, and perhaps even licking his lips, he gave me that look he sometimes gave me and asked innocently: "Do you also think Thomas Mann is such an important writer?"

One night, years later, I missed the last bus back from Rehovot to the kibbutz at Hulda and had to take a taxi. All day long the radio had been talking about the Nobel Prize that had been shared between Agnon and the poet Nellie Sachs, and the taxi driver asked me if I'd ever heard of a writer called, what was it, Egnon. "Think about it," he said in amazement. "We've never heard of him before, and suddenly he gets us into the world finals. Problem is, he ends up tying with some woman."

For several years I endeavored to free myself from Agnon's shadow. I struggled to distance my writing from his influence, his dense, ornamented, sometimes Philistine language, his measured rhythms, a certain midrashic self-satisfaction, a beat of Yiddish tunes, juicy ripples of Hasidic tales. I had to liberate myself from the influence of his sarcasm and wit, his baroque symbolism, his enigmatic labyrinthine games, his double meanings, and his complicated, erudite literary games.

Despite all my efforts to free myself from him, what I have learned from Agnon no doubt still resonates in my writing.

What is it, in fact, that I learned from him?

Perhaps this. To cast more than one shadow. Not to pick the raisins from the cake. To rein in and polish pain. And one other thing, that my grandmother used to say in a sharper way than I have found it expressed by Agnon: "If you have no more tears left to weep, then don't weep. Laugh."

12

SOMETIMES I was left with my grandparents for the night. My grandmother used to point suddenly at a piece of furniture or an item of clothing or a person and say to me:

"It's so ugly, it's almost beautiful."

Sometimes she said:

"He's become so clever, he can't understand anything anymore."

Or:

"It hurts so much, it almost makes me laugh."

All day long she hummed tunes to herself that she had brought with her from places where she lived apparently without fear of germs and without the rudeness that she complained also infected everything here.

"Like animals," she would suddenly hiss disgustedly, for no visible reason, with no provocation or connection, without bothering to explain whom she was comparing to animals. Even when I sat next to her on a park bench in the evening, and there was no one in the park, and a slight breeze gently touched the tips of the leaves or perhaps made them tremble without really touching them with its invisible fingertips, Grandma could suddenly erupt, quivering with shocked loathing:

"Really! How could they! Worse than animals!"

A moment later she was humming to herself gentle tunes that were unfamiliar to me.

She was always humming, in the kitchen, in front of the mirror, on her deck chair on the veranda, even in the night.

Sometimes, after I had had my bath and brushed my teeth and cleaned out my ears with an orange stick with its tip wrapped in cotton wool, I was put to bed next to her, in her wide bed (the double bed that Grandpa had abandoned, or been evicted from, before I was born).

Grandma read me a story or two, stroked my cheek, kissed my forehead, and immediately rubbed it with a little handkerchief moistened with perfume, which she always kept in her left sleeve and which she used to wipe away or squash germs, and then she turned out the light. Even then she went on humming in the dark, or rather she expelled from inside her a distant, dreamy voice, a chestnut-colored voice, a pleasant, dark voice that was gradually refined into an echo, a color, a scent, a gentle roughness, a brown warmth, lukewarm amniotic fluid. All night long.

But all these nocturnal delights she made you scrub off furiously first thing in the morning, even before your cup of cocoa without the skin. I would wake up in her bed to the sound of Grandpa's carpet beater as he fought his regular dawn battle with the bedding.

Before you even opened your eyes, there was a steaming hot bath waiting for you, smelling like a medical clinic because of the antiseptic solution that had been added to the water. On the edge of the bath a toothbrush was laid out, with a curly white worm of Ivory toothpaste already lying along the bristles. Your duty was to immerse yourself, soap yourself all over and rub yourself with the loofah, and rinse yourself, and then Grandma came, got you up on your knees in the bathtub, held you firmly by the arm, and scrubbed you all over, from head to toe and back again, with the dreaded brush, reminiscent of the iron combs that the wicked Romans used to tear the flesh of Rabbi Akiva and the other martyrs of the Bar Kochba Revolt, until your skin was pink like raw flesh, and then Grandma told you to close your eyes tight as tight, while she shampooed and pummeled your head and scratched your scalp with her sharp nails like Job scraping himself with a potsherd, and all the while she explained to you in her brown, pleasant voice about the filth and mire that the body's glands secrete while you sleep, such as sticky sweat and all sorts of fatty discharges and flakes of skin and fallen hairs and millions of dead cells and various kinds of slimy secretions you'd better not know about, and while you were fast asleep all this refuse and effluent smeared itself all over your body and mixed itself up together and invited, yes, positively invited, bacteria and bacilli and viruses too to come and swarm all over you, not to mention all the things that science has not yet discovered, things that cannot be seen even with the most powerful microscope, but even if they can't be seen, they crawl all over your body all night with trillions of horrible hairy little legs, just like a cockroach's but so tiny you can't see them, even scientists can't see them yet, and on these legs that are covered with disgusting bristles they creep back inside our bodies through the nose and the mouth and through I don't need to tell you where else they crawl in through, especially when people never wash themselves there in those not nice places they just wipe, but wiping isn't cleaning, on the contrary, it just spreads the filthy secretions into the millions of tiny holes we have all over our skin, and it all gets more and more filthy and disgusting, especially when the internal filth that the body is constantly excreting, day and night, gets mixed up with the external filth that comes from touching unhygienic things that have been handled by who knows whom before you, like coins or newspapers or handrails or door-knobs or even bought food, after all who can tell who has sneezed over what you're touching, or even, excuse me, wiped their nose or even dripped from their nose precisely on those sweet wrappers that you pick up in the street and put straight on the bed where people sleep, not to mention those corks you pick straight out of the garbage cans, and that corn on the cob your mother, God preserve her, buys straight from the hand of that man who may not even have washed and dried his hands after he has excuse me, and how can we be so sure that he's a healthy man? That he hasn't got TB or cholera, or typhus or jaundice or dysentery? Or an abscess or enteritis or eczema or psoriasis or impetigo or a boil? He might not even be Jewish. Have you any idea how many diseases there are here? How many Levantine plagues? And I'm only talking about known diseases, not the ones that are not known yet and that medical science doesn't recognize yet, not a day goes by after all here in the Levant that people don't die like flies from some parasite or bacillus or microbe, or from all kinds of microscopic worms that the doctors can't even identify especially here in this country where it's so hot and full of flies, mosquitoes, moths, ants, cockroaches, midges, and who knows what else, and people here perspire all the time and they are always touching and rubbing each other's inflammations and discharges and sweat and all their bodily fluids, better at your age you shouldn't know from all these foul fluids, and anyone can easily wet someone else so the other one doesn't even feel what's stuck to him in all the crush there is here, a handshake is enough to transmit all sorts of plagues, and even without touching, just by breathing the air that someone else has breathed into his lungs before you with all the germs and bacilli of ring-worm and trachoma and bilharzia. And the sanitation here is not at all

European, and, as for hygiene, half the people here have never even heard of it, and the air is full of all kinds of Asiatic insects and revolting winged reptiles that come here straight from the Arab villages or even from Africa, and who knows what strange diseases and inflammations and discharges they bring with them all the time, the Levant here is full of germs. Now you dry yourself very well all on your own like a big boy, don't leave anywhere damp, and then put some talcum powder all by yourself in your you-know-where, and in your other you-know-where, and all around about, and I want you to rub some Velveta cream from this tube all over your neck, and then get dressed in the clothes I'm putting out for you here, which are the clothes that your mother, God preserve her, has prepared for you only I've gone over them with a hot iron that disinfects and kills anything that might be breeding there better than the laundering does, and then come to me in the kitchen, with your hair nicely combed, and you'll get a nice cup of cocoa from me and then you'll have your breakfast.

As she left the bathroom, she would mutter to herself, not angrily but with a kind of deep sadness:

"Like animals. Or worse."

A door with a pane of frosted glass decorated with geometrical flower shapes separated Grandma's bedroom from the little cubicle that was known as "Grandpa Alexander's study." From here Grandpa had his own private way out into the veranda and from there into the garden and finally outside, to the city, to freedom.

In one corner of this tiny room stood the sofa from Odessa, as narrow and hard as a plank, on which Grandpa slept at night. Underneath this sofa, like recruits on parade, seven or eight pairs of shoes stood in a neat row, all black and shiny; just like Grandma Shlomit's collection of hats, in green and brown and maroon, that she guarded as her prize possession in a round hatbox, so Grandpa Alexander liked to be in command of a whole fleet of shoes that he polished until they shone like crystal, some hard and thick-soled, some round-toed or pointed, some brogued, some fastened with laces, some with straps, and others with buckles.

Opposite the sofa stood his small desk, always neat and tidy, with an inkwell and an olivewood blotter. The blotter always looked to me like a tank or a thick-funneled boat sailing toward a jetty formed by a trio of bright silvery containers, one full of paper clips, the next of thumbtacks, while in the third, like a nest of vipers, the rubber bands coiled and swarmed. There was a rectangular metal nest of trays on the desk, one for incoming mail, one for outgoing mail, a third for newspaper cuttings, another for documents from the municipality and the bank, and yet another for correspondence with the Herut Movement, Jerusalem Branch. There was also an olivewood box full of stamps of different values, with separate compartments for express, registered, and airmail stickers. And there was a container for envelopes and another for postcards, and behind them a revolving silvery stand in the form of the Eiffel Tower that contained an assortment of pens and pencils in different colors, including a wonderful pencil with a point at either end, one red and the other blue.

In one corner of Grandpa's desk, next to the files of documents, there stood a tall dark bottle of foreign liqueur and three or four green goblets that looked like narrow-waisted women. Grandpa loved beauty and hated everything ugly, and he liked to fortify his passionate, lonely heart occasionally with a little sip of cherry brandy, on his own. The world did not understand him. His wife did not understand him. Nobody really understood him. His heart always longed for what was noble, but everyone conspired to clip his wings: his wife, his friends, his business partners, they were all part of a plot to force him to plunge into two score and nine different kinds of breadwinning, hygiene, tidying up, business dealings, and a thousand petty nuisances and obligations. He was an even-tempered man, irascible but easily calmed. Whenever he saw some duty on the ground, whether a family or public or moral duty, he always bent down, picked it up, and shouldered it. But then he would sigh and complain about the weight of his burden and say that everyone, especially Grandma, took advantage of his good nature and loaded him with a thousand and one tasks that stifled his poetic spark and used him like an errand boy.

During the day, Grandpa Alexander worked as a commercial representative and salesman of garments, being the Jerusalem agent of the Lodzia textile factory and a number of other well-respected firms. In a large number of cases piled up on shelves that ran the full height of the wall of his study, he kept a colorful collection of samples of cloths, shirts, and trousers in tricot and gabardine, socks, and all kinds of towels, napkins, and curtains. I was allowed to use these sample cases, provided I did not open them, to construct towers, forts, and defensive walls. Grandpa sat on his chair with his back to the desk, his legs stuck out in front of him, and his pink face, generally beaming with kindness and contentment, smiling happily at me as though the tower of cases and boxes that was growing under my hands would soon put the pyramids, the hanging gardens of Babylon, and the great wall of China in the shade. It was Grandpa Alexander who told me about the great wall, the pyramids, the hanging gardens, and the other wonders of the human spirit, such as the Parthenon and the Coliseum, the Suez and Panama Canals, the Empire State Building, the churches of the Kremlin, the Venetian canals, the Arc de Triomphe, and the Eiffel Tower.

At night, in the solitude of his study, at his desk, over a goblet of cherry brandy, Grandpa Alexander was a sentimental poet who cast over an alien world poems of love, delight, enthusiasm, and longing, all in Russian. His good friend Joseph Kohen-Tsedek translated them into Hebrew. Here is an example:

> After many years of slumber
> Gracious lord my corpse upraise;
> Lovingly my eyelids open,
> Let me live for three more days.
> From northern Dan down to Beersheva
> Let me tour my fatherland,
> Let me roam each hill and valley
> And in beauty see it stand:
> Every man shall dwell in safety
> Each beneath his fig and vine,
> As the earth bestows its bounty,
> Full of joy this land of mine . . .

He wrote poems of praise, celebrating such figures as Vladimir Jabotinsky, Menachem Begin, and his famous brother, my great-uncle Joseph, and also poems of wrath against the Germans, the Arabs, the British, and all the other Jew haters. Among all these I also found three or four poems of loneliness and sorrow with lines like: "Such gloomy thoughts surround me / In the evening of my days: / Farewell to youthful vigor / And to sunshine's hopeful rays— / Now icy winter stays . . ."

But usually it was not icy winter that beset him: he was a nationalist, a patriot, a lover of armies, victories, and conquests, a passionate,
innocent-minded hawk who believed that if only we Jews girded ourselves with courage, boldness, iron resolve, etc., if only we finally rose up
and stopped worrying about the Gentiles, we could defeat all our foes
and establish the Kingdom of David from the Nile to the great river, the
Euphrates, and the whole cruel, wicked Gentile world would come and
bow down before us. He had a weakness for everything grand, powerful, and gleaming—military uniforms, brass bugles, banners and lances
glinting in the sun, royal palaces and coats of arms. He was a child of
the nineteenth century, even if he did live long enough to see three-
quarters of the twentieth.

I remember him dressed in a light-cream flannel suit, or a sharply
creased pinstripe suit under which he sometimes sported a piqué vest
with a fine silver chain that hugged him and led into a pocket of the said
vest. On his head he wore a loosely woven straw hat in summer, and in
winter a Borsalino with a dark silk band. He was terribly irascible, liable
to erupt suddenly in billows of resounding thunder, but he would very
quickly brighten up, forgive, apologize, be contrite, as though his anger
was just a sort of bad coughing fit. You could always tell the state of his
temper from a distance, because his face changed color like a traffic
light: pink-white-red and back to pink. Most of the time his cheeks were
a contented pink, but when he was offended they would turn white, and
when he was angry they went red, but after a short time they resumed
their pink hue that informed the whole world that the thunderstorm
had ended, the winter was over, the flowers had appeared on the earth,
and Grandpa's habitual cheeriness was beaming and radiating from him
again after a short interruption; and in an instant he would have forgotten who or what it was that had angered him, and what all the commotion had been about, like a child who cries for a moment and at once
calms down, smiles, and goes back to playing happily.

13

RAV ALEXANDER ZISKIND of Horodno (at that time in Russia, but later
Poland, Belarus . . .), who died in 1794, is known in rabbinic tradition
as YVShH, after the initials of his best-known work, *Yesod Ve-Shoresh*

Ha-'Avodah ("The Foundation and Root of Worship"). He was a mystic, kabbalist, ascetic, the author of several influential ethical writings. It was said of him that "He spent his life shut away in a small room studying Torah; he never kissed or held his children and never had any conversation with them that was not directed to heavenly things." His wife ran the household and brought up the children on her own. Nevertheless, this outstanding ascetic taught that one should "worship the Creator with great joy and fervor." (Rabbi Nahman of Bratslav said of him that he was a hasid *avant la lettre.*") But neither joy nor fervor prevented Rabbi Alexander Ziskind from leaving instructions in his will that after his death "the Burial Society shall perform on my corpse the four death penalties entrusted to the Sanhedrin," until all his limbs were crushed. For example: "Let them raise me to the height of the ceiling and throw me violently to the ground with no intervening sheet or straw, and let them repeat this seven times, and I solemnly admonish the Burial Society under pain of excommunication to afflict me with these seven deaths, and not to spare my humiliation, for my humiliation is my honor, that I may be released somewhat from the great Judgment on high." All this in atonement for sins or for purification, "for the spirit or soul of Alexander Ziskind who was born of the woman Rebecca." It is also known about him that he wandered through the German towns collecting money to settle Jews in the Holy Land, and he was even imprisoned for this. His descendants bear the family name Braz, which is an abbreviation for "Born of Rabbi Alexander Ziskind."

His son, Rav Yossele Braz, one of those whom their father never kissed or held, was considered a consummate Righteous Man who studied the Torah all his days and never left the house of study on a weekday even to sleep: he would permit himself to doze off as he sat, with his head on his arms and his arms on the desk, for four hours each night, with a lighted candle held between his fingers so that when it burned down, the flame would wake him. Even his snatched meals were brought to him in the house of study, which he left only at the onset of Sabbath and to which he returned as soon as the Sabbath was over. He was an ascetic like his father. His wife kept a draper's shop, and she kept him and his offspring until the day he died and beyond, as his mother too had done in her day, because Rav Yossele's humility did not allow him to assume the position of a rabbi, but he taught Torah for nothing to the children of the poor. Nor did he leave any books behind him, because he considered himself inadequate to say anything new that his predecessors had not said before him.

Rav Yossele's son, Rav Alexander Ziskind Braz (my grandfather Alexander's grandfather), was a successful businessman who dealt in grain, linen, and even hogs' bristles; he traded as far afield as Königsberg and Leipzig. He was a scrupulously observant Jew, but so far as is known he distanced himself from his father's and grandfather's zealotry: he did not turn his back on the world, did not live by the sweat of his wife's brow, and did not hate the Zeitgeist and the Enlightenment. He allowed his children to learn Russian and German and a little "alien wisdom," and even encouraged his daughter, Rasha-Keile Braz, to study, to read, and to be an educated woman. He certainly did not admonish the burial society with dire threats to crush his body after his death.

Menahem Mendel Braz, son of Alexander Ziskind, grandson of Rav Yossele, great-grandson of Rabbi Alexander Ziskind the author of the *Yesod Ve-Shoresh Ha-'Avodah,* settled in the early 1880s in Odessa where, together with his wife Perla, he owned and ran a small glass factory. Previously, in his youth, he had worked as a government clerk back in Königsberg. Menahem Braz was a well-to-do, good-looking bon vivant, and a strong-willed nonconformist even by the very tolerant standards of late-nineteenth-century Jewish Odessa. An undisguised atheist and well-known hedonist, he abhorred both religion and religious fanatics with the same whole-hearted devotion with which his grandfather and great-grandfather had insisted on observing every jot and tittle of the Law. Menahem Braz was a freethinker to the point of exhibitionism: he smoked publicly on the Sabbath, consumed forbidden foods with gay abandon, and pursued pleasure out of a gloomy vision of the brevity of human life and a passionate denial of the afterlife and divine judgment. This admirer of Epicurus and Voltaire believed that a man should reach out and help himself to whatever life put in his way and give himself over to the unrestrained enjoyment of whatever his heart desired, provided that in doing so he inflicted neither injury, injustice, nor suffering on others. His sister, Rasha-Keila, that educated daughter of Rav Alexander Ziskind Braz, was, on the other hand, affianced to a simple Jew back in the village of Olkieniki in Lithuania (not far from Vilna), whose name was Yehuda Leib Klausner, the son of Ezekiel Klausner, a tenant farmer.*

The Klausners of Olkieniki, unlike their learned cousins from the nearby town of Trakai, were mostly simple village Jews, stubborn and naive. Ezekiel Klausner had raised cattle and sheep and grown fruit and vegetables, first in a village named Popishuk (or Papishki), and later in another village called Rudnik, and finally in Olkieniki itself. All three villages were near Vilna. Yehuda Leib, like his father Ezekiel before him, had learned a little Torah and Talmud from a village teacher, and observed the commandments, although he loathed exegetical subtleties. He loved the outdoor life and hated being cooped up indoors.

After trying his hand at dealing in agricultural produce and failing because other traders soon discovered and took advantage of his naïveté and edged him out of the market, Yehuda Leib used the rest of his money to buy a horse and cart and cheerfully carried passengers and goods from village to village. He was an easygoing, gentle-natured carter, who was contented with his lot and enjoyed good food, singing table songs on Sabbaths and festivals, and a drop of schnapps on winter nights; he never beat his horse or recoiled from danger. He liked traveling alone, at a slow, relaxed pace, his cart weighed down with timber or sacks of grain through the dark forests, over empty plains, through snowstorms, and across the thin layer of ice that covered the river in winter. Once (so Grandpa Alexander loved to relate over and over again on winter evenings) the ice broke under the weight of his cart, and Yehuda Leib jumped into the icy water, grabbed the horse's bridle with his strong hands, and pulled his horse and cart to safety.

Rasha-Keila Braz bore three sons and three daughters to her husband the carter. But in 1884 she fell seriously ill, and the Klausners decided to

---

*Names run in families. My elder daughter is named Fania after my mother, Fania. My son is Daniel Yehuda Arie, after Daniel Klausner, my first cousin, who was born the year before me and was murdered together with his parents, David and Malka, by Germans in Vilna when he was three, and also after my father Yehuda Arieh Klausner, who in turn was named after his grandfather Yehuda Leib Klausner from the village of Olkieniki in Lithuania, the son of Rav Ezekiel, the son of Rav Kadish, the son of Rav Gedaliah Klausner-Olkienicki, a descendant of Rabbi Abraham Klausner the author of the *Sefer Haminhagim* ("Book of Customs"), who lived in Vienna in the late fourteenth century. My brother David was named after Uncle David, my father's brother, the one who was murdered by Germans in Vilna. Three of my grandchildren bear the name of one of their grandparents (Maccabi Salzberger, Lote Salzberger, Riva Zuckerman). And so it goes.

leave their out-of-the-way village in Lithuania and move hundreds of miles to Odessa, where Rasha-Keila came from and where her affluent brother lived: Menahem Mendel Braz would surely take care of them and see that his sick sister was treated by the best physicians.

At the time the Klausners settled in Odessa, in 1885, their eldest son, my great-uncle Joseph, was an infant prodigy of eleven, compulsively hard-working, a lover of Hebrew and thirsty for knowledge. He seemed to take after his cousins, the sharp-minded Klausners of Trakai, rather than his ancestors the farmers and carters from Olkieniki. His uncle, the Epicurean, Voltairian Menahem Braz, declared that little Joseph was destined for great things and supported his studies. His brother Alexander Ziskind, on the other hand, who was only four years old or so when they moved to Odessa, was a somewhat unruly and emotional child, who soon displayed an affinity with his father and grandfather, the rustic Klausners. He was not drawn to studying, and from an early age displayed a fondness for staying out of doors for extended periods, observing people's behavior, sniffing and feeling the world, being alone in the meadows and woods, and dreaming dreams. His liveliness, generosity, and kindness endeared him to all whom he met. He was universally known as Zusia or Zissel. And that was Grandpa Alexander.

There was also their younger brother, my great-uncle Bezalel, and three sisters, Sofia, Anna, and Daria, none of whom ever made it to Israel. So far as I have been able to ascertain, after the Russian Revolution Sofia was a literature teacher and later the headmistress of a school in Leningrad. Anna died before World War II, while Daria, or Dvora, and her husband Misha attempted to escape to Palestine after the Revolution but "got stuck" in Kiev because Daria was pregnant.*

Despite the help of their prosperous uncle Menahem and of other Odessa relations on the Braz side of the family, the Klausners fell on hard times soon after arriving in the city. The carter, Yehuda Leib, a strong, patient man who enjoyed life and loved joking, faded away after having to invest what was left of his savings in the purchase of a small, airless

---

*Daria's daughter, Yvetta Radovskaya, a woman in her eighties, still corresponds with me. Aunt Yvetta, my father's cousin, left St. Petersburg after the collapse of the Soviet Union and settled in Cleveland, Ohio. Her only child, Marina, who was about my age, died in St. Petersburg in the prime of life. Nikita, Marina's only son, who is my children's generation, went to America with his grandmother but changed his mind after a short while and returned to Russia or Ukraine, where he married and now works as a country vet. His daughters are the same generation as my grandchildren.

grocery shop from which he and his family eked out a precarious living. He longed for the open plains, the forests, the snowfields, his horse and cart, the inns and the river that he had left behind in Lithuania. After a few years he fell ill and soon died in his mean little shop when he was only fifty-seven. His widow, Rasha-Keila, for whose sake they had come all that way, lived on for twenty-five years after his death. She eventually died in the Bukharian Quarter of Jerusalem in 1928.

While great-uncle Joseph was pursuing his brilliant student career in Odessa and later in Heidelberg, Grandpa Alexander left school at fifteen and turned his hand to a variety of petty trading ventures, buying something here and selling something there, scribbling passionate poems in Russian by night, casting covetous eyes into shop windows and at the mountains of melons, grapes, and watermelons, as well as the sensual southern women, dashing home to compose yet another emotional poem, then cycling around the streets of Odessa once more, carefully dressed in the latest flashy style, smoking cigarettes like a grown-up, with his carefully waxed black mustache; he sometimes went down to the port to feast his eyes on the ships, stevedores, and cheap whores, or he watched excitedly as a troop of soldiers marched past to the accompaniment of a military band, and sometimes he would spend an hour or two in the library, eagerly reading whatever came to hand, resolving not to try to compete with the bookishness of his elder brother, the prodigy. Meanwhile he learned how to dance with well-bred young ladies, how to drink several glasses of brandy without losing his wits, how to cultivate acquaintances in coffeehouses, and how to pay court to the little dog so as to woo the lady.

As he made his way around the sun-washed streets of Odessa, a harbor town with a heady atmosphere colored by the presence of several different nationalities, he made friends of various kinds, courted girls, bought and sold and sometimes made a profit, sat down in a corner of a café or on a park bench, took out his notebook, wrote a poem (four stanzas, eight rhymes), then cycled around again as the unpaid errand boy of the leaders of the Lovers of Zion Society in pre-telephone Odessa: carrying a hasty note from Ahad Ha'am to Mendele Mokher Seforim, or from Mendele Mokher Seforim to Mr. Bialik, who was fond of saucy jokes, or to Mr. Menahem Ussishkin, from Mr. Ussishkin to Mr. Lilienblum, and while he waited in the drawing room or the hall for the reply, poems in Russian in the spirit of the Love of Zion movement played in his heart: Jerusalem whose streets are paved with onyx and jasper, an angel standing at every street corner, the sky above shining with the radiant light of the Seven Heavens.

He even wrote love poems to the Hebrew language, praising its beauty and its musicality, pledging his undying faithfulness—all in Russian. (Even after he had been living in Jerusalem for more than forty years, Grandpa was unable fully to master Hebrew: to his dying day he spoke a personal Hebrew that broke every rule, and he made horrific mistakes when he wrote it. In the last postcard he sent us to Kibbutz Hulda shortly before his death, he wrote, more or less: "My very dear grandchildrens and greatgrandchildrens, I mist you lots and lots. I want to sea you all lots and lots!")

When he finally arrived in Jerusalem in 1933 with a fear-ridden Grandma Shlomit, he stopped writing poems and devoted himself to commerce. For a few years he successfully sold dresses imported from Vienna in the fashion of the previous year to Jerusalemite women who longed for the delights of Europe. But eventually another Jew appeared who was cleverer than Grandpa, and began to import dresses from Paris in the fashion of the previous year, and Grandpa with his Viennese dresses had to admit defeat: he was forced to abandon the business and his love of dresses, and found himself supplying Jerusalem with hosiery by Lodzia in Holon and towels from a small firm called Szczupak and Sons in Ramat Gan.

Failure and want brought back the muse, who had abandoned him during his years of commercial success. Once more he shut himself away in his "study" at night and penned passionate verses in Russian about the splendors of the Hebrew language, the enchantments of Jerusalem, not the poverty-stricken, dusty, heat-stifled city of zealots but a Jerusalem whose streets are fragrant with myrrh and frankincense, where an angel of God floats over every one of its squares. At this point I entered the picture, in the role of the brave little boy in the story of the emperor's new clothes, and attacked Grandpa with exasperated realism for these poems of his: "You've been living in Jerusalem for years now, and you know perfectly well what the streets are paved with, and what really floats over Zion Square, so why do you keep writing about something that simply doesn't exist? Why don't you write about the real Jerusalem?"

Grandpa Alexander, furious at my impertinent words, turned in an instant from a pleasant pink hue to a blazing red, thumped the table with his fist, and roared: "The real Jerusalem? What on earth does a little bed-wetter like you know about the real Jerusalem?! The real Jerusalem is the one in my poems!!"

"And how long will you go on writing in Russian, Grandpa?"

"What do you mean, *ty durak,* you fool, you little bed-wetter? I do sums in Russian! I curse myself in Russian! I dream in Russian! I even—" (but here Grandma Shlomit, who knew exactly what was coming next, interrupted him: "*Shto s toboi? Ty ni normalni?! Vidish malchik ryadom s nami!!*"—What's the matter with you? Are you crazy? You can see the boy is right here!!)

"Would you like to go back to Russia, Grandpa? For a visit?"

"It doesn't exist anymore. *Propali!*"

"What doesn't exist anymore?"

"What doesn't exist anymore, what doesn't exist anymore—Russia doesn't exist anymore! Russia is dead. There is Stalin. There is Dzherzhinsky. There is Yezhov. There is Beria. There is one great big prison. Gulag! Yevsektsia! Apparatchiks! Murderers!"

"But surely you still love Odessa a little?"

"*Nu.* Love, don't love—what difference does it make. *Chort ego znayet.* The Devil knows."

"Don't you want to see it again?"

"*Nu, sha,* little bed-wetter, that's enough now. *Sha. Chtob ty propal. Sha.*"

One day, in his study, over a glass of tea and *kichelakh,* after the discovery of one of those scandals of embezzlement and corruption that shook the country, Grandpa told me how, when he was fifteen, in Odessa, "on my bike, very fast, I once carried a dispatch, a message, to Mr. Lilienblum, a committee member of the Lovers of Zion." (Besides being a well-known Hebrew writer, Lilienblum served in an honorary capacity as treasurer of the Lovers of Zion in Odessa.) "He, Lilienblum, was really our first finance minister," Grandpa explained to me.

While he was waiting for Lilienblum to write the reply, the fifteen-year-old man-about-town took out his cigarettes and reached for the ashtray and matchbox on the drawing room table. Mr. Lilienblum quickly put his hand on Grandpa's to stop him, then went out of the room and returned a moment later with another matchbox that he had brought from the kitchen, explaining that the matches on the drawing room table had been bought out of the budget of the Lovers of Zion, and were to be used only at committee meetings, and then only by members of the committee. "So, you see. In those days public property was public property, not a free-for-all. Not the way it is in the country at the moment, when after two thousand years we've established a state so as to have someone to steal from. In those days every child knew what was permitted and what was not, what was ownerless property and what was not, what was mine and what was not."

Not always, however. Once, it may have been in the late 1950s, a fine new ten-lira note came into circulation bearing a picture of the poet Bialik.* When I got hold of my first Bialik note, I hurried straight to Grandpa's to show him how the state had honored the man he had known in his youth. Grandpa was indeed excited, his cheeks flushed with pleasure, he turned the note this way and that, held it up to the lightbulb, scrutinized the picture of Bialik (who seemed to me suddenly to be winking mischievously at Grandpa, as if to say "*Nu?!*"). A tiny tear sparkled in Grandpa's eye, but while he reveled in his pride his fingers folded up the new note and tucked it away in the inside pocket of his jacket.

Ten liras was a tidy sum at that time, particularly for a kibbutznik like me. I was startled:

"Grandpa, what are you doing? I only brought it to show you and to make you happy. You'll get one of your own in a day or two, for sure."

"*Nu,*" Grandpa shrugged, "Bialik owed me twenty-two rubles."

14

BACK IN ODESSA, as a mustachioed seventeen-year-old, Grandpa had fallen in love with a well-respected young woman by the name of Shlomit Levin, who loved nice things and was drawn to high society. She

*Hayyim Nahuran Bialok (1873–1934), the Russian-born Hebrew poet, recognized as Israel's national poet, though he did not live to see the birth of the State of Israel.

longed to entertain famous people, to be friendly with artists and "live a cultured life."

It was a terrible love: she was eight or nine years older than her pocket Casanova, and moreover she also happened to be his first cousin.

At first the startled family did not want to hear about a marriage between the maiden and the boy. As if the difference in their ages and their blood tie were not enough, the young man had no education worthy of the name, no fixed employment, and no regular income beyond what he could earn from buying and selling here and there. Over and above all these catastrophes, Tsarist Russian law forbade the marriage of first cousins.

According to the photos, Shlomit Levin—the daughter of a sister of Rasha-Keila Klausner, née Braz—was a solidly built, broad-shouldered young woman, not particularly good-looking but elegant, haughty, tailored with severity and restraint. She wears a felt trilby, which cuts a fine slanting line across her brow, its brim coming down on the right over her neat hair and her left ear and sweeping upward on the left like the stern of a boat, while in front a bunch of fruit is held in place by a shiny hat pin, and to the left a feather waves proudly over the fruit, the hat, everything, like an arrogant peacock's tail. The lady's left arm, clad in a stylish kid glove, holds an oblong leather handbag, the other arm being firmly crossed with that of the young Grandpa Alexander, while her fingers, also gloved, hover lightly above the sleeve of his black overcoat, barely touching him.

He is standing to her right, nattily dressed, stiff, well turned out, his height enhanced by thick soles, yet he looks slighter and shorter than she is, despite the tall black homburg on his head. His young face is serious, resolute, almost lugubrious. His lovingly tended mustache tries in vain to dispel the boyish freshness that still marks his face. His eyes are elongated and dreamy. He is wearing an elegant, wide-lapeled overcoat with padded shoulders, a starched white shirt, and a narrow silk tie, and on his right arm hangs or perhaps even swings a stylish cane with a carved handle and shiny ferrule. In the old photograph it glints like the blade of a sword.

A shocked Odessa turned its back on this Romeo and Juliet. Their two mothers, who were sisters, engaged in a war of the worlds that began with mutual accusations of culpability and ended in everlasting silence. So Grandpa withdrew his meager savings, sold something here and something there, added one ruble to another, both families may have contributed something, if only to drive the scandal out of sight and out of mind, and my grandparents, the love-struck cousins, set sail for New York, as hundreds of thousands of other Jews from Russia and other Eastern European countries were doing at that time. Their intention was to marry in New York and take American citizenship, in which case I might have been born in Brooklyn or in Newark, New Jersey, and written clever novels in English about the passions and inhibitions of top-hatted immigrants and the neurotic ordeals of their agonized progeny.

But on board the ship, somewhere between Odessa and New York, on the Black Sea or off the coast of Sicily, or as they glided through the night toward the twinkling lights of the Straits of Gibraltar, or maybe as their love boat was passing over the lost continent of Atlantis, there was a further drama, a sudden twist to the plot: love raised its awesome dragon's head once more.

To cut a long story short, my grandfather, the bridegroom-to-be who had not yet reached his eighteenth birthday, fell in love again, passionately, heart-breakingly, desperately, up on deck or somewhere in the bowels of the ship, with another woman, a fellow passenger, who was also, as far as we know, a full decade older than he, give or take a year.

But Grandma Shlomit, so the family tradition has it, never entertained for a moment the thought of giving him up. She immediately took hold of him by the earlobe and held fast, she did not relax her grip day or night until they emerged from the premises of the New York rabbi who had married them to each other according to the laws of Moses and of Israel. ("By the ear," my family would say in a hilarious whisper, "she pulled him by the ear all the way, and she didn't let go till they were well and truly hitched." And sometimes they said: "Till they were hitched? Naah. She never let go of him. Ever. Not till her dying day, and maybe even a little bit longer than that, she held fast to his ear, and sometimes gave him a little tug.")

And then, a great puzzle followed. Within a year or two this odd couple had paid for another passage—or perhaps their parents helped them again—and embarked on another steamship, and without a backward glance they returned to Odessa.

It was utterly unheard of: some two million Jews migrated from east to west and settled in America in fewer than two score years between 1880 and 1917, and for all of them it was a one-way trip, except for my grandparents, who made the return journey. It must be supposed that they were the only passengers, so that there was no one for my passionate grandfather to fall in love with, and his ear was safe all the way back to Odessa.

Why did they return?

I was never able to extract a clear answer from them.

"Grandma, what was wrong with America?"

"There was nothing wrong. Only it was so crowded."

"Crowded? In America?"

"Too many people in such a small country."

"Who decided to go back, Grandpa? You or Grandma?"

"*Nu, shto,* what do you mean? What sort of a question is that?"

"And why did you decide to leave? What didn't you like about it?"

"What didn't we like? What didn't we like? We didn't like anything about it. *Nu,* well. It was full of horses and Red Indians."

"Red Indians?"

"Red Indians."

More than this I was never able to get out of him.

Here is a translation of a poem called "Winter" that Grandpa wrote in Russian, as usual:

> Springtime has fled, now it's winter instead,
> The storm winds do rage and the skies have turned black.
> Joy and gladness depart from my gloom-laden heart,
> I wanted to weep but my tears are held back.
>
> My soul feels weak and my spirit is bleak,
> My heart is as dark as the heavens above.
> My days have grown old, I'll no longer behold
> The joys of the spring and the pleasures of love.

In 1972, when I first went to New York, I looked for and found a woman who looked like a Native American; she was standing, as I recall, on the corner of Lexington and Fifty-third Street handing out leaflets. She was neither young nor old, had wide cheekbones, and she wore an old man's overcoat and a kind of shawl against the biting cold wind. She held out a leaflet and smiled; I took it and said thank you. "Love awaits you," it promised, under the address of a singles bar. "Don't waste another minute. Come now."

In a picture taken back in Odessa in 1913 or 1914 my grandfather is wearing a bowtie, a gray hat with a shiny silk band, and a three-piece suit whose open jacket reveals, running across the buttoned-up vest, a fine line of silver apparently connected to a pocket watch. The dark silk bow stands out against his brilliant white shirt, there is a high shine on his black shoes, his smart cane hangs, as usual, from his arm, just below the elbow; he is holding hands with a six-year-old boy on his right and a pretty four-year-old girl on his left. The boy has a round face, and a carefully combed lock of hair peeps endearingly from under his cap and cuts a straight line across his forehead. He is wearing a magnificent double-breasted coat with two rows of huge white buttons. From the bottom of the coat sprouts a pair of short trousers beneath which peeps a narrow band of white knee that is immediately swallowed up in long white socks presumably held up by garters.

The little girl is smiling at the photographer. She looks as though she is well aware of her charms, which she is projecting very deliberately at the lens of the camera. Her soft, long hair, which comes down over her shoulders and rests on her coat, is neatly parted on the right. Her round face is plump and happy, her eyes are elongated and slanted, almost Chinese-looking, and there is a half smile on her full lips. She has been dressed in a tiny double-breasted coat over her dress, identical to her brother's in every respect, only smaller, and wonderfully sweet. She too is wearing little socks that go up to her knees. On her feet she has shoes whose buckles sport cute little bows.

The boy in the picture is my uncle David, who was always called Ziuzya or Ziuzinka. And the girl, that enchanting, coquettish little woman, the little girl is my father.

From his infancy until the age of seven or eight—though sometimes he told us that it went on until he was nine—Grandma Shlomit used to dress him exclusively in dresses with collars, or in little pleated and starched skirts that she ran up for him herself, and girls' shoes, often in red. His magnificent long hair cascaded down onto his shoulders and was tied with a red, yellow, pale blue, or pink bow. Every evening his mother washed his hair in fragrant solutions, and sometimes she washed it again in the morning, because night grease is well known to harm hair and rob it of its freshness and sheen and serve as a hothouse for dandruff. She made him wear pretty rings on his fingers and bracelets on his pudgy arms. When they went to bathe in the sea, Ziuzinka—Uncle David—went to the men's changing rooms with Grandpa Alexander, while Grandma Shlomit and little Lionichka—my father—headed for the women's showers, where they soaped themselves thoroughly, yes, there, and there too, and especially there please, and wash twice down there.

After she gave birth to Ziuzinka, Grandma Shlomit had set her heart on having a daughter. When she gave birth to what was apparently not a daughter, she decided on the spot that it was her natural and indisputable right to bring this child, flesh of her flesh and bone of her bones, up as her heart desired, according to her own choice and taste, and no power in the world had the right to interfere and dictate her Lonia or Lionichka's education, dress, sex, or manners.

Grandpa Alexander apparently saw no cause for rebellion: behind the closed door of his little den, inside his own nutshell, he enjoyed a relative autonomy and was even permitted to pursue some of his own interests. Like some Monaco or Liechtenstein, he never would have thought to make a fool of himself and jeopardize his frail sovereignty by poking his nose into the internal affairs of a more extensive neighboring power, whose territory enclosed that of his own Lilliputian duchy on all sides.

As for my father, he never protested. He rarely shared his memories of the women's showers and his other feminine experiences, except when he took it into his head to try to joke with us.

But his jokes always seemed more like a declaration of intent: look, watch how a serious man like me can step outside himself for you and volunteer to make you laugh.

My mother and I used to smile at him, as though to thank him for his efforts, but he, excitedly, almost touchingly, interpreted our smiles as an invitation to go on amusing us, and he would offer us two or three jokes that we had already heard from him a thousand times, about the Jew and the Gentile on the train, or about Stalin meeting the Empress Catherine, and we had already laughed ourselves to tears when Father, bursting with pride at having managed to make us laugh, charged on to the story of Stalin sitting on a bus opposite Ben Gurion and Churchill, and about Bialik meeting Shlonsky in paradise, and about Shlonsky meeting a girl. Until Mother said to him gently:

"Didn't you want to do some more work this evening?"

Or:

"Don't forget you promised to stick some stamps in the album with the child before he goes to bed."

Once he said to his guests:

"The female heart! In vain have the great poets attempted to reveal its mysteries. Look, Schiller wrote somewhere that in the whole of creation there is no secret as deep as a woman's heart, and that no woman has ever revealed or will ever reveal to a man the full extent of the female mystique. He could simply have asked me: after all, I've been there."

Sometimes he joked in his unfunny way: "Of course I chase skirts sometimes, like most men, if not more so, because I used to have plenty of skirts of my own, and suddenly they were all taken away from me."

Once he said something like this: "If we had a daughter, she would almost certainly be a beauty." And he added: "In the future, in generations to come, the gap between the sexes may well narrow. This gap is generally considered to be a tragedy, but one day it may transpire that it is nothing but a comedy of errors."

15

IT WAS Grandma Shlomit, the distinguished lady who loved books and understood writers, who turned their home in Odessa into a literary salon—perhaps the first Hebrew literary salon ever. With her sensitivity she grasped that the sour blend of loneliness and lust for recognition, shyness and extravagance, deep insecurity and self-intoxicated egomania that drives poets and writers out of their rooms to seek one another out, to rub shoulders with one another, bully, joke, condescend, feel one another, lay a hand on a shoulder or put an arm around a waist, to chat and argue with little nudges, to spy a little, sniff out what is cooking in other pots, flatter, disagree, collide, be right, take offense, apologize, make amends, avoid one another, and seek one another's company again.

She was the perfect hostess, and she received her guests unpretentiously but graciously. She offered everyone an attentive ear, a supportive shoulder, curious, admiring eyes, a sympathetic heart, homemade fish delicacies or bowls of thick, steaming stew on winter evenings, poppy-seed cakes that melted in the mouth, and rivers of scalding tea from the samovar.

Grandpa's job was to pour out liqueurs expertly, and keep the ladies supplied with chocolates and sweet cakes, and the men with *papirosi*, those pungent Russian cigarettes. Uncle Joseph, who at the tender age of twenty-nine had inherited from Ahad Ha'am the editorship of *Hashiloach,* the leading periodical of modern Hebrew culture (the poet Bialik himself was the literary editor), ruled Hebrew literature from Odessa and promoted or demoted writers by his word. Aunt Zippora accompanied him to his brother and sister-in-law's "soirées," careful to wrap him well in woolen scarves, warm overcoats, and earmuffs. Menahem Ussishkin, the leader of those forerunners of Zionism, the Lovers of Zion, smartly turned out, his chest puffed out like a buffalo's, his voice as coarse as a Russian governor's, as effervescent as a boiling samovar, reduced the room to silence with his entrance: everyone stopped talking out of respect, someone or other would leap up to offer him a seat, Ussishkin would stride across the room with the gait of a general, seat himself expansively with his large legs spread wide, and tap the floor twice with his cane to indicate his consent that the conversations in the salon should continue. Even Rabbi Czernowitz (whose nom de plume was Rav Tsair) was a regular visitor. There was also a plump young historian who had once paid court to my grandmother ("But it was hard for a decent woman to be close to him—he was extremely intelligent and interesting, but he always had all sorts of disgusting stains on his collar, and his cuffs were grimy, and sometimes you could see bits of food caught in the folds of his trousers. He was a total *shlump, shmutsik, fui!*").

Occasionally Bialik would drop in for an evening, pale with grief or shivering with cold and anger—or quite the contrary: he could also be the life and soul of the party. "And how!" said my grandmother. "Like a kid, he was! A real scalawag! No holds barred! So risqué! Sometimes he would joke with us in Yiddish till he made the ladies blush, and Chone Rawnitski would shout at him: '*Nu, sha!* Bialik! What's up with you! *Fui!* That's enough, now!'" Bialik loved food and drink, he loved having a good time, he stuffed himself with bread and cheese, followed by a handful of cakes, a glass of scalding tea, and a little glass of liqueur, and then he would launch into entire serenades in Yiddish about the wonders of the Hebrew language and his deep love for it.

The poet Tchernikhowsky, too, might burst into the salon, flamboyant but shy, passionate yet prickly, conquering hearts, touching in his childlike innocence, as fragile as a butterfly but also hurtful, wounding people left, right, and center without even noticing. The truth? "He never meant to give offense—he was so innocent! A kind soul! The soul of a baby who has never known sin! Not like a sad Jewish baby, no! Like a *goyish* baby! Full of *joie de vivre*, naughtiness, and energy! Sometimes he was just like a calf! Such a happy calf! Leaping around! Playing the fool in front of everybody! But only sometimes. Other times he would arrive so miserable it immediately made every woman want to make a fuss over him! Every single one! Young and old, free or married, plain or pretty, they all felt some kind of hidden desire to make a fuss over him. It was a power he had. He didn't even know he had it—if he had, it simply would never have worked on us the way it did!"

Tchernikhowsky stoked his spirits with a *glazele* or two of vodka, and sometimes he would start to read those poems of his that overflowed with hilarity or sorrow and made everybody in the room melt with him and for him: his liberal ways, his flowing locks, his anarchic mustache, the girls he brought with him, who were not always too bright, and not even necessarily Jewish, but were always beauties who gladdened every eye and caused not a few tongues to wag and whetted the writers' envy—"I'm telling you as a woman (Grandma again), women are never wrong about such things, Bialik used to sit and stare at him like this . . . and at the *goyish* girls he brought along . . . Bialik would have given an entire year of his life if only he could have lived for a month as Tchernikhowsky!"

Arguments raged about the revival of the Hebrew language and literature, the limits of innovation, the connection between the Jewish cultural heritage and that of the nations, the Bundists, the Yiddishists (Uncle Joseph, in polemical vein, called Yiddish *jargon,* and when he was calm he called it "Judeo-German"), the new agricultural settlements in Judaea and Galilee, and the old troubles of the Jewish farmers in Kherson or Kharkov, Knut Hamsun and Maupassant, the great powers and *Sozialismus,* women's rights and the agrarian question.

In 1921, four years after the October Revolution, after Odessa had changed hands several times in the bloody fighting between Whites and Reds, two or three years after my father finally changed from a girl to a boy, Grandma and Grandpa and their two sons fled the city for Vilna, which at that time was part of Poland (long before it became Vilnius in Lithuania).

Grandpa loathed the Communists. "Don't talk to me about the Bolsheviks," he used to grumble. "*Nu,* what, I knew them very well, even before they seized power, before they moved into the houses they stole from other people, before they dreamed of becoming *apparatchiks, yevseks, politruks,* and commissars. I can remember them when they were still hooligans, the *Unterwelt* of the harbor district in Odessa, hoodlums, bullies, pickpockets, drunkards, and pimps. *Nu,* what, they were nearly all Jews, Jews of a sort, what can you do. Only they were Jews from the simplest families—*nu,* what, families of fishmongers from the market, straight from the dredgings that clung to the bottom of the pot, that's what we used to say. Lenin and Trotsky—what Trotsky, which Trotsky, Leibele Bronstein, the crazy son of some *gonef* called Dovidl from Janowka—this riffraff they dressed up as revolutionaries, *nu,* what, with leather boots and revolvers in their belts, like a filthy sow in a silk dress. And that's how they went around the streets, arresting people, confiscating property, and anyone whose apartment or girlfriend they fancied, *pif-paf,* they murdered him. *Nu,* what, this whole filthy *khaliastra* (gang), Kameneff was really Rosenfeld, Maxim Litvinoff was Meir Wallich, Grigory Zinoviev was originally Apfelbaum, Karl Radek was Sobelsohn, Leiser Kaganovich was a cobbler, the son of a butcher. *Nu,* what, I suppose there were one or two *goyim* who went along with them, also from the bottom of the pot, from the harbor, from the dredgings, they were riffraff, *nu,* what, riffraff with smelly socks."

He had not budged from this view of Communism and the Communists even fifty years after the Bolshevik Revolution. A few days after the Israeli army conquered the Old City of Jerusalem in the Six Days' War, Grandpa suggested that the international community should now assist Israel in returning all the Arabs of the Levant "very respectfully, without harming a hair of their heads, without robbing them of a single chicken," to their historic homeland, which he called "Arabia Souadia": "Just the way we Jews are returning to our homeland, so they ought to go back honorably to their own home, to Arabia Souadia, where they came here from."

To cut the argument short, I inquired what he proposed doing if Russia attacked us, in a desire to spare their Arab allies the hardships of the journey back to Arabia.

His pink cheeks turned red with rage, he puffed himself up and roared:

"Russia?! What Russia do you mean?! There is no more Russia, bedwetter! Russia doesn't exist! Are you talking about the Bolsheviks, maybe? *Nu,* what. I've known the Bolsheviks since they were pimping in the harbor district in Odessa. They're nothing but a gang of thieves and hooligans! Riffraff from the bottom of the pot! The whole of Bolshevism is just one gigantic bluff! Now that we've seen what wonderful Hebrew airplanes we have, and guns, *nu,* what, we ought to send these young lads and planes of ours across to Petersburg, two weeks there, two weeks back, then one decent bombing—what they've deserved from us a long time now—one big *phoosh*—and the whole of Bolshevism will fly away to hell there just like dirty cotton wool!"

"Are you suggesting Israel should bomb Leningrad, Grandpa? And for a world war to break out? Haven't you ever heard of atom bombs? Hydrogen bombs?"

"It's all in Jewish hands, *nu,* what, the Americans, the Bolsheviks, all these newfangled bombs of theirs are all in the hands of Jewish scientists, and they're bound to know what to do and what not to do."

"What about peace? Is there any way to bring peace?"

"Yes there is: we have to defeat all our enemies. We have to beat them up so they'll come and beg us for peace—and then, *nu*, what, of course we'll give it to them. Why should we deny it to them? After all, we are a peace-loving people. We even have such a commandment, to pursue peace—*nu*, what, so we'll pursue it as far as Baghdad if we have to, as far as Cairo even. Shouldn't we? How so?"

Bewildered, impoverished, censored, and terrified after the October Revolution, the Civil War, and the Red victory, the Hebrew writers and Zionist activists of Odessa scattered in every direction. Uncle Joseph and Aunt Zippora, together with many of their friends, left for Palestine at the end of 1919 on board the *Ruslan*, whose arrival in the port of Jaffa announced the beginning of the Third Aliyah. Others fled from Odessa to Berlin, Lausanne, and America.

Grandpa Alexander and Grandma Shlomit with their two sons did not emigrate to Palestine—despite the Zionist passion that throbbed in Grandpa's Russian poems, the country still seemed to them too Asiatic, too primitive and backward, lacking in minimal standards of hygiene and elementary culture. So they went to Lithuania, which the Klausners, the parents of Grandpa, Uncle Joseph, and Uncle Betsalel, had left more than twenty-five years earlier. Vilna was still under Polish rule, and the violent anti-Semitism that had always existed there was growing by the year. Poland and Lithuania were in the grip of nationalism and xenophobia. To the conquered and subdued Lithuanians the large Jewish minority appeared as the agent of the oppressive regimes. Across the border, Germany was in the grip of the new, cold-blooded, murderous Nazi brand of Jew hatred.

In Vilna, too, Grandpa was a businessman. He did not set his sights high; he bought a little here and sold a little there, and in between he sometimes made some money, and he sent his two sons first to Hebrew school and then to the classical gymnasium. The brothers David and Arieh, otherwise known as Zyuzia and Lonia, had brought three languages with them from Odessa: at home they had spoken Russian and Yiddish, in the street Russian, and at the Zionist kindergarten they had learned to speak Hebrew. Here, in the classical gymnasium in Vilna, they added Greek and Latin, Polish, German, and French. Later, in the European literature department at the university, English and Italian were added to the list, and in the Semitic philology department my father also learned Arabic, Aramaic, and cuneiform writing. Uncle David soon got a teaching job in literature, and my father, Yehuda Arieh, who took his first degree at Vilna University in 1932, was hoping to follow in his footsteps, but the anti-Semitism by now had become unbearable. Jewish students had to endure humiliation, blows, discrimination, and sadistic abuse.

"But what exactly did they do to you?" I asked my father. "What sort of sadistic abuse? Did they hit you? Tear up your exercise books? And why didn't you complain about them?"

"There's no way," Father said, "that you can understand this. And it's better that way. I'm glad, even though you can't understand this either, that is to say, why I'm glad that you can't understand what it was like: I definitely don't want you to understand. Because there's no need, there's simply no need anymore. Because it's all over. It's all over once and for all. That is to say, it won't happen here. Now let's talk about something else: shall we talk about your album of planets? Of course we still have enemies. And there are wars. There is a siege and no small losses. Definitely. I'm not denying it. But not persecution. That—no. Neither persecution nor humiliation nor pogroms. Not the sadism we had to endure there. That will never come back, for sure. Not here. If they attack us, we'll give as good as we get. It seems to me you've stuck Mars between Saturn and Jupiter. That's wrong. No, I'm not telling you. You can look it up yourself and see where you went wrong, and you can put it right all by yourself."

A battered photo album survives from Vilna days. Here is Father, with his brother David, both still at school, both looking very serious, pale, with their big ears sticking out from under peaked caps, both in suits, ties, shirts with stiff collars. Here is Grandpa Alexander, starting to go a little bald, still mustached, nattily turned out, looking a little like a minor Tsarist diplomat. And here are some group photographs, perhaps a graduation class. Is it Father's year or his brother David's? It's hard to tell: the faces are rather blurred. The boys are wearing caps and the girls round berets. Most of the girls have dark hair, and some are smiling a

Mona Lisa smile that knows something that you're dying to know but that you won't discover because it's not meant for you.

Who for, then? It is almost certain that virtually all the young people in these group photographs were stripped naked and made to run, whipped and chased by dogs, starved and frozen, into the large pits in the Ponar Forest. Which of them survived, apart from my father? I study the group photograph under a bright light and try to discern something in their faces: some hint of cunning or determination, of inner toughness that might have made this boy in the second row on the left guess what was in store for him, mistrust all the reassuring words, climb down into the drains under the ghetto while there was still time, and join the partisans in the forests. Or how about that pretty girl in the middle, with the clever, cynical look, no, my dear, they can't deceive me, I may still be a youngster but I know it all, I know things that you don't even dream I know. Perhaps she survived? Did she escape to join the partisans in the Rudnik Forest? Did she manage to go into hiding in a district outside the ghetto, thanks to her "Aryan" appearance? Was she sheltered in a convent? Or did she escape while there was time, manage to elude the Germans and their Lithuanian henchmen, and slip across the border into Russia? Or did she emigrate to the Land of Israel while there was still time, and live the life of a tight-lipped pioneer till the age of seventy-six, introducing beehives or running the chicken farm in a kibbutz in Jezreel Valley?

And here is my young father, looking very much like my son Daniel (whose middle names are Yehuda Arieh, after him), a spine-chilling resemblance, seventeen years old, long and thin as a cornstalk, wearing a bowtie, with his innocent eyes looking at me through his round spectacles, partly embarrassed and partly proud, a great talker and yet, with no contradiction, terribly shy, with his dark hair combed neatly back over his head and a cheerful optimism on his face, Don't worry, pals, everything's going to be fine, we shall overcome, somehow we'll put everything behind us, what more can happen, it's not so bad, it'll all be OK.

My father in this picture is younger than my son. If only it were possible, I would get into the photo and warn him and his cheerful chums. I would try to tell them what's in store. It's almost certain they wouldn't believe me if I told them: would just make fun of me.

Here is my father again, dressed for a party, wearing a *shapka*, a Russian hat, rowing a boat, with two girls who are smiling at him coquettishly. Here he is wearing slightly ridiculous knickers, showing his socks, embracing from behind a smiling girl with a neat center parting. The girl is about to post a letter in a box marked "Skrzynka Pocztowa" (the words are clearly legible in the picture). Who is the letter to? What happened to the addressee? What was the fate of the other girl in the picture, the pretty girl in a striped dress, with a little black handbag tucked under her arm and white socks and shoes? For how long after the picture was taken did this pretty girl go on smiling?

And here is my father, smiling too, suddenly reminiscent of the sweet little girl his mother made him into when he was a child, in a group of five girls and three boys. They are in a forest, but are dressed in their best town clothes. The boys, however, have removed their jackets and are standing in their shirts and ties, in a bold, laddish posture, daring fate—or the girls. And here they are constructing a human pyramid, with two boys carrying a rather plump girl on their shoulders and the third holding her thigh rather daringly, and two other girls looking on and laughing. The bright sky too looks merry, and so does the railing of the bridge over the river. Only the surrounding forest is dense, serious, dark: it extends from one side of the picture to the other and presumably a good deal farther. A forest near Vilna: the Rudnik Forest? Or the Ponar Forest? Or is it perhaps the Popishok or Olkieniki Forest, which my father's grandfather, Yehuda Leib Klausner, loved to cross on his cart, trusting to his horse, his strong arms, and his good luck in the dense darkness, even on rainy, stormy winter nights?

Grandpa yearned for the Land of Israel that was being rebuilt after its two thousand years of desolation; he yearned for Galilee and the valleys, Sharon, Gilead, Gilboa, the hills of Samaria and the mountains of Edom, "Flow, Jordan flow on, with your roaring billows"; he contributed to the Jewish National Fund, paid the Zionist shekel, eagerly devoured every scrap of information from the Land of Israel, got drunk on the speeches of Jabotinsky, who occasionally passed through Jewish Vilna and attracted an enthusiastic following. Grandpa was always a wholehearted supporter of Jabotinsky's proud, uncompromising nationalist politics and considered himself a militant Zionist. However, even as the ground of Vilna burned underneath his and his family's feet he was still inclined—or perhaps Grandma Shlomit inclined him—to seek a new homeland somewhere a little less Asiatic than Palestine and a little more European than ever-darkening Vilna. During 1930–32 the Klausners attempted to obtain immigration papers for France, Switzerland, America (Red Indians notwithstanding), a Scandinavian country, and England. None of these countries wanted them: they all had enough Jews already. ("None is too many," ministers in Canada and Switzerland said at the time, and other countries felt the same without advertising the fact.)

Some eighteen months before the Nazis came to power in Germany, my Zionist grandfather was so blinded by despair at the anti-Semitism in Vilna that he even applied for German citizenship. Fortunately for us, he was turned down by Germany too. So there they were, these over-enthusiastic Europhiles, who could speak so many of Europe's languages and recite its poetry, who believed in its moral superiority, appreciated its ballet and opera, cultivated its heritage, dreamed of its postnational unity, and adored its manners, clothes, and fashions, who had loved it unconditionally and uninhibitedly for decades, since the beginning of the Jewish Enlightenment, and who had done everything humanly possible to please it, to contribute to it in every way and in every domain, to become part of it, to break through its cool hostility with frantic courtship, to make friends, to ingratiate themselves, to be accepted, to belong, to be loved . . .

And so in 1933 Shlomit and Alexander Klausner, those disappointed lovers of Europe, together with their younger son Yehuda Arieh, who had just completed his first degree in Polish and world literature, emigrated halfheartedly, almost against their will, to Asiatic Asia, to the Jerusalem that Grandpa's sentimental poems had longed for ever since his youth.

They sailed from Trieste to Haifa on the *Italia*, and on the way they were photographed with the captain, whose name, recorded on the edge of the picture, was Beniamino Umberto Steindler. Nothing less.

And in the port of Haifa, so runs the family story, a British Mandatory doctor or sanitary officer in a white coat was waiting for them, to spray all the passengers with disinfectant. When it was Grandpa Alexander's turn, so the story goes, he was so furious that he grabbed the spray from the doctor and gave him a good dousing, as if to say: Thus shall it be done unto the man who dares to treat us here in our own homeland as though we were still in the Diaspora; for two thousand years we have borne everything in silence, but here, in our own land, we shall not put up with a new exile, our honor shall not be trampled underfoot—or disinfected.

Their elder son, David, a committed and conscientious Europhile, stayed behind in Vilna. There, at a very early age, and despite being Jewish, he was appointed to a teaching position in literature at the university. He had no doubt set his heart on the glorious career of Uncle Joseph, just as my father did all his life. There in Vilna he would marry a young woman called Malka, and there, in 1938, his son Daniel would be born. I never saw this son, born a year and a half before me, nor have I ever managed to find a photograph of him. There are only some postcards and a few letters left, written in Polish by Aunt Malka (Macia), Uncle David's wife. *10.2.39: The first night Danush slept from nine in the evening to six in the morning. He has no trouble sleeping at night. During the day he lies with his eyes open with his arms and legs in constant motion. Sometimes he screams . . .*

Little Daniel Klausner would live for less than three years. Soon they would come and kill him to protect "Europe" from him, to prevent in advance Hitler's "nightmare vision of the seduction of hundreds and thousands of girls by repulsive, bandy-legged Jew bastards . . . With satanic joy in his face, the black-haired Jewish youth lurks in wait for the unsuspecting girl whom he defiles with his blood . . . The final Jewish goal is denationalization . . . by the bastardization of other nations, lowering the racial level of the highest . . . with the secret . . . aim of ruining the . . . white race . . . If 5,000 Jews were transported to Sweden, within a short time they would occupy all the leading positions . . . the universal poisoner of all races, international Jewry."*

But Uncle David thought otherwise: he despised and dismissed such hateful views as these, refused to consider solemn Catholic anti-Semitism

*Hitler, quoted in Joachim C. Fest, *Hitler,* trans. Richard and Clara Winston (New York: Harcourt, 2002), pp. 40, 204, 533, and 746 (Hitler's testament); see also Hermann Rauschning, *Hitler Speaks: A Series of Political Conversations with Adolf Hitler on his Real Aims* (London: Thornton Butterworth Ltd., 1939).

echoing among the stone vaults of high cathedrals, or coldly lethal Protestant anti-Semitism, German racism, Austrian murderousness, Polish Jew-hatred, Lithuanian, Hungarian, and French cruelty, Ukrainian, Rumanian, Russian, and Croatian love of pogroms, Belgian, Dutch, British, Irish, and Scandinavian fear of Jews. All these seemed to him an obscure relic of savage, ignorant eons, remains of yesteryear, whose time was up.

A specialist in comparative literature, he found in the literatures of Europe his spiritual homeland. He did not see why he should leave where he was and emigrate to western Asia, a place that was strange and alien to him, just to please ignorant anti-Semites and narrow-minded nationalist thugs. So he stayed at his post, flying the flag of progress, culture, art, and spirit without frontiers, until the Nazis came to Vilna: culture-loving Jews, intellectuals, and cosmopolitans were not to their taste, and so they murdered David, Malka, and my little cousin Daniel, who was nicknamed Danush or Danushek. In their penultimate letter, dated 15.12.40, his parents wrote that "he has recently started walking . . . and he has an excellent memory."

Uncle David saw himself as a child of his time: a distinguished, multicultural, multilingual, fluent, enlightened European and a decidedly modern man. He despised prejudices and ethnic hatreds, and he was resolved never to give in to lowbrow racists, chauvinists, demagogues, and benighted, prejudice-ridden anti-Semites, whose raucous voices promised "death to the Jews" and barked at him from the walls: "Yids, go to Palestine!"

To Palestine? Definitely not: a man of his stamp would not take his young bride and infant son, defect from the front line and run away to hide from the violence of a noisy rabble in some drought-stricken Levantine province, where a few desperate Jews tried their hand at establishing a segregationist armed nationhood that, ironically, they had apparently learned from the worst of their foes.

No, he would definitely stay here in Vilna, at his post, in one of the most vital forward trenches of that rational, broad-minded, tolerant, and liberal European enlightenment that was now fighting for its existence against the waves of barbarism that were threatening to engulf it. Here he would stand, for he could do no other.

To the end.

16

GRANDMA CAST a single startled look around her and pronounced the famous sentence that was to become her motto for the twenty-five years she lived in Jerusalem: The Levant is full of germs.

Henceforth Grandpa had to get up at six or six thirty every morning, attack the mattresses and bedding violently for her with a carpet beater, air the bedspreads and pillows, spray the whole house with DDT, help her in her ruthless boiling of vegetables, fruit, linen, towels, and kitchen utensils. Every two or three hours he had to disinfect the toilet and washbasins with chlorine. These basins, whose drains were normally kept stoppered, had a little chlorine or Lysol solution at the bottom, like the moat of a medieval castle, to block any invasion by the cockroaches and evil spirits that were always trying to penetrate the apartment through the plumbing. Even the nostrils of the basins, the overflow holes, were kept blocked with improvised plugs made of squashed soap, in case the enemy attempted to infiltrate that way. The mosquito nets on the windows always smelled of DDT, and an odor of disinfectant pervaded the whole apartment. A thick cloud of disinfecting spirit, soap, creams, sprays, baits, insecticides, and talcum powder always hung in the air, and something of it may also have wafted from Grandma's skin.

Yet here too occasionally in the early evening some minor writers, two or three intellectually inclined businessmen, or some promising young scholars were invited over. Admittedly there was no more Bialik or Tchernikhowsky, there were no more large, jolly dinner parties. Their limited budget, cramped conditions, and daily hardships forced Grandma to lower her sights: Hannah and Chaim Toren, Esther and Israel Zarchi, Zerta and Jacob-David Abramski, and occasionally one or two of their friends from Odessa or Vilna, Mr. Scheindelevitch from Isaiah Street, Mr. Katchalsky the shopkeeper from David Yellin Street, whose two sons were already considered to be famous scientists with some enigmatic position in the Hagganah, or the Bar-Yitzhars (Itzeleviches) from Mekor Baruch, he a lugubrious haberdasher and she a maker of women's wigs and corsets to order, both of them devout right-wing Zionist Revisionists who loathed the Labor Party heart and soul.

Grandma would lay out the food in military fashion in the kitchen, dispatching Grandpa into the fray over and over again, laden with trays, to serve cold borscht with a hefty iceberg of sour cream floating on it, peeled fresh clementines, seasonal fruit, walnuts, almonds, raisins, dried figs, candied fruits, candied orange peel, various jams and preserves, poppy-seed cakes, jam sponges, apple strudel, and an exquisite tart that she made from puff pastry.

Here too they discussed current affairs and the future of the Jewish people and the world, and reviled the corrupt Labor Party and its defeatist, collaborationist leaders who ingratiated themselves obsequiously with the Gentile oppressor. As for the kibbutzim, from here they looked like dangerous Bolshevik cells that were anarcho-nihilist to boot, permissive, spreading licentiousness and debasing everything the nation held sacred, parasites who fattened themselves at the public expense and spongers who robbed the nation's land. Not a little of what was later to be said against the kibbutzim by their enemies from among radical Middle Eastern Jews was already "known for a fact," in those years, to visitors to my grandparents' home in Jerusalem. Apparently the discussions did not bring much joy to the participants; otherwise why did they often fall silent the moment they caught sight of me, or change to Russian, or shut the door between the sitting room and the castle of sample cases I was building in Grandpa's study?

Here is what their little apartment in Prague Lane was like. There was a single, very Russian sitting room, crammed with heavy furniture and with various objects and glass cases, thick smells of boiled fish, boiled carrot and pasties mingled with the odors of DDT and Lysol; around the walls were huddled chests, stools, a dark masculine wardrobe, a thick-legged table, a sideboard covered with ornaments and souvenirs. The whole room was full of white muslin mats, lace curtains, embroidered cushions, souvenirs, and on every available surface, on the windowsill were crowds of little knickknacks, such as a silver crocodile that opened its jaws to crack a nut when you raised its tail, or the life-size white poodle, a gentle, silent creature with a black nose and round glass eyes that always lay at the foot of Grandma Shlomit's bed and never barked or asked to be let out into the Levant, from which it might have brought in who knew what, insects, bedbugs, fleas, ticks, worms, lice, eczema, bacilli, and other plagues.

This amiable creature, whose name was Stakh or Stashek or Stashinka, was the mildest and most obedient dog ever, because he was made of wool and stuffed with rags. He had followed the Klausners faithfully in all their migrations from Odessa to Vilna and from Vilna to Jerusalem. For the sake of his health this poor dog was made to swallow several mothballs every few weeks. Every morning he had to put up with being sprayed by Grandpa. Now and again, in the summer, he was placed in front of the open window to get some air and sunlight.

For a few hours Stakh would sit motionless on the windowsill, raking the street below with unfathomable longing in his melancholy black eyes, his black nose raised in vain to sniff at the bitches in the little street, his woolen ears pricked up, straining to catch the myriad sounds of the neighborhood, the wail of a lovesick cat, the cheerful chirruping of the birds, noisy shouting in Yiddish, the rag-and-bone man's bloodcurdling cry, the barking of free dogs whose lot was better by far than his own. His head was cocked thoughtfully to one side, his short tail tucked sadly between his hind legs, his eyes had a tragic look. He never barked at passersby, never cried for help to dogs in the street, never burst out howling, but his face as he sat there expressed a silent despair that tugged at my heartstrings, a dumb resignation that was more piercing than the most dreadful howl.

One morning Grandma, without a second thought, wrapped her Stashinka up in newspaper and threw him in the trash, because all of a sudden she was smitten with suspicions of dust or mold. Grandpa was no doubt upset but didn't dare utter a peep. And I never forgave her.

This overcrowded living room, whose smell, like its color, was dark brown, doubled as Grandma's bedroom, and from it opened Grandpa's monastic cell of a study, with its hard couch, its office shelves, the piles of sample cases, the bookcase, and the little desk that was always as neat and tidy as the morning parade of a bright and shiny troop of Austro-Hungarian hussars.

Here in Jerusalem, too, they eked out an existence on Grandpa's precarious earnings. Once again he bought here and sold there, storing up in the summer to bring out and sell in the autumn, going around the clothes shops on Jaffa Road, King George V Avenue, Agrippa Street, Luncz Street, and Ben-Yehuda Street with his cases of samples. Once a month or so he went off to Holon, Ramat Gan, Netanya, Petah Tikva, sometimes as far as Haifa, to talk to towel manufacturers, or haggle with underwear makers or suppliers of ready-made clothing.

Every morning, before he went out on his rounds, Grandpa made up parcels of clothes or cloth for the mail. Sometimes he was awarded, lost, or regained the position of local sales representative for some wholesaler or factory. He did not enjoy trading and was not successful at it—he barely made enough to keep himself and Grandma alive—but what he did enjoy was walking the streets of Jerusalem, always elegant in his Tsarist diplomat's suit, with a triangle of white handkerchief protruding from his top pocket, with his silver cufflinks, and he loved to spend hours sitting in cafés, ostensibly for business purposes but in reality for the conversations and arguments and steaming tea and leafing through the newspapers and magazines. He also liked eating in restaurants. He always treated waiters like a very particular yet magnanimous gentleman.

"Excuse me. This tea is cold. I ask you bring me right away hot tea: hot tea, that means the essence also must be very very hot. Not just the water. Thank you very much."

What Grandpa loved best were the long trips out of town and the business meetings in the offices of the firms in the coastal towns. He had an impressive business card, with a gold border and an emblem in the form of intertwined rhombuses, like a little heap of diamonds. The legend on the card read: "Alexander Z. Klausner, Importer, Authorized Representative, General Agent and Accredited Wholesaler, Jerusalem and District." He would hold out his card with an apologetic, childlike little laugh:

"*Nu*, what. A man has to live somehow."

His heart was not in his business but in innocent, illicit love affairs, romantic yearnings, like a seventy-year-old schoolboy, vague longings and dreams. If he had only been allowed to live his life again, according to his choice and the real inclination of his heart, he would certainly have chosen to love women, to be loved, to understand their hearts, to enjoy their company in summer retreats in the bosom of nature, to row with them on lakes beneath snow-capped mountains, to write passionate poetry, to be good-looking, curly-haired, and soulful yet masculine, to be loved by the masses, to be Tchernikhowsky. Or Byron. Or, better still, Vladimir Jabotinsky, sublime poet and prominent political leader combined in a single wonderful figure.

All his life he longed for worlds of love and emotional generosity. (He never seems to have made the distinction between love and admiration, thirsting for an abundance of both.)

Sometimes in desperation he rattled his chains, champed at the bit, drank a couple of glasses of brandy in the solitude of his study, or on bitter, sleepless nights particularly, he drank a glass of vodka and smoked sadly. Sometimes he went out alone after dark and roamed the empty streets. It was not easy for him to go out. Grandma had a highly developed, supersensitive radar screen on which she kept track of us all: at any given moment she could check the inventory, to know precisely where each of us was, Lonya at his desk in the National Library on the fourth floor of the Terra Sancta Building, Zussya at Café Atara, Fania sitting in the B'nai B'rith Library, Amos playing with his best friend Eliyahu next door at Mr. Friedmann the engineer's, in the first building on the right. Only at the edge of her screen, behind the extinguished galaxy, in the corner from which her son Zyuzya, Zyuzinka, with Malka and little Daniel, whom she had never seen or washed, were supposed to flicker back at her, all she could see by day or night was a terrifying black hole.

Grandpa would stroll down the Street of the Abyssinians with his hat on, listening to the echo of his footsteps, breathing in the dry night air, saturated with pine trees and stone. Back at home, he would sit down at his desk, have a little drink, smoke a cigarette or two, and write a soulful Russian poem. Ever since that shameful lapse when he had fallen for someone else on the boat to New York, and Grandma had had to drag him off by force to the rabbi, it had never crossed his mind to rebel again: he stood before his wife like a serf before a lady, and he served her with boundless humility, admiration, awe, devotion, and patience.

She, for her part, called him Zussya, and on rare occasions of profound gentleness and compassion she called him Zissel. Then his face would suddenly light up as though the seven heavens had opened before him.

17

HE LIVED for another twenty years after Grandma Shlomit died in her bath.

For several weeks or months he continued to get up at daybreak and drag the mattresses and bedclothes to the balcony railing, where he beat them mercilessly to crush any germs or goblins that might have insinuated themselves into the bedding overnight. Perhaps he found it hard to break the habit; perhaps it was his way of paying his respects to the departed; perhaps he was expressing his longing for his queen; or perhaps he was afraid of provoking her avenging spirit if he stopped.

He did not immediately stop disinfecting the toilet and washbasins, either.

But slowly, with the passage of time, Grandpa's smily cheeks grew pink as they had never done before. They always had a cheerful look. Although he remained very particular to his last day about cleanliness and tidiness, being by nature a dapper man, the violence had gone out of him: there were no more furious beatings or frantic sprays of Lysol or chlorine. A few months after Grandma's death his love life began to blossom in a tempestuous and wonderful way. At about the same time, I have the impression that my seventy-seven-year-old grandfather discovered the joy of sex.

Before he had managed to wipe the dust of Grandma's burial off his shoes, Grandpa's home was full of women offering condolences, encouragement, freedom from loneliness, sympathy. They never left him alone, nourishing him with hot meals, comforting him with apple cake, and he apparently enjoyed not letting them leave him alone. He was always attracted to women—all women, both the beautiful ones and those whose beauty other men were incapable of seeing. "Women," my grandfather once declared, "are all very beautiful. All of them without exception. Only men," he smiled, "are blind! Completely blind! *Nu*, what. They only see themselves, and not even themselves. Blind!"

After my grandmother's death Grandpa spent less time on his business. He would still sometimes announce, his face beaming with pride and joy, "a very important business trip to Tel Aviv, to Grusenberg Street," or "an extremely important meeting in Ramat Gan, with all the heads of the company." He still liked to proffer to anyone he met one of his many impressive business cards. But now he was busy most days with his tempestuous affairs of the heart: issuing or receiving invitations to tea, dining by candlelight in some select but not too expensive restaurant ("with Mrs. Tsitrine, *ty durak,* not Mrs. Shaposhnik!").

He sat for hours at his table on the discreet upstairs floor of Café Atara in Ben Yehuda street, dressed in a navy blue suit, with a polka-dot tie, looking pink, smiling, gleaming, well groomed, smelling of shampoo, talcum powder, and aftershave. A striking sight in his starched white shirt, his gleaming white handkerchief in his breast pocket, his silver cufflinks, always surrounded by a bevy of well-preserved women in their fifties or sixties: widows in tight corsets and nylons with seams running down the back, well made up divorcees, adorned with an abundance of rings, earrings, and bracelets, finished off with a manicure, a pedicure, and a perm, matrons who spoke massacred Hebrew with a Hungarian, Polish, Romanian, or Bulgarian accent. Grandpa loved their company, and they were melted by his charms: he was a fascinating, entertaining conversationalist, a gentleman in the nineteenth-century mold, who kissed ladies' hands, hurried forward to open doors for them, offered his arm at every stairway or slope, never forgot a birthday, sent bouquets of flowers and boxes of sweets, noticed and made a subtle compliment on the cut of a dress, a change of hair style, elegant shoes, or a new handbag, joked tastefully, quoted a poem at the appropriate moment, chatted with warmth and humor. Once I opened a door and caught sight of my ninety-year-old grandfather kneeling before the jolly, dumpy brunette widow of a certain notary. The lady winked at me over my enamored grandfather's head, and smiled gaily, revealing two rows of teeth too perfect to be her own. I left, closing the door gently, before Grandpa was aware of my presence.

What was the secret of Grandpa's charm? I began to understand only years later. He possessed a quality that is hardly ever found among men, a marvelous quality that for many women is the sexiest in a man:

He listened.

He did not just politely pretend to listen, while impatiently waiting for her to finish what she was saying and shut up.

He did not break into his partner's sentence and finish it for her.

He did not cut in to sum up what she was saying so as to move on to another subject.

He did not let his interlocutress talk into thin air while he prepared in his head the reply he would make when she finally finished.

He did not pretend to be interested or entertained, he really was. *Nu,* what: he had an inexhaustible curiosity.

He was not impatient. He did not attempt to deflect the conversation from her petty concerns to his own important ones.

On the contrary: he loved her concerns. He always enjoyed waiting for her, and if she needed to take her time, he took pleasure in all her contortions.

He was in no hurry, and he never rushed her. He would wait for her to finish, and even when she had finished, he did not pounce or grab but enjoyed waiting in case there was something more, in case she was carried along on another wave.

He loved to let her take him by the hand and lead him to her own places, at her own pace. He loved to be her accompanist.

He loved getting to know her. He loved to understand, to get to the bottom of her. And beyond.

He loved to give himself. He enjoyed giving himself up to her more than he enjoyed it when she gave herself up to him.

Nu, what: they talked and talked to him to their heart's content, even about the most private, secret, vulnerable things, while he sat and listened, wisely, gently, with empathy and patience.

Or rather with pleasure and feeling.

There are many men around who love sex but hate women.

My grandfather, I believe, loved both.

And with gentleness. He never calculated, never grabbed. He never rushed. He loved setting sail, he was never in a hurry to cast anchor.

He had many romances in his twenty-year Indian summer after my grandmother's death, from when he was seventy-seven to the end of his life. He would sometimes go away with one or another of his lady friends for a few days to a hotel in Tiberias, a guesthouse in Gedera, or a "holiday resort" by the seaside in Netanya. (His expression "holiday resort" was apparently his translation of some Russian phrase with

Chekhovian overtones of dachas on the Crimean coast.) Once or twice I saw him walking down Agrippa Street or Bezalel Street arm in arm with some woman, and I did not approach them. He did not take any particular pains to conceal his love affairs from us, but he did not boast about them either. He never brought his lady friends to our house or introduced them to us, and he rarely mentioned them. But sometimes he seemed as giddy with love as a teenager, with veiled eyes, humming to himself, an absentminded smile playing on his lips. And sometimes his face fell, the baby pink left his cheeks like an overcast autumn day, and he would stand in his room furiously ironing shirts one after the other, he even ironed his underwear and sprayed it with scent from a little flask. and occasionally he would speak harshly but softly to himself in Russian, or hum some mournful Ukrainian melody, from which we deduced that some door had shut in his face, or, on the contrary, he had become embroiled again, as on his amazing trip to New York when he was engaged, in the anguish of two simultaneous loves.

Once, when he was already eighty-nine, he announced to us that he was thinking of taking an "important trip" for two or three days, and that we were on no account to worry. But when he had not returned after a week, we were beset with worries. Where was he? Why didn't he phone? What if something had happened to him, heaven forbid? After all, a man of his age . . .

We agonized: should we involve the police? If he was lying sick in some hospital, heaven forbid, or had got into some sort of trouble, we would never forgive ourselves if we hadn't looked for him. On the other hand, if we rang the police and he turned up safe and sound, how could we face his volcanic fury? If Grandpa didn't appear by noon on Friday, we decided after a day and a night of dithering, we would have to call the police. There was no alternative.

He turned up on Friday, about half an hour before the deadline, pink with contentment, brimming with good humor, amusement, and enthusiasm, like a little child.

"Where did you disappear to, Grandpa?"

"*Nu*, what. I was traveling."

"But you said you'd only be away for two or three days."

"So what if I did? *Nu*, I was traveling with Mrs. Hershkovich, and we were having such a wonderful time we didn't notice how the time was flying."

"But where did you go?"

"I've told you, we went away to enjoy ourselves for a little. We discovered a quiet guesthouse. A very cultured guesthouse. A guesthouse like in Switzerland."

"A guesthouse? Where?"

"On a high mountain in Ramat Gan."

"Couldn't you at least have phoned us? So we wouldn't be so worried about you?"

"We didn't find a phone in the room. *Nu*, what. It was such a wonderfully cultured guesthouse!"

"But couldn't you have phoned us from a public telephone? I gave you the tokens myself."

"Tokens. Tokens. *Nu, shto takoye*, what are tokens?"

"Tokens for the public phone."

"Oh, those *jetons* of yours. Here they are. *Nu*, take them, little bed-wetter, take your *jetons* along with the holes in the middle of them, take them, only be sure to count them. Never accept anything from anyone without counting properly first."

"But why didn't you use them?"

"The *jetons*? *Nu*, what. I don't believe in *jetons*."

And when he was ninety-three, three years after my father died, Grandpa decided that the time had come and that I was old enough for a man-to-man conversation. He summoned me into his den, closed the windows, locked the door, sat down solemnly and formally at his desk, motioned to me to sit facing him on the other side of the desk. He didn't call me "little bed-wetter," he crossed his legs, rested his chin in his hands, mused for a while, and said:

"The time has come we should talk about women."

And at once he explained:

"*Nu*. About woman in general."

(I was thirty-six at the time, I had been married fifteen years and had two teenage daughters.)

Grandpa sighed, coughed into his palm, straightened his tie, cleared his throat a couple of times, and said:

"*Nu*, what. Women have always interested me. That is to say, always.

Don't you go understanding something not nice! What I am saying is something completely different, *nu*, I am just saying that *woman* has always interested me. No, not the 'woman question'! Woman as a person."

He chuckled and corrected himself:

"—interested me in every way. All my life I am all the time looking at women, even when I was no more than a little *chudak, nu,* no, no, I never looked at a woman like some kind of *paskudniak,* no, only looking at her with all respect. Looking and learning. *Nu,* and what I learned, I want to teach you now also. So you will know. So now you, listen carefully please: it is like this."

He paused and looked around, as though to make certain that we were really alone, with no one to overhear us.

"Woman," Grandpa said, "*nu,* in some ways she is just like us. Exactly the same. But in some other ways," he said, "a woman is entirely different. Very very different."

He paused here and pondered it for a while, maybe conjuring up images in his mind, his childlike smile lit his face, and he concluded his lesson:

"But you know what? In which ways a woman is just like us and in which ways she is very very different—*nu,* on this," he concluded, rising from his chair, "I am still working."

He was ninety-three, and he may well have continued to "work" on the question to the end of his days. I am still working on it myself.

He had his own unique brand of Hebrew, Grandpa Alexander, and he refused to be corrected. He always insisted on calling a barber (*sapar*) a sailor (*sapan*), and a barber's shop (*mispara*) a shipyard (*mispana*). Once a month, precisely, this bold seafarer strode off to the Ben Yakar Brothers' shipyard, sat down on the captain's seat, and delivered a string of detailed, stern orders, instructions for the voyage ahead. He used to tell me off sometimes: "*Nu,* it's time you went to the *sailor,* what do you look like! A pirate!" He always called shelves *shlevs,* even though he could manage the singular, shelf, perfectly well. He never called Cairo by its Hebrew name, *Kahir,* but always Cairo; I was called, in Russian, either *khoroshi malchik* (good boy) or *ty durak* (you fool); Hamburg was

Gamburg; a habit was always a habitat: sleep was *spat,* and when he was asked how he had slept, he invariably replied "excellently!" and because he did not entirely trust the Hebrew language, he would add cheerfully in Russian "*Khorosho! Ochen khorosho!!*" He called a library *biblioteka,* a teapot *chainik,* the government *partats,* the people *oilem goilem,* and the ruling Labor Party, Mapai, he sometimes called *geshtankt* (stink) or *iblaikt* (decay).

And once, a couple of years before he passed away, he spoke to me about his death: "If, heaven forbid, some young soldier dies in battle, nineteen-years-old, maybe twenty-years-old boy, *nu,* it is a terrible disaster but it's not a tragedy. To die at my age though—that's a tragedy! A man like me, ninety-five years old, nearly a hundred, so many years getting up every morning at five o'clock, taking a cold *douche* every morning every morning since nearly hundred years, even in Russia cold *douche* in the morning, even in Vilna, hundred years now eating every morning every morning slice of bread with salty herring, drinking glass of *chai* and going out every morning every morning always to stroll half an hour in the street, summer or winter, morning stroll, this is for the *motion,* it gets the circulation going so well! And right away after that coming home every day every day and reading a bit newspaper and meanwhile drinking another glass *chai, nu,* in short, it's like this, dear boy, this *bakhurchik* of nineteen, if he is killed, Heaven forbid, he still hasn't had time to have all sorts of regular habitats. When would he have them? But at my age it is very difficult to stop, very very difficult. To stroll in the street every morning—this is for me old habitat. And cold *douche*—also habitat. Even to live—it's a habitat for me, *nu,* what, after hundred years who can all at once suddenly change all his habitats? Not to get up anymore at five in the morning? No *douche,* no salt herring with bread? No newspaper no stroll no glass hot *chai*? Now, that's tragedy!'

18

IN THE YEAR 1845 the new British Consul James Finn together with his wife Elizabeth Anne arrived in Ottoman-ruled Jerusalem. They both knew Hebrew, and the consul even wrote books about the Jews, for whom he always harbored a sympathy. He belonged to the London Society for Promoting Christianity among the Jews, although so far as is known he was not directly involved in missionary work in Jerusalem. Consul Finn and his wife believed fervently that the return of the Jewish people to their homeland would hasten the salvation of the world. More than once he protected Jews in Jerusalem from harassment by the Ottoman authorities. James Finn also believed in the need to make the Jews lead "productive" lives—he even helped Jews gain a proficiency in building work and adapt themselves to agriculture. To this end he purchased in 1853, at a cost of £250 sterling, a desolate rocky hill a few miles from Jerusalem *intra muros*, to the northwest of the Old City, an uninhabited and untilled piece of land that the Arabs called Karm al-Khalil, which translated means "Abraham's Vineyard." Here James Finn built his home and set up an "Industrial Plantation" that was intended to provide poor Jews with work and train them for "useful" lives. The farm extended over some ten acres, James and Elizabeth Anne Finn erected their house on the summit of the hill, and around it extended the agricultural colony, the farm buildings, and the workshops. The thick walls of the two-story house were built of dressed stone, and the ceilings were constructed in oriental style, with crossed vaults. Behind the house, around the edge of the walled garden, wells were sunk, and stables, a sheep pen, a granary, storehouses, a wine press and cellar, and an olive oil press were constructed.

Some two hundred Jews were employed on the Industrial Plantation in Finn's farm in work such as removing stones, building walls, fencing, planting an orchard, and growing fruit and vegetables, as well as developing a small stone quarry and engaging in various building trades. In the course of time, after the consul's death, his widow set up a soap factory in which she also employed Jewish workers. Not far from Abraham's Vineyard, almost at the same time, the German Protestant missionary Johann Ludwig Schneller founded an educational institute for Christian Arab orphans fleeing from the fighting between Druse and Christians in the Lebanon mountains. It was a large property surrounded by a stone wall. The Schneller Syrian Orphanage, like Mr. and Mrs. Finn's Industrial Plantation, was based on a desire to train its inmates for a productive life in handicrafts and agriculture. Finn and Schneller, in their different ways, were both pious Christians who were moved by the poverty, suffering, and backwardness of Jews and Arabs in the Holy Land. Both believed that training the inhabitants for a productive life of work, building, and agriculture would wrest the "Orient" from the clutches of degeneration, despair, indigence, and indifference. They may indeed have believed, in their different ways, that their generosity would light the way of Jews and Muslims into the bosom of the Church.*

In 1920 the suburb of Kerem Avraham, Abraham's Vineyard, was founded below Finn's farm: its huddled little houses were built among the plantations and orchards of the farm and progressively ate into them. The consul's house itself underwent various transformations after the death of his widow Elizabeth Anne Finn: first it was turned into a British institute for young offenders, then it became a property of the British administration, and finally an army HQ.

Toward the end of World War II the garden of Finn's house was surrounded by a high barbed-wire fence, and captured Italian officers were imprisoned in the house and the garden. We used to creep out at nightfall to tease the POWs. The Italians greeted us with cries of *Bambino! Bambino! Buon giorno bambino!* and we responded by shrieking *Bambino! Bambino! Il Duce morte! Finito il Duce!* Sometimes we shouted *Viva Pinocchio!* and from beyond the fences and the barriers of language, war, and Fascism there always echoed like the second half of some ancient slogan the cry: *Gepetto! Gepetto! Viva Gepetto!*

In exchange for the sweets, peanuts, oranges, and biscuits that we threw to them over the barbed-wire fence, as though to monkeys in the zoo, some of them passed us Italian stamps or displayed to us from a distance family photographs with smiling women and tiny children stuffed into suits, children with ties, children with jackets, children of our age with perfectly combed dark hair and a forelock shining with brilliantine.

One of the POWs once showed me, from behind the wire, in return for an Alma chewing gum in a yellow wrapper, a photo of a plump woman wearing nothing but stockings and a suspender belt. I stood staring, for a moment, wide-eyed and struck dumb with horror, as though someone in the middle of the synagogue on the Day of Atonement had suddenly stood up and shouted out the Ineffable Name. Then

*Based on the Hebrew book *Architecture in Jerusalem: European Christian Building outside the Walls, 1855–1918,* by David Kroyanker (Keter: Jerusalem, 1987), pp. 419–21.

I spun around and fled, terrified, sobbing, hardly seeing where I was running. I was six or seven at the time, and I ran as though there were wolves on my tail, I ran and ran and did not stop fleeing from that picture until I was eleven and a half or so.

After the establishment of the State of Israel in 1948 the Finns' house was used successively by the Home Guard, the Border Patrol, the Civil Defense, and the paramilitary youth movement, before becoming a religious Jewish girls' school by the name of Beit Bracha. I occasionally stroll around Kerem Avraham, turning from Geula Street, which has been renamed Malkei Israel Street, into Malachi Street, then left into Zechariah Street, walk up and down Amos Street a few times, then up to the top end of Obadiah Street, where I stand at the entrance to Consul Finn's house for a few minutes and gaze at the house. The old house has shrunk over the years, as though its head has been pushed down into its shoulders with an ax blow. It has been Judaized. The trees and shrubs have been dug up, and the whole area of the garden has been asphalted over. Pinocchio and Gepetto have vanished. The paramilitary youth movement has also disappeared without a trace. The old frame of a broken *sukkah* left over from the last Sukkot festival stands in the front yard. There are sometimes a few women wearing snoods and dark dresses standing at the gate; they stop talking when I look at them. They do not look back at me. They start whispering as I move away.

When he arrived in Jerusalem in 1933, my father registered for an MA at the Hebrew University on Mount Scopus. At first he lived with his parents in the dark little apartment in Kerem Avraham, in Amos Street, about two hundred yards east of Consul Finn's house. Then his parents moved to another apartment. A couple named Zarchi moved into the Amos Street apartment, but that young student, whose parents pinned such high hopes on him, paid rent to go on living in his room, which had its own entrance through the veranda.

Kerem Avraham was still a new district: most of the streets were unpaved, and the vestiges of the vineyard that gave it its name were still visible in the gardens of the new houses, in the form of vines and pomegranate bushes, fig and mulberry trees, that whispered to each other whenever there was a breeze. At the beginning of summer, when the windows were opened, the smell of greenery flooded the tiny rooms. From the rooftops and at the ends of the dusty streets you could catch sight of the hills that surrounded Jerusalem.

One after the other, simple square stone houses sprang up, two- or three-story buildings that were divided up into large numbers of cramped apartments each with two tiny rooms. The gardens and verandas had iron railings that soon rusted. The wrought-iron gates incorporated a six-pointed star or the word ZION. Gradually dark cypresses and pines supplanted the pomegranates and vines. Here and there, pomegranates grew wild, but the children snuffed them out before the fruit had a chance to ripen. Among the untended trees and the bright outcrops of rock in the gardens some people planted oleander or geranium bushes, but the garden beds were soon forgotten, as washing lines were strung out over them and they were trampled underfoot or filled with thistles and broken glass. If they did not die of thirst, the oleanders and geraniums grew wild, like scrub. All sorts of storehouses were erected in the gardens, sheds, corrugated-iron shacks, improvised huts made from the planks of the packing cases in which the residents brought their belongings here, as though they were trying to create a replica of the shtetl in Poland, Ukraine, Hungary, or Lithuania.

Some fixed an empty olive can to a pole, set it up as a dovecote, and waited for the doves to come—until they gave up hope. Here and there somebody tried to keep a few hens, someone else tended a little vegetable patch, with radishes, onions, cauliflower, parsley. Most of them longed to get out of here and move somewhere more cultured, like Rehavia, Kiryat Shmuel, Talpiot, or Beit Hakerem. All of them tried hard to believe that the bad days would soon be over, the Hebrew state would be established, and everything would change for the better: surely their cup of sorrow was full to overflowing? Shneour Zalman Rubashov, who later changed his name to Zalman Shazar and was elected President of Israel, wrote something like this in a newspaper at that time: "When the free Hebrew state finally arises, nothing will be the same as it was! Even love will not be what it was before!"

Meanwhile the first children were born in Kerem Avraham, and it was almost impossible to explain to them where their parents had come from, or why they had come, or what it was that they were all waiting for. The people who lived in Kerem Avraham were minor bureaucrats in the Jewish Agency, or teachers, nurses, writers, drivers, shorthand typists, world reformers, translators, shop assistants, theorists, librarians, bank tellers or cinema ticket sellers, ideologues, small shopkeepers, lonely old bachelors who lived on their meager savings. By eight o'clock in the evening the grilles on the balconies were closed, the apartments were locked, shutters were barred, and only the streetlamp cast a gloomy yellow puddle on the corner of the empty street. At night you could hear the piercing shrieks of night birds, the barking of distant dogs, stray shots, the wind in the trees of the orchard: for at nightfall Kerem Avraham went back to being a vineyard. Fig trees, mulberries and olives, apple trees, vines and pomegranates rustled their leaves in every garden. The stone walls reflected the moonlight back up into the branches in a pale, skeletal glow.

Amos Street, in one or two pictures in my father's photograph album, looks like an unfinished sketch for a street. Square stone buildings with iron shutters and iron grilles on the verandas. Here and there on the windowsills pale geraniums bloom in pots between the sealed jars of cucumbers or peppers pickling in garlic and dill. In the center between the buildings there is no road yet but only a temporary building site, a dusty track scattered with building materials, gravel, piles of half-finished stones, sacks of cement, metal drums, floor tiles, heaps of sand, coils of wire for fencing, a mound of wooden scaffolding. Some spiny prosopis still sprout among the mess of building materials, covered with whitish dust. Stonemasons sit on the ground in the middle of the track, barefoot, naked from the waist up, with cloths draped around their heads, in baggy trousers, the sound of their hammers striking the chisels and cutting grooves in the stones filling the air with the drumbeats of some strange, stubborn atonal music. Hoarse shouts ring out from time to time from the end of the street, "*Ba-rud! Ba-rud*" (explosion), followed by the thunderous haul of shattered stones.

In another, formal picture, as though taken before a party, there stands right in the center of Amos Street, in the midst of all this commotion, a rectangular black hearse-like automobile. A taxi or a hired car? Impossible to tell from the photo. It is a gleaming, polished car of the 1920s, with thin tires like a motorcycle, and metal spokes, and a strip of chrome running along the edge of the hood. The hood has louvers on the side to let in the air, and on the tip of its nose the shiny chrome radiator cap protrudes like a pimple. In front, two round headlights hang from a sort of silvery bar, and the headlights too are silvery and gleam in the sun.

By the side of this magnificent automobile the camera has caught Alexander Klausner, General Agent, resplendent in a cream-colored tropical suit and a tie, with a panama hat on his head, looking rather like Errol Flynn in a film about European aristocrats in equatorial Africa or in Burma. At his side, stronger, taller, and wider than he, stands the imposing figure of his elegant wife Shlomit, his cousin and mistress, a grande dame, stately as a battleship, in a short-sleeved summer frock, wearing a necklace and a splendid fedora hat with muslin veil set at a precise angle on her perfectly coiffed hairdo, and clutching a parasol. Their son Lonia, Lionichka, is standing at their side like a nervous bridegroom on his wedding day. He looks faintly comical, with his mouth slightly open, his round spectacles slipping down his nose, his shoulders drooping, confined, and almost mummified in a tight suit, and a stiff black hat that looks as though it has been forced onto his head: it comes halfway down his forehead like an upturned pudding basin, and gives the impression that only his overlarge ears prevent it from slipping down to his chin and swallowing up the rest of his head.

What was the solemn event for which the three of them had dressed up in their finery and ordered a special limousine? There is no way of knowing. The date, to judge by other photographs on the same page of the album, is 1934, the year after they arrived in the country, when they all still lived in the Zarchis' apartment on Amos Street. I can make out the number of the automobile without difficulty, M 1651. My father would have been twenty-four, but in the picture he looks like a fifteen-year-old disguised as a respectable middle-aged gentleman.

When they first arrived from Vilna, all three Klausners lived for a year or so in the two-and-a-half-room apartment in Amos Street. Then Grandma and Grandpa found themselves a little place to rent, with a single room plus a tiny room that served as Grandpa's "den," his safe haven from his wife's fits of rage and from the hygienic scourge of her war on germs. The new apartment was the one in Prague Lane, between Isaiah Street and Chancellor Street, now renamed Strauss Street.

The front room in the old apartment on Amos Street now became my father's student sitting room. Here he installed his first bookcase, containing the books he had brought with him from his student days in Vilna; here stood the old, spindly-legged plywood table that served as his desk, here he hung his clothes behind a curtain that concealed the packing case that did duty as his wardrobe. Here he invited his friends for intellectual conversations about the meaning of life, literature, the world, and local politics.

In one photograph, my father sits comfortably behind his desk, thin, young, and stern, his hair combed back, wearing those serious, black-framed spectacles and a long-sleeved white shirt. He is sitting in a relaxed pose, at an angle to the desk, with his legs crossed. Behind him is a double window, one half of which is open inward, but the shutters are still closed so that only thin fingers of light penetrate between the slats. In the picture my father is deeply engrossed in a big book that he is holding up in front of him. On the desk in front of him another book lies open, and there is something else that looks like an alarm clock with its back to the camera, a round tin clock with little slanting legs. To Father's left stands a small bookcase laden with books, one shelf bowing under the weight of the thick tomes it is carrying, foreign books apparently that have come from Vilna and are clearly feeling rather cramped, warm, and uncomfortable here.

On the wall above the bookcase hangs a framed photograph of Uncle Joseph, looking authoritative and magnificent, almost prophetic with his white goatee and thinning hair, as though he were peering down from a great height on my father and fixing him with a watchful eye, to make sure he does not neglect his studies, or let himself be distracted by the dubious delights of student life, or that he doesn't forget the historic condition of the Jewish nation or the hopes of generations, or—heaven forbid!—underestimate those little details out of which, after all, the big picture is made up.

Hanging on a nail underneath Uncle Joseph is the collecting box of the Jewish National Fund, painted with a thick Star of David. My father looks relaxed and pleased with himself, but as serious and resolute as a monk: he is taking the weight of the open book on his left hand, while his right hand rests on the pages to the right, the pages he has already read, from which we may deduce that it is a Hebrew book, read from right to left. At the place where his hand emerges from the sleeve of his white shirt I can see the thick black hair that covered his arms from elbow to knuckles.

My father looks like a young man who knows what his duty is and intends to do it come what may. He is determined to follow in the footsteps of his famous uncle and his elder brother. Out there, beyond the closed shutters, workmen are digging a trench under the dusty roadway to lay pipes. Somewhere in the cellar of some old Jewish building in the winding alleyways of Sha'arei Hesed or Nahalat Shiv'a the youths of the Jerusalem Hagganah are training in secret, dismantling and reassembling an ancient illicit Parabellum pistol. On the hilly roads that wind among menacing Arab villages, Egged bus drivers and Tnuva van drivers are steering their vehicles, their hands strong and suntanned on the wheel. In the wadis that go down to the Judaean desert, young Hebrew scouts in khaki shorts and khaki socks, with military belts and white *kaffiyeh*s, learn to recognize with their feet the secret pathways of the Fatherland. In Galilee and the Plains, in the Beth Shean Valley and the Valley of Jezreel, in the Sharon and the Hefer Valley, in the Judaean lowlands, the Negev and the wilderness around the Dead Sea, pioneers are tilling the land, muscular, silent, brave, and bronzed. And meanwhile he, the earnest student from Vilna, plows his own furrow here.

One fine day he too would be a professor on Mount Scopus, he would help push back the frontiers of knowledge and drain the swamps of exile in the people's hearts. Just as the pioneers in Galilee and the Valleys made the desert places bloom, so he too would labor with all his strength, with enthusiasm and dedication, to plow the furrows of the national spirit and make the new Hebrew culture bloom. The picture says it all.

19

EVERY MORNING Yehuda Arieh Klausner took the No. 9 bus from the stop in Geula Street via the Bukharian Quarter, Prophet Samuel Street, Simeon the Righteous Street, the American Colony, and the Sheikh

Jarrah district to the university buildings on Mount Scopus, where he diligently pursued his MA studies. He attended lectures on history by Professor Richard Michael Kobner, who never succeeded in learning Hebrew; Semitic linguistics by Professor Hans Jacob Polotsky; Biblical studies from Professor Umberto Moshe David Cassuto; and Hebrew literature from Uncle Joseph, alias Professor Dr. Joseph Klausner, the author of *Judaism and Humanism.*

While Uncle Joseph definitely encouraged my father, who was one of his star pupils, he never chose him, when the time came, as a teaching assistant, so as not give malicious tongues anything to wag about. So important was it for Professor Klausner to avoid aspersions on his good name that he may have behaved unfairly to his brother's son, his own flesh and blood.

On the front page of one of his books the childless uncle inscribed the following words: "To my beloved Yehuda Arieh, my nephew who is as dear to me as a son, from his uncle Joseph who loves him like his own soul." Father once quipped bitterly: "If only we had not been related, if only he loved me a little less, who knows, I might have been a lecturer in the literature department by now instead of a librarian."

All those years it was like a running sore in my father's soul, because he really deserved to be a professor like his uncle and his brother David, the one who had taught literature in Vilna and died of it. My father was amazingly knowledgeable, an excellent student with a prodigious memory, an expert in world literature as well as Hebrew literature, who was at home in many languages, utterly familiar with the Tosefta, the Midrashic literature, the religious poetry of the Jews of Spain, as well as Homer, Ovid, Babylonian poetry, Shakespeare, Goethe, and Adam Mickiewicz, as hard-working as a honey bee, as straight as a die, a gifted teacher who could give a simple and accurate explanation of the barbarian invasions, *Crime and Punishment,* the workings of a submarine, or the solar system. Yet he never earned the chance to stand up before a class or to have pupils of his own, but ended his days as a librarian and bibliographer who wrote three or four scholarly books and contributed a few entries to the *Hebrew Encyclopedia,* mainly on comparative and Polish literature.

In 1936 he was found a modest post in the newspaper department of the National Library, where he worked for twenty years or so, first on

Mount Scopus and after 1948 in the Terra Sancta Building, beginning as a simple librarian and eventually rising to deputy to the head of the department, Dr. Pfeffermann. In a Jerusalem that was full of immigrants from Poland and Russia and refugees from Hitler, among them distinguished luminaries from famous universities, there were more lecturers and scholars than students.

In the late 1950s, after receiving his doctorate from London University, my father tried unsuccessfully to secure a foothold in the literature department in Jerusalem as an outside lecturer. Professor Klausner, in his day, had been afraid of what people would say if he employed his own nephew. Klausner was succeeded as professor by the poet Shimon Halkin, who attempted to make a fresh start by eliminating the heritage, the methods, and the very smell of Klausner and certainly did not want to take on Klausner's nephew. In the early 1960s Father tried his luck at the newly opened Tel Aviv University, but he was not welcome there either.

In the last year of his life he negotiated for a literature post in the academic institute that was being set up in Beer Sheva and was eventually to become Ben Gurion University. Sixteen years after my father's death I myself became an adjunct professor of literature at Ben Gurion University; a year or two later I was made a full professor, and eventually I was appointed to the Agnon Chair. In time I received generous invitations from both Jerusalem and Tel Aviv Universities to be a full professor of literature, I, who am neither an expert nor a scholar nor a mover of mountains, who have never had any talent for research and whose mind always turns cloudy at the sight of a footnote.* My father's little finger was more professorial than a dozen "parachuted in" professors like me.

The Zarchis' apartment had two and a half small rooms, and was on the ground floor of a three-story building. The rear part of the apartment

*My father's books are rich in footnotes. As for me, I have only used them freely in one book, *The Silence of Heaven: Agnon's Fear of God* (Jerusalem: Keter, 1993; Princeton University Press, New Jersey, 2000). I introduced my father into note 92 on page 192 of the Hebrew edtion of that book. That is to say, I referred the reader to his book *The Novella in Hebrew Literature*. In writing that note, some twenty years after his death, I hoped to afford him a small pleasure yet at the same time feared that instead of being pleased he might be waving an admonishing finger at me.

was occupied by Israel Zarchi, his wife Esther, and his two aged parents. The front room, where my father lived, first with his parents, then on his own, and eventually with my mother, had its own door, leading onto the veranda, then down a few steps into the narrow front garden, and out into Amos Street, which was still no more than a dusty track, with no roadway or pavements, still scattered with heaps of building materials and dismantled scaffolding among which hunger-weary cats roamed and a few doves pecked. Three or four times a day a cart drawn by a donkey or mule came down the road, a cart bearing long iron rods for building, or the paraffin seller's cart, the iceman's cart, the milkman's cart, the cart of the rag-and-bone man, whose hoarse cry *"alte sachen"* always made my blood freeze: all the years of my childhood I imagined that I was being warned against illness, old age, and death, which though still distant from me were gradually and inexorably approaching, creeping secretly like a viper through the tangle of dark vegetation, ready to strike me from behind. The Yiddish cry *alte sachen* sounded to me just like the Hebrew words *al-tezaken,* "do not age." To this day, the cry sends a cold shiver up my spine.

Swallows nested in the fruit trees in the gardens, while lizards, geckos, and scorpions crept in and out of the clefts of the rocks. Occasionally we even saw a tortoise. The children burrowed under the fences, creating a network of shortcuts that spread through the backyards of the neighborhood, or climbed up on the flat rooftops to watch the British soldiers in the Schneller Barracks or to look out at the distant Arab villages on the surrounding hillsides: Isawiya, Shuafat, Beit Iksa, Lifta, Nebi Samwil.

Today the name of Israel Zarchi is almost forgotten, but in those days he was a prolific young writer whose books sold many copies. He was about my father's age, but by 1937, when he was twenty-eight, he had published no fewer than three books. I revered him because I was told that he was not like other writers: the whole of Jerusalem wrote scholarly books, put together from notes, from other books, from booklists, dictionaries, weighty foreign tomes, and ink-stained index cards, but Mr. Zarchi wrote books "out of his own head." (My father used to say: "If you steal from one book, you are condemned as a plagiarist, but if you steal from ten books, you are considered a scholar, and if you steal from thirty or forty books, a distinguished scholar.")

On winter evenings a few members of my parents' circle used to get together sometimes at our place or at the Zarchis' in the building across the road: Hayim and Hannah Toren, Shmuel Werses, the Breimans, flamboyant Mr. Sharon-Shvadron, who was a great talker, Mr. Haim Schwarzbaum the red-headed folklorist, Israel Hanani, who worked at the Jewish Agency, and his wife Esther Hananit. They arrived after supper, at seven or half past, and left at half past nine, which was considered a late hour. In between, they drank scalding tea, nibbled honey cake or fresh fruit, discussed with well-bred anger all kinds of topics that I could not understand; but I knew that when the time came, I would understand them, I would participate in the discussions and would produce decisive arguments that they had not thought of. I might even manage to surprise them, I might end up writing books out of my own head like Mr. Zarchi, or collections of poems like Bialik and Grandpa Alexander and Levin Kipnis and Dr. Saul Tchernikhowsky, the doctor whose smell I shall never forget.

The Zarchis were not only Father's former landlords but also dear friends, despite the regular arguments between my Revisionist father and Zarchi the "Red": my father loved to talk and explain, and Zarchi liked to listen. My mother would interpose a quiet sentence or two from time to time. Esther Zarchi, for her part, tended to ask questions, and my father enjoyed giving her extensively detailed replies. Israel Zarchi would turn to my mother sometimes, with downcast eyes, and ask her opinion as though begging her in coded language to take his side in the argument: my mother knew how to cast a new light on everything. She did this with a few brief words, after which the conversation sometimes took on a pleasant, relaxed tone, a new calm, a cautious or hesitant note entered the argument, until after a while tempers became inflamed again and voices were once more raised in a civilized fury, which simmered with exclamation marks.

In 1947 the Tel Aviv publisher Joshua Chachik brought out my father's first book, *The Novella in Hebrew Literature, from Its Origins to the End of the Haskalah*. This book was based on my father's MA dissertation. The title page declared that the book had been awarded the Klausner Prize of Tel Aviv Municipality and was published with the assistance of the Municipality and that of the Zippora Klausner Memorial Fund. Professor Dr. Joseph Klausner in person contributed a foreword:

> It is a twofold pleasure for me to see the publication of a Hebrew book on the novella that was submitted to me in my capacity as Professor of Literature in our one and only Hebrew University as a final dissertation in Modern Hebrew Literature by my long-standing pupil, my nephew Yehuda Arieh Klausner. This is no ordinary work . . . It is a comprehensive and all-embracing study . . . Even the style of the book is both rich and lucid, and is in keeping with the important subject matter . . . I am unable therefore to forbear from rejoicing . . . The Talmud says "Pupils are like sons" . . .

and on a separate page, after the title page, my father dedicated his book to the memory of his brother David:

To my first teacher of literary history—
my only brother
David
whom I lost in the darkness of exile.
Where art thou?

For ten days or a fortnight, as soon as my father got home from work at the library on Mount Scopus, he hurried to the local post office at the eastern end of Geula Street, opposite the entrance to Mea Shearim, eagerly awaiting copies of his first book, which he had been informed had been published and which someone or other had seen in a bookshop in Tel Aviv. So every day he rushed to the post office, and every day he returned empty-handed, and every day he promised himself that if the parcel from Mr. Gruber at Sinai Printers had not arrived by the next day, he would definitely go to the pharmacy and telephone forcefully to Mr. Chachik in Tel Aviv: This is simply unacceptable! If the books did not arrive by Sunday, by the middle of the week, by Friday at the latest—but the parcel did arrive, not by mail but by personal delivery, brought to our home by a smiling Yemenite girl, not from Tel Aviv but straight from Sinai Printers (Jerusalem, tel. no. 2892).

The parcel contained five copies of *The Novella in Hebrew Literature*, hot from the press, virginal, wrapped in several layers of good-quality white paper (on which the proofs of some picture book had been printed) and tied up with string. Father thanked the girl, and despite his excitement did not forget to give her a shilling (a handsome sum in those days, sufficient for a vegetarian meal at the Tnuva Restaurant). Then he asked me and my mother to step into his study to be with him while he opened the packet.

I remember how my father mastered his trembling enthusiasm, and did not forcibly snap the string holding the parcel together or even cut it with scissors but—I shall never forget this—undid the strong knots, one after another, with infinite patience, making alternate use of his strong fingernails, the tip of his paper knife, and the point of a bent paper clip. When he had finished, he did not pounce on his new book but slowly wound up the string, removed the wrapping of glossy paper, touched the jacket of the uppermost copy lightly with his fingertips, like a shy lover, raised it gently to his face, ruffled the pages a little, closed his eyes and sniffed them, inhaling deeply the fresh printing smells, the pleasure of new paper, the delightful, intoxicating odor of glue. Only then did he start to leaf through his book, peering first at the index, scrutinizing the list of addenda and corrigenda, reading and rereading Uncle Joseph's foreword and his own preface, lingering on the title page, caressing the cover again, then, alarmed that my mother might be secretly making fun of him, he said apologetically:

"A new book fresh from the press, a first book, it's as though I've just had another baby."

"When it's time to change its nappy," my mother replied, "I expect you'll call me."

So saying, she turned and left the room, but she returned a few moments later carrying a bottle of sweet, sacramental Tokay and three tiny liqueur glasses, saying that we must drink the health of Father's first book. She poured some wine for the two of them and a little drop for me, she may even have kissed him on the forehead, while he stroked her hair.

That evening my mother spread a white cloth on the kitchen table, as though it were Sabbath or a festival, and served up Father's favorite dish, hot borscht with an iceberg of pure white cream floating in it. She congratulated him. Grandpa and Grandma joined us to share our modest celebration, and Grandma remarked to my mother that the borscht was really very nice and almost tasty, but that—God preserve her from giving advice, but it was well known, every little girl knew, even Gentile women who cooked in Jewish homes knew, that borscht should be sour and just slightly sweet, certainly not sweet and just slightly sour, the way the Poles make it, because they sweeten everything, without rhyme or reason, and if you didn't watch them, they would drown salt herring in sugar, or even put jam on *chreyn* (horseradish sauce).

Mother, for her part, thanked Grandma for sharing her expertise with us and promised that in the future she would serve her only bitter and sour food, as that would be sure to suit her. As for Father, he was too pleased to notice such pinpricks. He presented one inscribed copy to his parents, another he gave to Uncle Joseph, a third to his dear friends Esther and Israel Zarchi, another to I cannot remember whom, and the last copy he kept in his library, on a prominent shelf, snuggled up close to the works of his uncle Professor Joseph Klausner.

Father's happiness lasted for three or four days, and then his face fell. Just as he had rushed to the post office every day before the packet arrived, so he now rushed every day to Achiasaph's bookshop in King George V Avenue, where three copies of *The Novella* were displayed for sale. The next day the same three copies were there, not one of them had been purchased. And the same the next day, and the day after that.

"You," Father said with a sad smile to his friend Israel Zarchi, "write a new novel every six months, and instantly all the pretty girls snatch you off the shelves and take you straight to bed with them, while we scholars, we wear ourselves out for years on end checking every detail, verifying every quotation, spending a week on a single footnote, and who bothers to read us? If we're lucky, two or three fellow prisoners in our own discipline read our books before they tear us to shreds. Sometimes not even that. We are simply ignored."

A week passed, and none of the three copies at Achiasaph's was sold. Father no longer spoke of his sorrow, but it filled the apartment like a smell. He no longer hummed popular songs out of tune while he shaved or washed the dishes. He no longer told me by heart of the doings of Gilgamesh or the adventures of Captain Nemo or Engineer Cyrus Smith in *The Mysterious Island,* but immersed himself furiously in the papers and reference books scattered on his desk, from which his next learned book would be born.

And then suddenly, a couple of days later, on Friday evening, he came home beaming happily and all atremble like a boy who has just been kissed in front of everyone by the prettiest girl in the class. "They're sold! They've all been sold! All in one day! Not one copy sold! Not two copies sold! All three sold! The whole lot! My book is sold out— Shakhna Achiasaph is going to order more copies from Chachik in Tel Aviv! He's ordered them already! This morning! By telephone! Not three copies, another five! And he thinks that's not going to be the end of the story!"

My mother left the room again and came back with the sickly sweet Tokay and the three tiny liqueur glasses. This time, though, she did not bother with the borscht or the white tablecloth. Instead she suggested the two of them go out to the Edison Cinema the next evening to the early showing of a famous film starring Greta Garbo, whom they both admired.

I was left with the novelist Zarchi and his wife, to have my supper there and behave myself until they got back, at nine or half past. Behave yourself, you hear?! Don't let us hear the tiniest complaint about you! When they set the table, don't forget to offer to help. After supper, but only once everyone has got up from the table, clear away your dishes and put them carefully on the draining board. Carefully, you hear?! Don't you break anything there. And take a dishcloth as at home and wipe the oil-cloth nicely when the table's cleared. And only speak when you're spoken to. If Mr. Zarchi is working, just find yourself a toy or a book and sit as quietly as a mouse! And if heaven forbid Mrs. Zarchi complains of a headache again, don't bother her with anything. Anything, you hear?!

And so they went off. Mrs. Zarchi may have shut herself up in the other room, or gone to visit a neighbor, and Mr. Zarchi suggested I go into his study, which, as in our apartment, was also the bedroom and the sitting room and everything. That was the room that had once been my father's room when he was a student, that was also my parents' room and where apparently I was conceived, since they lived there from their wedding up to a month before I was born.

Mr. Zarchi sat me down on the sofa and talked to me for a bit, I don't remember what about, but I shall never forget how I suddenly noticed on the little coffee table by the sofa no fewer than four identical copies of *The Novella in Hebrew Literature,* one on top of the other, as in a shop, one copy that I knew Father had given to Mr. Zarchi with an inscription, and three more whose existence I just couldn't understand, and it was on the tip of my tongue to ask Mr. Zarchi, but at the last moment I remembered the three copies that had just been bought today, at long last, in Achiasaph's bookshop, and I felt a rush of gratitude inside me that almost brought tears to my eyes. Mr. Zarchi saw that I had noticed them and he did not smile, but shot me a sidelong glance through half-closed eyes, as though he were silently accepting me into his band of conspirators, and without saying a word he leaned over, picked up three of the four copies on the coffee table, and secreted them in a drawer of his desk. I too held my peace, and said nothing either to him or to my parents. I did not tell a soul until after Zarchi died in his prime and after my father's death, I did not tell anyone except, many years later, his daughter Nurit Zarchi, who did not seem overly impressed by what I had told her.

I count two or three writers among my best friends, friends who have been close to me and dear to me for decades, yet I am not certain that I could do for one of them what Israel Zarchi did for my father. Who can say if such a generous ruse would have even occurred to me. After all, he, like everyone else in those days, lived a hand-to-mouth existence, and the three copies of *The Novella in Hebrew Literature* must have cost him at least the price of some much-needed clothes.

Mr. Zarchi left the room and came back with a cup of warm cocoa without skin on it, because he remembered from his visits to our apartment that that was what I drank in the evening. I thanked him as I had been told to, politely, and I really wanted to say something else, but I could not, and so I just sat there on the sofa in his room not uttering a peep, so as not to distract him from his work, even though in fact he did not work that evening but just skimmed backward and forward through the newspaper until my parents returned from the cinema, thanked the Zarchis, and hurriedly said good-night and took me home, because it was very late and I had to brush my teeth and go straight to bed.

That must have been the same room where, one evening some years earlier, in 1936, my father had first brought home a certain reserved, very pretty student, with olive skin and black eyes, who spoke little but whose very presence caused men to talk and talk.

She had left Prague University a few months previously and come to Jerusalem to study history and philosophy at the university on Mount Scopus. I do not know how or when or where Arieh Klausner met Fania Mussman, who was registered here by her Hebrew name, Rivka, although on some documents she is called Zippora and in one place she is registered as Feiga, but her family and her girlfriends always called her Fania.

He loved talking, explaining, analyzing, and she knew how to listen and hear even between the lines. He was very erudite, and she was sharp-eyed and something of a mind reader. He was a straightforward, decent, hard-working perfectionist, while she always understood why someone who clung firmly to a particular view did so, and why someone else who furiously opposed him felt such a powerful need to argue. Clothes interested her only as a peephole into their wearers' inner selves. When she was sitting in a friend's home, she always cast an appraising glance at the upholstery, the curtains, the sofas, the souvenirs on the window ledge, and the knicknacks on the bookshelf, while everyone else was busy talking: as though she were on a spying mission. People's secrets always fascinated her, but when there was gossip going on, she mostly listened with her faint smile, that hesitant smile that looked as though it was about to snuff itself out, and said nothing. She was often silent. But whenever she broke her silence and spoke a few sentences, the conversation was never the same as it had been before.

When Father spoke to her, there was sometimes something in his voice that suggested a mixture of timidity, distance, affection, respect, and fear. As though he had a fortune-teller living in his home under an assumed identity. Or a clairvoyant.

20

THERE WERE three wicker stools around our kitchen table with its flower-patterned oilcloth. The kitchen itself was small, low-ceilinged, and dark; its floor had sunk a little, its walls were sooty from the paraffin cooker and the Primus stove, and its one little window looked out on the basement yard surrounded by gray concrete walls. Sometimes, when my father had gone off to work, I used to sit on his stool so as to be opposite my mother, and she told me stories while she peeled and sliced vegetables or sorted lentils, picking out the black ones and putting them in a saucer. Later I would feed these to the birds.

My mother's stories were strange: they were nothing like the stories that were told in other homes at that time, or the stories I told my own children, but were veiled in a kind of mist, as though they did not begin at the beginning or end at the end but emerged from the undergrowth, appeared for a while, arousing alienation or pangs of fear, moved in front of me for a few moments like distorted shadows on the wall, amazed me, sometimes sent shivers up my spine, and slunk back to the forest they had come from before I knew what had happened. I can remember some of my mother's stories almost word for word to this day. For instance, there's the one about the very old man, Alleluyev:

Once upon a time, beyond the high mountains, beyond deep rivers and desolate steppes, there was a tiny, out-of-the-way village, with tumbledown huts. At the edge of this village, in a dark fir forest, lived a poor, dumb, blind man. He lived all on his own, without any family or friends, and his name was Alleluyev. Old Alleluyev was older than the oldest men in the village, older than the oldest men in the valley or the steppe. He was not just old, he was ancient. So old was he that moss had begun to grow on his bent back. Instead of hair, black mushrooms grew on his head, and instead of cheeks he had hollows where lichens spread. Brown roots had begun to sprout from his feet, and glowing fireflies had settled in his sunken eyesockets. This old Alleluyev was older than the forest, older than the snow, older than Time himself. One day a rumor spread that in the depths of his hut, whose shutters had never been opened, lodged another old man, Chernichortyn, who was much, much older than old Alleluyev, and even blinder and poorer and more silent, more bent, deafer, more motionless, and worn as smooth as a Tartar coin. They said in the village, on the long winter nights, that old Alleluyev looked after the ancient Chernichortyn, washing his wounds, setting the table for him, and making his bed, feeding him on berries from the forest washed down with well water or melted snow, and sometimes at night he sang to him, as one sings to a baby: Lula, lula, lula, don't be scared my trea-sure, lula, lula, lula, don't tremble my darling. And so they slept, the two of them, snuggled up together, the old man and the even older man, while outside there was nothing but wind and snow. If they have not been eaten by wolves, they are still living there, the two of them, to this day, in their miserable hut, while the wolf howls in the forest and the wind roars in the chimney.

Alone in bed before I fell asleep, trembling with fear and excitement, I whispered to myself over and over again the words "old," "ancient," "older then Time himself." I closed my eyes and saw in my mind's eye, with delicious dread, the moss slowly spreading over the old man's back, the black mushrooms and lichens, and those greedy brown wormlike roots growing in the darkness. I tried to visualize behind my closed eyes the meaning of "worn as smooth as a Tartar coin." And so I swathed my-self in sleep to the sound of the wind shrieking in the chimney, a wind that could never come near our home, sounds I had never heard, the chimney I had never seen except in the pictures in children's books where every house had a tiled roof and a chimney.

I had no brothers or sisters, my parents could hardly afford to buy me any toys or games, and television and computers had not yet been born. I spent my whole childhood in Kerem Avraham in Jerusalem, but where I really lived was on the edge of the forest, by the huts, the steppes, the meadows, the snow in my mother's stories, and in the illustrated books that piled up on my low bedside table: I was in the east, but my heart was in the farthermost west. Or the "farthermost north," as it said in those books. I wandered dizzily through virtual forests, forests of words, huts of words, meadows of words. The reality of the words thrust aside the suffocating backyards, the corrugated iron spread on top of stone houses, balconies laden with washtubs and washing lines. What sur-rounded me did not count. All that counted was made of words.

We had elderly neighbors in Amos Street, but their appearance as they walked slowly, painfully past our house was only a pale, sad, clumsy imitation of the spine-chilling reality of old, ancient Alleluyev, just as the Tel Arza woods were a miserable, amateurish sketch of the impenetrable, primeval forest. My mother's lentils were a disappointing reminder of the mushrooms and forest fruits, the blackberries and blueberries, in the stories she told me. The whole of reality was just a vain attempt to imitate the world of words. Here is the story my mother told me about the woman and the blacksmiths, not choosing her words but laying bare before my eyes with no thought for my tender age the full extent of the faraway many-colored provinces of language, where few children's feet had trodden before, the haunt of linguistic birds of paradise:

Many years ago, in a peaceful little town in the Land of Enularia, in the region of the innermost valleys, there lived three brothers who were blacksmiths, Misha, Alyosha, and Antosha. They were all thickset, hairy, bearlike men. All the winter long they slept, and only when summer came did they forge plows, shoe horses, whet knives, sharpen blades, and hammer out metal tools. One day Misha, the eldest brother, arose and went to the region of Troshiban. He was gone for many a day, and when he returned he was not alone, but with him he brought a laughing girlish woman named Tatiana, Tanya, or Tanichka. She was a beautiful woman, no one more beautiful than she was to be found in all the width and breadth of Enularia. Misha's two younger brothers ground their teeth and kept silent all day long. If ever one of them looked at her, this Tanichka would laugh her rippling laugh until the man was forced to lower his gaze. Or if she looked at one of them, then the brother she had chosen to look at trembled and lowered his eyes. There was only a single big room in the brothers' hut, and in this room dwelt Misha and Tanichka and the furnace and the bellows and the anvil and the wild brother Alyosha and the silent brother Antosha surrounded by heavy iron hammers and axes and chisels and poles and chains and coils of metal. So it befell that one day Misha was pushed into the furnace and Alyosha took Tanichka to himself. For seven weeks the beautiful Tanichka was the bride of the wild brother Alyosha until the heavy hammer fell on him and flattened his skull, and Antosha the silent brother buried his brother and took his place. When seven weeks had passed as the two of them were eating a mushroom pie, Antosha suddenly turned pale and went blue in the face, and he choked and died. And from that day on, young wandering blacksmiths from all the length and breadth of Enularia come and stay in that hut, but not one of them has dared to stay there for seven whole weeks. One might stay for a week, another for a couple of nights. And what of Tanya? Well, every blacksmith throughout the length and breadth of Enularia knew that Tanichka loved smiths who came for a week, smiths who came for a few days, smiths who stayed for a night and a day, half-naked they labored for her, farrowing, hammering, and forging, but she could never abide a smith who forgot to get up and leave. A week or two would do, but seven weeks? How could they?

Herz and Sarah Mussman, who lived in the early nineteenth century in the small village of Trope or Tripe near the town of Rovno in Ukraine, had a fine son named Ephraim. From his childhood on, so the family story ran,* this Ephraim loved playing with wheels and running water. When Ephraim Mussman was thirteen years old, twenty days after his bar mitzvah, some more guests were invited and entertained, and this time Ephraim was betrothed to a twelve-year-old girl named Haya-Duba: in those days boys were married to girls on paper to prevent their being carried off to serve in the Tsar's army and never being seen again.

My aunt Haya Shapiro (who was named after her grandmother, the child bride) told me many years ago about what happened at this wedding. After the ceremony and the festive meal, which took place in the late afternoon opposite the rabbi's house in the village of Trope, the little bride's parents stood up to take her home to bed. It was getting late, and the child, who was tired after the excitement of the wedding and a little tipsy from the sips of wine she had been given, had fallen asleep with her head in her mother's lap. The bridegroom was running around, hot and sweaty, among the guests, playing catch and hide-and-seek with his

*I heard this and other tales, which I tell on the following pages, from my mother when I was young and partly also from my grandparents and my mother's cousins Shimshon and Michael Mussman. In 1979 I wrote down some of my Aunt Haya's childhood memories, and between 1997 and 2001 I occasionally noted down some of the many things that Aunt Sonia told me. I have also been helped by my mother's cousin Shimshon Mussman's book *Escape from Horror*, published in Hebrew in Tel Aviv, 1996.

little school friends. So the guests started to take their leave, the two families began to say their farewells, and the groom's parents told their son to hurry up and get on the cart to go home.

But the young bridegroom had other ideas: the child Ephraim stood in the middle of the courtyard, all puffed up suddenly like a young cockerel, stamped his foot, and obstinately demanded his wife. Not in three years' time, not even in three months' time, but right here and now. This very evening.

When the remaining guests burst out laughing, he turned his back on them angrily and strode across the road, thumped on the rabbi's door, stood in the doorway face to face with the grinning rabbi, and started quoting texts from the Bible, the Mishnah, the law codes, and the commentators. The boy had clearly prepared his ammunition and done his homework well. He demanded that the rabbi judge immediately between him and the whole world, and give a ruling one way or the other. What was written in the Torah? What did the Talmud and the jurists say? Was it or was it not his right? Was she or was she not his wife? Had he or had he not married her according to the law? And so, which was it to be: either let him take his bride or he must have his *ketubba*, his marriage contract, back, and let the marriage be null and void.

The rabbi, so the story goes, hemmed and hawed and cleared his throat, fingered his mustache and scratched his head a few times, tugged his sidelocks and pulled at his beard, and eventually he heaved a sigh and ruled that there was nothing for it, the boy was not only skillful at marshaling his texts and his arguments, he was also perfectly right: the youthful bride had no alternative but to follow him and no other course but to obey him.

And so the little bride was woken and, at midnight, when all the deliberations were concluded, they had to accompany the bridal pair to his parents' home. The bride wept for fear all the way. Her mother held her tight and wept with her. The bridegroom, too, wept all the way, because of the guests' jeers and sneers. As for his mother and the rest of his family, they too wept all the way, from shame.

The nocturnal procession lasted an hour and a half. It was a cross between a tearful funeral procession and a raucous party, because some of the participants, delighted by the scandal, insisted on recounting at the tops of their voices the well-known joke about the male chick and the female chick, or the one about how to thread a needle, treating themselves to schnapps to the accompaniment of obscene snorts and neighs and shouts.

Meanwhile the youthful bridegroom's courage abandoned him, and he began to regret his victory. And so the young couple were led, bewildered, tearful, and deprived of sleep, like sheep to the slaughter, to the improvised bridal chamber, into which, in the early hours of the morning, they had to be pushed almost by force. The door, it is said, was locked from the outside. Then the wedding party retreated on tiptoe and spent the rest of the night sitting up in another room, drinking tea and finishing up the remains of the feast, while endeavoring to console one another.

In the morning, who knows, the mothers may have burst into the room, armed with towels and washbasins, anxious to discover whether or how their children had survived their wrestling bout, and what damage they had inflicted on each other.

But a few days later the husband and wife were to be seen happily running around the yard and playing together barefoot and noisily. The husband even built a little treehouse for his wife's dolls, while he himself went back to playing with wheels and watercourses that he channeled across the yard into streams, lakes, and waterfalls.

His parents, Herz and Sarah Mussman, supported the young couple until they reached the age of sixteen. *Kest-Kinder* was the Yiddish name given in those days to young couples who relied on their parents' support. When he came of age, Ephraim Mussman combined his love of wheels with his love of running water and set up a flour mill in the village of Trope. The mill wheel was turned by running water power. His business never prospered: he was dreamy and childishly naive, an idler and a spendthrift, argumentative and yet never stuck to his guns. He was inclined to engage in idle conversations that lasted from morning till evening. Haya-Duba and Ephraim lived a life of poverty. His little bride bore Ephraim three sons and two daughters. She trained to be a midwife and domestic nurse. She was in the habit of treating poor patients for nothing, secretly. She died in the prime of her life, of consumption. My great-grandmother was twenty-six at her death.

The handsome Ephraim swiftly married another child bride, a sixteen-year-old who was named Haya like her predecessor. The new

Haya Mussman lost no time in banishing her stepchildren from her home. Her weak husband made no attempt to stop her: he seemed to have expended his entire modest share of boldness and resolution all at one go, the evening when he knocked heroically on the rabbi's door and demanded in the name of the Torah and all the jurists the right to consummate his marriage. From that night of bloodshed until the end of his days he always behaved unassertively: he was meek and mild, always yielding to his wives, happy to defer to anyone who resisted his will, yet with strangers he acquired over the years the enigmatic manner of a man of hidden depths of mystery and sanctity. His bearing suggested a certain self-importance wrapped in humility, like a rustic wonder worker or a Russian Orthodox holy man.

And so his firstborn, my grandfather, Naphtali Hertz, at the age of twelve, became an apprentice on the Vilkhov estate, near Rovno, which belonged to an eccentric unmarried noblewoman named Princess Ravzova. Within three or four years the princess had discovered that the young Jew whom she had acquired virtually for nothing was agile, sharp-witted, charming, and amusing, and in addition to all these qualities he had also learned a thing or two about flour milling as a result of growing up in his father's mill. There was possibly something else about him, too, that aroused maternal feelings in the shriveled, childless princess.

And so she decided to buy a plot of land on the outskirts of Rovno, opposite the cemetery at the end of Dubinska Street, and build a flour mill. She placed in charge of this mill one of her nephews and heirs, Konstantin Semyonovich Steletsky, an engineer, and appointed the sixteen-year-old Hertz Mussman as his assistant. My grandfather very soon revealed the organizing abilities, tact, and empathy that endeared him to all who met him, and that sensitivity to others that enabled him to divine what people were thinking or what they wanted.

By the age of seventeen my grandfather was the real manager of the mill. ("So very quick he rose in the favor of that princess! Just like in that story about the righteous Joseph in Egypt and that what's her name? Lady Potiphar, wasn't it? That Engineer Steletsky, everything he fixed he smashed up again himself when he was drunk. He was a terrible alcoholic! I can still remember him beating his horse furiously and crying at the same time out of pity for dumb animals, he was weeping tears big like grapes, but still he went on beating his horse. All day long he was inventing new machines, systems, gear wheels, just like Stephenson. He had a sort of spark of genius. But as soon as he invented anything, he would get angry, that Steletsky, and destroy it all!")

And so the young Jew got in the habit of maintaining and repairing the machinery, haggling with the peasants who brought in their wheat and barley, paying the workers their wages, bargaining with dealers and customers. Thus he became a miller like his father, Ephraim. Unlike his idle, childlike father, however, he was clever, hardworking, and ambitious. And he was successful.

Meanwhile, Princess Ravzova in the evening of her life became increasingly pious: she wore nothing but black, multiplied vows and fasts, was in perpetual mourning, conversed in whispers with Jesus, traveled from monastery to monastery in search of illumination, squandered her wealth on gifts to churches and shrines. ("And one day she picked up a great hammer and hammered a nail into her own hand, because she wanted to feel exactly what Jesus had felt. And then they came and tied her up, took care of her hand, shaved her hair off, and shut her up for the rest of her days in a convent near Tula.")

The wretched engineer, Konstantin Steletsky, the Princess's nephew, subsided into drunkenness after his aunt's demise. His wife, Irina Matveyevna, ran off with Anton, the son of Philip the coachman. ("She was a great *pianitsa*—drunkard—too. But it was he, Steletsky, who made her a *pianitsa*. He used to lose her at cards sometimes. That is, he would lose her for one night, get her back in the morning, and the next night he would lose her again.")

And so Steletsky drowned his sorrows in vodka and cards. ("But he also wrote beautiful poetry, such wonderful poetry full of feeling, full of repentance and compassion! He even wrote a philosophical treatise, in Latin. He knew all the works of the great philosophers by heart, Aristotle, Kant, Soloviev, and he used to go off on his own in the forest. To abase himself he used to dress up as a beggar sometimes, and wander the streets in the early hours of the morning rooting around in the rubbish heaps like a starving beggar.")

Gradually Steletsky made Hertz Mussman his right-hand man at the mill, and then his deputy, and eventually his partner. When my grandfather was twenty-three, some ten years after he was "sold into slavery" to Princess Ravzova, he bought up Steletsky's share of the mill.

His business soon expanded, and among other acquisitions he swallowed up his father's little mill.

The young mill owner did not bear a grudge on account of his eviction from his parents' house. On the contrary: he forgave his father, who in the meantime had managed to become a widower for the second time, and installed him in the office, the so-called *kontora*, and even paid him a decent monthly salary to the end of his days. The handsome Ephraim sat there for many years, sporting an impressive long white beard, doing nothing: he passed his days slowly, drinking tea, and conversing pleasantly and at great length with the dealers and agents who came to the mill. He loved to lecture them, calmly and expansively, on the secret of longevity, the nature of the Russian soul as compared to the Polish or Ukrainian soul, the secret mysteries of Judaism, the creation of the world, or his own original ideas for improving the forests, for sleeping better, for preserving folk tales, or for strengthening the eyesight by natural means.

My mother remembered her Grandpa Ephraim Mussman as an impressive patriarchal figure. His face seemed sublime to her on account of the long snowy beard that flowed down majestically like that of a prophet and the thick white eyebrows that gave him a biblical splendor. His blue eyes sparkled like pools in this snowy landscape, with a happy, childlike smile. "Grandpa Ephraim looked just like God. I mean the way every child imagines God. He gradually came to appear before the whole world like a Slavic saint, a rustic wonder worker, something between the image of the old Tolstoy and that of Santa Claus."

Ephraim Mussman was in his fifties when he became an impressive if somewhat vague old sage. He was less and less capable of distinguishing between a man of God and God himself. He started to mind-read, tell fortunes, spout morality, interpret dreams, grant absolution, perform pious acts, and take pity. From morning to evening he sat over a glass of tea at the desk in the mill office and simply took pity. Apart from taking pity, he did virtually nothing all day.

He always had a smell of expensive scent about him, and his hands were soft and warm. ("But I," my Aunt Sonia said at eighty-five with ill-disguised jubilation, "I was the one he loved best of all his grandchildren! I was his favorite! That's because I was such a little *krasavitsa,* such a little coquette, like a little Frenchwoman, and I knew how to twist him around my little finger, though actually any girl could twist his handsome head around her little finger, he was so sweet and absentminded, so childish, and so emotional, the slightest thing brought tears to his eyes. And as a little girl I used to sit on his lap for hours on end, combing his magnificent white beard over and over, and I always had enough patience to listen to all the rubbish he used to spout. And on top of everything else I was given his mother's name. That's why Grandpa Ephraim loved me the best of all, and sometimes he used to call me Little Mother.")

He was quiet and good-tempered, a gentle, amiable man, rather a chatterbox, but people liked to look at him because of an amused, child-like, captivating smile that constantly flicked across his wrinkled face. ("Grandpa Ephraim was like this: the moment you looked at him, you started to smile yourself! Everybody started smiling, willy nilly, the moment he came into the room. Even the portraits on the walls started smiling the moment he came into the room!") Fortunately for him, his son Naphtali Hertz loved him unconditionally, and always forgave him or pretended not to notice whenever he got the accounts mixed up or opened the cash box in the office without permission and took out a couple of notes to hand out, like God in Hasidic folk tales, to grateful peasants after telling their fortunes and treating them to a moralizing sermon.

For days on end the old man used to sit in the office staring out the window, contentedly watching his son's mill at work. Perhaps because he looked "just like God," he actually saw himself in his later years as a kind of deity. He was humble yet arrogant, perhaps a little feeble-minded in his old age. He sometimes offered his son all kinds of advice and suggestions for improving and expanding the business, but most of the time he forgot what he had said after an hour or so and proffered new advice instead. He drank one glass of tea after another, glanced absentmindedly at the accounts, and if strangers mistook him for the boss, he did not correct them but chatted to them pleasantly about the wealth of the Rothschilds or the terrible hardships of the coolies in China (which he called *Kitai*). His conversations normally lasted for seven or eight hours.

His son indulged him. Wisely, cautiously, and patiently Naphtali Hertz expanded the business, opening branches here and there, making a little money. He married off one sister, Sarah, took in another sister, Jenny, and finally managed to marry her off too. ("To a carpenter, Yasha! A nice boy, even if he was very simple! But what other choice was there for Jenny? After all, she was nearly forty!") He employed his nephew Shimshon at a decent wage, and Jenny's Yasha the carpenter too, he spread his largesse over all his brothers and sisters and kinsfolk; his business prospered, and his Ukrainian and Russian customers bowed to him respectfully, with their hats pressed to their chests, and addressed him as Gertz Yefremovich (Hertz son of Ephraim). He even had a Russian assistant, an impoverished young aristocrat who suffered from ulcers. With his help my grandfather extended his business even further, and opened branches as far away as Kiev, Moscow, and St. Petersburg.

In 1909 or 1910, at the age of twenty-one, Naphtali Hertz Mussman married Itta Gedalyevna Schuster, the capricious daughter of Gedaliah Schuster and his wife Pearl (née Gibor). Of my great-grandmother Pearl, I was informed by Aunt Haya that she was a tough woman, "as shrewd as seven traders," with a sixth sense for village intrigues, sharp-tongued, fond of money and power, and desperately mean. ("The story goes that she always collected every lock of hair that was cut off at the hairdresser's for stuffing cushions. She cut every lump of sugar into four precise little cubes with a knife.") As for great-grandfather Gedaliah, his granddaughter Sonia remembered him as a grumpy, thickset man, over-flowing with appetites. His beard was black and unkempt, and his manner was noisy and domineering. It was said of him that he could belch loud enough to rattle the windowpanes, and that his roar was like the sound of rolling barrels. (But he was scared to death of animals, including dogs, cats, and even kids and calves.)

Their daughter Itta, my grandmother, always behaved like a woman whom life had not treated as gently as she deserved. She was pretty when she was young, and had many suitors, and it seems she was pampered.

She ruled her own three daughters with an iron hand, and yet behaved as though she wanted them to treat her like a younger sister or a sweet little child. Even in her old age she continued to treat her grandchildren to all sorts of little bribes and coquettish gestures, as though begging us to make a fuss of her, to be captivated by her charms, to pay court to her. At the same time, she was capable of behaving with polite ruthlessness.

The marriage of Itta and Hertz Mussman endured, with gritted teeth, through sixty-five years of insults, wrongs, humiliations, truces, shame, restraint, and pursed-lipped mutual politeness. My maternal grandparents were desperately different and remote from each other, yet this desperation was always kept under lock and key. Nobody in my family talked about it, and if I ever managed to sense it in my childhood, it was like a faint whiff of flesh being singed on the other side of a wall.

Their three daughters, Haya, Fania, and Sonia, sought ways to relieve the misery of their parents' married life. All three unhesitatingly took their father's side against their mother. All three loathed and feared their mother; they were ashamed of her and considered her a depressingly vulgar and domineering mischief maker. When they quarreled, they would say to each other accusingly: "Just look at yourself! You're becoming exactly like Maman!"

Only when her parents were old and when she was getting old herself did Aunt Haya manage finally to separate her parents, putting her father in a home for the elderly in Givatayim and her mother in a nursing home near Nes Tsiyona. She did this despite the protests of Aunt Sonia, who thought such enforced separation was totally wrong. But by then the schism between my two aunts was at its height. They did not speak a single word to each other for nearly thirty years, from the late 1950s until Aunt Haya's death in 1989. Aunt Sonia did attend her sister's funeral, where she remarked to us sadly: "I forgive her for everything. And I pray in my heart that God too will forgive her—and it won't be easy for Him, because he will have an awful lot to forgive her for." Aunt Haya, a year before her death, had said the very same thing to me about her sister Sonia.

The fact is that all three Mussman sisters, in their different ways, were in love with their father. My grandfather, Naphtali Hertz (whom we all, his daughters, sons-in-law, and grandchildren, called Papa), was a warmhearted, paternal, kindly, fascinating man. He had a swarthy complexion and a warm voice, and he had inherited his father's clear blue eyes, those piercing sharp eyes that concealed a smile. Whenever he spoke to you, you had the impression that he could plumb the depth of your feelings, guessing between the lines, grasping instantly what you had said and why you had said it, and at the same time discerning whatever it was you were trying unsuccessfully to conceal from him. He would sometimes shoot you an unexpected, mischievous smile, almost accompanied by a wink, as though to embarrass you slightly while being embarrassed on your behalf, but forgiving you because after all, when it comes down to it, a human being is only human.

He considered all human beings to be reckless children who brought great disappointment and suffering upon themselves and each other, all of us trapped in an unending, unsubtle comedy that would generally end badly. All roads led to suffering. Consequently virtually everyone, in Papa's view, deserved compassion, and most of their deeds were worthy of forgiveness, including all sorts of machinations, pranks, deceptions, pretensions, manipulations, false claims, and pretenses. From all these he would absolve you with his faint, mischievous smile, as though saying (in Yiddish): *Nu*, what.

The only thing that tested Papa's amused tolerance were acts of cruelty. These he abhorred. His merry blue eyes clouded over at the news of wicked deeds. "An evil beast? What does the expression mean?" he would reflect in Yiddish. "No beast is evil. No beast is capable of evil. The beasts have yet to invent evil. That is our monopoly, the lords of creation. So maybe we ate the wrong apple in the Garden of Eden after all? Maybe between the tree of life and the tree of knowledge there was another tree growing there in the Garden of Eden, a poisonous tree that is not mentioned in scripture, the tree of evil" (the tree of *rishes*, he called it in Yiddish) "and that was the one we accidentally ate from? That scoundrel of a serpent deceived Eve, he promised her that this was definitely the tree of knowledge, but it was really the tree of *rishes* he led her to. Perhaps if we had stuck to the trees of life and knowledge, we would never have been thrown out of the garden?"

And then, with his eyes restored to their merry sparkling blue, he went on to explain clearly, in his slow, warm voice and his picturesque, orotund Yiddish, what Jean-Paul Sartre was to discover only years later: "But what is hell? What is paradise? Surely it is all inside. In our homes. You can find hell and paradise in every room. Behind every door. Under every double blanket. It's like this. A little wickedness, and people are hell to each other. A little compassion, a little generosity, and people find paradise in each other.

"I said a little compassion and generosity, but I didn't say love: I'm not such a believer in universal love. Love of everybody for everybody— we should maybe leave that to Jesus. Love is another thing altogether. It is nothing whatever like generosity and nothing whatever like compassion. On the contrary. Love is a curious mixture of opposites, a blend of extreme selfishness and total devotion. A paradox! Besides which, love, everybody is always talking about love, love, but love isn't something you choose, you catch it, like a disease, you get trapped in it, like a disaster. So what is it that we do choose? What do human beings have to choose between every minute of the day? Generosity or meanness. Every little child knows that, and yet wickedness still doesn't come to an end. How can you explain that? It seems we got it all from the apple that we ate back then: we ate a poisoned apple."

21

THE CITY of Rovno (Polish Rowne, German Rowno), an important railway junction, grew up around the palaces and moated parks of the princely family of Lubomirsky. The River Uste crossed the city from south to north. Between the river and the marsh stood the citadel, and in the days of the Russians there was still a beautiful lake with swans. The skyline of Rovno was formed by the citadel, the Lubomirsky palace, and a number of Catholic and Orthodox churches, one adorned with twin towers. The city boasted some sixty thousand inhabitants before the Second World War, of whom Jews constituted the majority, and the rest were Ukrainians, Poles, Russians, and a handful of Czechs and Germans. Several thousand more Jews lived in the nearby towns and villages. The villages were surrounded by orchards and vegetable gardens, pastures and fields of wheat and rye that sometimes shuddered or rippled in the breeze. The silence of the fields was broken from time to time by the howl of a locomotive. Occasionally you could hear Ukrainian peasant girls singing in the gardens. From a distance it sounded like wailing.

Wide, flat plains extended as far as the eye could see, here and there arching up in gentle hills, crisscrossed by rivers and pools, dappled with marshes and forests. In the city itself there were three or four "European" streets with a handful of official buildings in neoclassical style and an almost unbroken facade of two-story apartment buildings with wrought-iron balconies, where the middle class lived. A row of small shops occupied the ground floor of these merchants' homes. But most of the side roads were unpaved tracks; they were muddy in winter and dusty in summer. Here and there they were edged with rickety wooden walkways. No sooner had you turned into one of these side roads than you were surrounded by low, broad-shouldered Slavic houses, with thick walls and deep eaves, surrounded by allotments and innumerable ramshackle wooden huts, some of which had sunk up to their windows in the earth and had grass growing on their roofs.

In 1919 a Hebrew secondary school was opened in Rovno by Tarbuth, a Jewish educational organization, together with a primary school and several kindergartens. My mother and her sisters were educated in Tarbuth schools. Hebrew and Yiddish newspapers were published in Rovno in the 1920s and 1930s, ten or twelve Jewish political parties contended frantically with each other, and Hebrew clubs for literature, Judaism, science, and adult education flourished. The more anti-Semitism increased in Poland in the 1920s and 1930s, the stronger Zionism and Hebrew education grew, and at the same time (with no contradiction) the stronger became the pull of secularism and of non-Jewish culture.*

Every evening, at ten o'clock precisely, the night express pulled out of Rovno Station, bound for Zdolbunowo, Lvov, Lublin, and Warsaw. On Sundays and Christian holidays all the church bells rang out. The winters were dark and snowy, and in summer warm rain fell. The cinema in Rovno was owned by a German named Brandt. One of the pharmacists was a Czech by the name of Mahacek. The chief surgeon at the hospital was a Jew called Dr. Segal, whose rivals nicknamed him Mad

---

*Menahem Gelehrter, *The Tarbuth Hebrew Gymnasium in Rovno* (in Hebrew) (Jerusalem, 1973). The Tarbuth schools were Zionist and secular.

Segal. A colleague of his at the hospital was the orthopedic surgeon Dr. Joseph Kopejka, who was a keen Revisionist Zionist. Moshe Rotenberg and Simcha-Hertz Majafit were the town's rabbis. Jews dealt in timber and grain, milled flour, worked in textiles and household goods, gold and silver work, hides, printing, clothing, grocery, haberdashery, trade, and banking. Some young Jews were driven by their social conscience to join the proletariat as print workers, apprentices, and day laborers. The Pisiuk family had a brewery. The Twischor family were well-known craftsmen. The Strauch family made soap. The Gendelberg family leased forests. The Steinberg family owned a match factory. In June 1941 the Germans captured Rovno from the Soviet Army, which had taken over the city two years earlier. In two days, November 7 and 8, 1941, Germans and their collaborators murdered more than twenty-three thousand of the city's Jews. Five thousand of those who survived were murdered later, on July 13, 1942.

My mother sometimes talked to me nostalgically, in her quiet voice that lingered on the ends of the words, about the Rovno she had left behind. In six or seven sentences she could paint me a picture. I repeatedly put off going to Rovno, so that the pictures my mother gave me do not have to make way for others.

The eccentric mayor of Rovno in the second decade of the twentieth century, Lebedevski, never had any children; he lived in a large house surrounded by more than an acre of land, with a garden, a kitchen garden, and an orchard, at 14 Dubinska Street. He lived there with a single servant and her little daughter, who was rumored to be his own daughter. There was also a distant relation of his, Lyubov Nikitichna, a penniless Russian aristocrat who claimed also to be somehow distantly related to the ruling Romanov family. She lived in Lebedevski's house with her two daughters by two different husbands, Anastasia Sergeyevna, or Tasia, and Antonina Boleslavovna, or Nina. The three of them lived crowded into a tiny room that was actually the end of a corridor, curtained off. The three noblewomen shared this tiny space with a huge, magnificent eighteenth-century piece of furniture made of mahogany and carved with flowers and ornaments. Inside it and behind its glazed doors were crammed masses of antiques, silver, porcelain, and crystal.

They also had a wide bed adorned with colorful embroidered cushions, where apparently the three of them slept together.

The house had a single, spacious story, but underneath it there was a vast cellar that served as workshop, larder, storage room, wine cellar, and repository of thick smells: a strange, slightly scary but also fascinating mixture of smells of dried fruit, butter, sausages, beer, cereals, honey, different kinds of jams, *varinnye, povidlo,* barrels of pickled cabbage and cucumbers and all sorts of spices, and strings of dried fruits hung across the cellar, and there were several kinds of dried pulses in sacks and wooden tubs, and smells of tar, paraffin, pitch, coal, and firewood, and also faint odors of mold and decay. A small opening close to the ceiling let in a slanting, dusty ray of light, which seemed to intensify rather than dispel the darkness. I came to know this cellar so well from my mother's stories that even now as I write this, when I close my eyes, I can go down there and inhale its dizzying blend of smells.

In 1920, shortly before Marshal Pilsudski's Polish troops captured Rovno and all of western Ukraine from the Russians, Mayor Lebedevski fell from grace and was expelled from office. His successor was a crass hoodlum and drunkard named Bojarski, who on top of everything else was a ferocious anti-Semite. Lebedevski's house in Dubinska Street was bought at a bargain price by my grandfather, the mill owner Naphtali Hertz Mussman. He moved in with his wife Itta and his three daughters, Haya, or Nyusya, the eldest, who had been born in 1911, Rivka-Feiga, or Fania, who was born two years later, and the daughter of his old age, Sarah, or Sonia, who was born in 1916. The house, I was told recently, is still standing.

On one side of Dubinska Street, whose name was changed by the Poles to Kazarmowa (Barracks) Street, stood the mansions of the wealthier inhabitants of the city, while the other side was occupied by the army barracks (the *kazarmy*). The fragrance of gardens and orchards filled the street in springtime, mingled sometimes with smells of washing or of baking, of fresh bread, cakes, biscuits, and pies, and scents of strongly seasoned dishes that wafted from the kitchens of the houses.

In that spacious house with its many rooms various lodgers whom the Mussmans had "inherited" from Lebedevski continued to dwell. Papa did not have the heart to turn them out. So the old servant, Xenia Demitrievna, Xenietchka, continued to live behind the kitchen, with her daughter Dora, who may or may not have been sired by Lebedevski himself; everyone called her simply Dora, with no patronymic. At the end of the corridor, behind the heavy curtain, the impoverished aristocrat Lyubov Nikitichna, Lyuba, still claiming to be somehow related to the imperial family, remained in undisturbed possession of her tiny space, together with her daughters Tasia and Nina; all three were very thin, erect, and proud, and always elaborately got up, "like a muster of peacocks."

In a light, spacious room at the front of the house that he rented on a monthly basis and that was known as the *Kabinett* lived a Polish colonel (*polkovnik*) by the name of Jan Zakrzewski. He was a boastful, lazy, and sentimental man in his fifties, solidly built, manly, broadshouldered, and not bad looking. The girls addressed him as "Panie Polkovnik." Every Friday, Itta Mussman would send one of her daughters with a tray of fragrant poppy cakes straight from the oven; she had to tap politely on Panie Polkovnik's door, curtsey, and wish him a good Sabbath on behalf of all the family. The colonel would lean forward and stroke the little girl's hair or sometimes her back or shoulder; he called them all *cyganka* (Gypsy) and promised each of them that he would wait for her faithfully, and marry no one but her when she was old enough.

Bojarski, the anti-Semitic mayor who had replaced Lebedevski, would sometimes come to play cards with Retired Colonel Zakrzewski. They drank together and smoked "until the air was black." As the hours passed, their voices became thick and hoarse, and their loud laughter filled with grunts and wheezes. Whenever the mayor came to the house, the girls were sent to the back or out into the garden, to prevent their ears picking up remarks that were unsuitable for well-brought-up girls to hear. From time to time the servant would bring the men hot tea, sausages, herring, or a tray of fruit compote, biscuits, and nuts. Each time she would respectfully convey the request of the lady of the house that they should lower their voices as she had a "blinding headache." What the gentlemen replied to the old servant we shall never know, as the servant was "as deaf as ten walls" (or sometimes they said "as deaf as God Almighty"). She would cross herself piously, curtsey, and leave the room dragging her tired, painful feet.

And once, in the early hours of a Sunday morning, before first light, when everyone else in the house was still in bed fast asleep, Colonel Zakrzewski decided to try out his pistol. First he fired into the garden through the closed window. By chance, or in some mysterious way, he managed in the dark to hit a pigeon, which was found wounded but still alive in the morning. Then, for some reason, he took a pot shot at the wine bottle on his table, shot himself in the thigh, fired twice at the chandelier but missed, and with his last bullet shattered his own forehead and died. He was a sentimental, garrulous man, who wore his heart on his sleeve; often he would suddenly burst out singing or weeping, sad as he was about the historic tragedy of his people, sad about the pretty piglet that the neighbor bludgeoned to death with a pole, sad about the bitter fate of songbirds when winter came, about the suffering of Jesus nailed to the cross, he was even sad about the Jews, who had been persecuted for fifty generations and had still not managed to see the light, he was sad about his own life, which was flowing on without rhyme or reason, and desperately sad about some girl, Vassilisa, whom he had once allowed to leave him, many years before, for which he would never cease to curse his stupidity and his empty, useless life. "My God, my God," he used to declaim in his Polish Latin, "why hast Thou forsaken me? And why hast Thou forsaken us all?"

That morning they took the three girls out of the house by the back door, through the orchard, and past the stable gate, and when the girls returned, the front room was empty, clean and tidy and aired, and all the colonel's belongings had been bundled into sacks and taken away. Only the smell of wine, from the bottle that had been smashed, Aunt Haya remembered, lingered for a few days.

And once the girl who was to be my mother found a note there tucked into a crack in the wardrobe, written in rather simple Polish, in a female hand, in which somebody wrote to her very precious little wolf cub to say that in all the days of her life she had never ever met a better or more generous man than he, and that she was not worthy to kiss the soles of his feet. Little Fania noticed two spelling mistakes in the Polish. The note was signed with the letter N, beneath which the writer had drawn a pair of full lips extended for a kiss. "Nobody," my mother said, "knows anything about anyone else. Not even about a close neighbor. Not even about the person you are married to. Or about your parent or your child. Nothing at all. Or even about ourselves. We know nothing. And if we sometimes imagine for an instant that we do know something after all, that's even worse, because it's better to live without knowing anything than to live in error. Although in fact, who knows? Maybe on second thought it's much easier to live in error than to live in the dark?"

From her stuffy, gloomy, clean and tidy, overfurnished, always shuttered two-room apartment on Wessely Street in Tel Aviv (while a damp, oppressive September day gradually gathers outside), Aunt Sonia takes me to visit the mansion in the Wolja quarter in northwest Rovno. Kazarmowa Street, formerly Dubinska, crossed the main street of Rovno, which used to be called Shossejna, but after the arrival of the Poles was renamed Trzecziego Maya, Third of May Street, in honor of the Polish national day.

When you approach the house from the road, Aunt Sonia describes to me, precisely and in detail, you first cross the small front garden, which is called a *palisadnik,* with its neat jasmine bushes ("and I can still remember a little shrub on the left that had a very strong and particularly pungent smell, which is why we called it 'love-struck'. . ."). And there were flowers called *margaritki,* that now you call daisies. And there were rose bushes, *rozochki,* we used to make a sort of *konfitura* from their petals, a jam that was so sweet and fragrant that you imagined it must lick itself when no one was looking. The roses grew in two circular beds surrounded by little stones or bricks that were laid diagonally and whitewashed, so that they looked like a row of snow white swans leaning on one another.

Behind these bushes, she says, we had a small green bench, and next to it you turned left to the main entrance: there were four or five wide steps, and a big brown door with all kinds of ornaments and carvings, left over from Mayor Lebedevski's baroque taste. The main entrance led to a hall with mahogany furniture and a large window with curtains that reached the floor. The first door on the right was the door of the *Kabinett* where Polkovnik Pan Jan Zakrzewski lived. His manservant or *denshchik,* a peasant boy with a broad red face like a beet, covered with the kind of acne you get from thinking not nice thoughts, slept in front of his door at night on a mattress that was folded away in the daytime. When this *denshchik* looked at us girls, his eyes popped out as though he were going to die of hunger. I'm not talking about hunger for bread, actually bread we used to bring him all the time from the kitchen, as much as he wanted. The *polovnik* used to beat his *denshchik* mercilessly, and then he used to regret it and give him pocket money.

You could enter the house through the wing on the right—there was a path paved with reddish stones that was very slippery in winter. Six trees grew along this path, in Russian they are called *siren*, I don't know what you call them, maybe they don't even exist here. These trees sometimes had little clusters of purple flowers with such an intoxicating scent, we used to stop there on purpose and breathe it in deeply until we sometimes felt light-headed, and we could see all kinds of bright dots in front of our eyes, in all kinds of colors that don't have names. In general, I think there are far more colors and smells than there are words. The path on this side of the house takes you to six steps that led up to a little open porch where there was a bench—the love bench, we all called it, because of something not very nice that they didn't want to tell us about but we knew it had to do with the servants. The servants' entrance opened off this porch; we called it *chyorny khod*, which means the black door.

If you didn't come into the house through the front door or the *chyorny khod*, you could follow the path around the side of the house and reach the garden. Which was gigantic: at least as big as from here, from Wessely Street, to Dizengoff Street. Or even as far as Ben Yehudah Street. In the middle of the garden there was an avenue with a lot of fruit trees on either side, all sorts of plum trees and two cherry trees whose blossoms looked like a wedding dress, and they used to make *vishniak* and *piroshki* from the fruit. *Reinette* apples, *popirovki*, and *grushi*—huge juicy pears, *pontovki* pears, that the boys called by names that are not very nice to repeat. On the other side there were more fruit trees, succulent peaches, apples that resemble the ones we call Peerless, and little green pears that again the boys said something about that made us girls press our hands hard against our ears so we wouldn't hear. And long plums for making jam, and among the fruit trees there were raspberry canes and blackberries and black currant bushes. And we had special apples for winter, which we used to put under straw in the *cherdak*—the loft— to ripen slowly for the winter. They put pears there too, also wrapped in straw, to sleep for a few more weeks and only wake up in the winter, and that way we had good fruit right through the winter, when other people only had potatoes to eat, and not always potatoes even. Papa used to say that wealth is a sin and poverty is a punishment but that God apparently wants there to be no connection between the sin and the punishment. One man sins and another is punished. That's how the world is made.

He was almost a Communist, Papa, your grandfather. He always used to leave his father, Grandpa Ephraim, eating with a knife and fork and a white napkin at the desk in the mill office, while he sat with his workers down by the wood-burning stove and ate with them, using his hands, rye bread and pickled herring, a slice of onion with some salt, and a potato in its jacket. On a piece of newspaper on the floor they used to eat, and they washed their food down with a swig of vodka. Every festival, the day before every festival, Papa used to give each worker a sack of flour, a bottle of wine, and a few rubles. He would point to the mill and say—*Nu*, all this isn't mine, it's ours! He was like Schiller's Wilhelm Tell, your grandfather, that socialist president who drank wine from the same goblet as the simplest soldiers.

That must surely be the reason that in 1919, when the Communists came into the town and immediately lined up all the capitalists and *Fabrikanten*—factory owners—against the wall, Papa's workers opened up the cover of the big engine, I can't remember what it was called, the main motor that gave power to the *Walzen*—the wheels—to grind the corn, and they hid him inside and locked him in, and they sent a delegation to the Red *povodir* and said to him, Listen to us real good, please, Comrade Governor, our Gerz Yefremovich Mussman, you're not to touch him, not even a hair on his head, right! Herz Mussman—*on nash bachka* (which is Ukrainian for "he's our father").

And the Soviet authorities in Rovno really did make your grandfather the *upravlayushi*—the boss—of the mill, they didn't interfere with his authority, on the contrary, they came and said to him something like this: Dear Comrade Mussman, listen please, from now on, if you have any trouble with a lazy worker or a *sabotazhnik*—just point him out to us and we'll put him up against the wall. To be sure, your grandfather did just the opposite: he was very crafty at protecting his workers from this workers' government. And at the same time he supplied flour to the entire Red Army in our district.

One time it so happened that the Soviet governor apparently took delivery of a huge consignment of totally moldy corn, and he was in a panic because for this they could put *him* up against the wall right away, What's this, why did you accept it without checking? So what did he do, the governor, to save his skin? Late at night he ordered the whole consignment to be unloaded near Papa's mill, and gave him an order to grind it into flour urgently by five in the morning.

In the dark Papa and the workers didn't even notice that the corn was moldy, they set to work and ground the lot, they worked all through the night, and in the morning they had foul-smelling flour full of maggots. Papa understood at once that this flour was his responsibility now, and it was his choice whether to accept the responsibility or to blame without any proof the Soviet governor who sent him the moldy corn: either way it was the firing squad.

What choice did he have? To put all the blame on his workers? So he simply threw away all the moldy flour with the maggots, and in its place he brought out from his stores a hundred and fifty sacks of best quality flour, not army flour but white flour, for baking cakes and *cholla,* and in the morning without saying a word he presented this flour to the governor. The governor didn't say a word either, even though in his heart he was maybe a bit ashamed that he tried to shift the blame onto your grandfather. But what could he do now? After all, Lenin and Stalin never accepted explanations or apologies from anyone: they just put them up against the wall and shot them.

Of course the governor understood that what Papa was giving him was definitely not his filthy corn, and therefore that Papa had saved both their skins at his own expense. And his workers' too.

This story has a sequel. Papa had a brother, Mikhail, Michael, who had the good fortune to be as deaf as God. I say good fortune, because Uncle Michael had a terrible wife, Rakhil, who was so nasty, she used to shout and curse at him all day and all night with her rough, hoarse voice, but he heard nothing: he lived in silent calm, like the moon in the sky.

All those years Mikhail hung around Papa's mill and did nothing, drinking tea with Grandpa Ephraim in the office and scratching himself, and for this Papa paid him a fairly handsome monthly salary. One day, a few weeks after the moldy flour incident, the Soviets suddenly took Mikhail away and conscripted him into the Red Army. But the same night Mikhail saw his mother Haya in a dream, and she was saying to him in the dream, Hurry, my son, hurry and flee, because tomorrow they plan to kill you. So he got up early in the morning and ran away from the barracks as if they were on fire: a deserter, *rastralki*. But the Reds caught him at once and court-martialed him and sentenced him to be put up against the wall. Just the way his mother had warned him in the dream! Only in the dream she forgot to say that it was the opposite, that he should on no account run away and desert!

Papa went to the square to take leave of his brother, there was nothing to be done, when all of a sudden, in the middle of the square, where the soldiers had already loaded their rifles for Mikhail—all of a sudden this governor of the moldy flour turns to the condemned man and shouts: Tell me please, *ty brat* of Gertz Yefremovich? Are you by any chance the brother of Hertz son of Ephraim? And Mikhail answers him: *Da*, Comrade General! And the governor turns to Papa and asks: Is he your brother? And Papa also answers, Yes, yes, Comrade General! He's my brother! Definitely my brother! So the general simply turns and says to Uncle Mikhail: *Nu, idi domoy! Poshol!* Go home! Off with you! And he leans toward Papa, so they can't hear, and this is what he says to him, quietly: "*Nu*, what, Gertz Yefremovich? Did you think you were the only one who knows how to turn shit into pure gold?"

Your grandfather was a Communist in his heart, but he was not a red Bolshevik. He always considered Stalin to be another Ivan the Terrible. He himself was, how should I say, a kind of pacifist Communist, a *narodnik*, a *Tolstoyshchik* Communist who was opposed to bloodshed. He was very frightened of the evil that lurks in the soul, in men of all stations: he always used to say to us that there ought someday to be a popular regime common to all decent people in the world. But that first of all it will be necessary to eliminate gradually all the states and armies and secret polices, and only after that will it be possible to start gradually creating equality between rich and poor. To take tax from one lot and give to the other, only not all at once, because that makes bloodshed, but slowly and gradually. He used to say: *Mit aroapfalendiker.* Downhill. Even if it takes seven or eight generations, so the rich almost don't notice how slowly they're not so rich anymore. The main thing in his opinion was that we had to start to convince the world at last that injustice and exploitation are a disease of mankind and that justice is the only medicine: true, a bitter medicine, that's what he always used to say to us, a dangerous medicine, a strong medicine that you have to take drop by drop until the body becomes accustomed to it. Anyone who tries to swallow it all at one go only causes disaster, sheds rivers of blood. Just look what Lenin and Stalin did to Russia and to the whole world! It's true that Wall Street really is a vampire that sucks the world's blood, but you can never get rid of the vampire by shedding blood, on the contrary, you only strengthen it, you only feed it more and more fresh blood!

The trouble with Trotsky and Lenin and Stalin and their friends, your grandfather thought, is that they tried to reorganize the whole of life, at a stroke, out of books, books by Marx and Engels and other great thinkers like them; they may have known the libraries very well, but they didn't have any idea about life, about malice or about jealousy, envy, *rishes*, or gloating at others' misfortunes. Never, never will it be possible to organize life according to a book! Not our *Shulhan Arukh*, not Jesus of Nazareth, and not Marx's *Manifesto*! Never! In general, Papa always used to say to us, better a little less to organize and reorganize and a little more to help one another and maybe to forgive, too. He believed in two things, your grandpa: compassion and justice, *der-baremen un gerechtigkeit*. But he was of the opinion that you always have to make the connection between them: justice without compassion isn't justice, it's an abattoir. On the other hand, compassion without justice may be all right for Jesus but not for simple mortals who have eaten the apple of evil. That was his view: a little less organizing, a little more pity.

Opposite the *chyorny khod* there grew a beautiful *kashtan*, a magnificent old chestnut tree that looked a bit like King Lear, and underneath it Papa had a bench put up for the three of us—we called it the "sisters' bench." On fine days we used to sit there and dream aloud about what would happen to us when we grew up. Which of us would be an engineer, a poet, or a famous inventor like Marie Curie? That was the kind of thing we dreamed about. We didn't dream, like most girls of our age, about marrying a rich or famous husband, because we came from a rich family and we weren't at all attracted by the idea of marrying someone even richer than we were.

If we ever talked about falling in love, it wasn't with some nobleman or famous actor but only with someone with elevated feelings, like a great artist for example, even if he didn't have a kopek. Never mind. What did we know then? How could we possibly know what scoundrels, what beasts great artists are? (Not all of them—definitely not all of them!) Only today I really don't think that elevated feelings and such-like are the main thing in life. Definitely not. Feelings are just a fire in a field of stubble: it burns for a moment, and then all that's left is soot and ashes. Do you know what the main thing is—the thing a woman should look for in her man? She should look for a quality that's not at all excit-ing but that's rarer than gold: decency. And maybe kindness too. Today, you should know this, I rate decency more highly than kindness. De-cency is the bread, kindness is the butter. Or the honey.

In the orchard, halfway down the avenue, there were two benches facing each other, and that was a good place to go when you felt like being alone with your thoughts in the silence between the birdsong and the whispering of the breeze in the branches.

Beyond that, at the edge of the field, was a little building we called the *ofitsina,* where, in the first room, there was a black boiler for the laundry. We played at being prisoners of the wicked witch Baba Yaga who puts little girls in the boiler. Then there was a little back room where the gardener lived. Behind the *ofitsina* were the stables, where Papa's phaeton was kept, and a big chestnut horse lived there too. Next to the stable stood a sleigh with iron runners in which Philip, the coach-man, or his son Anton, drove us to the hairdresser on icy or snowy days. Sometimes Hemi came with us—he was the son of Rucha and Arie Leib Pisiuk, who were very rich. The Pisiuks owned a brewery and supplied the whole district with beer and yeast. The brewery was enormous, and it was managed by Hertz Meir Pisiuk, Hemi's grandfather. The famous men who visited Rovno always stayed with the Pisiuks: Bialik, Jabotin-sky, Tchernikhowsky. I think that boy, Hemi Pisiuk, was your mother's first love. Fania must have been about thirteen or fifteen, and she always wanted to ride in the carriage or the sleigh with Hemi but without me, and I always deliberately came between them; I was nine or ten, I didn't let them be alone, I was a silly little girl. That's what I was called at that time. When I wanted to irritate Fania, I called her, in front of everybody, Hemuchka, which comes from Hemi. Nehemiah. Hemi Pisiuk went to study in Paris, and that's where they killed him. The Germans.

Papa, your grandfather, was fond of Philip, the coachman, and he was very fond of the horses, he even liked the smith who used to come and grease the carriage, but the one thing he really hated was to ride in the carriage, wearing a fur coat with a fox-fur collar, like a squire, behind his Ukrainian coachman. He preferred to walk. Somehow he didn't enjoy being a wealthy man. In his carriage, or in his *fauteuil*, surrounded by *buffets* and crystal chandeliers, he felt a bit like a *komediant*.

Many years later, when he had lost all his possessions, when he came to Israel almost empty-handed, he actually didn't think it was too terrible. He didn't miss his possessions at all. On the contrary: he felt lightened. He didn't mind sweating in the sun, with a gray vest on, with a thirty-kilo sack of flour on his back. Only Mama suffered terribly, she cursed, she shouted at him and insulted him, why had he come down in the world? Where were the *fauteuils*, the crystal and the chandeliers? Did she deserve at her age to live like a *mujik*, like a *hoholka*, without a cook or a hairdresser or a seamstress? When would he finally pull himself together and build a new flour mill in Haifa, so that we could recover our lost position? Like the fisherman's wife in the story, that's what Mama was like. But I forgave her for everything. May God forgive her too. And he will have plenty to forgive! May God forgive me too for talking about her like this, may she rest in peace. May she rest in peace the way she never gave Papa a moment's peace in his life. For forty years they lived in this country, and every day, morning to night, she did nothing but poison his life. They found themselves a sort of tumbledown hut in a field of thistles behind Kiriat Motskin, a one-room hut with no water and no toilet, roofed with tar paper—do you remember Papa and Mama's hut? Yes? The only faucet was outside among the thistles, the water was full of rust, and the toilet was a hole in the ground in a makeshift shelter at the back that Papa built himself out of bits of wood.

Maybe it's not entirely Mama's fault that she poisoned his life so. After all, she was very unhappy there. Desperately! She was an unhappy woman altogether. She was born unhappy. Even the chandeliers and the crystal did not make her happy. But she was the kind of unhappy person who has to make other people miserable too; that was your grandfather's bad luck.

As soon as he came to Israel, Papa found work in Haifa, in a bakery. He used to go around Haifa Bay with a horse and cart: they saw that he knew something about corn, flour, and bread, so instead of giving him a job milling or baking they made him carry sacks of flour and deliver bread with his horse and cart. After that he worked for many years with the Vulcan iron foundry, transporting all sorts of round and long bits of iron for building.

Sometimes he used to take you with him in his cart around Haifa Bay. Do you still remember? Yes? When he was old, your grandpa made a living carrying around wide planks for scaffolding or sand from the seashore for new buildings.

I can remember you sitting next to him, a skinny little kid, as taut as a rubber band; Papa used to give you the reins to hold. I can still see the picture clearly in front of my eyes: you were a white child, as pale as a piece of paper, and your grandpa was always very suntanned, a strong man, even when he was seventy he was strong, as dark as an Indian, some kind of Indian prince, a maharajah with blue eyes that sparkled with laughter. And you sat on the plank that served as the driver's seat in a little white vest, and he sat next to you in a sweaty gray workman's vest. He was actually happy, content with his lot, he loved the sunshine and the physical labor. He rather enjoyed being a carter, he had always had proletarian leanings, and in Haifa he felt good being a proletarian again, as at the beginning of his journey, when he was just an apprentice on the Vilkhov estate. Perhaps he enjoyed life much more as a carter than he had as a rich mill owner and man of property in Rovno. And you were such a serious little boy, a boy who couldn't stand the sunshine, too serious, seven or eight years old, all stiff on the driver's seat next to him, anxious about the reins, suffering from the flies and heat, afraid of being lashed by the horse's tail. But you behaved bravely and didn't complain. I remember it as if it were today. The big gray vest and the little white one. I thought then that you would surely be much more of a Klausner than a Mussman. Today I'm not so sure . . .

22

I REMEMBER we used to argue a lot, Aunt Sonia says with our girlfriends, with the boys, with teachers at school, and at home too, among ourselves, about questions like what is justice, what is fate, what is beauty, what is God? Of course we also argued about Palestine, assimilation, political parties, literature, socialism, or the ills of the Jewish people. Haya and Fania and their friends were especially argumentative. I argued less, because I was the little sister, and they would always say to me: You just listen. Haya was big in the Zionist youth movement. Your mother was in Hashomer Hatsair, and I joined Hashomer Hatsair too, three years later. In your family, the Klausners, it was best not to mention Hashomer Hatsair. It was too far left for them. The Klausners didn't even want the name mentioned because they were scared stiff you might get a sprinkling of red just from hearing it.

Once, it may have been in the winter, at Hannukah, we had a huge argument that lasted off and on for several weeks, about heredity versus free will. I remember as if it were yesterday how your mother suddenly came out with this strange sentence, that if you open up someone's head and take out the brains, you see at once that our brains are nothing but cauliflower. Even Chopin or Shakespeare: their brains were nothing but cauliflower.

I don't even remember in what connection Fania said this, but I remember that we couldn't stop laughing, I laughed so much I cried, but she didn't even smile. Fania had this habit of saying in deadly earnest things that would make everyone laugh, and she knew they would, but she didn't join in the laughter. Fania would laugh only when it suited her, not together with everyone else, just when nobody thought there was anything funny in what we were talking about—that's when your mother would suddenly burst out laughing.

Nothing but cauliflower, she said, and she showed us the size of the cauliflower with her hands, and what a miracle it is, she said—into this cauliflower you can get heaven and earth, the sun and all the stars, the ideas of Plato, the music of Beethoven, the French Revolution, Tolstoy's novels, Dante's *Inferno*, all the deserts and oceans, there's room in there for the dinosaurs and the whales, everything can get into that cauliflower, and all the hopes, desires, and errors and fantasies of mankind, there's room for everything there, even that puffy wart with the black hairs in it that grows on Bashka Durashka's chin. The moment Fania introduced Bashka's revolting wart right in the middle of Plato and Beethoven, we all burst out laughing again, except for your mother, who just stared at us all in amazement, as though it wasn't the cauliflower that was so funny, but us.

Later Fania wrote me a philosophical letter from Prague. I was about sixteen and she was a nineteen-year-old student, her letters to me were perhaps a bit too much *de haut en bas*, because I was always considered a silly little girl, but I can still remember that it was a long, detailed letter about heredity versus environment and free will.

I'll try to tell you what she said, but of course it will be in my own words, not Fania's: I don't know many people who are capable of expressing what Fania could express. So this is more or less what Fania wrote to me: that heredity and the environment that nurtures us and our social class—these are all like cards that are dealt out at random before the game begins. There is no freedom about this: the world gives, and you just take what you're given, with no opportunity to choose. But, she wrote to me from Prague, the question is what each person does with the cards that are dealt out to him. Some people play brilliantly with poor cards, and others do the opposite: they squander and lose everything even with excellent cards. And that is what our freedom amounts to: how to play with the hand we have been dealt. But even the freedom to play well or badly, she wrote, depends ironically on each person's luck, on patience, intelligence, intuition, or adventurousness. And in the last resort surely these too are simply cards that are or are not dealt to us before the game begins. And if so, then what is left of our freedom of choice?

Not much, your mother wrote, in the last resort maybe all we are left with is the freedom to laugh at our condition or to lament it, to play the game or to throw in our hand, to try more or less to understand what is and isn't the case, or to give up and not try to understand—in a nutshell, the choice is between going through this life awake or in a kind of stupor. That is, roughly, what Fania, your mother, said, but in my words. Not in her words. I can't say it in her words.

Now that we're talking about fate versus freedom of choice, now that we're talking about cards, I have another story for you . . . Philip, the Mussman family's Ukrainian coachman, had a dark, good-looking son called Anton: black eyes that sparkled like black diamonds, a mouth that turned down slightly at the corners, as if from contempt, and strength, broad shoulders, a bass voice like a bull's, the glasses in the *kommoda* tinkled when Anton roared. Every time he passed a girl in the street, this Anton deliberately walked more slowly, and the girl unconsciously walked a little faster, and her breath came a little faster too. I remember that we used to make fun of one another, we sisters and our girlfriends: who had arranged her blouse just so for Anton? Who had put a flower in her hair for Anton? And who had gone out walking in the street for Anton with a starched pleated skirt and snow-white short socks?

Next door to us on Dubinska Street lived Engineer Steletsky, the nephew of Princess Ravzova whom your grandfather was sent to work for when he was twelve. It was the same poor engineer who founded the flour mill that Papa started out working for and finally bought him out. Steletsky's wife simply ran off clutching a little blue suitcase straight to the little hut opposite, which Anton had built for himself beyond our front garden, at the edge of the built-up area. Actually it was a field where cows grazed. It's true she had reasons to run away from her husband: he may have been a bit of a genius, but he was a drunken genius, and sometimes he lost her at cards, that is, he handed her over for a night in lieu of payment, if you see what I mean.

I remember asking my mother about it, and she turned pale and said to me, Soniechka! *Oy vey!* You should be ashamed of yourself! Just you stop, do you hear me?! Just you stop even thinking about nasty things like that this minute and start thinking about beautiful things instead! Because it's well known, Soniechka, that a girl who thinks nasty thoughts in her heart starts growing hair in all sorts of parts of her body, and she develops an ugly deep voice like a man, and after that no one will ever want to marry her!

That was the way we were brought up in those days. And the truth? I myself didn't *want* to think thoughts like that at all, about a woman who had to go off with some drunken wretch to some filthy hut at night as his prize. Thoughts about the fate of many women whose husbands lose us. Because there are other ways of losing a woman. Not just at cards! But thoughts are not like television, where if you see unpleasant things you simply press the button and run away to another program. Nasty thoughts are more like worms in the cauliflower!

Aunt Sonia remembers Ira Steletskaya as a frail, miniature woman with a sweet, slightly surprised expression. "She always looked as though she'd just been told that Lenin was waiting for her outside in the courtyard."

She lived in Anton's hut for several months, maybe half a year, and her husband forbade the children to go to her or even to answer her if she addressed them, but they could see her every day in the distance and she could see them. Her husband could also see her all the time, in the distance, in Anton's hut. Anton liked to pick Ira up off the ground—after giving birth to two children she still had the slim, beautiful body of a sixteen-year-old—and he liked to lift her in his hands like a puppy, swing her in circles, throw her up and catch her, hop hop hop, and Ira used to scream with fear and pummel him with her tiny fists that must hardly have tickled him. Anton was as strong as an ox: he could straighten out the shaft of our carriage with his bare hands if it got bent. It was simply a tragedy without words: every day Ira Steletskaya could see her home and her children and her husband opposite, and every day they could see her in the distance.

Once this unfortunate woman, who already drank more than was good for her—she started drinking in the morning too—well, once she simply hid by the gate of their house and waited for her younger daughter, Kira, to come home from school.

I happened to be passing and I saw from close up how Kiruchka wouldn't let her mother pick her up in her arms, because her father forbade any contact. The child was afraid of her father, she was afraid even to say a few words to her mother, she pushed her away, kicked her, called for help, until Kasimir, Engineer Steletsky's manservant, heard her cries and came out on the steps. At once he started waving his hands at her, like that, and making noises as if shooing a chicken away. I shall never forget how Ira Steletskaya went away and cried, not quietly, like a lady, no, she cried like a servant, like a muzhik she cried, with terrifying, inhuman howls, like a bitch whose whelp is taken away and killed in front of her eyes.

There's something like it in Tolstoy, you surely remember, in *Anna Karenina,* when one day Anna slips into her house while Karenin is away at his office, she manages to slip inside the house that was once hers, and even manages to see her son for a moment, but the servants drive her away. Except in Tolstoy it is much less cruel than what I saw when Irina Matveyevna ran away from Kasimir the servant, she passed me, as close as I am to where you are sitting—after all, we were neighbors—but she didn't greet me, and I heard her broken howls and I smelled her breath and I saw from her face that she was no longer entirely sane. In her look, the way she cried, her walk, I could see clearly the signs of her death.

And after a few weeks or months Anton threw her out, or rather he went off to another village, and Irina went home, she went down on her knees to her husband, and apparently Engineer Steletsky took pity on her and took her back, but not for long: they kept taking her off to the hospital, and in the end male nurses came and bound her eyes and arms and took her away by force to a lunatic asylum in Kovel. I can remember her eyes, even now as I am talking to you I can see her eyes, and it's so strange, eighty years have passed, and there was the Holocaust, and there were all the wars here and our own tragedy, and illnesses, everyone apart from me is dead, and even so her eyes still pierce my heart like a pair of sharp knitting needles.

Ira came home to Steletsky a few times, calmed; she looked after the children, she even planted new rosebushes in the garden, fed the birds, fed the cats, but one day she ran away again, to the forest, and when they caught her, she took a can of petrol and went to the little hut that Anton had built himself in the pasture. The hut was roofed with tar paper— Anton hadn't lived there for a long time—and she lit a match and burned down the hut with all his rags and herself too. In the winter, when everything was covered with white snow, the blackened beams of the burned hut rose out of the snow, pointing to the clouds and the forest like sooty fingers.

Some time later Engineer Steletsky went off the rails and made a complete fool of himself; he remarried, lost all his money, and finally sold Papa his share of the mill. Your grandfather had managed to buy Princess Ravzova's share even before that. And to think that he started out as her apprentice, just a serf, a poor twelve-and-a-half-year-old boy who had lost his mother and been thrown out of the house by his stepmother.

Now see for yourself what strange circles fate draws for us: weren't you exactly twelve and a half when you lost your mother? Just like your grandfather. Although they didn't farm you out to some half-crazed landowner. You were sent to a kibbutz instead. Don't imagine I don't know what it means to come to a kibbutz as a child who wasn't born there: it was no paradise. By the age of fifteen your grandfather was virtually managing Princess Ravzova's mill for her, and at the same age you were writing poems. A few years later the whole mill belonged to Papa, who in his heart always despised property. He didn't just despise it, it choked him. My father, your grandfather, had persistence and vision, generosity, and even a special worldly wisdom. The one thing he didn't have was luck . . .

23

AROUND THE garden, Aunt Sonia says, we had a picket fence that was painted white every spring. Every year too the trunks of the trees were whitewashed to keep off the insects. The fence had a little *kalitka,* a wicket gate, through which you could go out into the *ploshchadka,* a sort of square or open space. Every Monday the *tsiganki,* the Gypsy women, came. They used to park their painted caravan there, with its large wheels, and erect a big tent of tarpaulin on the side of the square. Beautiful Gypsy women went barefoot from door to door: they came to the kitchens to read the cards, to clean the toilets, to sing songs for a few kopeks, and if you weren't watchful, to pilfer. They came into our house by the servants' entrance, the *chyorny khod* I told you about, which was to one side, in the wing.

That back door opened straight into our kitchen, which was enormous, bigger than this whole apartment, with a table in the middle and chairs for sixteen people. There was a kitchen range with twelve hobs of different sizes, and cupboards with yellow doors, and quantities of porcelain and crystal. I remember that we had a huge long dish on which you could serve a whole fish wrapped in leaves on a bed of rice and carrots. What happened to that dish? Who knows? It may still be adorning the sideboard of some fat *hohol.* And there was a kind of podium in one corner with an upholstered rocking chair and a little table next to it where there was always a glass of sweet fruit tea. This was Mama's—your grandmother's—throne, where she would sit, or sometimes stand with her hands on the back of the chair, like a captain on the bridge, giving orders to the cook and the maid and anyone who came into the kitchen. And not only the kitchen: her podium was arranged in such a way that she had a clear view to the left, through the door into the corridor, so that she could survey the doors to all the rooms, and to the right she could see through the hatch into the wing, to the dining room and the maid's room, where Xenia lived with her pretty daughter Dora.

From this vantage point, which we all called Napoleon's Hill, she could command all her battlefields.

Sometimes Mama stood there breaking eggs into a basin, and she made Haya, Fania, and me swallow the raw yolks, in such quantities that we loathed them, because there was a theory at that time that egg yolks made you resistant to all illnesses. It may even be true. Who knows? It's a fact that we were rarely ill. Nobody had heard of cholesterol in those days. Fania, your mother, was made to swallow the most egg yolks, because she was always the weakest, palest child.

Of the three of us, your mother was the one who suffered most from our mother, who was a strident, rather military woman, like a *Feldwebel*, a sergeant. From morning to evening she kept sipping her fruit tea and giving instructions and orders. She had some mean habits that exasperated Papa, she was obsessively mean, but mostly he was wary of her and gave way to her, and this irritated us: we were on his side because he had right on his side. Mama used to cover the *fauteuils* and the fine furniture with dustcovers, so that our drawing room always looked as though it were full of ghosts. Mama was terrified of the tiniest speck of dust. Her nightmare was that children would come and walk on her beautiful chairs with dirty shoes.

Mama hid the porcelain and crystal, and only when we had important guests or at New Year or Passover did she bring it all out and remove the dustcovers in the drawing room. We hated it so. Your mother especially detested the hypocrisy: that sometimes we kept kosher and sometimes we didn't, sometimes we went to synagogue and sometimes we didn't, sometimes we vaunted our wealth and sometimes we kept it hidden under white shrouds. Fania took Papa's side even more than we did, and resisted Mama's rule. I think that he, Papa, was also especially fond of Fania. I can't prove it, though—there was never any favoritism—he was a man with a very strong sense of fairness. I've never known another man like your grandpa, who so hated hurting people's feelings. Even with scoundrels he always tried very hard not to hurt their feelings. In Judaism, upsetting someone is considered worse than shedding their blood, and he was a man who would never hurt a soul. Never.

Mama quarreled with Papa in Yiddish. Most of the time they conversed in a mixture of Russian and Yiddish, but when they fought, it was only in Yiddish. To us daughters, to Papa's business partner, to the lodgers, the maid, the cook, and the coachman they spoke only Russian.

With the Polish officials they spoke Polish. (After Rovno was annexed by Poland, the new authorities insisted that everyone speak Polish.)

In our Tarbuth school all the pupils and teachers spoke almost exclusively Hebrew. Among the three of us sisters, at home, we spoke Hebrew and Russian. Mostly we spoke Hebrew, so that our parents wouldn't understand. We never spoke Yiddish to each other. We didn't want to be like Mama: we associated Yiddish with her complaints and bossiness and arguments. All the profits that Papa made by the sweat of his brow from his mill she extorted from him and spent on expensive dressmakers who made her luxurious dresses. But she was too mean to wear them: she saved them up at the back of her closet, and most of the time she wore an old mouse-colored housecoat. Only a couple of times a year she got herself up like the Tsar's carriage to go to synagogue or to some charity ball, so the whole town could see her and burst with envy. Yet she shouted at us that we were ruining Papa.

Fania, your mother, wanted to be talked to quietly and reasonably, not shouted at. She liked to explain, and she wanted to be explained to. She couldn't stand commands. Even in her bedroom she had her own special way of ordering things—she was a very tidy girl—and if someone disturbed the order, she was very upset. Yet she held her peace. Too much: I don't recall her ever raising her voice. Or telling someone off. She responded with silence even to things that she shouldn't have.

In one corner of the kitchen there was a big baking oven, and sometimes we were allowed as a treat to take the *lopata*, the paddle, and put the Sabbath *chollas* in the oven. We pretended we were putting the wicked witch Baba Yaga and the black devil, *chyorny chyort*, in the fire. There were smaller cookers too, with four cooktops and two *dukhovki*, for baking biscuits and roasting meat. The kitchen had three huge windows looking out on the garden and the orchard, and they were nearly always steamed up. The bathroom opened off the kitchen. Hardly anybody in Rovno had a bathroom inside their house at that time. The rich families had a little shed in the yard, behind the house, with a wood-burning boiler that served for baths and also for the laundry. We were the only ones who had a proper bathroom, and all our little friends were green with envy. They used to call it the "sultan's delight."

When we wanted to take a bath, we would put some logs and saw-dust in the opening under the big boiler, then light the fire and wait an hour or an hour and a half for the water to heat up. There was enough hot water for six or seven baths. Where did the water come from? There was a *kolodets*, a well, in the neighbor's yard, and when we wanted to fill our boiler, they shut off their water and Philip or Anton or Vassia pumped the water up with the squeaky hand pump.

I remember how once, on the eve of the Day of Atonement, after the meal, two minutes before the fast began, Papa said to me: *Sureleh, mein Tochterl*, please bring me a glass of water straight from the well. When I brought him the water, he dropped three or four sugar lumps in it and stirred it with his finger, and when he had drunk it, he said: Now thanks to you, Sureleh, the fast will be lighter for me. (Mama called me Sonichka, my teachers called me Sarah, but to Papa I was always Sureleh.)

Papa liked to stir with his finger and eat with his hands. I was a little girl then, maybe five or six. And I can't explain to you—I can't even explain to myself—what joy, what happiness his words brought me, and the thought that thanks to *me* the fast would be lighter for him. Even now, eighty years later, I feel happy, just as I did then, whenever I remember it.

But there's also an upside-down sort of happiness, a black happi-ness, that comes from doing evil to others. Papa used to say that we were driven out of paradise not because we ate from the tree of knowl-edge but because we ate from the tree of evil. Otherwise, how can you explain black happiness? The happiness we feel not because of what we have but because of what we have and others haven't got? That others will be jealous of? And feel bad? Papa used to say, every tragedy is something of a comedy and in every disaster there is a grain of enjoy-ment for the bystander. Tell me, is it true there's no word for *Schaden-freude* in English?

Opposite the bathroom, on the other side of the kitchen, was the door that led to the room that Xenia shared with her daughter Dora, whose father was rumored to be the previous owner of the house, Mayor Lebe-devski. Dora was a real beauty, she had a face like the Madonna, a full body but a very thin wasplike waist, and big brown doe's eyes, but she was already a little weak in the head. When she was fourteen or sixteen, she fell in love with an older Gentile called Krynicki, who was also said to be her mother's lover.

Xenia made her Dora only one meal a day, in the evening, and then she would tell her a story in installments, and the three of us would run there to listen, because Xenia knew how to tell such strange stories, they sometimes made your hair stand on end, I've never met anyone who could tell stories like her. I still remember one story she told. Once upon a time there was a village idiot, Ivanuchka, Ivanuchka Durachok, whose mother sent him every day across the bridge to take a meal to his elder brothers working in the fields. Ivanuchka himself, who was foolish and slow, was given only a single piece of bread for the whole day. One day a hole suddenly appeared in the bridge, or the dam, and the water started to come through and threatened to flood the whole valley. Ivanuchka took the single piece of bread that his mother had given him and stopped the hole in the dam with it, so the valley would not be flooded. The old king happened to be passing and was amazed, and he asked Ivanuchka why he had done such a thing. Ivanuchka replied, What do you mean, Your Majesty? I did it so there wouldn't be a flood, otherwise the people would all be drowned, heaven forbid! And was that your only piece of bread? asked the old king. So what will you eat all day? *Nu*, so if I don't eat today, Your Majesty, so what? Others will eat, and I shall eat tomorrow! The old king had no children, and he was so impressed by what Ivanuchka had done and by his answer that he decided there and then to make him his Crown Prince. He became King Durak (which means King Fool), and even when Ivanuchka was king, all his subjects still laughed at him, and he even laughed at himself, he sat on his throne all day making faces. But gradually it transpired that under the rule of King Ivanuchka the Fool there were never any wars, because he did not know what it was to take offense or to seek revenge. Of course eventually the generals killed him and seized power, and of course at once they took offense at the smell of the cattle pens that the wind carried across the border from the next-door kingdom, and they declared war, and they were all killed, and the dam that King Ivanuchka Durak had once stopped with his bread was blown up, and they all drowned happily in the flood, both kingdoms submerged.

Dates. My grandfather, Naphtali Hertz Mussman, was born in 1889. My grandmother Itta was born in 1891. Aunt Haya was born in 1911. Fania, my mother, was born in 1913. Aunt Sonia was born in 1916. The three Mussman girls went to the Tarbuth school in Rovno. Then Haya and Fania, each in turn, were sent for a year to a private Polish school that issued matriculation certificates. These enabled Haya and Fania to attend the university in Prague, because in anti-Semitic Poland in the 1920s hardly any Jews gained admittance to the universities. Aunt Haya came to Palestine in 1933 and obtained a public position in the Zionist Workers' Party and in the Tel Aviv branch of the Working Mothers' Organization. Through this activity she met some of the leading Zionist figures. She had a number of keen suitors, including rising stars in the Workers' Council, but she married a cheerful, warm-hearted worker from Poland, Tsvi Shapiro, who later became an administrator in the Health Fund and eventually ended up as executive director of the Donnolo-Tsahalon Hospital in Jaffa. One of the two rooms in Haya and Tsvi Shapiro's ground-floor apartment at 175 Ben Yehuda Street in Tel Aviv was sublet to various senior commanders of the Haganah. In 1948, during the War of Independence, Major General Yigael Yadin, who was head of operations and deputy chief of staff of the newly established Israeli army, lived there. Conferences were held there at night, with Israel Galili, Yitzhak Sadeh, Yaakov Dori, leaders of the Haganah, advisers and officers. Three years later, in the same room, my mother took her own life.

Even after little Dora fell in love with her mother's lover, Pan Krynicki, Xenia did not stop cooking the evening meal and telling her stories, but the food she made was drenched with tears and so were the stories. The two of them would sit there in the evening, one weeping and eating, the other weeping and not eating; they never quarreled, on the contrary, they embraced each other and wept together, as if they had both caught the same incurable disease. Or as if the mother had unintentionally infected the daughter, and now she was nursing her lovingly, compassionately, with endless devotion. At night we would hear the creaking of the wicket gate, that little *kalitka* in the garden fence, and we knew that Dora had returned and that soon her mother would slip away to the same house. Papa always said that every tragedy is something of a comedy.

Xenia watched over her daughter assiduously, to make sure she did not fall pregnant. She explained to her endlessly, do this, don't do that, and if he says this, you say that, and if he insists on this, you do that. In this way we also heard something and learned, because no one had ever explained such not-nice things to us. But it was all to no avail: little Dora became pregnant, and it was said that Xenia had gone to Pan Krynicki to ask for money, and he had refused to give her anything and pretended he didn't know either of them. That's how God created us: wealth is a crime and poverty is a punishment, though the punishment is given not to the one who sinned but to the one who hasn't got the money to escape the punishment. The woman, naturally, cannot deny that she is pregnant. The man denies it as much as he likes, and what can you do? God gave men the pleasure and us the punishment. To the man He said, in the sweat of thy face shalt thou eat bread, which is a reward not a punishment, anyway, take away a man's work and he goes out of his mind—and to us women He gave the privilege of smelling their sweat of thy face close up, which is not such a big pleasure, and also the added promise of "in sorrow thou shalt bring forth children." I know that it is possible to see it differently.

Poor Dora, when she was nine months pregnant, they came and took her away to a village, to some cousin of Xenia's. I think that Papa gave them some money. Xenia went with Dora to the village, and a few days later she came back sick and pale. Xenia, not Dora. Dora came back after a month, neither sick nor pale but red-faced and plump, like a juicy apple, she came back without a baby and she did not seem in the least sad, only, as it were, even more childish than she had been before. And she had been very childish before. After she came back from the village, Dora spoke to us only in baby talk, and she played with dolls, and when she cried, it sounded just like the crying of a three-year-old. She started sleeping the hours a baby sleeps too: that girl slept for twenty hours a day.

And what happened to the baby? Who knows. We were told not to ask and we were very obedient daughters: we did not ask questions and nobody told us anything. Only once, in the night, Haya woke me and

Fania saying that she could hear very clearly from the garden, in the dark—it was a rainy, windy night—the sound of a baby crying. We wanted to dress and go out but we were frightened. By the time Haya went and woke Papa, there was no baby to be heard, but still Papa took a big lantern and went out in the garden and checked every corner, and he came back and said sadly, Hayunia, you must have been dreaming. We did not argue with our father, what good would it do to argue? But each of us knew very well that she had not been dreaming, but that there really had been a baby crying in the garden: such a thin high-pitched cry so piercing, so frightening, not like a baby that is hungry and wants to suck, or a baby that's cold, but like a baby in terrible pain.

After that pretty Dora fell ill with a rare blood disease, and Papa paid again for her to go and be examined by a great professor in Warsaw, a professor as famous as Louis Pasteur, and she never came back. Xenia Dimitrovna went on telling stories in the evening, but her stories ended up wild, that is to say not very proper, and occasionally words crept into her stories that were not so nice and that we didn't want to hear. Or if we did want to, we denied ourselves, because we were well-brought-up young ladies.

And little Dora? We never spoke about her again. Even Xenia Dimitrovna never pronounced her name, as though she forgave her for taking her lover but not for disappearing to Warsaw. Instead Xenia raised two dear little birds in a cage on the porch and they thrived until the winter, and in the winter they froze to death. Both of them.

24

MENAHEM GELEHRTER, who wrote the book about the Tarbuth gymnasium (secondary school) in Rovno, was a teacher there himself. He taught Bible, literature, and Jewish history. Among other things in his book I found something of what my mother and her sisters and friends studied as part of their Hebrew curriculum in the 1920s. It included stories from the rabbis, selected poems from the Jewish Golden Age in Spain, medieval Jewish philosophy, collected works of Bialik and Tchernikhowsky and selections from other modern Hebrew writers, and also translations from world literature, including such authors as Tolstoy,

Dostoevsky, Pushkin, Turgenev, Chekhov, Mickiewicz, Schiller, Goethe, Heine, Shakespeare, Byron, Dickens, Oscar Wilde, Jack London, Tagore, Hamsun, the Epic of Gilgamesh in Tchernikhowsky's translation, and so on. The books on Jewish history included Joseph Klausner's *History of the Second Temple.*

Every day (Aunt Sonia continues), before the day begins, at six or even earlier, I go slowly down the stairs to empty the liner in the garbage can outside. Before I climb up again, I have to rest there for a moment, I have to sit on the low wall by the garbage cans because the stairs leave me breathless. Sometimes I bump into a new immigrant from Russia, Varia, who sweeps the pavement in Wessely Street each morning. Over there, in Russia, she was a big boss. Here—she sweeps the pavements. She has hardly learned any Hebrew. Sometimes the two of us stay for a few minutes by the garbage cans and talk a little in Russian.

Why is she a street sweeper? To keep two talented daughters at the university, one in chemistry, one in dentistry. Husband—she has none. Family in Israel—she has none either. Food—they save on that too. Clothes—they save on. Accommodation—they share a single room. All so that for tuition and textbooks they won't be short. It was always like that with Jewish families: they believed that education was an investment in the future, the only thing that no one can ever take away from your children, even if, heaven forbid, there's another war, another revolution, another migration, more discriminatory laws—your diploma you can always fold up quickly, hide it in the seams of your clothes, and run away to wherever Jews are allowed to live.

The Gentiles used to say about us: the diploma—that's the Jews' religion. Not money, not gold. The diploma. But behind this faith in the diploma there was something else, something more complicated, more secret, and that is that girls in those days, even modern girls, like us, girls who went to school and then to university, were always taught that women are entitled to an education and a place outside the home—but only until the children are born. Your life is your own only for a short time: from when you leave your parents' home to your first pregnancy. From that moment, from the first pregnancy, we had to begin to live our lives only around the children. Just like our mothers. Even to sweep pavements for our children, because your child is the chick and you are—what? When it comes down to it, you are just the yolk of the egg, you are what the chick eats so as to grow big and strong. And when your child grows up—even then you can't go back to being yourself, you simply change from being a mother to being a grandmother, whose task is simply to help her children bring up their children.

True, even then there were quite a few women who made careers for themselves and went out into the world. But everybody talked about them behind their backs: look at that selfish woman, she sits in meetings while her poor children grow up in the street and pay the price.

Now it's a new world. Now at last women are given more opportunity to live lives of their own. Or is it just an illusion? Maybe in the younger generations too women still cry into their pillows at night, while their husbands are asleep, because they feel they have to make impossible choices? I don't want to be judgmental: it's not my world anymore. To make a comparison I'd have to go from door to door checking how many mothers' tears are wept every night into the pillow when husbands are asleep, and to compare the tears then with the tears now.

Sometimes I see on television, sometimes I see even here, from my balcony, how young couples after a day's work do everything together—wash the clothes, hang them out, change diapers, cook, once I even heard in the grocer's a young man saying that the next day he and his wife were going—that's what he said, tomorrow *we're* going—for an amniocentesis. When I heard him say that, I felt a lump in my throat: maybe the world is changing a little after all?

It's certain that malice, *rishes*, hasn't lost ground in politics, between religions, nations, or classes, but maybe it's receding a little in couples? In young families? Or maybe I'm just deceiving myself. Maybe it's all just play-acting, and in fact the world carries on as before—the mother cat suckles her kittens, while Mr. Puss-in-Boots licks himself all over, twitches his whiskers, and goes off in search of pleasures in the yard?

Do you still remember what is written in the book of Proverbs? A wise son maketh a glad father, but a foolish son is the heaviness of his mother! If the son turns out wise, then the father rejoices, boasts of his son, and scores full marks. But if, heaven forbid, the son turns out unsuccessful, or stupid, or problematic, or deformed, or a criminal—*nu*, then it's bound to be the mother's fault, and all the care and suffering falls on her. Once your mother said to me: Sonia, there are just two things—no, I've got a lump in my throat again. We'll talk about this another time. Let's talk about something else.

Sometimes I'm not quite sure that I remember correctly whether that princess, Lyubov Nikitichna, who lived behind the curtain in our house with her two girls, Tasia and Nina, and slept with them in the same antique bed, I'm not quite sure: was she really their mother? Or was she just the *gouvernantka*, the governess, of the two girls? Who apparently had two different fathers? Because Tasia was Anastasia Sergeyevna, while Nina was Antonina Boleslavovna. There was something a bit foggy. Something we didn't talk about much, and when we did, it was an awkward subject. I remember that the two girls both called the Princess "Mama" or "Maman," but it might have been because they couldn't remember their real mother. I can't tell you for certain, either way, because the cover-up already existed. There were many cover-ups in life two or three generations ago. Today perhaps there are fewer. Or have they just changed? Have new ones been invented?

Whether the cover-up is a good thing or a bad thing I really don't know. I am not qualified to judge today's habits because I may well have been brainwashed, like all the girls of my generation. Still, I sometimes think that "between him and her," as they say, perhaps in these times it has all become simpler. When I was a girl, when I was what they called a young lady from a good home, it was full of knives, poison, terrifying darkness. Like walking in the dark in a cellar full of scorpions with no shoes on. We were completely in the dark. It simply wasn't talked about.

But they did talk all the time—chatter, jealousy, and *rishes*, malicious gossip—they talked about money, about diseases, they talked about success, about a good family versus who knows what sort of family, this was an endless topic, and about character they talked endlessly too, this one has such and such a character and that one has such and such a character. And how much they talked about ideas! It's unimaginable today! They talked about Judaism, Zionism, the Bund, Communism, they talked about anarchism and nihilism, they talked about America, they talked about Lenin, they even talked about the "woman question," women's emancipation. Your aunt Haya was the most daring of the three of us about women's emancipation—but only when it came to talking and arguing, naturally—Fania was a bit of a suffragette too, but she had some doubts. And I was the silly little girl who is always being told, Sonia don't talk, Sonia don't interrupt, you wait till you grow up, then you'll understand. So I closed my mouth and listened.

All young people in those days bandied notions of freedom about: this kind of freedom, that kind of freedom, another kind of freedom. But when it came to "between him and her" there was no freedom: there was just walking in the dark in a cellar full of scorpions with no shoes on. Not a week went by without our hearing horrifying rumors about a young girl who experienced what happens to girls who aren't careful; or a respectable woman who fell in love and went out of her mind; or a maid who was seduced; or a cook who ran off with her employer's son and came back alone with a baby; or a respectable woman who fell in love and threw herself at her beloved's feet only to be cast out and scoffed at. Do you say scoffed? No? When we were girls, chastity was both a cage and the only railing between you and the abyss. It lay on a girl's chest like a thirty-kilo stone. Even in the dreams she dreamed at night, chastity stayed awake and stood beside the bed and watched over her, so she could be very ashamed when she woke up in the morning, even if nobody knew.

All that business "between him and her" may be a bit less in the dark nowadays. A bit simpler. In the darkness that covered things then, it was much easier for men to abuse women. On the other hand, the fact that it's so much simpler and less mysterioius now—is that a good thing? Doesn't it turn out too ugly?

I'm surprised at myself that I'm talking to you about this at all. When I was still a girl, we would sometimes whisper to one another. But with a boy? Never in my life have I talked about such things with a boy. Not even with Buma, and we've been married now for nearly sixty years. How did we end up here? We were talking about Lyubov Nikitichna and her Tasia and Nina. If you go to Rovno someday, you can have a detective adventure. Maybe you could try to check if they still have in the town hall any documents that can shed light on that cover-up. Discover whether that countess, or princess, was or wasn't the mother of her two daughters. And whether she really was a princess or a countess. Or maybe whether Lebedevski, the mayor, was also the father of Tasia and Nina, just as he was said to be the father of poor Dora.

But on second thought, any documents there must have been burned by now ten times over, when we were conquered by the Poles, by the Red Army, and then by the Nazis, when they simply took us all and shot us in ditches and covered us with earth. Then there was Stalin again, with the NKVD, Rovno was thrown from hand to hand like a puppy being teased by Russia–Poland–Russia–Germany–Russia. And now it doesn't belong to Poland or to Russia but to Ukraine, or is it Belarus? Or some local gangs? I don't know myself who it belongs to now. And I don't even really care: what there was doesn't exist anymore, and what there is now will in a few more years also turn to nothing.

The whole world, if you just look at it from a distance, will not go on forever. They say one day the sun will go out and everything will return to darkness. So why do men slaughter one another throughout history? What does it matter so much, who rules Kashmir or the Tombs of the Patriarchs in Hebron? Instead of eating the apple from the tree of life or the tree of knowledge, it seems we ate the apple from the tree of *rishes,* and we ate it with pleasure. That's how paradise came to an end and this hell began.

There's so much either-or: you know so little even about people who live under the same roof as you do. You think you know a lot—and it turns out you know nothing at all. Your mother, for example—no, I'm sorry, I simply can't talk about her directly. Only in a roundabout way. Otherwise the wound starts to hurt. I won't talk about Fania. Only about what there was around her. What there was around Fania is also maybe a little bit Fania. We used to have a kind of proverb, that when you really love someone, then you love even their handkerchief. It loses something in translation. But you can see what I'm getting at.

Take a look at this, please: I've got something here that I can show you and you can feel it with your fingers, so you'll know that everything I've told you isn't just stories. Look at this please—no, it's not a tablecloth, it's a pillowcase, embroidered the way young ladies from good homes learned to embroider in the old days. It was embroidered for me as a present by the Princess—or Countess?—Lyubov Nikitichna. The head that's embroidered here, she told me herself, is the silhouette of the head of Cardinal Richelieu. Who he was, that Cardinal Richelieu, I don't remember anymore. Perhaps I never knew, I'm not clever like Haya and

Fania: they were sent off to get their matriculation, and then to Prague, to study at the university. I was a bit thick. People always said about me: that Sonichka, she is so cute but she's a bit thick. I was sent to the Polish military hospital to learn how to be a qualified nurse. But still I remember very well, before I left home, that the princess told me it was the head of Cardinal Richelieu.

Perhaps you know who Cardinal Richelieu was? Never mind. Tell me another time, or don't bother. At my age, it's not so important to me if I end my days without the honor of knowing who Cardinal Richelieu was. There are plenty of cardinals, and most of them are none too fond of our people.

Deep down in my heart I'm a bit of an anarchist. Like Papa. Your mother was also an anarchist at heart. Of course, among the Klausners she could never express it: they thought her pretty strange as it was, although they always behaved politely toward her. In general with the Klausners manners were always the most important thing. Your other grandfather, Grandpa Alexander, if I didn't snatch my hand away quickly, would have kissed it. There's a children's story about Puss-in-Boots. In the Klausner family your mother was like a captive bird in a cage hanging in Puss-in-Boots's drawing room.

I'm an anarchist for the very simple reason that nothing good ever came from any Cardinal Richelieu. Only Ivanuchka Durachok, do you remember, the village idiot in our maid Xenyuchka's story who took pity on the ordinary people and didn't begrudge the little bread he had to eat, but used it to stop the hole in the bridge and because of that he was made king—only someone like him might take pity on us, too, occasionally. All the rest, the kings and rulers, have no pity on anyone. In fact, we ordinary people don't have much pity for each other either: we didn't exactly have pity for the little Arab girl who died at the road block on the way to the hospital because apparently there was some Cardinal Richelieu of a soldier there, without a heart. A Jewish soldier—but still a Cardinal Richelieu! All he wanted was to lock up and go home, and so that little girl died, whose eyes should be piercing our souls so none of us can sleep at night, though I didn't even see her eyes because in the papers they only show pictures of our victims, never theirs.

Do you think ordinary people are so wonderful? Far from it! They are just as stupid and cruel as their rulers. That's the real moral of Hans Christian Andersen's story about the emperor's new clothes, that ordinary people are just as stupid as the king and the courtiers and Cardinal Richelieu. But Ivanuchka Durachok didn't care if they laughed at him; all that mattered to him was that they should stay alive. He had compassion for people, all of whom without exception need some compassion. Even Cardinal Richelieu. Even the Pope, and you must have seen on television how sick and feeble he is, and here we were so lacking in compassion, we made him stand for hours in the sun on those sick legs of his. They had no pity on an old, very sick man, who you could see even on TV could stand upright only with terrible pain, but he made a supreme effort and stood in front of us saying nothing at Yad Vashem (the Holocaust memorial) for half an hour without a break, in a heat wave, just so as not to bring us dishonor. It was quite hard for me to watch. I felt sorry for him.

Nina was a very good friend of your mother Fania, they were exactly the same age, and I made friends with the little one, Tasia. For many years they lived in our house with the princess, Maman they called her. Maman is the French for Mama, but who knows if she was really their Mama? Or just their nanny? They were very poor, I don't think they paid us even a kopek in rent. They were allowed to come into the house not through the servants' entrance, the *chyorny khod,* but through the main entrance, which was called *paradny khod.* They were so poor that the princess, the Maman, used to sit at night by the lamp sewing paper skirts for rich girls who were learning ballet. It was a kind of corrugated paper, and she glued lots of glittering stars on, made from golden paper.

Until one fine day that princess, or countess, Lyubov Nikitichna, left her two girls and suddenly went off to Tunis, of all places, to look for some long-lost relative called Yelizaveta Franzovna. And now just look how my memory is making an idiot of me! Where have I put my watch? I can't remember. But the name of some Yelizaveta Franzovna that I've never seen in my life, some Yelizaveta Franzovna that maybe eighty years ago our Princess Lyubov Nikitichna went off to Tunis, of all places, to look for, that I can remember as clear as the sun in the sky! Perhaps I lost my watch in Tunis, too?

In our dining room hung a picture in a gilded frame by some very expensive *khudozhnik* (artist): I remember that in the picture you could see a good-looking boy with fair hair, all disheveled, looking more like a spoiled girl than a boy, like something between a boy and a girl. I can't remember his face but I do remember very well that he was wearing a kind of embroidered shirt with puffy sleeves, a big yellow hat hanging by a string on her shoulder—perhaps it was a little girl after all—and you could see her three skirts, one under the other, because one side was raised a little and the lace peeped out from underneath, first a yellow underskirt, a very strong yellow like in a Van Gogh, then under that a white lace underskirt, and the bottom one—her legs were covered apparently by a third underskirt in sky blue. A picture like that, it seemed modest but it wasn't really. It was a life-size picture. And that girl who looked so much like a boy was standing there in the middle of the field, surrounded by pasture and white sheep, there were some light clouds in the sky, and in the distance you could see a strip of forest.

I remember once Haya said that a beauty like that shouldn't go out herding sheep but should stay inside the walls of the palace, and I said that the bottommost skirt was painted the same color as the sky, as though the skirt had been cut straight from the sky. And suddenly Fania burst out in fury against us and said, Be quiet, both of you, why are you talking such nonsense, it's a lying painting that is covering a very great moral decay. She used more or less these words, but not exactly, I can't repeat your mother's way of speaking, nobody could—can you still remember a little how Fania spoke?

I can't forget that outburst of hers, or her face at that moment. She was maybe fifteen or sixteen at the time. I remember it all precisely because it was so unlike her: Fania never raised her voice, ever, even when she was hurt, she would just withdraw inward. And anyway, with her you always had to guess what she was feeling, what she didn't like. And here suddenly—I remember it was Saturday night or the end of some festival, maybe Sukkot? or Shavuot?—she suddenly burst out and shouted at us. Never mind me, all my life I've been just the silly little one, but to shout at Haya! Our big sister! The leader of the youth group! With her charisma! Haya, who was admired by the whole school!

But your mother, as though suddenly rebelling, started to pour scorn on that artistic painting that had been hanging there in our dining room all those years. She ridiculed it for sweetening reality! For lying! She said that in real life, shepherdesses are dressed in rags, not in silk, and they have faces scarred by cold and hunger, not angelic faces, and dirty hair with lice and fleas, not golden locks. And that to ignore suffering is almost as bad as inflicting it, and that the picture turned real life into some kind of Swiss chocolate box scene.

Maybe the reason your mother was in such a rage about the picture in the dining room was that the *khudozhnik* who painted it had made it seem as if there were no more disasters in the world. I think that's what made her angry. At the time of this outburst she must have been more miserable than anyone could have imagined. Forgive me for crying. She was my sister and she loved me a lot and she's been ravaged by scorpions. That's enough: I've finished crying now. Sorry. Every time I remember that prettified picture, every time I see a picture with three underskirts and a feathery sky, I see scorpions ravaging my sister and I start to cry.

25

SO THE eighteen-year-old Fania, following in the footsteps of her elder sister Haya, was sent in 1931 to study at the university in Prague, because in Poland the universities were virtually closed to Jews. Mother studied history and philosophy. Her parents, Hertz and Itta, like all the Jews of Rovno, were witnesses and victims of the anti-Semitism that was growing among their Polish neighbors and among the Ukrainians and Germans, Catholic and Orthodox Christians—acts of violence by Ukrainian hooligans and increasingly discriminatory measures by the Polish authorities. And, like the rumble of distant thunder, echoes reached Rovno of deadly incitement to violence and the persecution of Jews in Hitler's Germany.

My grandfather's business affairs were also in crisis: the inflation of the early 1930s wiped out all his savings overnight. Aunt Sonia told me about "loads of Polish banknotes for millions and trillions that Papa gave me, that I wallpapered my room with. All the dowries that he had been saving for ten years for the three of us went down the drain in two months." Haya and Fania soon had to abandon their studies in Prague because the money, their father's money, had almost run out.

And so the flour mill, the house and orchard in Dubinska Street, the carriage, horses, and sleigh were all sold in a hasty, unfavorable deal. Itta and Hertz Mussman reached Palestine in 1933 almost penniless. They rented a miserable little hut covered with tar paper. Papa, who had always enjoyed being near flour, managed to find work in the Pat bakery. Later, when he was about fifty, as Aunt Sonia recalled, he bought a horse and cart and made his living first delivering bread, then transporting building materials around Haifa Bay. I can see him clearly, a darkly suntanned, thoughtful man, in his work clothes and sweaty gray vest, his smile rather shy but his blue eyes shooting sparks of laughter, the reins slack in his hands, as though from his seat on a board set across the cart he found some charming and amusing side to the views of Haifa Bay, the Carmel range, the oil refineries, the derricks of the port in the distance, and the factory chimneys.

Now that he had stopped being a wealthy man and returned to the proletariat, he seemed rejuvenated. A sort of perpetual suppressed joy seemed to have descended on him, a joie de vivre in which an anarchistic spark flickered. Just like Yehuda Leib Klausner of Ulkieniki in Lithuania, the father of my other grandfather, Alexander, my grandfather Naphtali Hertz Mussman enjoyed the life of a carter, the lonely, peaceful rhythm of the long slow journeys, the feel of the horse and its pungent smells, the stable, the straw, the harness, the shafts, the oat bag, the reins, and the bit.

Sonia, who was a girl of sixteen when her parents emigrated and her sisters were studying in Prague, stayed on in Rovno for five years, until she had qualified as a nurse at the nursing college attached to the Polish military hospital. She reached the port of Tel Aviv, where her parents, her sisters, and Tsvi Shapiro, Haya's "fresh" husband, were waiting for her, two days before the end of 1938. After a few years she married in Tel Aviv the man who had been her leader in the youth movement in Rovno, a strict, pedantic, opinionated man named Avraham Gendelberg. Buma.

And in 1934, a year or so after her parents and her elder sister Haya and four years before her younger sister Sonia, Fania too reached the Land of Israel. People who knew her said that she had had a painful love affair in Prague; they couldn't give me any details. When I visited Prague and on several successive evenings walked in the warren of ancient cobblestone streets around the university, I conjured up images and composed stories in my head.

A year or so after she arrived in Jerusalem, my mother registered to continue her history and philosophy studies at the Hebrew University on Mount Scopus. Forty-eight years later, apparently with no notion of what her grandmother had studied in her youth, my daughter Fania decided to study history and philosophy at Tel Aviv University.

I do not know if my mother broke off her studies at Charles University only because her parents' money had run out. How far was she pushed to emigrate to Palestine by the violent hatred of Jews that filled the streets of Europe in the mid-1930s and spread to the universities, or to what extent did she come here as the result of her education in a Tarbuth school and her membership in a Zionist youth movement? What did she hope to find here, what did she find, what did she not find? What did Tel Aviv and Jerusalem look like to someone who had grown up in a mansion in Rovno and arrived straight from the Gothic beauty of Prague? What did spoken Hebrew sound like to the sensitive ears of a young lady coming with the refined, book-learned Hebrew of the Tarbuth school and possessing a finely tuned linguistic sensibility? How did my young mother respond to the sand dunes, the motor pumps in the citrus groves, the rocky hillsides, the archaeology field trips, the biblical ruins and remains of the Second Temple period, the headlines in the newspapers and the cooperative dairy produce, the wadis, the hamsins, the domes of the walled convents, the ice-cold water from the *jarra,* the cultural evenings with accordion and harmonica music, the cooperative bus drivers in their khaki shorts, the sounds of English (the language of the rulers of the country), the dark orchards, the minarets, strings of camels carrying building sand, Hebrew watchmen, suntanned pioneers from the kibbutz, construction workers in shabby caps? How much was she repelled, or attracted, by tempestuous nights of arguments, ideological conflicts, and courtships, Saturday afternoon outings, the fire of party politics, the secret intrigues of the various underground groups and their sympathizers, the enlisting of volunteers for agricultural tasks, the dark blue nights punctuated by howls of jackals and echoes of distant gunfire?

By the time I reached the age when my mother could have told me about her childhood and her early days in the Land, her mind was elsewhere and set on other matters. The bedtime stories she told me were peopled by giants, fairies, witches, the farmer's wife and the miller's daughter, remote huts deep in the forest. If she ever spoke about the past, about her parents' house or the flour mill or the bitch Prima, something bitter and desperate would creep into her voice, something ambivalent or vaguely sarcastic, a kind of suppressed mockery, something too complicated or veiled for me to catch, something provocative and disconcerting.

Maybe that is why I did not like her to talk about these things and begged her to tell me simple stories I could relate to instead, like that of Matvey the Water Drawer and his six bewitched wives, or the dead horseman who went on crossing continents and cities in the form of a skeleton wearing armor and blazing spurs.

I have hardly any idea about my mother's arrival in Haifa, her first days in Tel Aviv, or her first years in Jerusalem. Instead, I can hand you back to Aunt Sonia to tell her story of how and why she came here, what she hoped to find and what she really found.

At the Tarbuth school we not only learned to read and write and speak very good Hebrew, which my subsequent life has corrupted. We also learned Bible and Mishnah and medieval Hebrew poetry, as well as biology, Polish literature and history, Renaissance art and European history. And above all we learned that beyond the horizon, beyond the rivers and forests, there was a land that we would all soon have to go to because the days of the Jews in Europe, at least those of us who lived in Eastern Europe, were numbered.

Our parents' generation were much more aware than we were that time was running out. Even those who had made money, like our father, or those who had built modern factories in Rovno or turned to medicine, law, or engineering, those who enjoyed good social relations with the local authorities and intelligentsia, felt that we were living on a volcano. We were right on the borderline between Stalin and Grajewski and Pilsudski. We already knew that Stalin wanted to put an end to Jewish existence by force; he wanted all the Jews to become good Komsomolniks who would inform on one another. On the other hand, the Polish attitude toward the Jews was one of disgust, like someone who has bitten into a piece of bad fish and can neither swallow it nor spit it out. They didn't feel like spewing us forth in the presence of the Versailles nations, in the atmosphere of minority rights, in front of Woodrow Wilson, the

League of Nations: in the 1920s the Poles still had some shame, they were keen to look good. Like a drunk trying to walk straight, so that no one can see he's weaving. They still hoped to appear outwardly more or less like other countries. But under the table they oppressed and humiliated us, so that we would gradually all go off to Palestine and they wouldn't have to see us anymore. That's why they even encouraged Zionist education and Hebrew schools: by all means let us become a nation, why not, the main thing was that we should scram to Palestine, and good riddance.

The fear in every Jewish home, the fear that we never talked about but that we were unintentionally injected with, like a poison, drop by drop, was the chilling fear that perhaps we really were not clean enough, that we really were too noisy and pushy, too clever and money-grubbing. Perhaps we didn't have proper manners. There was a terror that we might, heaven forbid, make a bad impression on the Gentiles, and then they would be angry and do things to us too dreadful to think about.

A thousand times it was hammered into the head of every Jewish child that we must behave nicely and politely with the Gentiles even when they were rude or drunk, that whatever else we did, we must not provoke them or argue with them or haggle with them, we must not irritate them, or hold our heads up, and we must speak to them quietly, with a smile, so they shouldn't say we were noisy, and we must always speak to them in good, correct Polish, so they couldn't say we were defiling their language, but we mustn't speak in Polish that was too high, so they couldn't say we had ambitions above our station, we must not give them any excuse to accuse us of being too greedy, and heaven forbid that they should say we had stains on our skirts. In short, we had to try very hard to make a good impression, an impression that no child must mar, because even a single child with dirty hair who spread lice could damage the reputation of the entire Jewish people. They could not stand us as it was, so heaven forbid we should give them more reasons not to stand us.

You who were born here in Israel can never understand how this constant drip-drip distorts all your feelings, how it corrodes your human dignity like rust. Gradually it makes you as fawning and dishonest and full of tricks as a cat. I dislike cats intensely. I don't like dogs much either, but if I had to choose, I prefer a dog. A dog is like a Gentile, you can see at once what it's thinking or feeling. Diaspora Jews became cats, in the bad sense, if you know what I mean.

But most of all they dreaded the mobs. They were terrified of what might happen in the gap between governments, for instance if the Poles were thrown out and the Communists came in, they were afraid that in the interval gangs of Ukrainians or Belarussians or the inflamed Polish masses or, farther north, the Lithuanians, would raise their heads once more. It was a volcano that kept dribbling lava all the time and smelling of smoke. "They're sharpening their knives for us in the dark," people said, and they never said who, because it could be any of them. The mobs. Even here in Israel, it turns out, Jewish mobs can be a bit of a monster.

The only people we were not too afraid of were the Germans. I can remember in 1934 or 1935—I'd stayed behind in Rovno to finish my nursing training when the rest of the family had left—there were quite a few Jews who said if only Hitler would come, at least in Germany there's law and order and everyone knows his place, it doesn't matter so much what Hitler says, what matters is that over there in Germany he imposes German order and the mob is terrified of him. What matters is that in Hitler's Germany there is no rioting in the streets and they don't have anarchy—we still thought then that anarchy was the worst state. Our nightmare was that one day the priests would start preaching that the blood of Jesus was flowing again, because of the Jews, and they would start to ring those scary bells of theirs and the peasants would hear and fill their bellies with schnapps and pick up their axes and pitch-forks, that's the way it always began.

Nobody imagined what was really in store, but already in the 1920s almost everyone knew deep down that there was no future for the Jews either with Stalin or in Poland or anywhere in Eastern Europe, and so the pull of Palestine became stronger and stronger. Not with everyone, naturally. The religious Jews were very much against it, and so were the Bundists, the Yiddishists, the Communists, and the assimilated Jews who thought they were already more Polish than Paderewski or Wojciechow-ski. But many ordinary Jews in Rovno in the 1920s were keen that their children should learn Hebrew and go to Tarbuth. Those who had enough money sent their children to study in Haifa, at the Technion, or at the Tel Aviv gymnasium, or the agricultural colleges in Palestine, and the echoes that came back to us from the Land were simply wonderful—the young people were just waiting, when would your turn come? Meanwhile everyone read newspapers in Hebrew, argued, sang songs from the Land of Israel, recited Bialik and Tchernikhowsky, split up into rival factions and parties, ran up uniforms and banners, there was a kind of tremendous excitement about everything national. It was very similar to what you see here today with the Palestinians, only without their penchant for bloodshed. Among us Jews you hardly see such nationalism nowadays.

Naturally we knew how hard it was in the Land: we knew it was very hot, a wilderness, and we knew there was unemployment, and we knew there were poor Arabs in the villages, but we could see on the big wall map in our classroom that there weren't many Arabs, there may have been half a million altogether then, certainly less than one million, and there was total certainty that there would be enough room for another few million Jews, and that maybe the Arabs were just being stirred up to hate us, like the simple people in Poland, but surely we'd be able to explain to them and persuade them that our return to the Land represented only a blessing for them, economically, medically, culturally, in every way. We thought that soon, in a few years, the Jews would be the majority here, and as soon as that happened, we'd show the whole world how to treat a minority—our own minority, the Arabs. We, who had always been an oppressed minority, would treat our Arab minority justly, fairly, generously, we would share our homeland with them, share everything with them, we would certainly never turn them into cats. It was a pretty dream.

In every classroom in the Tarbuth kindergarten, the Tarbuth primary school, and the Tarbuth secondary school there hung a large picture of Theodor Herzl, a large map of the Land from Dan to Beer Sheba with the pioneering villages highlighted, a Jewish National Fund collecting box, pictures of pioneers at work, and all sorts of slogans with snatches of verse. Bialik visited Rovno twice and Tchernikhowsky came twice too, and Asher Barash as well, I think, or it may have been some other writer. Prominent Zionists from Palestine came too, almost every month, Zalman Rubashov, Tabenkin, Yaakov Zerubavel, Vladimir Jabotinsky.

We used to put on big processions for them, with drums and banners, decorations, paper lanterns, passion, slogans, armbands, and songs. The Polish mayor himself went out to meet them in the square, and in that way we could sometimes begin to feel that we were also a nation, not just some kind of scum. It may be a little hard for you to understand, but in those days all the Poles were drunk on Polishness, the Ukrainians were drunk on Ukrainianness, not to mention the Germans, the Czechs, all of them, even the Slovaks, the Lithuanians, and the Latvians, and there was no place for us in that carnival, we didn't belong and we weren't wanted. Small wonder that we too wanted to be a nation, like the rest of them. What alternative had they left us?

But our education was not chauvinistic. Actually the education at Tarbuth was humanistic, progressive, democratic, and also artistic and scientific. They tried to give boys and girls equal rights. They taught us always to respect other peoples: every man is made in the image of God, even if he has a tendency to forget it.

From a very early age our thoughts were with the Land of Israel. We knew by heart the situation in every new village, what was grown in Beer Tuvia and how many inhabitants there were in Zichron Yaakov, who built the metaled road from Tiberias to Tsemach, and when the pioneers climbed Mount Gilboa. We even knew what people ate and wore there.

That is, we thought we knew. In fact our teachers did not know the whole truth, so even if they had wanted to tell us about the bad aspects, they couldn't have. They didn't have the faintest idea. Everybody who came from the Land—emissaries, youth leaders, politicians—and everyone who went and came back painted a rosy picture. And if anyone came back and told us less pleasant things, we didn't want to hear. We simply silenced them. We treated them with contempt.

Our headmaster was a delightful man. *Charmant.* He was a first-rate teacher with a sharp mind and the heart of a poet. His name was Reiss, Dr. Issachar Reiss. He came from Galicia and soon became the idol of the young people. The girls secretly adored him, including my sister Haya, who was involved in communal activities and was a natural leader, and Fania, your mother, on whom Dr. Reiss had a mysterious influence, gently steering her in the direction of literature and art. He was so handsome and manly, a bit like Rudolph Valentino or Ramon Navarro, full of warmth and natural empathy, he hardly ever lost his temper, and when he did, he never hesitated to send for the student afterward to apologize.

The whole town was under his spell. I think the mothers dreamed of him at night and the daughters swooned at the sight of him by day. And the boys, no less than the girls, tried to imitate him, to speak like him, to cough like him, to stop in the middle of a sentence like him and go and stand by the window for a few moments, deep in thought. He could have been a successful seducer. But no, so far as I know he was married—not particularly happily, to a woman who barely came up to his ankles—and behaved like an exemplary family man. He could also have been a great leader: he had a quality that made people long to follow him through fire and water, to do anything that would make him smile appreciatively and praise them afterward. His thoughts were our thoughts. His humor became our style. And he believed that the Land of Israel was the only place where the Jews could be cured of their mental illnesses and prove to themselves and to the world that they had some good qualities too.

We had some other wonderful teachers too. There was Menahem Gelehrter, who taught Bible studies as though he had been personally present at the Valley of Elah or Anathoth or the Philistine temple in Gaza. Every week he took us on a trip "in the Land," one day in Galilee, another in the new villages in Judaea, another day in the plain of Jericho, another through the streets of Tel Aviv. He would bring maps and photographs, newspaper cuttings and bits of poetry and prose, examples from the Bible, geography, history, and archaeology, until you ended up feeling pleasantly tired, as if you had really been there, not just in your thoughts but as if you'd really walked in the sun and the dust, among the citrus trees and the lodge in the vineyard and the cactus hedges and the pioneers' tents in the valleys. And so I came to the Land long before I actually arrived here.

26

IN ROVNO, your mother had a boyfriend, a deep, sensitive student whose name was Tarla or Tarlo. They had a sort of little union of Zionist students that included your mother, Tarlo, my sister Haya, Esterka Ben Meir, Fania Weissmann, possibly also Fania Sonder, Lilia Kalisch, who was later called Lea Bar-Samkha, and a few others. Haya was the natural leader until she went off to Prague. They would sit around concocting all sorts of plans, how they would live in the Land of Israel, how they would work there to reinvigorate the artistic and cultural life, how they would keep the Rovno connection alive. After the other girls left Rovno, either to study in Prague or to emigrate to the Land, Tarlo started courting me. He would wait for me every evening at the entrance to the Polish Military Hospital. I would come out in my green dress and white headband, and we would stroll together down Trzecziego Maya and Topolyova Streets, which had been renamed Pilsudski Street, in the Palace Gardens, in Gravni Park, sometimes we walked toward the River Ostia and the old quarter, the Citadel District, where the Great Synagogue and the Catholic cathedral stood. There was never anything more between us than words. We may have held hands two or three times at most. Why? That's hard for me to explain to you because your generation would never understand anyway. You might even make fun of us. We had a terrible sense of modesty. We were buried under a mountain of shame and fear.

That Tarlo, he was a great revolutionary by conviction, but he used to blush at everything: if ever he happened to utter a word like "women" or "suckle" or "skirt," or even "legs," he would flush red to his ears, like a hemorrhage, and he'd start apologizing and stuttering. He would talk to me endlessly about science and technology, whether they were a blessing or a curse for mankind. Or both. He would talk enthusiastically about a future where there would soon be no more poverty or crime or illness or even death. He was a bit of a Communist, but it didn't help him much: when Stalin came in '41, Tarlo was simply taken away, and he disappeared.

Of the whole of Jewish Rovno there's barely a soul left alive—only those who came to the Land while there was still time, and the few who fled to America, and those who somehow managed to survive the knives of the Bolshevik regime. All the rest were butchered by the Germans, apart from those who were butchered by Stalin. No, I have no desire to go back for a visit: what for? To start longing again from there for a Land of Israel that no longer exists and may never have existed outside our youthful dreams? To grieve? If I want to grieve, I don't have to leave Wessely Street or even set foot outside my own apartment. I sit here in my armchair and grieve several hours a day. Or I look out the window and grieve. Not for what once was and is no more, but for what never was. I have no reason now to grieve for Tarlo, it was nearly seventy years ago, he wouldn't be alive now anyway: if Stalin hadn't killed him, he'd be dead from this place, from a war or a terrorist bomb, or else from cancer or diabetes. I only grieve for what never was. Only for those pretty pictures we made for ourselves, and now they've faded.

I embarked from Trieste on a Romanian cargo boat, the *Constanţa* it was called, and I remember that, even though I didn't believe in any religion, I didn't want to eat pork—not because of God, after all God created pigs, they don't disgust him, and when a piglet is killed and it squeals and pleads with the voice of a tortured child, God sees and hears every grunt and has about as much pity for the tortured piglet as He does for human beings. He has neither more nor less pity for the piglet than He does for all His rabbis and Hasidim who keep all the commandments and worship Him all their lives.

So it wasn't because of God but merely because it didn't seem appropriate, on my way to the Land of Israel, to gobble smoked pork and salt pork and pork sausages on board that boat. So I ate wonderful white bread instead, bread that was so fine and rich. At night I slept belowdecks, in third class, in a dormitory, next to a Greek girl with a baby who must have been no more than three weeks old. Every evening the two of us used to rock the baby in a sheet so that she'd stop crying and go to sleep. We didn't speak to each other because we had no common language, and maybe that's the reason we parted from each other with great affection.

I even remember that at one moment I had a fleeting thought, why did I have to go to the Land of Israel at all? Just to be among Jews? Yet this Greek girl, who probably didn't even know what a Jew was, was closer to me than the entire Jewish people. The entire Jewish people seemed to me at that moment like a great sweaty mass whose belly I was being tempted to enter, so it could consume me entirely with its digestive juices, and I said to myself, Sonia, is that what you really want? It's curious that in Rovno I'd never experienced this fear, that I was going to be consumed by the digestive juices of the Jewish people. It never came back once I was here, either. It was just then, for a moment, on that boat, on the way, when the Greek baby fell asleep in my lap and I could feel it through my dress as though at that moment she really was flesh of my flesh, even though she wasn't Jewish, and despite the wicked Jew-hating Antiochus Epiphanes.

Early one morning, I can even tell you the precise date and time—it was exactly three days before the end of 1938, Wednesday, December 28, 1938, just after Hanukkah—it happened to be a very clear, almost cloudless day, by six in the morning I'd already dressed warmly, a sweater and light coat, and I went up on deck and looked at the gray line of clouds ahead. I watched for maybe an hour and all I saw was a few seagulls. And suddenly, almost in an instant, above the line of the clouds the winter sun appeared and below the clouds there was the city of Tel Aviv: row after row of square, white-painted houses, quite unlike houses in a town or a village in Poland or Ukraine, quite unlike Rovno or Warsaw or Trieste, but very like the pictures on the wall in every classroom at Tarbuth, and the drawings and photographs that our teacher Menahem Gelehrter used to show us. So I was both surprised and not surprised.

I can't describe how all at once the joy rose up in my throat; suddenly all I wanted to do was shout and sing, This is mine! All mine! It really is all mine! It's a funny thing, I'd never experienced such a strong feeling before in my life, of belonging, of ownership, if you know what I mean, not in our house, our orchard, the flour mill, never. Never in my life, either before that morning or after it, have I known that kind of joy: at long last this would be my home, at long last here I'd be able to draw my curtains and forget about the neighbors and do exactly as I pleased. Here I didn't need to be on my best behavior the whole time, I didn't have to be shy because of anyone, I didn't have to worry about what the peasants would think of us or what the priests would say or what the intelligentsia would feel, I didn't have to try to make a good impression on the Gentiles. Even when we bought our first apartment, in Holon, or this one in Wessely Street, I didn't feel so strongly how good it felt to own your own home. And that was the feeling that filled me at maybe seven in the morning, looking out at a city I'd never even been to, and a land where I'd never set foot, and funny little houses the like of which

I'd never seen before in my life! I don't suppose you can understand this. It must seem rather ludicrous to you, doesn't it? Or foolish?

At eleven o'clock we climbed down with our luggage into a little motorboat, and the sailor who was there, a big hairy Ukrainian, all sweaty and slightly scary, the moment I thanked him nicely in Ukrainian and wanted to give him a coin, he laughed and suddenly said in pure Hebrew, Darling, what's the matter with you, there's no need for that, why don't you give me a little kiss instead?

It was a pleasant, slightly cool day, and what I remember most is an intoxicating, strong smell of boiling tar, and out of the thick smoke coming from the tar barrels—they must have just asphalted some square or pavement—there suddenly burst my mother's face, laughing, and then Papa's, in tears, and my sister Haya with her husband, Tsvi, whom I hadn't met yet, but right from the first glance I had a flash of a thought like this: what a boy she's found herself here! He's quite good-looking, good-hearted, and jolly too! And it was only after I'd hugged and kissed everyone that I saw that my sister Fania, your mother, was there too. She was standing slightly to one side, away from the burning barrels, in a long skirt and a blue hand-knitted sweater, standing quietly there, waiting to hug and kiss me after all the others.

Just as I saw at once that my sister Haya was blooming here, she was so animated, pink-cheeked, confident, assertive—I also saw that Fania was not feeling so good: she seemed very pale and was even more silent than usual. She had come from Jerusalem especially to greet me, she apologized for Arieh, your father, but he hadn't been able to get a day off, and she invited me to come to Jerusalem.

It was only after a quarter of an hour or so that I saw that she was uncomfortable standing up for so long. Before she or some other member of the family told me, I realized suddenly for myself that she was finding it hard to bear her pregnancy—that is to say, you. She must only have been in her third month, but her cheeks seemed slightly sunken, her lips pale, and her forehead clouded. Her beauty had not vanished, on the contrary, it just seemed to have been covered with a gray veil, which she never removed right to the end.

Haya was always the most glamorous and impressive of the three of us, she was interesting, brilliant, a heartbreaker, but to any sharp-eyed observer who looked carefully it was clear that the most beautiful of us was Fania. Me? I didn't count for anything: I was just the silly little sister. I think our mother admired Haya most and was proudest of her, while Papa almost managed to hide the truth, that he was fondest of Fania. I was not the pet of either my father or my mother, maybe only Grandpa Ephraim, yet I loved them all: I wasn't jealous and I wasn't resentful. Maybe it's the people who are the least loved, provided they're not envious or bitter, who find the most love in themselves to give to others. Don't you think? I'm not too sure about what I've just said. It may just be one of those stories I tell myself before I go to sleep. Maybe everybody tells themselves stories before they go to sleep, so it'll be a bit less frightening. Your mother hugged me and said, Sonia, it's so good you're here, so good we're all together again, we're going to have to help one another a lot here, we'll especially have to help our parents.

Haya and Tsvi's apartment was maybe a quarter of an hour's walk from the port, and Tsvi was a hero and carried most of my luggage himself. On the way we saw some workmen building a great big building, it was the teachers' training college that still stands in Ben Yehuda Street just before the corner of Nordau Avenue. At first sight I took the builders for Gypsies or Turks, but Haya said they were just suntanned Jews. I'd never seen Jews like that before, except in pictures. Then I started crying—not just because the builders were so strong and happy, but also because among them there were some small children, twelve years old at most, and each one was carrying a sort of wooden ladder on his back laden with heavy building blocks. I wept a little when I saw that, from joy but also from sorrow. It's hard for me to explain.

In Haya and Tsvi's tiny apartment, Yigal was waiting with a neighbor who was looking after him until we got there. He must have been about six months, a lively, smily little boy, just like his father, and I washed my hands, picked up Yigal, and hugged him to me, ever so gently, and this time I didn't feel any desire to cry, and I didn't feel a wild joy as on the boat, I only felt a sort of reassurance, from inside, from the innermost depth of my being, as though from the bottom of the well, that it was very good that we were all here and not in the house in Dubinska Street. And I also felt that it was a great pity after all that the cheeky, sweaty sailor had not got the little kiss from me that he'd asked for. What was the connection? I don't know to this day. But that's how I felt there at that moment.

That evening Tsvi and Fania took me out to see Tel Aviv. We walked to Allenby Street and Rothschild Boulevard, because Ben Yehuda Street was not considered really part of Tel Aviv then. I remember how clean and nice everything looked at first glance, in the evening, with the benches and street lights and all the signs in Hebrew: as if the whole of Tel Aviv was just a very nice display in the playground of the Tarbuth school.

It was late December 1938, and since then I have never been abroad, except maybe in my thoughts. And I shall never go. It's not because the Land of Israel is so wonderful, it's because I now believe that all journeys are ridiculous: the only journey from which you don't always come back empty-handed is the journey inside yourself. Inside me there are no frontiers or customs, and I can travel as far as the farthest stars. Or walk in places that no longer exist, visit people who no longer exist. Inside, I can even go to places that never existed, that could never have existed, but where I like being. Or at least, don't dislike being. Now can I make you a fried egg before you go, with some tomato and cheese and a slice of bread? Or some avocado? No? You're in a hurry again? Won't you have another glass of tea, at least?

It was at the Hebrew University on Mount Scopus, or perhaps in one of those cramped rooms in Kerem Avraham, Geula, or Ahva, where poor students crowded in those days two or three to a room, that Fania Mussman met Yehuda Arieh Klausner. It was in 1935 or 1936. I know that my mother was living at the time in a room at 42 Zephaniah Street that she shared with two friends from Rovno who were also students, Esterka Weiner and Fania Weissmann. I know she was much courted. But, so I heard from Esterka Weiner, she had also had one or two passing affairs.

As for my father, I've been told that he was very keen on the company of women, he spoke a lot, brilliantly, wittily, he attracted attention and perhaps some mockery. "A walking dictionary," the other students called him. If anyone needed to know, or even if they didn't, he always liked to impress on them all that he knew—the name of the president of Finland, the Sanskrit word for "tower," or where oil is mentioned in the Mishnah.

If he fancied any student, he would take a fussy pleasure in helping her with her work, he would take her out walking at night in Mea Shearim or the lanes of Sanhedriya, buy her a fizzy drink, join trips to holy sites or archaeological digs, he enjoyed taking part in intellectual discussions, and he would read aloud, with pathos, from the poems of Mickiewicz or Tchernikhowsky. But apparently most of his relationships with girls only got as far as serious discussions and evening strolls: it seemed that girls were attracted only to his brains. Probably his luck was no different from that of most boys in those days.

I do not know how or when my parents became close, and I do not know whether there was still any love between them before I knew them. They were married at the beginning of 1938 on the roof of the Rabbinate building on Jaffa Road, he in a black pinstripe suit and a tie, with a triangle of white handkerchief peeping from his top pocket, she in a long white dress that accentuated the pallor of her skin and the beauty of her black hair. Fania moved with her few belongings from her shared room in Zephaniah Street to Arieh's room in the Zarchi family's apartment in Amos Street.

A few months later, when my mother was pregnant, they moved to a building across the road, to the two-room semibasement apartment. Here their only child was born. Sometimes my father joked in his rather anemic way that in those days the world was decidedly not a fit place to bring babies into (he was fond of the word "decidedly," as well as "nevertheless," "indeed," "in a certain sense," "unmistakably," "promptly," "on the other hand," and "utter disgrace"). In saying that the world was not a fit place to bring babies into, he may have been uttering an implied reproach to me, for being born so recklessly and irresponsibly, contrary to his plans and expectations, decidedly before he had achieved what he had hoped to achieve in his life, and hinting that because of my birth he had missed the boat. Or he may not have been hinting anything, just being clever in his usual way: quite often my father made some joke or other just to break the silence. He always imagined that silence was somehow directed against him. Or that it was his fault.

27

WHAT DID poor Ashkenazim eat in Jerusalem in the 1940s? We ate black bread with slices of onion and olives cut in half, and sometimes also with anchovy paste; we ate smoked fish and salt fish that came from the depths of the fragrant barrels in the corner of Mr. Auster's grocery; on special occasions we ate sardines, which were considered a delicacy.

We ate squash and eggplant, boiled or fried or made into an oily salad with slivers of garlic and chopped onion.

In the morning there was brown bread with jam, or occasionally with cheese. (The first time I went to Paris, straight from Kibbutz Hulda, in 1969, my hosts were amused to discover that in Israel there were only two kinds of cheese: white cheese and yellow cheese.) In the morning I was given Quaker Oats that tasted of glue, and when I went on strike, they replaced it with semolina and a sprinkling of cinnamon. My mother drank lemon tea in the morning, and sometimes she dunked a dark biscuit in it. My father's breakfast consisted of a slice of brown bread with thick yellow jam, half a hard-boiled egg with olives, slices of tomato, green pepper, and cucumber, and some Tnuva sour cream that came in a thick glass jar.

My father always got up early, an hour or an hour and a half before my mother and me. By five-thirty he was already standing at the bathroom mirror, brushing the snow on his cheeks into a thick lather, and while he shaved he softly sang a folk song that was hair-raisingly offkey. Afterward he would drink a glass of tea alone in the kitchen while he read the paper. In the citrus season he would squeeze some oranges with a little hand squeezer and bring my mother and me a glass of orange juice in bed. And because the citrus season was in the winter, and because in those days it was thought that you could catch a chill from drinking cold drinks on a cold day, my diligent father used to light the Primus stove before he squeezed the oranges and put a pan of water on, and when the water was almost boiling he carefully lowered the two glasses of juice into the pan and stirred them well with a spoon so that the juice close to the edge was not warmer than the juice in the middle of the glass. Then, shaved and dressed, with my mother's checked kitchen apron tied around his waist over his cheap suit, he would wake my mother (in the book room) and me (in the little room at the end of the corridor) and hand each of us a glass of warmed orange juice. I used to drink this lukewarm juice as though it were poison, while Father stood next to me in his checked apron and his quiet tie and his threadbare suit, waiting for me to give him back the empty glass. While I drank the juice, he would look for something to say: he always felt guilty about silence. He would rhyme in his unfunny way:

"Drink the juice my boy, I don't wish to annoy."

Or:

"If you drink your juice each day, you'll end up feeling merry and gay."

Or even:

"Every sip, so I've been tol', builds the body and the soul."

Or sometimes, on mornings when he was feeling more discursive than lyrical:

"Citrus fruit is the pride of our land! Jaffa oranges are appreciated all over the world. By the way, the name Jaffa, like the biblical name Japheth, apparently derives from the word for beauty, *yofi*, a very ancient word that may come from the Akkadian *faya*, and in Arabic has the form *wafi*, while in Amharic, I believe, it is *tawafa*. And now, my young *beauty*"—by now he would be smiling modestly, taking quiet satisfaction in his play on words—"finish your *boo-tiful* Jaffa juice and permit me to take the glass back to the kitchen as my *booty*."

Such puns and witticisms, that he called *calembours* or paronomasia, always aroused in my father a kind of well-intentioned good-humor. He felt that they had the power to dispel gloom or anxiety and spread a pleasant mood. If my mother said, for instance, that our neighbor Mr. Lemberg had come back from the hospital looking more emaciated than when he went in and they said he was in dire straits, Father would launch into a little lecture on the origin and meaning of the words "dire" and "straits," replete with biblical quotations. Mother expressed amazement that everything, even Mr. Lemberg's serious illness, sparked off his childish pleasantries. Did he really imagine that life was just some kind of school picnic or stag party, with jokes and clever remarks? Father would weigh her reproach, apologize, but he had meant well, and what good would it do Mr. Lemberg if we started mourning for him while he was still alive? Mother said, Even when you mean well, you somehow manage to do it with poor taste: either you're condescending or you're obsequious, and either way you always have to crack jokes. At which they would switch to Russian and talk in subdued tones.

When I came home from Mrs. Pnina's kindergarten at midday, my mother fought with me, using bribery, entreaties, and stories about princesses and ghosts, to distract my attention until I had swallowed some runny-nose squash and mucous squash (which we called by its Arabic name, *kusa*), and rissoles made from bread mixed with a little mince (they tried to disguise their breadiness with bits of garlic).

Sometimes I was forced to eat, with tears, disgust, and fury, all sorts of spinach rissoles, leaf spinach, beetroot, beetroot soup, sauerkraut, pickled cabbage, or carrots, raw or cooked. At other times I was condemned to cross wastelands of grits and bran, to chew my way through tasteless mountains of boiled cauliflower and all kinds of depressing pulses such as dried beans and peas and lentils. In summer Father chopped a fine salad of tomatoes, cucumbers, green peppers, spring onions, and parsley, gleaming with olive oil.

Every now and then a piece of chicken made a guest appearance, sunk in rice or run aground on a sandbank of potato purée, its mast and sails adorned with parsley and with a tight guard of boiled carrots with rickets-smitten squash standing around its deck. A pair of pickled cucumbers served as the flanks of this destroyer, and if you finished it all up, you were rewarded with a pink milk pudding made from powder, or a yellow jelly made from powder, which we called by its French name gelée, which was only a step away from Jules Verne and the mysterious submarine *Nautilus,* under the command of Captain Nemo, who despaired of the whole human race and set off for the depths of his mysterious realm under the oceans and where, so I had decided, I should be joining him soon.

In honor of Sabbaths and festivals my mother would get a carp, which she bought early, in the middle of the week. All day long the fish would swim relentlessly back and forth in the bathtub, from side to side to side, searching tirelessly for some secret underwater passage from the bath to the open sea. I fed it on breadcrumbs. Father taught me that in our own secret language a fish was called Noon. I quickly made friends with Noonie: he could distinguish my footsteps from a distance and hurried to the side of the bath to greet me, raising out of the water a mouth that reminded me of things it's best not to think about.

Once or twice I got up and crept along in the dark to check whether my friend really slept in the cold water all night, which seemed to me strange and even contrary to the laws of nature, or whether maybe after lights out Noonie's working day was over and he wriggled out and crawled slowly on his belly into the laundry basket and curled up and slept in the warm embrace of the towels and underwear, till in the morning he secretly slipped back into the bath to serve his time in the navy.

Once, when I was left at home on my own, I decided to enrich this poor bored carp's life with islands, straits, headlands, and sandbanks made from various kitchen utensils that I dropped in the bath. As patient and persistent as Captain Ahab I hunted my Moby Dick with a ladle for a long time, but time and again he wriggled away and escaped to the submarine lairs that I had scattered for him myself on the seabed. At one point I touched his cold, sharp scales, and I shuddered with disgust and fear at this new, spine-chilling discovery: until that morning, every living thing, whether chick, child, or cat, was always soft and warm; only what was dead turned cold and hard. And now this paradox of the carp, cold and hard but alive, all damp, slippery, and oily, scaly, with gills, wriggling and struggling strongly, stiffening and chill between my fingers, stabbed me with such a sudden panic that I hurriedly released my catch and shook my fingers, then washed, soaped, and scrubbed them three times. So I gave up the chase. Instead of hunting Noonie, I spent a long time trying to look at the world through the round, still eyes of a fish, without eyelids, without eyelashes, without moving.

And that's how Father, Mother, and retribution found me, because they came home and crept into the bathroom without my hearing them, and they caught me sitting motionless like a Buddha on the toilet lid, my mouth slightly open, my face frozen, my glazed eyes staring unblinkingly like a pair of glass beads. At once the kitchen utensils that the crazy child had sunk to the bottom of the carp water to serve as an archipelago or the underwater defenses of Pearl Harbor came to light. "His Highness," Father said sadly, "will once again be compelled to suffer the consequences of his deeds. I am sorry."

On Friday night, Grandpa and Grandma came, and so did Mother's friend Lilenka with her rotund husband Mr. Bar-Samkha, whose face was covered with a thick curly beard like steel wool. His ears were different sizes, like an Alsatian that has pricked up one ear and let the other flop.

After the chicken soup with kneidlach, Mother suddenly placed on the table the corpse of my Noonie, complete with head and tail but bearing a series of seven knife gashes along its side, as splendid as the body of a king being borne on a gun carriage to the Pantheon. The regal corpse reposed in a rich cream-colored sauce upon a couch of gleaming rice, embellished with stewed prunes and slices of carrot, scattered with decorative green flakes. But Noonie's alert, accusing, gaze was fixed unyieldingly on all his murderers in motionless reproach, in silent torment.

When my eyes met his terrifying gaze, his piercing eye cried Nazi betrayer and murderer, and I began to cry silently, dropping my head on my chest, trying not to let them see. But Lilenka, my mother's best friend and confidante, the soul of a kindergarten teacher in a china doll body, was alarmed and hastened to comfort me. First she felt my forehead and declared, No, he hasn't got a temperature. Then she kept stroking my arm and said, But yes, he is shivering a little. Then she bent over me until her breath almost took my breath away, and said: It looks as though it's something psychological, not physical. With that she turned to my parents and concluded, with self-righteous pleasure, that as she had already told them a long time ago, this child, like all vulnerable, complicated, sensitive future artists, was apparently entering puberty very early, and the best thing was simply to let him be.

Father mulled this over, weighed it, and pronounced judgment:

"Very well. But first of all you will please eat your fish like everyone else."

"No."

"No? And why not? Is His Highness by any chance contemplating sacking his team of cooks?"

"I can't."

At this point Mr. Bar-Samkha, overflowing with sweetness and the urge to mediate, started to wheedle in his reedy, placatory voice:

"Well, why don't you just have a tiny bit? Just one symbolic piece, eh? For the sake of your parents and the Sabbath day?"

But Lilka, his wife, a soulful, emotional person, cut in on my behalf:

"There's no point in forcing the child! He has a psychological block!"

Lea Bar-Samkha, also known as Lilenka, formerly Lilia Kalisch,* was a frequent visitor to our apartment during most of my childhood in Jerusalem. She was a small, sad, pale, frail woman with drooping shoul-

*I have changed some of the names, for various reasons.

ders. She had worked for many years as a schoolmistress and had even written two books about the mentality of the child. From behind she looked like a slim twelve-year-old girl. She and my mother spent hours whispering together, sitting on the wicker stools in the kitchen or on chairs that they had taken out into the garden, chatting or poring over some open book or a picture book of artistic gems, head to head and hand to hand.

Mostly Lilka came when my father was out at work. I have a feeling that she and my father maintained that polite mutual loathing that is commonly found between husbands and their wives' best friends. If I approached my mother when she was chatting to Lilenka, they both shut up at once and only resumed their conversation when I was out of earshot. Lilia Bar-Samkha looked at me with her wistful, I-understand-and-forgive-everything-on-emotional-grounds smile, but my mother asked me to buck up and say what I needed and leave them alone. They had a lot of shared secrets.

Once Lilenka came when my parents were out. She eyed me for a while with understanding and sorrow, nodded her head as though she was definitely agreeing with herself, and began a conversation. She had truly, but truly, been so fond of me since I was so small, and interested in me. Not interested like those boring grown-ups who always asked if I was good at school, if I liked soccer, or if I still collected stamps, and what did I want to be when I grew up, and silly things like that. No! She was interested in my thoughts! My dreams! My mental life! She considered me such a unique, original child! The soul of an artist in the making! She would like to try one day—not necessarily right now—to make contact with the inner, vulnerable side of my young personality (I was about ten at the time). For example, what did I think about when I was completely alone? What happened in the secret life of my imagination? What really made me happy and sad? What excited me? What frightened me? What repelled me? What kinds of scenery did I find attractive? Had I ever heard of Janusz Korczak? Had I ever read his book *Yotam the Magician*? Did I have any secret thoughts yet about the fair sex? She would love to be my, how to put it, my listening ear. My confidante. Despite the difference in our ages, etc.

I was a compulsively polite child. To her first question, what did I think about, I therefore replied politely: All sorts of things. To the volley of questions What-excited-me-What-frightened-me I answered: Nothing in particular. While to her offer of friendship I responded tactfully: "Thank you, Auntie Lilia, that's very kind of you."

"If ever you feel a need to talk about something that you don't find it easy to talk to your parents about, you won't hesitate? You'll come to me? And tell me? And of course I'll keep the secret. We can discuss it together."

"Thank you."

"The things you have nobody to talk to about? Thoughts that make you feel a bit lonely?"

"Thank you. Thank you truly. Would you like me to fetch you a glass of water? My mother will be home soon. She's just around the corner at Heinemann the pharmacist's. Or would you like to read the paper while you're waiting, Auntie Lilia? Shall I put the fan on for you?"

28

TWENTY YEARS later, on July 28, 1971, a few weeks after my book *Unto Death* was published, I received a letter from this friend of my mother's, who was then in her sixties:

I feel I haven't behaved properly to you since your late father's death. I have been very depressed and am unable to do anything. I have shut myself up at home (our apartment is frightening . . . but I have no energy to change anything) and I am afraid to go out—that's the simple truth. In the man in your story "Late Love" I recognized some common traits—he seemed so familiar and so close. "Crusade" I heard dramatized on the radio once, and you read some excerpts in a television interview. It was wonderful to see you so unexpectedly on the television in the corner of my room. I am curious to know what the sources of the story are—it is unique. It's hard for me to imagine what was going on inside you when you wrote those descriptions of horror and dread. It's chilling. The descriptions of the Jews—strong figures, definitely not victims . . . impressed me. And also the description of water eating away iron . . . and the picture of a Jerusalem that is not a reality nor is it the journey's end, it is just longing and yearning for something that is not a place in the world. Death appears to me from the pages of your book as something I had never imagined—and yet I craved it not so long ago . . . I am reminded now more than usually of your mother's words—she foresaw my failure in life. And I prided myself that my weakness was only superficial, that I was resilient. Now I feel disintegration—strange, for so many years I dreamed of returning to the Land, and now that it has become a reality—I am living here as in a nightmare. Don't pay any attention to what I'm saying. It just slipped out. Don't react. The last time I saw you, in your heated exchange with your father, I didn't sense in you the gloomy man . . . All my family send regards to yours. I'm going to be a grandma soon! With friendship and affection, Lilia (Lea).

And in another letter, from August 5, 1979, Lilka wrote to me:

. . . but enough of that for the time being, maybe some day we'll meet after all and then we'll chat about lots of questions that your words have raised for me. What are you hinting at now, in the "Autobiographical Note" in your book . . . when you talk of your mother dying "out of disappointment or longing. Something had gone wrong"? Please forgive me, I'm touching a wound. Your late father's wound, your wound especially, and even—my own. You can't know how much I miss Fania, especially lately. I am left so much on my own in my narrow little world. I long for her. And for another friend of ours, Stefa she was called, who departed this world from grief and suffering in 1963 . . . She was a pediatrician, and her life consisted of one disappointment after another, maybe because she trusted men. Stefa simply refused to grasp what some men are capable of. The three of us were very close in the 1930s. I am one of the last of the Mohicans—of friends who no longer exist. Twice I tried, in '71 and '73, to take my own life, and I didn't succeed. I won't try again . . . The time has not yet come for me to talk to you about things to do with your parents . . . Years have gone by since . . . No, I'm not ready yet to express in writing everything I'd like to say. To think that once I could only express myself in writing. Maybe we'll meet again—and many things may change before then . . . And by the way, you ought to know that your mother and I and some other members of our group in Hashomer Hatsair in Rovno considered

the petite bourgeoisie to be the worst of all things. We all came from similar backgrounds. Your mother was never a "rightist"...
Although when she married into the Klausner family, she may have pretended she was like them.

And again, in a letter dated September 28, 1980:

Your mother came from an unhappy family, and she damaged your family. But she is not to blame . . . I recall that once, in 1963, you sat in our apartment . . . and I promised you that I would write to you about your mother someday . . . But it's very hard for me to carry it out. Even to write a letter is hard for me . . . If you only knew how much your mother wanted to be an artist, to be a creative person— from her childhood! If only she could see you now! And why didn't she manage it? Maybe in a personal conversation I could be more daring and tell you things that I don't dare put in writing. Yours affectionately, Lilia.

My father, before he died (in 1970), was able to read my first three books, which he did not entirely enjoy. My mother was able to see only some stories I wrote at school and a few childish verses that I penned in the hope of touching the Muses, whose existence she liked to tell me about. (My father did not believe in the Muses, just as he always despised fairies, witches, wonder-working rabbis, elves, any kind of saint, intuition, miracles, and ghosts. He saw himself as a man with a secular worldview; he believed in rational thought and hard intellectual work.)

If my mother had read the two stories in *Unto Death*, would she, too, have responded to them with words similar to those written by her friend Lilenka Kalisch, "longing and yearning for something that is not a place in the world"? It is hard to know. A misty veil of dreamy sadness, unexpressed emotions, and romantic suffering enfolded those well-to-do Rovno young ladies, as though their lives there were painted forever within the walls of their secondary school with a palette that contained only two colors: either melancholy or festive. Although my mother sometimes rebelled against this upbringing.

Something in the curriculum of that school in the 1920s, or maybe some deep romantic mustiness that seeped into the hearts of my mother and her friends in their youth, some dense Polish-Russian emotionalism, something between Chopin and Mickiewicz, between the *Sorrows of Young Werther* and Lord Byron, something in the twilight zone between the sublime, the tormented, the dreamy, and the solitary, all kinds of will-o'-the-wisps of "longing and yearning" deluded my mother most of her life and seduced her until she succumbed and committed suicide in 1952. She was thirty-eight when she died. I was twelve and a half.

In the weeks and months that followed my mother's death I did not think for a moment of her agony. I made myself deaf to the unheard cry for help that remained behind her and that may have always hung in the air of our apartment. There was not a drop of compassion in me. Nor did I miss her. I did not grieve at my mother's death: I was too hurt and angry for any other emotion to remain. When, for example, I noticed her checked apron, which still hung on a hook on the back of the kitchen door several weeks after her death, I was as angry as though it were pouring salt on my wounds. My mother's toilet things, her powder box, her hairbrush on her green shelf in the bathroom hurt me as though they had remained there deliberately to mock me. Her books. Her empty shoes. The echo of her smell that continued for some time to waft in my face every time I opened "Mother's side" of the closet. Everything moved me to impotent rage. As though one of her sweaters, which had somehow crept into my pile of sweaters, was gloating at me with a vile grin.

I was angry with her for leaving without saying good-bye, without a hug, without a word of explanation: after all, my mother had been incapable of parting even from a total stranger, a delivery man or a pedlar at the door, without offering him a glass of water, without a smile, without a little apology and two or three pleasant words. All through my childhood, she had never left me alone at the grocer's or in a strange courtyard or in a public garden. How could she have done it? I was angry with her on Father's behalf too, whose wife had shamed him thus, had shown him up, had suddenly vanished like a woman running away with a stranger in a comic film. Throughout my childhood, if I ever disappeared even for an hour or two, I was shouted at and punished: it was a fixed rule that anyone who went out always had to say where they were going and for how long and what time they would be back. At least they had to leave a note in the usual place, under the vase.

All of us.

Is that the way to leave, rudely, in the middle of a sentence? She herself had always insisted on tact, politeness, considerate behavior, a constant effort not to hurt others, attentiveness, sensitivity! How could she?

I hated her.

After a few weeks the anger subsided. And with the anger I seemed to lose a protective layer, a kind of lead casing that had protected me in the early days against the shock and pain. From now on I was exposed.

As I stopped hating my mother, I began to hate myself.

I still had no free corner in my heart for my mother's pain, her loneliness, the suffocation that had closed in around her, the terrible despair of the last nights of her life. I was still living out my own crisis rather than hers. Yet I was no longer angry with her, but rather the opposite, I blamed myself: if only I had been a better, more devoted, son, if I had not scattered my clothes all over the floor, if I had not pestered and nagged her, if I had done my homework on time, if I had taken the rubbish out every evening willingly, without being shouted at to do it, if I had not made a nuisance of myself, made a noise, forgotten to turn out the light, come home with a torn shirt, left muddy footprints all around the kitchen. If I had been more considerate of her migraines. Or if at least I had tried to do what she wanted, and been a bit less weak and pale, eaten everything she cooked for me and put on my plate and not been so difficult, if for her sake I had been a more sociable child and a bit less of a loner, a bit less skinny and more suntanned and athletic, as she had wanted me to be!

Or perhaps the opposite? If I had been much weaker, chronically ill, confined to a wheelchair, consumptive, or even blind from birth? Surely her kindliness and her generous nature would never have allowed her to abandon such a disadvantaged child, leave him to his misery and just disappear? If only I had been a handicapped child with no legs, if only while there was still time I had run under a passing car and been run over and had both my legs amputated, perhaps my mother would have been filled with compassion? Would not have left me? Would have stayed to go on looking after me?

If my mother had abandoned me like that, without a backward glance, surely it was a sign that she had never loved me: if you love someone, she herself had taught me, you forgive them for everything, except betrayal. You even forgive them for nagging, for losing their cap, for leaving the squash on their plate.

To forsake is to betray. And she had forsaken both of us, Father and me. I would never have left her like that, despite her migraines, even though I now knew that she had never loved us, I would never have left her, despite all her long silences, her shutting herself up in a darkened room, and all her moods. I'd have lost my temper sometimes, maybe even not talked to her for a day or two, but not abandoned her forever. Never.

All mothers love their children: that's a law of nature. Even a cat or a goat. Even mothers of criminals and murderers. Even mothers of Nazis. Or of drooling retards. Even mothers of monsters. The fact that only I couldn't be loved, that my mother had run away from me, only proved that there was nothing in me to love, that I didn't deserve love. There was something wrong with me, something very terrible, something repulsive and truly horrifying, more loathsome than a physical or mental defect, or even madness. There was something so irreparably detestable about me, something so terrible, that even a sensitive woman like my mother, who could lavish love on a bird or a beggar or a stray puppy, couldn't stand me anymore and had to run away from me as far as she could go. There is an Arabic saying, *Kullu qirdin bi-'ayni ummihi ghazalun*—"Every monkey is a gazelle to its mother." Except for me.

If only I were also sweet, just a little, as all children in the world are to their mothers, even the ugliest and naughtiest children, even those violent, disturbed children who are always being thrown out of school, even Bianca Schor who stabbed her grandfather with a kitchen knife, even Yanni the pervert, who has elephantiasis and unzips his fly in the street and takes out his thing and shows it to the girls—if only I were good, if only I had behaved the way she asked me to a thousand times, and like an idiot I didn't listen to her—if only after Seder night I hadn't broken her blue bowl that had come down to her from her great-grandmother—if only I'd brushed my teeth properly every morning, top and bottom and all around and in the corners, without cheating—if only I hadn't pinched that half-pound note from her handbag and then lied and denied I'd taken it—if only I'd stopped thinking those wicked thoughts and never let my hand stray inside my pajama bottoms at night—if only I'd been like everyone else, deserving a mother, too—

After a year or two, when I'd left home and gone to live in Kibbutz Hulda, I slowly started to think about her, too. At the end of the day, after school and work and a shower, when all the kibbutz kids had showered and dressed for the evening and gone to spend time with their parents, leaving me all alone and odd among the empty children's houses, I would go and sit on my own on the wooden bench inside the reading room.

I would sit there in the dark for half an hour or an hour, conjuring up, picture by picture, the end of her life. In those days I was already trying to imagine a little of what had never been spoken about, either between my mother and me, or between me and my father, or apparently even between the two of them.

My mother was thirty-eight when she died: younger than my elder daughter and a little older than my younger daughter on the day these lines were written. Ten or twenty years after they completed their studies at the Tarbuth secondary school, when my mother, Lilenka Kalisch, and their group of friends experienced the buffeting of reality in a Jerusalem of heat waves, poverty, and malicious gossip, when those emotional Rovno schoolgirls suddenly found themselves in the rough terrain of everyday life, diapers, husbands, migraines, queues, smells of mothballs and kitchen sinks, it transpired apparently that the curriculum of the school in Rovno in the 1920s was of no help to them. It only made things worse.

Or it may have been something else, something neither Byronic nor Chopinic but closer to that haze of melancholy loneliness that surrounds introverted, well-born young ladies in the plays of Chekhov and in the stories of Gnessin, a sort of childhood promise that is inevitably frustrated, trampled underfoot, and even ridiculed by the monotony of life itself. My mother grew up surrounded by an angelic cultural vision of misty beauty whose wings were finally dashed on a hot dusty pavement of Jerusalem stone. She had grown up as the pretty, refined miller's daughter, she had come of age in the mansion in Dubinska Street, with an orchard, a cook, and maids, where she was probably brought up just like the shepherdess in that picture that she hated, that prettified pink-cheeked shepherdess with three petticoats.

The outburst that Aunt Sonia recalled seventy years later, when the sixteen-year-old Fania with an uncharacteristic access of rage suddenly poured scorn and almost spat on the picture of the gentle shepherdess with the dreamy expression and the profusion of silk petticoats, may have been the spark of my mother's life-force vainly trying to free itself from the darkness that was already beginning to enfold it.

Behind the curtained windows that protected Fania Mussman's childhood so well, Pan Zakrzewski one night shot a bullet into his thigh and another into his brain. Princess Ravzova hammered a rusty nail into her hand to receive some of the Savior's pain and bear it in His stead. Dora the housekeeper's daughter was pregnant by her mother's lover, drunk Steletsky lost his wife at cards, and she, Ira, his wife, was eventually burned to death when she set fire to the handsome Anton's empty hut. But all these things happened on the other side of the double glazing, outside the pleasant, illuminated circle of the Tarbuth school. None of them could break in and seriously harm the pleasantness of my mother's childhood, which was apparently tinged with a hint of melancholy that did not mar but merely colored and sweetened it.

A few years later, in Kerem Avraham, in Amos Street, in the cramped, damp basement apartment, downstairs from the Rosendorffs and next door to the Lembergs, surrounded by zinc tubs and pickled gherkins and the oleander that was dying in a rusty olive drum, assailed all day by smells of cabbage, laundry, boiled fish, and dried urine, my mother began to fade away. She might have been able to grit her teeth and endure hardship and loss, poverty, or the cruelty of married life. But what she couldn't stand, it seems to me, was the tawdriness.

By 1943 or 1944, if not earlier, she knew that everybody had been murdered there, just outside Rovno. Somebody must have come and reported how Germans, Lithuanians, and Ukrainians, armed with submachine guns, had marched the whole city, young and old alike, to Sosenki

Forest, where they had all loved to go for walks on fine days, for scout games, for sing-songs around campfires, to sleep in sleeping bags on the banks of a stream under starry skies. There, among boughs, birds, mushrooms, currants, and berries, the Germans opened fire and slaughtered on the edge of pits, in two days, some twenty-five thousand souls.* Almost all my mother's classmates perished. Together with their parents, and all of their neighbors, acquaintances, business rivals, and enemies; well-to-do and proletarian, pious, assimilated, and baptized, communal leaders, synagogue functionaries, pedlars and drawers of water, Communists and Zionists, intellectuals, artists, and village idiots, and some four thousand babies. My mother's schoolteachers also died there, the headmaster, Issachar Reiss, with his charismatic presence and hypnotic eyes, whose look had pierced the dreams of so many adolescent schoolgirls, sleepy, absentminded Isaac Berkowski, hot-tempered Eliezer Buslik, who had taught Jewish culture, Fanka Zeidmann, who had taught geography and biology and also PE, and her brother Shmuel the painter, and pedantic, embittered Dr. Moshe Bergmann, who through almost clenched teeth had taught general and Polish history. All of them.

Not long afterward, in 1948, when the Arab Legion was shelling Jerusalem, another friend of my mother's, Piroshka, Piri Yannai, was also killed, by a direct hit from a shell. She had only gone outside to fetch a bucket and floorcloth.

Perhaps something of the childhood promise was already infected by a kind of poisonous, romantic crust that associated the Muses with death? Something in the overrefined curriculum of the Tarbuth school? Or perhaps it was a melancholy Slavic bourgeois trait that I encountered a few years after my mother's death in the pages of Chekhov, Turgenev, Gnessin, and even some of the poetry of Rahel. Something that made my mother, when life failed to fulfill any of the promises of her youth, envisage death as an exciting but also protective, soothing lover, a last, artistic lover, who would finally heal the wounds of her lonely heart.

For many years now I have been trailing this old murderer, this cunning ancient seducer, this revolting old rake, deformed by old age yet

*Roughly the population of Arad, where I now live, and more than the total number killed on the Jewish side in a hundred years of war against the Arabs.

disguising himself time and again as a youthful prince charming. This crafty hunter of the broken-hearted, this vampire wooer with a voice as bittersweet as that of a cello on a lonely night, a subtle, velvety charlatan, a master of stratagems, a magic piper who draws the desperate and lonely into the folds of his silken cloak. The ancient serial killer of disappointed souls.

29

WHAT DOES my memory begin with? The very first memory is a shoe, a little brown fragrant new shoe, with a soft warm tongue. It must have been one of a pair, but memory has only salvaged the one. A new, still slightly stiff shoe. I was so entranced by its delightful smell of new, shiny, almost living leather, and of pungent, dizzying glue that apparently I first tried to put my new shoe on my face, on my nose, like a sort of snout. So I could get drunk on the smell.

My mother came into the room, followed by my father with various uncles and aunts or mere acquaintances. I must have looked cute but funny, with my little face stuck inside the shoe, because they all burst out laughing and pointed at me, and somebody roared and slapped his knees with both hands, and somebody else grunted and called hoarsely, Quick, quick, somebody fetch a camera!

There was no camera in our apartment, but I can still see that baby: all of two or two and a quarter, his hair flaxen and his eyes big, round, and surprised. But immediately under the eyes, instead of the nose, mouth, and chin, sprouted the heel of a shoe, and a shiny new virgin sole that had never been walked on. From the eyes up it was a pale-faced infant, and from the cheeks down what looked like a hammerfish or some kind of primeval, heavy-cropped bird.

What was the baby feeling? I can answer that question quite precisely, because I have inherited from that baby what he felt at that moment: a piercing joy, a wild, dizzying joooy, springing from the fact that the whole crowd of people was focused on him alone, surprised at him, enjoying him, pointing at him. At the same time, without any contradiction, the infant was also frightened and alarmed by the abundance of their attention, which he was too small to contain, because his parents and strangers and all of them were bellowing-laughing-pointing at him and his snout, and laughing again as they shouted to one another, a camera, quick, fetch a camera.

And also disappointed because they cut off right in the middle the intoxicating sensual pleasure of inhaling the fresh smell of leather and the dizzying fragrance of glue that made his insides tremble.

In the next picture there is no audience. Just my mother putting a soft warm sock on me (because it was cold in the room), and then encouraging me, push, push hard, harder, as if she were a midwife helping the fetus of my tiny foot travel down the virginal birth canal of my fragrant new shoe.

To this day, whenever I strain to push my foot into a boot or shoe, and even now as I sit and write this, my skin reexperiences the pleasure of my foot tentatively entering the inner walls of that first shoe, the trembling of the flesh as it entered for the first time in its life this treasure cave whose stiff yet soft walls enfolded it caressingly as it thrust deeper and deeper while my mother's voice, soft and patient, encouraged me, push, push just a bit more.

One hand gently pushed my foot deeper inside while the other, holding the sole lightly, thrust against me, apparently opposing my movement but really helping me get right inside, until that delicious moment when, as if overcoming a final obstacle, my heel made one last effort and slid in so that the foot entirely filled the space, and from now on you were all there, inside, enfolded, held, secure, and already Mother was pulling the laces, tying them, and finally, like a last delicious lick, the warm tongue stretched under the laces and the knot, that stretching that always gives me a kind of tickling sensation along the instep. And here I was. Inside. Clasped, held in the tight, pleasurable embrace of my very first shoe.

That night I begged to be allowed to sleep in my shoes: I didn't want it to end. Or begged at least to be allowed to have my new shoes next to my head, on the pillow, so that I could fall asleep with that scent of leather and glue. Only after protracted and tearful negotiations did they finally agree to put the shoes on a chair by the head of my bed—on condition you didn't so much as touch them till morning, because you've washed your hands, you can just look, you can peep every minute into their dark jaws that are smiling at you and inhale their smell until you drop off facing them, smiling to yourself in your sleep with a sensual pleasure, as if you are being stroked.

In my third memory I am locked in, alone, in a dark kennel.

When I was three and a half, nearly four, I was entrusted several times a week for a few hours to a middle-aged widowed neighbor who had no children of her own, a woman who smelled of damp wool and, less strongly, of washing soap and frying. Her name was Mrs. Gat, but we always called her Auntie Greta, except for my father, who occasionally put his arm around her shoulder and called her Gretchen, or Gret, and he would make up joky rhymes, as was his custom, in the manner of an old-world schoolboy: "Never let us forget that dear Gret is a pet!" (This was apparently his way of paying court to women.) Auntie Greta would blush, and because she was ashamed of blushing, she would immediately blush a deeper blood red, verging on purple.

Auntie Greta's blond hair was arranged in a thick plait that she coiled like a rope around her round head. The hair at her temples was turning gray, like thistles growing at the edge of a field of yellow. Her plump, soft arms were dotted with masses of pale brown freckles. Under the rustic cotton dresses she liked to wear she had heavy, very wide thighs that suggested a carthorse. An embarrassed, apologetic smile sometimes hung around her lips as though she had been caught doing something very naughty, or telling a fib, and she was frankly shocked at herself. She always had two of her fingers bandaged, or at least one, and occasionally three, either because she had cut herself while chopping vegetables or slammed her hand in the kitchen drawer or brought the lid of the piano down on her fingers; despite her constant misadventures with her fingers, she gave private piano lessons. She was also a private child sitter.

After breakfast my mother would stand me on a wooden stool in front of the basin in the bathroom, wipe the traces of porridge off my cheeks and chin with a damp towel, moisten my hair, and comb a sharp, straight side parting, then hand me a brown paper bag containing a banana, an apple, a piece of cheese, and some biscuits. And so, scrubbed, combed, and miserable, I was taken to the backyard of the

fourth building to the right of ours. On the way there I had to promise to be good, to do whatever Auntie Greta said, not to make a nuisance of myself, and above all on no account to scratch the brown crust
that had grown on the wound on my knee, because the crust, which is
called a scab, is part of the healing process and it will soon fall off by
itself, but if you touch it, heaven forbid, it might get infected and then
there will be nothing for it, they'll have to give you another injection.

At her door my mother wished me and Auntie Greta a good time
together and left. At once Auntie Greta took off my shoes and put me
down in my socks to play nicely and quietly on a mat, in one corner of
which I was awaited every morning by bricks, teaspoons, cushions, napkins, an agile felt tiger, and some dominoes, as well as a threadbare princess doll that smelled a little musty.

This inventory sufficed me for several hours of battles and of heroic
deeds. The princess had been captured by a wicked wizard (the tiger),
who had imprisoned her in a cave (under the piano). The teaspoons were
a fleet of airplanes that were all flying in search of the princess over the
sea (the mat) and beyond the mountains (cushions). The dominoes
were the dreaded wolves that the wizard had scattered around the cave
of the imprisoned princess.

Or the other way around: the dominoes were tanks, the napkins
Arab tents, the soft doll was transformed into the English High Commissioner, the cushions were built into the walls of Jerusalem, while the
teaspoons, under the command of the tiger, were promoted by me to
become Hasmonean fighters or the guerrilla troops of Bar Kochba.

Halfway through the morning Auntie Greta would bring me thick,
slimy raspberry juice in a heavy cup that was unlike any we had at home.
Sometimes she carefully lifted the hem of her dress and sat down next
to me on the mat. She made all sorts of chirruping sounds and other
signs of affection that always ended in sticky, jammy kisses. Sometimes
she allowed me to dabble—gently!—on the piano. If I finished up all
the food Mummy had put in my paper bag, Auntie Greta would treat
me to a couple of squares of chocolate or cubes of marzipan. The shutters in her apartment were always closed because of the sunlight. The
windows were shut because of the flies. As for the flowery curtains, they
were always kept drawn and firmly joined together, like a pair of chaste
knees, for greater privacy.

Sometimes Auntie Greta would put on my shoes, put on my head a little khaki cap with a stiff peak like an English policeman's or a Hamekasher bus driver's. Then she would scrutinize me with a quizzical look, rebutton my shirt, lick her finger and scrape off the encrusted remains of chocolate or marzipan around my mouth, and put on her round straw hat, which hid half her face but accentuated the roundness of her body. When all these preparations were concluded, the two of us would go out together for a couple of hours, "to see what's going on in the wide world."

30

FROM OUR suburb of Kerem Avraham you could reach the wide world by taking either the No. 3A bus, which stopped in Zephaniah Street, next to Mrs. Hasia's kindergarten, or the No. 3B bus, which stopped at the other end of Amos Street, on the corner of Geula Street at Malachi Street. The wide world itself extended along Jaffa Road, down King George V Avenue toward the Ratisbonne Convent and the Jewish Agency Buildings, in and around Ben Yehuda Street, in Hillel Street and Shammai Street, around the Studio Cinema and the Rex Cinema, which were down Princess Mary's Way, and also up Julian's Way, which led to the King David Hotel.

At the junction of Julian's Way, Mamilla Road, and Princess Mary's Way there was always a busy policeman in shorts and white armbands. He ruled firmly over a little concrete island sheltered by a round tin umbrella. From atop his island he directed the traffic, an all-powerful divinity armed with a piercing whistle; his left hand stopped the traffic and his right moved it on. From this junction the wide world branched out and continued toward the Jewish commercial center beneath the walls of the Old City, and sometimes its extensions reached as far as the Arab parts around the Damascus Gate, in Sultan Suleiman Road, and even into the bazaar inside the walls.

On every one of these expeditions Auntie Greta would drag me to three or four clothes shops, where she liked to try on, take off, and try on again, in the privacy of a changing cubicle, a number of beautiful dresses and a range of magnificent skirts, blouses, and nightgowns, and a mass of colorful housecoats that she termed "negligées." Once she even tried on a fur: the look in the tortured eyes of the slain fox terrified me. The fox's face stirred my soul because it looked both cunning and heart-rendingly wretched.

Time and again Auntie Greta would plunge into the little cubicle, from which she emerged after what seemed like years. Time and again this broad-beamed Aphrodite was reborn from the foam, bursting from behind the curtain in a new and ever more glamorous incarnation. For my benefit and for that of the salesperson and the other shoppers she would turn on her heel a couple of times in front of the mirror. Despite her heavy thighs she enjoyed executing a coquettish pirouette, and inquired of us each in turn whether it suited her, whether it flattered her, whether it clashed with the color of her eyes, whether it hung well, didn't it make her look fat, wasn't it rather common, a bit brash? As she did so, her face reddened, and because she was embarrassed at blushing, she blushed again, that blood red verging on purple. Finally she promised the salesperson earnestly that she would almost certainly be back the same day, in fact very shortly, after lunch, by the end of the afternoon, when she'd had time just to look around some other shops, tomorrow at the very latest.

So far as I can recall, she never went back. On the contrary, she was always very careful not to visit the same shop twice until several months had elapsed.

And she never bought anything. At any rate, from all the excursions on which I accompanied her in the role of escort, *arbiter elegantiarum,* and confidant she returned empty-handed. Perhaps she did not have enough money. Perhaps the curtained changing cubicles in all the women's clothes shops in Jerusalem were for Auntie Greta what the wizard's castle I built from bricks at the edge of the mat was for the shabby princess doll.

Until one day, one windy winter's day when throngs of rustling leaves eddied in the gray light, Auntie Greta and I, hand in hand, arrived at a splendid large clothes store, perhaps in one of the Christian Arab streets. As usual, Auntie Greta, laden with dressing gowns, nightgowns, and colorful dresses, disappeared into the fitting rooms, though not before giving me a sticky kiss and sitting me down to wait for her on a wooden stool in front of her solitary confinement cell, which was protected by a thick curtain. Promise me now you won't go anywhere, on any account, heaven forbid, just sit here and wait for me, and above all don't talk to any stranger until Auntie Greta comes out again even prettier than ever, and if you're a good boy, you'll get a little surprise from Auntie Greta, guess what it is!

While I was sitting waiting for her, sadly but obediently, all of a sudden a little girl tripped by, dressed up as though for a carnival, or else just dolled up. She was very young but older than me. For an instant I had the impression she was wearing lipstick, but how could she be? And they'd made her a sort of chest like a woman's with a cleft down the middle. The shape of her waist and hips was not like a child's, but violin-like. On her little legs I managed to see nylons with a seam at the back, ending in a pair of pointy red high-heeled shoes. I had never seen such a child-woman: too little to be a woman and too dressed up to be a child. So I stood up, fascinated and bewildered, and started to follow her to see what I had seen, or rather what I had almost not seen, because the girl had darted out from the rail of skirts behind me and walked past very fast. I wanted to see her close up. I wanted her to see me. I wanted to do or say something that would make her notice me: I already had a little repertoire that could draw cries of admiration from grown-ups, and one or two that worked quite well with children too, especially little girls.

The dressed-up little girl floated lightly between rows of shelves weighed down with bales of cloth and disappeared down a tunnel-like passage lined on either side with tall tree trunks festooned with dresses, branches almost broken under the weight of their colorful cloth foliage. Despite their weight, these trunks could be turned around with a light push.

It was a women's world, a dark, fragrant maze of warm paths, a deep, seductive silky, velvety labyrinth that ramified into ever more dress-lined paths. Smells of wool, mothballs, and flannel mingled with a vague hint of elusive scents that wafted through a dense thicket of frocks, sweaters, blouses, skirts, scarves, shawls, lingerie, dressing gowns, and all kinds of corsets and garter belts, petticoats and nightgowns, and assorted jackets and tops, coats and furs, while rustling silk stirred like a gentle sea breeze.

Here and there little dark cubicles draped in dark curtains gaped at me on my way. Here and there at the end of a winding tunnel a shadowy lightbulb winked faintly. Here and there mysterious secondary alleys opened up, alcoves, narrow winding jungle tracks, little niches, sealed fitting rooms, and all kinds of cupboards, shelves, and counters. And there were many corners hidden by thick screens or curtains.

The footsteps of the high-heeled infant were rapid and confident, ti-ta-tak ti-ta-tak (in my fever I heard "come to chat, come to chat," or, mockingly, "tiny tot, tiny tot!"), not at all those of a little girl, and yet I could see for myself that she was shorter than I was. My heart went out to her. I yearned with all my being, whatever the cost, to make her eyes open wide in admiration.

I quickened my pace. I was almost running after her. With a soul steeped in fairy tales about princesses that knights like me galloped to rescue from the teeth of dragons or the spells of wicked wizards, I just had to overtake her, to get a good look at the face of this wood nymph, perhaps rescue her a little, slay a dragon or two for her, earn her undying gratitude. I was afraid of losing her forever in the darkness of the labyrinth.

But I had no way of knowing whether the girl who was winding her way with such agility through the forest of clothes had noticed that a valiant knight was close on her heels, lengthening his little strides so as not to fall behind. If she had, why had she not given any sign: not once had she turned toward me or looked around.

All of a sudden the little fairy dived under a many-branched raincoat tree, stirred it this way and that, and in an instant vanished from my sight, swallowed up in its thick foliage.

Flooded by an uncharacteristic bravery, electrified by knightly daring, I plunged fearlessly into the thicket of cloth after her, and swimming against the tide, I fought my way through the mass of rustling garments. And so, finally, panting with excitement, I emerged—almost stumbled—into a sort of poorly lit clearing in the forest. Here I resolved to wait as long as I had to for the little wood nymph, whose sound and indeed whose scent I imagined I could perceive among the nearest branches. I would risk my life to take on bare-handed the wizard who had imprisoned her in his cellar. I would defeat the monster, smash the iron chains from her hands and feet, set her free, then stand at a distance, my head bowed in mute modesty, and wait for my reward, which would not be long in coming, and her tears of gratitude, after which I did not know what would follow, but I did know that it would surely come and that it would overwhelm me.

She was tiny, chicklike, her frame fragile as a matchstick, almost a baby, and she had cascading brown curls. And red high-heeled shoes. And a woman's dress with a low neckline that revealed a woman's breast with a real woman's cleavage. And she had wide, slightly parted lips, painted a garish red.

When I finally found the courage to look up at her face, a wicked, mocking crack suddenly opened between her lips, a kind of twisted, poisonous smile that disclosed sharp little teeth among which a single gold incisor glinted. A thick layer of powder mottled with islands of rouge covered her forehead and whitened her terrifying cheeks, which were slightly hollow, sunken like those of a wicked witch, as though she had suddenly put on the face of the killed fox fur, that face that had seemed both malicious and heartrendingly sad.

That elusive infant, the fleet-footed fairy, the enchanted nymph that I had pursued as though bewitched through the length and breadth of the forest, was not a child at all. She was neither fairy nor wood nymph but a sardonic-looking, almost elderly woman. A midget. A little hunchbacked. From close up her face had something of the look of a crooked-beaked, beady-eyed raven. To me she was frightening, dwarfish, shrunken, with a wrinkled old neck and hands that she suddenly opened wide and extended toward me, with a terrifying low laugh, like a witch who must be trying to touch me so as to trap me, with bony, wrinkled fingers like the claws of a bird of prey.

Instantly I turned and fled, breathless, terrified, sobbing, I ran, too petrified to shout aloud, I ran, screaming a choked scream inside me, help, help me, I ran crazily among the rustling tunnels in the dark, losing my way, becoming more and more lost in that labyrinth. Never before or since have I experienced such terror. I had discovered the terrible secret that she was not a child, that she was a witch disguised as a child, and now she would never let me escape alive from her dark forest.

As I ran I suddenly fell into a small entrance, with a wooden door that was neither open nor shut; in fact it was not a full-sized door but just a low opening like that of a dog kennel. I dragged myself inside with my last breath and there I hid from the witch, cursing myself, why hadn't I closed the door of my hiding place behind me? But I was paralyzed by horror, too frightened to emerge even for a moment from my shelter, too petrified even to reach out and close the door behind me.

And so I curled up in a corner of this kennel, which may have been no more than a storeroom, a kind of enclosed triangular space under a staircase. There, among some vague twisting metal pipes and crumbling cases and piles of moldy cloth, shrunk and curled up fetus-like, my hand covering my head, my head burrowing between my knees, trying to blot out my very existence, to withdraw inside my own womb, I lay trembling, perspiring, afraid to breathe, careful not to let out so much as a squeak, frozen with panic because of the bellows-like breathing that would soon give me away since it must surely be audible out there.

Over and over again I fancied I heard the tapping of her heels, "traitor die, traitor die, traitor die," getting closer, she was chasing me with her killed fox's face, here she was now right on top of me, any moment now she would catch me, drag me out, touch me with fingers that felt like a frog's, groping at me, hurting me, and suddenly she would stoop over me laughing with her sharp teeth and inject some terrifying magic spell into my blood to make me too turn suddenly into a killed fox. Or into stone.

After seven years somebody went past. Someone who worked in the shop? I stopped breathing and clenched my trembling fists. But the man did not hear my pounding heart. He hurried past my kennel and on the way he closed the door and inadvertently shut me in. Now I was locked in. Forever. In total darkness. At the bottom of a quiet ocean.

I have never been in such darkness and quiet either before or since. It was not the darkness of night, which is usually a dark blue darkness where you can generally make out various glimmers of light, with stars and glow-worms, lanterns of distant wayfarers, the window of a house here and there, and everything that punctuates night darkness, where you can always navigate from one block of darkness to the next by means of the various glimmers and shimmers and flickers, and you can always try to grope in the darkness at some shadows that are a little darker than the night itself.

Not here: I was at the bottom of a sea of ink.

Nor was the silence that of the night, where there is always some far-away pump pounding away, and you can hear the crickets and a chorus of frogs, dogs barking, dimly rumbling motors, the whine of a mosquito, and from time to time the wail of a jackal goes right through you.

But here I was not in a living, shivering dark purple night, I was locked into the darkest darkness. And silent silence enfolded me there, the silence you can find only at the bottom of a sea of ink.

How long was I there?

There is no one left to ask now. Greta Gat was killed in the siege of Jewish Jerusalem in 1948. An Arab Legion sniper with a diagonal black belt and a red *kaffieh* fired an accurate shot at her from the direction of the Police Academy that was on the cease-fire line. The bullet, so locals related, went in through Auntie Greta's left ear and came out of her eye. To this day, when I try to imagine what her face was like, I have nightmares about one spilled eye.

Nor have I any means to establish where in Jerusalem that clothes shop was, with its abundance of warrens, caves, and forest tracks, some sixty years ago. Was it an Arab shop? An Armenian one? And what stands on the site now? What happened to those forests and winding tunnels? And the alcoves behind the curtains, the counters, and all the changing cubicles? And the kennel where I was buried alive? Or the witch disguised as a wood nymph, whom I pursued and then fled in terror? What happened to my very first temptress, who drew me into her forest hideaway until I found myself inside her secret lair where suddenly she deigned to show me her face, which with nothing more than a look I managed to transform into a horror, the face of a slain fox, both vicious and desperately sad.

It is possible that Auntie Greta, when *she* finally deigned to reemerge glittering anew from her limbo, clad in a shiny dress, was alarmed not to find me waiting for her in the place where she had fixed me, on the wicker stool opposite the fitting room. No doubt she was startled and her face blushed so deeply that it turned almost purple. What has happened to the child? He is usually such a responsible and obedient child, a very cautious child, not at all adventurous, not even particularly brave.

We must imagine that at first Auntie Greta tried to find me on her own: perhaps she imagined that the child had waited and waited until he got bored and now was playing hide-and-seek with her to punish her for being away so long. Maybe the little scamp was hiding here behind the shelves? No? Or here among the coats? Perhaps he was standing and staring at waxwork models of half-dressed girls? Perhaps he was looking out at the people in the street from the inside of the shopwindow? Or had he simply found the toilet all by himself? Or a faucet to drink some water? A clever boy, quite a responsible boy, no question of that, only a bit absentminded, muddled, lost in all sorts of daydreams, always getting lost in the stories I tell him or he tells himself. Perhaps he's gone out in the street, after all? Frightened I might have forgotten him, trying to find his own way home? What if a strange man appeared and held out his hand and promised him all sorts of wonderful things? And what if the child let himself be tempted? And went off? With a stranger?

As Auntie Greta's apprehension intensified, she stopped blushing and turned white instead, and she started to shiver as though she had caught a cold. Eventually no doubt she raised her voice, she burst out crying, and everyone in the shop, assistants and shoppers alike, came to help and set to work looking for me. They may have called my name, combed the maze-like alleys of the shop, searched all the forest tracks in vain. And because apparently it was an Arab shop, one may imagine that crowds of children a little older than me were summoned and sent out to search for me in the neighborhood, in the narrow streets, in pits, in the nearby olive grove, in the courtyard of the mosque, in the goat pasture on the hillside, in the passages leading to the bazaar.

Was there a telephone? Did Auntie Greta phone Mr. Heinemann's pharmacy on the corner of Zephaniah Street? Did she or did she not manage to apprise my parents of the terrible news? Apparently not, otherwise my parents would have reminded me of it over and over again, for years to come, at any sign of disobedience they would have brandished a reenactment of that terrible experience of loss and mourning, however short-lived, that the crazy child had inflicted on them, and how in an hour or two their hair had almost turned white.

I remember that I did not shout there in the total darkness. I did not make a sound. I did not try to shake the locked door or hammer on it with my little fists, maybe because I was still trembling with fear that the witch with the killed fox's face was still sniffing around after me. I remember that the fear was replaced there, at the bottom of that silent sea of ink, by a strange sweetness: being there was a little like snuggling up warmly to my mother under a winter blanket while gusts of cold and darkness touched the windowpanes from the outside. And a bit like playing at being a deaf and blind child. And a bit like being free of all of them. Completely.

I hoped they would soon find me and get me out of there. But only soon. Not right away.

I even had a small, solid object there, a sort of round metal snail, smooth and pleasant to touch. Its dimensions exactly matched my hand, and my fingers thrilled as they closed around it, felt it, stroked it, clenched a little and relaxed a little, and sometimes pulled and drew out—only a little—the tip of the thin, lithe lodger within, like the head of a snail that peeps out for a moment, curiously, curls this way and that, and instantly retreats inside its shell.

It was a retractable measuring tape, a thin, lithe strip of steel, coiled within a steel case. I amused myself with this snail for a long while in the dark, unsheathing it, stretching it, extending it, letting go suddenly and causing the steel snake to dart back into the shelter of its lair with the speed of lightning until the case had drawn it all back into its belly, received its entire length, and responded with a final slight shudder, a quivering click that was very pleasant to my enfolding hand.

And again unsheathing, releasing, stretching, and this time I extended the steel snake to its full length, sending it far away into the depth of the dark space, feeling with it for the end of the darkness, listening to the popping of its delicate joints as it stretched and its head moved farther and farther away from its shell. Eventually I allowed it to come home gradually, releasing just a tiny bit and stopping, another tiny bit and stopping again, trying to guess—because I'd seen nothing, literally nothing—how many soft *puk-puk* pulses there would be before I heard the decisive *tluk* of the final locking that indicated that the snake had vanished from head to tail back into the womb from which I had allowed it to emerge.

How had this good snail suddenly come into my possession? I can't remember whether I had snatched it as I went past, in my knight-errant journey, in one of the twists and turns of the maze, or if my fingers had come across it inside that kennel, after the stone was rolled back to seal the mouth of my tomb.

One may reasonably imagine that, on reflection, Auntie Greta decided that from every angle it would be best not to tell my parents. She certainly saw no reason to alarm them after the event, when everything had ended well and safely. She may have feared that they would judge her to be an insufficiently responsible child sitter, and that she would thereby lose a modest but regular and much-needed source of income.

Between me and Auntie Greta the story of my death and resurrection in the Arab clothes shop was never mentioned or even hinted at. There was not so much as a conspiratorial wink. She may have hoped that in time the memory of that morning would fade and we would both come to think that it had never happened, that it had been only a bad dream. She may even have been a little ashamed of her extravagant excursions to clothes shops: after that winter's morning she never again made me her partner in crime. She may even have managed, thanks to me, to recover somewhat from her addiction to dresses. A few weeks or months later I was taken away from Auntie Greta and sent to Mrs. Pnina Shapiro's kindergarten in Zephaniah Street. We continued, however, for a few years to hear the sound of Auntie Greta's piano dimly in the distance, at dusk, a persistent, lonely sound beyond the other noises of the street.

It had not been a dream. Dreams dissolve with time and make way for other dreams, while that dwarf witch, that elderly child, the face of the killed fox, still sniggers at me with sharp teeth, among which is a single gold incisor.

And there was not only the witch: there was also the snail I had brought back from the forest, the snail I hid from my father and mother, and that sometimes, when I was alone, I dared to take out and play with under the bedclothes, causing it long erections and lightning retreats back into the depth of its lair.

A brown man with big bags under his kind eyes, neither young nor old, with a green-and-white tailor's tape measure around his neck and both ends dangling down onto his chest. He moved in a weary sort of way. His brown face was wide and sleepy, and a shy smile flickered for a moment and died under his soft gray mustache. The man leaned over me and said something to me in Arabic, something I could not understand but that I nevertheless translated into words in my heart, Don't be frightened, child, don't be frightened anymore now.

I remember that my rescuer had square, brown-framed reading glasses, which suited not an assistant in a women's clothes shop but rather, perhaps, a heavily built carpenter getting on in years, who hums to himself as he walks along dragging his feet, with a dead cigarette butt between his lips and a worn folding ruler peeping out of his shirt pocket.

The man eyed me for a moment, not through the lenses of his glasses, which had slipped down his nose, but over the top of them, and after scrutinizing me closely and hiding another smile or shadow of a smile behind his neat mustache, he nodded to himself two or three times and then reached out and took my hand, which was cold with fear, into his warm hand, as though he were warming a freezing chick, and drew me out of that dark recess, raised me high in the air, and squeezed me quite hard to his chest, and at that I began to cry.

When the man saw my tears, he pressed my cheek against his slack cheek, and said, in his low, dusty voice, pleasantly reminiscent of a shaded dirt road in the country at dusk, in Arabs' Hebrew, question, answer, and summing up:

"Everything all right? Everything all right. OK."

And he carried me in his arms to the office, which was located in the bowels of the shop, and there the air was full of smells of coffee and cigarettes and woolen cloth and the aftershave lotion of the man who had found me, different from my father's, much sharper and fuller, a smell that I wanted my father to have too. And the man who had found me said a few more words to the assembled company in Arabic, because there were people in the office standing and sitting between me and Auntie Greta, who was weeping in a corner, and he said one sentence to Auntie Greta too, and she blushed very deeply, and with that, with a long, slow, responsible movement, like a doctor feeling to find out where exactly it hurts, the man passed me over into Auntie Greta's arms.

But I was not so keen to be in her arms. Not quite yet. I wanted to stay a little longer pressed to the chest of the man who had rescued me.

After that they talked for a while, the others, not my man, he did not talk but just stroked my cheek and patted me twice on the shoulder and left. Who knows what he was called? Or if he's still alive? Is he living in his home? Or in dirt and poverty, in some refugee camp?

Then we went home on the No. 3A bus. Auntie Greta washed her face and mine too, so that it wouldn't show that we'd been crying. She gave me some bread and honey, a bowl of boiled rice, and a glass of luke-warm milk, and for dessert she gave me two pieces of marzipan. Then she undressed me and put me to bed in her bed, and she gave me lots of cuddles and mewing sounds that ended in sticky kisses, and as she tucked me in, she said, Sleep, sleep a little, my darling child. Perhaps she was hoping to wipe away the evidence. Perhaps she was hoping that when I woke from my siesta, I would think that it had all happened in a dream and wouldn't tell my parents, or if I did, she could smile and say that I always had such dreams in the afternoon, someone really ought to write them down and publish them in a book, with pretty color pictures, so that all the other children could enjoy them too.

But I didn't go to sleep, I lay quietly under the blanket playing with my metal snail.

I never told my parents about the witch, the bottom of the inky sea, or the man who rescued me: I didn't want them to confiscate my snail. And I didn't know how I would explain to them where I'd found it. I could hardly say I'd brought it back as a souvenir from my dream. And if I told them the truth, they would be furious with Auntie Greta and me. What's that?! His Highness?! A thief?! Has His Highness gone out of his mind?

And they would take me straight back there and force me to give my snail back and say I was sorry.

And then the punishment.

Later in the afternoon Father came to pick me up from Auntie Greta's. As usual, he said, "His Highness looks a little pale today. Has he had a hard day? Have his ships been shipwrecked, heaven forbid? Or have his castles been captured by foes?"

I did not reply, even though I could definitely have made him un-happy. For instance, I could have told him that since that morning I had another father apart from him. An Arab father.

While he was putting on my shoes, he joked with Auntie Greta. He always courted women with witticisms. And he always chatted on endlessly so as not to allow any room for a moment's silence. All his life my father was afraid of silence. He always felt himself to be responsible for the life of the conversation and saw it as a sign of failure and guilt on his part if it flagged for an instant. So he made up a rhyme in honor of Auntie Greta, something like this:

"It's not illegal yet, I bet, to flirt and pet with Gret."

Perhaps he went even further and said:

"Greta dear, Greta dear, you have really touched me here," pointing at his heart.

Auntie Greta blushed immediately, and because she was embarrassed at blushing, she blushed even more deeply, and her neck and chest turned purple like an eggplant, despite which she managed to mutter:

"*Nu*, but really, Herr Doktor Klausner," but her thighs nodded to him slightly, as though they longed to execute a little pirouette for him.

That same evening Father took me on a long, detailed tour of the remains of Inca civilization: eager for knowledge, we crossed oceans and mountains, rivers and plains together in the big German atlas. With our own eyes we saw the mysterious cities and the remains of palaces and temples in the encyclopedia and in the pages of a Polish book with pictures. All evening Mother sat in an armchair reading, with her legs tucked under her. The paraffin heater burned with a quiet, deep blue flame.

And every few minutes the silence of the room was emphasized by three or four soft mutters as air bubbled through the veins of the heater.

31

THE GARDEN wasn't a real garden, just a smallish rectangle of trampled earth as hard as concrete, where even thistles could scarcely grow. It was always in the shade of the concrete wall, like a prison yard. And in the shade of the tall cypress trees on the other side of the wall, in the Lembergs' garden next door. In one corner a stunted pepper tree struggled to survive, with gritted teeth; I loved to rub its leaves between my fingers and inhale its exciting smell. Opposite, near the other wall, was a single pomegranate tree or bush, a disillusioned survivor of the days when Kerem Avraham was still an orchard, which obstinately flowered year after year. We children did not wait for the fruit but ruthlessly cut off the vase-shaped unripe buds, into which we would insert a stick that was a finger's length or so, and thus make them into pipes like those the British smoked, and a few better-off people in our neighborhood who wanted to imitate the British. Once a year we opened a pipe shop in a corner of the yard. Because of the color of the buds it sometimes looked as though there was a reddish glow at the tip of each of our pipes.

Some agriculturally minded visitors, Mala and Staszek Rudnicki from Chancellor Street, once brought me a gift of three little paper bags containing radish, tomato, and cucumber seeds. So Father suggested we should make a vegetable patch. "We'll both be farmers," he said enthusiastically. "We'll make a little kibbutz in the space by the pomegranate tree, and bring forth bread from the earth by our own efforts!"

No family in our street had a spade, fork, or hoe. Such things belonged to the new, suntanned Jews, who lived over the hills and far away—in the villages and kibbutzim in Galilee, the Sharon, and the Valleys. So Father and I set out to conquer the wilderness and make a vegetable garden almost with our bare hands.

Early on Saturday morning, when Mother was still asleep and the whole neighborhood too, the two of us crept outside, wearing white vests and khaki shorts and hats, skinny, narrow-chested, townies to our slim fingertips, as pale as two sheets of paper but well protected by the thick coating of cream that we had rubbed into each other's shoulders. (The cream, called Velveta, was calculated to frustrate all the wiles of the spring sun.)

Father led the parade, wearing boots and armed with a hammer, a screwdriver, a kitchen fork, a ball of string, an empty sack, and the letter opener from his desk. I marched behind, all excited, full of the fierce joys of agriculture, carrying a bottle of water, two glasses, and a small box containing a plaster, a little bottle of iodine, a little stick to apply the iodine with, a strip of gauze, and a bandage, first aid in case of mishaps.

First Father brandished the letter opener ceremoniously, bent down, and drew four lines on the ground. In this way he marked out once and for all the boundaries of our plot, which was about two meters square, or just a little larger than the world map that hung on the wall of our corridor between the doors of the two rooms. Then he instructed me to get down on my knees and hold tightly, with both hands, a sharpened stick that he called a peg. His plan was to hammer a peg into each corner of the plot and surround it all with a border of taut string. The trodden earth, however, was as hard as cement and resisted all Father's efforts to hammer in the pegs. So he put down the hammer, with a martyred expression removed his glasses, deposited them carefully on the kitchen windowsill, returned to the battlefield, and redoubled his efforts. He sweated profusely as he battled, and without his glasses he once or twice narrowly missed my fingers, which were holding the peg for him. The peg, meanwhile, was fast becoming flattened.

By dint of hard work we finally managed to pierce the top crust and make a shallow depression. The pegs were embedded to the depth of half a finger's length and refused to go any farther. We were obliged to support each peg with two or three large stones and to compromise on the tautness of the string, because every time we tightened the string, the pegs threatened to come out of the ground. So the plot was marked out with four lines of slack string. Despite everything we had managed to create something out of nothing: from here to here was inside, in fact our vegetable garden, and everything beyond was outside, in other words the rest of the world.

"That's it," said Father modestly, and nodded his head several times, as though to agree with himself and confirm the validity of what he had done.

And I repeated after him, unconsciously imitating his nods:

"That's it."

This was Father's way of announcing a short break. He instructed me to wipe off my sweat, drink some water, sit down on the step, and take a rest. He himself did not sit down next to me but put his glasses back on, stood beside our square of string, inspected the progress of our project so far, mulled it over, considered the next stage of the campaign, analyzed our mistakes, drew the conclusions, and instructed me to remove the pegs and string provisionally and lay them neatly next to the wall: it would be better, in fact, to dig the plot first and mark it out afterward, otherwise the string would get in our way. It was also decided to pour four or five buckets of water on the soil and wait for twenty minutes or so for it to work its way in and soften the iron plating, and only then to renew our onslaught.

Father struggled on until midday, heroically, against the compacted earth. Bent double, with an aching back, pouring with sweat, gasping for breath like a drowning man, his eyes looking bare and helpless without the glasses, time after time he brought his hammer down on the stubborn ground. But the hammer was too light: it was a domestic hammer, meant not for storming fortifications but for cracking nuts or hammering a nail into the back of the kitchen door. Time after time Father brandished his pathetic hammer, like David with his sling against the mighty armor of Goliath, or as though he were assailing the battlements of Troy with a frying pan. The forked part of the hammer, intended for pulling nails out, served as spade, fork, and hoe rolled into one.

Large blisters soon rose on the soft cushions of his hands, but Father gritted his teeth and ignored them, even when they burst and released their fluid and became open wounds. Nor did he take any notice of the blisters that appeared on the sides of his scholar's fingers. Time and again he raised his hammer, brought it down, pounded and smote and raised it again, and as he wrestled with the elements of nature and the primeval wilderness, his lips muttered fevered imprecations to the unyielding soil in Greek and Latin and for all I know in Amharic, Old Slavonic, and Sanskrit.

At one point he brought the hammer down with all his force on the toe of his shoe and groaned with pain; he bit his lip, took a rest, used the word "decidedly" or "definitely" to reproach himself for his carelessness, wiped his brow, sipped some water, wiped the mouth of the bottle with his handkerchief, and insisted that I take a swig, returned to the field of combat limping but determined, and heroically renewed his unrelenting efforts.

Eventually the compacted earth took pity on him, or perhaps it was just astonished at his dedication, and began to crack. Father lost no time in inserting the tip of his screwdriver into the cracks, as though he was afraid the soil might change its mind and turn to concrete once again. He worked at the cracks, deepened and widened them, and with his bare fingers turning white with effort he detached thick clods that he piled up one by one at his feet, like slain dragons belly up. Severed roots protruded from these clods of earth, twisting and turning like sinews torn from living flesh.

My task was to advance in the rear of the assault echelon, open up the clods of earth with the letter opener, detach the roots and put them in the sack, remove any stones or bits of gravel, break up and crumble each clod, and finally, using the kitchen fork as a rake or harrow, comb the hair of the loosened soil.

Now came the time to fertilize. We had no animal or poultry manure, and the pigeon droppings on the roof were out of the question because of the risk of infection, so Father had prepared in advance a saucepanful of leftover food. It was a murky swill of grit water, fruit and vegetable peelings, rotten pumpkins, muddy coffee grounds with tea leaves floating on them, remains of porridge and borscht and boiled vegetables, fish trimmings and burnt frying oil, sour milk and various other viscous liquids and murky slops full of dubious lumps and particles in a sort of thick soup that had turned rancid.

"This will enrich our poor soil," Father explained to me as we rested side by side on the step in our sweat-soaked vests, feeling like a pair of real working men, and fanned our faces with the khaki hats. "We absolutely must feed the soil with anything that may turn from kitchen waste into a humus rich in organic substances, to give our plants the nourishment without which they will grow stunted and sickly."

He must have guessed correctly at a horrible idea that had come into my mind, because he hastened to add reassuringly: "And don't make the mistake of worrying that we might end up eating through the vegetables that we grow what may now appear to be disgusting rubbish. No, and no again! On no account! Manure is not filth, it is a hidden treasure—generations upon generations of peasants and farmers have sensed this mysterious truth instinctively. Tolstoy himself speaks somewhere about the mystical alchemy that is constantly taking place within the womb of the earth, that wonderful metamorphosis that translates rot and decay into compost, compost into rich soil and thence into cereals, vegetables, fruit, and all the rich produce of field, garden, and orchard."

While we fixed the pegs back in the four corners of our plot and stretched the string carefully between them, Father explained the words to me simply, precisely, and in order: rot and decay, compost, organic, alchemy, metamorphosis, produce, Tolstoy, mystery.

By the time Mother came out to warn us that lunch would be ready in half an hour, the project of conquering the wilderness was complete. Our new garden extended from peg to peg and from string to string, surrounded on all sides by the barren earth of the backyard, but distinguished from it by its dark, brown color and its crumbly, tilled soil. Our vegetable plot was beautifully hoed and raked, manured and sown, divided into three equal, elongated waves or hillocks, one for the tomatoes, one for the cucumbers, and one for the radishes. And as temporary labels, like those that are put up at the head of graves that have not yet been covered with a tombstone, we placed a stick at the end of each row with an empty seed packet on each stick. Thus we had, for the time being, at least until the vegetables themselves grew, a colorful garden of pictures: a vivid image of a fiery red tomato with two or three transparent dewdrops trickling down its cheeks; a picture of some cucumbers in an attractive shade of green; and an appetizing illustration of a bunch of radishes, washed and bursting with health, gleaming in red, white, and green.

After spreading the fertilizer and sowing the seeds, we watered and rewatered each of the pregnant hillocks gently with an improvised watering can made from a water bottle and the little strainer from the kitchen that in civilian life hung on the kettle and caught the tea leaves when we made tea.

Father said:

"So from now on every morning and every evening we'll water our vegetable beds, we mustn't overwater or underwater them, and you will no doubt run and check every morning, as soon as you get up, for the first signs of germination, because in a few days' time tiny shoots will start to raise their heads and shake the grains of soil aside, like a naughty boy shaking his cap off his head. Every plant, the Rabbis say, has its own private angel that stands over it, taps it on the head, and says, 'Grow!'"

Father also said:

"Now Your sweaty, grubby Honor will kindly take out clean underwear, shirt, and trousers and jump in the bath. Your Highness will remember to use plenty of soap, especially you-know-where. And don't fall asleep in the bath as usual, because your humble servant is waiting patiently for his turn."

In the bathroom I stripped down to my underpants and then climbed on the toilet seat and peeped out through the little window. Was there anything to see yet? A first shoot? A green sprout? Even if it was just the size of a pinhead?

As I peeped out, I saw my father lingering for a few minutes beside his new garden, modest and humble, as happy as an artist posing beside his latest creation, tired, still limping from when he hit his toe with the hammer, but as happy as a conquering hero.

My father was a tireless talker, always overflowing with quotations and proverbs, always happy to explain and to quote, eager to treat you on the spot to the benefit of his extensive knowledge. Had you ever reflected on the way the Hebrew language links certain roots together by their sounds, for instance, to uproot and to rend, to stone and to drive away, to till and to be lacking, to plant and to dig up, or the etymological link between earth-red-man-blood-silence? A regular torrent of allusions, associations, connotations, and wordplays poured out of him, whole forests of facts and analogies, piles upon piles of explanations, rebuttals, and arguments, desperately straining to entertain or amuse those present, to spread happiness, even to play the fool, not sparing his own dignity, so long as silence had no dominion, even for a moment.

A lean, tense figure, in a sweat-drenched T-shirt and khaki shorts that were too wide and reached almost down to his nobby knees. His thin arms and legs were very pale and covered with thick black hair. He looked like a dazed Talmud student who had suddenly been dragged out of the darkness of the house of study, dressed up in the khaki garb of the pioneer, and ruthlessly led out into the dazzling blue of midday. His hesitant smile fixed you for a moment as though begging, as though plucking your sleeve and beseeching you to show him some affection. His brown eyes stared at you absentmindedly or even in a panic through his round-framed glasses, as though he had just remembered that he had forgotten something, who knows what, but it was the most important and urgent thing of all, something that he must not at any cost forget. But what it was that he had forgotten he completely failed to recall. Excuse me, perhaps you happen to know what I've forgotten? Something important. Something that can't be delayed. Would you be kind enough to remind me what it was? If I may make so bold.

The following days I ran to our vegetable garden every two or three hours, impatient to discover signs of germination, if only some tiny movement in the loosened soil. Again and again I watered the plot, until the soil turned to mud. Every morning I leaped out of bed and ran barefoot in my pajamas to check whether the longed-for miracle had occurred during the night. And after a few days, early one morning, I found that the radishes had taken the lead and put up their tiny, closely packed periscopes.

I was so happy that I watered them again and again.

And I erected a scarecrow dressed in an old slip of my mother's, with an empty tin can for a head, on which I drew a mouth and a mustache and a forehead with black hair falling across it like Hitler, and eyes one of which came out slightly crooked, as though he was winking or mocking.

A couple of days later the cucumbers came up too. But whatever it was the radishes and cucumbers saw must have saddened or terrified them, because they changed their minds, turned pale, their bodies bent double overnight as though in deep dejection, their tiny heads touched the ground, and they became shriveled, thin, gray, until they were no more than miserable threads of straw. As for the tomatoes, they never even sprouted: they examined the prevailing conditions, discussed what to do, and decided to give us up. Maybe our yard was incapable of growing anything, since it was so low-lying, surrounded by high walls and shaded by tall cypress trees, so that not a ray of sunlight reached it. Or perhaps we had overdone the watering. Or the fertilizer. It is possible that my Hitler scarecrow, which left the birds completely unimpressed, terrified the tiny shoots to death. So that was the end of our attempt to create a kind of little kibbutz in Jerusalem and someday to eat the fruit of the labor of our own hands.

"From this," my father said sadly, "follows the grave but inescapable conclusion that we must decidedly have gone wrong somewhere along the line. So now we are definitely under an obligation to labor tirelessly and uncompromisingly to determine the root and cause of our failure. Did we put on too much fertilizer? Did we water excessively? Or, on the contrary, did we omit some essential step? When all is said and done, we are not peasants and sons of peasants but mere amateurs, inexperienced suitors paying court to the earth but unfamiliar as yet with the golden mean."

That very day, when he came back from his work in the National Library on Mount Scopus, he brought with him two thick tomes he had borrowed about gardening and vegetable growing (one of them was in German) and studied them carefully. His attention soon turned to other matters, and to totally different books, the decline of certain minority languages in the Balkans, the influence of medieval courtly poetry on the origins of the novella, Greek words in the Mishnah, the interpretation of Ugaritic texts.

But one morning, as he was setting off to work with his rather battered briefcase, Father saw me bent over the dying shoots with tears in my eyes, absorbed in a last desperate effort to rescue them by means of some nose or ear drops that I had taken without permission from the medicine chest in the bathroom and was now administering to the withered shoots, one drop each. At that moment Father's pity was stirred toward me. He picked me up and hugged me, but lost no time in putting me down again. He was perplexed, embarrassed, at a loss. Before he left, as though fleeing the field of combat, he nodded his head three or four times and muttered thoughtfully, to himself rather than to me, the words: "We'll see what else can be done."

On Ibn Gabirol Street in Rehavia there used to stand a building called Pioneering Women's House, or it may have been Working Women's Farm, or something of the sort. Behind it there was a small agricultural reserve, a kind of commune, a women's farm, just a quarter of an acre or so of fruit trees, vegetables, poultry, and beehives. On this site in the early 1950s President Ben-Zvi's famous official prefab would be erected.

Father went to this experimental farm after work. He must have explained to Rachel Yannait or one of her assistants the whole story of our agricultural defeat, sought advice and guidance, and finally left and came home by bus bearing a small wooden box in whose soil there were some twenty or thirty healthy seedlings. He smuggled his booty into the apartment and hid it from me behind the laundry basket or under the kitchen cupboard, waited till I was asleep, and then crept outside, armed with his flashlight, his screwdriver, his heroic hammer, and his letter opener.

When I got up in the morning, Father addressed me in a matter-of-fact voice, as though reminding me to tie my shoelaces or button up my shirt. Without taking his eyes off his paper he said:

"Right. I have the impression your medicine from yesterday has done some good to our ailing plants. Why don't you go and have a look for yourself, Your Highness, and see if there's any sign of recovery? Or was it just my impression? Please go and check, and come back to let me know what you think, and we'll see if we both share the same opinion, more or less, shall we?"

My tiny shoots, which the day before had been so withered and yellowed that they were no more than sad threads of straw, had suddenly overnight, as though by magic, into sturdy, vigorous plants, bursting with health, full of sap and a deep green color. I stood there stunned, overwhelmed by the magical power of ten or twenty nose or ear drops.

As I went on staring, I realized that the miracle was even greater than it had appeared at first glance. The radish seedlings had jumped over into the cucumber bed in the night. While in the radishes' bed some plants I didn't recognize at all had settled, perhaps eggplants or carrots. And the most wondrous thing of all: all along the left-hand row, where we had put the tomato seeds that had not germinated, the row where I had not seen any point in using my magic drops at all, there were now three or four bushy young plants, with yellow buds among their upper shoots.

A week later disease struck our garden again, the death throes began all over again, the saplings bowed their heads and once more started looking as sickly and weak as persecuted Diaspora Jews, their leaves dropped, the shoots withered, and this time neither nose drops nor cough syrup did any good: our vegetable patch was drying out and dying. For two or three weeks the four pegs continued to grow there, joined by the grubby strings, and then they too died. Only my Hitler scarecrow flourished for a little longer. Father sought consolation in the exploration of the sources of the Lithuanian romance or the birth of the novel from troubadour poetry. As for me, I scattered the yard with galaxies crammed with strange stars, moons, suns, comets, and planets, and set out on a perilous journey from star to star, in search of other signs of life.

32

LATE ONE summer afternoon. It is the end of the first grade, or maybe the beginning of the second grade, or the summer between the two. I am alone in the yard. The others have all gone off without me, Danush, Alik, Uri, Lulik, Eitan, and Ammi, they've gone to look for those things among the trees on the slope of the Tel Arza woods, but they wouldn't have me in the Black Hand gang because I wouldn't blow. Danush found one among the trees, full of smelly sticky stuff that had dried up, and he washed it out under the tap, and anyone who didn't have the guts to blow it up wasn't fit to belong to the Black Hand, and anyone who didn't have the guts to put it on and pee into it a bit, like an English soldier, there was no question of his being admitted to the Black Hand. Danush explained how it worked. Every night English soldiers take girls to the Tel Arza woods and there, in the dark, it goes like this. First they kiss a long time, on the mouth. Then he touches her body in all sorts of places, even under her clothes. Then he pulls both their pants down and puts one of those things on and he lies on top of her and so on and in the end he wets. And this thing was invented so that she wouldn't get wet from him at all. And that's the way it goes every night in Tel Arza woods, and that's the way it goes every night with everyone. Even Mrs. Sussmann, the teacher, her husband does it to her at night. Even your parents. Yes, yours too. And yours. All of them. And it gives you all sorts of nice feelings in your body and it builds up your muscles and it's also good for cleansing the blood.

They've all gone off without me and my parents are out too. I'm lying on my back on the concrete at the end of the yard behind the washing lines and watching the remains of the day. The concrete is cold and hard under your body in a vest. Thinking, but not right to the end, that everything that's hard and everything that's cold will stay hard and cold forever and everything that's soft and everything that's warm is only soft and warm for the time being. In the end everything has to pass over to the cold, hard side. Over there you don't move, you don't think, you don't feel, you don't warm anything. Forever.

You're lying on your back, and your fingers find a small stone and put it inside your mouth, which can taste dust and plaster and something else that's kind of salty but not exactly salty. The tongue explores all sorts of little projections and depressions as though the stone is a world like ours and it has mountains and valleys. And what if it turns out that our earth, or even our whole universe, is just a little stone on the concrete in the yard of some giants? What will happen if, in the next moment, some huge child, it's impossible to imagine how big he is, and his friends have made fun of him and gone off without him and that child simply picks up our whole universe between two of his fingers and puts it all in his mouth and also starts exploring us with his tongue? And he also thinks that maybe this stone that's inside his mouth is really a whole universe with Milky Ways and suns and comets and children and cats and washing hanging on the line? And who knows, maybe that huge boy's universe, the boy in whose mouth we are just a tiny stone, is actually nothing more than a little stone on the ground in the yard of an even bigger boy, and he and his universe, and so on and so forth, like Russian dolls, a whole universe inside a tiny stone inside a universe inside a stone, and it's just the same when it gets smaller as when it gets bigger? Every universe is a stone, and every stone is a universe. Until it begins to make your head spin, and meanwhile your tongue explores the stone as though it were a sweet, and now your tongue itself has a chalky taste. Danush, Alik, Uri, Lulik, Eitan, and Ammi and the rest of the Black Hand, in another sixty years they'll be dead and then everyone who remembers them will die and then everyone who remembers everyone who remembers everyone who remembers them. Their bones will turn to stone like this stone that's in my mouth. Maybe the stone in my mouth was children who died trillions of years ago? Maybe they went to look for those things in the woods too and there was someone they made fun of because he didn't have the guts to blow it up and put it on? And they left him alone in his yard too, and he also lay on his back and put a stone in his mouth, and the stone was also a boy once and the boy was once a stone. Dizzy. And meanwhile this stone is getting a bit of life and it's not quite so cold and hard anymore, it's become wet and warm, it's even beginning to stir in your mouth and gently return the tickles it's getting from the tip of your tongue.

Behind the cypress trees behind the fence at the Lembergs' someone's put the electric light on, but lying here you can't see who's there, Mrs. Lemberg or Shula or Eva, who put the light on, but you can see the yellow electricity pouring out like glue that's so thick it's hard to spill, it can hardly move, it can barely make its heavy way, the way viscous liquids do; dull and yellow and slow, it advances like heavy motor oil across the evening, which is a little gray-blue now, and the breeze stirs and licks it for a moment. And fifty-five years later, as I sit and write that evening in an exercise book at the garden table in Arad, that very same evening breeze stirs and from the neighbors' window again this evening too there flows a thick, slow, yellow electric light like heavy motor oil—we know each other, we've known each other for a long time, it's as if there are no more surprises. But there are. That evening of the stone in the mouth in the yard in Jerusalem didn't come here to Arad to remind you of what you've forgotten or to revive old longings, but the opposite: it's come to assault this evening. It's like a woman you've known for a long time, you no longer find her attractive or unattractive, whenever you bump into each other, she always says more or less the same few worn-out words, always offers you a smile, always taps you on the chest in a familiar way, only now, only this time, she doesn't, she suddenly reaches out and grabs your shirt, not casually but with her all, her claws, lustfully, desperately, eyes tight shut, her face twisted as though in pain, determined to have her way, determined not to let go, she doesn't care anymore about you, about what you are feeling, whether or not you want to, what does she care, now she's got to, she can't help herself, she reaches out now and strikes you like a harpoon and starts pulling and tearing you, but actually she's not the one who's pulling, she just digs her claws in and you're the one who's pulling and writing, pulling and writing, like a dolphin with the barb of the harpoon caught in his flesh, and he pulls as hard as he can, pulls the harpoon and the line attached to it and the harpoon gun that's attached to the line and the hunters' boat that the harpoon gun is fixed to, he pulls and struggles, pulls to escape, pulls and turns over and over in the sea, pulls and dives down into the dark depths, pulls and writes and pulls more; if he pulls one more time with all his desperate strength, he may manage to free himself from the thing that is stuck in his flesh, the thing that is biting and digging into you and not letting go, you pull and you pull and it just bites into your flesh, the more you pull, the deeper it digs in, and you can never inflict a pain in return for this loss that is digging deeper and deeper, wounding you more and more because it is the catcher and you are the prey, it is the hunter and you are the harpooned dolphin, it gives and you have taken, it is that evening in Jerusalem and you are in this evening here in Arad, it is your dead parents, and you just pull and go on writing.

———

The others have all gone to the Tel Arza woods without me, and because I didn't have the guts to blow, I'm lying here on my back on the concrete at the end of the yard behind the washing lines. Watching the light of day gradually surrendering. Soon it will be night.

Once I watched from the Ali Baba's cave I had in the space between the wardrobe and the wall when Grandma, my mother's mother, who had come to Jerusalem from the tar-papered shack on the edge of Kiriat Motskin, lost her temper with my mother, gesticulating at her with the iron, her eyes flashing, and spat terrible words at her in Russian or Polish mixed with Yiddish. Neither of them imagined that I was squeezed into that space holding my breath, peering out, seeing and hearing everything. My mother didn't reply to her mother's thunderous curses but just sat on the hard chair that had lost its back, which stood in the corner, she sat up straight with her knees pressed together and her hands motionless on her knees and her eyes also fixed on her knees, as though everything depended on her knees. My mother sat there like a scolded child, and as her mother shot one venomous question at her after another, all of them soaked and sizzling with sibilants, she said nothing in reply, but her eyes focused even more fixedly on her knees. Her continued silence only redoubled Grandma's fury, she seemed to have gone right out of her mind: her eyes flashing, her face wolflike with rage, flecks of foam whitening the corners of her open lips, and her sharp teeth showing, she hurled the hot iron she was holding, as though to smash it against the wall, then kicked the ironing board over and stormed out of the room, slamming the door so hard that the windowpanes, the vase, and the cups all rattled.

My mother, unaware that I was watching, suddenly stood up and began punishing herself, she slapped her cheeks and tore her hair, she grabbed a clothes hanger and hit her head and back with it until she wept, and I too in my space between the wardrobe and the wall began to cry silently and to bite both my hands so hard that painful marks appeared. That evening we all ate sweetened gefilte fish that Grandma had brought with her from the tar-papered shack on the edge of Kiriat Motskin, in a sweet sauce with sweet boiled carrot, and they all talked to each other about speculators and the black market, about the state construction company and free enterprise and the Ata textile factory near Haifa, and they finished the meal with a cooked fruit salad that we called compote, which was also made by my mother's mother and which had also turned out sweet and sticky like a syrup. My other grandma, the one from Odessa, Grandma Shlomit, politely finished her compote, wiped her lips on a white paper napkin, took a lipstick and pocket mirror out of her leather handbag, and redrew the line of her lips, and then, while she carefully retracted her red dog's erection of a lipstick into its sheath, she observed:

"What can I say to you? I have never tasted sweeter food in my whole life. The Almighty must be very fond of Vohlynia, to have soaked it so in honey. Even your sugar is much sweeter than ours, and your salt is sweet, and your pepper, and even the mustard in Vohlynia has a taste of jam, and your horseradish, your vinegar, your garlic, they're all so sweet you could sweeten the Angelofdeath himself with them."

As soon as she had spoken these words, she fell silent, as though in fear of the wrath of the angel whose name she had dared to take so lightly.

At which my other grandma, my mother's mother, adopted a pleasant smile, not at all vindictive or gloating, but a well-meaning smile as pure and innocent as the singing of the cherubs, and to the charge that her cooking was sweet enough to sweeten vinegar or horseradish and even the angel of death Grandma Ita replied to Grandma Shlomit with a sing-song lilt:

"But not you, dear mother-in-law of my daughter!"

The others are not back yet from the Tel Arza woods and I am still on my back on the concrete, which seems to have become a little less cold and hard. The evening light is growing cooler and grayer above the points of the cypresses. As though someone is surrendering there, on the awesome heights above the treetops, the rooftops, and everything that is stirring here in the street, the backyards and kitchens, high above the smells of dust, cabbage, and rubbish, high above the twittering of the birds, as high as the sky is above the earth, above the wailing sounds of prayer coming in ragged tatters from the synagogue down the road.

Lofty, clear, and indifferent it is unfolding now above the water heaters and the washing hung out on every roof here and above the abandoned junk and the alley cats and above all sorts of longings and above all the corrugated iron lean-tos in the yards and above the schemes, the omelettes, the lies, the washtubs, the slogans pasted up by the Underground, the borscht, the desolation of ruined gardens and remains of fruit trees from the times when there was an orchard here, and now, right now, it is spreading and creating the calm of a clear, even evening, making peace in the high heavens above the garbage cans and above the hesitant, heartrending piano notes repeatedly attempted by a plain girl, Menuchele Schtich, whom we nicknamed Nemucheleh, Shortie, trying over and over again to play a simple ascending scale, stumbling over and over again, always in the same place, and each time trying again. While a bird replies to her, over and over again, with the first five notes of Beethoven's *Für Elise*. A wide, empty sky from horizon to horizon at the end of a hot summer day. There are three cirrus clouds and two dark birds. The sun has set beyond the walls of the Schneller Barracks, though the firmament has not let go of the sun but has seized it in its claws and managed to tear the train of its many-colored cloak and now is trying on its booty, using the cirrus clouds as a dressmaker's dummy, putting on light like a garment, removing it, checking how well necklaces of greenish radiance suit it, or the coat of many colors with its golden glow and its halo of bluish purple, or how some fragile strips of silver curl along their length, shivering like the broken lines sketched underwater by a fast-moving school of fish. And there are some flashes of purple-tinged pink and lime green, and now it strips quickly and dresses in a reddish mantle from which trail rivers of dull crimson light and after a moment or two puts on a different robe, the color of bare flesh that is suddenly stabbed and stained by several strong hemorrhages while its dark train is being gathered up beneath folds of black velvet, and all at once it is no longer height upon height but depth upon depth upon depth, like the valley of death opening up and expanding in the firmament, as if it were not overhead and the one lying on his back underneath, but the opposite, all the firmament an abyss and the one lying on his back no longer lying but floating, being sucked, plunging rapidly, falling like a stone toward the velvety depth. You will never forget this evening: you are only six or at most six and a half, but for the first time in your little life something enormous and very terrible has opened up for you, something serious and grave, something that extends from infinity to infinity, and it takes you, and like a mute giant it enters you and opens you, so that you too for a moment seem wider and deeper than yourself, and in a voice that is not your voice but may be your voice in thirty or forty years' time, in a voice that allows no laughter or levity, it commands you never to forget a single detail of this evening: remember and keep its smells, remember its body and light, remember its birds, the notes of the piano, the cries of the crows and all the strangeness of the sky running riot from one horizon to the other before your eyes, and all of this is for you, all strictly for the attention of the addressee alone. Never forget Danush, Ammi, and Lulik, or the girls with the soldiers in the woods, or what your grandma said to your other grandma, or the sweet fish floating, dead and seasoned, in a sauce of carrots. Never forget the roughness of the wet stone that was in your mouth more than half a century ago, an echo of whose grayish taste of chalk, plaster, and salt still seduces the tip of your tongue. And all the thoughts that stone conjured up you are never to forget, a universe inside a universe inside a universe. Remember the vertiginous sense of time within time within time, and the whole host of heaven trying on, blending, and hurting the innumerable hues of light just after the sun has set, purple lilac lime orange gold mauve crimson scarlet blue and dull red with gushing blood, and slowly there descends over all a deep dim blue-gray color like the color of silence with a smell like that of the repeated notes on the piano, climbing and stumbling over and over again up a broken scale, while a single bird answers with the five opening notes of *Für Elise*: Ti-da-di-da-di.

33

MY FATHER had a weakness for the momentous, whereas my mother was fascinated by yearning and surrender. My father was an enthusiastic admirer of Abraham Lincoln, Louis Pasteur, and the speeches of Churchill, "blood, sweat, and tears," "never have so many owed so much," "we shall fight them on the beaches." My mother, with a gentle smile, identified with the poetry of Rahel, "I have not sung to you, my land, or praised your name with deeds of heroism, only a path have my feet trodden down . . ." My father, at the kitchen sink, would suddenly erupt into a spirited recital, with no prior warning, of Tchernikhowsky:

". . . and in this Land will rise a brood / that breaks its iron chains / looking the light straight in the eye!" Or sometimes Jabotinsky: ". . . Jotapata, Masada / and captured Beitar / shall rise again in might and splendor! O Hebrew—whether pauper, / slave, or wanderer / you were born a prince / crowned with David's royal diadem." When the spirit descended upon him, Father would roar out, with a tunelessness that would startle the dead, Tchernikhowsky's "My country, oh my land, bare rock-covered highland!" Until Mother had to remind him that the Lembergs next door and probably the other neighbors, the Buchovskis and the Rosendorffs, must be listening to his recital and laughing, whereupon father would stop sheepishly, with an embarrassed smile, as though he had been caught stealing sweets.

As for my mother, she liked to spend the evening sitting on the bed that was disguised as a sofa, with her bare feet folded underneath her, bent over a book on her knees, wandering for hours on end along the paths of autumnal gardens in the stories of Turgenev, Chekhov, Iwaszkewicz, André Maurois, and U. N. Gnessin.

Both my parents had come to Jerusalem straight from the nineteenth century. My father had grown up on a concentrated diet of operatic, nationalistic, battle-thirsty romanticism (the Springtime of Nations, Sturm und Drang), whose marzipan peaks were sprinkled, like a splash of champagne, with the virile frenzy of Nietzsche. My mother, on the other hand, lived by the other Romantic canon, the introspective, melancholy menu of loneliness in a minor key, soaked in the suffering of broken-hearted, soulful outcasts, infused with vague autumnal scents of fin de siècle decadence.

Kerem Avraham, our suburb, with its street hawkers, shopkeepers and little middlemen, its fancy-goods sellers and Yiddishists, its pietists with their wailing chants, its displaced petite bourgeoisie and its eccentric world reformers, suited neither of them. There was always a hesitant dream hovering over our home of moving to a more cultured neighborhood, such as Beit Hakerem or Kiryat Shemuel, if not to Talpiot or Rehavia, not right away but someday, in the future, when it was a possibility, when we'd put something by, when the child was a bit older, when Father had managed to get his foot on the academic ladder, when Mother had a regular teaching position, when the situation improved, when the country was more developed, when the English left, when the Hebrew State came into being, when it was clearer what was going to happen here, when things finally got a little easier for us.

"There, in the land our fathers loved," my parents used to sing when they were young, she in Rovno and he in Odessa and Vilna, like thousands of other young Zionists in Eastern Europe in the early decades of the twentieth century, "all our hopes will be fulfilled. There to live in liberty, there to flourish, pure and free."

But what were all the hopes? What sort of "pure and free" life did my parents expect to find here?

Perhaps they vaguely thought they would find in the renewed Land of Israel something less petit-bourgeois and Jewish and more European and modern; something less crudely materialistic and more idealistic; something less feverish and voluble and more settled and reserved.

My mother may have dreamed of living the life of a bookish, creative teacher in a village school in the Land of Israel, writing lyric poetry in her spare time, or perhaps sensitive, allusive stories. I think that she hoped to forge gentle relationships with subtle artists, relationships marked by baring one's breast and revealing one's true feelings, and so to break free at last of her mother's noisy, domineering hold on her, and to escape from the stifling puritanism, poor taste, and base materialism that were apparently rampant where she came from.

My father, on the other hand, saw himself as destined to become an original scholar in Jerusalem, a bold pioneer of the renewal of the Hebrew spirit, a worthy heir to Professor Joseph Klausner, a gallant officer in the cultured army of the Sons of Light battling against the forces of darkness, a fitting successor to a long and glorious dynasty of scholars that began with the childless Uncle Joseph and continued with his devoted nephew who was as dear to him as a son. Like his famous uncle, and no doubt under his inspiration, my father could read scholarly works in sixteen or seventeen languages. He had studied in the universities of Vilna and Jerusalem (and even wrote a doctoral thesis later, in London). For years, neighbors and strangers had addressed him as "Herr Doktor," and then, at the age of fifty, he finally had a real doctorate. He had also studied, mostly on his own, ancient and modern history, the history of literature, Hebrew linguistics and general philology, biblical studies, Jewish thought, archaeology, medieval literature, philosophy, Slavonic studies, Renaissance history, and Romance studies: he was equipped and ready to become an assistant lecturer and to advance through the ranks to senior lecturer and eventually professor, to be a path-breaking scholar, and indeed to end up sitting at the head of the table every Saturday afternoon and delivering one monologue after another to his awestruck tea-time audience of admirers and devotees, just like his esteemed uncle.

But nobody wanted him, or his learned accomplishments. So this Treplev had to eke out a wretched existence as a librarian in the newspaper department of the National Library, writing his books about the history of the novella and other subjects of literary history at night, with what remained of his strength, while his Seagull spent her days in a basement apartment, cooking, laundering, cleaning, baking, looking after a sickly child, and when she wasn't reading novels, she stood staring out of the window while her glass of tea grew cold in her hand. Whenever she could, she gave private lessons.

I was an only child, and they both placed the full weight of their disappointments on my little shoulders. First of all, I had to eat well and sleep a lot and wash properly, so as to improve my chances of growing up to fulfill something of the promise of my parents when they were young. They expected me to learn to read and write even before I reached school age. They vied with each other to offer me blandishments and bribes to make me learn the letters (which was unnecessary, as letters fascinated me anyway and came to me of their own accord). And once I learned to read, at the age of five, they were both anxious to provide me with a tasty but also nutritious diet of reading, rich in cultural vitamins.

They frequently conversed with me about topics that were certainly not considered suitable for young children in other homes. My mother liked telling me stories about wizards, elves, ghouls, enchanted cottages in the depths of the forest, but she also talked to me seriously about crimes, emotions, the lives and sufferings of brilliant artists, mental illness, and the inner lives of animals. ("If you just look carefully, you'll see that every person has some dominant characteristic that makes him resemble a particular animal, a cat or a bear or a fox or a pig. A person's physical features also point to the animal he most closely resembles.") Father, meanwhile, introduced me to the mysteries of the solar system, the circulation of the blood, the British White Paper, evolution, Theodor Herzl and his astonishing life story, the adventures of Don Quixote, the history of writing and printing, and the principles of Zionism. ("In the Diaspora the Jews had a very hard life; here in the Land of Israel it's still not easy for us, but soon the Hebrew State will be established, and then everything will be made just and rejuvenated. The whole world will come and marvel at what the Jewish people is creating here.")

My parents and grandparents, sentimental family friends, well-meaning neighbors, all sorts of gaudy aunties, with their bear hugs and greasy kisses, were constantly amazed at every word that came out of my mouth: the child is so *marvelously* intelligent, so original, so sensitive, so special, *so* precocious, he's so thoughtful, he understands everything, he has the vision of an artist.

For my part, I was so amazed at their amazement that I inevitably ended up amazing myself. After all, they were grown-ups, in other words creatures who knew everything and were permanently right, and if they were always saying that I was so clever, then, of course, I must be. If they found me interesting, I was not unnaturally inclined to agree with them. And if they thought I was a sensitive, creative child and rather something and quite something else (both in some foreign language), and also so original, so advanced, so intelligent, so logical, so cute, etc., well . . .

Being conformist and respectful as I was of the grown-up world and its prevailing values, and having no brothers or sisters or friends to counterbalance the personality cult that surrounded me, I had no alternative but to concur, humbly but thoroughly, with the grown-ups' opinion of me.

And so, unconsciously, by the age of four or five I had become a little show-off whose parents together with the rest of the adult world had invested a considerable fortune in me and offered generous fuel to my arrogance.

Sometimes on winter evenings the three of us would sit and chat around the kitchen table after supper. We spoke softly because the kitchen was so small and cramped, and we never interrupted each other. (Father considered this a precondition of any conversation.) We would talk, for instance, about what a blind man or a creature from another planet would make of our world. Perhaps fundamentally we were all rather like some blind alien? We talked about children in China and India, children of Bedouin and Arab peasants, children of the ghetto, children of the illegal immigrants, and children in the kibbutzim who did not belong to their parents but by my age were already living independent communal lives that they were themselves responsible for, cleaning their own rooms by rotation and deciding by vote what time they would turn the lights out and go to sleep.

The pale-yellow electric light lit the shabby little kitchen even in the daytime. Outside in the street, which was already empty by eight in the evening, whether because of the British curfew or simply out of habit, a hungry wind whistled on winter nights. It rattled the garbage can lids outside the houses, terrified the cypresses and the stray dogs, and with its dark fingers tested the washtubs suspended on balcony railings. Sometimes a distant echo of gunfire or a muffled explosion reached us from the heart of darkness.

After supper the three of us stood in line, as though on parade, first Father then Mother then me, facing the wall that was stained black from the Primus stove and the paraffin cooker, with our backs to the room. Father bent over the sink, washed and rinsed each plate and glass in turn, and placed each one on the draining board, from where mother picked them up and dried them and put them away. I was responsible for drying the forks and spoons, and I also sorted them out and put them away in the drawer. From the time I was six, I was allowed to dry the table knives, but I was absolutely forbidden to handle the bread knife or the kitchen knives.

For them it was not enough for me to be intelligent, rational, good, sensitive, creative, and thoughtful with the dreamy vision of an artist. In addition, I also had to be a seer and a fortune-teller, a kind of family oracle. After all, everyone knew that children were closer to nature, to the magical bosom of creation, not having been corrupted yet by lies or poisoned by selfish considerations.

And so I had to play the role of the Delphic oracle or the holy fool.

As I climbed the consumptive pomegranate tree in the yard, or ran from wall to wall without treading on the lines between the paving stones, they called out to me to give them and their guests some spontaneous sign from heaven to help them to settle a dispute, whether or not to go and visit their friends in Kibbutz Kiriat Anavim, whether or not to buy (in installments) a round brown table with four chairs, whether or not to endanger the lives of the survivors by smuggling them into the country on decrepit boats, or whether or not to invite the Rudnickis to supper on Friday night.

My task was to utter some vague, ambiguous thought, beyond my years, some obscure sentence based on fragments of ideas that I had heard from the grown-ups and shaken up and stirred well, something that could be taken either way, something that was open to all sorts of interpretations. If possible, it should include some vague simile, or feature the phrase "in life." For example: "Every journey is like opening a drawer." "In life there is morning and evening, summer and winter." "Making small concessions is like avoiding treading on little creatures."

Such enigmatic sentences, "out of the mouths of babes and sucklings," made my parents overflow with emotion; their eyes sparkled, they turned my words this way and that, discovering in them an oracular expression of the pure, unconscious wisdom of nature itself.

Mother would clasp me warmly to her breast on hearing such beautiful sayings, which I always had to repeat or reproduce in the presence of astonished relatives or friends. I soon learned how to mass-produce such utterances to order, at the request of my excited public. I succeeded in extracting not one but three separate pleasures from each prophecy. First, the sight of my audience fixing their hungry eyes on my lips, waiting excitedly for what would come out, and then plunging into a mass of contradictory interpretations. Second, the dizzying experience of sitting in judgment like Solomon between these grown-ups ("Didn't you hear what he said to us about small concessions? So why do you keep insisting we shouldn't go to Kiriat Anavim tomorrow?"). The third pleasure was the most secret and delicious of all: my generosity. There was nothing I enjoyed more in the world than the delight of giving. They were thirsty, they needed me, and I gave them what they wanted. How fortunate that they had me! What would they do without me?

34

I WAS ACTUALLY a very easy child, obedient, hard-working, unknowingly supporting the established social order (Mother and I were subject to Father, who sat at the feet of Uncle Joseph, who in turn—despite his critical opposition—obeyed Ben-Gurion and the "authorized institutions"). Apart from which I was tireless in my quest for words of praise from grown-ups, my parents and their visitors, aunts, neighbors, and acquaintances.

Nevertheless, one of the most popular performances in the family repertoire, a favorite comedy with a set plot, revolved around a transgression followed by a session of soul-searching and then a fitting punishment. After the punishment came remorse, repentance, pardon, remission of part or most of the punishment, and, finally, a tearful scene of forgiveness and reconciliation, accompanied by hugs and mutual affection.

One day, for example, driven by love of science, I sprinkle black pepper into my mother's coffee.

Mother takes one sip, chokes, and spits the coffee out into her napkin. Her eyes are full of tears. Already full of regret, I say nothing, I know very well that the next scene belongs to Mother.

Father, in his role of unbiased investigator, cautiously tastes Mother's coffee. He may just wet his lips with it. At once he gives his diagnosis:

"Somebody has decided to season your coffee. It is my suspicion that this is the work of some high-ranking personage."

Silence. Like a supremely well-behaved child I shovel spoonful after spoonful of porridge from my plate into my mouth, wipe my lips with my napkin, pause for a moment, and then eat another two or three spoonfuls. Composed. Sitting up straight. As though acting out an etiquette book. Today I shall finish all my porridge. Like a model child. Until the plate is sparkling clean.

Father continues, as though deep in thought, as though sharing with us the general outlines of the mysteries of chemistry, without looking at me, talking only to Mother, or to himself:

"There might have been a disaster, though. As is well known, there are a number of compounds made up of substances that in themselves are completely harmless and fit for human consumption, but that when combined are liable to pose a threat to the life of anyone who tastes them. Whoever it was who put whatever it is in your coffee might well have mixed in some other ingredient. And then? Poisoning. Hospital. Life-threatening, even."

A deathly silence fills the kitchen. As though the worst has already happened.

Mother, unconsciously, pushes the poisoned chalice away from her with the back of her hand.

"And then what?" Father continues, thoughtfully, nodding his head a few times as though he knows very well what almost happened but is too tactful to name the horror.

Silence.

"I therefore suggest that whoever performed this prank—no doubt inadvertently, as a misplaced joke—should have the courage to stand up at once. So that we should all know that if there is such a frivolous miscreant in our midst, at least we're not harboring a coward. A person bereft of all honesty and self-respect."

Silence.

It is my turn.

I get to my feet and say in a grown-up tone just like my father's:

"It was me. I'm sorry. It was a really stupid thing to do. It won't ever happen again."

"Are you sure?"

"Definitely."

"On your word of honor as a self-respecting man?"

"On my word of honor as a self-respecting man."

"Confession, regret, and promise all point to a reduction of the penalty. We shall content ourselves on this occasion with your kindly drinking it. Yes, now. Please."

"What, this coffee? With the black pepper in it?"

"Yes, indeed."

"What, me, drink it?"

"Yes, please."

But after a first hesitant sip Mother intervenes. She suggests that will be enough. There is no need to exaggerate. The child has such a sensitive stomach. And he has surely learned his lesson by now.

Father does not hear the plea for compromise. Or pretends not to. He asks:

"And how does Your Highness find his beverage? Does it taste like manna from heaven?"

I screw up my face in utter revulsion. Expressing suffering, remorse, and heart-wrenching sadness. So Father declares:

"Very well, then. that's enough. We shall make do with that on this occasion. Your Highness has expressed his contrition. So let us draw a line under what has been done. And let us underline it with the help of a piece of chocolate, to take away the bad taste. Then, if you like, we can sit at my desk and sort some more stamps. Right?"

Each of us enjoyed his fixed part in this comedy. Father was fond of acting the part of a vengeful deity, all-seeing and punishing wrongdoing, a sort of domestic Jehovah flashing sparks of rage and rumbling terrible thunder, but also compassionate and merciful, long-suffering and abundantly loving.

But occasionally he was overcome with a blind wave of real fury, not just theatrical anger, especially if I did something that might have been dangerous for me, and then, without any foreplay, he would hit me across the face two or three times.

Sometimes, after I had been playing with electricity or climbing onto a high branch, he even ordered me to pull my trousers down and get my bottom ready (he called it "The seat, if you please!"), then he beat me ruthlessly six or seven times with his belt.

But generally Father's anger was expressed not through pogroms but through courtly politeness and icy sarcasm:

"Your Highness has deigned to tread mud from the street all down the corridor again: apparently it is beneath Your Honor's dignity to wipe his feet on the doormat as we poor mortals take the trouble to do on rainy days. On this occasion I fear Your Excellency will have to condescend to wipe away his royal footprints with his own fair hands. And then Your Supreme Highness will kindly submit to being locked in the bathroom for an hour in the dark so as to have an opportunity to reflect on the error of his ways and resolve to make amends for the future."

Mother immediately protested at the severity of the sentence:

"Half an hour will do. And not in the dark. What's the matter with you? You'll be forbidding him to breathe next."

"How very fortunate for His Excellency that he always has such an enthusiastic counsel to leap to his defense."

Mother said:

"If only there was a punishment for having a warped sense of humor—" but she never finished the sentence.

A quarter of an hour later it was time for the final scene. Father himself would come to fetch me from the bathroom. Reaching out to give me a quick, embarrassed hug, he would mutter a sort of apology:

"Of course I realize you didn't leave the mud on purpose, it's just that you're absentminded. But of course you also realize that we only punished you for your own good, so that you don't grow up to be another absentminded professor."

I looked straight into his innocent, sheepish brown eyes and promised him that from now on I would always be careful to wipe my shoes when I came in. Moreover, my fixed part in the drama was to say at this point, with an intelligent, grown-up expression on my face and words borrowed from my father's arsenal, that naturally I understood full well that I was only punished for my own good. My set part even included an address to Mother, in which I begged her not to be so quick to forgive me, because I accepted the consequences of my actions and was perfectly capable of taking the punishment I deserved. Even two hours in the bathroom. Even in the dark. I didn't care.

And I really didn't care, because there was hardly any difference between being locked in the bathroom and my usual solitude, in my room or the yard or the kindergarten: for most of my childhood I was a solitary child, with no brother or sister and with hardly any friends.

A handful of toothpicks, a couple of bars of soap, three toothbrushes and a half-squeezed tube of Shenhav toothpaste, plus a hairbrush, five of Mother's hairpins, Father's toilet bag, the bathroom stool, an aspirin packet, some sticky plasters, and a roll of toilet paper were enough to last me for a whole day of wars, travels, mammoth construction projects, and grand adventures in the course of which I was, by turns, His Highness, His Highness's slave, a hunter, the hunted, the accused, a fortune-teller, a judge, a seafarer, and an engineer digging the Panama and Suez Canals through difficult hilly terrain to join up all the seas and lakes in the tiny bathroom and to launch on voyages from one end of the world to the other merchant ships, submarines, warships, pirate corsairs, whalers, and boatloads of explorers who would discover continents and islands where no man had ever set foot.

Even if I was condemned to solitary confinement in the dark, I was not alarmed. I would lower the cover of the toilet, sit myself on it, and conduct all my wars and journeys with empty hands. Without any soap or combs or hairpins, without stirring from my place. I sat there with my eyes closed and switched on all the light I wanted inside my head, leaving all the darkness outside.

You might even say I loved my punishment of solitary confinement. "Whoever doesn't need other human beings," Father quoted Aristotle, "must be a god or an animal." For hours on end, I enjoyed being both. I didn't mind.

When Father mockingly called me Your Highness or Your Excellency, I didn't take offense. On the contrary: I inwardly agreed with him. I adopted these titles and made them my own. But I said nothing. I gave him no hint of my enjoyment. Like an exiled king who has managed to slip back across the border and walks around his city disguised as an ordinary person. Every now and again one of his startled subjects recognizes him and bows down before him and calls him Your Majesty, in the line for the bus or in the crowd in the main square, but I simply ignore the bow and the title. I give no sign. Maybe the reason I decided to behave in this way was that Mother had taught me that you can tell real kings and nobles by the fact that they despise their titles and know full well that true nobility consists in behaving toward the simplest people with humility, like an ordinary human being.

And not just like any ordinary human being, but like a good-natured, benevolent ruler, who always tries to do whatever his subjects want. They seem to enjoy dressing me and putting my shoes on: so let them. I gladly extend all four limbs. After some time they suddenly change their mind and prefer me to dress myself and put on my own shoes: I am only too pleased to slip into my clothes all by myself, enjoying the sight of their beaming delight, occasionally getting the buttons wrong, or sweetly asking them to help me tie my shoelaces.

They almost fall over each other as they claim the privilege of kneeling down in front of the little prince and tying his shoelaces, as he is in the habit of rewarding his subjects with a hug. No other child is as good at thanking them regally and politely for their services. Once he even promises his parents (who look at each other with eyes misting over with pride and joy, patting him as they inwardly melt with pleasure) that when they are very old, like Mr. Lemberg next door, he will do up their buttons and shoelaces. For all the goodnesses they're always doing for him.

Do they enjoy brushing my hair? Explaining to me how the moon moves? Teaching me to count to a hundred? Putting one sweater on me on top of another? Even making me swallow a teaspoon of revolting cod liver oil every day. I happily let them do whatever they want to me, I enjoy the constant pleasure that my tiny existence affords them. So even if the cod liver oil makes me want to throw up, I gladly overcome my disgust and swallow the whole spoonful at one go, and even thank them for making me grow up healthy and strong. At the same time I also enjoy their amazement: it's clear this is no ordinary child—this child is so special!

And so for me the expression "ordinary child" became a term of utter contempt. It was better to grow up to be a stray dog, better to be a cripple or a mental retard, better to be a girl even, provided I didn't become an "ordinary child" like the rest of them, provided I could go on being "so very special!" or "really out of the ordinary!"

So there I was, from the age of three or four, if not earlier, already a one-child show. A nonstop performance. A lonely stage star, constantly compelled to improvise, and to fascinate, excite, amaze, and entertain his public. I had to steal the show from morning to evening. For example, we go to visit Mala and Staszek Rudnicki one Saturday morning in their home on Chancellor Street, at the corner of the Street of the Prophets. As we walk along, my parents impress on me that I am on no account to forget that Uncle Staszek and Auntie Mala have no children, so I am not even to think of asking them, for instance, when they are going to have a baby. And in general I must be on my best behavior. Uncle and

Auntie have such a high opinion of me already, so I mustn't do anything, anything at all, that might damage their good opinion.

Auntie Mala and Uncle Staszek may not have any children, but they do of course have their pair of plump, lazy, blue-eyed Persian cats, Chopin and Schopenhauer (and as we make our way up Chancellor Street, I am treated to two thumbnail sketches, of Chopin from my mother and of Schopenhauer from my father). Most of the time the cats doze curled up together on the sofa or on a pouffe, like a pair of hibernating polar bears. And in the corner, above the black piano, hangs the cage containing the ancient, bald bird, not in the best of health and blind in one eye. Its beak always hangs half open, as though it is thirsty. Sometimes Mala and Staszek call it Alma, and sometimes they call it Mirabelle. In its cage, too, is the other bird that Auntie Mala put there to relieve its solitude, made from a painted pinecone, with matchsticks for legs and a dark red sliver of wood for a beak. This new bird has wings made from real feathers that have fallen or been plucked from Alma-Mirabelle's wings. The feathers are turquoise and mauve.

Uncle Staszek is sitting smoking. One of his eyebrows, the left one, is always raised, as though expressing a doubt: is that really so, aren't you exaggerating a little? And one of his incisors is missing, giving him the look of a rough street kid. My mother hardly speaks. Auntie Mala, a blond woman who wears her hair in two plaits that sometimes fall elegantly over her shoulders and at other times are wrapped tightly around her head like a wreath, offers my parents a glass of tea and some apple cake. She can peel apples in a single spiral that winds around itself like a telephone cord. Both Staszek and Mala once dreamed of being farmers. They lived on a kibbutz for a couple of years, and then tried living on a cooperative farm for another couple of years, until it became clear that Auntie Mala was allergic to most wild plants, while Uncle Staszek was allergic to the sun (or, as he put it, the sun itself was allergic to him). So now Uncle Staszek works as a clerk in the Head Post Office, while Auntie Mala works as an assistant to a well-known dentist on Sundays, Tuesdays, and Thursdays. When she serves us the apple cake, Father cannot resist complimenting her in his usual jocular fashion:

"Dear Mala, you bake the most heavenly cake, and I always adore the tea that you pour."

Mother says:

"That's enough, Arieh."

And for me, on condition I eat up a thick slice of cake like a big boy, Auntie Mala has a special treat: homemade cherryade. Her homemade cherryade compensates for being short on bubbles (evidently the soda bottle has suffered the consequences of standing around for too long with its hat off) by being so rich in red syrup that it is almost unbearably sweet.

So I politely eat all my cake (not bad at all), careful not to chew with my mouth open, to eat properly with a fork and not dirty my fingers, fully aware of the various dangers of stains, crumbs, and an overfull mouth, spearing each piece of cake on the fork and moving it through the air with extreme care, as though taking into account enemy aircraft that might intercept my cargo flight on the way from plate to mouth. I chew nicely, with my mouth closed, and swallow discreetly and without licking my lips. On the way I pluck the Rudnickis' admiring glances and my parents' pride and pin them to my air-force uniform. And I finally earn the promised prize: a glass of homemade cherryade, short on bubbles but very rich in syrup.

So rich in syrup, indeed, that it is completely, utterly, and totally undrinkable. I can't take a single gulp. Not even a sip. It tastes even worse than Mother's pepper-flavored coffee. It is revoltingly thick and sticky, like cough medicine.

I put the cup of sorrows to my lips, pretending to drink, and when Auntie Mala looks at me—with the rest of my audience, eager to hear what I shall say—I hastily promise (in Father's words and Father's tone of voice) that both her creations, the apple cake and the syrupy drink, are "truly very excellent."

Auntie Mala's face lights up:

"There's more! There's plenty more! Let me pour you another glass! I've made a whole jugful!"

As for my parents, they look at me with mute adoration. In my mind's ears I can hear their applause, and from my mind's waist I bow to my appreciative audience.

But what to do next? First of all, to gain some time, I must distract their attention. I must pronounce some utterance, something deep beyond my years, something they will like:

"Something as tasty as this in life needs to be drunk in tiny sips."

The use of the phrase "in life" particularly helps me: the Pythian has spoken again. The pure, clear voice of nature itself has sounded from my mouth. Taste your life in little sips. Slowly, thoughtfully.

Thus, with a single dithyrambic sentence, I manage to distract their attention. So they won't notice I still haven't drunk any of their wood glue. Meanwhile, while they are still in a trance, the cup of horrors stays on the floor beside me, because life must be drunk in little sips.

As for me, I am deep in thought, my elbows resting on my knees and my hands under my chin, in a pose that precisely represents a statue of the Thinker's little son. I was shown a picture of the original once in the encyclopedia. After a moment or two their attention leaves me, either because it is not fitting to stare at me when my soul is floating up to higher spheres, or because more visitors have arrived and a heated discussion gets going about the refugee ships, the policy of self-restraint, and the High Commissioner.

I seize the opportunity with both hands, slip out into the hallway with my poisoned chalice, and hold it up to the nose of one of the Persian cats, the composer or the philosopher, I'm not sure which. This plump little polar bear takes a sniff, recoils, lets out an offended mew, twitches its whiskers, No thank you very much, and retreats with a bored air to the kitchen. As for its partner, the portly creature does not even bother to open its eyes when I hold out the glass but merely wrinkles its nose, as if to say No, really, and flicks a pink ear toward me. As though to chase away a fly.

Could I empty the lethal potion into the water container in the birdcage, which blind, bald Alma-Mirabelle shares with her winged pinecone? I weigh the pros and cons: the pinecone might tell on me, whereas the philodendron will not give me away even if it is interrogated under torture. My choice therefore falls on the plant rather than the pair of birds (who, like Auntie Mala and Uncle Staszek, are childless, and whom one must therefore not ask when they are planning to lay an egg).

After a while Auntie Mala notices my empty glass. It immediately becomes apparent that I have made her really and truly happy by appreciating her drink. I smile at her and say, just like a grown-up, "Thank you, Auntie Mala, it was just lovely." Without asking or waiting for confirmation she refills my glass and reminds me to remember that that isn't all, she's made a whole jug. Her cherryade might not be as fizzy as it could be, but it is as sweet as chocolate, isn't it?

I concur and thank her once again and settle down to wait for another opportunity; then I slink out again unobserved, like an underground fighter on his way to the British fortified radar installations, and poison their other plant, a cactus.

But at that moment I sense a powerful urge, like a sneeze you can't hold back, like an irresistible laugh in class, to confess, to stand up and announce in public that their drink is so foul that even their cats and their birds find it disgusting, that I have poured the whole lot into their flowerpots, and now their plants are going to die.

And be punished, and take my punishment like a man. With no regrets.

Of course I won't do it: my desire to charm them is much stronger than my urge to shock them. I am a saintly rabbi, not a Genghis Khan.

On the way home Mother looks me straight in the eye and says with a conspiratorial smile:

"Don't think I didn't see you. I saw it all."

All innocence and purity, my sinful heart thumping in my chest like a startled rabbit, I say:

"What did you see?"

"I saw that you were terribly bored. But you managed not to show it, and that made me happy."

Father says:

"The boy really did behave well today, but after all he got his reward, he got a piece of cake and two glasses of cherryade, which we never buy him although he's always asking us to, because who knows if the glasses in the kiosk are really clean?"

Mother:

"I'm not so sure you really liked that drink, but I noticed that you drank it all, so as not to offend Auntie Mala, and I'm really proud of you for that."

"Your mother," Father says, "can see right into your heart. In other words she knows at once not only what you've said and done but also the things you think no one else knows. It's not necessarily easy to live with someone who can see right into your heart."

"And when Auntie Mala offered you a second glass," Mother continues, "I noticed that you thanked her and you drank it all up, just to make her happy. I want you to know that there are not many children of your age, in fact there aren't that many people of any age, who are capable of such consideration."

At that moment I almost admit that it was the Rudnickis' plants, not I, that deserve the compliment, since it was they who drank the syrupy mess.

But how can I tear off the medals that she has just pinned to my chest and fling them at her feet? How can I cause my parents such undeserved hurt? I have just learned from Mother that if you have to choose between telling a lie and hurting someone's feelings, you should choose sensitivity over truthfulness. Faced with a choice between making someone happy and telling the truth, between not causing pain and not lying, you should always prefer generosity over honesty. In so doing you raise yourself above the common herd and earn a bouquet from all of them: a very special child.

Father then patiently explains to us that in Hebrew the word for childlessness is not unrelated to the word for darkness, because both imply a lack, a lack of children or a lack of light. There is another related word that means to spare or to save. "'He who spares the rod hates his child,' it says in the book of Proverbs, and I fully agree with that statement." By way of digression into Arabic, he goes on to suggest that the word for darkness is related to the word for forgetting. "As for the pinecone, its Hebrew name, *itstrubal,* derives from a Greek word, *strobilos,* which denotes anything that spins or whirls, from *strobos,* the act of revolving. And that word comes from the same root as words like 'strophe' and 'catastrophe.' A couple of days ago I saw a truck that had overturned on the way up to Mount Scopus: the people inside were hurt and the wheels were still going around—so there was *strobos* and also catastrophe. As soon as we get home, would Your Honor kindly pick up all the toys you left scattered on the floor and put them back where they belong?"

35

MY PARENTS put on my shoulders everything that they had not managed to achieve themselves. In 1950, on the evening of the day they first met by chance on the steps of Terra Sancta College, Hannah and Michael (in the novel *My Michael*) meet again in Café Atara in Ben Yehuda Street in Jerusalem. Hannah encourages shy Michael to talk about himself, but he tells her instead about his widowed father:

> His father cherished high hopes for him. He refused to recognize that his son was an ordinary young man. . . . His father's greatest wish was for Michael to become a professor in Jerusalem, because his paternal grandfather had taught natural sciences in the Hebrew teachers' seminary in Grodno. . . . It would be nice, Michael's father thought, if the chain could pass on from one generation to another.
>
> "A family isn't a relay race, with a profession as the torch," [Hannah] said.*

For many years my father did not abandon the hope that eventually the mantle of Uncle Joseph would alight on him, and that he might pass it on to me when the time came, if I followed the family tradition and became a scholar. And if, because of his dreary job that left him only the night hours for his research, the mantle passed over him, perhaps his only son would inherit it.

I have the feeling that my mother wanted me to grow up to express the things that she had been unable to express.

In later years they repeatedly reminded me, with a chuckle combined with pride they reminded me, in the presence of all their guests they reminded me, in front of the Zarchis and the Rudnickis and the Hananis and the Bar Yitzhars and the Abramskis they always reminded me how, when I was only five years old, a couple of weeks after I learned the letters of the alphabet, I printed in capital letters on the back of one of

*My Michael, trans. Nicholas de Lange (New York: Random House, 1972), p. 6.

Father's cards the legend AMOS KLAUSNER WRITER, and pinned it up on the door of my little room.

I knew how books were made even before I knew how to read. I would sneak in and stand on tiptoe behind my father's back as he bent over his desk, his weary head floating in the pool of yellow light from his desk lamp, as he slowly, laboriously made his way up the winding valley between the two piles of books on the desk, picking all sorts of details from the tomes that lay open in front of him, plucking them out, holding them up to the light, examining them, sorting them, copying them onto little cards, and then fitted each one in its proper place in the puzzle, like stringing a necklace.

In fact, I work rather like him myself. I work like a watchmaker or an old-fashioned silversmith: one eye screwed up, the other fitted with a watchmaker's magnifying glass, with fine tweezers between my fingers, with bits of paper rather than cards in front of me on my desk on which I have written various words, verbs, adjectives, and adverbs, and bits of dismantled sentences, fragments of expressions and descriptions and all kinds of tentative combinations. Every now and again I pick up one of these particles, these molecules of text, carefully with my tweezers, hold it up to the light and examine it carefully, turn it in various directions, lean forward and rub or polish it, hold it up to the light again, rub it again slightly, then lean forward and fit it into the texture of the cloth I am weaving. Then I stare at it from different angles, still not entirely satisfied, and I take it out again and replace it with another word, or try to fit it into another niche in the same sentence, then remove it, file it down a tiny bit more, and try to fit it in again, perhaps at a slightly different angle. Or deploy it differently. Perhaps farther down the sentence. Or at the beginning of the next one. Or should I cut it off and make it into a one-word sentence on its own?

I stand up. Walk around the room. Return to the desk. Stare at it for a few moments, or longer, cross out the whole sentence or tear up the whole page. I give up in despair. I curse myself aloud and curse writing in general and the language as a whole, despite which I sit down and start putting the whole thing together all over again.

Writing a novel, I said once, is like trying to make the Mountains of Edom out of Lego blocks. Or to build the whole of Paris, buildings, squares, and boulevards, down to the last street bench, out of matchsticks.

If you write an eighty-thousand-word novel, you have to make about a quarter of a million decisions, not just decisions about the outline of the plot, who will live or die, who will fall in love or be unfaithful, who will make a fortune or make a fool of himself, the names and faces of the characters, their habits and occupations, the chapter divisions, the title of the book (these are the simplest, broadest decisions); not just what to narrate and what to gloss over, what comes first and what comes last, what to spell out and what to allude to indirectly (these are also fairly broad decisions); but you also have to make thousands of finer decisions, such as whether to write, in the third sentence from the end of that paragraph, "blue" or "bluish." Or should it be "pale blue"? Or "sky blue"? Or "royal blue"? Or should it really be "blue-gray"? And should this "grayish blue" be at the beginning of the sentence, or should it only shine out at the end? Or in the middle? Or should it simply be caught up in the flow of a complex sentence, full of subordinate clauses? Or would it be best just to write the three words "the evening light," without trying to color it in, either "gray-blue" or "dusty blue" or whatever?

From my early childhood on I was the victim of a thorough, protracted brainwashing: Uncle Joseph's temple of books in Talpiot, Father's straitjacket of books in our apartment in Kerem Avraham, my mother's refuge of books, Grandpa Alexander's poems, our neighbor Mr. Zarchi's novels, my father's index cards and word play, and even Saul Tchernikhowsky's pungent hug, and Mr. Agnon, who cast several shadows at once, with his currants.

But the truth is that secretly I turned my back on the card I had pinned to the door of my room. For several years I dreamed only of growing up and escaping from these warrens of books and becoming a fireman. The fire and water, the uniform, the heroism, the shiny silver helmet, the wail of the siren, and the stares of the girls and the flashing lights, the panic in the street, the thunderous charge of the red engine, leaving a trail of terror in its wake.

And then the ladders, the hose uncoiling endlessly, the glow of the flames reflected like gushing blood in the red of the engine, and finally, the climax, the girl or woman carried unconscious on the shoulder of her gallant rescuer, the self-sacrificing devotion to duty, the scorched skin, eyelashes, and hair, the infernal suffocating smoke. And then immediately afterward—the praise, the rivers of tearful love from dizzy women swooning toward you in admiration and gratitude, and above all the fairest of them all, the one you bravely rescued from the flames with the tender strength of your own arms.

But who was it that through most of my childhood I rescued in my fantasies over and over again from the fiery furnace and whose love I earned in return? Perhaps that is not the right way to ask the question, but rather: What terrible, incredible premonition came to the arrogant heart of that foolish, dreamy child and hinted to him, without revealing the outcome, signaled to him without giving him any chance to interpret, while there was still time, the veiled hint of what would happen to his mother one winter's evening?

Because already at the age of five I imagined myself, over and over again, as a bold, calm fireman, resplendent in uniform and helmet, bravely darting on his own into the fierce flames, risking his life, and rescuing her, unconscious, from the fire (while his feeble, verbal father merely stood there stunned, helplessly staring at the conflagration).

And so, while embodying in his own eyes the fire-hardened heroism of the new Hebrew man (precisely as prescribed for him by his father), he dashes in and saves her life, and in doing so he snatches his mother forever from his father's grasp and spreads his own wings over her.

But from what dark threads could I have embroidered this oedipal fantasy, which did not leave me for several years? Is it possible that somehow, like a smell of faraway smoke, that woman, Irina, Ira, infiltrated my fantasy of the fireman and the rescued woman? Ira Steletskaya, the wife of the engineer from Rovno whose husband used to lose her every night at cards. Poor Ira Steletskaya, who fell in love with Anton the coachman's son and lost her children, until one day she emptied a can of paraffin and burned herself to death in his tar-papered shack. But all that happened fifteen years before I was born, in a country I had never seen. And surely my mother would never have been so crazy as to tell a terrible story like that to a four- or five-year-old child?

When my father was not at home, as I sat at the kitchen table sorting lentils while my mother stood with her back to me, peeling vegetables or squeezing oranges or shaping meatballs on the work surface, she would tell me all sorts of strange and, yes, frightening stories. Little Peer, the orphan son of Jon, the grandson of Rasmus Gynt, must have been just like me, as he and his poor widowed mother sat alone in their mountain cabin on those long, windy, snowy nights, and he absorbed and stored in his heart her mystical, half-crazed stories, about Soria-Moria Castle beyond the fjord, the snatching of the bride, the trolls in the hall of the mountain king, and the green ghouls, the button-molder, and the imps and pixies and also about the terrible Boyg.

The kitchen itself, with its smoke-blackened walls and sunken floor, was as narrow and low as a solitary confinement cell. Next to the stove we had two matchboxes, one for new matches and one for used matches, which, for reasons of economy, we used to light a burner or the Primus from a burner that was already lit.

My mother's stories may have been strange, frightening, but they were captivating, full of caves and towers, abandoned villages and broken bridges suspended above the void. Her stories did not begin at the beginning or conclude with a happy ending but flickered in the half light, wound around themselves, emerged from the mists for a moment, amazed you, sent shivers up your spine, then disappeared back into the darkness before you had time to see what was in front of your eyes. That is how her story about the old man Alleluyev was, and the one about Tanitchka and her three husbands, the blacksmith brothers who killed one another, the one about the bear who adopted a dead child, the ghost in the cave that fell in love with the woodman's wife, or the ghost of Nikita the waggoner that came back from the dead to charm and seduce the murderer's daughter.

Her stories were full of blackberries, blueberries, wild strawberries, truffles, and mushrooms. With no thought for my tender years my mother took me to places where few children had ever trodden before, and as she did so, she opened up before me an exciting fan of words, as though she were picking me up in her arms and raising me higher and higher to reveal vertiginous heights of language: her fields were sun-dappled or dew-drenched, her forests were dense or impenetrable, the trees towered, the meadows were verdant, the mountain, a primeval mountain, loomed up, the castles dominated, the turrets towered, the plains slumbered and sprawled, and in the valleys, which she called vales, springs, streams, and rivulets were constantly gushing, babbling, and purling.

My mother lived a solitary life, shut up at home for most of the time. Apart from her friends Lilenka, Esterka, and Fania Weissmann, who had also been at the Tarbuth gymnasium in Rovno, my mother found no sense or interest in Jerusalem; she did not like the holy places and the many ancient sites. The synagogues and rabbinic academies, churches, convents, and mosques all seemed much of a muchness to her, dreary and smelling of religious men who did not wash often enough. Her sensitive nostrils recoiled from the odor of unwashed flesh, even under a thick cloud of incense.

My father did not have much time for religion either. He considered the priests of every faith as rather suspect, ignorant men who fostered antique hatreds, promoted fears, devised lying doctrines, shed crocodile tears, and traded in fake holy objects and false relics and all kinds of vain beliefs and prejudices. He suspected everyone who made a living from religion of some kind of sugared charlatanism. He enjoyed quoting Heine's remark that the priest and the rabbi both smell (or in Father's toned-down version, "Neither of them has a rosy smell! And nor has the Muslim Mufti, Haj Amin the Nazi-lover!"). On the other hand, he did believe at times in a vague providence, a "presiding spirit of the people" or "Rock of Israel," or in the wonders of the "creative Jewish genius," and he also pinned his hopes on the redeeming and reviving powers of art: "The priests of beauty and the artists' brush," he used to recite dramatically from Tchernikhowsky's sonnet cycle, "and those who master verse's mystic charm / redeem the world by melody and song." He believed that artists were superior to other human beings, more perceptive, more honest, unbesmirched by ugliness. The question of how some artists, despite all this, could have followed Stalin, or even Hitler, troubled and saddened him. He often argued with himself about this: artists who were captivated by the charms of tyrants and placed themselves at the service of repression and wickedness did not deserve the title "priests of beauty." Sometimes he tried to explain to himself that they had sold their souls to the devil, like Goethe's Faust.

The Zionist fervor of those who built new suburbs, who purchased and cultivated virgin land and paved roads, while it intoxicated my father to some extent, passed my mother by. She would usually put the newspaper down after a glance at the headlines. Politics she considered a disaster. Chitchat and gossip bored her. When we had visitors, or when we went to call on Uncle Joseph and Aunt Zippora in Talpiot, or the Zarchis, the Abramskis, the Rudnickis, Mr. Agnon, the Hananis, or Hannah and Hayim Toren, my mother rarely joined in the conversation. Yet sometimes her mere presence made men talk and talk with all their might while she just sat silent, smiling faintly, as though she was trying to decipher from their argument why Mr. Zarchi maintained that particular view and Mr. Hanani the opposite one: would the argument be any different if they suddenly changed around, and each defended the other's position while attacking the one he had argued for previously?

Clothes, objects, hairdos, and furniture interested my mother only as peepholes through which she could peer into people's inner lives. Whenever we went into someone's home, or even a waiting room, my mother would always sit up straight in a corner, with her hands folded across her chest like a model pupil in a boarding school for young ladies, and stare carefully, unhurriedly, at the curtains, the upholstery, the pictures on the walls, the books, the china, the objects displayed on the shelves, like a detective amassing details, some of which might eventually combine to yield a clue.

Other people's secrets fascinated her, but not on the level of gossip—who fancied whom, who was going out with whom, who had bought what. She was like someone studying the placing of tiles in a mosaic or of the pieces in a huge jigsaw puzzle. She listened attentively to conversations, and with that faint smile hovering unawares on her lips she would observe the speaker carefully, watching the mouth, the wrinkles on the face, what the hands were doing, what the body was saying or trying to hide, where the eyes were looking, any change of position, and whether the feet were restless or still inside the shoes. She rarely contributed to the conversation, but if she came out of her silence and spoke a sentence or two, the conversation usually did not go back to being as it was before she intervened.

Maybe it was that in those days women were allotted the role of the audience in conversations. If a woman suddenly opened her mouth and said a sentence or two, it caused some surprise.

Now and then my mother gave private lessons. Occasionally she went to a lecture or a literary reading. Most of the time, though, she stayed at home. She did not sit around, but worked hard. She worked silently and efficiently. I never heard her humming or grumbling while she was doing the housework. She cooked, baked, did the washing, put the shopping away, ironed, cleaned, tidied, washed the dishes, sliced vegetables, kneaded dough. But when the apartment was perfectly tidy, the washing up was done, and the laundry had been folded and put away neatly, then my mother curled up in her corner and read. At ease with her body, breathing slowly and gently, she sat on the sofa and read. With her bare feet tucked under her legs, she read. Bent over the book that was propped on her knees, she read. Her back curved, her neck bent forward, her shoulders drooping, her whole body shaped like a crescent moon, she read. With her face, half hidden by her dark hair, leaning over the page, she read.

She read every evening, while I played outside in the yard and my father sat at his desk writing his research on cramped index cards, and she also read after the supper things were washed up, she read while my father and I sat together at his desk, my head slanting, lightly resting on his shoulder, while we sorted stamps, checked them in the catalogue, and stuck them in the album, she read after I had gone to bed and Father had gone back to his little cards, she read after the shutters had been shut and the sofa had been turned over to reveal the double bed that was hidden inside it, and she went on reading even after the ceiling light had been switched off and my father had taken off his glasses, turned his back to her, and fallen into the sleep of well-meaning people who firmly believe that everything will turn out well, and she went on reading: she suffered from insomnia that grew worse with time, until in the last year of her life various doctors saw fit to prescribe strong pills and all sorts of sleeping potions and solutions and recommended a fortnight's real rest in a family hotel in Safed or the Health Fund sanatorium in Arza.

Consequently my father borrowed a few pounds from his parents and volunteered to look after the child and the house, and my mother really did go off alone to the sanatorium in Arza. But even there she did not stop reading; on the contrary, she read almost day and night. From morning to evening she sat in a deck chair in the pine woods on the flank of the hill and read, and in the evening she read on the lit veranda while the other guests danced or played cards or took part in all sorts of other activities. And at night she would go down to the little sitting room next to the reception desk and read for most of the night, so as not to disturb the woman who shared her room. She read Maupassant, Chekhov, Tolstoy, Gnessin, Balzac, Flaubert, Dickens, Chamisso, Thomas Mann, Iwaszkiewicz, Knut Hamsun, Kleist, Moravia, Hermann Hesse, Mauriac, Agnon, Turgenev, as well as Somerset Maugham, Stefan Zweig, and André Maurois—she hardly took her eyes off a book for the whole of her break. When she came back to Jerusalem, she looked tired and pale, with dark shadows under her eyes, as if she had been living it up every night. When Daddy and I asked her how she had enjoyed her holiday, she smiled and said: "I haven't really thought about it."

Once, when I was seven or eight, my mother said to me, as we sat on the last seat but one on the bus to the clinic or the shoe shop, that while it was true that books could change with the years just as much as people could, the difference was that whereas people would always drop you when they could no longer get any advantage or pleasure or interest or at least a good feeling from you, a book would never abandon you. Naturally you sometimes dropped them, maybe for several years, or even forever. But they, even if you betrayed them, would never turn their backs on you: they would go on waiting for you silently and humbly on their shelf. They would wait for ten years. They wouldn't complain. One night, when you suddenly needed a book, even at three in the morning, even if it was a book you had abandoned and erased from your heart for years and years, it would never disappoint you, it would come down from its shelf and keep you company in your moment of need. It would not try to get its own back or make excuses or ask itself if it was worth its while or if you deserved it or if you still suited each other, it would come at once as soon as you asked. A book would never let you down.

What was the title of the very first book I read on my own? That is, Father read me the book in bed so often that I must have ended up knowing it by heart, word for word, and once when Father could not read to me, I took the book to bed with me and recited the whole of it to myself, from beginning to end, pretending to read, pretending to be Father, turning the page at the precise gap between two words where Father used to turn it every night.

Next day I asked Father to follow with his finger as he read, and I followed his finger, and by the time we had done this five or six times, I could identify each word by its shape and its place in the line.

Then the moment came to surprise them both. One Saturday morning I appeared in the kitchen, still in my pajamas, and without saying a word I opened the book on the table between them, my finger pointed to each word in turn and I said the word aloud just as my finger touched it. My parents, dizzy with pride, fell into the trap, unable to imagine the enormity of the deception, both convinced that the special child had taught himself to read.

But in the end I really did teach myself. I discovered that each word had its own special shape. As though you could say, for instance, that "dog" looks like a round face, with a nose drawn in profile on one side and a pair of glasses on the other; while "eye" actually looks like a pair of eyes with the bridge of a nose between them. In this way I managed to read lines and even whole pages.

After another couple of weeks I started making friends with the letters themselves. The F of Flag looks like a flag waving at the beginning of the flag. The S of Snake looks just like a snake. Daddy and Mummy are the same at the end, but the rest is quite different: Daddy has a pair of boots in the middle with legs sticking up from them, while Mummy has a row of teeth that look like a smile.

The very first book I can remember was a picture book about a big, fat bear who was very pleased with himself, a lazy, sleepy bear that looked a bit like our Mr. Abramski, and this bear loved to lick honey even when he wasn't supposed to. He didn't just lick honey, he stuffed himself with it. The book had an unhappy ending followed by a very unhappy ending, and only after that did it come to the happy ending. The lazy bear was horribly stung by a swarm of bees, and in case that was not enough, he was punished for being so greedy by suffering from toothache, and there was a picture of him with his face all swollen, and a white cloth tied right around his head and ending with a big knot on top, just between his ears. And the moral was written in big red letters:

IT'S NOT GOOD TO EAT TOO MUCH HONEY!

In my father's world there was no suffering that did not lead to redemption. Were the Jews miserable in the Diaspora? Well, soon the Hebrew State would be established and then everything would change for the better. Had the pencil sharpener got lost? Well, tomorrow we'd buy a new and better one. Did we have a bit of a tummy ache today? It would get better before your wedding. And as for the poor, stung bear, whose eyes looked so miserable that my own eyes filled with tears looking at him? Well, here he was on the next page healthy and happy, and he was no longer lazy because he had learned his lesson: he had made a peace treaty with the bees, to the benefit of both sides, and there was even a clause in it granting him a regular supply of honey, admittedly a reasonable, moderate amount, but forever and ever.

And so on the last page the bear looked jolly and smiling, and he was building himself a house, as though after all his exciting adventures he had decided to join the ranks of the middle class. He looked a bit like my father in a good mood: he looked as though he was about to make up a rhyme or pun, or call me Your Honorable Highness ("only in fun!").

All this more or less was written there, in a single line on the last page, and this may actually have been the first line in my life that I read not by the shapes of the words but letter by letter, the proper way, and from now on every letter would be not a picture but a different sound:

TEDDY BEAR IS VERY HAPPY!
TEDDY BEAR IS FULL OF JOY!

Except that within a week or two my hunger had turned into a feeding frenzy. My parents were unable to separate me from books, from morning till evening and beyond.

They were the ones who had pushed me to read, and now they were the sorcerer's apprentice: I was the water that couldn't be stopped. Just come and look, your son is sitting half naked on the floor in the middle of the corridor, if you please, reading. The child is hiding under the table, reading. That crazy child has locked himself in the bathroom again and he's sitting on the toilet reading, if he hasn't fallen in, book and all, and drowned himself. The child was only pretending to fall asleep, he was actually waiting for me to leave, and after I left the room, he waited a few moments, then switched the light on without permission, and now he seems to be sitting with his back against the door so that you and I can't get in, and guess what he's doing. The child can read fluently without vowels. Do you really want to know what he's doing? Well, now the child says he'll just wait for me to finish part of the newspaper. Now we've got another newspaper addict in the house. That child didn't get out of bed the whole weekend, except to go to the toilet. And even then he took his book with him. He reads all day long, indiscriminately, stories by Asher Barash or Shoffmann, one of Pearl Buck's Chinese novels, *The Book of Jewish Traditions, The Travels of Marco Polo, The Adventures of Magellan and Vasco da Gama, Advice for the Elderly in Case of Influenza,* the *Newsletter of the Beit Hakerem District Council, The Kings of Israel and Judah, Notable Events of 1929,* pamphlets about agricultural settlement, back issues of *Working Women's Weekly,* if it goes on like this, he'll soon be eating bindings and drinking compositor's ink. We're going to have to step in and do something. We must put a stop to this: it's already becoming odd and in fact rather worrying.

36

THE BUILDING down Zechariah Street had four apartments. The Nahlielis' apartment was on the first floor, at the back. Its windows overlooked a neglected backyard, partly paved and the other part overgrown with weeds in winter and thistles in summer. The yard also housed washing lines, garbage cans, traces of a bonfire, an old suitcase, a corrugated iron lean-to, and the wooden remains of a ruined sukkah. Pale blue passionflowers bloomed on the wall.

The apartment contained a kitchen, a bathroom, an entrance passage, two rooms, and eight or nine cats. After lunch Isabella, who was a teacher, and her husband Nahlieli the cashier used the first room as their living room, and at night they and their army of cats slept in the tiny second room. They got up early every morning and pushed all the furniture out into the passage and set out three or four school desks in each of the rooms, with three or four benches, each of which could seat two children.

Thus between eight A.M. and noon their home became the Children's Realm Private Elementary School.

There were two classes and two teachers at Children's Realm, which was all the small apartment could hold, with eight pupils in the first grade and another six in the second grade. Isabella Nahlieli was the proprietor of the school and served as headmistress, storekeeper, treasurer, syllabus organizer, sergeant major of discipline, school nurse, maintenance woman, cleaner, class teacher of the first grade, and responsible for all practical activities. We always called her Teacher Isabella.

She was a loud, jolly, broad woman in her forties, with a hairy mole that looked like a stray cockroach above her upper lip. She was irascible, temperamental, strict, yet overflowing with a rough warmheartedness. In her plain loose cotton-print frocks with their many pockets she looked like a thickset, sharp-eyed matchmaker from the shtetl, who could weigh your character, inside and out, with a single look of her experienced eye and a couple of well-aimed questions. In a moment she had got to the bottom of who you were, with all your secrets. While she interrogated you, her raw red hands would be fidgeting restlessly in her innumerable pockets, as though she was just about to pull out the perfect bride for you, or a hairbrush, or some nose drops, or at least a clean hankie to wipe away that embarrassing green booger on the end of your nose.

Teacher Isabella was also a cat herder. Wherever she went, she was surrounded by a flock of admiring cats that got under her feet, clung to the hem of her dress, impeded her progress, and almost tripped her up, so devoted were they to her. They were of every possible color, and they would claw their way up her dress and lie down on her broad shoulders, curl up in the book basket, settle like broody hens on her shoes, and fight among themselves with desperate wails for the privilege of snuggling in her bosom. In her classroom there were more cats than pupils, and they kept perfectly quiet so as not to disturb the students; as tame as dogs, as well brought up as young ladies from good families, they sat on her desk, on her lap, on our little laps, on our satchels, on the windowsill and the box that held equipment for PE, art, and crafts.

Sometimes Teacher Isabella reprimanded the cats or issued orders. She would wave her finger at one or another of them and threaten to tweak its ears or pull its tail out if it did not improve its behavior instantly. The cats, for their part, always obeyed her promptly, unconditionally, and without a murmur. "Zerubbabel, you should be ashamed of yourself!" she would suddenly shout. Immediately some poor wretch would detach himself from the huddled mass on the rug beside her desk and creep away in disgrace, his belly almost touching the floor, his tail between his legs and his ears pressed back, making his way to the corner of the room. All eyes—children's and cats' alike—were fixed on him, witnessing his disgrace. So the accused would crawl into the corner, miserable, humiliated, ashamed of himself, repenting his sins, and perhaps hoping humbly up to the last minute for some miraculous reprieve.

From the corner the poor thing sent us a heartrending look of guilt and supplication.

"You child of the muck heap!" Teacher Isabella snarled at him contemptuously, and then she would pardon him with a wave of her hand:

"All right. That's enough. You can come back now. But just remember that if I catch you once more—"

She had no need to finish her sentence, because the pardoned criminal was already dancing toward her like a suitor, determined to make her head spin with his charms, barely mastering his joy, tail erect, ears pricked forward, with a spring in the pads of his dainty paws, aware of the secret power of his charm and using it to heartbreaking effect, his whiskers gleaming, his coat shiny and bristling slightly, and with a flicker of sanctimonious feline slyness in his glowing eyes, as though he were winking at us while swearing that from now on there would be no more pious or upright cat than he.

Teacher Isabella's cats were schooled to lead productive lives, and indeed they were useful cats. She had trained them to bring her a pencil, some chalk, or a pair of socks from the closet, or to retrieve a stray teaspoon that was lurking under some piece of furniture; to stand at the window and give a wail of recognition if an acquaintance approached, but to issue a cry of alarm at the approach of a stranger. (Most of these wonders we did not witness with our own eyes, but we believed her. We would have believed her if she had told us that her cats could solve crossword puzzles.)

As for Mr. Nahlieli, Teacher Isabella's little husband, we hardly ever saw him. He had usually gone to work before we arrived, and if for any reason he was at home, he had to stay in the kitchen and do his duty there quietly during school hours. If it had not been for the fact that both we and he occasionally had permission to go to the toilet, we would never have discovered that Mr. Nahlieli was actually only Getzel, the pale boy who took the money at the cooperative store. He was nearly twenty years younger than his wife, and if they had wanted to, they could have passed for mother and son.

Occasionally when he had to (or dared to) call out to her during a class, because he had either burned the beef patties or scalded himself, he did not call her Isabella but Mum, which is presumably what her herd of cats also called her. As for her, she called her youthful husband some name taken from the world of birds: Sparrow or Finchy or Thrush or Warbler. Anything except Wagtail, which was the literal meaning of the name Nahlieli.

There were two primary schools within half an hour's walk for a child from our home. One was too socialist, and the other was too religious. The Berl Katznelson House of Education for Workers' Children, at the north end of Haturim Street, flew the red flag of the working class on its roof side by side with the national flag. They celebrated May Day there with processions and ceremonies. The headmaster was called Comrade by teachers and pupils alike. In summer the teachers wore khaki shorts and biblical sandals. In the vegetable garden in the yard pupils were prepared for farming life and personal pioneering in the new villages. In the workshops they learned productive skills such as woodwork, metalwork, building, mending engines and locks, and something vague but fascinating called fine mechanics.

In class the pupils could sit anywhere they liked; boys and girls could even sit together. Most of them wore blue shirts fastened at the chest with the white or red laces of the two youth movements. The boys wore shorts with the legs rolled up as far as the crotch, while the girls' shorts, which were also shamelessly short, were secured to their thighs with elastic. The pupils called the teachers by their first names. They were taught arithmetic, homeland studies, Hebrew and history, but also subjects like the history of Jewish settlement in the Land, history of the workers' movement, principles of collective villages, or key phases in the evolution of the class war. And they sang all kinds of working class anthems, starting with the Internationale and ending with "We are all pioneers" and "The blue shirt is the finest jewel."

The Bible was taught at the House of Education for Workers' Children as a collection of pamphlets on current affairs. The prophets fought for progress and social justice and the welfare of the poor, whereas the kings and priests represented all the iniquities of the existing social order. Young David, the shepherd, was a daring guerrilla fighter in the ranks of a national movement to liberate the Israelites from the Philistine yoke, but in his old age he turned into a colonialist-imperialist king who conquered other countries, subjugated peoples, stole the poor man's ewe-lamb, and ruthlessly exploited the sweat of the working people.

Some four hundred yards away from this red House of Education, in the parallel street, stood the Tachkemoni national-traditional school, founded by the Mizrahi religious Zionist movement, where the pupils were all boys who kept their heads covered during class. Most of the pupils came from poor families, apart from a few who came from the old Sephardi aristocracy, which had been thrust aside by the more assertive Ashkenazi newcomers. The pupils here were addressed only by their surnames, while the teachers were called Mr. Neimann, Mr. Alkalai, and so forth. The headmaster was addressed as Mr. Headmaster. The first lesson every day began with morning prayers, followed by study of the Torah with Rashi's commentary, classes where the skullcapped pupils read the *Ethics of the Fathers* and other works of rabbinic wisdom, the Talmud, the history of the prayers and hymns, all sorts of commandments and good deeds, extracts from the code of Jewish law, the *Shulhan Arukh,* the cycle of the Jewish high days and holidays, the history of the Jewish communities around the world, lives of the great Jewish teachers down the ages, some legends and ethics, some legal discussions, a little poetry by Judah Hallevi or Bialik, and among all this they also taught some Hebrew grammar, mathematics, English, music, history, and elementary geography. The teachers wore jackets even in summer, and the headmaster, Mr. Ilan, always appeared in a three-piece suit.

My mother wanted me to go to the House of Education for Workers' Children from the first grade on, either because she did not approve of the rigorous religious separation of boys and girls or because Tachkemoni, with its heavy old stone buildings, which were built under Turkish rule, seemed antiquated and gloomy compared to the House of

Education for Workers' Children, which had big windows, light, airy classrooms, cheerful beds of vegetables, and a sort of infectious youthful joy. Perhaps it reminded her in some way of the Tarbuth gymnasium in Rovno.

As for my father, he worried himself about the choice. He would have preferred me to go to school with the professors' children in Rehavia or at least with the children of the doctors, teachers, and civil servants who lived in Beit Hakerem, but we were living in times of riots and shooting, and both Rehavia and Beit Hakerem were two bus rides away from our home in Kerem Avraham. Tachkemoni was alien to my father's secular outlook and to his skeptical, enlightened mind. The House of Education, on the other hand, he considered a murky source of leftist indoctrination and proletarian brainwashing. He had no alternative but to weigh the black peril against the red peril and choose the lesser of two evils.

After a difficult period of indecision Father decided, against my mother's choice, to send me to Tachkemoni. He believed that there was no fear that they would turn me into a religious child, because in any case the end of religion was nigh, progress was driving it out fast, and even if they did succeed in turning me into a little cleric there, I would soon go out into the wide world and shake off that archaic dust, I would give up any religious observance just as the religious Jews themselves with their synagogues would disappear off the face of the earth in a few years, leaving nothing behind but a vague folk memory.

The House of Education, on the other hand, presented in Father's view a serious danger. The red tide was on the upsurge in our land, it was sweeping through the whole world, and socialist indoctrination was a one-way road to disaster. If we sent the child there, they would instantly brainwash him and stuff his head full of all sorts of Marxist straw and turn him into a Bolshevik, one of Stalin's little soldiers, they would pack him off to one of their kibbutzim and he would never come back ("None that go into her return again," as Father put it).

But the way to Tachkemoni, which was also the way to the House of Education for Workers' Children, ran along the side of the Schneller Barracks. From sandbagged positions on top of the walls, nervous, Jew-hating, or simply drunken British soldiers sometimes fired on passersby in the street below. Once they opened fire with a machine gun and killed the milkman's donkey because they were afraid that the milk churns were full of explosives, as had happened in the bombing of the King David Hotel. Once or twice British drivers even ran pedestrians over with their jeeps, because they had not got out of the way fast enough.

These were the days after the World War, the days of the underground and terrorism, the blowing up of the British headquarters, infernal devices planted by the Irgun in the basement of the King David Hotel, attacks on CID HQ in Mamilla Road and on army and police installations.

Consequently my parents decided to postpone the frustrating choice between the darkness of the Middle Ages and the Stalinist trap for another two years and send me for the time being to Mrs. Isabella Nahlieli's Children's Realm. The great advantage of her cat-ridden school was that it was literally within hailing distance of our home. You went out of our yard and turned left, passed the entrance to the Lembergs' and Mr. Auster's grocery shop, carefully crossed Amos Street opposite the Zahavis' balcony, went down Zechariah Street for thirty yards, crossed it carefully, and there you were: a wall covered with passionflowers, and a gray-white cat, the sentry cat, announcing your arrival from the window. Up twenty-two steps, and you were hanging up your water bottle on the hook in the entrance to the smallest school in Jerusalem: two classes, two teachers, a dozen pupils, and nine cats.

37

WHEN I FINISHED my year in the first grade, I passed from the volcanic realm of Teacher Isabella the cat herder into the cool, calm hands of Teacher Zelda in the second grade. She had no cats, but a sort of blue-gray aura surrounded her and at once beguiled and fascinated me.

Teacher Zelda talked so softly that if we wanted to hear what she was saying, we not only had to stop talking, we had to lean forward on our desks. Consequently we spent the whole morning leaning forward, because we did not want to miss a word. Everything that Teacher Zelda said was enchanting and rather unexpected. It was as if we were learning another language from her, not very different from Hebrew and yet distinctive and touching. She would call stars the "stars of heaven," the abyss was "the mighty abyss," and she spoke of "turbid rivers" and "nocturnal deserts." If you said something in class that she liked, Teacher Zelda would point to you and say softly: "Look, all of you, there's a child who's flooded with light." If one of the girls was daydreaming, Teacher Zelda explained to us that just as nobody can be blamed for being unable to sleep, so you couldn't hold Noa responsible for being unable to stay awake at times.

Any kind of mockery Teacher Zelda called "poison." A lie she called "a Fall." Laziness was "leaden," and gossip "the eyes of the flesh." She called arrogance "wing-scorching," and giving anything up, even little things like an eraser or your turn to hand out the drawing paper, she called "making sparks." A couple of weeks before the festival of Purim, which was our favorite festival in the whole year, she suddenly announced: There may not be a Purim this year. It may be put out before it gets here.

Put out? A festival? We were all in a panic: we were not only afraid of missing Purim, but we felt a dark dread of these powerful, hidden forces, whose very existence we had not been told about before, that were capable, if they so wished, of lighting or putting out festivals as though they were so many matches.

Teacher Zelda did not bother to go into details but just hinted to us that the decision of whether to extinguish the festival depended mainly on her: she herself was somehow connected to the invisible forces that distinguished between festival and nonfestival, between sacred and profane. So if we didn't want the festival to be put out, we said to each other, it would be best for us to make a special effort to do at least the little we could to make sure Teacher Zelda was in a good mood with us. There is no such thing as a little, Teacher Zelda used to say, to someone who has nothing.

I remember her eyes: alert and brown, secretive, but not happy. Jewish eyes that had a slightly Tatar set to them.

Sometimes she would cut the lesson short and send everyone out into the yard to play, but keep back a couple of us who were found worthy to continue. The exiles in the yard were not so much pleased at the free time as jealous of the elect.

And sometimes when time was up, when Teacher Isabella's class had long been sent home, when the cats, set free, had spread all over the apartment, the staircase, and the yard, and only we seemed forgotten under the wings of Teacher Zelda's stories, leaning forward on our desks so as not to miss a word, an anxious mother, still wearing her apron, would come and stand in the doorway, hands on her hips, and wait at first impatiently, then with surprise that turned into curiosity, as though she too had become a little girl full of wonderment, reaching out, with the rest of us, to hear and not miss what would happen at the end of the story to the lost cloud, the unloved cloud whose cloak had got caught on the rays of the golden star.

If you said in class that you had something to say to everyone, even in the middle of a lesson, Teacher Zelda would immediately seat you on her own desk, while she sat down on your little bench. So she would promote you in a single wonderful bound to the role of teacher, on condition that the story you told made sense, or that you had an interesting argument to put forward. So long as you managed to hold her interest, or the class's, you could go on sitting in the saddle. If, on the other hand, you said something stupid or were just trying to attract attention, if you did not really have anything to say, then Teacher Zelda would cut in, in her coldest, quietest voice, a voice that brooked no levity:

"But that's very silly."

Or:

"That's enough of playing the fool."

Or even:

"Stop it: you're just lowering yourself in our estimation."

So you went back to your place covered with shame and confusion.

We quickly learned to be careful. Silence is golden. Best not to steal the show if you have nothing sensible to say. True, it was pleasant and could even go to your head, to be raised up above the others and sit on the teacher's desk, but the fall could be swift and painful. Poor taste or overcleverness could lead to humiliation. It was important to prepare before any public utterance. You should always think twice, and ask yourself if you would not be better off keeping quiet.

She was my first love. An unmarried woman in her thirties, Teacher Zelda, Miss Schneersohn. I was not quite eight, and she swept me away, she set in motion some kind of inner metronome that had not stirred before and has not stopped since.

When I woke up in the morning, I conjured up her image even be-fore my eyes were open. I dressed and ate my breakfast in a flash, eager to finish, zip up, shut, pick up, run straight to her. My head melted with the effort to prepare something new and interesting for her every day so that I would get the light of her look and so that she would point to me and say, "Look, there's a boy among us this morning who's flooded with light."

I sat in her class each morning dizzy with love. Or sooty with jeal-ousy. I was constantly trying to discover what charms of mine would draw her favors to me. I was always plotting how to frustrate the charms of the others and get between them and her.

At noon I would come home from school, lie down on my bed, and imagine how just she and I—

I loved the color of her voice and the smell of her smile and the rustle of her dresses (long-sleeved and usually brown or navy or gray, with a simple string of ivory-colored beads or occasionally a discreet silk scarf). At the end of the day I would close my eyes, pull the blanket up over my head, and take her with me. In my dreams I hugged her, and she kissed me on my forehead. An aura of light surrounded her and il-luminated me too, to make me a boy who's flooded with light.

Of course, I already knew what love was. I had devoured so many books, books for children, books for teenagers, and even books that were considered unsuitable for me. Just as every child loves his mother and father, so everyone falls in love, when he is a little older, with some-one from outside the family. Someone who was a stranger before, but suddenly, like finding a treasure in a cave in the Tel Arza woods, the lover's life is different. And I knew from the books that in love, as in sick-ness, you neither eat nor sleep. And I really did not eat much, although I slept very well at night, and during the day I waited for it to get dark so I could go to sleep. This sleep did not match the symptoms of love as described in the books, and I was not quite sure if I was in love the way grown-ups are, in which case I should have suffered from insomnia, or if my love was still a childish love.

And I knew from the books and from the films I had seen at the Edi-son Cinema and simply out of the air that beyond falling in love, like beyond the Mountains of Moab, which we could see from Mount Sco-pus, there was another, rather terrifying, landscape, not visible from here, and it was probably just as well that it wasn't. There was something lurking there, something furry, shameful, something that belonged in the darkness. Something that belonged to that picture I had tried so hard to forget (and yet also to remember some detail of it that I had not managed to get a good look at), the photo that the Italian prisoner showed me that time through the barbed-wire fence, and I ran away almost before I'd seen it. It also belonged to items of women's clothing that we boys didn't have and neither did the girls in our class yet. In the darkness there was something else living and moving, stirring, and it was moist and full of hair, something that on the one hand it was much better for me not to know anything about but on the other hand if I didn't know anything about it, it followed that my love was nothing more than that of a child.

A child's love is something different, it doesn't hurt and it's not embarrassing, like Yoavi with Noa or Ben-Ammi with Noa or even like Noa with Avner's brother. But in my case it wasn't a girl in my class or someone from the neighborhood, a girl of my own age or just a little older, like Yoezer's big sister: I had fallen in love with a woman. And it was much worse, because she was a teacher. My class teacher. And there was no one in the whole world I could approach and ask about it without being made fun of. She called mockery poison. Lying she regarded as falling. She called disappointment sorrow, or dreamers' sorrow. And arrogance was certainly wing-scorching. And she actually called being ashamed the image of God.

And what about me, whom she sometimes used to point to in class and call a boy flooded with light, and who now, because of her, was flooded with darkness?

All of a sudden I didn't want to go to Children's Realm school anymore. I wanted to go to a real school, with classrooms and a bell and a playground, not in the Nahlielis' apartment with its swarms of cats everywhere, even in the toilet, that clung to your body under your clothes, and without the perpetual smell of old cats' pee that had dried under some piece of furniture. A real school, where the head teacher didn't suddenly come up and pull a booger out of your nose and wasn't married to a cashier in a cooperative store, and where I wouldn't be called flooded with light. A school without falling in love and that sort of thing.

And indeed, after a row between my parents, a whispered row in Russian, a *tichtikhchavoyniy* kind of row, which Father apparently won, it was decided that at the end of the second grade, when I finished at Children's Realm, after the summer holiday, I would start in the third grade at Tachkemoni, and not at the House of Education for Workers' Children: of the two evils, the red was worse than the black.

But between me and Tachkemoni there still stretched a whole summer of love.

"What are you off to Teacher Zelda's house again for? At half past seven in the morning? Don't you have any friends of your own age?"

"But she invited me. She said I could come whenever I liked. Even every morning."

"That's very nice. But just you tell me, please, don't you think it's a little unnatural for an eight-year-old child to be tied to his teacher's apron strings? His ex-teacher, in fact? Every day? At seven o'clock in the morning? In the summer holidays? Don't you think that's overdoing it a bit? Isn't it a bit impolite? Think about it please. Rationally!"

I shifted my weight from one foot to the other, impatiently, waiting for the sermon to be finished, and I blurted out: "Fine, all right! I'll think about it! Rationally!"

I was already running as I spoke, borne on eagles' wings to the yard of her ground-floor apartment on Zephaniah Street, across the road from the No. 3 bus stop, opposite Mrs. Hassia's kindergarten, behind the milkman Mr. Langermann, with his big iron milk churns, which came to our gloomy little streets straight from the highlands of Galilee "from the sun-drenched plains, with the dew beneath us and the moon overhead." But the moon was here: Teacher Zelda was the moon. Up there in the Valleys and Sharon and Galilee there stretched the lands of the sun, the realm of those tough, tanned pioneers. Not here. Here in Zephaniah Street even on a summer morning there was still the shadow of a moonlit night.

I was standing outside her window before eight every morning, with my hair plastered down with some water and my clean shirt tucked neatly into the top of my shorts. I had willingly volunteered to help her with her morning chores. I ran off to the shops for her, swept the yard, watered her geraniums, hung her little washing out on the line and brought in the clothes that had dried, fished a letter for her out of the letter box, whose lock was rusted up. She offered me a glass of water, which she called not simply water but limpid water. The gentle west wind she called the "westerly," and when it stirred the pine needles, it dabbled among them.

When I had finished the few household chores, we would take two rush stools out into the backyard and sit under Teacher Zelda's window facing north toward the Police Training School and the Arab village of Shuafat. We traveled without moving. Being a map child, I knew that beyond the mosque of Nebi Samwil, which was on top of the farthest and highest hills on the horizon, was the valley of Beit Horon, and I knew that beyond it were the territories of Benjamin and Ephraim, Samaria, and then the Mountains of Gilboa, and after them the Valleys, Mount Tabor and Galilee. I had never been to those places: once or twice a year we went to Tel Aviv for one of the festivals; twice I had been to Grandma-Mama and Grandpa-Papa's tar-papered shack on the edge of Kiryat Motskin behind Haifa, once I went to Bat Yam, and apart from that I had not seen anything. Certainly not the wonderful places that Teacher Zelda described to me in words, the stream of Harod, the mountains of Safed, the shores of Kinneret.

The summer after our summer, Jerusalem would be shelled from the tops of the hills facing which we sat all through the morning. Next to the village of Beit Iksa and by the hill of Nebi Samwil the guns of the British artillery battery, which was at the service of the Transjordanian Arab Legion, would be dug in and would rain thousands of shells on the besieged and starving city. And many years later all the hilltops we could see would be covered with densely packed housing, Ramot Eshkol, Ramot Alon, Ma'alot Dafna, Ammunition Hill, Giv'at Hamivtar, French Hill, "and all the hills shall melt." But in the summer of 1947 they were all still abandoned rocky hills, slopes dappled with patches of light rock and dark bushes. Here and there the eye lingered over a solitary, stubborn old pine tree, bent by the powerful winter winds that had bowed its back forever.

She would read to me what she might have been intending to read anyway that morning: Hasidic tales, rabbinic legends, obscure stories about holy kabbalists who succeeded in combining the letters of the alphabet and working wonders and miracles. Sometimes, if they did not take all the necessary precautions, while these mystics were endeavoring to save their own souls or those of the poor and oppressed or even those of the entire Jewish people, they caused terrible disasters that always resulted from an error in the combinations or a single grain of impurity that got into the sacred formulae of mental direction.

She replied to my questions with strange, unexpected answers. Sometimes they seemed quite wild, threatening to undermine in a terrifying way my father's firm rules of logic.

Sometimes, however, she surprised me by giving me an answer that was predictable, simple yet as nutritious as black bread. Even the most expected things came out of her mouth in an unexpected way, though. And I loved her and was fascinated by her, because there was something strange and disturbing, almost frightening, in virtually everything she said and did. Like the "poor in spirit," of whom she said that they belong to Jesus of Nazareth but that there is a lot of poverty of spirit among us Jews here in Jerusalem too, and not necessarily in the sense that "That Man" intended. Or the "dumb of spirit" who appear in Bialik's poem "May My Lot Be with You," who are actually the thirty-six hidden just men who keep the universe in existence. Another time she read me Bialik's poem about his pure-spirited father whose life was mired in the squalor of the taverns but who was himself untouched by squalor and impurity. It was only his son the poet who was touched by them, and how, as Bialik himself writes in the first two lines of "My Father," in which he talks only about himself and his impurity, even before he moves on to tell us about his father. She found it strange that scholars had not noticed that the poem about the pure life of the father actually opens with such a bitter confession about the impurity of the son's life.

Or maybe she did not say all this; after all, I didn't sit there with a pencil and notebook writing down everything she said to me. And more than fifty years have passed since then. Much of what I heard from Zelda that summer was beyond my comprehension. But day by day she raised the crossbar of my comprehension. I remember, for example, that she told me about Bialik, about his childhood, his disappointments, and his unfulfilled yearnings. Even things that were beyond my years. Among other poems she certainly read "My Father" to me, and talked to me about cycles of purity and impurity.

———

But what precisely did she say?

Now in my study in Arad on a summer day at the end of June 2001 I am trying to reconstruct, or rather to guess, to conjure up, almost to create out of nothing: like those paleontologists in the natural history museum who can reconstruct a whole dinosaur on the basis of two or three bones.

I loved the way Teacher Zelda placed one word next to another. Sometimes she would put an ordinary, everyday word next to another word that was also quite ordinary, and all of a sudden, simply because they were next to each other, two ordinary words that did not normally stand next to each other, a sort of electric spark jumped between them and took my breath away.

> For the first time I am thinking
> about a night when the constellations are only a rumor . . .

That summer Zelda was still unmarried, but sometimes a man appeared in the yard; he did not look young to me, and his appearance marked him out as a religious Jew. As he passed between us, he tore unawares the mass of invisible morning webs that had spun themselves between the two of us. Sometimes he shot me a nod with the fag end of a smile, and standing with his back to me, he had a conversation with Teacher Zelda that lasted seven years, if not seventy-seven. And in Yiddish, so that I should not understand a single word. Once or twice he even managed to draw out of her a peal of girlish laughter such as I had never managed to extract from her. Not even in my dreams. In my despair I conjured up a detailed image of the noisy cement mixer that had been stirring away at the bottom of Malachi Street for several days: I would hurl the body of this jester into the belly of that mixer at dawn, after murdering him at midnight.

I was a word child. A ceaseless, tireless talker. Even before my eyes opened in the morning, I had embarked on an oration that continued almost without interruption until lights out in the evening, and beyond, into my sleep.

But I had no one to listen to me. To the other children of my age everything I said sounded like Swahili or Double Dutch, while as for the grown-ups, they were all delivering lectures too, just like me, from morning till night, none of them listening to the others. Nobody listened to anybody else in Jerusalem in those days. And perhaps they did not even really listen to themselves (apart from good old Grandpa Alexander, who could listen attentively, and even derived a lot of pleasure from what he heard, but he listened only to ladies, not to me).

Consequently there was not a single ear in the whole world open to listen to me, except very rarely. And even if anyone did deign to listen to me, they got tired of me after two or three minutes, although they politely pretended to go on listening and even feigned enjoyment.

Only Zelda, my teacher, listened to me. Not like a kindly aunt wearily lending an experienced ear out of pity to a frantic youngster who had suddenly boiled over on her. No, she listened to me slowly and seriously, as if she was learning things from me that pleased her or aroused her curiosity.

Furthermore, Zelda, my teacher, did me the honor of gently fanning my flames when she wanted me to speak, putting twigs on my bonfire, but when she had had enough, she did not hesitate to say:

"That's enough for now. Please stop talking."

Other people stopped listening after three minutes but let me go prattling on to my heart's content for an hour or more, all the time pretending to listen while they thought their own thoughts.

All this was after the end of the second grade, after I'd finished at Children's Realm School and before I started at Tachkemoni. I was only eight, but I had already got into the habit of reading newspapers, newsletters, and all sorts of magazines, on top of the hundred or two hundred books I had devoured by then (almost anything that fell into my hands, quite indiscriminately: I scoured my father's library and whenever I found a book written in modern Hebrew, I dug my teeth into it and took it off to gnaw on it in my corner).

I wrote poetry too: about Hebrew battalions, about the underground fighters, about Joshua the conqueror, even about a squashed beetle or the sadness of autumn. I presented these poems to Zelda, my teacher, in the morning, and she handled them carefully, as though conscious of her responsibility. What she said about each poem I don't remember. In fact, I have forgotten the poems.

But I do remember what she said to me about poems and sounds: not the sound of voices from above speaking to the poet's soul, but about the different sounds that various words make: "rustling," for example, is a whispering word, "strident" is a screeching word, "growl" has a deep, thick sound, while "tone" has a delicate sound and the word "noise" is itself noisy. And so forth. She had a whole repertoire of words and their sounds, and I am asking more of my memory now than it is capable of yielding.

I may also have heard this from Zelda, my teacher, that summer when we were close: if you want to draw a tree, just draw a few leaves. You don't need to draw them all. If you draw a man, you don't have to draw every hair. But in this she was not consistent: one time she would say that at such and such a place I had written a bit too much, while another time she would say that actually I should have written a little more. But how do you tell? I am still looking for an answer to this day.

Teacher Zelda also revealed a Hebrew language to me that I had never encountered before, not in Professor Klausner's house or at home or in the street or in any of the books I had read so far, a strange, anarchic Hebrew, the Hebrew of stories of saints, Hasidic tales, folk sayings, Hebrew leavened with Yiddish, breaking all the rules, confusing masculine and feminine, past and present, pronouns and adjectives, a sloppy, even disjointed Hebrew. But what vitality those tales had! In a story about snow, the writing itself seemed to be formed of icy words. In a story about fires, the words themselves blazed. And what a strange, hypnotic sweetness there was in her tales about all sorts of miraculous deeds! As though the writer had dipped his pen in wine: the words reeled and staggered in your mouth.

Teacher Zelda also opened up books of poetry to me that summer, books that were really, but really, unsuitable for someone of my age: poems by Leah Goldberg, Uri Tzvi Greenberg, Yocheved Bat-Miriam, Esther Raab, and Y. Z. Rimon.

It was from her that I learned that there are some words that need to have total silence all around them, to give them enough space, just as when you hang pictures there are some that cannot abide having neighbors.

I learned a great deal from her, in class and also in her courtyard. Apparently she did not mind sharing some of her secrets with me.

Only some of them, though. For instance, I had not the slightest idea, and she never gave me the faintest hint, that besides being my teacher, my beloved, she was also Zelda the poet, some of whose poems had been published in literary supplements and in one or two obscure magazines. I did not know that, like me, she was an only child. Nor did I know that she was related to a famous dynasty of Hasidic rabbis, that she was a first cousin of the Lubavitcher Rebbe, Menachem Mendel Schneersohn (their fathers were brothers). And I did not know that she had also studied drawing, or that she belonged to a drama group, or that even then she enjoyed a modest reputation among small circles of poetry lovers. I did not imagine that my rival, her other suitor, was Rabbi Chayim Mishkowsky, or that two years after our summer, hers and mine, he would marry her. I knew almost nothing about her.

At the beginning of the autumn in 1947 I entered the third grade of the Tachkemoni Religious Boys' School. New thrills filled my life. And anyway, it wasn't appropriate for me to go on being tied like a baby to the skirts of a teacher from the elementary classes: neighbors were raising their eyebrows, their children had begun to make fun of me, and I even made fun of myself. What's wrong with you that you keep running to her every morning? What will you look like when the whole neighborhood starts talking about the crazy little boy who takes down her washing and sweeps her yard and probably even dreams of marrying her in the middle of the night when the stars are shining?

A few weeks after that, violent clashes broke out in Jerusalem, then came the war, the shelling, the siege and starvation. I drifted away from Teacher Zelda. I no longer ran around at seven o'clock in the morning, washed and scrubbed with my hair plastered down, to sit with her in her yard. I no longer took her poems I had written the night before. If we met in the street, I would mumble hurriedly, "Good morning, how are you, Teacher Zelda," without a question mark, and run away without waiting for an answer. I was ashamed of everything that had happened. And I was also ashamed of the way I had ditched her so suddenly, without even bothering to tell her I had ditched her and without even offering an explanation. And I was ashamed of her thoughts, because she must surely know that in my thoughts I had not ditched her yet.

After that we were finally freed from Kerem Avraham. We moved to Rehavia, the area my father had dreamed of. Then my mother died and I went to live and work in the kibbutz. I wanted to leave Jerusalem behind me once and for all. All the links were severed. Now and then I would come across a poem by Zelda in a magazine and so I knew that she was still alive and that she was still a person with feelings. But after my mother's death I had recoiled from all feelings, and I especially wanted to put a distance between myself and women with feelings. In general.

The year my third book, *My Michael*, the action of which takes place more or less in our neighborhood, was published, Zelda's first collection, *Leisure*, also appeared. I thought of writing her a few words to congratulate her, but I didn't. I thought of sending her my book, but I didn't. How could I know if she still lived in Zephaniah Street or if she had moved somewhere else? In any case, I had written *My Michael* to draw a line between myself and Jerusalem, not to reconnect with her. Among the poems in *Leisure* I discovered Teacher Zelda's family and I also met some of our neighbors. Then two more books of poems appeared, *The Invisible Carmel* and *Neither Mountain nor Fire*, which aroused the love of thousands of readers and earned her eminent literary prizes and salvos of acclaim, which Teacher Zelda, a solitary woman, seems to have dodged, and to which she appeared indifferent.

All Jerusalem in my childhood, in the last years of British rule, sat at home and wrote. Hardly anyone had a radio in those days, and there was no television nor video nor CD player nor Internet nor e-mail, not even the telephone. But everyone had a pencil and a notebook.

The whole town was locked indoors at eight o'clock in the evening because of the British curfew, and on evenings when there was no curfew, Jerusalem locked itself in of its own accord, and nothing stirred outside except the wind, the alley cats, and the puddles of light from the street lamps. And even these hid themselves in the shadows whenever an English jeep went past, patrolling the streets with its searchlight and its gun. The evenings were longer because the sun and the moon moved more slowly, and the electric light was dim because everyone was poor: they saved on bulbs and they saved on lighting. And sometimes the power was cut off for several hours or several days, and life continued by the light of sooty paraffin lamps or candles. The winter rains were also much stronger than they are now, and with them the fists of the wind and the echoes of the thunder and lightning also beat on the barred shutters.

We had a nightly ritual of locking up. Father would go outside to close the shutters (they could be closed only from the outside); bravely he went out into the jaws of the rain and the dark and the unknown perils of the night, like those shaggy Stone Age men who used to emerge boldly from their warm caves to look for food or to defend their women and children, or like the fisherman in *The Old Man and the Sea,* so Father went out on his own to brave the ferocious elements, covering his head with an empty bag as he confronted the unknown.

Each evening, when he returned from Operation Shutters, he locked the front door from the inside and put the bar in place: iron brackets were set into both doorposts, and into those Father fixed the flat iron bar that guarded the door against marauders or invaders. The thick stone walls defended us from evil, along with the iron shutters, and the dark mountain that stood heavily just on the other side of our back wall, guarding us like a gigantic, taciturn wrestler. The whole outside world was locked out, and inside our armored cabin there were just the three of us, the stove, and the walls covered with books upon books from floor to ceiling. So the whole apartment was sealed off every evening and slowly sank, like a submarine, beneath the surface of the winter. Because right next to us the world suddenly ended: you turned left outside the front yard, two hundred yards farther on at the end of Amos Street you turned left again, you walked three hundred yards as far as the last house on Zephaniah Street, and that was also the end of the road and the end of the city and the end of the world. Beyond that there were just empty rocky slopes in the thick darkness, ravines, caves, bare mountains, valleys, dark rain-swept stone villages: Lifta, Shuafat, Beit Iksa, Beit Hanina, Nebi Samwil.

And so each evening all the residents of Jerusalem locked themselves away in their homes like us, and wrote. The professors and scholars in Rehavia, Talpiot, Beit Hakerem, and Kiriat Shemuel, the poets and writers, the ideologues, the rabbis, the revolutionaries, the apocalypticists, and the intellectuals. If they did not write books, they wrote articles. If they did not write articles, they wrote verses or composed all sorts of pamphlets and leaflets. If they did not write illegal wall posters against the British, they wrote letters to the newspaper. Or letters to each other. The whole of Jerusalem sat each evening bent over a sheet of paper, correcting, erasing, writing, and polishing. Uncle Joseph and Mr. Agnon, on either side of their little street in Talpiot. Grandpa Alexander and Teacher Zelda. Mr. Zarchi, Mr. Abramski, Professor Buber, Professor Scholem, Professor Bergman, Mr. Toren, Mr. Netanyahu, Mr. Wislawski, and perhaps even my mother. My father researched and laid bare Sanskrit motifs that had crept into the Lithuanian national epic, or Homeric influences on White Russian poetry. As though he were raising a periscope from our little submarine at night and looking toward Danzig or Slovakia. Our neighbor to the right, Mr. Lemberg, sat and wrote his memoirs in Yiddish, while our neighbors to the left, the Bukhovskis, probably also wrote each evening, and the Rosendorffs upstairs and the Stichs across the road. Only the mountain, the neighbor beyond our back wall, always kept silent and did not write a single line.

Books were the slender lifeline that attached our submarine to the outside world. We were surrounded on all sides by mountains, caves, and deserts, the British, the Arabs, and the underground fighters, salvos of machine-gun fire in the night, explosions, ambushes, arrests, house-to-house searches, stifled dread of what awaited us in the days to come. Among all these the slender lifeline still wound its way to the real world. In the real world there were the lake and the forest, the cottage, the field and the meadow, and also the palace with its turrets, cornices, and gables. There the foyer, embellished with gold, velvet, and crystal, was lit by chandeliers with a mass of lights like the seven heavens.

In those years, as I said, I hoped I would grow up to be a book.

Not a writer but a book. And that was from fear.

Because it was slowly dawning on those whose families had not arrived in Israel that the Germans had killed them all. There was fear in Jerusalem, but people tried as hard as they could to bury it deep inside their chests. Rommel's tanks had reached almost to the gateway of the Land of Israel. Italian planes had bombed Tel Aviv and Haifa during the war. And who knew what the British might do to us before they left?

And after they had left, hordes of bloodthirsty Arabs, millions of fanatical Muslims, would be bound to butcher the whole lot of us in a few days. They would not leave a single child alive.

Naturally the grown-ups tried hard not to talk about these horrors in the presence of children. At any rate, not in Hebrew. But sometimes a word slipped through, or somebody cried out in his sleep. All our apartments were as tiny and cramped as cages. In the evening after lights out I could hear them whispering in the kitchen, over tea and biscuits, and I caught Chelmno, Nazis, Vilna, partisans, *Aktionen,* death camps, death trains, Uncle David and Aunt Malka and little cousin David who was the same age as me.

Somehow the fear got into me. Children of your age don't always grow up. Sometimes bad people come and kill them in the cradle, or in kindergarten. In Nehemiah Street once there was a bookbinder who had a nervous breakdown, and he went out on his balcony and screamed, Jews, help, hurry, soon they'll burn us all. The air was heavy with dread. And I may have already gathered how easy it is to kill people.

Books are not difficult to burn either, it's true, but if I grew up to be a book, there was a good chance that at least one copy might manage to survive, if not here then in some other country, in some city, in some remote library, in a corner of some godforsaken bookcase. After all, I had seen with my own eyes how books manage to hide in the dusty darkness between the crowded rows, underneath heaps of offprints and journals, or find a hiding place behind other books—

38

SOME THIRTY years later, in 1976, I was invited to spend a couple of months in Jerusalem and give some guest lectures at the Hebrew University. I was offered a studio room in the campus on Mount Scopus, and every morning I sat and wrote the story "Mr. Levi" in *The Hill of Evil Counsel.* The story takes place on Zephaniah Street at the end of the British Mandate, and so I went for a walk on Zephaniah Street and the adjoining streets, to see what had changed since then. The Children's Realm Private School had long since closed. The yards were full of junk. The fruit trees had died. The teachers, clerks, translators, and cashiers, bookbinders, domestic intellectuals, and writers of letters to the newspaper had mostly disappeared, and the district had filled up over the years with poor ultra-Orthodox Jews. Almost all our neighbors' names had disappeared from the letter boxes. The only familiar person I saw was Mrs. Stich, the invalid mother of Menuchele Stich, the girl with the stoop that we called Nemuchele, "Shortie"; I caught sight of her in the distance, sitting dozing on a stool in an out-of-the-way yard, not far from the garbage cans. Every wall was festooned with strident handbills that waved puny fists in the air and threatened sinners with various forms of unnatural death: "The bounds of modesty have been breached," "We have suffered a great loss," "Touch not mine anointed," "Stones cry out from the wall for the evil decree," "Heavens behold the dreadful abomination the like of which has never been seen in Israel," and so forth.

For thirty years I had not set eyes on my teacher from the second grade in Children's Realm Private School, and now here I was suddenly standing on her doorstep. Instead of the dairy that belonged to Mr. Langermann, who used to sell us milk out of heavy round metal milk churns, the front of the building was occupied now by an ultra-Orthodox shop selling all kinds of haberdashery, cloth, buttons, fasteners, zippers, and curtain hooks. Surely Teacher Zelda didn't live here anymore?

But there was her letter box, the one out of which I used to fish her mail when I was little, because the lock had rusted up and it was impossible to open it. Now the door hung open: somebody, certainly a man, must have been more impatient than Teacher Zelda and me, and had smashed the lock once and for all. The wording had changed too: instead of "Zelda Schneersohn" it now said "Schneersohn Mishkowsky." No more Zelda, but no hyphen or "and" either. And what would I do if it was her husband who opened the door to me? What could I say to him? Or to her?

I almost turned tail and fled, like a startled suitor in a comedy film. (I hadn't known she was married, or that she had been widowed, I had not worked it out that I was eight when I left her apartment and now I was thirty-seven, older than she had been when I left her.)

This time, as then, it was quite early in the morning.

I really should have phoned her before coming to see her. Or written her a note. Perhaps she was angry with me? Perhaps she had not forgiven me for walking out on her? For this long silence? For not congratulating her on either the publication of her books or the literary prizes she had won? Perhaps, like some other Jerusalemites, she resented my spitting in the well from which I had drunk, in *My Michael.* Suppose she had changed beyond recognition? What if she was an entirely different woman now, twenty-nine years later?

I stood in front of the door for some ten minutes, I went out into the yard, I smoked a cigarette or two, I touched the washing lines from which I once used to pluck her modest brown or gray skirts. I identified the cracked paving stone that I cracked myself once when I tried to break almonds open with a stone. And I looked out beyond the red roofs of the Bukharian Quarter, toward the desolate hills there used be to the north. Now, though, the hills were no longer desolate but smothered in housing developments: Ramot Eshkol, Ma'alot Dafna, Givat Hamivtar, French Hill, and Ammunition Hill.

But what should I say to her? Hello, Dear Teacher Zelda? I hope I'm not disturbing you. My name is, ahem, such and such? Good morning Mrs. Schneersohn-Mishkowsky? I was a pupil of yours once, I don't know if you remember? Excuse me, may I take just a few minutes of your time? I like your poetry? You still look marvelous? No, I haven't come to interview you?

I must have forgotten how dark little ground-floor apartments in Jerusalem could be, even on a summer morning. Darkness opened the door to me: darkness full of brown smells. And out of the darkness the fresh voice that I remembered, the voice of a confident girl who loved words, said to me:

"Come on in, Amos."

And immediately afterward:

"You probably want us to sit outside in the yard?"

And then:

"You like your iced lemonade weak."

And then:

"I have to correct myself: you used to like your lemonade weak. But maybe there has been a change since then?"

Naturally I am reconstructing that morning and our conversation from memory—like trying to restore an ancient ruined building on the basis of seven or eight stones that are still left standing. But among the few stones left standing exactly as they were, neither reconstructed nor invented, are these words: "I have to correct myself: . . . But maybe there has been a change since then?" That is exactly what Zelda said to me on that summer morning in late June 1976. Twenty-nine years after our honey summer. And twenty-five years before the summer morning that I am writing this page (in my study in Arad, in an exercise book full of crossings out, on July 30, 2001: this is therefore a recollection of a visit that was also meant, in its day, to conjure up a recollection or to scratch at old wounds. In all these recollections, my task is a bit like that of someone trying to build something out of old stones that he is digging out of the ruins of something that was also, in its day, built out of stones from a ruin).

"I have to correct myself," Teacher Zelda said. "Maybe there has been a change since then?"

She could have said it in so many different ways. For instance, she might have said: Maybe you don't like lemonade anymore? Or: Maybe you like it very strong now? Or she might have asked, quite simply: What would you like to drink?

She was a person of precision. Her intention was to allude at once, happily, without a hint of bitterness, to our private past, hers and mine (lemonade, not too strong), but to do so without subordinating the present to the past ("Maybe there has been a change since then?"—with a question mark—thus offering me the choice, and also shouldering me with the responsibility for the continuation, for the rest of the visit. Which I had initiated).

I said (certainly not without a smile):

"Thank you. I'd love to have some lemonade like before."

She said:

"That's what I thought, but I felt I ought to ask."

Then we both drank iced lemonade (instead of the icebox there was now a little refrigerator, an obsolete model that was showing signs of its age). We reminisced. She had indeed read my books, and I had read hers, but we passed over all that in five or six sentences, as though hurrying past an unsafe stretch of road.

We talked about what had happened to the Nahlielis, Isabella and Getzel. About other common acquaintances. About the changes that had taken place in Kerem Avraham. My parents and her late husband, who had passed away some five years before my visit, we also mentioned at a run, then went back to walking pace to talk about Agnon and perhaps also about Thomas Wolfe (*Look Homeward, Angel* was translated into Hebrew around that time, although it is possible that we had both read it in English). As my eyes became accustomed to the darkness, I was amazed to see how little the apartment had changed. The dreary brown dresser with its thick coat of varnish was still crouching in its usual corner like an old dog. The china tea set still dozed behind its glass panes. On the dresser there were photographs of Zelda's parents, who looked younger than she did, and a picture of a man who I imagined must be her husband, but I still asked who he was. Her eyes suddenly lit up and sparkled mischievously; she grinned at me as though we had just done something naughty together, then she pulled herself together and said simply:

"That's Chayim."

The round brown table seemed to have shrunk over the years. In the bookcase there were old prayer books in battered dark covers, and a few big new religious books in splendid leather bindings with gold tooling, as well as Schirmann's history of Hebrew poetry in Spain, a lot of books of poetry and modern Hebrew novels, and a row of paperbacks. When I was a child, this bookcase had loomed very, very large; now it only loomed shoulder-height. On the dresser and various shelves there were silver Sabbath candlesticks, a number of Hanukkah lamps, little ornaments made of olive wood or copper, and a sad potted plant on the chest of drawers and a couple more on the windowsill. The whole scene was dominated by a dim light saturated with brown smells: it was unmistakably the room of a religious woman. Not an ascetic place, but one that was withdrawn and reserved, and also somehow depressing. There had indeed been, as she had put it, a change. Not because she had aged, or because she had become loved and famous, but perhaps because she had become earnest.

Yet she had always been a person of precision, earnestness, and inner seriousness. It's hard to explain.

I never saw her again after that morning. I heard that she finally moved to a new area. I heard that over the years she had a number of close women friends who were younger than herself and younger than me. I heard that she had cancer, and that one Friday night in 1984 she died in terrible pain. But I never went back to see her, I never wrote to her, I never sent her any of my books, and I never set eyes on her again except a couple of times in literary supplements and once more, on the day of her death, for less than half a minute, toward the end of the TV news (and I wrote about her, and her room, in *The Same Sea*).

When I stood up to go, it turned out that the ceiling had become lower over the years. It almost touched my head.

The years had not changed her much. She had not become ugly, or fat, or shriveled, the lightning of her eyes still flashed out occasionally while we talked, like a beam sent to search all my hidden recesses. Yet even so, something had changed. As though over the decades that I had not seen her, Teacher Zelda had grown to resemble her old-fashioned apartment.

She was like a silver candlestick, like a candlestick glowing dimly in a dark void. And I should like to be as precise here as it is possible to be: in that last meeting Zelda seemed to me like the candle, the candlestick, and the dark void.

39

EVERY MORNING, a little before or a little after sunrise, I am in the habit of going out to discover what is new in the desert. The desert begins here in Arad at the end of our road. An easterly morning breeze comes from the direction of the Mountains of Edom, stirring little eddies of sand here and there that try unsuccessfully to rise up from the ground. Each of them struggles, loses its whirlwind shape, and dies down. The hills themselves are still hidden by the mist that comes up from the Dead Sea and covers the rising sun and the highlands with a gray veil, as though it were autumn already instead of summer. But it is a false autumn: in another couple of hours it will be dry and hot again here. Like yester-day. Like the day before yesterday, like a week ago, like a month ago.

In the meantime the cool of the night is still holding its own. There is a pleasant smell of dust that has soaked up a lot of dew, blended with a faint smell of sulfur, goat droppings, thistles, and dead campfires. This is the smell of the Land of Israel from time immemorial. I go down into the wadi and advance along a winding path to the edge of the cliff from which I have a view of the Dead Sea, nearly three thousand feet below, fifteen and a half miles away. The shadow of the hills to the east falls on the water and gives it the color of old copper. Here and there a sharp needle of light manages to pierce the cloud for a moment and touch the sea. The sea responds with a dazzling shimmer, as though there is an electric storm raging under the surface.

From here to there stretch empty slopes of limestone dappled with black rocks. Among these rocks, exactly on the horizon at the top of the hill facing me, suddenly there are three black goats and with them a human figure standing motionlessly draped in black from head to foot. A Bedouin woman? And is that a dog next to her? And suddenly they've all disappeared beyond the line of the hills, the woman, the goats, and the dog. The gray light casts doubt on every movement. Meanwhile other dogs give voice in the distance. A little farther on, among the rocks by the side of the path, lies a rusty shell casing. How did it end up here? Maybe one night a camel caravan of smugglers passed here on their way from Sinai to the southern part of Mount Hebron, and one of the smugglers lost the shell casing, or threw it away after wondering what he would do with it.

Now you can hear the full depths of the desert silence. It isn't the quiet before the storm, or the silence of the end of the world, but a silence that only covers another, even deeper, silence. I stand there for three or four minutes inhaling silence like a smell. Then I turn back. I walk back up from the wadi to the end of my road, arguing with an angry chorus of dogs that start barking at me from every garden. Perhaps they imagine that I'm threatening to help the desert invade the town.

In the branches of the first tree in the garden of the first house a whole parliament of sparrows are deep in a noisy argument, all interrupting each other with deafening shrieks: they seem to be roaring rather than chirping. As though the departure of the night and the breaking of the day are unprecedented developments that justify an emergency meeting.

Along the road an old car is starting up with a hoarse coughing fit, like a heavy smoker. The newspaper boy vainly tries to make friends with an uncompromising dog. A thickset, tanned neighbor, with a thicket of gray hair on his bare chest, a retired colonel, whose foursquare body reminds me of a tin trunk, is standing half naked in blue running shorts, watering the bed of roses in front of his house.

"Your roses are looking wonderful. Good morning, Mr. Shmuelevich."

"What's so good about it?" he assails me. "Has Shimon Peres finally stopped selling out the whole country to Arafat?"

And when I remark that some people see it differently, he adds bitterly:

"It seems one holocaust wasn't enough to teach us a lesson. Do you really call this disaster peace? Have you ever heard of the Sudetenland? Or Munich? Or Chamberlain? Well?"

I do indeed have a detailed, reasoned reply to this, but thanks to the reserves of calm I have built up earlier, in the wadi, I bring up the words:

"Somebody was playing the Moonlight Sonata in your house about eight o'clock last night. I was walking past and I even stopped to listen for a few minutes. Was it your daughter? She played beautifully. Tell her."

He moved the hose to the next bed and smiled at me like a shy schoolboy who has suddenly been chosen as class monitor by secret ballot. "That wasn't my daughter," he says, "she's gone off to Prague. That was *her* daughter. My granddaughter, Daniella. She came third out of the whole Southern Region in the Young Talent Competition. Though everyone without exception says she should have been second. She writes beautiful poems too. So sensitive. Would you have time to take a look at them? Maybe you could give her some encouragement. Or even send them to a newspaper, for publication. They'd be bound to publish them if you sent them."

I promise Mr. Shmuelevich that I'll read Daniella's poems when I have a chance. Gladly. Certainly. Why not. Don't mention it.

In my heart I enter this promise as my contribution to the advancement of peace. Back in my study, with a mug of coffee in my hand and the morning paper spread out on the sofa, I stand at the window for another ten minutes. I hear on the news about a seventeen-year-old Arab girl who has been seriously injured by a round of bullets after she tried to stab an Israeli soldier with a knife at a roadblock outside Bethlehem. The early morning light, which was blended with a gray mist, has begun to glow and turned to a harsh, uncompromising blue.

At my window there is a little garden, a few shrubs, a vine, and a sickly lemon tree: I don't know yet if it will live or die, its foliage is pale, its trunk is bent like an arm that someone is forcing backward. The Hebrew word for "bent," which happens to begin with the letters AK, reminds me of what my father used to say, that every word that begins with AK signifies something bad. "And you must have noticed yourself, Your Highness, that your own initials, whether by chance or not, are also AK."

Maybe I should write an article today for *Yediot Aharonot*, to try to explain to Mr. Shmuelevich that getting out of the conquered territories will not weaken Israel but actually strengthen us. And that it's a mistake to see the Holocaust and Hitler and Munich everywhere.

Mr. Shmuelevich told me once, on one of those long summer evenings when you think the evening light will never fade, when the two of us were sitting in vests and sandals on his garden wall, how he was taken to the Maidanek death camp when he was about twelve with his parents, his three sisters, and their grandmother, and he was the only one who survived. He didn't want to tell me how he survived. He promised he'd tell me some other time. But every other time he chose instead to open my eyes, so I shouldn't believe in peace, so I should stop being naive, so I should get it firmly in my head that their only aim is to butcher us all and all their talk of peace is a trap, or a sleeping draught that the whole world has helped them brew and given us to lull us to sleep. Just as then.

I decide to put off writing the article. An unfinished chapter of this book is waiting for me on my desk in a heap of scribbled drafts, crumpled notes, and half pages full of crossings out. It's the chapter about Teacher Isabella Nahlieli from Children's Realm School and her army of cats. I'm going to have to make some concessions there and delete some incidents about cats and about Getzel Nahlieli, the cashier. They were quite amusing incidents, but they do not contribute anything to the progress of the story. Contribute? Progress? I don't know what can contribute to the progress of the story, because as yet I have no idea where this story wants to go, and in fact why it needs contributions. Or progress.

Meanwhile the eleven o'clock news has finished and I've had a second mug of coffee and I'm still staring out the window. A pretty little turquoise-colored bird peers at me for a moment out of the lemon tree:

it moves to and fro, leaps from a branch to a twig, and shows off the lightning of its feathers in the dappled light and shade. Its head is nearly violet, its neck is a dark metallic blue, and it is wearing a delicate yellow waistcoat. Welcome back. What have you come to remind me about this morning? The Nahlielis? Bialik's poem "A twig fell on a wall and dozed"? My mother, who used to spend hours standing at the window, with a glass of tea getting cold in her hand, with her face to the pomegranate bush and her back to the room? That's enough. I must get down to work. Now I have to use the rest of the calm I stored up in the wadi this morning before the sun rose.

Just before noon I drive into town to sort out one or two things at the post office, the bank, the clinic, and the stationer's. A tropical sun is scorching the streets and their dusty, thin-looking trees. The desert light is white-hot now and so cruel to your eyes that they turn of their own accord into two narrow slits.

There is a short line at the cash dispenser and another one at Ouaknine's newspaper stand. In Tel Aviv, in the summer holiday of 1950 or 1951, not far from Auntie Haya and Uncle Tsvi's apartment at the north end of Ben Yehuda Street, my cousin Yigal pointed out to me a newspaper kiosk that was kept by David Ben-Gurion's brother and told me that anyone who wanted to could simply go up and talk to him, to this brother of Ben-Gurion's, who really looked a lot like him. You could even ask him questions. Like, How are you, Mr. Gruen? How much is a chocolate wafer, Mr. Gruen? Is there going to be another war soon, Mr. Gruen? The only thing you mustn't do is ask him about his brother. That's the way it is. He really doesn't like being asked questions about his brother.

I was very jealous of the people in Tel Aviv. In Kerem Avraham we didn't have any celebrities or even brothers of celebrities. All we had were the Minor Prophets in our street names: Amos Street, Obadiah Street, Zephaniah Street, Haggai, Zechariah, Nahum, Malachi, Joel, Habakkuk, Hosea, Micah, and Jonah. The lot.

A Russian immigrant is standing on the corner of the square in the center of Arad. His violin case lies open on the pavement in front of him, for coins. The tune is quiet, poignant, reminiscent of fir forests with cottages, streams, and meadows, which bring back to me my mother's stories when she and I used to sit together sorting lentils or shelling peas in our soot-blackened little kitchen.

But here in the square at the center of Arad the desert light banishes ghosts and dispels any memory of fir forests and misty autumns. The musician, with his shock of gray hair and his thick white mustache, reminds me a little of Albert Einstein, and a little too of Professor Samuel Hugo Bergman, who taught my mother philosophy on Mount Scopus; in fact I attended some unforgettable lectures of his myself at the Givat Ram Campus in 1961, on the history of dialogical philosophy from Kierkegaard to Martin Buber.

There are two young women, possibly of North African extraction, one of them very thin and wearing a semitransparent top and a red skirt, the other in a trouser suit replete with belts and buckles. They stop in front of the musician and listen to his playing for a minute or two. He is playing with his eyes closed and doesn't open them. The women exchange whispers, open their handbags, and each puts a shekel in the case.

The thin woman, whose upper lip is slightly drawn up toward her nose, says:

"But how can you tell they're real Jews? Half the Russians who come here, I've heard they're simply *goyim* who just take advantage of us to get the hell out of Russia and come here for the free handouts."

Her friend says:

"What do we care, let them all come, let him play in the street, Jew, Russian, Druze, Georgian, what difference is it to you? Their children will be Israelis, they'll go in the army, eat meatballs in pita with pickles, take out a mortgage, and moan all day long."

The red skirt remarks:

"What's the matter with you, Sarit? If they let in anyone who wants to come for free, including foreign workers and Arabs from Gaza and the territories, who's going to—"

But the rest of the discussion drifts away from me toward the parking lot of the shopping mall. I remind myself that I have not made any progress yet today and the morning is no longer young. Back in my study. The heat is beginning to be too much, and a dusty wind brings the desert indoors. I close the windows and shutters and draw the curtain, block every crack, just as Greta Gat, my child sitter, who was also a piano teacher, always used to seal her apartment and turn it into a submarine.

This study was built by Arab workers not many years ago. They laid the floor and checked it with a spirit level. They erected the door and window frames. They concealed the plumbing and electrical wiring in the walls and put in an outlet for the telephone. A large-bodied carpenter, an opera lover, made the cupboards and put up the bookshelves. A contractor who emigrated from Romania in the late 1950s sent for a truckload of rich topsoil from somewhere for the garden and laid it over the lime, chalk, flint, and salt that have always lain on these hills, like putting a plaster on a wound. In this good topsoil the previous occupant planted shrubs and trees and a lawn, which I do my best to look after but without overdoing the love, so that this garden doesn't suffer the same fate as the one my father and I planted with such good intentions.

A few dozen pioneers, including loners who loved the desert or were searching for solitude and also a few young couples, came and settled here in the early 1960s: miners, quarry workers, regular army officers, and industrial workers. Lova Eliav, with a handful of other town planners seized by Zionist enthusiasm, planned, sketched out, and immediately constructed this town, with its streets, squares, avenues, and gardens, not far from the Dead Sea, in an out-of-the-way place that at that time, in the early 1960s, was not served by any main road, water pipeline, or power supply, where there were no trees, no paths, no buildings, no tents, no signs of life. Even the local Bedouin settlements mostly came into being after the town was built. The pioneers who founded Arad were passionate, impatient, talkative, and busy. Without a second thought, they vowed to "conquer the wilderness and tame the desert."

Somebody is passing the house now in a little red van; he stops at the mailbox on the corner and extracts the letters I posted yesterday. Somebody else has come to replace the broken curbstone of the pavement opposite. I must find some way to thank them all, the way a bar mitzvah boy publicly thanks everyone who has helped him come this far: Aunt Sonia, Grandpa Alexander, Greta Gat, Teacher Zelda, the Arab man with bags under his eyes who rescued me from the dark cell where I was trapped in that clothes shop, my parents, Mr. Zarchi, the Lembergs next door, the Italian prisoners of war, Grandma Shlomit with her war on germs, Teacher Isabella and her cats, Mr. Agnon, the Rudnickis, Grandpa Papa the carter from Kiriat Motskin, Saul Tchernikhowsky, Auntie Lilenka Bar Samkha, my wife, my children, my grandchildren, the builders and electricians who made this house, the carpenter, the newspaper boy, the man in the red mail van, the musician playing his violin on the corner of the square who reminded me of Einstein and Bergman, the Bedouin woman and the three goats I saw this morning before dawn, or did I just imagine them, Uncle Joseph who wrote *Judaism and Humanity,* my neighbor Shmuelevich who is afraid of another Holocaust, his granddaughter Daniella who played the Moonlight Sonata yesterday, Minister Shimon Peres who went to talk to Arafat again yesterday in the hope of finding some compromise formula despite everything, and the turquoise bird that sometimes visits my lemon tree. And the lemon tree itself. And especially the silence of the desert just before sunrise, that has more and more silences wrapped up inside it. That was my third coffee this morning. That's enough. I put the empty mug down at the edge of the table, taking particular care not to make the slightest noise that would injure the silence that has not vanished yet. Now I will sit down and write.

40

I HAD NEVER seen a house like it in my life before that morning.

It was surrounded by a thick stone wall that concealed an orchard shady with vines and fruit trees. My astonished eyes looked instinctively for the tree of life and the tree of knowledge. There was a well in front of the house set in a wide terrace paved with blocks of smooth pinkish stone with delicate pale-blue veins. An arbor of thick vines shaded a corner of this terrace. Some stone seats and a low, wide stone table tempted you to linger in this arbor, to take your ease, to rest in the shade of the vines and listen to the buzzing of the summer bees, the singing of the birds in the orchard, and the trickle of the fountain—because at one end of the arbor there was a little pool in the form of a five-pointed star made of stone and lined with blue tiles decorated with Arabic writing. In the middle of the pool a fountain bubbled quietly. Groups of goldfish swam slowly to and fro among the clumps of water lilies.

From the terrace the three of us, excited, polite, and humble, walked up the stone steps to a wide veranda with a view of the northern walls of the Old City with the minarets and domes beyond. Wooden chairs with cushions and footstools and some mosaic-covered tables were scattered around the veranda. Here too, as in the arbor, one felt an urge to sprawl facing the view of the city walls, to doze in the shade of the foliage or calmly drink in the silence of the hills and the stone.

We did not linger in the orchard or in the arbor or on the veranda but pulled the bell pull next to the double iron doors, which were painted the color of mahogany and skillfully carved in relief with all sorts of pomegranates, grapes, winding tendrils, and symmetrical flowers. While we waited for the door to open, Uncle Staszek turned his head to us again and put his finger to his lips one more time, as though to signal a final warning to Auntie Mala and me: manners! composure! diplomacy!

Along all four walls of the spacious reception room stood soft sofas, their carved wooden backs adjacent and touching one another. The furniture was carved with leaves, buds, and flowers, as though to represent inside the house the garden and orchard that surrounded it on the outside. The sofas were upholstered in a variety of striped fabrics in shades of red and sky blue. On each sofa there was a mass of colorful embroidered cushions. There were rich carpets on the floor, one of them woven with a scene of birds of paradise. In front of each sofa there was a low table, the top of which was formed by a wide round metal tray, and each tray was richly engraved with abstract designs of interwoven forms that recalled Arabic writing; in fact, they may well have been stylized Arabic inscriptions.

On each side of the room six or eight doors opened. The walls were draped with rugs, and between the rugs the plaster was visible; it too was patterned with flowers, and colored pink, lilac, and pale green. Here and there, beneath the high ceiling, ancient weapons were hung as decorations: Damascus swords, a scimitar, daggers and spears, pistols, long-barreled muskets and double-barreled rifles. Facing the entrance, and flanked by a burgundy-covered sofa on one side and a lemon-colored one on the other, stood a huge, heavily ornamented brown sideboard in baroque style looking like a small palace, with many glass-fronted compartments containing porcelain cups, crystal goblets, silver and brass goblets, and numerous ornaments of Hebron or Sidon glass.

In a deep recess in the wall between two windows nestled a green vase inlaid with mother-of-pearl from which rose several peacocks' feathers. Other recesses housed large brass pitchers and glass or earthenware beakers. Four fans hung from the ceiling, constantly making a wasplike buzz and stirring the smoke-laden air. In between the fans a huge, splendid brass chandelier sprouted from the ceiling, resembling a great tree with a profusion of branches, boughs, twigs, and tendrils all blooming with shining stalactites of crystal and quantities of pear-shaped lightbulbs that were all lit despite the summer morning light streaming through the open windows. The arches of the windows were fitted with stained glass representing wreaths of trefoils, each of which colored the daylight a different color: red, green, gold, and purple.

Two cages hung from brackets on facing walls, each containing a pair of solemn parrots whose feathers were a riot of orange, turquoise, yellow, green, and blue. Every now and again one of them would exclaim in a hoarse voice like that of a heavy smoker: "*Tfaddal! S'il vous plaît!* Enjoy!" And from the other cage, at the other end of the room, a wheedling soprano voice replied at once in English: "Oh, how very, very sweet! How lovely!"

Above the lintels of the doors and windows and on the flowery plaster Quranic verses or lines of poetry were inscribed in curling green Arabic writing, and between the rugs on the wall there were family portraits. Some were of portly, plump-faced, clean-shaven effendis, wearing red fezzes with black tassels, and squeezed into heavy blue suits, with gold chains suspended across their bellies and disappearing into their vest pockets. Their predecessors were mustachioed men with an authoritative air and a sullen mien, robed in responsibility, awe-inspiring, with a commanding presence, wearing embroidered robes and gleaming white keffiyehs held in place by black rings. There were also two or three mounted figures, ferocious-looking bearded men riding on magnificent horses, galloping at such speed that their keffiyehs trailed behind and their horses' manes streamed; they had long daggers thrust through their belts and curved scimitars tied at the side or brandished aloft.

The deep-set windows of this reception hall faced north and east toward Mount Scopus and the Mount of Olives, a pine copse, rocky slopes, the Ophel, and the Augusta Victoria hospice, its tower crowned like an imperial helmet with a sloping gray Prussian roof. A little to the left of Augusta Victoria stood a fortified building with narrow loopholes topped with a dome: this was the National Library, where my father worked, and around it were ranged the other buildings of Hebrew University and Hadassah Hospital. Below the skyline could be seen some small stone houses scattered over the hillside, small flocks among the boulders and fields of thorns, and the occasional old olive tree that seemed to have long since abandoned the living world and joined the realm of the inanimate.

In the summer of 1947 my parents went to stay with some acquaintances in Netanya, leaving me with Uncle Staszek, Auntie Mala, and Chopin and Schopenhauer Rudnicki for the weekend. ("Just you behave yourself there! Impeccably, do you hear! And give Auntie Mala a hand in the kitchen and don't disturb Uncle Staszek, and keep yourself occupied, take a book to read and keep out of their way, and let them sleep late on Saturday morning! Be as good as gold! You can do it when you really want to!")

The writer Hayyim Hazaz once decreed that Uncle Staszek should get rid of his Polish name, "that smelt of the pogroms," and persuaded him to take the first name of Stav, meaning "autumn" in Hebrew, because it sounded a little like Staszek but had a certain flavor of the Song of Songs. And that is how they appeared in Auntie Mala's handwriting on the card that was attached to the door of their apartment:

Malka and Stav Rudnicki
Please do not knock
during the usual rest times.

Uncle Staszek was a thickset, compact man with powerful shoulders, dark, hairy nostrils like caverns, and bushy eyebrows, one of which was always raised quizzically. He had lost one of his incisors, which sometimes gave him a villainous look, particularly when he smiled. He worked for a living in the registered mail department of the main post office in Jerusalem, and in his spare time he was collecting material on little cards for an original piece of research on the medieval Hebrew poet Immanuel of Rome.

Ustaz Najib Mamduh al-Silwani, a resident of Sheikh Jarrah in the northeast of the city, was a wealthy businessman and the local agent of a number of large French firms whose business extended as far as Alexandria and Beirut and from there branched off to Haifa, Nablus, and Jerusalem. It so happened that at the beginning of the summer a considerable money order or bank draft, or it may have been some share certificates, went missing. Suspicion fell on Edward Silwani, Ustaz Najib's eldest son and his partner in the firm of Silwani and Sons. The young man was questioned, so we were told, by the assistant head of the CID in person, and he was subsequently taken to the remand center in Haifa for further questioning. Ustaz Najib, after attempting to rescue his son in various ways, eventually turned in desperation to Mr. Kenneth Orwell Knox-Guildford, the postmaster general, and begged him to renew the search for a lost envelope that he had, he swore, sent in person, the previous winter, by registered post.

Unfortunately he had mislaid the receipt. It had vanished as though the Devil himself had swallowed it.

Mr. Kenneth Orwell Knox-Guildford, for his part, after assuring Ustaz Najib of his sympathy but informing him candidly and sadly that there was not much hope of the search resulting in a positive outcome, nevertheless entrusted Staszek Rudnicki with the task of investigating the matter and discovering whatever there was to learn about the possible fate of a registered letter sent several months previously, a letter that might or might not have existed, that might or might not have been mislaid, a letter of which there was no trace either in the possession of the sender or in the post office ledger.

Uncle Staszek lost no time in investigating, and discovered that not only was there no entry for the letter in question, but that the whole page had been carefully torn out of the ledger. There was no sign of it. Staszek's suspicions were immediately aroused. He made inquiries, found out which clerk was on duty at the registered counter at the time, and questioned the other clerks too until he discovered when the page had last been seen in the ledger. Once he had done this, it was not long before he identified the culprit (the youngster had held the envelope up to the light and seen the draft, and the temptation had been too much for him).

So the lost property was restored to its owner, young Edward al-Silwani was released from custody, the honor of the respectable firm of

Silwani and Sons once more shone forth from the company's letterhead without blot or stain, while dear Mr. Stav was invited together with his wife to partake of coffee at Silwani Villa in Sheikh Jarrah on Saturday morning. As for the dear child, their friends' son who would be staying with them, whom they had no one to leave with on Saturday morning, of course, what a question, he must come with them, the whole Silwani family was impatient to express their gratitude to Mr. Stav for his efficiency and integrity.

After breakfast on Saturday therefore, just before we set out, I put on my best clothes, which my parents had left with Auntie Mala especially for the visit ("The Arab attaches great importance to outward appearances!" Father insisted): a gleaming white shirt, freshly ironed, its sleeves rolled up with splendid precision; navy blue trousers with cuffs and a neat crease down the front; and a serious-looking black leather belt with a shiny metal buckle that, for some reason, bore the image of the two-headed imperial Russian eagle. On my feet I wore a pair of sandals that Uncle Staszek had polished for me with the same brush and black polish that he had used for his own best shoes and Auntie Mala's.

Despite the heat of the August day, Uncle Staszek insisted on wearing his dark woolen suit (it was his only one), his snow-white silk shirt, which had made the journey with him fifteen years ago from his parents' home in Lodz, and the unobtrusive blue silk tie he had worn on his wedding day. As for Auntie Mala, she agonized for three quarters of an hour in front of the mirror, tried out her evening dress, changed her mind, tried a dark pleated skirt with a light cotton blouse, changed her mind again, and looked at herself in the girlish summer frock she had bought recently, with a brooch and a silk scarf, or with a necklace and without the brooch and the scarf, or with the necklace and a different brooch but without the scarf, with or without drop earrings?

Suddenly she decided that the airy summer frock with the embroidery around the neck was too frivolous, too folksy for the occasion, and she went back to the evening dress she had started with. In her predicament Auntie Mala turned to Uncle Staszek and even to me, and made us swear to tell the truth and nothing but the truth, however painful: wasn't this outfit too dressy, too theatrical for an informal visit on a hot day? Wasn't it wrong for her hairdo? And while we were looking at her hair, what did we think, really and truly, should she tie her plaits up around her head, or should she undo them and let her hair fall loose over her shoulder, and if so which one?

Finally, reluctantly, she opted for a plain brown skirt, a long-sleeved blouse set off with a pretty turquoise brooch, and a pair of pale blue drop earrings to match her beautiful eyes. And she unplaited her hair and let it fall freely over both shoulders.

On the way, Uncle Stav, his thickset body crammed uncomfortably into his heavy suit, explained to me some of the facts of life resulting from the historical difference between cultures. The Silwani family, he said, was a highly respected Europeanized family whose menfolk had been educated in excellent schools in Beirut and Liverpool and could all speak Western languages well. We ourselves, for our part, were definitely Europeans, although perhaps in rather a different sense of the word. We, for example, attached no importance to outward appearances but only to inner cultural and moral values. Even a universal genius like Tolstoy had not hesitated to walk around dressed as a peasant, and a great revolutionary like Lenin had mostly despised bourgeois dress and preferred to wear a leather jacket and a worker's cap.

Our visit to Silwani Villa was not like Lenin visiting the workers or like Tolstoy among the simple folk: it was a special occasion. In the eyes of our more respectable and enlightened Arab neighbors, who adopted a more Western European culture most of the time, Uncle Staszek explained, we modern Jews were mistakenly portrayed as a sort of rowdy rabble of rough paupers, lacking manners and not yet fit to stand on the lowest rung of cultural refinement. Even some of our leaders were apparently portrayed in a negative light among our Arab neighbors, because they dressed in a very simple way and their manners were crude and informal. Several times in his work at the post office, both at the public counters and behind the scenes, he had had the opportunity to observe that the new Hebraic style, sandals and khaki, rolled-up sleeves and open neck, which we considered pioneer-like and democratic and egalitarian, was viewed by the British and particularly by the Arabs as uncouth, or as a vulgar kind of display, showing a lack of respect for others and contempt for the public services. Of course this impression was fundamentally mistaken, and there was no need to repeat that we believed in the simple life, in making do with little and in renouncing all outward show. But in the present circumstances, a visit to the mansion of a well-known and highly respected family, and on other similar occasions, it was proper for us to behave as though we had been entrusted with a diplomatic mission. Consequently we had to take great care about our appearance, our manners, and our way of talking.

For instance, Uncle Staszek insisted, in such gatherings children and even teenagers were not expected on any account to join in the grownups' conversation. If, and only if, they were spoken to, they should reply politely and as briefly as possible. If refreshments were being served, the child should choose only things that would not spill or make crumbs. If he was offered a second helping, he should refuse very politely, even if he was dying to help himself. And throughout the visit the child should kindly sit up straight and not stare, and above all he must on no account make faces. Any inappropriate behavior, particularly in Arab society, which was, he assured us, well known to be extremely sensitive, easily hurt, and inclined to take offense (and even, he was inclined to believe, vengeance), would not only be impolite and a breach of trust but might also impair future mutual understanding between the two neighboring peoples; thus—he warmed to his theme—exacerbating hostility during a period of anxiety about the danger of bloody warfare between the two nations.

In brief, Uncle Staszek said, a great deal, maybe far more than an eight-year-old child can carry on his shoulders, depends on you too this morning, on your intelligence and good behavior. By the way, you too, Malenka my dear, had better not say anything there, just say nothing beyond the necessary courtesies: as is well known, in the tradition of our Arab neighbors, as it was for our forefathers too, it is not considered acceptable for a woman suddenly to open her mouth in male company. Consequently you would do well, my darling, to let your innate good breeding and feminine charm speak for you on this occasion.

And so this little diplomatic mission set forth at ten o'clock in the morning, resplendent and fully briefed, from the Rudnickis' one-and-a-half-room apartment on the corner of the Street of the Prophets and Chancellor Street, just above Blooms Galore, the florist, leaving Chopin and Schopenhauer, the lame bird Alma-Mirabelle and the painted pine-cone bird behind, and began to wend its way eastward toward Silwani

Villa on the northern side of Sheikh Jarrah, up the road that leads to Mount Scopus.

The first thing we passed on our way was the wall of the house named Thabor, which was once the home of an eccentric German architect named Conrad Schick, a devout Christian who was in love with Jerusalem. Above his gate Schick had built a small turret around which I used to weave all sorts of tales peopled by knights and princesses. From there we walked down the Street of the Prophets to the Italian Hospital, which, to judge by its castellated tower and its tiled domes, was modeled on a Florentine palace.

At the Italian Hospital, without saying a word, we turned north toward St. George's Street, skirting the ultra-Orthodox Jewish quarter of Mea Shearim, pressing on into the world of cypresses, grilles, cornices, and stone walls. This was the opposite Jerusalem, the Jerusalem I hardly knew, the Abyssinian, Arab, pilgrim, Ottoman, missionary, German, Greek, brooding, Armenian, American, monastic, Italian, Russian Jerusalem, thick with pine trees, menacing yet fascinating, with its bells and winged enchantments that were forbidden to you because they were alien and hostile, a veiled city, concealing dangerous secrets, heavy with crosses, turrets, mosques, and mysteries, a dignified and silent city, through whose streets ministers of alien cults shrouded in black cloaks and priestly garb flitted like dark shadows, monks and nuns, kadis and muezzins, notables, worshippers, pilgrims, veiled women, and cowled priests.

It was a Saturday morning in the summer of 1947, a few months before the bloody clashes broke out in Jerusalem, less than a year before the British left, before the siege, the shelling, the water stoppage, and the partition of the city. The Saturday that we walked to the Silwani family's house in Sheikh Jarrah a pregnant calm still lay on all these northeastern suburbs. But already within the calm you could sense a faint hint of impatience, a whiff of suppressed hostility. What were three Jews, a man, a woman, and a child, doing here, where had they suddenly sprung from? And now that you're here, on this side of the city, you'd better not linger longer than necessary. Slip swiftly through these streets. While there is still—

———

There were already some fifteen or twenty guests and members of the family in the hall when we arrived, as though hovering on a cloud of cigarette smoke, most of them seated on the rows of sofas along the four walls, a few standing in little clusters in the corners. Among them was Mr. Cardigan, and also Mr. Kenneth Orwell Knox-Guildford, the postmaster general and Uncle Staszek's boss, who was standing with some other gentlemen and greeted Uncle Staszek by raising his glass slightly. Most of the doors leading into inner rooms were closed, but through one that was ajar I could see three girls of my own age, wearing long dresses, huddled together on a little bench, eyeing the guests and whispering among themselves.

Ustaz Najib Mamduh al-Silwani, our host, introduced a few members of the family and some of the other guests, men and women, including a pair of middle-aged English ladies in gray suits, an elderly French scholar, and a Greek priest in a robe and a curly square beard. To all alike our host praised his guest, in English and sometimes in French, and explained in a couple of sentences how dear Mr. Stav had dispelled the great trouble that had hung over the heads of the Silwani family for several dark weeks.

We, in turn, shook hands, chatted, smiled, made little bows, and murmured "How nice!," "*Enchanté*," and "Good to meet you." We even presented a modest symbolic gift to the al-Silwani family: a book of photographs of life in the kibbutz, with pictures of everyday scenes in the communal dining room, pioneers in the fields and the dairy, naked children happily splashing around under the sprinklers, and an old Arab peasant, holding fast to his donkey's halter as he stared at a gigantic tractor on tracks going past in a cloud of dust. Each photograph was accompanied by a few words of explanation in Hebrew and English.

Ustaz al-Silwani leafed through the book of photographs, smiling pleasantly, and nodding a few times as though he had finally understood what the photographers had meant to say in the pictures. He thanked his guests for the present and put it down in one of the recesses in the wall, or was it a windowsill. The parrot with the high voice suddenly chanted in English from its cage: "Who will be my destiny? Who will be my prince?" and from the other end of the room the hoarse parrot replied: "*Kalamat, ya sheikh! Kalamat, ya sheikh! Kalamat!*"

Two crossed swords hung on the wall above our heads in the corner where we sat. I tried unsuccessfully to guess who were the guests and who were family. Most of the men were in their fifties or sixties, and one was a very old man in a threadbare brown suit that was a little frayed at the cuffs. He was a wrinkled old man, his cheeks were hollow, his silvery mustache was yellowed from tobacco smoke, as were his lined plasterer's hands. He closely resembled some of the portraits hanging on the wall in their gilt frames. Was he the grandfather? Or even the great-grandfather? Because to the left of Ustaz al-Silwani there appeared another old man, veined, tall, and stooped, looking like a broken tree trunk, his brown head covered with prickly bristles. He was sloppily dressed, in a striped shirt that was buttoned up only halfway and trousers that seemed too big for him. I was reminded of the old man Alleluyev in my mother's story, who looked after an even older man in his cottage.

There were a few young people in white tennis clothes, and a pair of pot-bellied men in their mid-forties who looked like twins; they sat sleepily side by side, with their eyes half closed, and one of them fingered a string of amber worry beads while his brother chain-smoked, making his contribution to the gray pall of smoke that hung in the air. Apart from the two English ladies there were some other women sitting on the sofas, or circulating around the room, taking care not to collide with the servants in bow ties carrying trays laden with cold drinks, sweetmeats, glasses of tea, and tiny cups of coffee. Which of the women was the mistress of the house was hard to say: several of them seemed to be at home here. A large woman in a flowery silk dress the same color as the vase containing the peacock feathers, whose fleshy arms were so festooned with silver bracelets and bangles that they jangled with every movement, stood talking eagerly to some young men in tennis shorts. Another lady, in a cotton dress printed with a profusion of fruit that seemed to accentuate the roundness of her bust and thighs, extended her hand for her host to kiss and immediately repaid him with three kisses on the cheek, right, left, and right again. There was also an older matron with a gray mustache and flared hairy nostrils, as well as some charming young girls, slim-hipped, red-nailed, ceaselessly whispering-pspispering, with elegant hairdos and sporty skirts. Staszek Rudnicki in his ministerial dark suit that had emigrated with him from Lodz some fifteen years previously and his wife Mala in her brown skirt, long-sleeved blouse, and drop earrings seemed to be the most formally dressed people in the room (apart from the waiters). Even the postmaster general, Mr. Knox-Guildford, was wearing a plain blue shirt with no jacket or tie. Suddenly the parrot who sounded like an inveterate smoker called out from his cage at one end of the hall: "*Mais oui, mais oui, chère mademoiselle, mais oui, absolument, naturellement.*" From the other end of the room the pampered soprano immediately answered: "*Bas! Bas, ya 'eini! Bas min fadlak! Usqut! Bas wahalas!*"

Every now and then the servants in their black, white, and red materialized out of the cloud of smoke and tried to tempt us with bowl after bowl of almonds, walnuts, peanuts, pumpkin and melon seeds, and trays laden with warm pastries, fruit, slices of watermelon, more little cups of coffee, glasses of tea and tall frost-ringed glasses containing fruit juices and pomegranate juice with lumps of ice, and little bowls of blancmange smelling deliciously of cinnamon and decorated with chopped almonds. But I made do with two biscuits and a single glass of fruit juice, and politely but firmly refused all subsequent delicacies, mindful of the obligations that stemmed from my status as a junior diplomat accepting the hospitality of an important power that was scrutinizing my behavior with suspicion.

Mr. Silwani stopped next to us and chatted in English for a few minutes with Auntie Mala and Uncle Staszek, joking, smiling, perhaps complimenting Auntie on her drop earrings. Then, as he was excusing himself and about to move on to his other guests, he hesitated, suddenly turned to me, and said with a pleasant smile in stumbling Hebrew:

"If the young sir would like to go out in the garden. There are some children in the garden."

Apart from Father, who liked to call me Your Highness, nobody had ever called me sir before. For one glorious moment I really did see myself as a young Hebrew gentleman whose status was not one whit less exalted than that of the young foreign gentlemen who were outside in the garden. When the free Hebrew state was finally established, Father used to quote enthusiastically from Vladimir Jabotinsky, our nation would be able to join the comity of nations, "like a lion confronting other lions."

Like a lion confronting other lions I therefore left the smoke-filled room. From the spacious veranda I took in the view of the walls of the Old City, the towers and domes. Then slowly, imperiously, with a strong sense of national awareness, I descended the flight of stone steps and walked toward the arbor of vines and beyond, into the orchard.

41

OUT IN THE arbor there was a group of five or six girls in their mid-teens. I gave them a wide berth. Then some rowdy boys sauntered past me. A young couple were strolling under the trees, deep in whispered conversation but not touching each other. At the other end of the orchard, near the corner of the wall, around the rough trunk of a leafy mulberry tree, someone had erected a kind of bench without legs, and here a pale-faced girl was sitting with her knees together. Her hair and eyelashes were black, her neck was slim, her shoulders were frail, and her bobbed hair fell over a brow that seemed to me to be illuminated from within by a light of curiosity and joy. She was dressed in a cream blouse under a long navy blue dress with broad straps. On the lapel of her blouse she wore an ivory brooch that reminded me of one that belonged to my Grandma Shlomit.

At first sight this girl seemed to be my age, but from the slight curve of her blouse and the unchildlike look of curiosity and also of warning in her eyes as they met mine (for an instant, before my eyes looked away), she must have been two or three years older, perhaps eleven or twelve. Still, I managed to see that her eyebrows were rather thick and joined in the middle, in contrast with the delicacy of her other features. There was a little child at her feet, a curly-haired boy of about three who may have been her brother; he was kneeling on the ground and was absorbed in picking up fallen leaves and arranging them in a circle.

Boldly and all in one breath I offered the girl a quarter of my entire vocabulary of foreign words, perhaps less like a lion confronting other lions and more like the parrots in the room upstairs. Unconsciously I even bowed a little bow, eager to make contact and thus to dispel any prejudices and to advance the reconciliation between our two peoples:

"*Sabah al-heir*, Miss. *Ana ismi* Amos. *Wa-inti, ya bint? Votre nom s'il vous plaît, Mademoiselle?* Please your name kindly?"

She eyed me without smiling. Her joined eyebrows gave her a severe look beyond her years. She nodded a few times, as though making a decision, agreeing with herself, ending the deliberation, and confirming the findings. Her navy blue dress came down below her knees, but in the gap between the dress and her shoes with the butterfly buckles I caught sight of the skin of her calves, brown and smooth, feminine, already grown up; my face reddened, and my eyes fled again, to her little brother, who looked back at me quietly, unsuspectingly, but also unsmilingly. Suddenly he looked very much like her with his dark, calm face.

Everything I had heard from my parents, from neighbors, from Uncle Joseph, from my teachers, from my uncles and aunts, and from rumors came back to me at that moment. Everything they said over glasses of tea in our backyard on Saturdays and on summer evenings about mounting tensions between Arab and Jew, distrust and hostility, the rotten fruit of British intrigues and the incitement of Muslim fanatics who painted us in a frightening light to inflame the Arabs to hate us. Our task, Mr. Rosendorff once said, was to dispel suspicions and to explain to them that we were in fact a positive and even kindly people. In brief, it was a sense of mission that gave me the courage to address this strange girl and try to start a conversation with her: I meant to explain to her in a few convincing words how pure our intentions were, how abhorrent was the plot to stir up conflict between our two peoples, and how good it would be for the Arab public—in the form of this graceful-lipped girl—to spend a little time in the company of the polite, pleasant Hebrew people, in the person of me, the articulate envoy aged eight and a half. Almost.

But I had not thought out in advance what I would do after I had used up most of my supply of foreign words in my opening sentence. How could I enlighten this oblivious girl and get her to understand once and for all the rightness of the Jewish return to Zion? By charades? By dance gestures? And how could I get her to recognize our right to the Land without using words? How, without any words, could I translate for her Tchernikhowsky's "O, my land, my homeland"? Or Jabotinsky's "There Arabs, Nazarenes and we / shall drink our fill in happy manner, / when both the banks of Jordan's stream / are purged by our unsullied banner"? In a word, I was like that fool who had learned how to advance the king's pawn two squares, and did so without any hesitation, but after that had no idea at all about the game of chess, not even the names of the pieces, or how they moved, or where, or why.

Lost.

But the girl answered me, and actually in Hebrew, without looking at me, her hands resting open on the bench on either side of her dress, her eyes fixed on her brother, who was laying a little stone in the center of each leaf in his circle:

"My name is Aisha. That little one is my brother. Awwad."

She also said:

"You're the son of the guests from the post office?"

And so I explained to her that I was definitely not the son of the guests from the post office, but of their friends. And that my father was a rather important scholar, an *ustaz,* and that my father's uncle was an even more important scholar, who was even world famous, and that it was her honored father, Mr. Silwani, who had personally suggested that I should come out in the garden and talk to the children of the house.

Aisha corrected me and said that Ustaz Najib was not her father but her mother's uncle: she and her family did not live here in Sheikh Jarrah but in Talbieh, and she herself had been going to lessons from a piano teacher in Rehavia for the past three years, and she had learned a little Hebrew from the teacher and the other pupils. It was a beautiful language, Hebrew, and Rehavia was a beautiful area. Well kept. Quiet.

Talbieh was well kept and quiet, too, I hastened to reply, repaying one compliment with another. Would she be willing for us to talk a little?

Aren't we talking already? (A little smile flickered for an instant around her lips. She straightened the hem of her dress with both her hands, and uncrossed and recrossed her legs. And for an instant her knees appeared, the knees of a grown-up woman already, then her dress straightened again. She looked slightly to my left now, where the garden wall peered at us among the trees.)

I therefore adopted a representative position, and expressed the view that there was enough room in this country for both peoples, if only they had the sense to live together in peace and mutual respect. Somehow, out of embarrassment or arrogance, I was talking to her not in my own Hebrew but in that of Father and his visitors: formal, polished. Like a donkey dressed up in a ballgown and high-heeled shoes: convinced for some reason that this was the only proper way to speak to Arabs and girls. (I had hardly ever had an occasion to talk to a girl or an Arab, but I imagined that in both cases a special delicacy was required: you had to talk on tiptoe, as it were.)

It transpired that her knowledge of Hebrew was not extensive, or perhaps her views were not the same as mine. Instead of responding to my challenge, she chose to sidestep it: her elder brother, she told me, was in London, studying to be a "solicitor and a barrister."

Puffed up with representativity, I asked her what she was thinking of studying when she was older.

She looked straight into my eyes, and at that moment, instead of blushing, I turned pale. Instantly I averted my eyes, and looked down at her serious little brother Awwad, who had already laid out four precise circles of leaves at the foot of the mulberry tree.

How about you?

Well, you see, I said, still standing, facing her, rubbing my clammy palms against the sides of my shorts, well, you see, it's like this—

You'll be a lawyer too. From the way you speak.

What makes you think that exactly?

Instead of replying, she said: I'm going to write a book.

You? What kind of a book will you write?

Poetry.

Poetry?

In French and English.

You write poetry?

She also wrote poetry in Arabic, but she never showed it to anyone. Hebrew was a beautiful language, too. Had anyone written any poetry in Hebrew?

Shocked by her question, swollen with indignation and a sense of mission, I began there and then to give her an impassioned recital of snatches of poetry. Tchernikhowsky. Levin Kipnes. Rahel. Vladimir Jabotinsky. And one poem of my own. Whatever came to mind. Furiously, describing circles in the air with my hands, raising my voice, with feeling and gestures and facial expressions and occasionally even closing my eyes. Even her little brother Awwad raised his curly head and fixed me with brown, innocent lamblike eyes, full of curiosity and slight apprehension, and suddenly he recited in clear Hebrew: Jest a minute! Rest a minute! Aisha, meanwhile, said nothing. Suddenly she asked me if I could climb trees.

All excited and perhaps a little in love with her and yet trembling with the thrill of national representativity, eager to do anything she wanted, I instantly transformed myself from Jabotinsky into Tarzan. Taking off the sandals that Uncle Staszek had polished for me that morning till the leather gleamed like jet, oblivious of my neatly pressed best clothes, I took a jump and swung myself up onto a low branch, scrabbled with my bare feet against the gnarled trunk, and without a moment's hesitation climbed up into the tree, from one fork to the next and upward, toward the topmost branches, not caring about scratches, ignoring bruises, grazes, and mulberry stains, up beyond the line of the wall, beyond the tops of the other trees, out of the shade, up to the top-most part of the tree, until my tummy was clinging to a sloping branch that bent under my weight like a spring, and I groped and suddenly discovered a rusty iron chain with a heavy iron ball, also rusty, attached to the end of it, the devil only knew what it was for and how it had got to the top of the mulberry tree. Little Awwad looked at me thoughtfully, doubtfully, and called again: Jest a minute! Rest a minute!

These were apparently the only Hebrew words he knew.

I held on to my sighing branch with one hand, and with the other, uttering wild war cries, I waved the chain and whirled the iron ball in quick circles, as though brandishing some rare fruit for the young woman underneath. For sixty generations, so we had learned, they had considered us a miserable nation of huddled yeshiva students, flimsy moths who start in a panic at every shadow, *awlad al-mawt*, children of death, and now at last here was muscular Judaism taking the stage, the resplendent new Hebrew youth at the height of his powers, making everyone who sees him tremble at his roar: like a lion among lions.

But this awesome tree lion that I was exultantly acting the part of in front of Aisha and her brother was unaware of approaching doom. He was a blind, deaf, foolish lion. Eyes had he but he saw not, ears neither did he hear. He just whirled the chain, straddling his swaying branch, piercing the air with stronger and stronger revolutions of his iron apple, like those heroic cowboys he had seen in the cinema, describing loops in the air with their lassos as they rode along.

He did not see or hear or imagine or beware, this eager brother's keeper, this flying lion, even though nemesis was well on the way, and everything was ready for the horror to come. The rusty iron ball at the end of the rusty chain was whirling in the air, threatening to wrench his arm out of his shoulder socket. His arrogance. His folly. The poison of his rising virility. The intoxication of vainglorious chauvinism. The branch he was lying on to perform his demonstration was already groaning under his weight. And the delicate, thoughtful girl with the thick black eyebrows, the poetess, was looking up at him with a pitying smile, not a smile of admiration or awe for the new Hebrew man but a faintly contemptuous expression, an amused, indulgent smile, as if to say, that's nothing, all those efforts of yours, it's nothing at all, we've seen much more than that already, you can't impress us with that, if you really want to surprise me someday, you'll have to try seven times as hard.

(And from the depth of some dark well there may have flashed before him for a brief instant a faint memory of a thick forest in a women's clothes shop, a primeval jungle through which he had once pursued a little girl, and when he finally caught up with her, she turned out to be a horror.)

And her brother was still there, at the foot of the mulberry tree, he had finished making his precise, mysterious circles out of fallen leaves and now, tousled, serious, responsible-looking, and sweet, he was toddling after a white butterfly in his shorts and red shoes when suddenly from the top of the mulberry tree someone called his name in a terrified roar, Awwad Awwad run, and he may just have had time to look up into the tree with his round eyes, he may just have had time to see the rusty iron apple that had broken free from the end of the chain and was rushing toward him like a shell straight toward him getting darker and bigger and flying straight at the child's eyes, and it would surely have smashed his skull in if it had not missed his head by an inch and whizzed right down past the child's nose to land with a heavy dull thud crushing his little foot through his tiny red shoe, the doll-like shoe that was suddenly covered with blood and started to fountain blood through the lace holes and to gush out through the seams and over the top of the shoe. Then a single long, piercing, heartrending shriek of pain rose above the tops of the trees and then your whole body was seized with trembling like frosty needles and everything was silent all around you in an instant as though you had been shut up inside an iceberg.

———

I don't remember the unconscious child's face when his sister carried him away in her arms, I don't remember if she screamed too, if she called for help, if she spoke to me, and I don't remember when or how I got down from the tree or if I fell down with the branch that collapsed beneath me, I don't remember who dressed the cut on my chin that trickled blood down onto my best shirt (I still have a mark on my chin), and I can hardly remember anything that happened between the injured boy's only shriek and the white sheets that evening, as I lay still shivering all over curled up fetus-like with several stitches in my chin in Uncle Staszek and Auntie Mala's double bed.

But I do remember to this day, like two sharp burning coals, her eyes beneath the mourning border of her black eyebrows that joined in the middle: loathing, despair, horror, and flashing hatred came from her eyes, and beneath the loathing and the hatred there was also a sort of gloomy nod of the head, as though she were agreeing with herself, as if to say I could tell right away, even before you opened your mouth I should have noticed, I should have been on my guard, you could sniff it from a long way away. Like a bad smell.

And I can remember, vaguely, somebody, a hairy, short man, with a bushy mustache, wearing a gold watch on a very wide bracelet, maybe he was one of the guests, or one of the host's sons, dragging me roughly out of there, pulling me by my torn shirt, almost at a run. And on the way I could see a furious man, standing by the well in the middle of the paved terrace, hitting Aisha, not punching her with his fists, not slapping her cheeks, but hitting her hard, repeatedly, with the flat of his hand, slowly, thoroughly, on her head, her back, her shoulder, across her face, not the way you punish a child but the way you vent your rage on a horse. Or an obstinate camel.

Of course my parents intended, and so did Staszek and Mala, to get in touch and ask how the child Awwad was and how serious his injuries were. Of course they intended to find some way to express their sorrow and shame. They might have considered offering suitable compensation. It might have been important to them to make our hosts see with their own eyes that our side had not come off unscathed either, but he had cut his chin and needed two or three stitches. It is possible that my parents and the Rudnickis even planned a return visit to Silwani Villa, in which they would bring presents for the injured youngster, while my task would be to express my humble remorse by prostrating myself on the threshold or putting on sackcloth and ashes, to demonstrate to the al-Silwani family in particular and to the Arab people in general how sorry and ashamed and embarrassed we were, but at the same time too high-minded to seek excuses or extenuating circumstances, and sufficiently responsible to shoulder the full burden of embarrassment, remorse, and guilt.

But while they were still conferring, arguing with each other about the timing and the manner, possibly suggesting that Uncle Staszek should go and ask his boss Mr. Knox-Guildford to put out some informal feelers on our behalf and find out how the land lay with the Silwani family, how angry they still were and how they could be mollified, how helpful a personal apology would be and in what spirit they would receive our offer to put matters right, while they were still laying plans and exploratory measures, the Jewish high holidays arrived. And even before that, on the first day of September 1947, the United Nations Special Committee on Palestine presented its recommendations to the General Assembly.

And in Jerusalem, even though no violence had broken out as yet, it felt as though all of a sudden an invisible muscle was suddenly flexed. It was not sensible to go to those areas anymore.

So Father bravely telephoned the offices of Silwani and Sons Ltd in Princess Mary Street, introduced himself in English and in French, and asked, in both languages, to be put through to Mr. al-Silwani senior. A young male secretary answered him with cold politeness, asked him in fluent English and in French to be kind enough to hold the line for a few moments, and came on again to say that he had been authorized to take a message for Mr. Silwani. So Father dictated a brief message about our feelings, our regrets, our anxiety for the health of the dear child, our readiness to meet any medical expenses in full, and our sincere wish to effect a meeting at an early date to clarify and to try to right the wrong. (Father had a pronounced Russian accent in English and in French. When he said "the," it sounded like "dzee," while "locomotive" came out as "locomotsif.")

We received no answer from the Silwani family, either directly or via Mr. Knox-Guildford, Staszek Rudnicki's boss. Did Father endeavor to discover by other means how serious little Awwad's injuries were? What

Aisha had or hadn't said about me? If he did indeed manage to find anything out, they didn't say a word to me. To the day my mother died and afterward, to the day of his own death, my father and I never talked about that Saturday. Not even incidentally. And even many years later, some five years after the Six Day War, at Mala Rudnicki's memorial service, when poor Staszek talked half the night in his wheelchair and reminisced about all sorts of good and terrible times, he did not mention that Saturday at Silwani Villa.

And once, in 1967, after we conquered East Jerusalem, I went there on my own, quite early one Saturday morning in the summer, along the same route that we had taken that earlier Saturday. There were new iron gates, and a shiny black German car was parked in front of the house, fitted with gray curtains. On top of the wall that surrounded the garden there was broken glass that I did not remember. The green treetops showed above the wall. The flag of a certain important consulate fluttered above the roof, and beside the new iron gates there was a gleaming brass plate bearing the name of the state in question, in Arabic and in Latin characters, and its coat of arms. A guard in plain clothes came and stared at me curiously; I mumbled something and walked on toward Mount Scopus.

The cut on my chin healed in a few days. Dr. Hollander, the pediatrician at the clinic on Amos Street, removed the stitches put in at the first-aid station that Saturday morning.

From the day the stitches came out, a veil descended over the entire episode. Auntie Mala and Uncle Staszek were also enlisted in the cover-up. Not a word. Neither about Sheikh Jarrah nor about little Arab children nor about iron chains nor about orchards and mulberry trees, nor about scars on the chin. Taboo. It never happened. Only Mother, in her usual way, challenged the walls of censorship. Once, in our own special place, at the kitchen table, at our own special time, when Father was out of the house, she told me an Indian fable:

Once upon a time there were two monks who imposed all sorts of disciplines and afflictions on themselves. Among other things, they resolved to cross the whole Indian subcontinent on foot. They also determined to make the journey in complete silence: they were not to utter a single word, even in their sleep. Once, however, when they were walking on the bank of a river, they heard a drowning woman crying for help. Without a word the younger monk leaped into the water, carried the woman to the bank on his back, and laid her down wordlessly on the sand. The two ascetics continued their journey in silence. Six months or a year passed, and suddenly the younger monk asked his companion: Tell me, do you think I sinned in carrying that woman on my back? His friend answered with a question: What, are you still carrying her?

Father, for his part, went back to his research. At that time he was deep in the literatures of the ancient Near East, Akkadia and Sumeria, Babylonia and Assyria, the discoveries of early archives in Tel el-Amarna and Hatushash, the legendary library of King Assurbanipal, whom the Greeks called Sardanapalus, the stories of Gilgamesh, and the short myth of Adapa. Monographs and reference works piled up on his desk, surrounded by a regular army of notes and index cards. He tried to amuse Mother and me with one of his usual wisecracks: If you steal from one book, you're a plagiarist; if you steal from five books, you're a scholar; if you steal from fifty books, you're a great scholar.

Day by day that invisible muscle under Jerusalem's skin was tensing. Wild rumors circulated in our neighborhood; some of them were blood-curdling. Some said that the British government in London was about to withdraw the army, so as to enable the regular forces of the member states of the Arab League, which was nothing but an arm of the British dressed up in desert robes, to defeat the Jews, conquer the land and then, once the Jews had gone, let the British in by the back door. Jerusalem, some of the strategists in Mr. Auster's grocery maintained, would soon be King Abdullah of Trans-Jordan's capital, and we Jewish residents would be put on board ships and taken to refugee camps in Cyprus. Or we might be dispersed to DP camps in Mauritius and the Seychelles.

Others did not hesitate to claim that the Hebrew underground movements, the Irgun, the Stern Gang, and the Haganah, by their bloody actions against the English, particularly by blowing up the British HQ in the King David Hotel, had brought disaster upon us. No empire in history had turned a blind eye to such humiliating provocations, and the British had already decided to punish us with a savage bloodbath. The overhasty outrages of our fanatical Zionist leaders had made us so hated by the British public that London had decided simply to allow the Arabs to slaughter the lot of us: so far the British armed forces had stood between us and a general massacre by the Arab nations, but now they would step aside, and our blood would be on our own heads.

Some people reported that various well-connected Jews, rich people from Rehavia, contractors and wholesalers with connections to the British, high-ranking civil servants in the Mandatory administration, had been tipped that they would be better off going abroad as soon as possible, or at least sending their families to some safe haven. They mentioned such and such a family that had pushed off to America, and various well-to-do business people who had quit Jerusalem overnight and settled in Tel Aviv with their families. They must know for certain something that the rest of us could only imagine. Or they could imagine what was just a nightmare for us.

Others told of groups of young Arabs who combed our streets at night, armed with pots of paint and brushes, marking the Jewish houses and allocating them in advance. They claimed that armed Arab gangs, under the orders of the Grand Mufti of Jerusalem, already controlled all the hills around the city, and the British turned a blind eye to them. They said that the forces of the Trans-Jordanian Arab Legion, under the command of the British Brigadier Sir John Glubb, Glubb Pasha, were already deployed in various key positions across the country so that they could crush the Jews before they could even try to raise their heads. And that the fighters of the Muslim Brotherhood, whom the British had allowed to come in from Egypt with their arms and set up fortified positions in the hills around Jerusalem, were digging themselves in just across from Kibbutz Ramat Rahel. Some expressed the hope that when the British left, the American president, Truman, would step in despite everything. He would send his army in quickly, two gigantic American aircraft carriers had already been spotted off Sicily heading east; President Truman surely wouldn't allow a second Holocaust to happen here less than three years after the Holocaust of the Six Million. Surely the rich and influential American Jews would put pressure on him. They couldn't just stand idly by.

Some believed that the conscience of the civilized world, or progressive public opinion, or the international working class, or widespread guilt feelings over the sorry fate of the Jewish survivors, would all act to thwart the "Anglo-Arab plot to destroy us." At the very least, some of our friends and neighbors encouraged themselves at the onset of that strange, threatening autumn with the comforting thought that even if the Arabs didn't want us here, the last thing the peoples of Europe wanted was for us to go back and flood Europe again. And since the Europeans were far more powerful than the Arabs, it followed that there was a chance that we might be left here after all. They would force the Arabs to swallow what Europe was trying to spew forth.

One way or another, virtually everyone prophesied war. The underground broadcast passionate songs on the short waves. Grits, oil, candles, sugar, powdered milk, and flour almost vanished from the shelves in Mr. Auster's grocery shop: people were beginning to stock up in readiness for what was to come. Mother filled the kitchen cupboard with bags of flour and matzo meal, packets of rusks, Quaker oats, oil, preserves, canned food, olives, and sugar. Father bought two sealed canisters of paraffin and stored them under the basin in the bathroom.

Father still went off every day, as usual, at half past seven in the morning, to work in the National Library on Mount Scopus, on the No. 9 bus that went from Geula Street along Mea Shearim and crossed Sheikh Jarrah not far from Silwani Villa. He came home a little before five, with books and offprints in his battered briefcase and more tucked under his arm. But Mother asked him several times not to sit by the window in the bus. And she added some words in Russian. We suspended our regular Saturday afternoon walks to Uncle Joseph and Aunt Zippora's house for the time being.

I was barely nine, and already I was a devout newspaper reader. An avid consumer of the latest news. A keen expositor and debater. A political and military expert whose views were valued by the neighbors' children. A strategist with matchsticks, buttons, and dominoes on the matting. I would dispatch troops, execute tactical outflanking movements, forge alliances with one foreign power or another, store up trenchant arguments that were capable of winning over the stoniest British heart, and compose speeches that would not only bring the Arabs to understanding and reconciliation and make them ask for our forgiveness, but could even bring tears of sympathy for our sufferings to their eyes, mixed with profound admiration for our noble hearts and moral grandeur.

I conducted proud yet pragmatic talks at that time with Downing

Street, the White House, the Vatican, the Kremlin, and the Arab rulers. "Hebrew state! Free immigration!" demonstrators from the affiliated community shouted in marches and public gatherings, one or two of which Mother let Father take me along to. While every Friday, Arab crowds, marching angrily after they came out of the mosques, roared "*Idbah al-Yahud!*" (Butcher the Jews!) and "*Falastin hi arduna wa al-Yahud kilbuna!*" (Palestine is our land, and the Jews are our dogs!). If I had the chance, I could easily convince them rationally that while our slogans contained nothing that could hurt them, their slogans, shouted by inflamed mobs, were not very nice or civilized, and in fact they showed up the people who were shouting them in rather a shameful light. In those days I was not so much a child as a bundle of self-righteous arguments, a little chauvinist dressed up as a peace lover, a sanctimonious, honey-tongued nationalist, a nine-year-old Zionist propagandist. We were the goodies, we were in the right, we were innocent victims, we were David against Goliath, a lamb among wolves, the sacrificial lamb, whereas they—the British, the Arabs, and the whole Gentile world— they were the wolves, the evil, hypocritical world that was always thirsting for our blood, more shame on them.

When the British government announced the intention of ending its rule in Palestine and returning the mandate to the United Nations Organization, the UN set up a Special Committee on Palestine (UNSCOP) to examine conditions in Palestine and also among the hundreds of thousands of displaced Jews, survivors of the Nazi genocide, who had been living for two years and more in DP camps in Europe.

At the beginning of September 1947, UNSCOP published its majority report, recommending that the British mandate should end at the earliest opportunity. Instead, Palestine should be partitioned into two independent states, one for the Arabs and one for the Jews. The area allocated to the two states was almost equal in size. The complicated, winding border that separated them was drawn roughly in accordance with the demographic distribution of the respective populations. The two states would be linked by a common economy, currency, etc. Jerusalem, the committee recommended, should be a neutral *corpus separatum,* under international trusteeship with a governor appointed by the UN.

These recommendations were submitted to the General Assembly for its approval, which required a two-thirds majority. The Jews gritted their teeth and agreed to accept the partition proposal: the territory allocated to them did not include Jerusalem or Upper and Western Galilee, and three quarters of the proposed Jewish state was uncultivated desert land. Meanwhile the Palestinian Arab leadership and all the nations of the Arab League declared at once that they would not accept any compromise, and that they intended "to resist by force the implementation of these proposals, and to drown in blood any attempt to create a Zionist entity on a single inch of Palestinian soil." They argued that the whole of Palestine had been Arab land for hundreds of years, until the British came and encouraged hordes of foreigners to spread all over it, flattening hills, uprooting ancient olive groves, purchasing land, plot by plot, by subterfuges from corrupt landlords, and driving out the peasants who had farmed it for generations. If they were not stopped, these crafty Jewish colonists would swallow up the whole of the land, eradicating every trace of Arab life, covering it with their red-roofed European colonies, corrupting it with their arrogant and licentious ways, and very soon they would take control of the holy places of Islam and then they would overflow into the neighboring Arab countries. In no time at all, thanks to their deviousness and technical superiority, and with the support of British imperialism, they would do here exactly what the whites had done to the indigenous populations in America, Australia, and elsewhere. If they were allowed to set up a state here, even a little one, they would undoubtedly use it as a bridgehead, they would flood in, millions of them, like locusts, settle on every hill and valley, rob these ancient landscapes of their Arab character, and swallow everything up before the Arabs had time to shake themselves out of their slumber.

In the middle of October the British High Commissioner, General Sir Alan Cunningham, uttered a veiled threat to David Ben-Gurion, who was the executive head of the Jewish Agency: "If troubles begin," he remarked sadly, "I fear that we will not be able to help you; we will not be able to defend you."*

Father said:

"Herzl was a prophet and he knew it. At the time of the First Zionist congress in 1897 he said that in five years, or at the latest in fifty years,

*Dov Joseph, *The Faithful City: The Siege of Jerusalem, 1948* (London, 1962), p. 31.

there would be a Jewish State in the Land of Israel. And now fifty years have passed, and the state is literally standing at the gate."

Mother said:

"It's not standing. There is no gate. There's an abyss."

Father's reprimand sounded like the crack of a whip. He spoke in Russian, so that I would not understand.

And I said, with a joy I could not conceal:

"There's going to be a war soon in Jerusalem! And we'll beat them all!"

But sometimes, when I was all alone in the yard toward sunset or early on Saturday morning when my parents and the whole neighborhood were still asleep, I would freeze with a stab of terror, because the picture of the girl Aisha picking up the unconscious child and silently carrying him in her arms suddenly seemed to me like a chilling Christian picture that Father showed me and explained to me in a whisper when we visited a church once.

I remembered the olive trees I saw from the windows of that house, which had left the world of the living ages before and become part of the realm of the inanimate.

Jest a minute rest a minute jest a rest a jesta resta.

By November a sort of curtain had begun to divide Jerusalem. The buses still ran there and back, and fruit sellers from the nearby Arab villages still did their rounds in our street, carrying trays of figs, almonds, and prickly pears, but some Jewish families had already moved out of the Arab neighborhoods, and Arabs families had begun to leave the west of the city for the southern and eastern parts.

Only in my thoughts could I sometimes go to the extension of St. George's Street northeastward, and stare wide-eyed at the other Jerusalem: a city of old cypress trees that were more black than green, streets of stone walls, interlaced grilles, cornices, and dark walls, the alien, silent, aloof, shrouded Jerusalem, the Abyssinian, Muslim, pilgrim, Ottoman city, the strange, missionary city of crusaders and Templars, the Greek, Armenian, Italian, brooding, Anglican, Greek Orthodox city, the monastic, Coptic, Catholic, Lutheran, Scottish, Sunni, Shi'ite, Sufi, Alawite city, swept by the sound of bells and the wail of the muezzin, thick with pine trees, frightening yet alluring, with all its concealed enchantments, its warrens of narrow streets that were forbidden to us and threatened us from the darkness, a secretive, malign city pregnant with disaster.

The whole Silwani family, I was told after the Six Day War, left Jordanian Jerusalem in the 1950s and early 1960s. Some went to Switzerland and Canada, others settled in the Gulf emirates, a few moved to London, and some others to Latin America.

And what about their parrots? "Who will be my destiny? Who will be my prince?"

And what about Aisha? And her lame brother? Where on earth is she playing her piano, assuming she still has one, assuming she has not grown old and worn out among the dusty, heat-blasted hovels in some refugee camp where the sewage runs down the unpaved streets.

And who are the fortunate Jews who now live in what was once her family home in Talbieh, a neighborhood built of pale blue and pinkish stone with stone vaults and arches?

It was not because of the approaching war but for some other, deeper reason that I would be suddenly seized with dread in those autumn days of 1947 and feel aching pangs of yearning mixed with shame and the certainty of impending punishment and also some ill-defined pain: a sort of forbidden longing, blended with guilt and sorrow. For that orchard. For that well that was covered with a sheet of green metal, and the blue-tiled pool where golden fish sparkled for an instant in the sunlight before disappearing into the forest of water lilies. For the soft cushions trimmed with fine lace. For the richly textured rugs, one of which showed birds of paradise among trees of paradise. For the stained-glass trefoils, each of which colored the daylight a different shade: red leaf, green leaf, gold leaf, purple leaf.

And for the parrot who sounded like an inveterate smoker: "*Mais oui, mais oui, chère mademoiselle,*" and its soprano counterpart that answered in a voice like a silver bell: "*Tfaddal! S'il vous plaît! Enjoy!*"

I was there once, in that orchard, before I was banished from it in disgrace, I did touch it once, with my fingertips—

"Bas! Bas, ya 'eini! Bas min fadlak! Usqut!"

Early in the morning I would wake to the smell of first light and see through the iron slats of the closed shutters the pomegranate tree that stood in our yard. Hidden in this tree every morning an invisible bird would repeat joyfully and precisely the first five notes of *Für Elise*.

Such an articulate fool, such a noisy little fool.

Instead of approaching her like the New Hebrew Youth approaching the Noble Arab People, or like a lion approaching lions, perhaps I could simply have approached her like a boy approaching a girl. Or couldn't I?

42

"JUST LOOK how that strategist of a child has occupied the whole apartment again. You can't move in the corridor, it's so full of fortifications and towers made out of building blocks, castles made out of dominoes, mines made out of corks, and borders made out of spillikins. In his room there are battlefields of buttons from wall to wall. We're not allowed in there, it's out of bounds. That's an order. And even in our room he's scattered knives and forks all over the floor, presumably to mark out some Maginot Line or navy or armored corps. If it goes on like this, you and I will have to move out into the yard. Or into the street. But the moment the paper arrived, your child dropped everything, he must have declared a general cease-fire, and he lay back on the sofa and read it from cover to cover, including the small ads. Now he's running a line from his HQ behind his wardrobe right through the apartment to Tel Aviv, which is apparently on the edge of the bathtub. If I'm not mistaken, he's about to use it to speak to Ben-Gurion. Like yesterday. To explain to him what we ought to be doing at this point and what we ought to watch out for. He might already have started giving Ben-Gurion orders."

In one of the bottom drawers here in my study in Arad I found a battered cardboard box last night, containing various notes that I made when I was writing the novellas that make up *The Hill of Evil Counsel*, more than twenty-five years ago. Among other things there are some messy notes that I made in a library in Tel Aviv in 1974 or 1975 from newspapers from September 1947. And so, in Arad, on a summer morning in 2001, like an image reflected in a mirror reflected in another mirror, my notes from twenty-seven years ago remind me of what the "strategist of a child" read in the paper of September 9, 1947:

Hebrew traffic police have started to operate in Tel Aviv with the consent of the British governor. They have eight policemen working in two shifts. A thirteen-year-old Arab girl is to stand trial before a military court, accused of possessing a rifle in the village of Hawara, Nablus District. The "illegal" immigrants from the *Exodus* are being deported to Hamburg, and they say they will fight to the last to resist disembarkation. Fourteen Gestapo men have been sentenced to death in Lübeck. Mr. Solomon Chmelnik of Rehovot has been kidnapped and badly beaten up by an extremist organization but has been returned safe and sound. The Voice of Jerusalem orchestra is going to be conducted by Hanan Schlesinger. Mahatma Gandhi's fast is in its second day. The singer Edis de Philippe will be unable to perform this week in Jerusalem, and the Chamber Theatre has been obliged to postpone its performance of *You Can't Take It with You*. On the other hand, two days ago the new Colonnade Building on the Jaffa Road was opened, containing, among other shops, Mikolinski, Freidmann & Bein, and the chiropodist Dr. Scholl. According to the Arab leader Musa Alami, the Arabs will never accept the partition of the country; after all, King Solomon ruled that the mother who was opposed to partition was the true mother, and the Jews ought to recognize the significance of the parable. And then again, Comrade Golda Myerson [later Meir] of the Jewish Agency Executive has declared that the Jews will fight for the inclusion of Jerusalem in the Hebrew State, because the Land of Israel and Jerusalem are synonymous in our hearts.

A few days later the paper reported:

Late last night, an Arab set upon two Jewish girls in the vicinity of the Bernardiya Café, between Beit Hakerem and Bayit Vagan. One of the girls escaped, and the other screamed for help, and some of the local residents heard and succeeded in preventing the suspect from escaping. In the course of investigations by Constable O'Connor, it emerged that the man is an employee of the Broadcasting Service and is distantly related to the influential Nashashibi family. Despite this, bail was refused, on account of the gravity of the alleged offense. In his defense the prisoner stated that he had come out of the café drunk and had been under the impression that the two girls were prancing around naked in the dark.

And another day in September 1947:

> Lieutenant-Colonel Adderley has presided over a military court hearing the case of Shlomo Mansoor Shalom, a distributor of illegal leaflets who was found to be of unsound mind. The probation officer, Mr. Gardewicz, requested that the prisoner should not be committed to a lunatic asylum, for fear of a deterioration in his condition, and pleaded with the judges that he should be isolated in a private institution instead, lest his weak intellect be exploited by fanatics for their own criminal ends. Lt.-Col. Adderley regretted that he was unable to accede to Mr. Gardewicz's request, since it was beyond his powers; he was obliged to commit the unfortunate man to custody pending a ruling by the High Commissioner, representing the Crown, on the possible exercise of special leniency or clemency. On the radio, Cilla Leibowitz is giving a piano recital, and after the news we are promised a commentary by Mr. Gordus; to round off the evening Miss Bracha Tsefira will give a rendition of a selection of folk songs.

One evening Father explained to his friends who had come over for a glass of tea that ever since the middle of the eighteenth century, long before the appearance of modern Zionism and unconnected with it, the Jews constituted a clear majority of the population of Jerusalem. At the beginning of the twentieth century, still before the beginning of the Zionist immigrations, Jerusalem, under Ottoman Turkish rule, was already the most populous city in the country: it had fifty-five thousand inhabitants, of whom some thirty-five thousand were Jews. And now, in the autumn of 1947, there were about a hundred thousand Jews living in Jerusalem and some sixty-five thousand non-Jews, made up of Muslim and Christian Arabs, Armenians, Greeks, British, and many other nationalities.

But in the north, east, and south of the city there were extensive Arab neighborhoods, including Sheikh Jarrah, the American colony, the Muslim and Christian Quarters in the Old City, the German Colony, the Greek Colony, Katamon, Bakaa, and Abu Tor. There were Arab towns, too, in the hills around Jerusalem, Ramallah and el-Bireh, Beit Jalla and Bethlehem, and many Arab villages: el-Azariya, Silwan, Abu-Dis, et-Tur, Isawiya, Qalandaria, Bir Naballah, Nebi Samwil, Biddu, Shuafat, Lifta, Beit Hanina, Beit Iksa, Qoloniya, Sheikh Badr, Deir Yassin, where more than a hundred inhabitants would be butchered by members of the Irgun and the Stern Gang in April 1948, Suba, Ein Karim, Beit Mazmil, el-Maliha, Beit Safafa, Umm Tuba, and Sur Bahir.

To the north, south, east, and west of Jerusalem were Arab areas, and only a few Hebrew settlements were scattered here and there around the city: Atarot and Neve Yaakov to the north, Kalya and Beit ha-Arava on the shore of the Dead Sea to the east, Ramat Rahel and Gush Etsion to the south, and Motsa, Kiriat Anavim and Maale ha-Hamisha to the west. In the war of 1948 most of these Hebrew settlements, together with the Jewish Quarter inside the walls of the Old City, fell into the hands of the Arab Legion. All the Jewish settlements that were captured by the Arabs in the War of Independence, without exception, were razed to the ground, and their Jewish inhabitants were murdered or taken captive or escaped, but the Arab armies did not allow any of the survivors to return after the war. The Arabs implemented a more complete "ethnic cleansing" in the territories they conquered than the Jews did: hundreds of thousands of Arabs fled or were driven out from the territory of the State of Israel in that war, but a hundred thousand remained, whereas there were no Jews at all in the West Bank or the Gaza Strip under Jordanian and Egyptian rule. Not one. The settlements were obliterated, and the synagogues and cemeteries were razed to the ground.

In the lives of individuals and of peoples, too, the worst conflicts are often those that break out between those who are persecuted. It is mere wishful thinking to imagine that the persecuted and the oppressed will unite out of solidarity and man the barricades together against a ruthless oppressor. In reality, two children of the same abusive father will not necessarily make common cause, brought close together by their shared fate. Often each sees in the other not a partner in misfortune but in fact the image of their common oppressor.

That may well be the case with the hundred-year-old conflict between Arabs and Jews.

The Europe that abused, humiliated, and oppressed the Arabs by means of imperialism, colonialism, exploitation, and repression is the same Europe that oppressed and persecuted the Jews, and eventually allowed or even helped the Germans to root them out of every corner of the continent and murder almost all of them. But when the Arabs look at us, they see not a bunch of half-hysterical survivors but a new offshoot of Europe, with its colonialism, technical sophistication, and exploitation, that has cleverly returned to the Middle East—in Zionist guise this time—to exploit, evict, and oppress all over again. And when we look at them, we do not see fellow victims either; we see not brothers in adversity but pogrom-making Cossacks, bloodthirsty anti-Semites, Nazis in disguise, as though our European persecutors have reappeared here in the Land of Israel, put keffiyehs on their heads, and grown mustaches, but they are still our old murderers, interested only in slitting Jews' throats for fun.

In September, October, and November 1947 nobody in Kerem Avraham knew whether to pray that the UN General Assembly would approve the UNSCOP majority report or to hope instead that the British would not abandon us to our fate, "alone and defenseless in a sea of Arabs." Many hoped that a free Hebrew state would be established at last, that the restrictions on immigration imposed by the British would be lifted, and the hundreds of thousands of Jewish survivors who had been languishing in displaced persons camps and detention camps in Cyprus since the downfall of Hitler would finally be allowed into the land that most of them considered their only home. Yet behind the back of these hopes, as it were, they feared (in whispers) that the million local Arabs, with the help of the regular armies of the countries of the Arab League, might rise up and slaughter the six hundred thousand Jews the moment the British pulled out.

At the grocer's, in the street, at the pharmacist's, people talked openly about an imminent redemption, they talked about Moshe Shertok and

Eliezer Kaplan becoming ministers in the Hebrew government to be set up by Ben-Gurion in Haifa or Tel Aviv, and they talked (in whispers) about famous Jewish generals from abroad, from the Red Army, the American Air Force, and even the Royal Navy, being invited to come and command the Hebrew armed forces to be created when the British left.

But secretly, at home, under the blankets, after lights out, they whispered to each that who knew—perhaps the British would still cancel their evacuation, perhaps they had no intention of leaving, and the whole thing was nothing but a cunning ploy on the part of Perfidious Albion, with the aim of getting the Jews themselves to turn to the British in the face of impending annihilation and beg them not to abandon them to their fate. Then London could demand, in exchange for continued British protection, that the Jews cease all terrorist activities, decommission some of their stockpiles of illegal weapons, and hand over the leaders of the underground armies to the CID. Perhaps the British would change their minds at the last minute and not surrender us all to the mercy of the Arabs' knives. Perhaps at least here in Jerusalem they might leave a regular force behind to protect us from an Arab pogrom. Or perhaps Ben-Gurion and his friends down there in comfortable Tel Aviv, which was not surrounded by Arabs on every side, might come to their senses at the last minute and give up this adventure of a Hebrew state in favor of some modest compromise with the Arab world and the Muslim masses. Or perhaps the United Nations would send some troops from neutral countries while there was still time to take over from the British and protect the Holy City at least, if not the whole Holy Land, from the threat of a bloodbath.

Azzam Pasha, the secretary general of the Arab League, warned the Jews that "if they dared to attempt to create a Zionist entity on a single inch of Arab land, the Arabs would drown them in their own blood," and the Middle East would witness horrors "compared to which the atrocities of the Mongol conquests would pale into insignificance." The Iraqi Prime Minister, Muzahim al-Bajaji, called on the Jews of Palestine to "pack their bags and leave while there was still time," because the Arabs had vowed that after their victory they would spare the lives only of those few Jews who had lived in Palestine before 1917, and even they "would be allowed to take refuge under the wings of Islam and be tolerated under its banner only on condition that they woke up once and for all from the poison of Zionism and became once more a religious community that knew its place under the protection of Islam and lived according to the laws and customs of Islam." The Jews, added a preacher at the great mosque in Jaffa, were not a people and not really a religion either: everyone knew that Allah, the compassionate, the merciful, himself detested them, and had therefore condemned them to be accursed and despised forever in all the lands of their dispersion. The Jews were the most stubborn of the stubborn: the Prophet had extended his hand to them, and they had spat at him; Issa (Jesus) had extended his hand to them, and they had murdered him; they had even regularly stoned to death the prophets of their own contemptible faith. Not in vain had all the nations of Europe resolved to be rid of them once and for all, and now Europe was planning to inflict them all upon us, but we Arabs would not permit the Europeans to dump their rubbish on us. We Arabs would frustrate with our swords this devilish plan to turn the holy land of Palestine into a midden for all the refuse of the world.

And what about the man from Aunt Greta's clothes shop? The compassionate Arab man who rescued me from the dark pit and carried me in his arms when I was only four or five? The man with big bags under his kind eyes, and a brown, soporific smell, with the green-and-white tailor's tape-measure around his neck, both ends dangling down onto his chest, with his warm cheek and pleasant gray stubble, that sleepy, kindly man with a shy smile that flickered for a moment and died under his soft gray mustache? With his square, brown-framed reading glasses, which he wore halfway down his nose, like a kindhearted, elderly carpenter, a sort of Gepetto, that man who walked so slowly, dragging his feet in a weary sort of way, through the thicket of women's clothes, and when he pulled me out of my solitary confinement, said to me in his husky voice, a voice that I will always remember with longing: "Enough child every thing all right child everything all right." What, him too? Was he "sharpening his curved dagger, whetting the blade and preparing to slaughter us all"? Would he too sneak into Amos Street in the middle of the night with a long curved knife between his teeth, to slit my throat and my parents' throats and "drown us all in blood"?

Balmy are the nights in Canaan
as the breeze blows over all.
From the Nile hyenas answer
the Syrian jackals' call.
Abd el-Qadr, Spears, and Khoury
stir their poison brew of gall.

. . .

Stormy March winds puff and bluster
sending clouds across the sky.
Youthful, fully armed, and bristling
Tel Aviv tonight lets fly,
Manara keeps a lofty vigil,
watchful is the Huleh's eye.*

But Jewish Jerusalem was neither youthful nor fully armed and bristling, it was a Chekhovian town, confused, terrified, swept by gossip and false rumors, at its wits' end, paralyzed by muddle and terror. On April 20, 1948, David Ben-Gurion wrote in his diary, following a conversation with David Shealtiel, the commander of the Haganah militia in Jerusalem, his impression of Jewish Jerusalem:

> The element in Jerusalem: 20% normal people, 20% privileged (university etc.), 60% weird (provincial, medieval, etc.).**

(It is hard to say whether Ben-Gurion smiled when he wrote this entry in his diary; either way, Kerem Avraham was not included in the first category, nor in the second either.)

At the greengrocer's, our neighbor Mrs. Lemberg said:

"But I don't trust them anymore already. I don't trust anybody. It's just one big intrigue."

Mrs. Rosendorff said:

"You absolutely mustn't speak like this. I'm sorry. You must please forgive me if I say this to you: speaking like this simply wrecks the morale of the entire nation. What are you thinking? That our boys will

---

*Natan Alterman, "Nights in Canaan," from *The Seventh Column*, vol. 1 (Tel Aviv, 1950), p. 364.
**David Ben-Gurion, *Diary of the War, 1948*, ed. G. Rivlin and Dr. E. Oren, vol. 1 (Tel Aviv, 1983), p. 359.

agree to go and fight for you, risk their young lives, if you are saying that it is all an intrigue?"

The greengrocer, Mr. Babaiof, said:

"I don't envy those Arabs. There are some Jews in America, they will soon send us here some atom bombs."

My mother said:

"These onions don't look too good. Neither do the cucumbers."

And Mrs. Lemberg (who always smelled faintly of hard-boiled eggs, perspiration, and stale soap) said:

"It's all just one big intrigue, I'm telling you! They're making theater! Comedy! Ben-Gurion has already agreed in secret to sell all of Jerusalem to the Mufti and the Arab gangs and King Abdullah, and for this the English and the Arabs have agreed maybe to leave him his kibbutzim and the Nahalal and Tel Aviv. And that's all they care about! And what will happen to us, if they will murder us or burn us all, they don't care about that at all. Jerusalem, the best thing they should all go *faifen*, so afterward in the state they want to make for themselves they should be left with a few less revisionists, a few less ultra-Orthodox, a few less intelligentsia."

The other women hurriedly silenced her: What's the matter with you! Mrs. Lemberg! *Sha! Bist du meshigge? Es shteit da a kind! A farshtandiker kind!* (Hush! Are you crazy? There is a child here! A child who understands!)

The *farshtandiker kind*, the child strategist, recited what he had heard from his father or his grandfather:

"When the British go home, the Haganah, the Irgun, and the Stern Gang will certainly unite and defeat the enemy."

Meanwhile, the unseen bird in the pomegranate tree held fast to its own line: it did not budge. "Ti-da-di-da-di." And over and over again: "Ti-da-di-da-di." And after a pause for reflection: "Ti-da-di-da-di!!"

43

IN SEPTEMBER and October 1947 the papers were full of guesses, analyses, assessments, and suppositions. Would there be a vote on partition at the General Assembly? Would the Arabs succeed in getting the recommendations changed or the vote canceled? And if it did go to the vote, where would we get a two-thirds majority?

Every evening Father would sit between Mother and me at the kitchen table, and after drying the oilcloth he would spread out some cards and start calculating, in pencil, in the sickly yellow light, the chances of winning the vote. Evening by evening his spirits fell. All his calculations indicated a certain and crushing defeat.

"All twelve Arab and Muslim states will naturally vote against us. And the Catholic Church is definitely putting pressure on the Catholic countries to vote against, because a Jewish state contradicts the fundamental belief of the Church, and there's no one like the Vatican when it comes to pulling strings behind the scenes. So we'll probably lose all twenty votes of the Latin American countries. And Stalin will undoubtedly instruct all his satellites in the Communist bloc to vote in accordance with his rigid anti-Zionist approach, so that makes another twelve votes against us. Not to mention England, which is always stirring up feeling against us everywhere and especially in her dominions, Canada, Australia, New Zealand, and South Africa, and they'll all be roped in to thwart any chance of a Hebrew state. What about France, and the countries that follow her? France will never dare to risk incurring the anger of the millions of Muslims in Tunisia, Algeria, and Morocco. Greece has close trade links with the whole Arab world, and there are big Greek communities in all the Arab countries. And what about America itself? Is America's support for the partition plan final? What happens if the intrigues of the giant oil companies and our enemies in the State Department tip the balance and outweigh President Truman's conscience?"

Over and over again Father calculated the balance of votes in the Assembly. Evening after evening he tried to soften the blow, to devise some coalition of countries that usually followed the United States, countries that might have reasons of their own to oppose the Arabs, and small, respectable countries like Denmark or Holland, countries that had witnessed the horrors of the genocide of the Jewish people and might now gird their loins and act according to the dictates of their conscience rather than considerations of self-interest and oil.

Was the Silwani family, in their villa in Sheikh Jarrah (a mere forty minutes' walk from here), also sitting around a piece of paper at their kitchen table this very minute, making the same calculations in reverse? Were they worrying, just like us, which way Greece would vote, and chewing the tip of a pencil over the final decision of the Scandinavian countries? Did they also have their optimists and pessimists, their cynics and their prophets of doom? Were they also trembling every night, imagining that we were scheming, stirring things up, cunningly pulling strings? Were they also all asking what would happen here, what would come to pass? Were they just as frightened of us as we were of them?

And how about Aisha, and her parents in Talbieh? Was her whole family sitting in a room full of men with mustaches and jeweled women with angry faces and eyebrows that met above their noses, gathered in a circle around bowls of sugared orange peel, whispering among themselves and planning to "drown us in blood"? Did Aisha still sometimes play tunes she had learned from her Jewish piano teacher? Or was she forbidden to?

Or perhaps they were standing in a silent circle around their little boy's bed? Awwad. His leg had been amputated. Because of me. Or he was dying from blood poisoning. Because of me. His curious, innocent puppy-dog eyes were closed. Pressed tight with suffering. His face drawn and pale as ice. His forehead racked with pain. His pretty curls lying on the white pillow. Jest a moment rest a moment. Groaning and shaking with pain. Or quietly crying in a high-pitched baby voice. And his sister sitting by his bedside hating me because it was my fault, everything was my fault, it was my fault she was beaten so cruelly, so thoroughly, over and over again, on her back, her head, her frail shoulders, not the way a girl who has done something wrong is sometimes beaten, but like a stubborn horse. It was my fault.

Grandpa Alexander and Grandma Shlomit used to come around sometimes on those September evenings in 1947 to sit with us and take part in Father's vote-counting stock exchange. Also Hannah and Hayim Toren, or the Rudnickis, Auntie Mala and Uncle Staszek, or the Abramskis, or our neighbors the Rosendorffs and Tosia and Gustav Krochmal. Mr. Krochmal had a tiny lock-up shop down Geula Street where he sat all day wearing a leather apron and horn-rimmed glasses, repairing dolls:

Reliable healer from Danzig, toy doctor

Once, when I was about five, Uncle Gustav mended my red-haired ballerina doll, Tsilly, for me for nothing, in his miniature workshop. Her freckled nose had broken off. Skillfully, with a special glue, Mr. Krochmal repaired her so well that you could hardly see the scar.

Mr. Krochmal believed in dialogue with our Arab neighbors. In his view, the residents of Kerem Avraham ought to get together a small, select deputation and go and hold talks with the mukhtars, sheikhs, and other dignitaries of the nearest Arab villages. After all, we had always enjoyed good neighborly relations, and even if the rest of the country was going out of its mind, there was no logical reason why here, in northwest Jerusalem, where there had never been any conflict or hostility between the two sides—

If he could only speak a little Arabic or English, he himself, Gustav Krochmal, who had applied his healing skills for many years to Arab and Jewish dolls alike, without distinction, would pick up his walking stick, cross the empty field that divided us from them, knock on their doors, and explain to them, in simple terms, from house to house—

Sergeant Wilk, Uncle Dudek, a handsome man who looked like an English colonel in a film and actually did serve the British at that time as a policeman, came around one evening and stayed for a while, bringing a box of *langues de chat* from a special chocolate factory. He drank a cup of coffee and chicory mixture, ate a couple of biscuits, and dazzled me with his smart black uniform with its row of silvery buttons, the leather belt that ran diagonally across his chest, and his black pistol that reposed in a gleaming holster on his hip, like a sleeping lion (only the butt protruded, giving me the shivers every time I looked at it). Uncle Dudek stayed a quarter of an hour or so, and it was only after my parents and their guests had begged him that he finally let out one or two veiled hints about what he had gathered from the veiled hints of some high-ranking British police officers who knew what they were talking about:

"It's a pity about all your calculations and guesses. There's not going to be any partition. There aren't going to be two states, seeing as what the whole of the Negev is going to remain in British hands so they can protect their bases in Suez, and the British will also hang on to Haifa, the town as well as the port, and the main airfields at Lydda, Ekron, and Ramat David, and their clump of army camps at Sarafand. All the rest, including Jerusalem, the Arabs will get, seeing as what America wants them to agree in return to let the Jews have a kind of pocket between Tel Aviv and Hadera. The Jews will be permitted to establish an autonomous canton in this pocket, a sort of Jewish Vatican City, and we'll gradually be allowed to bring into this pocket up to a hundred thousand or at most a hundred and fifty thousand survivors from the DP camps. If necessary, this Jewish pocket will be defended by a few thousand US marines from the Sixth Fleet, from their giant aircraft carriers, seeing as that they don't believe the Jews will be able to defend themselves under these conditions."

"But that's a ghetto!" Mr. Abramski shouted in a terrible voice. "A prison! Solitary confinement!"

Gustav Krochmal, for his part, smiled and suggested pleasantly:

"It would be much better if the Americans took this Lilliput they want to give us, and simply gave us their two aircraft carriers instead: we'd be more comfortable there, and safer too. And a bit less crowded."

Mala Rudnicki begged the policeman, implored him, as though she were pleading with him for our lives:

"What about Galilee? Galilee, dear Dudek? And the Valleys? Won't we even get the Valleys? Why can't they leave us that at least? Why must they take the poor man's last ewe-lamb?"

Father remarked sadly:

"There's no such thing as the poor man's last ewe-lamb, Mala: the poor man had only one ewe-lamb, and they came and took that away from him."

After a short silence Grandpa Alexander exploded furiously, going red in the face, puffing up as if he was about to boil over:

"He was quite right, that villain from the mosque in Jaffa! He was quite right! We really are just dung! *Nu*, what: this is the end! *Vsyo! Khvatit!* That's enough! All the anti-Semites in the world are very right. Khmelnicki was right. Petliura was right. Hitler was right also: *nu*, what. There really is a curse on us! God really does hate us! As for me," Grandpa groaned, flaming red, shooting flecks of saliva in every direction, thumping on the table till he made the teaspoons rattle in the glasses, "*nu*, what, *ty skazal*, the same way as God hates us so I hate him back! I hate God! Let him die already! The anti-Semite from Berlin is burnt, but up there is sitting another Hitler! Much worse! *Nu*, what! He's sitting there laughing at us, the rascal!"

Grandma Shlomit took hold of his arm and commanded: "Zisya! that's enough! *Shto ty govorish! Genug! Iber genug!*" They somehow calmed him down. They poured him a little brandy and put some biscuits in front of him.

But Uncle Dudek, Sergeant Wilk, apparently considered that words such as those that Grandpa had roared so desperately should not be uttered in the presence of the police, so he stood up, donned his splendid policeman's peaked cap, adjusted his holster on his left hip, and from the doorway offered us a chance of a reprieve, a ray of light, as though taking pity on us and condescending to respond positively to our appeal, at least up to a point:

"But there's another officer, an Irishman, a real character, who keeps repeating the same thing, that the Jews have more brains than the rest of the world put together, and they always end up landing on their feet. That's what he says. The question is, whose feet exactly do they land on? Good night, all. I must just ask you not to repeat anything I've told you, seeing as what it's inside information." (All his life, even as an old man, after living in Jerusalem for sixty years, Uncle Dudek always insisted on saying "seeing as what," and three generations of devoted sticklers for the language failed to teach him otherwise. Even his years of service as a senior police officer and eventually as chief of the Jerusalem police, and later as deputy director-general of the Ministry of Tourism, did not help. He always stayed just as he was—"seeing as what I'm just a stubborn Jew!").

44

FATHER EXPLAINED over supper one evening that at the General Assembly of the United Nations, which would meet on November 29, at Lake Success, near New York, a majority of at least two-thirds would be required if the UNSCOP report recommending the creation of two states on the territory of the British Mandate, one Jewish and one Arab, was to be adopted. The Muslim bloc, together with Britain, would do everything in their power to prevent such a majority. They wanted the whole territory to become an Arab state under British protection, just as some other Arab countries, including Egypt, Trans-Jordan, and Iraq, were de facto under British protection. On the other side, President Truman was working, contrary to his own State Department, for the partition proposal to be accepted.

Stalin's Soviet Union had surprisingly joined with the United States and also supported the establishment of a Jewish state side by side with an Arab one: he may have foreseen that a vote in favor of partition would lead to many years of bloody conflict in the region, which would enable the USSR to acquire a foothold in the area of British influence in the Middle East, close to the oil fields and the Suez Canal. Contorted calculations on the part of the superpowers coincided with one another, and apparently intersected with religious ambitions: the Vatican hoped to gain decisive influence in Jerusalem, which under the partition plan was to be under international control, i.e., neither Muslim nor Jewish. Considerations of conscience and sympathy intertwined with selfish, cynical ones: several European governments were seeking a way of somehow compensating the Jewish people for losing a third of its numbers at the hands of the German murderers and for generations of persecution. The same governments, however, were not averse to channeling the tide of hundreds of thousands of indigent displaced Eastern European Jews who had been languishing in camps since the defeat of Germany as far away as possible from their own territories and indeed from Europe.

Right up to the moment of the actual vote it was hard to foresee the outcome. Pressures and temptations, threats and intrigues and even bribes managed to sway the crucial votes of three or four little republics in Latin America and the Far East back and forth. The government of Chile, which had been in favor of partition, yielded to Arab pressure and instructed its representative at the UN to vote against. Haiti announced its intention of voting against. The Greek delegation was of a mind to abstain, but also decided at the last minute to support the Arab position. The Philippine representative refused to commit himself. Paraguay hesitated; its delegate to the UN, Dr. César Acosta, complained that he had not received clear instructions from his government. In Siam there had been a coup d'état, and the new government had recalled its delegation and not yet dispatched a new one. Liberia promised to support the proposal. Haiti changed its mind, under American pressure, and decided to vote in favor.* Meanwhile, in Amos Street, in Mr. Auster's grocery shop

*See Jorge García Granados, *The Birth of Israel: The Drama As I Saw It* (New York: Alfred A. Knopf, 1948).

or at Mr. Caleko's, the news agent and stationer, they told of a good-looking Arab diplomat who had exerted his charms on the female representative of a small state and managed to get her to vote against the partition plan, even though her government had promised the Jews their support. "But at once," Mr. Kolodny, the proprietor of Kolodny's Printing Press, chuckled, "they sent a clever Jew to spill the beans to the infatuated diplomat's husband, and a clever Jewess to spill the beans to the diplomatic Don Juan's wife, and in case that doesn't do the trick, they've also arranged . . ." (here the conversation switched to Yiddish, so I wouldn't understand).

On Saturday morning, they said, the General Assembly would convene at a place called Lake Success and there they would determine our fate. "Who is for life and who for destruction," said Mr. Abramski. And Mrs. Tosia Krochmal fetched the extension cord from the sewing machine in her husband's dolls' hospital to enable the Lembergs to bring their heavy black radio receiver outside and set it up on the table on the balcony. (It was the only radio in Amos Street, if not in the whole of Kerem Avraham.) They would put it on at full volume, and we would all assemble in the Lembergs' apartment, in the yard, in the street, on the balcony of the apartment upstairs and on the balcony opposite, and so the whole street would be able to hear the live broadcast, and learn the verdict and what the future held for us ("if indeed there is a future after this Saturday").

"The name Lake Success," Father remarked, "is the opposite of the Sea of Tears that symbolizes the fate of our people in Bialik. Your Highness," he continued, "will be allowed to take part on this occasion, as befits his new role as devout newspaper reader and as our political and military commentator."

Mother said:

"Yes, but with a sweater on: it's chilly out."

But on Saturday morning it turned out that the fateful meeting due to take place that afternoon at Lake Success would start here only in the evening, because of the time difference between New York and Jerusalem, or perhaps because Jerusalem was such an out-of-the-way place, so far from the great world, over the hills and far away, that everything that happened out there only reached us faintly, and always after a delay. The vote, they worked out, would be taken when it was very late in Jerusalem, close to midnight, an hour when this child ought to be long since tucked in bed, because we have to get up for school in the morning.

Some rapid sentences were exchanged between Mother and Father, a short exchange in shchphzhenic Polish and yanikhatchuic Russian, at the end of which Mother said:

"It might be best after all if you go to bed as usual tonight, but we'll sit outside by the fence and listen to the broadcast from the Lembergs' balcony, and if the result is positive, we'll wake you up even if it's midnight and tell you. We promise."

After midnight, toward the end of the vote, I woke up. My bed was underneath the window that looked out on the street, so all I had to do was kneel and peer through the slats of the shutters. I shivered.

Like a frightening dream, crowds of shadows stood massed together silently by the yellow light of the street lamp, in our yard, in the neighboring yards, on balconies, in the roadway, like a vast assembly of ghosts. Hundreds of people not uttering a sound, neighbors, acquaintances, and strangers, some in their nightclothes and others in jacket and tie, occasional men in hats or caps, some women bareheaded, others in dressing gowns with scarves around their heads, some of them carrying sleepy children on their shoulders, and on the edge of the crowd I noticed here and there an elderly woman sitting on a stool or a very old man who had been brought out into the street with his chair.

The whole crowd seemed to have been turned to stone in that frightening night silence, as if they were not real people but hundreds of dark silhouettes painted onto the canvas of the flickering darkness. As though they had died on their feet. Not a word was heard, not a cough or a footstep. No mosquito hummed. Only the deep, rough voice of the American presenter blaring from the radio, which was set at full volume and made the night air tremble, or it may have been the voice of the president of the Assembly, the Brazilian Oswaldo Aranha. One after another he read out the names of the last countries on the list, in English alphabetical order, followed immediately by the reply of their representative. United Kingdom: abstains. Union of Soviet Socialist Republics: yes. United States: yes. Uruguay: yes. Venezuela: yes. Yemen: no. Yugoslavia: abstains.

At that the voice suddenly stopped, and an otherworldly silence descended and froze the scene, a terrified, panic-stricken silence, a silence of hundreds of people holding their breath, such as I have never heard in my life either before or after that night.

Then the thick, slightly hoarse voice came back, shaking the air as it summed up with a rough dryness brimming with excitement: Thirty-three for. Thirteen against. Ten abstentions and one country absent from the vote. The resolution is approved.

His voice was swallowed up in a roar that burst from the radio, overflowing from the galleries in the hall at Lake Success, and after a couple more seconds of shock and disbelief, of lips parted as though in thirst and eyes wide open, our faraway street on the edge of Kerem Avraham in northern Jerusalem also roared all at once in a first terrifying shout that tore through the darkness and the buildings and trees, piercing itself, not a shout of joy, nothing like the shouts of spectators in sports grounds or excited rioting crowds, perhaps more like a scream of horror and bewilderment, a cataclysmic shout, a shout that could shift rocks, that could freeze your blood, as though all the dead who had ever died here and all those still to die had received a brief window to shout, and the next moment the scream of horror was replaced by roars of joy and a medley of hoarse cries and "The Jewish People Lives" and somebody trying to sing Hatikvah and women shrieking and clapping and "Here in the Land Our Fathers Loved," and the whole crowd started to revolve slowly around itself as though it were being stirred in a huge cement mixer, and there were no more restraints, and I jumped into my trousers but didn't bother with a shirt or sweater and shot out our door, and some neighbor or stranger picked me up so I wouldn't be trampled underfoot, and I was passed from hand to hand until I landed on my father's shoulders near our front gate. My father and mother were standing there hugging one another like two children lost in the woods, as I had never seen them before or since, and for a moment I was between them inside their hug and a moment later I was back on Father's shoulders and my very cultured, polite father was standing there shouting at the top of his voice, not words or wordplay or Zionist slogans, not even cries of joy, but one long naked shout like before words were invented.

Others were singing now, everyone was singing, but my father, who couldn't sing and didn't know the words of the popular songs, did not stop but went on with his long shout to the end of his lungs *aaaahhh,* and when he ran out of breath, he inhaled like a drowning man and went on shouting, this man who wanted to be a famous professor and deserved to become one, but now he was all just *aaahhhh.* And I was surprised to see my mother's hand stroking his wet head and the back of his neck, and then I felt her hand on my head and my back too because I might unawares have been helping my father shout, and my mother's hand stroked the two of us over and over again, perhaps to soothe us or perhaps not, perhaps out of the depths she was also trying to share with him and me in our shout and with the whole street, the whole neighborhood, the whole city, and the whole country, my sad mother was trying to participate this time—no, definitely not the whole city but only the Jewish areas, because Sheikh Jarrah, Katamon, Bakaa, and Talbieh must have heard us that night wrapped in a silence that might have resembled the terrified silence that lay upon the Jewish neighborhoods before the result of the vote was announced. In the Silwanis' house in Sheikh Jarrah and in Aisha's home in Talbieh and the home of the man in the clothes shop, the beloved man Gepetto with the bags under his compassionate eyes, there were no celebrations tonight. They must have heard the sounds of rejoicing from the Jewish streets, they may have stood at their windows to watch the few joyful fireworks that injured the dark sky, pursing their lips in silence. Even the parrots were silent. And the fountain in the pool in the garden. Even though neither Katamon, Talbieh, nor Bakaa knew or could know yet that in another five months they would fall empty, intact, into the hands of the Jews and that new people would come and live in those vaulted houses of pink stone and those villas with their many cornices and arches.

Then there was dancing and weeping on Amos Street, in the whole of Kerem Avraham and in all the Jewish neighborhoods; flags appeared, and slogans written on strips of cloth, car horns blared, and "Raise the Banner High to Zion" and "Here in the Land Our Fathers Loved," shofar blasts sounded from all the synagogues, and Torah scrolls were taken out of the holy arks and were caught up in the dancing, and "God Will Rebuild Galilee" and "Come and Behold How Great Is This Day," and later, in the small hours of the morning, Mr. Auster suddenly opened his shop, and all the kiosks in Zephaniah Street and Geula Street and Chancellor Street and Jaffa Road and King George opened, and the bars opened up all over the city and handed out soft drinks and snacks and even alcoholic drinks until the first light of dawn, bottles of fruit drink, beer, and wine passed from hand to hand and from mouth to mouth, strangers hugged each other in the streets and kissed each other with tears, and startled English policemen were also dragged into the circles of dancers and softened up with cans of beer and sweet liqueurs, and frenzied revelers climbed up on British armored cars and waved the flag of the state that had not been established yet, but tonight, over there in Lake Success, it had been decided that it had the right to be established. And it would be established 167 days and nights later, on Friday, May 14, 1948, but one in every hundred men, women, old folk, children, and babies in those crowds of Jews who were dancing, reveling, drinking, and weeping for joy, fully one percent of the excited people who spilled out onto the streets that night, would die in the war that the Arabs started within seven hours of the General Assembly's decision at Lake Success—to be helped, when the British left, by the regular armed forces of the Arab League, columns of infantry, armor, artillery, fighter planes, and bombers, from the south, the east, and the north, the regular armies of five Arab states invading with the intention of putting an end to the new state within one or two days of its proclamation.

But my father said to me as we wandered there, on the night of November 29, 1947, me riding on his shoulders, among the rings of dancers and merrymakers, not as though he was asking me but as though he knew and was hammering in what he knew with nails: Just you look, my boy, take a very good look, son, take it all in, because you won't forget this night to your dying day and you'll tell your children, your grandchildren, and your great-grandchildren about this night when we're long gone.

And very late, at a time when this child had never been allowed not to be fast asleep in bed, maybe at three or four o'clock, I crawled under my blanket in the dark fully dressed. And after a while Father's hand lifted my blanket in the dark, not to be angry with me because I'd got into bed with my clothes on but to get in and lie down next to me, and he was in his clothes too, which were drenched in sweat from the crush of the crowds, just like mine (and we had an iron rule: you must never, for any reason, get between the sheets in your outdoor clothes). My father lay beside me for a few minutes and said nothing, although normally he detested silence and hurried to banish it. But this time he did not touch the silence that was there between us but shared it, with just his hand lightly stroking my head. As though in this darkness my father had turned into my mother.

Then he told me in a whisper, without once calling me Your Highness or Your Honor, what some hooligans did to him and his brother David in Odessa and what some Gentile boys did to him at his Polish school in Vilna, and the girls joined in too, and the next day, when his father, Grandpa Alexander, came to the school to register a complaint, the bullies refused to return the torn trousers but attacked his father, Grandpa, in front of his eyes, forced him down onto the paving stones in the middle of the playground and removed his trousers too, and the girls laughed and made dirty jokes, saying that the Jews were all so-and-sos, while the teachers watched and said nothing, or maybe they were laughing too.

And still in a voice of darkness with his hand still losing its way in my hair (because he was not used to stroking me), my father told me under my blanket in the early hours of November 30, 1947, "Bullies may well bother you in the street or at school someday. They may do it precisely because you are a bit like me. But from now on, from the moment we have our own state, you will never be bullied just because you are a Jew and because Jews are so-and-sos. Not that. Never again. From tonight that's finished here. Forever."

I reached out sleepily to touch his face, just below his high forehead, and all of a sudden instead of his glasses my fingers met tears. Never in my life, before or after that night, not even when my mother died, did I see my father cry. And in fact I didn't see him cry that night either: it was too dark. Only my left hand saw.

A few hours later, at seven o'clock, while we and probably all our neighbors were asleep, shots were fired in Sheikh Jarrah at a Jewish ambulance that was on its way from the city center to Hadassah Hospital on Mount

Scopus. All over the country Arabs attacked Jewish buses on the highways, killed and wounded passengers, and fired with light arms and machine guns into outlying suburbs and isolated settlements. The Arab Higher Committee headed by Jamal Husseini declared a general strike and sent the crowds into the streets and mosques, where religious leaders called for a jihad against the Jews. A couple of days later, hundreds of armed Arabs came out of the Old City, singing bloodthirsty songs, roaring verses from the Qur'an, howling "*idbah al-Yahud*" (butcher the Jews), and firing volleys in the air. The English police accompanied them, and British armored cars, it was reported, led the crowd that burst into the Jewish shopping center at the eastern end of Mamilla Road and looted and set fire to the whole area. Forty shops were burned down. British soldiers and policemen formed barriers across Princess Mary Street and prevented the defense forces of the Haganah from coming to the help of the Jews who were caught in the shopping center, and even confiscated their arms and arrested sixteen of them. The following day, in retaliation, the paramilitary Irgun burned down the Rex Cinema, which was apparently under Arab ownership.

In the first week of the troubles some twenty Jews were killed. By the end of the second week about two hundred Jews and Arabs had died throughout the country. From the beginning of December 1947 until March 1948 the initiative was in the hands of the Arab forces; the Jews in Jerusalem and elsewhere had to content themselves with static defense, because the British thwarted the Haganah's attempts to launch counterattacks, arrested its men, and confiscated their weapons. Local semiregular Arab forces, together with hundreds of armed volunteers from the neighboring Arab countries and some two hundred British soldiers who had defected to the Arabs and fought beside them, blocked the highways and reduced the Jewish presence to a fragmented mosaic of beleaguered settlements and blocks of settlements that could be kept supplied with food, fuel, and ammunition only by means of convoys.

While the British still continued to govern and used their power mainly to help the Arabs in their war and to tie the Jews' hands, Jewish Jerusalem was gradually cut off from the rest of the country. The only road linking it with Tel Aviv was blocked by Arab forces, and convoys carrying food and supplies were able to make their way up from the coast only at irregular intervals and at the cost of heavy losses. By the end of December 1947, the Jewish parts of Jerusalem were de facto under siege. Regular Iraqi forces, whom the British administration had allowed to take control of the waterworks at Rosh ha-Ayin, blew up the pumping installations and Jewish Jerusalem was left without water, apart from wells and reservoirs. Isolated Jewish areas like the Jewish Quarter within the walls of the Old City, Yemin Moshe, Mekor Hayim, and Ramat Rahel underwent a siege within a siege as they were cut off from the other Jewish parts of the city. An "emergency committee" set up by the Jewish Agency supervised the rationing of food and the tankers that traveled the streets between bouts of shelling distributing a bucket of water per person every two or three days. Bread, vegetables, sugar, milk, eggs, and other foodstuffs were strictly rationed and were distributed to families under a system of food coupons, until supplies ran out and instead we received occasional meager rations of powdered milk, dry rusks, and strange-smelling egg powder. Drugs and medical supplies had almost run out. The wounded were sometimes operated on without anesthetic. The electricity supply collapsed, and since it was virtually impossible to obtain paraffin, we lived for several months in the dark, or by candlelight.

Our cramped basement-like apartment was turned into a kind of bomb shelter for the residents of the apartments above us, being safer from shelling and shooting. All the windowpanes were taken out, and we barricaded the windows with sandbags. We lived in uninterrupted cavelike darkness, night and day, from March 1948 until the following August or September. In this thick darkness, breathing fetid air that had no escape, we were joined at intervals by some twenty or twenty-five persons, neighbors, strangers, acquaintances, refugees from front-line neighborhoods, who slept on mattresses and mats. They included two very elderly women who sat all day on the floor in the corridor staring into space, a half-crazed old man who called himself the Prophet Jeremiah and constantly lamented the destruction of Jerusalem and foretold for all of us Arab gas chambers near Ramallah "where they've already started gassing 2,100 Jews per day," as well as Grandpa Alexander and Grandma Shlomit, and Grandpa Alexander's widowed elder brother

(Aunt Tsipora had died in 1946), Uncle Joseph himself—Professor Klausner—with his sister-in-law Haya Elitsedek: the two of them had managed, virtually at the last minute, to escape from Talpiot, which was cut off and encircled, and taken refuge with us. Now the two lay fully dressed, with their shoes on, alternately dozing and waking—because on account of the darkness it was hard to tell night from day—on the floor in our tiny kitchen, which was considered the least noisy place in the apartment. (Mr. Agnon, too, we were told, had left Talpiot with his wife and was staying with friends in Rehavia.)

Uncle Joseph was constantly lamenting, in his reedy, rather tearful voice, the fate of his library and his precious manuscripts, which he had had to leave behind in Talpiot and who knew if he would ever see them again. As for Haya Elitsedek, her only son, Ariel, had joined up and was fighting to defend Talpiot, and for a long time we did not know if he was alive or killed, wounded or taken prisoner.*

The Miudovniks, whose son Grisha was serving somewhere with the Palmach, had fled from their home on the front line in Beit Yisrael, and they too had landed up in our apartment, along with various other families who crowded together in the little room that had been my room before the war. I regarded Mr. Miudovnik with awe, because it emerged that he was the man who had written the greenish book that we all used at Tachkemoni School: *Arithmetic for Third-Graders* by Matityahu Miudovnik.

Mr. Miudovnik went out one morning and did not return by evening. He did not come back the next day either. So his wife went to the municipal mortuary, had a good look around, and came back happy and reassured because her husband was not among the dead.

When Mr. Miudovnik did not return the next day either, my father began to joke, as he usually did when he wanted to banish silence or dispel gloom. Our dear Matya, he declared, has obviously found himself some fighting beauty in a khaki skirt and now he's her comrade in arms (this was his feeble attempt at a pun).

But after a quarter of an hour of this labored jollity Father suddenly turned serious and went off to the morgue himself, where, thanks

---

*My father's cousin Ariel Elitsedek wrote about his experiences in the War of Liberation in his book *The Thirsty Sword* (Jerusalem: Ahiasaf, 1950).

to a pair of his own socks that he had lent to Matityahu Miudovnik, he managed to identify the body that had been smashed by an artillery shell; Mrs. Miudovnik had failed to recognize it because the face was missing.

During the months of the siege, my mother, my father, and I slept on a mattress at the end of the corridor, and all night long processions of people clambered over us on their way to the toilet, which stank to high heaven because there was no water to flush it and because the window was blocked with sandbags. Every few minutes, when a shell landed, the whole hill shook, and the stone-built houses shuddered too. I was sometimes woken by the sound of bloodcurdling cries whenever one of the other sleepers in the apartment had a nightmare.

On February 1 a car bomb exploded outside the building of the English-language Jewish newspaper, the *Palestine Post.* The building was completely destroyed and suspicion fell on British policemen who had deserted to the Arab cause. On February 10 the defenders of Yemin Moshe managed to repel a heavy attack by semiregular Arab troops. On Sunday, February 22, at ten past six in the morning, an organization calling itself the "British Fascist Army" blew up three trucks loaded with dynamite in Ben Yehuda Street, in the heart of Jewish Jerusalem. Six-story buildings were reduced to rubble and a large part of the street was left in ruins. Fifty-two Jewish residents were killed in their homes, and some hundred and fifty were injured.

That day my shortsighted father went to the National Guard HQ that had been set up in a narrow lane off Zephaniah Street and offered to enlist. He had to admit that his previous military experience was limited to composing some illegal posters in English for the Irgun ("Shame on Perfidious Albion!," "Down with Nazi British repression!," and such).

On March 11 the American consul general's familiar car, with the consul general's Arab driver at the wheel, drove into the courtyard of the Jewish Agency building, the site of the offices of the Jewish organizations in Jerusalem and the country as a whole. Part of the building was destroyed and dozens of people were killed or injured. In the third week of March attempts to bring convoys of food and supplies up from the coast failed: the siege grew worse, and the city was on the brink of starvation, short of water, and at risk of epidemic.

The schools in our area had been closed since mid-December 1947. We children from the third and fourth grades at Tachkemoni and the House of Education were assembled one morning in an empty apartment in Malachi Street. A suntanned youth casually dressed in khaki and smoking a cigarette, who was introduced to us only by his code name, Garibaldi, addressed us in very serious tones for some twenty minutes, with a kind of wry matter-of-factness that we had previously encountered only in grown-ups. Garibaldi gave us the task of searching all the yards and storage sheds for empty sacks ("We'll fill them with sand") and bottles ("Someone knows how to fill them with a cocktail that the enemy will find very tasty").

We were also taught to collect wild mallow, which we all called by its Arabic name, *khubeizeh,* on plots of wasteland or in neglected back-yards. This *khubeizeh* helped relieve the horrors of starvation somewhat. Mothers boiled or fried it and then used it to make rissoles or puree, which was green like spinach but tasted much worse. We also had a lookout round: every hour during daylight two of us kids had to keep watch from a suitable rooftop in Obadiah Street on the British army camp in Schneller Barracks, and every now and then one of us ran to the operations room in the apartment on Malachi Street to tell Garibaldi or one of his adjutants what the Tommies were up to and whether there were any signs of preparations for departure.

The bigger boys, from the fourth and fifth grades, were taught by Garibaldi to carry messages between the various Haganah posts at the end of Zephaniah Street and around the Bukharian Quarter. My mother begged me to "show real maturity and give up these childish games," but I couldn't do as she wanted. I was particularly good at collecting bottles: in a single week I managed to collect 146 empty bottles and take them in boxes and sacks to HQ. Garibaldi himself gave me a slap on the back and shot me a sidelong glance. I record here exactly the words he spoke to me as he scratched the hair on his chest through his open shirt: "Very nice. We may hear more of you one day." Word for word. Fifty-three years have gone by, and I have not forgotten to this day.

45

MANY YEARS later I discovered that a woman I knew as a child, Mrs. Abramski, Zerta, the wife of Yakov-David Abramski (both of them were frequent visitors to our home), kept a diary during those days. I vaguely remember that my mother sometimes sat on the floor in a corner of the corridor during bombardments, with an exercise book supported on a closed book on her knees, writing, ignoring the exploding shells and mortars and the bursts of machine-gun fire, deaf to the noise of a score of inmates who bickered all day long in our dark, smelly submarine, writing in her exercise book, indifferent to the Prophet Jeremiah's doom-laden mutterings and Uncle Joseph's lamentations, and the penetrating, babylike crying of an old woman whose mute daughter changed her wet diapers in front of all of us. I will never know what my mother was writing: no exercise book of hers has reached me. Maybe she burned them all before she killed herself. I do not have a single complete page in her handwriting.

In Zerta Abramski's diary I find written, among other things:

February 24, 1948
I am weary . . . so weary . . . the storeroom full of belongings of the killed and injured . . . Hardly anyone comes to claim these objects: there is no one to claim them, their owners are killed or lying wounded in the hospital. A man came in who had been wounded in the head and arm, but was able to walk. His wife had been killed. He found her clothes, her pictures, and some linen . . . And these things that were bought with such love and joie de vivre are piled up in this basement . . . And a young man, G., came in search of his belongings. He had lost his father and mother, his two brothers, and his sister in the Ben Yehuda Street car bombing. He himself escaped only because he did not sleep at home that night, he was on duty . . . Incidentally: he was not interested in objects so much as in photographs. Among the hundreds of photographs . . . that survived he was trying to find a few family photographs.

April 14, 1948
This morning they announced . . . that for a coupon from the paraffin book (the head of the household's book) you can receive a quarter of

a chicken per family at certain designated butchers. Some of my neighbors asked me to collect their ration, if I was in line anyway, as they had to work and could not wait in line. Yoni, my son, offered to keep me a place in line before he went to school, but I told him I would do it myself. I sent Yair off to kindergarten and went to "Geula," where the butcher was. I arrived at a quarter to eight and found a line of about six hundred people.

They said some people had arrived at three or four in the morning, because the rumor of the distribution of chicken started to spread before it was dark. I had no desire to stand in line, but I had promised my neighbors to bring them their ration, and I didn't like to go home without it. I decided to "stand" like the rest.

While I was in line, it turned out that the "rumor" that had been circulating since yesterday had been confirmed: yes, a hundred Jews were burned alive yesterday near Sheikh Jarrah; they were in a convoy going up to Hadassah and the university. A hundred people. They included distinguished scientists and scholars, doctors and nurses, workers and students, clerks and patients.

It is hard to believe it. There are so many Jews in Jerusalem, and they were unable to save these hundred people who were facing death only a kilometer away . . . They said the English would not let them. What is the point of a quarter of a chicken, if horrors like this happen in front of your very eyes? Yet people stood in line patiently. And all the time all you hear is: "The children are getting thin . . . they haven't tasted meat for months . . . there is no milk, there are no vegetables . . ." It is hard to stand in a line for six hours, yet it is worth it: there will be soup for the children . . . What happened in Sheikh Jarrah is terrible, but who knows what is awaiting us all here in Jerusalem . . . The dead are dead, and the living go on living . . . The line advances slowly. The "lucky ones" go home hugging their quarter of a chicken per family . . . Eventually a funeral went past . . . At two o'clock in the afternoon I received my ration and my neighbors' and I went home.*

---

*Zerta Abramski, "Excerpts from the Diary of a Woman from the Siege of Jerusalem, 1948," in *The Correspondence of Yakov-David Abramski*, edited and annotated by Shula Abramski (Tel Aviv: Sifriat Poalim, 5751/1991), pp. 288–89.

My father was supposed to go up to Mount Scopus in that very convoy, on April 13, 1948, in which seventy-seven doctors and nurses, professors and students were murdered and burned alive. He had been instructed by the National Guard, or perhaps by his superiors in the National Library, to go and lock up certain sections of the basement stores of the library, since Mount Scopus was cut off from the rest of the city. But the evening before he was due to go, he had a temperature, and the doctor absolutely forbade him to leave his bed. (He was shortsighted, and frail, and every time his temperature went up, his eyes clouded over until he was almost blind and he also lost his sense of balance.)

Four days after Irgun and Stern Gang forces captured the Arab village of Deir Yassin to the west of Jerusalem and butchered many of its inhabitants, armed Arabs attacked the convoy, which, at half past nine in the morning, was crossing Sheikh Jarrah on its way to Mount Scopus. The British secretary of state for the colonies, Arthur Creech-Jones, had personally promised the representatives of the Jewish Agency that as long as the British army was in Jerusalem, it would guarantee the regular arrangement of convoys to relieve the skeleton presence guarding the hospital and the university. (Hadassah Hospital served not just the Jewish population but all the inhabitants of Jerusalem.)

There were two ambulances in the convoy, three buses whose windows had been reinforced with metal plates for fear of snipers, several trucks carrying supplies, including medical supplies, and two small cars. At the approach to Sheikh Jarrah stood a British police officer who signaled to the convoy, as usual, that the road was open and safe. In the heart of the Arab neighborhood, almost at the feet of the villa of the Grand Mufti Haj Amin al-Husseini, the exiled pro-Nazi leader of the Palestinian Arabs, at a distance of 150 yards or so from Silwani Villa, the leading vehicle went over a land mine. Immediately a hail of fire assailed the convoy from both sides of the road, including hand grenades and Molotov cocktails. The firing continued right through the morning.

The attack took place less than two hundred yards away from the British military post whose task was to safeguard the road to the hospital. For several hours the British soldiers stood and watched the attack without lifting a finger. At 9:45 General Gordon H. A. MacMillan, the supreme commander of the British forces in Palestine, drove past without stopping. (He later claimed, without batting an eye, that he had the impression the attack had ended.)

At one o'clock, and again an hour later, some British vehicles drove past without stopping. When the Jewish Agency liaison officer contacted British military headquarters and requested permission to send in the Haganah to evacuate the injured and the dying, he was informed that "the army is in control of the situation" and that HQ forbade the Haganah to intervene. Haganah rescue forces nevertheless attempted to assist the trapped convoy, both from the city and from Mount Scopus. They were prevented from approaching. At 1:45 P.M. the president of the Hebrew University, Professor Judah Leon Magnes, telephoned General MacMillan and asked for help. The answer was that "the army is trying to reach the scene, but a large battle has developed."

There was no fighting. By three o'clock two of the buses had caught fire and almost all the passengers, most of whom were already wounded or dying, were burned alive.

The seventy-seven dead included the director of the Hadassah Medical Organization, Professor Chaim Yassky, Professors Leonid Doljansky and Moshe Ben-David, who were among the founders of the Faculty of Medicine at the university, the physicist Dr. Guenther Wolfsohn, Professor Enzo Bonaventura, head of the Department of Psychology, Dr. Abraham Chaim Freimann, an expert on Jewish law, and Dr. Binyamin Klar, a linguist.

The Arab Higher Committee later issued an official statement in which the slaughter was described as a heroic exploit carried out "under the command of an Iraqi officer." The statement censured the British for their last-minute intervention and declared: "Had it not been for Army interference, not a single Jewish passenger would have remained alive."* It was only through a coincidence, because of his high temperature, and perhaps also because my mother knew how to curb his patriotic fervor, that my father was not among those who were burned to death in that convoy.

Not long after this massacre, the Haganah launched major offensives for the first time all over the country and threatened to take up arms against

*Based on various sources, including Dov Joseph, *The Faithful City: The Siege of Jerusalem, 1948* (London, 1962), p. 78.

the British army if it dared to intervene. The main road from the coastal plain to Jerusalem was unblocked by means of a major offensive, then blocked again, then unblocked again, but the siege of Hebrew Jerusalem was renewed with the invasion by regular Arab armies. Through April and up to the middle of May, large Arab and mixed towns—Haifa, Jaffa, Tiberias, and Safed—as well as dozens of Arab villages in the north and the south were captured by the Haganah. Hundreds of thousands of Arabs lost their homes in those weeks and became refugees. Some of them have remained refugees to this day. Many fled, but many were driven out by force. Several thousand were killed.

There may not have been anyone at the time in besieged Jewish Jerusalem who mourned the fate of the Palestinian refugees. The Jewish Quarter in the Old City, which had been inhabited continuously by Jews for thousands of years (with the exception of a single interruption after they were all massacred or expelled by the Crusaders in 1099), fell to the Trans-Jordanian Arab Legion, all its buildings were looted and razed and the residents were killed, expelled, or taken prisoner. The settlements in the Etzion bloc were also taken and destroyed, and their residents were killed or taken prisoner. Atarot, Neve Yaakov, Kaliya, and Beit Ha-Arava were evacuated and destroyed. The hundred thousand Jewish inhabitants of Jerusalem feared that a similar fate awaited them. When the Voice of the Defender radio station announced the flight of the Arab residents from Talbieh and Katamon, I do not remember feeling sorry for Aisha and her brother. I merely extended, with my father, our matchstick frontier on the map of Jerusalem: the months of bombardment, hunger, and fear had hardened my heart. Where did Aisha go, with her little brother? To Nablus? Damascus? London? Or to the refugee camp at Deheisha? Today, if she is still alive, Aisha is a woman of sixty-five. And her little brother, whose foot I may have smashed, would be nearly sixty now. Perhaps I could set out to find them? To discover what happened to all the branches of the Silwani family, in London, South America, and Australia?

But suppose I found Aisha, somewhere in the world, or the person who was once that sweet little boy: how would I introduce myself? What could I say? What could I really explain? What could I offer?

Do they still remember? And if so, what do they remember? Or have the horrors they must have undergone since made them both forget the silly show-off in the tree?

It wasn't all my fault. Not all of it. All I did was talk, and talk, and talk. Aisha is to blame, too. It was Aisha who said to me, Come on, let's see you climb a tree. If she hadn't urged me on, it would never have occurred to me to climb the tree, and her brother—

It's gone forever. It can't be undone.

At the National Guard post in Zephaniah Street my father was given a very old rifle and put on night-watch duty in the streets of Kerem Avraham. It was a heavy, black rifle, with all sorts of foreign words and initials engraved on its worn butt. Father eagerly attempted to decipher the writing even before turning to study the rifle itself. It may have been an Italian rifle from the First World War, or an ancient American carbine. Father felt it all over, scrabbled around, pushed and pulled without success, and eventually put it down on the floor and turned to check the magazine. Here he scored an immediate and dazzling success: he managed to extract the bullets. He brandished a handful of bullets in one hand and the empty magazine in the other, and waved them exultantly at my tiny form as I stood in the doorway, while he made some sort of joke about the narrow-mindedness of those who had tried to discourage Napoleon Bonaparte.

But when he tried to press the bullets back into the magazine, his triumph turned to utter defeat: the bullets had got a whiff of freedom and obdurately refused to be reimprisoned. None of his stratagems and blandishments had the slightest effect. He tried to insert them the right way around and he tried them back to front, he tried doing it gently and he tried with all the force of his delicate scholar's fingers, he even tried putting them in alternately, one facing upward and the next downward and so on, but all in vain.

Undeterred, my father tried to charm the bullets into the magazine by reciting poetry at them in a voice laden with pathos: he gave them selections from Polish patriotic poetry, as well as Ovid, Pushkin, and Lermontov, entire Hebrew love poems from medieval Spain—all in the original languages with a Russian accent, and all without success. In a final paroxysm of rage he declaimed from memory extracts from Homer in ancient Greek, the *Nibelungenlied* in German, Chaucer in Middle English, and, for I know, from the *Kalevala* in Saul Tchernikhowsky's Hebrew translation, from the epic of Gilgamesh, in every possible language and dialect. All in vain.

Dejectedly, therefore, he wended his way back to the National Guard post in Zephaniah Street, with the heavy rifle in one hand, in the other the precious bullets in an embroidered bag originally intended for sandwiches, and in his pocket (pray God he did not forget it there) the empty magazine.

At the National Guard post they took pity on him and quickly showed him how easy it was to load the bullets into the magazine, but they did not give him the weapon or the ammunition back. Not that day, or in the days that followed. Or ever. Instead he was given an electric lamp, a whistle, and an impressive armband bearing the motto "National Guard." Father came back home beside himself with joy. He explained to me the meaning of "National Guard," flashed his lamp on and off, blew and blew on his whistle, till Mother touched his shoulder lightly and said, That's enough now, Arieh? Please?

At midnight between Friday, May 14, 1948, and Saturday, May 15, at the end of thirty years of the British Mandate, the state whose birth David Ben-Gurion had announced in Tel Aviv a few hours earlier came into being. After a gap of some nineteen hundred years, Uncle Joseph declared, Jewish rule was once more established here.

But at one minute past midnight, without war being declared, the infantry columns, artillery, and armor of the regular Arab armies poured into the country, from Egypt to the south, Trans-Jordan and Iraq to the east, and Lebanon and Syria to the north. On Saturday morning Tel Aviv was bombed by Egyptian planes. The Arab Legion, the half-British army of the Kingdom of Trans-Jordan, and regular Iraqi troops, as well as armed Muslim volunteers from several other countries, had all been invited in by the British to seize key points around the country before the formal ending of the Mandate.

The noose was tightening around us. The Trans-Jordanian Legion captured the Jewish Quarter of the Old City, cut off the highway to Tel Aviv and the coastal plain with massive forces, took control of the Arab districts of the city, stationed artillery on the hills around Jerusalem, and began a massive bombardment whose aim was to cause losses among the civilian population, break their spirit, and bring them to submission. King Abdullah, London's protégé, already saw himself as King of Jerusalem. The legion's gun batteries were commanded by British artillery officers.

At the same time the Egyptian army was reaching the southern outskirts of Jerusalem and attacked the kibbutz of Ramat Rahel, which changed hands twice. Egyptian planes dropped fire bombs on Jerusalem and, among other things, destroyed the old people's home in Romema, not far from us. Egyptian mortars joined the Trans-Jordanian artillery in bombarding the civilian population. From a hill close to the Mar Elias Monastery the Egyptians pounded Jerusalem with 4.2 inch shells. Shells fell on the Jewish areas at a rate of one every two minutes, and the streets were raked by continuous rifle fire. Greta Gat, my piano-playing child sitter who always smelled of wet wool and washing soap, Aunt Greta, who used to drag me off to clothes shops with her, for whom my father used to compose his silly rhymes, went out on her veranda one morning to hang out her washing. A Jordanian sniper's bullet, they said, went in her ear and came out her eye. Zippora Yannai, Piri, my mother's shy friend who lived in Zephaniah Street, went out in the yard for a moment to fetch a floor cloth and a bucket and was killed on the spot by a direct hit from a shell.

And I had a little tortoise. During the Passover holiday in 1947, some six months before the outbreak of war, Father joined some people from the Hebrew University for a day trip to Jerash in Trans-Jordan. He set off early in the morning, with a bag of sandwiches and a genuine army water bottle, which he wore proudly on his belt. He came back that evening, full of happy stories of the trip and the wonders of the large Roman theater, and he brought me a present of a little tortoise he found there "at the foot of an amazing Roman stone arch."

Although he had no sense of humor and possibly had no clear idea of what a sense of humor was, my father always loved jokes, witticisms, and wordplay, and whenever he made anyone smile with his remarks, his face would light up with modest pride. Thus he decided to call the tortoise by the comical name of Abdullah-Gershon, in honor of the king of Trans-Jordan and the city of Jerash (Gerash in Hebrew). Whenever we had visitors, he would call the tortoise solemnly by his full name, like a master of ceremonies announcing the arrival of some duke or ambassador, and he was always amazed that everyone present did not double up with laughter. Consequently he felt it necessary to enlighten them as to the reasons for the two names. Perhaps he hoped that, not having found the joke funny before the explanation, they would find it hilarious afterward. Sometimes he was so enthusiastic or absentminded that he told the whole story to guests who had already heard it at least twice before and knew it backward.

I loved that little tortoise, who used to crawl to my hideaway under the pomegranate bush every morning and eat lettuce leaves and juicy cucumber peel right out of my hand. He was not afraid of me and did not retract his head inside his shell, and while he was gobbling up his food, he would make funny movements with his head, as though he were nodding in agreement at what you were saying. He was like a certain bald professor from Rehavia, who also used to nod enthusiastically until you had finished talking, but then his approval turned to mockery, as he continued to nod at you while he tore your views to shreds.

I used to stroke my tortoise's head with my finger while he ate, amazed at the similarity between his nose holes and his ear holes. In my heart of hearts, and behind Father's back, I secretly called him Mimi instead of Abdullah-Gershon.

During the bombardment there were no cucumbers or lettuce leaves and I wasn't allowed out into the yard, but I still used to open the door sometimes and throw scraps of food out for Mimi. Sometimes I could see him in the distance, and sometimes he disappeared for several days on end.

The day that Greta Gat and my mother's friend Piri Yannai were killed, my tortoise Mimi was killed too. He was sliced in half by a piece of shrapnel. When I tearfully asked Father if I could at least bury him under the pomegranate and put up a tombstone to remember him by, Father explained to me that I could not, mainly for reasons of hygiene. He told me he had already gotten rid of the remains. He refused to tell me where he had gotten rid of them, but he took the opportunity to give me a little lecture on the meaning of irony: our Abdullah-Gershon was an immigrant from the Kingdom of Trans-Jordan, so it was ironic that the piece of shrapnel that killed him came from a shell fired from one of King Abdullah of Trans-Jordan's guns.

That night I could not get to sleep. I lay on my back on our mattress in the far corner of the corridor, surrounded by the snores, mutterings, and intermittent moans of old people. I was dripping with sweat as I lay between my parents, and by the faint trembling light of the single candle in the bathroom, in the fetid air, I suddenly thought I saw the form of a tortoise, not Mimi, the little tortoise I loved to stroke with my finger (there was no possibility of a cat or a puppy: forget it!), but a terrifying gigantic monster-tortoise, dripping blood and mashed bones, floating through the air, digging with its sharp-clawed paws and chuckling mockingly at me from above all the people sleeping in the corridor. Its face was horrible, crushed and torn by a bullet that had entered its eye and come out in the place where even a tortoise has a sort of ear hole, although it has no actual ear.

I may have tried to wake Father. He did not wake up: he was lying motionless on his back breathing deeply, like a contented baby. But Mother took my head and pressed it to her bosom. Like the rest of us, she was sleeping in her clothes, and the buttons of her blouse hurt my cheek a little. She hugged me hard but didn't try to comfort me; instead she sobbed with me, smothering her crying so that no one would hear, and her lips whispered over and over again: Piri, Piroshka, Piriii. All I could do was stroke her hair and her cheeks, and kiss her, and it was as though I was the grown-up and she was my child, and I whispered, There there, Mummy, it's all right, I'm here.

Then we whispered a little more, she and I. Tearfully. And later on, after the faint flickering candle at the end of the corridor went out and only the wails of the shells broke the silence and the hill on the other side of our wall shuddered with every shell that fell, instead of my head on her chest Mother put her wet head on my chest. That night I understood for the first time that I would die too. That everyone would die. And that nothing in the world, not even my mother, could save me. And I could not save her. Mimi had an armored shell, and at any sign of danger he would withdraw, hands, feet, and head, inside his shell. And that hadn't saved him.

In September, during a cease-fire that interrupted the fighting in Jeru-salem, we had visitors on Saturday morning: Grandpa and Grandma, the Abramskis, and maybe some others. They drank tea in the yard and discussed the successes of the Israeli army, and the terrible dangers of the peace plan put forward by the UN mediator, the Swede Count Bernadotte, a scheme behind which the British were undoubtedly lurk-ing and whose aim was to crush our young state to death. Somebody had brought a rather large, ugly new coin from Tel Aviv: it was the first Hebrew coin to be minted, and it was passed excitedly from hand to hand. It was a twenty-five *prutot* coin, and it had a picture of a bunch of grapes, a motif that Father said was taken straight from a Jewish coin of the Second Temple period, and above the bunch of grapes was a clear Hebrew legend: ISRAEL. To be on the safe side, it was written not just in Hebrew but in English and Arabic as well.

Mrs. Zerta Abramski said:

"If only our dear late parents, and their parents, and all the genera-tions, had been privileged to see and hold this coin. Jewish money—"

Her voice choked. Mr. Abramski said:

"It is fitting to give thanks with the appropriate benediction. *Blessed art thou, O Lord our God, King of the Universe, who hast given us life, pre-served us, and permitted us to reach this time.*"

Grandpa Alexander, my elegant, hedonistic grandfather, so beloved of the fair sex, said nothing, but simply touched the overlarge nickel coin to his lips and kissed it twice, gently, and his eyes brimmed. Then he passed it on. At that moment the street was startled by the wail of an ambulance on its way to Zephaniah Street, and ten minutes later the siren howled again on its way back, and Father may have seen in this a pretext to make some pallid joke about the last trump or something of the sort. They sat and chatted and may even have had another glass of tea, and after half an hour or so the Abramskis took their leave, wishing us all the best, and Mr. Abramski, who loved rhetorical flourishes, prob-ably uttered a few high-flown phrases. While they were still standing in the doorway, a neighbor arrived and gently called them over to a corner of the yard, and they were in such a hurry to follow him that Aunt Zerta forgot her handbag. A quarter of an hour later the Lembergs came, look-ing bewildered, to tell us that while his parents were visiting us, Yonatan Abramski, twelve-year-old Yoni, had been playing in Nehemiah Street, when a Jordanian sniper firing from the Police Training School had hit him with a single shot in the middle of his forehead, and the boy had lain there dying for five minutes, vomited, and expired before the ambulance reached him.

I found this in Zerta Abramski's diary:

September 23, 1948

On the eighteenth of September, at a quarter past ten on Saturday morning, my Yoni, Yoni my child, my whole life, was killed . . . He was hit by an Arab sniper, my angel, he only managed to say "Mummy," to run a few yards (my wonderful, pure boy was standing near the house) before he fell . . . I did not hear his last word, neither did I answer him when he called out to me. When I returned, my sweet, beloved child was no longer alive. I saw him at the mortuary. He looked so wonderfully beautiful, he seemed to be asleep. I embraced him and kissed him. They had put a stone under his head. The stone moved, and his head, his cherubic head, moved a little. My heart said, He is not dead, my son, look, he's moving . . . His eyes were half shut. Then "they" came—the mortuary workers—came and insulted me and reprimanded me rudely and disturbed me: I had no right to embrace and kiss him . . . I left.

But a few hours later I returned. There was a "curfew" (they were searching for the killers of Bernadotte). On every street corner policemen stopped me . . . They asked for my permit to be out during the curfew. He, my slain son, was my only permit. The policemen let me into the mortuary. I had brought a cushion with me. I removed the stone and put it to one side: I could not bear to see his dear, wonderful head resting on a stone. Then "they" came back and tried to make me leave. They said that I ought not to touch him. I did not heed them. I continued to embrace and kiss him, my treasure. They threatened to lock the door and leave me with him, with the essence of my whole life. This was all that I wanted. Then they reconsidered and threatened to call the soldiers. I was not afraid of them . . . I left the mortuary a second time. Before I left, I embraced and kissed him. The next morning I came to him again, to my child . . . Once more I embraced and kissed him. Once again I prayed to God for vengeance,

vengeance for my baby, and once again they drove me out . . . And when I came back again, my wonderful child, my angel, was in a closed coffin, yet I remember his face, all of him, everything about him I remember.*

46

TWO FINNISH missionary ladies lived in a little apartment at the end of Ha-Turim Street in Mekor Baruch, Aili Havas and Rauha Moisio. Aunt Aili and Aunt Rauha. Even when the conversation turned to the shortage of vegetables, they both spoke high-flown, biblical Hebrew, because that was the only Hebrew they knew. If I knocked at their door to ask for some wood that we could use for the Lag Baomer bonfire, Aunt Aili would say with a gentle smile, as she handed me an old orange crate: "And the shining of a flaming fire by night!" If they came around to our apartment for a glass of tea and a bookish conversation while I was fighting against my cod-liver oil, Aunt Rauha might say: "The fishes of the sea shall shake at His presence!"

Sometimes the three of us paid them a visit in their Spartan one-room apartment, which resembled an austere nineteenth-century girls' boarding school: two plain iron bedsteads stood facing each other on either side of a rectangular wooden table covered with a dark blue tablecloth, with three plain wooden chairs. Beside each of the matching beds was a small bedside table with a reading lamp, a glass of water, and some sacred books in black covers. Two identical pairs of bedroom slippers peered out from under the beds. In the middle of the table there was always a vase containing a bunch of everlasting flowers from the nearby fields. A carved olive-wood crucifix hung in the middle of the wall between the two beds. And at the foot of each bed stood a chest of drawers made from a thick shiny wood of a sort we did not have in Jerusalem, and Mother said it was called oak, and she encouraged me to touch it with my fingertips and run my hand over it. My mother always insisted that it was not enough to know the various names of objects but you

*Zerta Abramski, "Excerpts from the Diary of a Woman from the Siege of Jerusalem, 1948," in *The Correspondence of Yakov-David Abramski,* edited and annotated by Shula Abramski (Tel Aviv: Sifriat Poalim, 5751/1991), pp. 288–89.

should get to know them by sniffing them, touching them with the tip of your tongue, feeling them with your fingertips, to know their warmth and smoothness, their smell, their roughness and hardness, the sound they made when you tapped them, all those things that she called their "response" or "resistance." Every material, she said, every piece of clothing or furniture, every utensil, every object had different characteristics of response and resistance, which were not fixed but could change according to the season or the time of day or night, the person who was touching or smelling, the light and shade, and even vague propensities that we have no means of understanding. It was no accident, she said, that Hebrew uses the same word for an inanimate object and a desire. It was not only we who had or did not have a desire for one thing or another, inanimate objects and plants also had an inner desire of their own, and only someone who knew how to feel, listen, taste, and smell in an ungreedy way could sometimes discern it.

Father observed jokingly:

"Our Mummy goes one further than King Solomon. Legend says that he understood the language of every animal and bird, but our Mummy has even mastered the languages of towels, saucepans, and brushes."

And he went on, beaming mischievously:

"She can make trees and stones speak by touching them: Touch the mountains, and they shall smoke, as it says in the Psalms."

Aunt Rauha said:

"Or as the prophet Joel put it, The mountains shall drop down new wine, and the hills shall flow with milk. And it is written in the twenty-ninth Psalm: The voice of the Lord maketh the hinds to calve."

Father said:

"But coming from someone who is not a poet, such things are always liable to sound somewhat, how shall I put it, prettified. As if they are trying to sound very deep. Very mystical. Very hylozoical. Trying to make the hinds to calve. Let me explain the meaning of these difficult words, mystical and hylozoical. Behind them both is a clear, rather unhealthy, desire to blur realities, to dim the light of reason, to blunt definitions, and to muddle distinct domains."

Mother said:

"Arieh?"

And Father, in a conciliatory tone (because although he enjoyed teasing her, goading her, and even occasionally gloating, he enjoyed even more repenting, apologizing, and beaming with goodwill, just like his own father, Grandpa Alexander), said:

"*Nu*, that's enough, Fanitchka. I've finished. I was only having a bit of fun."

The two missionaries did not leave Jerusalem during the siege: they had a strong sense of mission. The Savior himself seemed to have charged them with the task of boosting the spirits of the besieged and helping as volunteers to treat the wounded at the Shaarei Tsedek Hospital. They believed that every Christian had a duty to try to atone, in deeds rather than words, for what Hitler had done to the Jews. They considered the establishment of the State of Israel as the finger of God. As Aunt Rauha put it, in her biblical language and gravely pronunciation: It is like the appearance of the rainbow in the cloud, after the flood. And Aunt Aili, with a tiny smile, no more than a twitch of the corner of her mouth: "For it repented the Lord of all that great evil, and He would no longer destroy them."

Between bombardments they used to walk around our neighborhood, in their ankle boots and headscarves, carrying a deep bag of grayish hessian, distributing a jar of pickled cucumbers, half an onion, a piece of soap, a pair of woolen socks, a radish, or a small quantity of black pepper to anyone prepared to receive it from them. Who knows how they got hold of all these treasures. Some of the ultra-Orthodox rejected these gifts in disgust, some drove the two ladies away from their doors contemptuously, others accepted the gifts but spat on the ground the missionaries' feet had trodden on the moment their backs were turned.

They did not take offense. They were constantly quoting verses of consolation from the Prophets, which seemed strange to us in their Finnish accent, which sounded like their heavy boots tramping on gravel. "For I will defend this city, to save it." "No enemy or foe shall come into the gates of this city." "How beautiful upon the mountains are the feet of him that bringeth good tidings, that publisheth peace . . . for the wicked shall no more pass through thee . . ." "Fear not, O Jacob my servant, saith the Lord: for I am with thee; for I will make a full end of all the nations whither I have driven thee."

Sometimes one of them would volunteer to take our place in the long line for water that was distributed from a tanker, half a bucket per family on Sundays, Tuesdays, and Thursdays only, assuming the tanker had not been pierced by shrapnel before it reached our street. Or else one of them would go around our tiny barricaded apartment handing out half a "mixed vitamin" tablet to each of the many inmates. Children received a whole tablet. Where did the two missionaries get hold of these wonderful gifts? Where did they replenish their gray hessian bag? Some said one thing and some another, and some warned me not to accept anything from them because their only objective was "to take advantage of our distress and make converts for that Jesus of theirs."

Once I plucked up my courage and asked Aunt Aili—even though I knew what the answer would be: "Who was Jesus?" Her lips quivered slightly as she replied hesitantly that he was still alive, and that he loved us all, particularly those who mocked or despised him, and if I filled my heart with love, he would come and dwell within my heart and bring me suffering but also great happiness, and the happiness would shine forth out of the suffering.

These words seemed so strange and full of contradictions that I felt a need to ask Father too. He took me by the hand and led me to the mattress in the kitchen, which was Uncle Joseph's refuge, and asked the famous author of *Jesus of Nazareth* to explain to me who and what Jesus was.

Uncle Joseph was lying on his mattress, looking exhausted, gloomy, and pale, his back resting on the blackened wall and his glasses raised onto his forehead. His answer was very different from Aunt Aili's: Jesus of Nazareth was, in his view, "one of the greatest Jews of all time, a wonderful moralist who loathed the uncircumcised of heart and fought to restore to Judaism its original simplicity and wrest it from the power of hair-splitting rabbis."

I did not know who the uncircumcised of heart or the hair-splitting rabbis were. Nor did I know how to reconcile Uncle Joseph's Jesus, who loathed and fought to wrest, with Aunt Aili's Jesus who neither loathed nor fought nor wrested but did the exact opposite, he especially loved sinners and those who despised him.

In an old folder I came across a letter that Aunt Rauha wrote to me from Helsinki in 1979, on behalf of both of them. She wrote in Hebrew, and among other things she said:

... We too were pleased that you won the Euro-Viseo Song Contest. And how about the song?

The faithful here were very glad that they from Israel sang: Hallelujah! There is no more fitting song ... I was able also to see the film *Shoah,* which caused tears and pains of conscience from the countries that persecuted to such an extent, without any end, without any sense. The Christian countries must ask much pardon from the Jews. Your father said once that he cannot understand why the Lord allows such terrible things ... I always said to him that the Lord's secret is on high. Jesus suffers with the people of Israel in all its sufferings. The faithful also have to bear their share of the sufferings of Jesus that he let them suffer ... Nevertheless the atonement of Christ on the cross covers all the sins of the world, of all mankind. But this you can never understand with your brain ... There were Nazis who received pains of conscience and repented before their death. But their repentance did not make the Jews who died come back to life. We all need atonement and grace each day. Jesus says: Do not fear those who kill the body, because they are not able to kill the soul. This letter is from me and from Aunt Aili. I received a heavy blow to my back six weeks ago when I fell inside the bus, and Aunt Aili does not see so well.

With love,
Rauha Moisio

And once when I went to Helsinki, because one of my books had been translated into Finnish, the two of them suddenly turned up in the cafeteria of my hotel, both wearing dark shawls that covered their heads and shoulders, like a pair of old peasant women. Aunt Rauha was leaning on a stick and was gently holding Aunt Aili's hand, as she was now almost blind. Aunt Aili helped her to a corner table. They both demanded the right to kiss me and bless me. It was not easy to get them to allow me to order them each a cup of tea, "but nothing else please!"

Aunt Aili smiled slightly: it was not so much a smile as a faint quivering of her lips; she was on the verge of saying something, changed her mind, placed her right fist inside her left hand, as though putting a diaper on a baby, moved her head once or twice as though in lament, and finally she said:

"Praise be to God for permitting us to see you here in our land, though I do not understand why your dear parents were not vouchsafed to be among the living. But who am I to understand? The Lord has the answers. We can merely wonder. Please, I'm sorry, will you allow me to feel your dear face? It is only because my eyes have failed."

Aunt Rauha said of my father: "Blessed be his memory, he was the dearest of men! He had such a noble spirit! Such a humane spirit!" And of my mother she said: "Such a suffering soul, peace be upon her! She had many sufferings, because she saw into the heart of people, and what she saw was not so easy for her to bear. As the prophet Jeremiah says, 'The heart is deceitful above all things, and desperately wicked: who can know it?'"

Outside, in Helsinki, sleet was falling. The daylight was low and murky, and the snowflakes were gray and did not settle. The two old women were wearing almost identical dark dresses and thick brown socks, like girls from a respectable boarding school. When I kissed them, they both smelled of plain washing soap, brown bread, and bedding. A small maintenance man hurried past us, with a battery of pencils and pens in the pocket of his overalls. Aunt Rauha took a brown paper packet out of a big bag that was under the table and handed it to me. I recognized the bag: it was the same gray hessian bag from which they used to hand out small bars of soap, woolen socks, rusks, matches, candles, radishes, or a precious packet of powdered milk during the siege of Jerusalem, thirty years previously.

I opened the packet, and there was a Bible printed in Jerusalem, in Hebrew and Finnish on facing pages, a tiny music box made of painted wood with a brass lid, and an assortment of dried flowers, unfamiliar Finnish flowers that were beautiful even in their death, flowers that I could not name and that I had never seen before that morning.

"We were very fond," Aunt Aili said, her unseeing eyes seeking mine, "of your dear parents. Their life on this earth was not easy, and they did not always dispense grace to each other. There was sometimes much shadow between them. But now that finally they dwell in the secret of Almighty in the shelter of the wings of the Lord, now there is certainly only grace and truth between your parents, like two innocent children who have known no thought of iniquity, only light, love, and compassion between them forever, his left hand under her head and her right hand embraces him, and every shadow has long since departed from them."

For my part, I had intended to present two copies of the Finnish translation of my book to the two aunts, but Aunt Rauha refused: A Hebrew book, she said, a book about Jerusalem written in the city of Jerusalem, we must please read it in Hebrew and not in any other language! And besides, she said with an apologetic smile, truly Aunt Aili can no longer read anything because the Lord has taken to himself the last of the light of her eyes. I read to her, morning and evening, only from the Old and New Testament, from our prayer book, and the books of the saints, although my eyes are also growing dim, and soon we shall both be blind.

And when I am not reading to her and Aunt Aili is not listening to me, then we both sit at the window and look out at trees and birds, snow and wind, morning and evening, daylight and night lights, and we both give thanks in all humility to the good Lord for all his mercies and all his wonders: His will be done on earth as it is in heaven. Do you not also see sometimes, only when you are at rest, how the sky and the earth, the trees and the stones, the fields and the woods, are all full of great wonders? They are all bright and shining and they all together like a thousand witnesses testify to the greatness of the miracle of grace.

47

IN THE winter between 1948 and 1949 the war ended. Israel signed an armistice agreement with the neighboring countries, first with Egypt, then with Trans-Jordan, and finally with Syria and Lebanon. Iraq withdrew its expeditionary force without signing any document. Despite all these agreements, all the Arab countries continued to proclaim that one day they would embark on a "second round" of the war so as to put an end to a state that they refused to recognize; they declared that its very existence was an act of continuing aggression, and they called it the "artificial state," "ad-dawla al-maz'uma."

In Jerusalem the Trans-Jordanian commander, Lieutenant-Colonel Abdullah al-Tall, and the Israeli commander, Lieutenant-Colonel Moshe Dayan, met several times to draw a demarcation line between the two parts of the city and to reach an agreement about the passage of convoys to the university campus on Mount Scopus, which remained as an isolated Israeli enclave within the area under the control of the Trans-Jordanian army. High concrete walls were erected along the line, to block streets that were half in Israeli Jerusalem and half in Arab Jerusalem. Here and there corrugated iron barriers were put up to conceal passersby in West Jerusalem from the view of the snipers on the rooftops of the eastern part of the city. A fortified strip of barbed wire, minefields, firing positions, and observation posts crossed the whole city, enclosing the Israeli section to the north, east, and south. Only the west was left open, and a single winding road linked Jerusalem to Tel Aviv and the rest of the new state. But as part of this road was still in the hands of the Arab Legion, it was necessary to build a bypass road and to lay a new water pipeline along it, in place of the pipeline laid by the British, parts of which had been destroyed, and to replace the pumping stations that remained under Arab control. The new road was called the Burma Road. A year or two later a new bypass road was laid and asphalted; it was named the Road of Heroism.

Nearly everything in the young state in those days was named for those who had died in battle, or for heroism, or for the struggle, the illegal immigration and the realization of the Zionist dream. The Israelis were very proud of their victory and entrenched in the justice of their cause and their feelings of moral superiority. People did not think much about the fate of the hundreds of thousands of Palestinian refugees and displaced persons, many of whom had fled and many others of whom had been driven out of the towns and villages conquered by the Israeli army.

War was a terrible thing, of course, and full of suffering, people said, but who asked the Arabs to start it? After all, we had accepted the partition compromise that was agreed by the United Nations, and it was the Arabs who had rejected any compromise and tried to butcher us all. In any case, it was well known that that every war claims its victims, millions of refugees from World War II were still wandering around Europe, entire populations had been uprooted and others had been settled in their place, the newly created states of Pakistan and India had exchanged millions of people, and so had Greece and Turkey. And after all, we had lost the Jewish Quarter in the Old City of Jerusalem, we had lost the Etzion bloc, Kfar Darom, Atarot, Kaliya, and Neve Yaakov, just as they had lost Jaffa, Ramla, Lifta, el-Maliha, and Ein Karim. Instead of the hundreds of thousands of displaced Arabs, hundreds of thousands of Jewish refugees who had been driven out of the Arab countries had arrived here. People were careful to avoid the word "expulsion." The massacre at Deir Yassin was laid at the door of "irresponsible extremists."

A concrete curtain came down and divided us from Sheikh Jarrah and the other Arab neighborhoods of Jerusalem.

From our roof I could see the minarets of Shuafat, Biddu, and Ramallah, the solitary tower atop Nebi Samwil, the Police Training School (from which a Jordanian marksman had shot and killed Yoni Abramski when he was playing in the yard outside his house), beleaguered Mount Scopus and the Mount of Olives, now held by the Arab Legion, and the roofs of Sheikh Jarrah and the American Colony.

Sometimes I imagined I could identify, among the thick treetops, a corner of the roof of Silwani Villa. I believed that they were much better off than we were: they had not been shelled for long months, they had not been subjected to hunger and thirst, they had not been made to sleep on mattresses in foul-smelling basements. And yet I often talked to them in my heart. Just like Mr. Gustav Krochmal, the doll repairer from Geula Street, I longed to put on my best clothes and go to them at the head of a deputation for peace and reconciliation, to prove to them that we were in the right, to apologize and receive their apology, to be treated to biscuits and sugared orange peel, to demonstrate our forgiveness and magnanimity, to sign an agreement of peace, friendship, and mutual respect with them, and maybe also to convince Aisha and her brother and all the Silwani family that the accident had not been entirely my fault, or not only my fault.

Sometimes we were woken in the early hours by machine-gun salvos from the direction of the armistice line, a mile or so from where we lived, or the wailing of the muezzin on the other side of the new border: like a hair-raising lament, the howl of his prayer penetrated our sleep.

Our apartment was emptied of all the visitors who had sought refuge in it. The Rosendorffs went back to their apartment on the next floor up; the vacant old lady and her daughter folded their bedding away into a sack and disappeared; Gita Miudovnik, the widow of the man who wrote the arithmetic textbook, whose mangled body had been identified by my father because of the socks he had lent him, also left. And Uncle Joseph with his sister-in-law Haya Elitsedek returned to the Klausner house in Talpiot, with the brass plate bearing the motto JUDAISM AND HUMANITY over the front door. They had to do some work on the house because it had been damaged in the fighting. For several weeks the old professor mourned the thousands of books that had been swept off the shelves and thrown on the floor or used to make barricades and shelters against bullets fired through the windows of the house, which had become firing positions. Ariel Elitsedek, the prodigal son, was found safe and sound after the war, but he kept arguing and cursing the wretched Ben-Gurion, who could have liberated the Old City and the Temple Mount and had not done so, who could have driven all the Arabs out to the Arab countries and had not done so, all because he and his fellow reds who had seized the leadership of our beloved state had been perverted by socialistic pacifism and Tolstoyan vegetarianism. Soon, he believed, a new, proud national leadership would arise, and our forces would be unleashed to liberate every part of the fatherland at last from the yoke of the Arab conqueror.

Most Jerusalemites, however, did not yearn for more war, and were not concerned about the fate of the Wailing Wall and Rachel's tomb, which had vanished behind the concrete curtain and the minefields. The shattered city licked its wounds. All through that winter and throughout the following spring and summer, long gray lines formed in front of the grocers, greengrocers, and butchers. The austerity regime had arrived. Lines formed behind the ice man's cart, lines formed behind the paraffin seller's cart. Food was distributed in exchange for coupons from ration books. The sale of eggs and a little bit of chicken was restricted to children and invalids with medical certificates. Milk was measured out in limited quantities. Fruit and vegetables were rarely seen in Jerusalem. Oil, sugar, grits, and flour appeared intermittently, monthly or fortnightly. If you wanted to buy simple clothes, shoes, or furniture you had to use up precious coupons from your dwindling ration books. Shoes were made from reused leather, and their soles were as thin as cardboard. The furniture was shoddy. Instead of coffee people drank ersatz coffee or chicory, and powdered eggs and milk replaced the real thing. And we all came to hate the frozen cod fillets we had to eat every day, surplus stock from Norway that the new government bought at a cut-rate price.

In the early months after the war you even needed a special permit to leave Jerusalem to go to Tel Aviv and the rest of the country. But all sorts of clever or pushy people, anyone with a bit of money who knew the way to the black market, anyone with connections to the new administration, hardly felt the shortages. And some people managed to grab themselves apartments and houses in the prosperous Arab neighborhoods whose residents had fled or been expelled, or in the closed zones where British army and civil service families had lived before the war: Katamon, Talbieh, Bakaa, Abu Tor, and the German Colony. The poorer Arabs from Musrara, Lifta, and el-Maliha were replaced by thousands and thousands of poor Jewish families who had fled or been thrown out of the Arab countries. Huge transit camps were set up in Talpiot, the Allenby Barracks, and Beit Mazmil, rows of corrugated iron shacks with no electricity, drains, or running water. In winter the paths between the huts became a gooey porridge, and the cold pierced the bone. Accountants from Iraq, goldsmiths from Yemen, tradesmen and shopkeepers from Morocco, and watchmakers from Bucharest were crowded into these huts and employed for a pittance on government schemes of rock clearing and reforesting in the Jerusalem hills.

Gone were the "heroic years" of World War II, the genocide of European Jewry, the partisans, mass enlistment in the British army and the Jewish Brigade, which the British set up for the war against Nazism, the years of the struggle against the British, the underground, the illegal immigration, the new "tower and stockade" villages settlements, the war to the death against the Palestinians and the regular armies of five Arab states.

Now that the years of euphoria were over, we were suddenly living in the "morning after": gray, gloomy, damp, mean, and petty. These were the years of blunt Okava razor blades, tasteless Shenhav toothpaste, smelly Knesset cigarettes, the roaring sports commentators Nehemia Ben-Avraham and Alexander Alexandroni on the Voice of Israel, cod-liver oil, ration books, Shmulik Rozen and his quiz shows, the political commentator Moshe Medzini, the Hebraization of surnames, food rationing, government work schemes, lines at the grocer's, larders built into kitchen walls, cheap sardines, Inkoda canned meat, the Mixed Israeli-Jordanian Armistice Committee, Arab infiltrators from the other side of the armistice line, the theater companies—Ohel, Habima, Doh-Re-Mi, Chisbatron—Djigan and Schumacher the comedians, the Mandelbaum Gate crossing, retaliatory raids, washing children's hair with paraffin to get rid of the lice, "Help for the Transit Camps," "abandoned property," the Defense Fund, no-man's-land, and "Our blood will no longer be shed with impunity."

And once more I went to school each morning at the Tachkemoni Religious Boys' School on Tachkemoni Street. The pupils were poor children, schooled to beatings, whose parents were artisans, manual workers, and small traders; they came from families of eight or ten, some of them were always hungry for my sandwiches; some had shaved heads, and we all wore black berets at an angle. They would gang up on me at the water fountains in the playground and splash me, because they quickly discovered that I was the only only child, the weakest among them, and that I was easily offended or upset. When they went out of their way to devise new humiliations for me, I sometimes stood panting in the middle of a circle of my sneering tormentors, beaten up, covered with dust, a lamb among wolves, and suddenly to the astonishment of my enemies I would start to beat myself, scratch myself hysterically, and bite my arm so hard that a bleeding watch shape appeared. Just as my mother did in my presence two or three times when she was overwhelmed.

But sometimes I made up stories of suspense for them in installments, breathtaking tales in the spirit of the action films we used to watch at the Edison Cinema. In these stories I never hesitated to introduce Tarzan to Flash Gordon or Nick Carter to Sherlock Holmes, or to mix the cowboys-and-Indians world of Karl May and Mayne Reid with Ben Hur or the mysteries of outer space or gangs of thugs in the suburbs of New York. I used to give them an installment each break, like Scheherazade postponing her fate with her tales, always stopping at the moment of greatest tension, just when it seemed as though the hero was doomed and beyond hope, leaving the sequel (which I had not invented yet) ruthlessly to the following day.

So I used to walk around in the playground during breaks like Rabbi Nahman with his flocks of students eager to drink in his teachings; I would turn this way and that surrounded by a tight crush of listeners afraid of missing a single word, and among them would sometimes be my leading persecutors, whom I would make a point of magnanimously inviting into the innermost circle and favoring with a precious clue to a possible twist in the plot or some hair-raising event that would figure in the next installment, thus promoting the recipient into an influential figure who had the power to reveal or withhold invaluable information at will.

My first stories were full of caves, labyrinths, catacombs, forests, ocean depths, dungeons, battlefields, galaxies inhabited by monsters, brave policemen and fearless warriors, conspiracies, terrible betrayals accompanied by wonderful acts of chivalry and generosity, baroque twists, unbelievable self-sacrifice, and highly emotional gestures of self-denial and forgiveness. As far as I recall, the characters in my early works included both heroes and villains. And there were a number of villains who repented and atoned for their sins by acts of self-sacrifice or by a heroic death. There were also bloodthirsty sadists, and all sorts of scoundrels and mean cheats, as well as unassuming characters who sacrificed their lives with a smile. The female characters, on the other hand, were all, without exception, noble: loving despite being exploited, suffering yet compassionate, tormented and even humiliated, yet always proud and pure, paying the price for male insanities yet generous and forgiving.

But if I tightened the string too much, or not enough, then after a few episodes, or at the end of the story, at the moment when wrong-doing was confounded and magnanimity finally received its reward, that was when this poor Scheherazade was thrown into the lions' den and showered with blows and insults to his ancestry. Why could he never keep his mouth shut?

Tachkemoni was a boys' school. Even the teachers were all male. Apart from the school nurse no woman ever appeared there. The bolder boys sometimes climbed onto the wall of the Laemel Girls' School to get a glimpse of life on the other side of the iron curtain. Girls in long blue skirts and blouses with short puffy sleeves, so the rumor went, walked around the playground in pairs during break, played hopscotch, braided each other's hair, and occasionally splashed each other with water from the fountains just like us.

Apart from me, almost all the boys at Tachkemoni had older sisters, sisters-in-law, and female cousins, and so I was the last of the last to hear the whispers about what it was that girls had and we didn't, and vice versa, and what the older brothers did to their girls in the dark.

At home not a word was spoken on the subject. Ever. Except, perhaps, if some visitor got carried away and joked about bohemian life, or about the Bar-Yizhar-Itselevitches who were so meticulous about observing the commandment to be fruitful and multiply, but he would immediately be silenced by the others with the rebuke: *Shto s toboi?! Vidish malchik ryadom s nami!!* (Can't you see the boy is here!)

The boy may have been there, but he understood nothing. If his classmates hurled the Arabic word for what girls have at him, if they huddled together and passed a picture of a scantily dressed woman from hand to hand, or if someone brought along a ballpoint pen inside which was a girl dressed for tennis, and when you turned it upside down, the clothes disappeared, they would all chortle hoarsely, elbowing each other in the ribs, trying hard to sound like their older brothers, and only I felt a terrible dread, as though some vague disaster was taking shape far away on the horizon. It was not here yet, it did not touch me yet, but it was already blood-curdlingly frightening, like a forest fire on the faraway hilltops. Nobody would escape from it unscathed. Nothing would be the same as it was before.

When they whispered breathlessly in recess about some "half-witted Tali who lives down the alley," who hangs around in the Tel Arza woods and gives it to anyone who hands her half a pound, or the fat widow from the kitchen goods shop who takes a few boys from class 8 to the storeroom behind her shop and shows what she's got in exchange for watching them jerk off, I felt a pang of sorrow nibbling at my heart, as though some great horror was lying in wait for everybody, men and women alike, a cruel, patient horror, a creeping horror that was slowly spinning a slimy invisible web, and maybe I was already infected without knowing it.

When we got to class 6 or 7, the school nurse, a gruff, military woman, suddenly came into our classroom, and stood there for a whole double lesson, alone in front of thirty-eight dazed boys, revealing to us all the facts of life. Fearlessly she described organs and functions, drew diagrams of the plumbing in colored chalks on the blackboard, she spared us nothing: seeds and eggs, glands, sheaths and tubes. Then she moved on to the horror show and treated us to terrifying descriptions of the two monsters lurking at the gateway, the Frankenstein's monster and the werewolf of the world of sex: the twin calamities of pregnancy and infection.

Dazed and shamefaced, we left the lecture and went out into the world, which now appeared to me as a gigantic minefield or a plague-ridden planet. The child I was then grasped, more or less, what was supposed to be pushed into what, what was supposed to receive what, but for the life of me I could not understand why a sane man or woman would want to get caught in those labyrinthine dragon's lairs. The bold nurse who had not hesitated to lay everything bare for us, from hormones to rules of hygiene, had forgotten to mention, even obliquely, that there might be some pleasure involved in all those complicated, dangerous procedures, either because she wanted to protect our innocence or because she simply did not know.

Our teachers at Tachkemoni mostly wore threadbare dark-gray or brown suits or ancient jackets and constantly demanded our respect and fear: Mr. Monzon, Mr. Avisar, Mr. Neimann Senior and Mr. Neimann Junior, Mr. Alkalai, Mr. Duvshani, Mr. Ophir, Mr. Michaeli, the imperious Mr. Ilan the headmaster, who always appeared in a three-piece suit, and his brother, also Mr. Ilan but only in a two-piece suit.

We had to get to our feet when each of these men entered the classroom, and we could not sit down until he had graciously indicated that we were worthy to do so. We addressed the teachers as "my teacher," and always in the third person. "My teacher asked me to bring a note from my parents, but my parents have gone to Haifa. Would he please let me bring the note on Sunday instead?" Or: "Please, my teacher, doesn't he think he's laying it on a bit thick here?" (The second "he" in this sentence does not, of course, refer to the teacher—whom none of us would ever have dared accuse of laying it on a bit thick—but merely the prophet Jeremiah, or the poet Bialik, whose blazing anger we were studying at the time.)

As for us, the pupils, we lost our first names completely from the moment we crossed the threshold of the school. Our teachers called us only Bozo, Saragosti, Valero, Ribatski, Alfasi, Klausner, Hajaj, Schleifer, De La Mar, Danon, Ben-Naim, Cordovero, and Axelrod.

They had a plethora of punishments, those teachers at Tachkemoni School. A slap on the face, a ruler blow across an outstretched hand, shaking us by the scruff of the neck and banishing us to the playground, summoning our parents, a black mark in the class register, copying out a chapter from the Bible twenty times, writing out five hundred lines: "I must not chatter during class" or "Homework must be done on time." Anyone whose handwriting was not neat enough was made to write pages upon pages at home in calligraphic writing "as pure as a mountain stream." Anyone whose fingernails were untrimmed, whose ears were not immaculate, or whose shirt collar was a bit grimy was sent home in disgrace, but not before being made to stand in front of the class and recite loud and clear: "I'm a dirty boy, being dirty is a sin; if I don't have a wash, I'll end up in the bin!"

The first lesson every morning at Tachkemoni began with the singing of "Modeh ani":

> I give thanks unto thee, O living and eternal King,
> who hast restored my soul unto me in mercy: great is thy faithfulness.

After which we all trilled shrilly but with gusto:

> O universal Lord, who reigned ere any creature yet was formed . . .
> And after all things pass away, alone the dreaded one shall reign . . .

Only when all the songs and the (abbreviated) morning prayers were complete did our teachers order us to open our textbooks and exercise books and prepare our pencils, and generally they launched straight into a long, boring dictation that went on until the bell for recess rang, or sometimes even longer. At home we had to learn by heart: chunks of the Bible, entire poems, and sayings of the rabbis. To this day you can wake me up in the middle of the night and get me to recite the prophet's reply to Rab-shakeh, the envoy of the king of Assyria: "The virgin, the daughter of Zion / hath despised thee, and laughed thee to scorn; / the daughter of Jerusalem / hath shaken her head at thee. / Whom hast thou reproached and blasphemed? / and against whom has thou exalted thy voice? . . . I will put my hook in thy nose, / and my bridle in

thy lips, / and I will turn thee back by the way by which thou camest."
Or the *Ethics of the Fathers*: "On three things the world stands ... Say
little and do much ... I have found nothing better for a body than silence ... Know what is above thee ... Separate thyself not from the
congregation, neither trust in thyself until the day of thy death, and do
not judge thine associate until thou comest to his place ... and in a
place where there are no men endeavor to be a man."

At Tachkemoni School, I studied Hebrew. It was as if the drill had struck
a rich vein of minerals, which I had touched for the first time in Teacher
Zelda's class and in her yard. I was powerfully drawn to the solemn id-
ioms, the almost forgotten words, the exotic syntax, and the linguistic
byways where barely a human foot had trodden for centuries, and the
poignant beauty of the Hebrew language: "And it came to pass, that in
the morning, behold, it was Leah"; "ere any creature yet was formed";
"uncircumcised of heart"; "a *seah* of suffering"; or "Warm thyself by the
fire of the wise; but beware of their glowing coals, lest thou be burnt, for
their bite is the bite of a fox, and their sting is the scorpion's sting ...
and all their words are like coals of fire."

Here, at Tachkemoni, I studied the Pentateuch with Rashi's witty,
light-winged commentary, here I soaked up the wisdom of the sages,
lore and law, prayers, hymns, commentaries, supercommentaries, Sabbath and festival prayer books and the laws of the *Prepared Table*. I also
encountered familiar friends from home, like the wars of the Maccabees, the Bar Kochba Revolt, the history of Jewish communities of the
Diaspora, lives of the great rabbis, and Hasidic tales with the moral attached. Something too of the rabbinic jurists, and of the Hebrew poetry
of Spain and Bialik, and occasionally, in Mr. Ophir's music lessons, some
song of the pioneers in Galilee and the Valley, which was as out of place
in Tachkemoni as a camel in the snows of Siberia.

Mr. Avisar, the geography teacher, would take us with him on
adventure-laden trips to Galilee, the Negev, Trans-Jordan, Mesopotamia,
the pyramids, and the hanging gardens of Babylon, with the aid of wall
maps and occasionally a battered magic lantern. Mr. Neimann Junior
declaimed the fury of the prophets at us in thunderous cascades, followed
at once by gentle rivulets of comfort and consolation. Mr. Monzon, the
English teacher, hammered into us the eternal difference between "I do,"

"I did," "I have done," "I have been doing," "I would have done," "I should have done," and "I should have been doing": "Even the King of England in person!" he would thunder like the Lord from Mount Sinai, "even Churchill! Shakespeare! Gary Cooper!—all obey these rules of language with no excuses, and only you, honorable sir, Mister Abulafia, are apparently above the law! What, are you above Churchill?! are you above Shakespeare?! are you above the King of England?! Shame on you! Disgrace! Now please note this, pay attention all the class, write it down, get it right: *It is* a shame, but you, the Right Honorable Master Abulafia, *you are* a disgrace!!!"

But my favorite teacher of all was Mr. Michaeli, Mordechai Michaeli, whose soft hands were always perfumed like a dancer's and whose face was sheepish, as though he was forever ashamed of something; he used to sit down, take off his hat, put it on the desk in front of him, adjust his little skullcap, and, instead of bombarding us with knowledge, he would spend hours telling us stories. From the Talmud he would move on to Ukrainian folk tales, and then he would plunge suddenly into Greek mythology, Bedouin stories, and Yiddish slapstick, and he would go on until he came to the tales of the Brothers Grimm and Hans Christian Andersen and his own stories, which he composed, just like me, by telling them.

Most of the boys in my class took advantage of sweet Mr. Michaeli's good nature and absentmindedness, and they dozed through his lessons with their heads resting on their arms on the desk. Or sometimes they passed notes around or even tossed a paper ball between the desks: Mr. Michaeli did not notice, or perhaps he did not care.

I did not care either. He fixed me with his weary, kindly eyes and told his stories to me alone. Or just to two or three of us, who did not take our eyes off his lips, which seemed to be creating entire worlds in front of us.

48

FRIENDS AND neighbors started appearing in our little yard again on summer evenings, to talk about politics or cultural affairs over a glass of tea and a piece of cake. Mala and Staszek Rudnicki, Hayim and Hannah Toren, the Krochmals, who had reopened their tiny shop in Geula Street and were once more repairing dolls and making hair grow on balding teddy bears. Yakov-David and Zerta Abramski were also regular visitors. (They had both gone very gray in the months since their son Yoni was killed. Mr. Abramski had become even more talkative than before, while Zerta had turned very quiet.) My father's parents, Grandpa Alexander and Grandma Shlomit, also came sometimes, very elegant and robed in Odessan self-importance. Grandpa Alexander would briskly dismiss everything his son said with a "*Nu,* what" and a scornful wave of his hand, but he never found the courage to disagree with Grandma Shlomit about anything. Grandma would plant two wet kisses on my cheeks, and immediately wipe her lips with a paper napkin and my cheeks with another one, wrinkle her nose at the refreshments Mother had prepared, or the napkins that weren't folded the right way, or her son's jacket, which seemed to her too loud and verging on Oriental bad taste:

"But really, Lonya, it's so *cheap!* Where did you find that rag? In some Arab shop in Jaffa?" And without favoring my mother with so much as a glance she added sadly: "Only in the tiniest shtetls, where culture was barely more than a rumor, might you have seen somebody dressing like that!"

They would sit in a circle around the black tea cart that had been taken outside to serve as a garden table, unanimously bless the cool evening breeze, and over tea and cakes analyze Stalin's latest devious move or President Truman's determination, discuss the decline of the British Empire or the partition of India, and from there the conversation moved on to the politics of the young state and became more animated. Staszek Rudnicki raised his voice while Mr. Abramski ridiculed him with expansive movements of his hand and in high-flown, biblical Hebrew. Staszek believed firmly in the kibbutzim and the new collective farms and maintained that the government ought to send all the new immigrants there en masse, straight off the ships, whether they wanted to go or not, to be cured once and for all of their Diaspora mentality and their persecution complexes; it was there, through hard work in the fields, that the New Hebrew Man would be molded.

My father expressed his resentment of the Bolshevik despotism of the Histadrut leadership who withheld work from those not in possession of their red card. Mr. Gustav Krochmal timidly advanced the view that Ben-Gurion, despite his faults, was the hero of the age: he had been sent to us providentially at a time when petty-minded party hacks might have been put off by the enormity of the undertaking and missed the opportune moment to establish a state. "It was our youth!" Grandpa Alexander shouted loudly, "It was our wonderful youth that gave us the victory and the miracle! Without no Ben-Gurion! The youth!" At which Grandpa leaned toward me and patted me absentmindedly a couple of times, as though to reward the younger generation for winning the war.

Women hardly ever joined in the conversation. In those days it was customary to compliment women on being "such marvelous listeners," on the cakes and biscuits, on the pleasant atmosphere, but not on their contribution to the conversation. Mala Rudnicki, for instance, would nod happily whenever Staszek spoke and shake her head if anyone interrupted him. Zerta Abramski clasped her shoulders with her hands as though she felt cold. Ever since Yoni's death she would sit, even on warm evenings, with her head inclined as though she was looking at the tops of the cypresses in the next-door garden, hugging her shoulders with her hands. Grandma Shlomit, who was a strong-minded, opinionated woman, would sometimes interpose in that deep alto voice of hers: "How very true!" or "It's much worse than you said, Staszek, much, much worse!" Or else: "N-o! What do you mean, Mr. Abramski! That is simply not possible!"

Only my mother sometimes subverted this rule. When there was a moment's silence, she would say something that at first might seem irrelevant but then could be seen to have gently shifted the center of gravity completely, without changing the subject or contradicting those who had spoken before, but rather as though she were opening a door in some back wall of the conversation that up to then had not seemed to have a doorway in it.

Once she had made her remark, she shut up, smiling agreeably and looking triumphantly not at the visitors or at my father but at me. After my mother had spoken, the whole conversation seemed to shift its weight from one foot to another. Soon afterward, still smiling her delicate smile that seemed to be doubting something while deciphering something else, she would get up and offer her guests another glass of tea: Please? How strong? And another slice of cake?

To the child I was then my mother's brief intervention in the men's conversation was rather distressing, perhaps because I sensed an invisible ripple of embarrassment among the speakers, an almost imperceptible search for a way out, as though there were a vague momentary fear that they might inadvertently have said or done something that had caused my mother to snigger at them, but none of them knew what it was. Maybe it was her withdrawn, radiant beauty that always embarrassed those inhibited men and made them fear she might not like them, or find them just a little repulsive.

As for the women, my mother's interventions stirred in them a strange mixture of anxiety and hope that one day she would finally lose her footing, and perhaps a mite of pleasure at the men's discomfiture.

Hayim Toren, the writer and writers' union hack, might say, for example:

"Surely everyone must realize that you cannot run a state the way you might run a grocer's shop. Or like the town council in some godforsaken shtetl."

My father says:

"It may be too early to judge, my dear Hayim, but everyone with eyes in his head occasionally discerns cause for profound disappointment in our young state."

Mr. Krochmal, the dolls' doctor, adds shyly:

"Apart from which, they don't even mend the pavement. Two letters I've written to the mayor, and I haven't had a single reply. I'm not saying that to disagree with what Mr. Klausner was saying, but in the self-same spirit."

My father ventures one of his puns:

"The only things that work in this country of ours are the road works."

Mr. Abramski quotes:

"'And blood toucheth blood,' saith the prophet Hosea, 'therefore shall the land mourn.' The remnant of the Jewish nation has come here to rebuild the kingdom of David and Solomon, to lay the foundation of the Third Temple, and we have all fallen into the sweaty hands of assorted bloated kibbutz treasurers of little faith, and other red-faced hacks of uncircumcised heart, 'whose world is as narrow as that of an ant.' Rebellious princes and companions of thieves the lot of them, who are sharing among themselves plot by plot the paltry strip of the Fatherland that the nations have left in our hands. It was to them and no one else that the prophet Ezekiel was referring when he said: 'The suburbs shall shake at the sound of the cry of thy pilots.'"

And Mother, with her smile hovering on her lips and barely touching them:

"Perhaps when they've finished sharing out the plots, they'll start mending the pavements? And then they'll mend the pavement in front of Mr. Krochmal's shop."

Now, fifty years after her death, I imagine I can hear in her voice as she says these words, or something like them, a tense mixture of sobriety, skepticism, sharp, fine sarcasm, and ever-present sadness.

In those years something gnawed at her. A slowness started to make itself felt in her movements, or something resembling a slight absence of mind. She had stopped giving private history and literature lessons. Sometimes, for a paltry payment, she would correct the grammar and style of articles written in limping Germanic Hebrew by professors from Rehavia and edit them for publication. She still did all the housework herself, ably and nimbly: she spent each morning cooking, frying, baking, shopping, slicing, mixing, drying, cleaning, scraping, washing, hanging out, ironing, folding, until the whole place was gleaming, and after lunch she sat in an armchair reading.

She had a strange way of sitting when she read: the book always rested on her knees, and her back and neck were bent over it. She looked like a young girl shyly lowering her eyes to her knees when she sat reading like that. Often she stood at the window looking out for a long time at our quiet street. Or she took her shoes off and lay on her back on the bedspread, fully dressed, with her open eyes fixed on a particular spot on the ceiling. Sometimes she would suddenly stand up, feverishly put on her outdoor clothes, promise to be back in a quarter of an hour, straighten her skirt, smooth down her hair without looking in the mirror, hang her plain straw handbag on her shoulder, and go out briskly, as though she was afraid of missing something. If I asked to go with her, or if I asked her where she was going, my mother would say:

"I need to be on my own for a bit. Why don't you be on your own too?" And again: "I'll be back in a quarter of an hour."

She always kept her word: she'd be back very soon, with a sparkle in her eyes and color in her cheeks, as though she had been in very cold air. As though she'd run all the way. Or as though something exciting had happened to her on the way. She was prettier when she returned than when she left.

Once I followed her out of the house without her noticing me. I trailed her at a distance, clinging to walls and bushes, as I'd learned to do from Sherlock Holmes and from films. The air was not very cold and my mother did not run, she walked briskly, as though afraid she'd be late. At the end of Zephaniah Street she turned right and stepped out jauntily in her white shoes until she reached the bottom of Malachi Street. There she stopped beside the mailbox and hesitated. The young detective who was trailing her came to the conclusion that she went out to mail letters secretly, and I was bristling with curiosity and vague apprehension. But my mother did not mail any letter. She stood for a moment beside the mailbox, lost in thought, and then she suddenly put a hand to her forehead and turned to go home. (Years later that red mailbox still stood there, set into a concrete wall, and inscribed with the letters GR, for King George V.) So I cut through a yard that led me to a shortcut through a second yard, and I got home a minute or two before she arrived, a little out of breath, her cheeks colored as though she'd been in snow, with a mischievous, affectionate sparkle in her piercing brown eyes. At that moment my mother looked very much like her father, Grandpa-Papa. She took my head and pressed it lightly to her tummy and said something like this to me:

"Of all my children, you're the one I love best. Can you tell me once and for all what it is about you that makes me love you the most?"

And also:

"It's especially your innocence. I've never encountered innocence like yours in all my life. Even when you've lived for many long years and had all sorts of experiences, your innocence will never leave you. Ever. You'll always stay innocent."

And also:

"There are some women who just devour the innocent, and there are others, and I'm one of them, who love innocent men and feel an inner urge to spread a protective wing over them."

And also:

"I think you will grow up to be a sort of prattling puppydog like your father, and you'll also be a man who is quiet and full and closed like a well in a village that has been abandoned by all its inhabitants. Like me. You can be both, yes. I do believe you can. Would you like us to play at making up a story now? We'll take it in turns to make up a chapter. Shall I start? Once upon a time there was a village that had been abandoned by all its inhabitants. Even the cats and dogs. Even the birds had abandoned it. So the village stood silent and abandoned for years upon years. The thatched roofs were lashed by the rain and the wind, the walls of the cottages were cracked by hail and snow, the vegetable gardens were overgrown, and only the trees and bushes went on growing, and with no one to prune them, they grew thicker and thicker. One evening, in the autumn, a traveler who had lost his way arrived in the abandoned village. Hesitantly he knocked at the door of the first cottage, and . . . would you like to carry on?"

Around that time, in the winter between 1949 and 1950, two years before her death, she began to have frequent headaches. She often had the flu and sore throats, and even when she recovered, the migraines did not go away. She put her chair near the window and sat for hours in a blue flannel dressing gown staring at the rain, with her book open upside-down on her lap, but instead of reading she drummed on its cover with her fingers. She sat stiffly staring at the rain or at some sodden bird for an hour or two hours and never stopped drumming on the book with all ten fingers. As though she were repeating the same piece over and over again on the piano.

Gradually she had to cut down on the housework. She still managed to put away the dishes, tidy up, and throw out every scrap of paper and crumb. She still swept the apartment every day and washed the floor once every two or three days. But she did not cook complicated meals anymore. She made do with simple food: boiled potatoes, fried eggs, raw vegetables. Occasionally bits of chicken floating in chicken soup. Or boiled rice with canned tuna. She hardly ever complained about her piercing headaches, which sometimes continued for days. It was my father who told me about them. He told me quietly, not in her presence, in a kind of man-to-man conversation. He put his arm around my shoulder and asked me to promise to keep my voice down from now on when Mother was at home. Not to shout or make a racket. And I must especially promise not to slam doors, windows, or shutters. I must be careful not to drop pots or cans or saucepan lids. And not to clap my hands indoors.

I promised, and I kept my word. He called me a bright boy, and once or twice he even called me "young man."

My mother smiled at me affectionately, but it was a smile without a smile. That winter she got more wrinkles at the corners of her eyes.

We had few visitors. Lilenka—Lilia Kalish, Lea Bar-Samkha, the teacher who wrote two popular books about child psychology—came over some days; she sat facing my mother, and the two of them chatted in Russian or Polish. I had the feeling they were talking about their hometown, Rovno, and about their friends and teachers who were shot by Germans in the Susenki Forest. Because occasionally they mentioned the name of Issachar Reiss, the charismatic headmaster whom all the girls in Tarbuth were in love with, and the names of some other teachers too—Buslik, Berkowski, Fanka Seidman—and of some of the streets and parks from their childhood.

Grandma Shlomit came around occasionally, inspected the icebox and the larder, screwed up her face, had a brief whispered conversation with Father at the end of the corridor, outside the door of the little bathroom that was also the toilet, then peeped into the room where Mother was resting and asked her in a sweetened voice:

"Do you need anything, my dear?"

"No, thank you."

"Then why don't you lie down?"

"I'm fine like this. Thank you."

"Aren't you cold? Shall I light the heater for you?"

"No thanks, I'm not cold. Thank you."

"What about the doctor? When did he call?"

"I don't need the doctor."

"Really? *Nu*, and how exactly do you know you don't need the doctor?"

Father said something to his mother in Russian, sheepishly, then immediately apologized to both of them. Grandma told him off:

"Be quiet, Lonya. Don't interfere. I'm talking to her, not to you. What an example, excuse me, you're setting for the child."

The child hurriedly got out of the way, although once he did manage to hear Grandma whispering to Father when he saw her to the door:

"Yes. Play-acting. As though she deserves the moon. Just stop arguing with me. You'd think she was the only one who has a hard time here. You'd think the rest of us are living in the lap of luxury. You should open her window a bit. A person could literally suffocate to death in there."

Nevertheless, the doctor was called. He was called again not long afterward. Mother was sent to the clinic for thorough tests and even had to spend a couple of nights at Hadassah Hospital, in its temporary premises at Davidka Square. The tests were inconclusive. A fortnight after she came back from the hospital, pale and drooping, our doctor was called again. Once he was even called out in the middle of the night, and I was woken by his kind voice, thick and rough like wood glue, joking with Father in the corridor. By the side of the sofa that opened out at night into a narrow double bed, on Mother's side, all sorts of packets and jars appeared, vitamin pills, migraine pills, something called APC, and bottles of medicine. She refused to lie in bed. She sat quietly on her chair by the window for hours on end, and sometimes she seemed in a very good mood. She spoke gently and kindly to Father that winter, as though he were the patient, as though he were the one who shuddered if anyone raised their voice. She got into the habit of speaking to him as though to a child, sweetly, affectionately, sometimes she even spoke to him in baby talk. Whereas to me she spoke as one might speak to a confidant.

"Please don't be angry with me, Amos," she would say, piercing my soul with her eyes. "I'm not having an easy time of it right now. You can see for yourself how hard I'm trying to make everything all right."

I got up early and swept the floor before I went to school, and twice a week I washed it with soapy water and wiped it dry. I learned how to chop up a salad, butter bread, fry an egg for my supper, because Mother generally suffered from slight evening sickness.

As for Father, he suddenly showed signs of cheerfulness at this time, for no apparent reason, which he made every effort to disguise. He hummed to himself, chuckled for no reason, and once, when he didn't notice me, I caught sight of him leaping and jumping in the yard as though he had been stung. He often went out in the evening and came back only after I was asleep. He had to go out, he said, because my light went out at nine and in their room Mother couldn't stand the electric light. Every evening she would sit in the dark in her chair by the window. He tried sitting with her, next to her, in silence, as though he were sharing her suffering, but his cheery, impatient nature didn't let him sit motionless like that for more than three or four minutes.

49

AT FIRST Father withdrew to the kitchen in the evenings. He tried to read, or to spread out his books and note cards on the worn oilcloth and work a little. But the kitchen was too small and cramped, and he felt confined there. He was a man who thrived on company, he loved arguing and joking, he loved light, and if he was made to sit on his own night after night in that depressing kitchen, with no clever wordplay, no historical or political debate, his eyes misted over with a sort of childish sulkiness.

Mother suddenly laughed and said to him:

"Go and play outside for a bit."

She added:

"Only take care. There are all sorts of people out there. They're not all as kindhearted and straightforward as you are."

"*Shto ty ponimayesh?*" Father exploded. "*Ty ne normalnaya? Vidish malchik!*"

Mother said:

"Sorry."

He always asked her permission before he went out. He never went out before he had finished all the chores: putting the shopping away, washing up, hanging out the wash, bringing in the wash. Then he would polish his shoes, take a shower, splash on some of the new aftershave he had bought for himself, put on a clean shirt, carefully choose a suitable tie, and, still holding his jacket, he would bend over my mother and say:

"Are you really sure you don't mind if I go out to see some friends? Have a chat about the political situation? Talk about work? Tell me the truth."

Mother never objected. But she adamantly refused to listen when he tried to tell her where he was going.

"Just try not to make too much noise when you come in, Arieh."

"I will."

"Good night. Off you go."

"You really don't mind if I go out? I won't stay out late."

"I really don't mind. And you can come home when you like."

"Do you need anything else?"

"Thank you. No, I don't need anything. Amos is here to look after me."

"I won't be late."

And after another little hesitant silence:

"All right then. So is that OK? I'm off? See you soon. Hope you feel better. Try to get into bed, don't fall asleep in the chair."

"I'll try."

"Good night then? See you? I promise I won't make a noise when I come in, it won't be late."

"Go."

He straightened his jacket, adjusted his tie, and left, humming as he walked past my window in a warm voice but hair-raisingly out of tune: "So long is the road and so winding the way, you're farther away than the moon . . ." Or "What are they saying, your eyes, your eyes, without ever saying a word . . ."

Her insomnia came from her migraine. The doctor prescribed all kinds of sleeping pills and tranquilizers, but none of them helped. She was afraid of going to bed, and spent every night in her chair, draped in a blanket, with a cushion under her head and another one hiding her face; perhaps she tried to sleep like that. The slightest disturbance made her start: the wailing of lovesick cats, distant gunfire in Sheikh Jarrah or Isawiya, the muezzin's call at dawn from a minaret in Arab Jerusalem, across the border. If Father turned out all the lights, she was afraid of the dark; if he left a light on in the corridor, it made her migraine worse. Apparently he would get back shortly before midnight, in high spirits but full of shame, to find her sitting awake in her chair, staring dry-eyed at the darkened window. He would ask if she wanted some tea or hot milk, beg her to get into bed and try to go to sleep, and offer to sit up on the chair instead, if that would help her to get some sleep at last.

Sometimes he felt so guilty that he got down on his knees to put some woolen socks on her, in case her feet were cold.

When he came home in the middle of the night, he probably showered thoroughly, singing to himself cheerfully, shamelessly out of tune, "I have a garden, and I have a well," catching himself in the middle and silencing himself at once, covered with shame and confusion, getting undressed in a guilty silence, putting on his striped pajamas, gently repeating his offer of tea or milk or a cold drink, and perhaps trying once more to induce her to lie down in bed, next to him or instead of him. And begging her to banish her bad thoughts and think pleasant thoughts instead. While he got into bed and curled up under the blanket, he suggested all sorts of pleasant thoughts that she might think, and ended up falling asleep like a baby with all those pleasant thoughts. But I imagine that he would wake up, responsibly, two or three times in the night to check on the patient in her chair, bring her her medicine and a glass of water, straighten her blanket, and go back to sleep.

By the end of the winter she had almost stopped eating. Sometimes she dunked a dry rusk in a glass of tea and said that was enough for her, she was feeling a little queasy and had no appetite. Don't worry about me, Arieh, I hardly ever go out. If I did eat, I'd get fat like my mother. Don't worry.

Father said sadly to me:

"Mother isn't well, and the doctors can't discover what's wrong with her. I wanted to call in some other doctors, but she wouldn't let me."

And once he said to me:

"Your mother is punishing herself. Just to punish me."

Grandpa Alexander said:

"*Nu,* what. Mental state. *Melancholia.* Whims. It's a sign that the heart is still young."

Auntie Lilenka said to me:

"It can't be easy for you either. You're such a bright, sensitive child. You'll be a writer one day. And your mother says you're a ray of sunshine in her life. You really are a ray of sunshine. Not like someone whose childish selfishness allows him to go out and gather rosebuds at such a time, without realizing that he's only making matters worse. Never mind. I was talking to myself there, not to you. You're a rather lonely child, and you may be even more lonely than usual right now, so whenever you need to have a heart to heart with me, don't hesitate, please remember that Lilia is not just a friend of Mother's but, if only you let me, a good friend of yours too. A friend who doesn't just see you the way grown-ups see children, but is a real kindred spirit."

I may have understood that when Aunt Lilia said "go out and gather rosebuds" she was referring to Father's habit of going to see friends in the evening, although I couldn't see what rosebuds she thought grew in the Rudnickis' cramped apartment, with the bald bird and the pinecone bird and the herd of raffia animals behind the glass doors of the sideboard, or in the miserable, run-down apartment that was all the Abramskis could afford, and that they had almost stopped cleaning and keeping tidy since they went into mourning for their son. Or perhaps in those rosebuds of Aunt Lilia's I guessed at something that was impossible. And that may be why I refused to understand it or to make a connection with Father's meticulous polishing of his shoes or his new aftershave.

Memory deludes me. I have just remembered something that I completely forgot after it happened. I remembered it again when I was about sixteen, and then I forgot it again. And this morning I remembered not the event itself but the previous recollection, which itself was more than forty years ago, as though an old moon were reflected in a windowpane from which it was reflected in a lake, from where memory draws not the reflection itself, which no longer exists, but only its whitened bones.

So here it is. Here and now, in Arad on an autumn day at half past six in the morning, I can suddenly see perfectly sharply the image of me and my friend Lolik walking down Jaffa Road near Zion Square, one cloudy lunchtime in the winter of 1950 or 1951, and Lolik punches me lightly in the ribs and whispers, Hey, take a look at that, isn't that your Dad sitting in there? Let's scamper before he spots us and realizes we've cut Avisar's class. So we made off, but as we went, I saw my father through the glass front of Sichel's Café, sitting just inside, laughing, with a young woman who had her back to the window, and holding her hand—she was wearing a bracelet—to his lips; and I ran away from there, I ran away from Lolik, and I haven't quite stopped running since.

Grandpa Alexander kissed every lady's hand. Father did it sometimes, but otherwise he just took her hand and bent over it to look at her wristwatch and compare it with his own, he was always doing that, to almost everybody, watches were his hobby. That was the only time I ever skipped a class, and I did it this time especially to go and see the burned-out Egyptian tank they put on display in the Russian Compound. I would never cut a class again. Ever.

I hated him. For a couple of days. Out of shame. And after a couple of days I started hating my mother, with her migraines and her play-acting and her sit-in in her chair by the window, she was the one who was to blame because she had pushed him to look for signs of life. Then I hated myself because I had let Lolik tempt me like the fox and the cat in *Pinocchio* to skip Mr. Avisar's class. Why didn't I have a single ounce of strength of character? Why was I so easily influenced? And a week later it had completely slipped my mind, and I recalled what I had seen through the window of Sichel's Café only one bad night at Kibbutz Hulda when I was about sixteen. I forgot, just as I forgot all about the morning I came home early from school and found my mother sitting quietly in her blue flannel dressing gown, not in her chair by the window but outside in the yard, in a deck chair, under the bare pomegranate tree, sitting there calmly with an expression on her face that looked like a smile but wasn't; her book was lying as usual upside down open on her lap and torrential rain was pouring down on her and must have been doing so for an hour or two because when I stood her up and dragged her indoors, she was soaked and frozen like a drenched bird that would never fly again. I got her to the bathroom and fetched her some dry clothes from her closet and I told her off like a grown-up and I gave her instructions, through the bathroom door, and she didn't answer but she did everything I told her to do, only she didn't stop smiling that smile that wasn't a smile. I didn't say a word to Father, because Mother's eyes asked me to keep it a secret. And to Aunt Lilia all I said was something like this:

"But you're completely wrong, Auntie Lilia. I'll never be a writer or a poet, or a scholar either, there's no way I will, because I haven't got any feelings. Feelings disgust me. I'm going to be a farmer. I'm going to live in a kibbutz. Or maybe someday I'll be a dog poisoner. With a syringe full of arsenic."

In the spring she felt better. On the morning of the spring festival of Tu Bishvat, the day that Chaim Weizmann, as president of the Provisional Council of State, opened the meeting of the Constituent Assembly that became the First Knesset, my mother put on her blue dress and asked Father and me to join her in a little outing to the Tel Arza woods. I thought she carried herself well and looked pretty in this dress, and when we finally left our book-laden basement and went out into the spring sunlight, there was a warm sparkle of affection in her eyes. Father put his arm in hers and I ran a little way ahead of them, like a puppy, to give them a chance to talk to each other, or maybe just because I was so happy.

Mother had made some cheese sandwiches with slices of tomato, hard-boiled egg, red pepper, and anchovy, and Father had made a flask of lukewarm orange juice that he had squeezed himself. When we got to the woods, we spread out a small tarpaulin and sprawled on it, inhaling the smell of the pines that had drunk their fill of the winter rains. Rocky slopes that had grown a deep fuzz of green peeped at us through the trees. We could see the houses of the Arab village of Shuafat across the border, and the minaret of Nebi Samwil rose slim and tall on the horizon. Father observed that the word for "woods" in Hebrew was similar to the words for "deaf," "silent," "industry," and "plowing," which led into a short lecture about the charms of language. Since Mother was in such a good mood, she gave him a list of other similar words.

Then she told us about a Ukrainian neighbor, an agile, good-looking boy who could predict exactly which morning the rye would start sprouting and the first shoots of beetroot would appear. All the Gentile girls were crazy about this boy, Stephan, Stepasha they called him, or Stiopa, but he was madly in love with a Jewish teacher at the Tarbuth school, so much so that he once tried to drown himself in a whirlpool in the river, but he was such a wonderful swimmer that he could not drown, he was carried along to an estate on the bank of the river, and the woman who owned the estate seduced him, and a few months later she bought an inn for him, and he's probably still there, ugly and gross from too much drinking and womanizing.

For once Father forgot to silence her when she used the word "womanizing," and didn't even shout, "*Vidish Malchik!*" He laid his head on her knee, stretched out on the tarpaulin, and chewed a blade of grass. I did the same: I lay down on the tarpaulin, put my head on Mother's other knee, chewed a blade of grass, and filled my lungs with the intoxicating warm air, full of fresh scents and the hum of insects drunk with the spring, and washed clean by the winter wind and rain. How good it would be to stop time, and to stop writing this too, a couple of years before her death, with the picture of the three of us in the Tel Arza woods on that spring festival: my mother in her blue dress, with a red silk scarf tied gracefully around her neck, sitting upright and looking pretty, then leaning back against the trunk of a tree, with my father's head on one knee and mine on the other, stroking our faces and hair with her cool hand, as throngs of birds shrilled overhead in the spring-cleaned pine trees.

She was really much better that spring. No longer did she sit day and night in her chair facing the window; she didn't recoil from the electric light or start at every noise. She no longer neglected the housework and the hours of reading that she loved. She had fewer migraines, and she almost recovered her appetite. And once again it was enough for her to spend five minutes in front of the mirror, a dab of powder, a touch of lipstick and eyeshadow, a brush of the hair, another couple of minutes carefully making her choice in front of the open closet door, to appear to all of us mysterious, pretty, and radiant. The usual visitors reappeared at our apartment, the Bar-Yitzhar-Itselevitches, the Abramskis, devout Revisionists who loathed the Labor government, Hannah and Hayim Toren, the Rudnickis, and Tosia and Gustav Krochmal from Danzig, who had the dolls' hospital in Geula Street. The men sometimes shot a hasty, embarrassed look at my mother and hurriedly looked away again.

And we resumed going on Friday evenings to light candles and eat gefilte fish or stuffed chicken neck sewn up with a needle and thread at Grandma Shlomit and Grandpa Alexander's round table. On Saturday mornings we sometimes went to visit the Rudnickis, and after lunch, almost every Sabbath, we crossed the whole of Jerusalem, from north to south, on the pilgrimage to Uncle Joseph in Talpiot.

Once, over supper, Mother suddenly told us about a standard lamp that had stood beside her armchair in her rented room in Prague when she was a student there. Father stopped on his way home from work the next day at two furniture shops in King George Street and an electrical goods shop in Ben Yehuda Street: he compared, went back to the first shop, and came home with the most beautiful standard lamp. It had cost him nearly a quarter of his monthly salary. Mother kissed us both on our foreheads and promised us with her strange smile that the lamp would give us light long after she had gone. Father, drunk on victory, did not hear these words of hers because he was never a good listener and because his torrent of verbal energy had already swept him on, to the proto-Semitic root meaning light, NWR, the Aramaic form *menarta* and the Arabic equivalent *manar*.

I heard but I didn't understand. Or I understood but I didn't grasp the significance.

Then the rain started again. Once again Father asked permission, after I had been sent to bed, to "go out and see some people." He promised to come back not too late, and not to make a noise, he brought her a cup of warm milk, and went out with his super-shiny shoes, with a triangle of white handkerchief peering out of his jacket pocket, like his father, trailing a scent of aftershave. As he went past my window, I heard him open his umbrella with a click, humming out of tune, "What delicate hands she had, no man dared to tou-ou-ouch her," or "Her eyes were like the northern star, but her heart was as hot as the de-e-e-sert."

But Mother and I deceived him while his back was turned. Although he was so strict about lights-out for me, "nine on the dot and not a second later," as soon as the sound of his footsteps faded down the wet street I leaped out of bed and ran to her, to hear more and more stories. She sat in her chair in a room whose walls were lined with row upon row of books, with more piled up on the floor, and I knelt on the rug at her feet in my pajamas, with my head resting on her warm thigh, listening with my eyes closed. There were no lights on in the apartment apart from the new standard lamp by her chair. The wind and rain pounded at the shutters. Occasional volleys of low thunder rolled across Jerusalem. Father had gone off and left me and Mother with her stories. Once, she told me about the empty apartment above her rented room in Prague when she was a student. No one had lived there for two years except, so the neighbors said, in a whisper, the ghosts of two little dead girls. There had been a big fire in the apartment, and it had been impossible to save the girls, Emilia and Jana. After the tragedy, the girls' parents had emigrated. The soot-blackened apartment was locked and shuttered. It was not renovated or rented. Sometimes, the neighbors whispered, muffled sounds of laughter and mischief were heard, or crying in the middle of the night. I never heard sounds like that, Mother said, but sometimes I was almost certain that faucets were turned on, furniture was moved, bare feet pattered from room to room. Perhaps somebody was using the empty apartment for secret love-making or for some other shady purpose. When you grow up, you'll discover that almost everything your ears hear at night can be interpreted in more than one way. In fact, not only at night and not only your ears. What your eyes see, too, even in broad daylight, can almost always be understood in various ways.

On other nights she told me about Eurydice and Orpheus. She told me about the eight-year-old daughter of a well-known Nazi, a brutal killer who was hanged by the Allies at Nuremberg after the war: his little daughter was sent to an institution for juvenile delinquents just because she was caught decorating his photograph with flowers. She told me about a young timber merchant from one of the villages near Rovno who got lost in the forest one stormy night in winter and disappeared, but six years later somebody secretly deposited his worn-out boots at the foot of his widow's bed in the middle of the night. She told me about old Tolstoy, who left his home at the end of his life and expired in a station master's cottage at a remote railway junction called Astapovo.

My mother and I were like Peer Gynt and his mother Ase on those winter nights:

> My young lad and I were companions in grief . . .
> As we sat in our home there, my young Peer and I—
> seeking solace from sorrow and blessed relief . . .
> So all sorts of adventures we started to spin

of princes and trolls and all manner of beasts;
and of bride-rapes as well. Oh, but who would have thought
that those devilish tales would have stuck in his head?*

Often we played a game on those nights, making up a story alternately: Mother would start a story, I would continue it, then the thread passed back to her, and then to me again, and so on. My father would get home just before or after midnight, and at the sound of his footsteps outside, we instantly switched off the lamp, jumped into bed like a pair of naughty children, and pretended to be sleeping the sleep of the just. Half asleep, I heard him moving about the little apartment, undressing, drinking some milk from the icebox, going to the bathroom, turning on the faucet, turning it off, flushing the toilet, turning the faucet on and off again, humming an old love song under his breath, drinking some more milk, and padding barefoot to the book room and the sofa, which had been opened into a double bed, presumably lying down next to Mother, who was feigning sleep, internalizing his humming, humming inside himself for another minute or two, then dropping off to sleep, and sleeping like a babe until six in the morning. At six he woke first, shaved, dressed, and put on Mother's apron to squeeze us both some oranges, warming the juice, as always, over a pan of boiling water, because cold juice is well known to give you a chill, then bringing each of us a glass of juice in bed.

One of those nights my mother couldn't sleep again. She didn't like lying on the sofa bed next to Father, who was sleeping soundly while his glasses slept quietly on the shelf next to him, so she got up and instead of going to sit in her chair facing the window or to the gloomy kitchen, she got into bed with me, cuddled me, and kissed me till I woke up. Then she asked me in a whisper, right into my ear, if I minded if we whispered together tonight. Just the two of us. I'm sorry I woke you up but I really need to talk to you tonight. And this time in the dark I heard in her voice a smile that was a real smile, not a shadow of one.

When Zeus discovered that Prometheus had managed to steal a spark from the fire that he had withheld from the mortals as a punishment,

*Henrik Ibsen, *Peer Gynt*, act II, scene 2.

he almost exploded with rage. Rarely had the other gods seen their king so sullen and angry. Day after day he let his thunder roll, and no one dared approach him. In his rage the furious father of the gods decided to bring a great disaster upon the race of mortals in the guise of a wonderful present. So he commanded Hephaestus, the blacksmith god, to form a beautiful woman out of clay. The goddess Athena taught her to spin and sew and clothed her in fine garments. The goddess Aphrodite endowed her with graceful charms that beguiled all men and enflamed their desires. Hermes, the god of merchants and thieves, taught her to lie without batting an eyelid, to captivate and to deceive. The beautiful temptress was named Pandora, meaning "She who possesses all gifts." And then Zeus, thirsty for vengeance, ordered her to be given as a bride to Prometheus's foolish brother. In vain did Prometheus warn his brother to beware of the gifts of the gods. When the brother saw this beauty queen, he leaped with joy upon Pandora, who had brought with her as a dowry a casket filled with gifts from all the gods of Olympus, which she was instructed never to open. One day Pandora lifted the lid of the casket of gifts, and out flew illness, loneliness, injustice, cruelty, and death. That is how all the troubles that we see around us came into this world. If you haven't fallen asleep, I wanted to tell you that in my opinion the troubles existed already. There were the troubles of Prometheus and Zeus, and the troubles of Pandora herself, not to mention simple people like us. The troubles did not come out of Pandora's box, Pandora's box was invented because of troubles. It was opened because of troubles, too. Will you go and have your hair cut after school tomorrow? Just look how long it's grown.

50

SOMETIMES MY parents took me with them when they went "into town," that is to say to King George Street or Ben Yehuda Street, to one of the three or four main cafés that may have been reminiscent of cafés in the cities of Central Europe in the interwar years. In these cafés Hebrew and foreign-language newspapers were at the disposal of customers, fixed into long sticks, as well as a selection of weeklies and monthlies in various languages. Beneath the brass and crystal chandeliers a subdued foreign murmur mingled with blue-gray cigarette smoke and a whiff of other worlds, in which tranquil lives of study and companionship proceeded at a peaceful pace.

Well-groomed ladies and distinguished-looking gentlemen sat at the tables, conversing quietly. Waiters and waitresses in white jackets with white tea towels folded neatly over their arms floated among the tables serving piping-hot coffee on top of which floated pure, curly angels of whipped cream, Ceylon tea with the essence served separately in little china pots, liqueur-filled pastries, croissants, apple strudel with cream, chocolate cake with vanilla icing, mulled wine on winter evenings, and little glasses of brandy and cherry brandy. (In 1949 and 1950 there still was only ersatz coffee, and the chocolate and cream were probably ersatz too.)

In these cafés my parents sometimes met a different group of acquaintances, far removed from their usual circle of doll menders or the post office. Here we conferred with such valuable acquaintances as Mr. Pfeffermann, who was Father's boss in the newspaper department at the library, Joshua Czaczik the publisher, who came to Jerusalem occasionally from Tel Aviv on business, promising young philologists and historians of my parents' age who were embarking on a university career, and other young scholars, including professors' assistants, whose future seemed assured. Sometimes my parents met a small group of Jerusalem writers whom Father felt honored to know: Dov Kimche, Shraga Kadari, Yitzhak Shenhar, Yehuda Yaari. Today they are almost forgotten, and even most of their readers have gone the way of all flesh, but in their time they were very well known, and their books were widely read.

Father would prepare for these meetings by washing his hair, polishing and buffing his shoes till they shone like jet, securing his favorite tie, the gray-and-white striped one, with a silver tie clip, and explaining to me not once but several times the rules of polite behavior and my duty to reply to any question with brevity and good taste. Sometimes he shaved before we left home, even though he had already shaved in the morning. My mother would mark the occasion by putting on her coral necklace, which set off her olive complexion perfectly and added an exotic touch to her rather withdrawn beauty, making her look Italian or possibly Greek.

The well-known scholars and writers were impressed by Father's acuity and erudition. They knew they could always rely on his extensive knowledge whenever their dictionaries and reference works let them down. But even more than they made use of my father and took advantage of his expertise, they were openly pleased by my mother's company. Her profound, inspirational attentiveness urged them on to tireless verbal feats. Something in her thoughtful presence, her unexpected questions, her look, her remarks, would shed a new, surprising light on the subject under discussion, and made them talk on and on as though they were slightly intoxicated, about their work, their creative struggles, their plans and their achievements. Sometimes my mother would produce an apposite quotation from the speaker's own writings, remarking on a certain similarity to the ideas of Tolstoy, or she would identify a stoic quality in what was being said, or observe with a slight inclination of the head—at such moments her voice would take on a dark, winelike quality—that here her ear seemed to catch an almost Scandinavian note in the work of a writer who was present, an echo of Hamsun or Strindberg, or even of the mystical writings of Emmanuel Swedenborg. Thereupon my mother would resume her previous silence and alert attentiveness, like a finely tuned instrument, while they enchantedly lavished on her whatever they did or did not have on their minds as they competed for her attention.

Years later, when I happened to bump into one or two of them, they informed me that my mother had been a very charming woman and a truly inspired reader, the sort of reader every writer dreamed of when hard at work in the solitude of his study. What a pity she left no writings of her own: it was possible that her premature death had deprived us of a highly talented writer, at a time when women writing in Hebrew could be counted on the fingers of one hand.

If these notables met my father at the library or in the street, they would chat with him briefly about Education Minister Dinur's letter to the heads of the university, or Zalman Shneour's attempt to become Walt Whitman in his old age, or who would get Professor Klausner's chair when he retired, and then they would pat him on the back and say, with a gleam in their eyes and a beaming expression, please greet your lady wife warmly from me, what a truly wonderful woman, such a cultivated, discerning woman! So artistic!

As they patted him affectionately on the shoulder, in their heart of hearts they may have envied him his wife and wondered what she had seen in him, that pedant, even if he was extraordinarily knowledgeable, industrious, and even, relatively speaking, a not insignificant scholar, but, between ourselves, a rather scholastic, totally uncreative person.

I had a specific role in these conversations at the café. First of all I had to give polite, intelligent answers, just like a grown-up, to such difficult questions as how old I was, what class I was in at school, did I collect stamps or have a scrapbook, what did they teach us these days in geography, what did they teach us in Hebrew, was I a good boy, what had I read by Dov Kimche (or Yaari, or Kadari, or Even-Zahav, or Shenhar), did I like all my teachers? And occasionally: had I started to take an interest in young ladies yet? And what would I be when I grew up—a professor too? Or a pioneer? Or a field marshal in the armies of Israel? (I came to the conclusion at that time that writers were phony and even somewhat ridiculous.)

Secondly, my task was not to get in the way.

I had to be nonexistent, invisible.

Their café talk lasted at least seventy hours at a time, and for the whole of this eternity I had to embody an even more silent presence than the softly humming fan on the ceiling.

The penalty for breach of trust in the presence of strangers might be complete house arrest, from the moment I got home from school, every day for a fortnight, or the loss of the privilege of playing with friends, or cancellation of the right to read in bed for the next twenty days.

The big prize for a hundred hours of solitude was an ice cream. Or even corn on the cob.

I was hardly ever allowed ice cream because it was bad for the throat and gave one a chill. As for corn on the cob, that was sold on street corners from a container of boiling water set on top of a Primus stove, the hot, fragrant corn on the cob that the unshaven man wrapped in a green leaf for you and sprinkled with cooking salt. I was hardly ever allowed it because the unshaven man looked distinctly unwashed, and his water was probably teeming with germs. "But if Your Highness behaves impeccably at Café Atara today, you will be allowed a free choice on our way home: ice cream or corn on the cob, whichever you prefer."

So it was in cafés, against a background of endless conversations be-tween my parents and their friends about politics, history, philosophy, and literature, about power struggles among professors and intrigues of editors and publishers, conversations whose content I was unable to un-derstand, that I gradually became a little spy.

I developed a secret little game that I could play for hours on end without moving, without speaking, with no accessories, not even a pen-cil and paper. I would look at the strangers in the café and try to guess, from their clothes and gestures, from the paper they were reading or the drinks they had ordered, who they all were, where they came from, what they did, what they had done just before they came here, and where they were going afterward. That woman over there who had just smiled to herself twice—I tried to deduce from her expression what she was thinking. That thin young man in a cap who had not taken his eyes off the door and was disappointed every time anyone came in: what was he thinking about? What did the person he was waiting for look like? I sharpened my ears and stole snatches of conversation out of the air. I leaned over and peeped to see what everyone was reading, I observed who was in a hurry to leave and who was just settling down.

On the basis of a few uncertain outward signs, I made up compli-cated but exciting life stories for them. That woman with the embittered lips and the low-cut dress, for example, sitting at a corner table in a thick cloud of cigarette smoke: three times in the space of an hour by the big clock on the wall behind the counter she has stood up, disappeared into the ladies', then returned to sit in front of her empty cup, chain smok-ing with her brown cigarette holder, casting an occasional glance at the tanned figure in the vest sitting at a table near the hat stand. Once she stood up and went over to the man in the vest, bent over, said a few words to which he replied only with a nod, and now she's sitting smok-ing again. How many possibilities there are! How dizzyingly rich the kaleidoscope of plots and stories I can weave from these fragments! Or maybe she just asked him if she could have the newspaper he was read-ing when he was finished with it.

My eyes attempt in vain to escape the profile of the woman's ample bosom, but when I close them, it comes closer, I can feel its warmth, it almost enfolds my face. My knees begin to shake. The woman is waiting for her lover, who has promised to come but forgotten, and that's why she's sitting there chain smoking so desperately, drinking one black coffee after another, to soothe the lump in her throat. She disappears to the ladies' from time to time to powder her face and hide the signs of her tears. The waitress has brought the man in the vest a goblet of liqueur, to drown his sorrow because his wife has left him for a younger man. Perhaps at this very moment the pair are sailing away on some love boat, dancing cheek to cheek by the light of the moon, which is reflected in the ocean, at a ball given by the captain, dreamy music from the Edison Cinema wafting around them as they dance, on their way to some outrageous resort: St. Moritz, San Marino, San Francisco, São Paulo, Sans Souci.

I go on weaving my web. The young lover, whom I visualize in the form of the proud, manly sailor depicted on the packet of Nelson Navy Cut, is actually the man who promised the chain-smoking woman to meet her here this evening, and now he's a thousand miles away. She is waiting in vain. "Have you, too, sir, been abandoned to your fate? Have you, like me, been left all alone?" That, in the language of old romantic stories, is how she addressed the man in the vest when she went over to his table a moment ago and bent over him, and he answered with a nod. Soon the forsaken couple will walk out of the café together, and outside in the street they will link arms without another word needing to be spoken.

Where will they go together?

My imagination paints avenues and parks, a moonlit bench, a lane leading to a little house behind a stone wall, candlelight, closed shutters, music, and here the story becomes too sweet and terrible for me to tell it to myself or to bear, and I hasten to take my leave of it. Instead I fix my eyes on two middle-aged men at a table close to ours, playing chess and talking Germanic Hebrew. One of them is sucking and stroking a cold pipe made of reddish wood, the other occasionally wipes invisible perspiration from his high brow with a checkered handkerchief. A waitress comes over and whispers something to the man with the pipe, and he begs the other's pardon in his Germanic Hebrew, apologizes to the waitress too, and goes across to the telephone next to the serving hatch. When he has finished talking, he hangs up, stands for a moment looking forlorn and lost, then stumbles back to his table and apparently asks his chess partner again to excuse him, then he explains something to him, in German this time, hurriedly puts some coins down on the table and turns to leave; his friend is angry and tries almost by force to put the coins back in his pocket, but the other resists, and suddenly the coins are rolling on the floor under several tables, and the two gentlemen have stopped parrying and have gone down on their knees to pick them up.

Too late: I have already decided for them that they are cousins, the only survivors of a family that was murdered by Germans. I have already enriched their story with an enormous legacy and an eccentric will under the terms of which the winner of the game of chess will receive two-thirds of the inheritance while the loser will have to make do with one-third. Then I introduce to the story an orphan girl of my own age, who has been sent from Europe with Youth Aliya to some kibbutz or educational institution, and she, not the chess players, is the real heir. At this point I step into the story myself, in the role of the knight in shining armor, the protector of orphans, who will wrest the legendary inheritance from those who are not entitled to it and restore it to its rightful owner, not for nothing but in exchange for love. But when I get to the love, my eyes close again and I have an urgent need to cut the story short and start spying on another table. Or on the lame waitress with her deep black eyes. This, it seems, was the beginning of my life as a writer: in cafés, waiting for ice cream or corn on the cob.

To this day I pickpocket in this way. Especially from strangers. Especially in busy public places. In line at the clinic, for instance, or in some bureaucratic waiting room, at the railway station or the airport. Even sometimes when I am driving, in a traffic jam, peeping into the car next to me. Peeping and making up stories. Peeping again, and making up more stories. Where does she come from, by her clothes, her expression, her gestures as she touches up her makeup? What is her home like? What is her man like? Or take that boy over there with the unfashionably long sideburns, holding his mobile phone in his left hand while his other hand describes slicing movements, exclamation marks, distress signals: why exactly is he getting ready to fly to London tomorrow? What is his failing business? Who is waiting for him there? What do his parents look like? Where do they come from? What was he like as a child? And how is he planning to spend the evening, and the night, after he lands in London? (Nowadays I no longer stop in terror at the bedroom door: I float invisibly in.)

If strangers intercept my inquisitive look, I smile absently at them by way of apology and look away. I have no desire to embarrass. I live in fear of being caught in the act and asked to explain myself. But, anyway, after a minute or two I have no need to keep peeping at the heroes of my casual stories: I've seen enough. Half a minute, and they're caught in my invisible paparazzi camera.

Waiting at the supermarket check-out, for instance: the woman in front of me is short and plump, in her mid-forties, very attractive because something in her pose or expression suggests that she's tried everything and is unshockable now, even the most bizarre experience will do no more than arouse her amused curiosity. The wistful-looking young soldier behind me, who is only about twenty, is staring at this knowing woman with a starved look in his eyes. I take half a step sideways, not to block his view, and prepare a room with a deep-pile carpet for them, I shut the shutters, stand leaning back against the door, and now the vision is in full flow, in all its details, including the comic touch of his coy feverishness, and the moving touch of her compassionate generosity. Until the woman at the till has to raise her voice: Next, please! In an accent that is not exactly Russian, but perhaps comes from one of the Central Asian republics? And already I'm in Samarkand, in beautiful Bukhara: Bactrian camels, pink stone mosques, round prayer halls with sensual domes, and soft, deep carpets accompany me out into the street with my shopping.

After my military service, in 1961, the Committee of Kibbutz Hulda sent me to Jerusalem to study for two years at the Hebrew University. I studied literature because the kibbutz needed a literature teacher urgently, and I studied philosophy because I insisted on it. Every Sunday, from four to six P.M., a hundred students gathered in the large hall in the Meiser Building to hear Professor Samuel Hugo Bergman lecture on "dialectical philosophy from Kierkegaard to Martin Buber." My mother Fania also studied philosophy with Professor Bergman, in the 1930s, when the university was still on Mount Scopus, before she married my father, and she had fond memories of him. By 1961 Bergman was already retired, he was an emeritus professor, but we were fascinated by his lucid, fierce wisdom. I was thrilled to think that the man standing in front of us had been at school with Kafka in Prague, and, as he once told us, had actually shared a bench with him for two years, until Max Brod turned up and took his place next to Kafka.

That winter Bergman invited five or six of his favorite or most interesting pupils to come to his house for a couple of hours after the lectures. Every Sunday, at eight o'clock, I took the No. 5 bus from the new campus on Givat Ram to Professor Bergman's modest apartment in Rehavia. A pleasant faint smell of old books, fresh bread, and geraniums always filled the room. We sat down on the sofa or on the floor at the feet of our great master, the childhood friend of Kafka and Martin Buber and the author of the books from which we learned the history of epistemology and the principles of logic. We waited in silence for him to pronounce. Samuel Hugo Bergman was a stout man even in old age. With his shock of white hair, the ironic, amused lines around his eyes, a piercing glance that looked skeptical yet as innocent as that of a curious child, Bergman bore a striking resemblance to pictures of Albert Einstein as an old man. With his Central European accent he walked in the Hebrew language not with a natural stride, as though he were at home in it, but with a sort of elation, like a suitor happy that his beloved has finally accepted him and determined to rise above himself and prove to her that she has not made a mistake.

Almost the only subject that concerned our teacher at these meetings was the survival of the soul, or the chances, if there were any, of existence after death. That is what he talked to us about on Sunday evenings through that winter, with the rain lashing at the windows and the wind howling in the garden. Sometimes he asked for our opinions, and he listened attentively, not at all like a patient teacher guiding his pupils' footsteps but more like a man listening for a particular note in a complicated piece of music, so as to decide if it was right or wrong.

"Nothing," he said to us on one of the Sunday evenings, and I have not forgotten, so much so that I believe I can repeat what he said almost word for word, "ever disappears. The very word 'disappears' implies that the universe is, so to speak, finite, and that it is possible to leave it. But no-o-othing" (he deliberately drew the word out) "can ever leave the universe. And nothing can enter it. Not a single speck of dust can appear or disappear. Matter is transformed into energy, and energy into matter, atoms assemble and disperse, everything changes and is transformed, but no-o-othing can ever change from being to not-being. Not even the tiniest hair growing on the tail of some virus. The concept of infinity is indeed open, infinitely open, but at the same time it is also closed and hermetically sealed. Nothing leaves and nothing enters."

Pause. A crafty, innocent smile spread like a sunrise across the wrinkled landscape of his rich, fascinating face: "In which case why, maybe someone can explain to me, why do they insist on telling me that the one and only exception to the rule, the one and only thing that is doomed to perdition, that can become nothing, the one and only thing that is destined for cessation in the whole wide universe in which not so much as an atom can be destroyed, is my poor soul? Will everything, every speck of dust, every drop of water continue to exist eternally, albeit in different forms, except for my soul?"

"Nobody," murmured a clever young genius from a corner of the room, "has ever seen the soul."

"No," Bergman agreed at once. "You don't meet the laws of physics or mathematics in a café either. Or wisdom, or foolishness, or desire or fear. No one has yet taken a little sample of joy or longing and put it in a test tube. But who is it, my young friend, who is talking to you right now? Is it Bergman's humors? His spleen? Is it perhaps Bergman's large intestine speaking? Who was it, if you will excuse my saying so, who spread that none-too-pleasant smile on your face? Was it not your soul? Was it your cartilages? Your gastric juices?"

On another occasion he said:

"What is in store for us after we die? No-o-obody knows. At any rate not with a knowledge that is susceptible of proof or demonstration. If I tell you this evening that I sometimes hear the voice of the dead and that it is much clearer and more intelligible to me than most of the voices of the living, you are entitled to say that this old man is in his dotage. He has gone out of his mind with terror at his impending death. Therefore I will not talk to you this evening about voices, this evening I will talk mathematics: since no-o-obody knows if there is anything on the other side of our death or if there is nothing there, we can deduce from this complete ignorance that the chances that there is something there are exactly the same as the chances that there is nothing there. Fifty percent for cessation and fifty percent for survival. For a Jew like me, a Central European Jew from the generation of the Nazi Holocaust, such odds in favor of survival are not at all bad."

Gershom Scholem, Bergman's friend and rival, was also fascinated and possibly even tormented by the question of life after death. The morning the news of his death was broadcast, I wrote:

Gershom Scholem died in the night. And now he knows.

Bergman too knows now. So does Kafka. So do my mother and father. And their friends and acquaintances and most of the men and women in those cafés, both those I used to tell myself stories about and those who are forgotten. They all know now. Someday we will know too. And in the meantime we will continue to gather little details. Just in case.

51

I WAS A fiercely nationalistic child when I was in the fourth and fifth grades at Tachkemoni School. I wrote a historical novel in installments called *The End of the Kingdom of Judah*, and several poems about conquest, and about national greatness, which resembled Grandpa Alexander's patriotic verses and aimed to imitate Vladimir Jabotinsky's nationalistic marching songs such as the Beitar Anthem: ". . . Spill your blood and offer up your soul! / Raise high the fire: / Repose is like mire; / We fight for a glorious goal!" I was also influenced by the song of the Jewish partisans in Poland and the ghetto rebels: ". . . What if our blood we spill? / Surely our spirit with heroic deeds shall thrive!" And poems by Saul Tchernikhowsky that Father used to read to me with wavering pathos in his voice: ". . . a tune of blood and fire! / So climb the hill and crush the vale, whate'er you see—acquire!" The poem that excited me most of all was "Nameless Soldiers," by Avraham Stern, alias Yair, the leader of the Stern Gang. I used to recite it with pathos but in a whisper in bed after lights out: "Nameless soldiers are we, we must fight to be free; / all around is the shadow of death. / We have signed up for life to do battle and strife— / we must fight till we breathe our last breath . . . / In the day that is red with our blood that is shed, / in the blackest despair of the night, / over village and town our flag shall be flown / for we fight to defend what is right!"

Torrents of blood, soil, fire, and iron intoxicated me. Over and over again I imagined myself falling heroically on the battlefield, I imagined my parents' sorrow and pride, and at the same time, with no contradiction, after my heroic death, after tearfully enjoying the rousing funeral orations pronounced by Ben-Gurion, Begin, and Uri Zvi, after grieving over myself and seeing with emotion and a lump in my throat the marble statues and songs of praise in my memory, I always arose healthy and sound from my temporary death, soaked in self-admiration, appointed myself commander-in-chief of Israel's armed forces, and led my legions to liberate in blood and fire everything that the effeminate, Diaspora-bred worm of Jacob had not dared to wrest from the hand of the foe.

Menachem Begin, the legendary underground commander, was my chief childhood idol at that time. Even earlier, in the last year of the British Mandate, the nameless commander of the underground had fired my imagination. In my mind I saw his form swathed in clouds of biblical glory. I imagined him in his secret headquarters in the wild ravines of the Judaean Desert, barefoot, with a leather girdle, flashing sparks like the prophet Elijah among the rocks of Mount Carmel, sending out orders from his remote cave with innocent-looking youths. Night after night his long arm reaches the heart of the British occupation force, dynamiting HQs and military installations, breaking through walls, blowing up ammunition dumps, pouring out its wrath on the strongholds of the enemy who was called, in the posters composed by my father, the "Anglo-Nazi foe," "Amalek," "Perfidious Albion." (My mother once said of the British: "Amalek or not, who knows if we won't miss them soon.")

Once the state of Israel was established, the supreme commander of the Hebrew underground forces finally emerged from hiding, and his picture appeared one day in the paper above his name: not something heroic like Ari Ben-Shimshon or Ivriahu Ben-Kedumim, but Menachem Begin. I was shocked: the name Menachem Begin might have suited a Yiddish-speaking haberdasher from Zephaniah Street or a gold-toothed *sheitel* and corset maker from Geula Street. Moreover, to my disappointment, my childhood hero was revealed in the photograph in the paper as a frail, skinny man with large glasses perched on his pale face. Only his mustache attested to his secret powers; but after a few months the mustache disappeared. Mr. Begin's figure, voice, accent, and diction did not remind me of the biblical conquerors of Canaan or of Judah Maccabee, but of my feeble teachers at Tachkemoni, who were also men flowing with nationalist fervor and righteous wrath, but from behind their heroism a nervous self-righteousness and latent sourness occasionally burst through.

And one day, thanks to Menachem Begin, I suddenly lost my desire to "spill my blood and offer up my son" and to "fight for a glorious goal." I abandoned the view that "repose is like mire"; after a while I came around to the opposite view.

Every few weeks half of Jerusalem assembled at eleven o'clock on a Saturday morning to hear fiery speeches by Menachem Begin at gatherings of the Herut movement in the Edison Auditorium, which was the largest hall in the city. Its facade bore posters announcing the imminent appearance of the Israel Opera under the baton of Fordhaus Ben-Zisi. Grandpa used to dress himself up for the occasion in his magnificent black suit and a light blue satin tie. A triangle of white handkerchief protruded from his breast pocket like a snowflake in a heat wave. When we entered the auditorium, half an hour before the meeting was due to start, he raised his hat in all directions in greeting and even bowed to his friends. I marched beside my grandfather, solemn and well combed, in a white shirt and polished shoes, straight to the second or third row, where seats of honor were reserved for people like Grandpa Alexander, members of the Jerusalem committee of the "Herut Movement— founded by the Irgun, the National Military Organization." We would sit between Professor Yosef Yoel Rivlin and Mr. Eliahu Meridor, or between Dr. Israel Sheib-Eldad and Mr. Hanoch Kalai, or next to Mr. Isak Remba, the editor of the newspaper *Herut.*

The hall was always packed with supporters of the Irgun and admirers of the legendary Menachem Begin, almost all of them men, among them the fathers of many of my classmates at Tachkemoni. But there was a fine invisible dividing line between the front three or four rows, which were reserved for prominent members of the intelligentsia, veterans of the National Front campaigns, activists in the Revisionist movement, former commanders of the Irgun, who mostly came from Poland, Lithuania, White Russia, and Ukraine, and the throngs of Sephardim, Bukharians, Yemenites, Kurds, and Aleppo Jews who filled the rest of the hall. This excitable throng packed the galleries and aisles, pressed against the walls, and spilled out into the foyer and the square in front of the auditorium. In the front rows they talked nationalist, revolutionary talk with a taste for glorious victories and quoted Nietzsche and Mazzini, but there was a dominant petit-bourgeois air of good manners: hats, suits, and ties, etiquette and a certain flowery salon formality that even then, in the early 1950s, had a whiff of mold and mothballs.

Behind this inner circle extended an ocean of fervent true believers, a loyal, devoted throng of tradesmen, shopkeepers, workmen, many of them sporting skullcaps, having come straight from synagogue to hear their hero, their leader Mr. Begin, shabbily dressed, hard-working Jews trembling with idealism, warmhearted, hot-tempered, excitable, and vocal.

At the beginning of the meeting they sang Beitar songs and at the end they sang the anthem of the Movement and the National Anthem, Hatikva. The dais was decorated with masses of Israeli flags, a gigantic photograph of Vladimir Jabotinsky, two razor-sharp rows of Beitar Youth resplendent in their uniforms and black ties—how I longed to join them when I was older—and stirring slogans such as "Jotapata, Masada, Beitar!," "If I forget thee O Jerusalem may my right hand lose its cunning!," and "In blood and fire Judaea fell, in blood and fire Judaea will rise again!"

After a couple of warm-up speeches by committee members of the Jerusalem branch, everyone suddenly left the stage. Even the Beitar Youth marched off. A deep, religious silence fell upon the Edison Auditorium like a quiet whirring of wings. All eyes were fixed on the empty stage, and all hearts were primed. This expectant silence lasted for a long moment, then something stirred at the back of the stage, the velvet curtains parted a crack, and a solitary small, thin man stepped daintily to the microphone and stood before the audience with his head humbly bowed, as though he was overwhelmed by his own shyness. Only after a few seconds of awestruck silence did a few hesitant claps rise from the audience, as if the crowd could hardly believe its eyes, as if they were stunned, every time, to discover that Begin was not a fire-breathing giant but a slightly built, almost frail-looking man. But at once they burst into applause, and at the back the applause quickly turned to roars of affection that accompanied Begin's speech almost from beginning to end.

For a couple of seconds the man stood motionless, with head bowed, shoulders drooping, as if to say: "I do not deserve this accolade," or "My soul is bowed down to the dust under the burden of your love." Then he stretched out his arms as if to bless the crowds, smiled shyly, silenced them, and began hesitantly, like a novice actor with stage fright:

"Good Sabbath to you all, brothers and sisters. Fellow Jews. People of Jerusalem, our eternal holy city."

And he stopped. Suddenly he said quietly, sadly, almost mournfully:

"Brothers and sisters. These are difficult days for our beloved young state. Exceptionally difficult days. Awesome days for all of us."

Gradually he overcame his sadness, gathered his strength, and continued, still quietly but with a controlled power, as though behind that veil of quietness there lurked a subdued but very serious warning:

"Once again our enemies are grinding their teeth in the dark and plotting vengeance for the shameful defeat we inflicted on them on the battlefield. The Great Powers are devising evil once again. There is nothing new. In every generation men rise up against us to annihilate us. But we, my brothers and sisters, we shall stand up to them again. As we have stood up to them not once or twice but many times in the past. We shall stand up to them with courage and devotion. Holding our heads up high. Never, never shall they see this nation on its knees. Never! To the last generation!"

At the words "Never, never" he raised his voice to a resounding cry from the heart, full of pained vibrations. This time the audience did not shout, it roared with rage and anguish.

"The Eternal One of Israel," he said in a quiet, authoritative voice, as though he had just come from an operational meeting at the Eternal One of Israel's headquarters, "the Rock of Israel shall rise up again and frustrate and dash to pi-eces all the schemes of our enemies!"

Now the crowd was flushed with gratitude and affection, which they expressed by a rhythmic chant of "Begin! Begin!" I too leaped to my feet and roared his name with all the power I could muster in my voice, which was breaking at the time.

"On one condition," the speaker said solemnly, sternly, raising his hand, and then he paused as though pondering the nature of this condition and wondering whether it was proper for him to share it with the audience. A deathly hush spread through the hall. "One sole, crucial, vital, fateful condition." He paused again. His head drooped. As though bent under the terrible weight of the condition. The audience listened so intently that I could hear the hum of the fans on the high ceiling of the hall.

"On condition that our leadership, brothers and sisters, is a national leadership and not a bunch of panic-stricken ghetto Jews who are scared of their own shadows! On condition that the feeble, enfeebling, defeated, defeatist, despicable Ben-Gurion government makes way at once for a proud, daring Hebrew government, an emergency government that knows how to make our foes quake with terror, just as the very name of our glorious army, the army of Israel, puts fear and trembling into the hearts of all the enemies of Israel wherever they may be!"

At this the whole audience boiled over and seemed to burst its banks. The mention of the "despicable Ben-Gurion government" roused snorts of hatred and contempt on every side. From one of the galleries someone shouted hoarsely "Death to the traitors!," and from another corner of the hall came a wild chant of "Begin for PM, Ben-Gurion go home!"

But the speaker silenced them and declared slowly, calmly, like a strict teacher rebuking his pupils:

"No, brothers and sisters. That is not the way. Shouting and violence are not the right way, but peaceful, respectful, democratic elections. Not with the methods of those Reds, not with deception and hooliganism, but with the upright and dignified way that we have learned from our great mentor Vladimir Jabotinsky. We shall soon send them packing, not with hatred among brothers, not with violent upheaval, but with cold contempt. Yes, we shall send them all packing. Those who sell the soil of our Fatherland and those who have sold their souls to Stalin. Those bloated kibbutz hacks, and the arrogant, condescending tyrants of the Bolshevik Histadrut, all the petty Zhdanovs together with all the big thieves. Off with them! Aren't they always spouting to us smugly about manual labor and draining the swamps? Very well then. We shall send them off, ve-ery respectfully, to do some manual labor. They've long since forgotten what the word labor means. It'll be interesting to see if any of them can still hold a shovel! We, my brothers and sisters, shall do a great job of draining swamps—very soon, brothers and sisters, very soon, just be patient—we shall drain the swamp of this Labor government once and for all! Once and for all, my brothers and sisters! We shall drain it irreversibly, with no return! Now repeat after me, my people, as one man, loud and clear, this solemn vow: Once and for all! Once and for all!! Once and for all!!! No return! No return!! No return!!!"*

The crowd went mad. So did I. As though we had all become cells in a single giant body, blazing with rage, boiling with indignation.

And it was at this point that it happened. The fall. The expulsion from Paradise. Mr. Begin went on to speak about the imminent war and the arms race that was in progress all over the Middle East. However, Mr. Begin spoke the Hebrew of his generation, and was evidently not aware that usage had changed. A dividing line separated those under the age of twenty-five or so, who were brought up in Israel, from those above that age or who had learned their Hebrew from books. The word that for Mr. Begin, as for others of his generation, of all parties, meant "weapon" or "arm," for the rest of us signified the male sexual organ and nothing else. And his verb "to arm" for us signified the corresponding action.

Mr. Begin took a couple of sips of water, scrutinized the audience, nodded his head a few times, as though agreeing with himself, or lamenting, and in a harsh, accusing voice, like a prosecutor sternly enumerating a series of unanswerable charges, launched into his tirade:

"President Eisenhower is arming the Nasser regime!

"Bulganin is arming Nasser!

"Guy Mollet and Anthony Eden are arming Nasser!!

"The whole world is arming our Arab enemies day and night!!!"

Pause. His voice filled with loathing and contempt:

"But who will arm the government of Ben-Gurion?"

A stunned silence fell on the hall. But Mr. Begin did not notice. He raised his voice and crowed triumphantly:

*Begin's speech is reconstructed from memory and experience.

"If only I were the prime minister today—everyone, everyone would be arming us!! Ev-ery-one!!!"

A few faint claps rose from the elderly Ashkenazim in the front rows. But the rest of the vast crowd hesitated, apparently unable to believe their ears, or perhaps they were shocked. In that moment of embarrassed silence there was just one nationalistic child, one twelve-year-old child who was politically committed to the roots of his hair, a devoted Beginite in a white shirt and highly polished shoes, who could not contain himself and burst out laughing.

This child tried with all his might and main to restrain his laughter, he wanted to die of shame on the spot, but his contorted, hysterical laughter was irrepressible: it was a choked, almost tearful laugh, a hoarse laugh with strident hoots, a laugh that resembled sobbing and also suffocation.

Looks of horror and alarm fixed on the child from every direction. On every side hundreds of fingers were laid on hundreds of lips, as he was hushed and shushed. Shame! Disgrace! All around important persons fumed reproachfully at a horror-smitten Grandpa Alexander. The child had the impression that far away at the back of the hall an unruly laugh echoed his, followed by another. But those laughs, if they occurred, had broken out in the outer suburbs of the nation, while his own outburst had struck in the middle of the third row, which was full of veterans of Beitar and dignitaries of Herut, all well-known and respectable figures.

And now the speaker had noticed him and interrupted his speech; he waited patiently, with an indulgent, tactful smile, while Grandpa Alexander, blushing, shocked, and seething like someone whose world had collapsed around him, seized the child's ear, lifted him furiously to his feet, and dragged him out by his ear, in front of the whole third row, in front of the massed lovers of the Fatherland in Jerusalem, bellowing desperately as he tugged and pulled. (It must have been rather like this that Grandpa himself was dragged by the ear to the rabbi in New York by the formidable Grandma Shlomit when, having been engaged to her, he suddenly fell in love with another lady on the boat to America.)

And once the three of them were outside the Edison Auditorium, the one who was doing the dragging, seething with rage, the one who was being dragged, choking and weeping with laughter, and the poor ear that was by now as red as a beet, Grandpa raised his right hand and administered the grandfather of a slap on my right cheek, then he raised his left hand and slapped my other cheek with all the force of his hatred for the Left, and because he was such a Rightist, he did not want to let the left have the last word, so he gave me another slap on the right, not a feeble, obsequious Diaspora slap in the spirit of the worm of Jacob, but a bold, hawkish, patriotic slap, proud, magnificent, and furious.

Jotapata, Masada, and besieged Beitar had lost: they might indeed rise again in glory and might, but without me. As for the Herut movement and the Likkud Party, they lost someone that morning who might have become in time a little heir, a fiery orator, perhaps an articulate member of the Knesset, or even a deputy minister without portfolio.

I have never again blended happily into an ecstatic crowd, or been a blind molecule in a gigantic superhuman body. On the contrary, I have developed a morbid fear of crowds. The line "Repose is like mire" seems to me now to attest to a widespread, dangerous illness. In the phrase "blood and fire" I can taste blood and smell burning human flesh. As on the plains of northern Sinai during the Six Day War and among the blazing tanks on the Golan Heights in the Yom Kippur War.

The autobiography of Professor Klausner, Uncle Joseph, which I have drawn on for much of what I have written here about the history of the Klausner family, is entitled *My Road to Resurrection and Redemption*. On that Saturday, while kindhearted Grandpa Alexander, Uncle Joseph's brother, was dragging me outside by my ear and making furious noises that sounded like sobs of horror and madness, I seem to have begun to run away from resurrection and redemption. I am still running.

But that was not the only thing I ran away from. The suffocation of life in that basement, between my father and mother and between the two of them and all those books, the ambitions, the repressed, denied nostalgia for Rovno and Vilna, for a Europe that was embodied by a black tea cart and gleaming white napkins, the burden of his failure in life, the wound of hers, failures that I was tacitly charged with the responsibility of converting into victories in the fullness of time, all this oppressed me so much that I wanted to run away from it. At other times young people left their parents' homes and went off to find themselves— or to lose themselves—in Eilat or the Sinai Desert, later on in New York or Paris, and later still in ashrams in India or jungles in South

America, or in the Himalayas (where the only child Rico went in my book *The Same Sea* following the death of his mother). But in the early 1950s the opposite pole to the oppressiveness of the parental home was the kibbutz. There, far from Jerusalem, "over the hills and far away," in Galilee, Sharon, the Negev, or the Valleys—so we imagined in Jerusalem in those days—a new, rugged race of pioneers was taking shape, strong, serious but not complicated, laconic, able to keep a secret, able to be swept away in a riot of heady dancing, yet also able to be lonely and thoughtful, fitted for life in the fields and under canvas: tough young men and women, ready for any kind of hard work yet with a rich cultural and intellectual life and sensitive, contained feelings. I wanted to be like them so as not to be like my father or my mother or any of those gloomy refugee scholars of whom Jewish Jerusalem was full. After a while I signed up for the scout movement, whose members in those days intended to enlist in the Nahal, the military formation that specialized in creating new kibbutzim along the border, when they had finished at school, and to go on to "labor, defense, and the kibbutz." My father was not pleased, but because he yearned to be a true liberal, he contented himself with remarking sadly: "The scout movement. Very well. So be it. Why not. But the kibbutz? The kibbutz is for simple, strong people, and you are neither. You are a talented child. An individualist. Surely it would be better for you to grow up to serve our beloved state with your talents, not with your muscles. Which are not all that developed."

My mother was far away by then. She had turned her back on us.

And I agreed with my father. That is why I forced myself to eat twice as much and to strengthen my feeble muscles with running and exercises.

Three or four years later, after my mother's death and my father's remarriage, in Kibbutz Hulda, at half past four one Saturday morning, I told Ephraim Avneri about Begin and the arms. We had gotten up early because we had been detailed for apple picking. I was fifteen or sixteen. Ephraim Avneri, like the other founder-members of Hulda, was in his mid-forties, but he and his friends were called—by us and even among themselves—the oldies.

Ephraim listened to the story and smiled, but for a minute it seemed he had trouble understanding what the point of it was, because he too belonged to the generation for whom "arming" was a matter of tanks and guns. After a moment he said: "Ah yes, I see, Begin was talking about 'arming' with weapons and you took it in the slang sense. It does come out rather funny. But listen here my young friend," (we were standing on ladders on opposite sides of the same tree, talking while we picked, but the foliage was in the way so we could not see each other) "it seems to me you missed the main point. The thing that's so funny about them, Begin and all his noisy crew, is not their use of the word 'arm' but their use of words in general. They divide everything up into 'obsequious Diaspora-Jewish' on the one hand and 'manly Hebrew' on the other. They don't notice how Diaspora-Jewish the division itself is. Their whole childish obsession with military parades and hollow machismo and weapons comes straight from the ghetto."

Then he added, to my great surprise:

"Basically he's a good man, that Begin. He's a demagogue, it's true, but he's not a fascist or a warmonger. Absolutely not. On the contrary, he's a rather soft man. A thousand times softer than Ben-Gurion. Ben-Gurion's as hard as granite, but Menachem Begin is made of cardboard. And he's so old-fashioned, Begin. So anachronistic. A sort of lapsed *yeshiva bocher*, who believes that if we Jews start shouting at the top of our voices that we're not the way Jews used to be, we're not sheep for the slaughter, we're not pale weaklings but the opposite, we're dangerous now, we're terrifying wolves now, then all the real beasts of prey will be scared of us and give us everything we want, they'll let us have the whole land, they'll let us take all the holy places, swallow up Trans-Jordan, and be treated with respect and admiration by the whole civilized world as well. They, Begin and his chums, talk from morning to evening about power, but they haven't the first idea what power is, what it's made of, what the weaknesses of power are. After all, power also has an element of terrible danger for those that wield it. Didn't that bastard Stalin once say that religion is the opium of the masses? Vell, just listen to little old me: I tell you, power is the opium of the ruling classes. And not only the ruling classes. Power is the opium of the whole of humanity. Power is the temptation of the Devil, I would say, if I believed in the Devil. As a matter of fact, I do believe in him a bit. Vell, where were we?" (Ephraim and some of his fellow Galicians always pronounced "well" as "vell.") "We were talking about Begin and your big laugh. You laughed at him for the wrong reason that day, my young friend. You laughed at him be-cause the word 'arm' can be taken in different ways. Vell, so be it. You know what you should really have laughed at? Laughed till the floor col-lapsed? I'll tell you what. You shouldn't have laughed at the 'arming' but because Menachem Begin truly believes that if he were prime minister, everybody, the whole world, would immediately leave the side of the Arabs and come over to his side. Why? Why would they do that? For what? For his beautiful eyes? For his polished language? In memory of Jabotinsky, perhaps? You should have laughed your head off at him, be-cause that's exactly the politics that all those layabouts in the shtetl used to like. All day long they would sit behind the stove in the house of study and talk that kind of politics. They used to wave their thumbs around like Talmud teachers: 'Foist of all, we send a delegation to Tsar Nikolai, an important delegation, that will speak to him very nicely and prom-ise the Tsar to fix for him what Russia wants most of all, a way out to the Mediterranean. Then, we ask the Tsar that in exchange for this he should put in a kind word for us with his friend Kaiser Wilhelm, so our Tsar should get this Kaiser to tell his good friend the Sultan of Turkey to give the Jews, right away, no arguments, the whole of Palestine from the Euphrates to the Nile. Only after that, when we've sorted out the whole redemption once for all, then we can decide according to how we feel if Ponya (that's what we called Tsar Nikolai) deserves that we should keep our promise and let him have a way out to the Mediterranean or not.' If you've finished there by any chance, vell, let's both go and empty our baskets into the bin and move on to the next tree. On the way we can check with Alec or Alyoshka if they remembered to bring a pitcher of water with them or if we'll have to go and complain to Tsar Nikolai."

A year or two later my class was already sharing night-watch duties in Hulda; we had learned to use a gun in our paramilitary training. These were the nights of the fedayeen and the reprisal raids before the Sinai campaign of 1956. Almost every night the fedayeen attacked a moshav or a kibbutz or a suburb of a town, blowing up houses with people inside them, shooting or throwing hand grenades through people's windows, and laying land mines behind them.

Every ten days it was my turn to keep watch along the perimeter fence of the kibbutz, which was only some three miles from the Israel-Jordan armistice line at Latrun. Every hour I would sneak into the empty clubhouse, against regulations, to listen to the news on the radio. The self-righteous, heroic rhetoric of a beleaguered society dominated those broadcasts as it dominated our kibbutz education. Nobody used the word "Palestinians" in those days: they were called "terrorists," "fedayeen," "the enemy," or "Arab refugees hungry for revenge."

One winter evening I happened to be on night duty with Ephraim Avneri. We were wearing boots, tattered army fatigues, and prickly woolly hats. We were tramping through the mud along the fence behind the storehouses and cowsheds. A stench of fermenting orange peels that were used for making silage mingled with other agricultural smells: compost, rotting straw, warm steam from the sheep sheds, feather dust from the chicken coops. I asked Ephraim if he had ever, in the War of Independence or during the troubles in the 1930s, shot and killed one of those murderers.

I could not see Ephraim's face in the dark, but there was a certain subversive irony, a strange sarcastic sadness in his voice as he replied, after a short pensive silence:

"Murderers? What d'you expect from them? From their point of view, we are aliens from outer space who have landed and trespassed on their land, gradually taken over parts of it, and while we promise them that we've come here to lavish all sorts of goodies on them—cure them of ringworm and trachoma, free them from backwardness, ignorance, and feudal oppression—we've craftily grabbed more and more of their land. Vell, what did you think? That they should thank us? That they should come out to greet us with drums and cymbals? That they should respectfully hand over the keys to the whole land just because our ancestors lived here once? Is it any wonder they've taken up arms against us? And now that we've inflicted a crushing defeat on them and hundreds of thousands of them are living in refugee camps—what, d'you expect them to celebrate with us and wish us luck?"

I was shocked. Even though I had come a long way from the rhetoric of Herut and the Klausner family, I was still a conformist product of a Zionist upbringing. Ephraim's nocturnal words startled and even enraged me. In those days this kind of thinking was seen as treachery. I was so stunned that I asked him sarcastically:

"In that case, what are you doing here with your gun? Why don't you emigrate? Or take your gun and go and fight on their side?"

I could hear his sad smile in the dark:

"Their side? But their side doesn't want me. Nowhere in the world wants me. Nobody in the world wants me. That's the whole point. It seems there are too many of my kind in every country. That's the only reason I'm here. That's the only reason I'm carrying a gun, so they won't kick me out of here the way they kicked me out of everywhere else. But you won't find me using the word 'murderers' about Arabs who've lost their villages. At least, not easily. About Nazis, yes. About Stalin, also. And about whoever steals other people's land."

"Doesn't it follow from what you're saying that we have also stolen other people's land? But didn't we live here two thousand years ago? Weren't we driven out of here by force?"

"It's like this," said Ephraim. "It's really very simple. Where is the Jewish people's land if not here? Under the sea? On the moon? Or is the Jewish people the only people in the world that doesn't deserve to have a little homeland of its own?"

"And what about what we've taken from them?"

"Vell, maybe you happen to have forgotten that in '48 they had a go at killing all of us? Then, in '48, there was a terrible war, and they themselves made it a simple question of either them or us, and we won and took it from them. It's nothing to boast about! But if they'd beaten us in '48, there would have been even less to boast about: they wouldn't have left a single Jew alive. And it's true that there isn't a single Jew living in the whole of their sector today. But that's the whole point: it's because we took what we did from them in '48 that we have what we have now. And because we have something now, we mustn't take anything else from them. That's it. And that's the whole difference between me and your Mr. Begin: if we take even more from them someday, now that we already have something, that will be a very big sin."

"And what if the fedayeen turn up here now?"

"If they do," Ephraim sighed, "vell, we'll just have to lie down in the mud and shoot. And we'll try our damnedest to shoot better and faster than them. But we won't shoot at them because they're a nation of murderers, but for the simple reason that we also have a right to live and for the simple reason that we also have a right to a land of our own. Not just them. And now thanks to you I'm going on like Ben-Gurion. Now if you'll just excuse me, I'm going into the cowshed to have a quiet smoke, and you keep a good lookout here while I'm gone. Keep a lookout for both of us."

52

A FEW YEARS after this nocturnal conversation, eight or nine years after the morning when Menachem Begin and his camp lost me at the Edison Auditorium, I met David Ben-Gurion. In those years he was prime minister and minister of defense but was thought of by many as the "great man of his day," the founder of the state, the great victor in the War of Independence and the Sinai Campaign. His enemies loathed him and ridiculed the cult of personality that surrounded him, while his admirers already saw him as the Father of the Nation, a sort of miraculous blend of King David, Judah Maccabee, George Washington, Garibaldi, a Jewish Churchill, and even the Messiah of God Almighty.

Ben-Gurion saw himself not only as a statesman but also—maybe primarily—as an original thinker and intellectual mentor. He had taught himself classical Greek so as to read Plato in the original, had dipped into Hegel and Marx, had taken an interest in Buddhism and Far Eastern thought, and had studied Spinoza so thoroughly that he considered himself a Spinozist. (The philosopher Isaiah Berlin, a man with a razor-sharp mind, whom Ben-Gurion used to enlist as his companion whenever he raided the great bookshops of Oxford for philosophy books, when he was already prime minister, once said to me: "Ben-Gurion went out of his way to depict himself as an intellectual. This was based on two mistakes. The first, he believed, wrongly, that Chaim Weizmann was an intellectual. The second, he also believed, wrongly, that Jabotinsky was an intellectual." In this way Isaiah Berlin ruthlessly killed three prominent birds with one clever stone.)

Every now and again Prime Minister Ben-Gurion filled the weekend supplement of *Davar* with lengthy theoretical reflections on philosophical questions. Once, in January 1961, he published an essay in which he claimed that equality between human beings was impossible, although they could achieve a measure of fraternity.

Considering myself a defender of kibbutz values, I penned a short response in which I asserted, with due humility and respect, that Comrade Ben-Gurion was mistaken.* When my article appeared, it provoked a great deal of anger in Kibbutz Hulda. The members were furious at my impertinence: "How dare you disagree with Ben-Gurion?"

Only four days later, however, the gates of Heaven opened for me: the Father of the Nation descended from his great heights and deigned to publish a long, courteous reply to my piece; extending over several prominent columns, it defended the views of the "great man of his day" against the criticisms of the lowest of the low.**

The same members of the kibbutz who only a couple of days earlier had wanted to send me away to some reeducation institution because of my impertinence now beamed delightedly and hurried over to shake my hand or pat me on the back: Vell, you've made it! You're immortal! Your name will be in the index of Ben-Gurion's collected writings someday! And the name of Kibbutz Hulda will be there too, thanks to you!"

But the Age of Miracles had only just begun.

A couple of days later came the phone call.

It didn't come to me—we didn't have telephones in our little rooms yet—it came to the kibbutz office. Bella P., a veteran member who happened to be in the office at the time, ran to find me, pale and trembling like a sheet of paper, as shaken as though she had just seen the chariots of the gods wreathed in flames of fire, and told me as though they were her dying words that the Prime-Minister-and-Minister-of-Defense's secretary had summoned me to appear early the next morning, at six-thirty precisely, at the minister of defense's office in Tel Aviv, for a personal meeting with the Prime-Minister-and-Minister-of-Defense, at David Ben-Gurion's personal invitation. She pronounced the words "Prime-Minister-and-Minister-of-Defense" as though she had said "The Holy One Blessed Be He."

Now it was my turn to go pale. Firstly, I was still in uniform, I was

*David Ben-Gurion, "Reflections," *Davar*, 27 Jan. 1961; Amos Oz, "Fraternity Is No Substitute for Equality," *Davar*, 20 Feb. 1961.
**David Ben-Gurion, "Further Reflections," *Davar*, 24 Feb. 1961.

a regular soldier, a staff sergeant in the army, and I was half afraid that I had broken some rule or regulation in embarking on an ideological dispute in the columns of the newspaper with my commander-in-chief. Secondly, I didn't possess a single pair of shoes apart from my heavy, studded army boots. How could I appear before the Prime-Minister-and-Minister-of-Defense? In sandals? Thirdly, there was no way in the world I could get to Tel Aviv by half past six in the morning: the first bus from Kibbutz Hulda didn't leave till seven and it didn't get to the Central Bus Station till half past eight, with luck.

So I spent the whole of the night praying silently for a disaster: a war, an earthquake, a heart attack—his or mine, either would do.

And at four-thirty I polished my studded army boots for the third time, put them on and laced them up tight. I wore well-pressed civilian khaki trousers, a white shirt, a sweater, and a windbreaker. I walked out onto the main road, and by some miracle I managed to get a lift and made it, half fainting, to the minister of defense's office. This was located not in the monstrous Ministry of Defense building, bristling with antennas, but in a courtyard at the back, in a charming, idyllic little Bavarian-style cottage on two floors, with a red-tiled roof, covered with a green vine, which had been built in the nineteenth century by German Templars, who created a tranquil agricultural colony in the sands north of Jaffa and ended up being thrown out of the country by the British at the outbreak of World War II.

The gentle-mannered secretary ignored my shaking body and strangled throat; he briefed me, with an almost intimate warmth, as though plotting with me behind the back of the divinity in the next room:

"The Old Man," he began, using the affectionate nickname that had been in common use since Ben-Gurion was in his fifties, "has, you understand, how shall we say, a tendency these days to get carried away by long philosophical conversations. But his time, I'm sure you can imagine, is like gold dust. He still deals with virtually all affairs of state himself, from preparations for war and relations with the Great Powers to the postal workers' strike. You will, of course, beat a tactful retreat after twenty minutes, so that we can somehow rescue his diary for the rest of the day."

There was nothing in the whole wide world that I wanted better than to "beat a tactful retreat," not after twenty minutes but right away. At once. The very thought that the Almighty himself was here, in person, just behind that gray door, and that in another minute I would be in his power, almost made me faint from awe and dread.

So much so that the secretary had no alternative but to push me gently from behind into the Holy of Holies.

The door was closed behind me, and I stood there, silently, with my back against the door I had just come in by, and my knees were shaking. King David's office was an ordinary, sparsely furnished room, hardly bigger than one of our modest kibbutz living rooms. Facing me was a window, covered with a rustic curtain, that added a little daylight to the electric light. On either side of the window stood a metal filing cabinet. A large glass-topped desk stood in the middle of the room, taking up about a quarter of its area; on it there were three or four piles of books, magazines, and newspapers, and various papers and folders, some open and some closed. On either side of the desk there was a bureaucratic gray metal chair, of the sort you could see in those days in every administrative or military office, and they were always inscribed, on the underside, with the words "Property of the State of Israel." There were no other chairs in the room. An entire wall, from ceiling to floor and from corner to corner, was taken up by a huge map of the whole Mediterranean basin and the Middle East, from the Straits of Gibraltar to the Persian Gulf. Israel, the size of a postage stamp, had been marked out with a thick line. Another wall had three shelves loaded and piled with books, as if someone might suddenly be seized here with an urgent reading frenzy that brooked no delay.

In this Spartan room there was a man pacing to and fro with rapid little steps, his hands clasped behind his back, his eyes on the floor, his big head thrust forward as though to butt. The man looked exactly like Ben-Gurion, but there was no way he could actually be Ben-Gurion. Every child in Israel, even in kindergarten, in those days knew in his sleep what Ben-Gurion looked like. But since there was no television yet, it was obvious to me that the Father of the Nation was a giant whose head reached the clouds, whereas this impostor was a short, tubby man whose height was less than five foot three.

I was alarmed. Almost offended.

Nevertheless, during the two or three minutes of uninterrupted silence that felt like an eternity, with my back still pressed against the door in terror, I feasted my eyes on the strange, hypnotic form of this compact, powerfully built little man, something between a tough, patriarchal highlander and an ancient, energetic dwarf, who was restlessly pacing to and fro with his hands behind his back, his head thrust forward like a battering ram, sunk in thought, remote, not bothering to give the slightest indication that he was aware that somebody, something, a speck of floating dust, had suddenly landed in his office. David Ben-Gurion was about seventy-five at the time, and I was barely twenty.

He had a prophetic shock of silvery hair that surrounded his bald patch like an amphitheater. At the lower margin of his massive brow were two thick, bushy gray eyebrows, beneath which a pair of sharp gray-blue eyes pierced the air. He had a wide, coarse nose, a shamelessly ugly nose, a pornographic nose, like an anti-Semitic caricature. His lips, on the other hand, were thin and indrawn, but his jaw looked to me like the prominent, defiant jaw of an ancient mariner. His skin was rough and red like raw meat. Under a short neck his shoulders were broad and powerful. His chest was massive. His open-necked shirt revealed a hand's-breadth of hairy chest. His shamelessly protruding belly, like a whale's hump, looked as solid as if it were made of concrete. But all this magnificence terminated, to my bewilderment, in a dwarf-like pair of legs that, if it were not blasphemous, one would be tempted to call almost ridiculous.

I tried to breathe as little as possible. I may have envied Gregor Samsa in Kafka's *Metamorphosis*, who managed to shrink himself into a cockroach. The blood fled from my extremities and collected in my liver.

The first words that broke the silence came in the piercing, metallic voice that we all heard virtually every day on the radio, and even in our dreams. The Almighty shot me an angry look, and said:

"*Nu!* So why aren't you sitting! Sit!"

I sat down in a flash on the chair facing the desk. I sat bolt upright, but only on the edge of the chair. There was no question of leaning back.

Silence. The Father of the Nation continued to pace to and fro, with hasty little steps, like a caged lion or someone who was determined not to be late. After half an eternity he suddenly said:

"Spinoza!"

And he stopped. When he had walked away as far as the window, he whirled around and said:

"Have you read Spinoza? You have. But maybe you didn't understand? Few people understand Spinoza. Very few."

And then, still pacing to and fro, to and fro, between the window and the door, he burst into a protracted dawn lecture on Spinoza's thought.

In the middle of the lecture, the door hesitantly opened a crack and the secretary poked his head in meekly, smiled, and tried to mumble something, but the roar of a wounded lion was unleashed on him:

"Get out of here! Go! Do not disturb! Can't you see that I'm having one of the most interesting conversations I've had in a long time? So be off with you!"

The poor man vanished in a flash.

So far I had not uttered a single word. Not a sound.

But Ben-Gurion, it turned out, was enjoying lecturing on Spinoza before seven o'clock in the morning. And he did indeed continue for a few minutes without interruption.

Suddenly he stopped in the middle of a sentence. I could almost feel his breath on the back of my petrified neck, but I dared not turn around. I sat rigid, my tightly pressed knees forming a right angle and my thighs at a right angle to my tense back. Without a hint of a question mark in his voice Ben-Gurion hurled at me:

"You haven't had any breakfast!"

He did not wait for an answer. I did not utter a sound.

All of a sudden Ben-Gurion sank out of sight behind his desk like a large stone in water; even his silvery mane vanished from view.

After a moment he resurfaced, holding two glasses in one hand and a bottle of cheap fruit drink in the other. Energetically he poured a glass for himself, then he poured one for me and declared:

"Drink it!"

I drank it all, in a single gulp. Down to the last drop.

David Ben-Gurion, meanwhile, took three noisy swallows, like a thirsty peasant, and resumed his lecture on Spinoza.

"As a Spinozist I say to you without a shadow of doubt that the whole essence of Spinoza's thought can be summed up as follows. A man should always stay composed! He should never lose his calm! All the rest is hair-splitting and paraphrase. Composure! Calm in any situation! And the rest—frippery!" (Ben-Gurion's peculiar intonation stressed the last syllable of each word with something like a little roar.)

By now I could not take the slur on Spinoza's honor any longer. I could not remain silent without betraying my favorite philosopher. So I summoned up all my courage, blinked, and by some miracle I dared to open my mouth in the presence of the Lord of All Creation, and even to squeak in a small voice:

"It's true that there is calm and composure in Spinoza, but surely it's not right to say that that's the whole essence of Spinoza's thought? Surely there's also—"

Then fire and brimstone and streams of molten lava erupted over me from the mouth of the volcano:

"I've been a Spinozist all my life! I've been a Spinozist since I was a young man! Composure! Calm! That is the essence of the whole of Spinoza's thought! That's the heart of it! Tranquility! In good or in evil, in victory or in defeat, a man must never lose his peace of mind! Never!"

His two powerful, woodcutter's fists landed furiously on the glass top of the desk, making our two glasses jump and rattle with fear.

"A man must never lose his temper!" The worlds were hurled at me like the thunder of judgment day. "Never! And if you can't see that, you don't deserve to be called a Spinozist!"

At this he calmed down. He brightened up.

He sat down opposite me and spread his arms out wide on his desk as though he was about to clasp everything on it to his breast. A pleasant, heart-melting light radiated from him when he suddenly smiled a simple, happy smile, and it seemed not only as though it was his face and his eyes that smiled but as though his whole fistlike body relaxed and smiled with him, and the whole room smiled too, and even Spinoza himself. Ben-Gurion's eyes, which had turned from a cloudy gray to bright blue, scrutinized me all over, with no thought for good manners, as though he were feeling me with his fingers. There was something mercurial about him, something restless and ferocious. His arguments were like punches. And yet when he suddenly brightened without warning, he was transformed from a vengeful deity to a delightful old grandfather, radiating good health and satisfaction. A seductive warmth gushed from him, and for a moment he displayed the charming quality of a cheeky child with an insatiable curiosity.

"And what about you? You write poetry? Yes?"

He winked mischievously. As though he had laid a playful little trap for me. And had won the game.

I was startled again. All I had authored at that time were two or three worthless poems in out-of-the-way quarterlies published by the kibbutz movement (which I hope have crumbled to dust by now together with my miserable attempts at poetry). But Ben-Gurion must have seen them. He was reportedly in the habit of poring over everything that was published: gardening monthlies, magazines for lovers of nature or chess, studies in agricultural engineering, statistical journals. His curiosity knew no bounds.

He also apparently had a photographic memory: once he had seen something, he never forgot it.

I mumbled something.

But the prime minister and minister of defense was no longer with me. His restless spirit had moved on. Now that he had explained once and for all, in one crushing blow, everything that had been left unexplained in the thought of Spinoza, he started to lecture me with passion about other matters: the loss of Zionistic fervor in our youth, or modern Hebrew poetry, which was dabbling in all kinds of weird experiments instead of opening its eyes and celebrating the miracle that was happening here daily in front of our eyes: the rebirth of the nation, the rebirth of the Hebrew language, the rebirth of the Negev Desert!

And suddenly, again without any warning, in the full flow of his monologue, almost in the middle of a sentence, he had had enough.

He leaped up from his chair as though shot from a gun, made me stand up too, and as he pushed me toward the door—pushed me physically, just as his secretary had pushed me in some three-quarters of an hour previously—he said warmly:

"It's good to chat! Very good! And what have you been reading lately? What is the youth reading? Please come and see me any time you're in town. Just drop in, don't be afraid!"

And while he pushed me, with my studded army boots and my white Sabbath-best shirt, through the door, he went on shouting cheerily:

"Drop in! Any time! My door is always open!"

More than forty years have passed since that Spinoza morning in Ben-Gurion's Spartan office. I have met famous people since then, including political leaders, fascinating personalities, some of whom exuded great personal charm, but nobody has left such a sharp impression of their physical presence on me, or of their electrifying willpower. Ben-Gurion had, at least on that morning, a hypnotic energy.

Isaiah Berlin was right in his cruel observation: Ben-Gurion was no intellectual, Plato and Spinoza notwithstanding. Far from it. As I see it, he was a visionary peasant. There was something primeval about him, something not of this day and age. His simplicity of mind was almost biblical; his willpower resembled a laser beam. As a young man in the shtetl of Plonsk in eastern Poland he had two simple ideas: that the Jews must reestablish their homeland in the Land of Israel, and that he was the right man to lead them. Throughout his life he never budged from these two decisions of his youth; everything else was subordinated to them.

He was an honest, cruel man; like most visionaries he did not stop to count the cost. Or perhaps he did stop for a moment and decided: let it cost whatever it costs.

As a child growing up among the Klausners and all their fellow anti-leftists in Kerem Avraham, I was always taught that Ben-Gurion was responsible for all the troubles of the Jewish people. Where I grew up he was the baddie, the embodiment of all the plagues of the leftist regime.

As I grew up, however, I opposed Ben-Gurion from the opposite angle, from the Left. Like many of the Israeli intelligentsia of my time, I saw him as an almost despotic personality, and I recoiled from the tough way he treated the Arabs in the War of Independence and the reprisal raids. It is only in recent years that I have begun to read about him and wonder whether I was right.

There is no simple way of summing him up.

And suddenly, as I write the words "the tough way," I can see again with perfect clarity the way Ben-Gurion held his glass of cheap fruit drink, which he had poured for himself first. The glass was cheap too, it was made of thick glass, and his tough fingers were thick and short as they clasped it like a hand grenade. I was alarmed: if I put a foot wrong and said something that would trigger his rage, Ben-Gurion might well dash the contents of the glass into my face, or hurl the glass at the wall. Or he might tighten his grip on the glass and crush it. That was the awesome way he held that glass. Until he suddenly brightened and showed me that he knew all about my attempts at writing poetry, and smiled with pleasure at the sight of my discomfiture, and for a brief moment he looked almost like a merry joker who had pulled off a little trick and was now asking himself: What next?

53

IN THE autumn, toward the end of 1951, my mother's condition took another turn for the worse. Her migraines came back, and so did her insomnia. Once again she sat all day at the window counting the birds or the clouds. She sat there at night too, with her eyes wide open.

My father and I shared the household chores. I peeled vegetables, and he chopped them up to make a fine salad. He sliced bread, and I spread it with margarine and cheese or margarine and jam. I swept and washed the floors and dusted all the surfaces, and my father emptied the garbage cans and bought a third of a block of ice for the icebox every two or three days. I went shopping at the grocer's and the greengrocer's, while Father took care of the butcher and the pharmacist. Both of us added items as necessary to the shopping list that we wrote on one of Father's index cards and pinned up on the kitchen door. As we bought items, we crossed them off the list. Every Saturday evening we started a new list:

Tomatoes. Cucumber. Onion. Potatoes. Radishes.
Bread. Eggs. Cheese. Jam. Sugar.
Find out if any clementines yet and when oranges start.
Matches. Oil. Candles for power failures.
Washing-up liquid. Washing soap. Shenhav toothpaste.
Paraffin.

A 40-watt lightbulb. Get iron mended. Batteries.

New washer for faucet in bathroom basin. Fix the faucet because it
    doesn't turn off completely.

Yogurt. Margarine. Olives.

Buy woolen socks for Mother.

At that time my handwriting grew more and more like my father's,
so that it was almost impossible to say which of us had written "paraffin" or who had added, "We need a new floorcloth." To this day my writing looks like my father's: vigorous, not always legible, but always
energetic, sharp, and revealing strong pressure on the pen, unlike my
mother's calm, rounded, pearl-like letters, leaning slightly backward,
precise and pleasant to look at, written with a light, disciplined hand,
letters as perfect and well-spaced as her teeth.

We were very close to one another at that time, Father and I: like a
pair of stretcher bearers carrying an injured person up a steep slope. We
took her a glass of water and made her take the tranquilizers that were
prescribed by two different doctors. We had one of Father's little cards
for that too: we wrote down the name of each medicine and the times
she had to take it, and we put a tick by each one that she took and a cross
by the ones she refused to swallow or that she brought up. Mostly she
was obedient and took her medicine even when she was feeling queasy.
Sometimes she forced herself to give us a little smile, which was even
more painful than her pallor or the dark half moons that appeared
under her eyes, because it was such a hollow smile, as if it had nothing
to do with her. And sometimes she motioned to us to lean over and she
stroked both our heads with a uniform circular movement. She stroked
us both for a long time, until Father gently removed her hand and laid
it on her bosom. And I did the same.

Every evening, at supper time, Father and I held a kind of daily staff
meeting in the kitchen. I filled him in on my day at school, and he told
me something about his day at work, at the National Library, or described an article he was trying to finish in time for the next issue of *Tar-
biz* or *Metsuda*.

We talked about politics, about the assassination of King Abdullah,
or about Begin and Ben-Gurion. We talked like equals. My heart filled
with love for this tired man when he concluded gravely:

"It seems there remain considerable areas of disagreement between us. So for the time being we shall have to agree to differ."

Then we would talk about household matters. We would jot down on one of Father's little cards what we still had to do, and cross out what we'd already seen to. Father even discussed money matters with me sometimes: still a fortnight to go till pay day, and we had already spent such and such a sum. Every evening he would ask me about my homework, and I would hand him my list of assignments from school and the exercise books in which I had completed the allotted tasks, for comparison. Sometimes he took a look at what I had done and made appropriate comments; he knew more about virtually every subject than my teachers and even than the authors of the textbooks. Mostly he would say:

"There's no need to check up on you. I know I can rely on you and trust you absolutely."

Secret pride and gratitude flooded through me when I heard these words. Sometimes I also felt a rush of pity.

For him, not for Mother. I had no pity for her at that time: she was just a long series of daily duties and demands. And a source of embarrassment and shame, because I had to explain somehow to friends why they could never come over to my place, and I had to answer neighbors who quizzed me sweetly at the grocer's about why they never saw her. What had happened to her? Even to uncles and aunts, even to Grandpa and Grandma, Father and I did not tell the whole truth. We played it down. We said she had the flu even when she didn't. We said: Migraine. We said: A particular sensitivity to daylight. Sometimes we said: She's very tired, too. We tried to tell the truth but not the whole truth.

We didn't know the whole truth. But we did know, even without exchanging notes, that neither of us told anyone everything we both knew; we only shared a few facts with the outside world. The two of us never discussed her condition. All we ever talked about was the work to do tomorrow, sharing the daily chores, and the needs of the household. Not once did we talk about what was wrong with her, apart from Father's repeated refrain: "Those doctors, they don't know anything. Not a thing." We didn't talk after her death, either. From the day of my mother's death to the day of my father's death, twenty years later, we did not talk about her once. Not a word. As if she had never lived. As if her life was just a censured page torn from a Soviet encyclopedia. Or as if, like Athena, I had been born straight from the head of Zeus. I was a sort of upside-down Jesus: born of a virgin man by an invisible spirit. And every morning, at dawn, I was awoken by the sound of a bird in the branches of the pomegranate tree in the yard, which greeted the day with the first five notes of Beethoven's *Für Elise*: "Ti-da-di-da-di!" And again, more excitedly: "Ti-da-di-da-di!" And under my blanket I completed it with feeling: "Da-di-da-da!" In my heart I called the bird Elise.

I was sorry for my father at that time. As though he had fallen victim, through no fault of his own, to some protracted act of abuse. As though my mother were maltreating him on purpose. He was very tired, and sad, even though as usual he tried to be cheery and chatty the whole time. He always hated silences and blamed himself for any silence that occurred. His eyes, like Mother's, had dark half moons beneath them.

Sometimes he left work during the day to take her for tests. What didn't they test in those months: her heart, lungs, and brain waves, digestion, hormones, nerves, women's problems, and circulation. To no effect. He spared no expense, he called various doctors and took her to see private specialists; he may even have had to borrow sums of money from his parents, although he hated having debts and loathed the way his mother, Grandma Shlomit, enjoyed being "put in the picture" and sorting out his marriage for him.

My father got up before dawn every morning to tidy the kitchen, sort the laundry, squeeze fruit, and bring Mother and me the juice at room temperature, to make us stronger, and he also managed to write hasty replies to a few letters from editors and scholars before he left for work. Then he rushed to the bus stop, with a string shopping bag folded up in his battered briefcase, to get to work on time at Terra Sancta Building, where the Newspaper Department of the National Library was transferred when the Mount Scopus campus of the university was cut off from the rest of the town in the War of Independence.

He would come home at five o'clock, having stopped on the way at the grocer's, the electrician's, or the pharmacist's, and would hurry straight in to Mother to see if she was feeling better, hoping that she might have dozed off for a bit while he was out. He would try to spoon-feed her some potato purée or boiled rice that he and I had somehow learned to cook. Then he locked the door on the inside, helped her to change, and tried to talk to her. He may even have attempted to entertain her with jokes that he had read in the paper or brought back from the library. Before it got dark, he would hurry out to the shops again, take care of various things, not resting, peering at the instructions that accompanied some new medicine, without even sitting down, trying to draw Mother into a conversation about the future of the Balkans.

Then he would come to my room to help me change my sheets or to put mothballs in my closet for the winter, while singing some sentimental ballad to himself, criminally out of tune, or try to draw me into an argument about the future of the Balkans.

After nightfall we sometimes had a visit from Auntie Lilenka—Aunt Lilia, Aunt Leah Kalish-Bar-Samkha—Mother's best friend, who came from the same town, Rovno, and had been in the same class at the Tarbuth gymnasium, the one who had written two books about child psychology.

Aunt Lilia brought some fruit and a plum cake. Father served tea and biscuits and her plum cake, while I washed and put out the fruit, with plates and knives, and then we left the two of them alone together. Aunt Lilia sat shut up with my mother for an hour or two, and when she emerged, her eyes were red. Whereas my mother was as calm and serene as always. Father overcame the dislike he felt toward this lady sufficiently to invite her politely to stay for supper. Why don't you give us a chance to spoil you a little? And it would make Fania happy too. But she always apologized embarrassedly, as though she had been asked to take part in an indecent act. She didn't want to be in the way, God forbid, and anyway she was expected at home, and they'd start worrying about her soon.

Sometimes Grandpa and Grandma came, dressed up as though for a ball. Grandma, in high heels and a black velvet dress with her white necklace, made a tour of the kitchen before she sat down next to Mother. Then she examined the packets of pills and the little bottles, pulled Father toward her and looked inside his collar, and screwed up her face in disgust as she inspected the state of my fingernails. She saw fit to remark sadly that medical science was now aware that most if not all illnesses had their origin in the mind rather than the body. Meanwhile, Grandpa

Alexander, always charming and restless like a playful puppy, kissed my mother's hand and praised her beauty, "even in sickness, and all the more so when you are restored to full health, tomorrow, if not this very evening. *Nu,* what! You're already blossoming! Perfectly enchanting! *Krasavitsa!*"

My father still insisted adamantly that my light had to be out by nine o'clock precisely every evening. He tiptoed into the other room, the book room, the living-room-study-and-bedroom, wrapped a shawl around my mother's shoulders because autumn was on the way and the nights were getting cooler, sat down beside her, took her cold hand into his hand, which was always warm, and tried to rouse her into a simple conversation. Like the prince in the story, he tried to wake Sleeping Beauty. But even if he kissed her, he was unable to wake her: the apple's spell could not be broken. Perhaps he did not kiss her right, or else she was not waiting in her dreams for a bespectacled chatterbox who was an expert in every branch of knowledge, never stopped cracking jokes, and worried about the future of the Balkans, but some other kind of prince entirely.

He sat next to her in the dark, because she could not stand the light at that time. Every morning before he went off to work or before I went to school, we had to close all the shutters and draw the curtains as though my mother had become the terrifying mad woman in the attic in *Jane Eyre.* He sat in the dark, silently holding my mother's hand, without moving. Or he may have held both her hands in his.

But he was unable to sit without moving for more than three or four minutes, either beside my sick mother or anywhere else apart from at his desk with his little cards. He was an active, busy man, always bustling, arranging things, talking nonstop.

When he could not take any more of the darkness and the silence, he took his books and his innumerable cards out to the kitchen, cleared himself a space on the oilcloth, sat down on a stool, and worked for a bit. But he was soon dispirited by this solitary confinement in the soot-blackened kitchen. So once or twice a week he would get up, sigh, change into his suit, comb his hair, brush his teeth well, splash on some of his aftershave, and peep quietly into my room to see if I was fast asleep (for his sake I always pretended I was). Then he went in to Mother, said whatever he said, promised her whatever he promised, and she certainly did not stop him, on the contrary, she used to stroke his head and say, Go, Arieh, go and play, they're not all as dozy as I am.

When he went out, with a Humphrey Bogart hat on his head and a just-in-case umbrella swinging on his arm, my father walked past my window singing to himself, terribly out of tune, and with a distinct Ashkenazi accent: ". . . my head found rest upon your breast, and my distant prayers found a nest," or "like a pair of doves your lovely eyes, and your voice like the s-ou-ou-nd of a be-e-ll!"

I did not know where he was going and yet I did know without knowing and yet I did not want to know and yet I forgave him. I hoped he enjoyed himself there a bit. I had absolutely no desire to picture to myself what went on there, in that "there" of his, but what I didn't want to picture to myself came to me in the night and threw me in a whirl and would not let me sleep. I was a twelve-year-old boy. My body had begun to be a pitiless foe.

Sometimes I had the feeling that when the house emptied every morning, Mother actually did get into bed and slept during the daylight hours. And sometimes she got up and walked around the house, always barefoot, despite my father's entreaties and the slippers he brought to her: to and fro, to and fro my mother sailed along the corridor that had been our shelter during the war and was now piled with books and with its wall maps served as the operations room from which my father and I supervised the security of Israel and the defense of the Free World.

Even during the day the corridor was pitch black, unless you switched the light on. In the black my mother floated to and fro, unvaryingly, for half an hour or an hour, as prisoners walk around their prison yard. And sometimes she began to sing, as though to compete with my father, but with far fewer wrong notes. Her singing voice was dark and warm, like the taste of mulled wine on a winter evening. She did not sing in Hebrew, but in sweet-sounding Russian, in dreamy Polish, or occasionally in Yiddish, with a sound like choked tears.

On the nights when he went out, my father always kept his promise and came back before midnight. I could hear him undressing down to his underwear, then making himself a glass of tea, sitting on a stool in the kitchen and humming quietly to himself as he dunked a biscuit in his sweet tea. Then he would take a cold shower (to get hot water, you had to heat the boiler three-quarters of an hour beforehand with wood that you had to sprinkle with paraffin first). Then he would come into my room on tiptoe to make sure I was asleep and to straighten my bed-clothes. Only then did he tiptoe to their room. Sometimes I could hear the two of them talking in low voices until I fell asleep at last. And some-times there was total silence as though there was no living being there.

Father began to fear that he himself was responsible for my mother's insomnia, because he was in the big bed. Sometimes he insisted on put-ting her to bed in the sofa bed every night (when I was little, we called it the "barking sofa" because when you opened it up, it looked like the jaws of an angry dog), and he himself slept on her chair. He said it would really be better for everyone if he slept on the chair and she in the bed, because he slept like a log wherever he was put, "even on a hot griddle." In fact, he would sleep much better on the chair knowing that she was sleeping in the bed, than he would in the bed knowing that she was awake for hours on end on the chair.

One night, toward midnight, the door of my room opened silently and Father's silhouette bent over me in the dark. As usual, I hastily feigned sleep. Instead of straightening my bedclothes, he lifted them and got into bed with me. Like that time. Like on November 29, after the vote for the creation of the state, when my hand saw his tears. I was terrified and hastily drew my knees up and pressed them hard against my stom-ach, hoping and praying that he would not notice what it was that had stopped me getting to sleep: if he did, I would die on the spot. My blood froze when Father got into bed with me, and I was in such a panic not to be caught out being filthy, that it was quite a while before I realized, as though in a nightmare, that the silhouette that had slipped into bed with me was not my father's.

She pulled the covers up over both our heads and cuddled me, and whispered, Don't wake up.

And in the morning she was not there. The next night she came to my room again, but this time she brought one of the two mattresses from the "barking sofa" with her and slept on the floor at the foot of my bed. The following night I firmly insisted, doing my best to imitate my father's authoritative manner, that she should sleep in my bed and I would sleep on the mattress at her feet.

It was as if we were all playing an improved version of musical chairs called musical beds. First round: normal—both my parents in their double bed and me in my bed. Then in the next round Mother slept in her chair, Father on the sofa, and I was still in my bed. In the third round Mother and I were in my single bed while Father was alone in the double bed. In the fourth round my father was unchanged and I was alone again in my bed and my mother on the mattress at my feet. Then she and I swapped over, she went up, I went down, and Father stayed where he was.

But we weren't finished yet.

Because after a few nights when I slept on the mattress in my room at my mother's feet, she frightened me in the middle of the night with broken sounds that were almost but not quite like coughing. Then she calmed down, and I went back to sleep. But a night or two later I was woken again by her coughs that weren't coughs. I got up, with my eyes stuck together, went down the corridor in a daze with my blanket wrapped around me, and climbed in with my father into the double bed. I fell asleep again at once. And I slept there the following nights, too.

Almost to her last days my mother slept in my room, in my bed, and I slept with my father. After a couple of days all her tablets and bottles of medicine and tranquilizers and migraine pills moved to her new place.

We did not exchange a word about the new sleeping arrangements. None of us mentioned them. It was as if it had happened all by itself.

And it really had. Without any family decision. Without a word.

But the week before the last one Mother did not spend the night in my bed but returned to her chair by the window, except that the chair was moved from our room—mine and Father's—to my room, which had become her room.

Even when it was all over, I did not want to go back to that room. I wanted to stay with my father. And when I did eventually return to my old room, I couldn't get to sleep: it was as if she were still there. Smiling at me without a smile. Coughing without a cough. Or as if she had bequeathed me the insomnia that had pursued her to the end and was now pursuing me. The night I went back to my own bed was so terrifying that the following nights my father had to drag one of the mattresses from the "barking sofa" to my room and sleep there with me. For a week or maybe two he slept at the foot of my bed. After that he went back to his place, and she, or her insomnia, followed him.

It was as though a great whirlpool had swept us up, thrown us together and apart, hurled us around and around and jumbled us up, until each of us was thrown up on a shore that was not our own. And we were all so tired that we silently accepted the move. Because we were very tired. It was not only my mother and father who had dark half moons under their eyes: in those weeks I saw them under my eyes, too, in the mirror.

We were bound and stuck together that autumn like three prisoners sharing the same cell. Yet each of us was on his or her own. For what could my parents know about the sordidness of my nights? The filthiness of my cruel body? How could my parents know that I warned myself over and over again, with my teeth clenched in shame, If you don't give that up, if you don't stop it tonight, then I swear by my life that I'll swallow all Mother's pills and that'll be the end of it.

My parents suspected nothing. A thousand light-years divided us. Not light-years: dark years.

But what did I know about what they were going through?

And how about the two of them? What did my father know about her ordeal? What did my mother understand about his suffering?

A thousand dark years separated everyone. Even three prisoners in a cell. Even that day in Tel Arza, that Saturday morning when Mother sat with her back against the tree and my father and I laid our heads on her knees, one head on each knee, and Mother stroked us both, even at that moment, which is the most precious moment of my childhood, a thousand lightless years separated us.

54

IN THE COLLECTED poems of Jabotinsky, after "With blood and sweat we'll raise a race," "Two banks has the Jordan," and "From the day I was called to the wonder / of Beitar, Zion, and Sinai," came his melodic translations from world poetry, including Edgar Allan Poe's "The Raven" and "Annabel Lee," Edmond Rostand's "The Princess Faraway," and Paul Verlaine's heartrending "Autumn Song."

Very soon I knew all these poems by heart and walked around all day drunk on the romantic anguish and macabre torments that enveloped them.

Side by side with the militaristic patriotic verses that I composed in the splendid black notebook that was a present from Uncle Joseph, I started to write poems of Weltschmerz as well, full of storm, forest, and sea. And some love poems too, before I even knew what was what. Or didn't know but vainly tried to find some accommodation between the westerns in which whoever slew the most Indians won the pretty girl as the prize and the tearful vows of Annabel Lee and her partner and their love beyond the grave. It was not easy to reconcile them. And much harder still to make some sort of peace between all of this and the school nurse's labyrinth of sheaths-eggs-and-Fallopian-tubes. And the nocturnal filth that tormented me so mercilessly that I wanted to die. Or to go back to being as I had been before I fell into the clutches of those jeering night hags: night after night I resolved to kill them off once and for all, and night after night those Scheherazades revealed to my startled gaze such uninhibited plots that all day long I waited impatiently to be in bed at night. Sometimes I could not wait and locked myself in the smelly toilets in the playground at Tachkemoni or our bathroom at home and emerged a few minutes later with my tail between my legs and as wretched as a rag.

The love of girls and everything associated with it seemed to me to be a catastrophe, a terrible trap from which there was no way out: you start out floating dreamily into an enchanted crystal palace, and you wake up immersed up to here in a cesspool.

I ran away and sought refuge in the fortress of sanity of books of mystery, adventure, and battle: Jules Verne, Karl May, James Fenimore Cooper, Mayne Reid, Sherlock Holmes, *The Three Musketeers, Captain Hatteras, Montezuma's Daughter, The Prisoner of Zenda, With Fire and Sword,* De Amicis's *The Heart of a Boy, Treasure Island, Twenty Thousand Leagues under the Sea, Through the Desert and Jungle, The Gold of Caxamalca, The Mysterious Island, The Count of Monte Cristo, The Last of the Mohicans, The Children of Captain Grant,* the darkest recesses of Africa, grenadiers and Indians, wrongdoers, cavalrymen, cattle thieves, robbers, cowboys, pirates, archipelagos, hordes of bloodthirsty natives in feathered headdresses and war paint, blood-chilling battle cries, magical spells, knights of the dragon and Saracen horsemen with curved scimitars, monsters, wizards, emperors, bad guys, hauntings, and especially stories about pale little adolescents who are destined for great things when they have managed to overcome their own wretchedness. I wanted to be like them and I wanted to be able to write like the people who wrote them. Perhaps I did not make a distinction yet between writing and winning.

Jules Verne's *Michael Strogoff* imprinted something on me that is with me to this day. The Russian tsar has sent Strogoff on a secret mission to take a fateful message to the beleaguered Russian forces in remotest Siberia. On the way he has to cross regions that are under Tartar control. Michael Strogoff is captured by Tartar guards and taken to their leader, the Great Khan, who orders his eyes to be put out by being touched with a white-hot sword, so that he will be unable to continue with his mission to Siberia. Strogoff has memorized the fateful message, but how can he slip through the Tartar ranks and reach Siberia if he cannot see? Even after the glowing iron touches his eyes, the faithful messenger continues to grope his way blindly eastward, until at a crucial moment in the plot it is revealed to the reader that he has not lost his sight after all: the white-hot sword as it approached his eyes was cooled by his tears! Because at the crucial moment Michael Strogoff thought of his beloved family whom he would never see again, and the thought filled his eyes with tears, which cooled the blade and saved his sight as well as his fateful mission, which is crowned with success and leads to the victory of his country over all its foes.

So it was Strogoff's tears that saved him and the whole of Russia. But where I lived, men were not allowed to shed tears! Tears were shameful! Only women and children were permitted to weep. Even when I was five, I was ashamed of crying, and at the age of eight or nine I learned to suppress it so as to be admitted to the ranks of men. That is why I was so astonished on the night of November 29 when my left hand in the dark encountered my father's wet cheek. That is why I never talked about it, either to Father himself or to any other living soul. And now here was Michael Strogoff, a flawless hero, a man of iron who could endure any hardship or torture, and yet when he suddenly thinks of love, he shows no restraint: he weeps. Michael Strogoff does not weep from fear, or from pain, but because of the intensity of his feelings.

Moreover, Michael Strogoff's crying does not demote him to the rank of a miserable wretch or a woman or a wreck of a man; it is acceptable both to the author, Jules Verne, and to the reader. And as if it were not enough that it is suddenly acceptable for a man to weep, both he and the whole of Russia are saved by his tears. And so this manliest of men defeats all his foes thanks to his "feminine side," which rose up from the depths of his soul at the crucial moment, without impairing or weakening his "masculine side" (as they brainwashed us to say in those days): on the contrary, it complemented it and made peace with it. So perhaps there was an honorable way out of the choice that tormented me in those days, the choice between emotion and manliness? (A dozen years later, Hannah in *My Michael* would also be fascinated by the character of Michael Strogoff.)

And then there was Captain Nemo in *Twenty Thousand Leagues under the Sea,* who detested exploitative regimes and the oppression of nations and individuals by heartless bullies and selfish powers. He had a hatred for the arrogant condescension of the northwestern countries that is reminiscent of Edward Said, if not Franz Fanon, so he decided to dissociate himself from all of it and to create a little utopia under the ocean.

This apparently aroused in me, among other things, a throb of Zionist responsiveness. The world always persecuted us and treated us unjustly: that was why we had retreated sideways, to create our own little independent bubble where we could live "a life of purity and freedom," far from the cruelty of our persecutors. But, like Captain Nemo, we would not go on being helpless victims but by the power of our creative genius we would arm our own *Nautilus* with sophisticated death rays. No one would ever dare to plot against us again. Our long arm would reach to the end of the world if necessary.

In Verne's *The Mysterious Island* a group of survivors from a shipwreck manage to create a tiny patch of civilization on a barren desert island. The survivors are all Europeans, all men, all rational, generous-hearted men of goodwill, they are all technologically minded, bold and resourceful: they are the very image of the way the nineteenth century wanted to see the future: sane, enlightened, virile, capable of solving any problem by the power of reason and in accordance with the tenets of the new religion of progress. (Cruelty, baser instincts, and evil were apparently banished to another, later island: the one in William Golding's *Lord of the Flies.*)

By their hard work, common sense, and pioneering enthusiasm the group manages to survive and to build up from scratch, with their bare hands, a prosperous homestead on the desert island. This delighted me, imbued as I was with the pioneering ethos of Zionism that I had received from my father: secular, enlightened, rationalistic, idealistic, militantly optimistic and progressive.

And yet, there were moments when the pioneers of *The Mysterious Island* were threatened by catastrophe from the forces of nature, moments when they had their backs to the wall and their brains were of no further use to them, and at such fateful moments a mysterious hand always intervened in the plot, a miraculous, all-powerful providence that time and again delivered them from certain destruction. "If there be justice, let it shine forth at once," Bialik wrote: in *The Mysterious Island* there was justice and it did shine forth at once, as quick as lightning, whenever all hope was lost.

But that was precisely the other ethos, the one diametrically opposed to my father's rationalism. It was the logic of the stories my mother used to tell me at night, tales of demons, of miracles, the tale of the ancient man who sheltered an even more ancient man under his roof, tales of evil, mystery, and grace, Pandora's box where at the end hope still remained beyond all despair. It was also the miracle-laden logic of the Hasidic tales that Teacher Zelda first exposed me to and that my storytelling teacher at Tachkemoni, Mordechai Michaeli, took up from the place where she had left off.

It was as if here, in *The Mysterious Island,* there was at last some kind of reconciliation between the two opposing windows through which the world had first been revealed to me, at the beginning of my life: my father's commonsensical, optimistic window, over against my mother's window, which opened onto grim landscapes and strange supernatural forces, of evil but also of pity and compassion.

At the end of *The Mysterious Island* it turns out that the providential force that intervened over and over again to rescue the "Zionist enterprise" of the survivors of the shipwreck whenever they were threatened with destruction was actually the discreet intervention of Captain Nemo, the angry-eyed captain from *Twenty Thousand Leagues under the Sea*. But that in no way diminished the pleasure of reconciliation that I got from the book, the elimination of the contradiction between my childish fascination with Zionism and my no less childish fascination with the Gothic.

It was as though my father and mother had finally made peace and were living together in perfect harmony. Admittedly not here in Jerusalem but on some desert island. But still, they could make peace.

Kindhearted Mr. Marcus, who sold new and secondhand books on Jonah Street, almost at the corner of Geula Street, also ran a lending library, and eventually he allowed me to change my book every day. Sometimes twice on the same day. At first he would not believe that I had really read the whole book, and when I brought a book back only a few hours after I had borrowed it, he used to test me on it with all sorts of crafty trick questions. Gradually his suspicion turned to astonishment and finally to devotion. He was convinced that with such an amazing memory and the ability to read so fast, particularly if I also learned the major languages, someday I could become the ideal private secretary for one of our great leaders. Who knew, I might end up as Ben-Gurion's secretary, or Moshe Sharet's. Consequently he decided that I was worth a long-term investment, that he should cast his bread upon the water: who knew, he might need some permit one day, he might need to jump a line or oil the wheels of the publishing business he was planning to join, and then surely his ties of friendship with the private secretary of one of the greatest of the great would be worth its weight in gold.

Mr. Marcus sometimes used to show my crowded reader's ticket proudly to selected customers, as though gloating over the fruits of his investment. Just look what we have here! A bookworm! A phenomenon! A child who devours not just books but whole shelves every month!

So I got special permission from Mr. Marcus to make myself at home in his library. I could borrow four books at a time so as not to go hungry over the holidays, when the shop was closed. I could leaf—carefully!—through books hot from the press that were intended for sale, not for lending. I could even look at books that were not meant for someone of my age, like the stories of Somerset Maugham, O. Henry, Stefan Zweig, and even spicy Maupassant.

In the winter I ran in the dark, through showers of piercing rain and driving wind, to get to Mr. Marcus's bookshop before it closed, at six o'clock. It was very cold in Jerusalem in those days, a sharp biting cold, and hungry polar bears came down from Siberia to roam the streets of Kerem Avraham on those late December nights. I ran without a coat, and so my sweater got drenched and gave off a depressing, itchy smell of wet wool all evening.

Occasionally it happened that I was left without a scrap to read, on those long empty Saturdays when by ten in the morning I had finished all the ammunition I had brought from the library. Frantically I grabbed whatever came to hand in my father's bookcases: *Till Eulenspiegel* in Shlonsky's translation, the *Arabian Nights* translated by Rivlin, the books of Israel Zarchi, Mendele Mocher Sforim, Sholem Aleichem, Kafka, Berdyczewski, Rahel's poetry, Balzac, Hamsun, Yigal Mossensohn, Feierberg, Natan Shaham, Gnessin, Brenner, Hazaz, even Mr. Agnon's books. I understood almost nothing, except perhaps for what I could see through my father's spectacles, namely that life in the shtetl was despicable, repulsive, and even ridiculous. In my foolish heart, I was not entirely surprised by its terrible end.

Father had most of the key works of world literature in the original languages, so I could hardly even read their titles. But whatever was there in Hebrew, if I didn't actually read it, at least I sniffed at it. I left no stone unturned.

Of course, I also read the weekly children's section of *Davar,* and those children's books that were on everyone's dessert menu: poems by Leah Goldberg and Fania Bergstein, *The Children's Island* by Mira Lobeh, and all the books by Nahum Guttmann. Lobengula's Africa, Beatrice's Paris, Tel Aviv surrounded by sand dunes, orchards, and sea, all these were destinations of my first hedonistic world cruises. The difference between Jerusalem and Tel-Aviv-that-was-joined-to-the-rest-of-the-big-wide-world seemed to me like the difference between our wintry, black-and-white life and a life of color, summer, and light. One book that particularly captured my imagination was *Over the Ruins* by Tsvi Liebermann-Livne, which I read and reread. Once upon a time, in the days of the Second Temple, there was a remote Jewish village, tucked away peacefully among hills, valleys, and vineyards. One day the Roman legionnaires arrived, slaughtered all the inhabitants, men, women, and old folk, looted their property, set fire to the buildings, and went on their way. But the villagers had managed before the massacre to hide their little children, the ones who were not yet twelve and could not take part in the defense of the village, in a cave in the hills.

After the calamity the children emerged from the cave, saw the destruction, and instead of despairing they decided, in a discussion that resembled a general assembly in a kibbutz, that life must go on and that they must rebuild the ruined village. So they set up committees, which girls sat on too, because these children were not only brave and industrious but also amazingly progressive and enlightened. Gradually, working like ants, they managed to recover the remaining livestock, repair the pens and cow sheds, restore the burned houses, start working the fields again, and set up a model community of children, a sort of idyllic kibbutz: a commune of Robinson Crusoes without a single Man Friday.

Not a cloud darkened the life of sharing and equality enjoyed by these children of the dream: neither power struggles nor rivalries and jealousies, neither filthy sex nor the ghosts of their dead parents. It was exactly the opposite of what happened to the children in *Lord of the Flies*. Tsvi Livne certainly intended to give the children of Israel an inspiring Zionist allegory: the generation of the wilderness had all died, and in its place there arose the generation of the Land, bold and brave, raising itself up by its own efforts from catastrophe to heroism and from darkness to great light. In my own, Jerusalem version, in the sequel that I composed in my head, the children were not content with milking the cows and harvesting the olives and grapes; they discovered an arms cache, or better still they managed to devise and construct machine guns, mortars, and armored vehicles. Or else it was the Palmach that managed to smuggle these weapons a hundred generations backward in time to the outstretched hands of the children of *Over the Ruins*. Armed with all these weapons, Tsvi Livne's (and my) children hurried to Masada and arrived at the very last minute. With a devastating barrage of fire, from the rear, with long, accurate salvos and deadly mortar fire they took the Roman legionnaires by surprise—the very same legionnaires who had killed their parents and were now engaged in building a ramp to storm the rocky citadel of Masada. And so, at the very moment when Eleazar Ben Yair was about to conclude his unforgettable farewell speech and the last defenders of Masada were on the point of falling on their swords so as not to be taken captive by the Romans, my young men and I burst onto the mountain and saved them from death, and our nation from the ignominy of defeat.

Then we carried the war to enemy territory: we positioned our mortars on the seven hills of Rome, smashed the Arch of Titus to smithereens, and brought the emperor to his knees.

There may well be another sick illicit pleasure concealed here, one that no doubt never occurred to Tsvi Livne when he was writing the book, a dark, oedipal pleasure. Because the children here buried their own parents. All of them. Not a single grown-up was left in the entire village. No parent, no teacher, no neighbor, no uncle, no grandpa, no grandma, no Mr. Krochmal, no Uncle Joseph, no Mala and Staszek Rudnicki, no Abramskis, no Bar-Yizhars, no Aunt Lilia, no Begin, and no Ben-Gurion. And so a well-repressed desire of the Zionist ethos, and of the child that I was then, was miraculously fulfilled: that the grown-ups should be dead. Because they were so alien, so burdensome. They belonged to the Diaspora. They were the generation of the wilderness. They were always full of demands and commands, they never let you breathe. Only when they are dead will we be able to show them at last how we can do everything ourselves. Whatever they want us to do, whatever they expect from us, we'll do the lot, magnificently: we'll plow and reap and build and fight and win, only without them, because the new Hebrew nation needs to break free from them. Because everything here was made to be young, healthy, and tough, while they are old and shattered and complicated and a bit repulsive, and more than a bit ridiculous.

So in *Over the Ruins* the whole generation of the wilderness has evaporated, leaving behind happy, light-footed orphans, as free as a flock of birds in the clear blue sky. There is no one left to nag them in a Diaspora accent, to speechify, to enforce musty manners, to spoil life with all kinds of depressions, traumas, imperatives, and ambitions. Not one of them has survived to moralize all day long—this is permitted, that is forbidden, that is disgusting. Just us. Alone in the world.

The death of all the grown-ups concealed a mysterious, powerful spell. And so at the age of fourteen and a half, a couple of years after my mother's death, I killed my father and the whole of Jerusalem, changed my name, and went on my own to Kibbutz Hulda to live there over the ruins.

55

I KILLED HIM particularly by changing my name. For many years my father had lived under the wide shadow of his learned uncle with his "worldwide reputation" (a concept that my father would voice in piously hushed tones). For many years Yehuda Arieh Klausner had dreamed of following in the footsteps of Professor Joseph Gedalyahu Klausner, the author of *Jesus of Nazareth, From Jesus to Paul, A History of the Second Temple, A History of Hebrew Literature,* and *When a Nation Fights for Its Freedom.* In his heart of hearts my father even dreamed of succeeding the childless professor when the time came. That is why he learned no fewer foreign languages than his uncle had mastered. That is why he sat huddled over his desk at night while the little cards piled up around him. And when he began to despair of being a famous professor some-day, he may have begun to pray in his heart of hearts that the torch would pass to me, and that he would be there to see it.

My father sometimes jokingly compared himself to the insignificant Mendelssohn, the banker Abraham Mendelssohn, whose fate it was to be the son of the famous philosopher Moses Mendelssohn and the father of the great composer Felix Mendelssohn-Bartholdy. ("First I was my father's son, then I became my son's father," Abraham Mendelssohn once said jokingly.)

As though in jest, as though he was making fun of me out of stunted feelings of affection, my father insisted on addressing me, from an early age, as "Your Honor," "Your Highness." It was only many years later, the night of the day he died, that it suddenly occurred to me that behind this fixed, irritating joke there may have lurked his own disappointed ambitions, and the sad necessity to reconcile himself to his own mediocrity, as well as the concealed wish to entrust me with the mission to achieve in his name, when the time came, the goals that had eluded him.

My mother, in her loneliness and depression, told me stories of wonders, horrors, and ghosts that were possibly not much different from those that the widow Åse told the young Peer Gynt on winter nights. My father, in his own way, was Jon Gynt, Peer's father, to my mother's Åse, hoping for "great things."

"The kibbutz," Father remarked sadly, "may be a not insignificant phenomenon, but it requires tough manual workers of average intelligence. You know by now that you are decidedly not average. I do not wish to cast aspersions on the kibbutz as such, kibbutzim have distinct merits in the life of the state, but you will not be able to develop there. Consequently I am afraid I cannot agree to this. In any way. And that's that. End of discussion."

After my mother's death, and his remarriage a year or so later, he and I talked almost only about the necessities of everyday life, politics, new scientific discoveries, or values and moral theories. (By now we were living in the new apartment, at 28 Ben Maimon Avenue, in Rehavia, the area of Jerusalem where he had longed to live for years.) The anxieties of my adolescent years, his remarriage, his feelings, my feelings, the last days of my mother's life, her death, her absence, these were topics about which we never spoke. We sometimes clashed, with a polite but very tense mutual hostility, about Bialik, Napoleon, and socialism, which had begun to fascinate me and which my father saw as the "red epidemic," and once we had a terrible row about Kafka. Most of the time, though, we behaved like two lodgers sharing a small apartment. The bathroom's free. We need margarine and toilet paper. Don't you think it's getting rather cold: shall I light the heater?

When I started to go away on weekends and during festivals to visit my mother's sisters, Haya and Sonia, in Tel Aviv, or to Grandpa Papa's house in Kiriat Motskin, my father gave me money for the fare and added a few pounds "So you won't have to ask anybody there for money." "And don't forget to tell somebody there that you mustn't eat anything fried." Or "Please remember to ask somebody there if they'd like me to put the things from her drawer in an envelope for the next time you go."

The word "her" covered my mother's memory like a slab of stone with no inscription. The words "anybody there" or "somebody there" signified the breaking of all ties between him and my mother's family, which had never been renewed. They blamed him. His relationships with other women, my mother's sisters in Tel Aviv believed, had cast a cloud over their sister's life. Plus all those nights when he had sat at his desk with his back to her and his mind on his research and his little cards. My father was shocked by this accusation and wounded to the quick. He viewed my trips to Tel Aviv and Haifa more or less the way the Arab states, in that time of boycott and denial, viewed visits to Israel by neutral individuals: we can't stop you going, go where you like, but please don't call that place by its name in our presence, and don't tell us anything about it when you get back. Anything good or bad. And don't tell them about us. We don't want to hear and we don't care to know. And make sure they don't put any unwanted stamps in your passport.

Some three months after my mother's suicide came the day of my bar mitzvah. There was no party. They made do with my being called up to the Torah on Saturday morning at Tachkemoni Synagogue and mumbling my way through the weekly reading. The whole Mussman family came, from Tel Aviv and Kiriat Motskin, but they found their own corner in the synagogue, as far as possible from the Klausners. Not a word was exchanged between the two camps. Zvi and Buma, my aunts' husbands, may have given a little, almost imperceptible nod. And I ran back and forth between the two cantons like a dizzy puppy dog, trying my best to look like a happy little boy, talking endlessly, in imitation of my father.

Only Grandpa Alexander unhesitatingly crossed the iron curtain, kissed my grandmother from Haifa and my mother's two sisters on both cheeks, three times, left right left, in the Russian manner, and pressed me to his side as he exclaimed delightedly: "*Nu*, what? A charming young man, is he not? A *molodyets* young man! And very talented, too! Very very talented! Very!"

Some time after my father's remarriage, my schoolwork went downhill so badly that there was a threat of expulsion from school (the year after my mother's death I had been moved from Tachkemoni to Rehavia

High School). My father took it as a personal affront, and was outraged; he punished me in various ways. Gradually he came to suspect that this was my form of guerrilla warfare, which would not stop until I had forced him to let me go to the kibbutz. He fought back: every time I entered the kitchen, he would get up and leave without saying a word. But one Friday he went out of his way to accompany me to the old Egged bus station halfway down Jaffa Road. Before I boarded the bus to Tel Aviv, he suddenly said:

"If you wish, please ask them there what they think about this kibbutz idea of yours. Needless to say their opinion is not binding on us and does not interest us that much, but for once I do not object to hearing what they think of this possibility over there."

Long before my mother's death, from the beginning of her illness and perhaps even earlier, my aunts from Tel Aviv saw my father as a selfish and maybe slightly domineering man; they were convinced that since her death I had been groaning under the yoke of his oppression and that since his marriage my stepmother, too, was mistreating me. Over and over again I annoyed my aunts by saying nice things about my father and his wife, how devotedly they looked after me and tried their very best to make sure I didn't lack for anything. My aunts refused to listen: they were surprised at me, they were angry, they were offended, as though I were singing the praises of Abdel Nasser and his regime, or defending the fedayeen. Both of them silenced me whenever I began to sing my father's praises. Aunt Haya said:

"That's enough. Please stop. You're hurting me. They seem to be brainwashing you properly."

Aunt Sonia did not reproach me at such moments: she simply burst into tears.

To their inquisitive eyes, the truth spoke for itself: I looked as thin as a rake, pale, nervous, and not properly washed. They must be neglecting me over there. If not something worse. And what's that wound on your check? Don't they send you to the doctor there? And that rag of a sweater—is that the only one you've got? And when was the last time they bought you any underwear? And how about money for the return fare? Did they forget to give you any? No? Why are you so obstinate? Why don't you let us put a few pounds in your pocket, to be on the safe side?

As soon as I arrived in Tel Aviv, my aunts pounced on the bag I'd packed for the weekend and took out the shirt, the pajamas, the socks, the underwear, and even the spare hankie, tut-tutting to themselves wordlessly and condemning the whole lot to be laundered, boiled, thoroughly aired for a couple of hours on the balcony, then there was violent ironing, and occasionally uncompromising destruction, as though they were eliminating the risk of plague or sending all my personal effects off for a course of reeducation. I was always sent off to the shower first thing, and secondly it was, Sit in the sun on the balcony for half an hour, you're as white as that wall, and won't you have a bunch of grapes? an apple? some raw carrot? Then we'll go and buy you some new underwear. Or a decent shirt. Or some socks. They both tried to feed me chicken liver, cod-liver oil, fruit juices, and masses of raw vegetables. As if I'd come straight from the ghetto.

On the question of my going to the kibbutz Aunt Haya immediately declared:

"Yes, definitely. You ought to get away from them for a bit. In a kibbutz you'll get bigger and stronger, and gradually you'll lead a healthier life."

Aunt Sonia suggested sadly, with her arm around my shoulder:

"Try the kibbutz, yes. And if, God forbid, you feel just as miserable there, simply move in with us here."

Towards the end of year nine (the fifth grade at Rehavia School) I suddenly gave up the scouts and almost stopped going to school. I lay on my back in my room all day in my underwear, devouring one book after another and piles of sweets, which were almost the only thing I ate at the time. I was already in love up to here, with stifled tears and without the ghost of a chance, with one of the princesses of my class: not bittersweet youthful love as in the books I was reading, where they described how the soul aches with love but is still uplifted and thrives, but as if I had been hit over the head with an iron rod. And to make matters worse, my body, at that time, didn't stop tormenting me at night and even during the day with its insatiable filth. I wanted to go free, to be liberated once and for all from these two enemies, the body and the soul. I wanted to be a cloud. To be a stone on the surface of the moon.

Every evening I got up, went out, and wandered the streets for two or three hours or walked to the empty fields outside the city. Sometimes I felt attracted to the barbed-wire fence and the minefields that divided the city, and once, in the dark, straying perhaps into one of the areas of no-man's-land, I accidentally trod on an empty can, which made a noise that sounded as loud as a landslide, and immediately two shots rang out from quite nearby in the dark and I ran away. Still, I went back the next evening and the following ones to the edge of no-man's-land as though I had had enough of it all. I even went down into the secluded wadis, till I couldn't see any lights, only the outline of the hills and a sprinkling of stars, the smell of fig and olive trees and thirsty summer earth. I got home at ten, eleven, or midnight, refusing to say where I'd been, ignoring my bedtime even though Father had extended it from nine o'clock to ten, ignoring all his complaints, not responding to his hesitant efforts to bridge the silence between us with his well-worn jokes:

"And where, if we may be permitted to ask, has Your Excellency spent the evening, until almost midnight? Did you have a rendezvous? With some beautiful young lady? Was Your Highness invited to an orgy in the Queen of Sheba's palace?"

My silence scared him even more than the burrs that clung to my clothes or the fact that I had stopped studying. When he realized that his anger and his punishments were having no effect, he replaced them with petty sarcasm. He muttered with a nod of the head: "If that's the way Your Highness wants it, that's the way it will be." Or: "When I was your age I had almost finished the gymnasium. Not the light entertainment of a school like yours! The classical gymnasium! With iron military discipline! With classical Greek and Latin lessons! I read Euripides, Ovid, and Seneca in the original! And what are you doing? Lying flat on your back for twelve hours on end reading rubbish! Comics! Dirty magazines! *Dwarf* and *Stalag!* Disgusting rags intended for the dregs of humanity! To think of the great-nephew of Professor Klausner ending up as a good-for-nothing! A hooligan!"

Eventually his sarcasm gave way to sorrow. At the breakfast table he would look at me for a moment with sad, warm, doglike eyes, and at once his gaze fled before mine and buried itself behind his paper. As though he were the one who had gone astray and should be ashamed of himself.

Finally, with a heavy heart, my feather suggested a compromise. Some friends in Kibbutz Sde Nehemia would be willing to have me stay for the summer months: I could try my hand at agricultural work and find out whether life with youngsters of my age sleeping in communal dormitories suited me. If it turned out that the experience of the summer was enough for me, I had to commit myself to coming back to school and tackle my studies with the seriousness they deserved. But if I still hadn't come to my senses by the end of the summer holidays, then the two of us would sit down together again and have a truly grown-up conversation and try to come up with a solution that was agreeable to both of us.

Uncle Joseph himself, the old professor whom the Herut Party put forward at that time as its candidate for the presidency of the State against Professor Chaim Weizmann, the candidate of the Center and the Left, heard about my distressing intention to join a kibbutz and was alarmed. He considered kibbutzim to be a threat to the national ethos, if not an extension of Stalinism. So he invited me to his house for a serious private conversation, a tête-à-tête, not on one of our Sabbath pilgrimages but, for the first time in my life, on a weekday. I prepared for this meeting with a pounding heart and even jotted down three or four notes. I would remind Uncle Joseph of what he himself always proclaimed: the need to swim against the tide. The determined individual must always stand up boldly for what he conscientiously believes in, even against strong resistance from those dearest to him. But Uncle Joseph was forced to withdraw his invitation at the last minute because of some urgent matter that had attracted his outrage.

And so it was without his blessing, and without this David and Goliath confrontation, that I got up at five o'clock on the first morning of the summer holidays to go to the Central Bus Station on Jaffa Road. My father had gotten up half an hour before me: by the time my alarm went off, he had already made me two thick cheese and tomato sandwiches, two egg and tomato sandwiches, some peeled cucumber, an apple, and a slice of sausage, and wrapped them in greaseproof paper, with a bottle of water with the top screwed on very tight so it wouldn't leak on the journey. He had cut his finger slicing the bread and was bleeding, so before I left, I bandaged it for him. At the door he gave me a hesitant hug, then a second, harder one, put his head to one side and said:

"If I have hurt you in any way lately, I apologize. I haven't had an easy time of it either."

Suddenly he changed his mind, hastily put on a jacket and tie, and walked me to the bus station. The two of us carried the bag that held all my worldly belongings through the streets of Jerusalem, which were deserted before dawn. All the way my father spouted old jokes and puns. He talked about the Hasidic origins of the term "kibbutz," which means "ingathering," and the interesting parallel between the kibbutz ideology and the Greek idea of *koinonia,* community, from *koinos,* meaning "common." He pointed out that *koinonia* was the origin of the Hebrew word *kenounia,* "collusion," and perhaps also of the musical term "canon." He got on the Haifa bus with me and argued about where I should sit, then he said good-bye again, and he must have forgotten that this was not one of my Saturday visits to the aunts in Tel Aviv because he wished me a good Sabbath, even though it was Monday. Before he got off the bus, he joked with the driver and asked him to drive with special care because he was carrying a great treasure. Then he ran off to buy a paper, stood on the platform, looked for me, and waved good-bye to the wrong bus.

56

AT THE END of that summer I changed my name and moved with my bag from Sde Nehemia to Hulda. To start with I was an external boarder at the local secondary school (which modestly called itself "continuation classes"). When I finished school, just before I started my military service, I became a member of the kibbutz. Kibbutz Hulda was to be my home from 1954 to 1985.

My father had remarried about a year after my mother's death, and then a year later, after I went to live in the kibbutz, he and his wife moved to London. He lived there for about five years. It was in London that my sister Marganita and brother David were born, that he finally—with immense difficulty—learned to drive, and that he gained a Ph.D. from London University for a dissertation on "an unknown manuscript by I. L. Peretz." Periodically we sent each other postcards. Occasionally he sent me copies of his articles. He sometimes sent me books and little objects intended as gentle reminders of my true destiny, such as pens and pen holders, handsome notebooks, and a decorative letter opener.

Every summer he used to come home on a visit, to see how I really was and if kibbutz life really suited me, and at the same time to check on the state of his apartment and how his library was feeling. In a detailed letter my father announced to me at the start of the summer of 1956:

On Wednesday of next week, provided it is not too much trouble for you, I plan to come and visit you in Hulda. I have made inquiries and ascertained that there is a local bus that leaves the Central Bus Station in Tel Aviv daily at 12 noon and arrives at Hulda at approximately 1:20. Now here are my questions: 1. Would you be able to come and meet me at the bus stop? (But if it is a problem for you, if you are busy for example, I can easily ask where you are and find you by myself.) 2. Should I eat something before I board the bus in Tel Aviv, or would it be possible for us to eat together when I reach the kibbutz? Only on condition that it is no trouble for you, naturally. 3. My inquiries show that in the afternoon there is only one bus from Hulda to Rehovot, from where I can take a second bus to Tel Aviv and then a third bus back to Jerusalem. But in that case we would only have some two and a half hours at our disposal. Would that be enough for us? 4. Or, alternatively, perhaps I could stay the night and leave Hulda on the 7 o'clock bus in the morning? That is, if three conditions are met: A. that you would have no difficulty finding me somewhere to stay (a very simple bed or even a mattress would suffice); B. that this would not be viewed askance in the kibbutz; and C. that you yourself feel comfortable with such a relatively long visit. Please let me know at once, either way. 5. What should I bring with me, apart from personal effects? (Towel? Sheets? I have never stayed on a kibbutz before!) Naturally I will give you all the news (there is not much) when we see each other. And I will tell you about my plans, if you are interested. And if you like you can tell me something of your plans. I hope you are in good health and spirits (there is a definite connection between the two!). As for the rest, we'll talk very soon. With love, yours, Dad.

———

That Wednesday I finished school at one, and I asked to be let off the two hours' work we had to do after lunch (I was working in the chicken coop at the time). Nevertheless, after my last class I dashed back to change into dusty blue work clothes and heavy work boots, then I ran to the tractor shed, found the keys of the Massey-Ferguson hidden under the seat cushion, started the engine, and roared up to the bus stop in a cloud of dust a couple of minutes after the Tel Aviv bus got in. My father, whom I had not seen for more than a year, was already there, sheltering his eyes from the sun with his hand and waiting nervously to see where his help would come from. He was dressed—to my utter amazement—in khaki trousers, a light-blue short-sleeved shirt and a kibbutz-type hat, without a trace of a jacket and tie. From a distance he almost looked like one of our "oldies." I imagine he had thought hard before dressing in this way, as a gesture of respect to a culture that he felt some esteem for, even if it did not conform to his own ethos and principles. In one hand he was carrying his battered briefcase, and in the other he held a handkerchief with which he was mopping his brow. I roared up to him, braked almost in front of his nose, and, leaning toward him with one hand on the wheel and the other posed proprietorially on the wing, I said: *Shalom*. He looked up at me with eyes magnified by his glasses so that he looked like a frightened child and hurriedly returned my greeting, although he was not entirely sure who I was. When he did identify me, he looked startled.

After a moment he said:

"Is that you?"

And after another moment:

"You've grown so much. You're looking healthier."

And finally, when he had recovered himself:

"Permit me to remark that it wasn't very safe, that stampede of yours. You might have run me over."

I asked him to wait there, out of the sun, and returned the Massey-Ferguson to the shed: its role in the drama was over. Then I took my father to the dining hall, where we suddenly both became aware that we were the same height now; we were embarrassed, and my father made a joke about it. He felt my muscles curiously, as though he was wondering whether to buy me, and he made another joke about the dark color of my skin, compared to his pale skin: "Little Black Sambo! You're as dark as a Yemenite!"

In the dining hall most of the tables had been cleared; there was only one that was laid, and I served my father some boiled chicken with carrots and potatoes and a bowl of chicken soup with croutons. He ate very carefully, with meticulous table manners, ignoring my own deliberately noisy, peasantlike way of eating. While we drank sweet tea from plastic cups, he struck up a polite conversation with Tsvi Butnik, one of the old-timers, who was sitting at our table. Father was very careful not to touch on any topic that might degenerate into an ideological argument. He inquired which country Tsvi had come from, and when he said he was from Romania, my father's face lit up and he started speaking Romanian, which for some reason Tsvi had trouble understanding from the way my father spoke it. Then he moved on to the beauty of the landscape of the coastal plain, the biblical prophetess Hulda and the Hulda Gates in the Temple, topics that must have seemed to him beyond any risk of disagreement. But before we parted from Tsvi, Father could not resist asking him how they were enjoying having his son here. Was he managing to acclimatize? Tsvi Butnik, who had not the faintest idea whether or how I was acclimatizing in Hulda, said:

"What a question! Very well!"

And Father replied:

"Well, for that I am most grateful to you all."

As we were leaving the dining hall, he remarked to Tsvi without sparing my feelings, like someone collecting a dog from a boarding kennels:

"He was rather out of condition in some ways when he came, and now he seems to be in tip-top form."

I dragged him off for a comprehensive tour of the length and breadth of Hulda. I did not bother to ask if he would rather rest. I did not bother to offer him a cold shower, or show him the toilets. Like a sergeant-major on a base for new recruits I rushed my poor father along, red-faced, panting, mopping his face all the time, from the sheep pens to the chicken coops and the barns, and then on to the carpentry shop and the locksmith's shop and the olive-oil plant at the top of the hill, and all the time I lectured him about the principles of the kibbutz, agricultural economy, the advantages of socialism, the contribution of the kibbutz to Israel's military victories. I didn't spare him a single detail. I was possessed by a kind of vindictive didactic zeal that was too strong to contain. I did not let him utter a word. I rebuffed his attempts to ask questions. I talked and I talked and I talked.

From the children's block I dragged him, with his last remaining strength, to see the veterans' quarters, the clinic, and the schoolrooms, until finally we reached the culture hall and the library, where we found the librarian Sheftel, the father of Nily, who was to become my wife a few years later. Kindhearted, smily Sheftel was sitting in blue work clothes, humming a Hasidic melody under his breath and typing something with two fingers on a wax stencil sheet. Like a dying fish that by some miracle has been thrown back into the water at the last minute, my father, who was gasping from the heat and dust and stifled by the smell of manure, revived: the sight of books and a librarian suddenly brought him back to life, and at once he started pouring forth opinions.

They chatted for ten minutes or so, the two future in-laws, about whatever librarians talk about. Then Sheftel's shyness got the better of him, and Father left him and turned to inspect the layout of the library and all its nooks and crannies, like an alert military attaché observing with a professional eye the maneuvers of a foreign army.

Then we walked around a bit longer, Father and I. We had coffee and cakes in the home of Hanka and Oizer Huldai, who had volunteered to be my adoptive family. Here Father displayed the full extent of his knowledge of Polish literature, and after studying their bookcase for a moment, he even had a lively conversation with them in Polish: he quoted from Julian Tuwim, and Hanka replied by quoting Slowacki; he mentioned Mickiewicz, and they responded with Iwaszkiewicz, he mentioned the name of Rejmont, and they answered with Wyspianski. Father seemed to be treading on tiptoe as he talked to the people in the kibbutz, as though being very careful not to let slip something terrible whose consequences might be irretrievable. He spoke to them with great delicacy, as though he saw their socialism as an incurable disease whose unfortunate carriers did not realize how grave their condition was, and he, the visitor from outside who saw and knew, had to be careful not to say something accidentally that might alert them to the seriousness of their plight.

So he took care to express admiration for what he had seen, he showed polite interest, asked a few questions ("Are your crops doing well?" "How is the livestock doing?"), and reiterated his admiration. He did not drown them in a display of his erudition, nor did he attempt any puns. He kept himself under control. Perhaps he was afraid he might harm me.

But toward evening a sort of melancholy descended upon him, as though his witticisms had run out and his fountain of anecdotes had dried up. He asked if we could sit down together on a shady bench behind the culture hall and wait for the sunset. When the sun was setting, he stopped talking and we sat together side by side in silence. My brown forearm, which already boasted a blond fuzz, rested on the back of the bench not far from his pale arm with its black hair. This time my father did not address me as Your Highness or Your Honor, he did not even behave as though he were responsible for banishing any silence. He looked so awkward and sad that I almost touched his shoulder. But I didn't. I thought he was trying to say something to me, something important and even urgent, and that he was unable to get started. For the first time in my life, my father seemed afraid of me. I would have liked to help him, even to start the conversation instead of him, but I was as inhibited as he was. Eventually he suddenly said:

"Well then."

And I repeated after him:

"Well."

And we fell silent again. I suddenly remembered the vegetable garden we had tried to create together in the concrete-hard ground of our backyard in Kerem Avraham. I remembered the letter opener and the household hammer that were his agricultural equipment. The seedlings he brought from the Pioneering Women's House or the Working Women's Farm and planted in the night behind my back to make up for the failure of the seeds we had sown.

My father brought me a present of two of his own books. On the title page of *The Novella in Hebrew Literature* he had written this dedication: "To my chicken-breeding son, from your (ex-)librarian father," while the inscription he wrote in his *History of Literature* may have contained a veiled reproach expressing his own disappointment: "To my son Amos, in the hope that he will carve out a place for himself in our literature."

We slept in an empty dormitory with two children's beds and a packing chest fitted with a curtain for hanging clothes. We undressed in the dark, and in the dark we talked for ten minutes or so. About the NATO alliance and the Cold War. Then we said good-night and turned our backs to each other. Perhaps, like me, my father found it hard to get to sleep. His breath sounded labored, as if he did not have enough air, or as if he were breathing through his mouth with his teeth clenched. We had not slept in the same room for several years, not since my mother's death, since her last days when she moved into my room and I ran away and slept next to him in the double bed, and the first nights after her death, when he had to come and sleep on a mattress on the floor in my room because I was so terrified.

This time, too, there was a moment of terror. I woke up in a panic in the early hours, imagining in the moonlight that my father's bed was empty and that he had silently pulled up a chair and was sitting by the window, quiet, motionless, his eyes open, staring all night at the moon or counting the passing clouds. My blood froze.

But in fact he was sleeping deeply and peacefully in the bed I had made up for him, and what had looked like someone sitting quietly on the chair with open eyes staring at the moon was not my father or a ghost but his clothes, the khaki trousers and plain blue shirt that he had chosen so thoughtfully so as not to seem superior to the kibbutz members. So as not to hurt their feelings, heaven forbid.

In the early 1960s my father returned to Jerusalem from London with his wife and children. They settled in a suburb called Beit Hakerem. Once more he went to work every day in the National Library, not in the newspaper department but in the bibliographical section, which was started at that time. Now that he finally had a doctorate from London University and a handsome yet modest visiting card attesting to the fact, he made another attempt to obtain a teaching post, if not in the Hebrew University in Jerusalem, his late uncle's fiefdom, then perhaps at least in one of the new universities: Tel Aviv, Haifa, Beersheba. He even tried his luck on one occasion at the religious university, Bar Ilan, though he saw himself as an avowed anticlericalist.

In vain.

In his fifties now, he was too old to become a teaching assistant or a junior lecturer, and not sufficiently well thought of to be in the running for a senior academic position. He was not wanted anywhere. (This was also a time when Professor Joseph Klausner's reputation suffered a dramatic decline. All Uncle Joseph's work on Hebrew literature had by the 1960s begun to seem antiquated and rather naive.) As Agnon writes about one of his characters, in the story "Forever":

> For twenty years Adiel Amzeh conducted research into the secrets of Gumlidatha, which was a great city and the pride of mighty nations until the Gothic hordes descended upon it and made it into a heap of dust and its inhabitants into eternal slaves, and all the years during which he labored he did not show his face to the sages of the universities or to their womenfolk and children; now that he came to ask them for a favor, their eyes radiated such cold anger that their spectacles glinted as they addressed him in these terms: Who are you, sir, we do not know you. His shoulders sagged and he departed from them a disappointed man. Nevertheless, the matter was not without benefit, for he had learned the lesson that if one wishes to be recognized by people, one must be close to them. He was not, however, a man who knew how to be close to people . . .*

My father never learned "how to be close to people," even though he always tried his hardest to do so, by means of jokes and wisecracks, displays of erudition and plays on words, a constant willingness to shoulder any task without counting the cost. He never knew how to flatter, and he did not master the art of attaching oneself to academic power groups and cabals; he was nobody's lackey, and he wrote in praise of people only after their death.

Eventually he seems to have accepted his fate. For another ten years or so he spent his days sitting meekly in a windowless cell in the bibliographical section in the new National Library building in Givat Ram,

*S. Y. Agnon, "Forever," in *Complete Works of S. Y. Agnon*, vol. 8 (Jerusalem/Tel Aviv, 1962), pp. 315–14.

accumulating footnotes. When he came home from work, he sat down at his desk and compiled entries for the *Hebrew Encyclopedia*, which was taking shape at the time. He mainly wrote about Polish and Lithuanian literature. Slowly he converted some chapters of his doctoral dissertation about I. L. Peretz into articles that he published in Hebrew journals, and once or twice he even managed to publish in French. Among the copies that I have here in my home in Arad I have found articles on Saul Tchernikhowsky ("The Poet in His Homeland"), Immanuel of Rome, Longus's *Daphnis and Chloë*, and one entitled "Mendele Studies," which my father dedicated

To the memory of my wife, a woman of discrimination and good taste, who left me on 8 Tebeth 5712*

In 1960, just a few days before Nily and I were married, my father had his first heart attack. It prevented him from attending the ceremony, which took place in Hulda under a canopy held up on the points of four pitchforks. (It was a fixed tradition in Hulda to support the bridal canopy on two rifles and two pitchforks, symbolizing the union of work, defense, and the kibbutz. Nily and I caused quite a scandal by refusing to marry in the shadow of rifles. In the kibbutz assembly Zalman P. called me a "bleeding heart," while Tzvi K. inquired mockingly whether the army unit I was serving in allowed me to go on patrol armed with a pitchfork or a broom.)

My father recovered two or three weeks after the wedding, but his face did not look the same: he was gray and tired. From the mid-1960s on, his liveliness gradually left him. He still got up early in the morning enthusiastic and eager for work, but after lunch his head would start drooping wearily onto his chest, and he would lie down and rest at the end of the afternoon. Then his stamina began to ebb at midday. In the end he only had the first two or three hours of the morning, after which he became gray and faded.

He still liked jokes and wordplay, and he still got pleasure from explaining to me, for example, that the Hebrew word for a faucet, *berez*, was derived from the Modern Greek *vrisi*, a spring, and that Hebrew

*January 6, 1952, in the Roman calendar.

mahsan, a store, like the English word "magazine," came from Arabic *mahzan,* a storeroom, which may be derived from a Semitic root HSN meaning strong. As for the word *balagan,* mess or confusion, he said, which was wrongly considered by many to be a Russian word, it actually came from Persian *balakan,* denoting an unobtrusive veranda where unwanted rags were thrown, from which the English word "balcony" was derived.

He repeated himself more and more. Despite his once-sharp memory, he would now repeat a joke or explanation twice in the same conversation. He was tired and withdrawn and sometimes found it hard to concentrate. In 1968, when my third book, *My Michael,* came out, he read it in a few days and then phoned me in Hulda to say that "there were some quite convincing descriptions, but in the end the book lacks a certain spark of inspiring vision, it lacks a central idea." And when I sent him my story "Late Love," he wrote me a letter in which he expressed his joy that

> your daughters are so splendid, and the main thing is that we shall see each other soon . . . As for the story, it is not bad. Apart from the main character, however, the rest are mere caricatures in my humble opinion. But the main character, unappealing and ridiculous as he is, is alive. A few observations: 1. p. 3, "the mighty river of the galaxies": "Galaxy" comes from Greek *gala,* milk, and means "the milky way." The singular is preferable. To the best of my knowledge there is no basis for the plural. 2. p. 3 (and elsewhere), "Liuba Kaganov*ska*": This is the *Polish* form; in Russian it should be "Kaganov*skaya.*" 3. On p. 7 you have written *viazhma*: it should be *viazma* (z, not zh!).

And so on and so forth, up to observation no. 23, by which time he only had a tiny space left at the end of the page to write "Regards from all of us, Dad."

But a few years later Hayim Toren said to me: "Your father used to run from room to room in the National Library, beaming, and showing us what Gershom Shaked had written about your book *Where the Jackals Howl* and how Avraham Shaanan had praised *Elsewhere, Perhaps.* Once he explained to me angrily how blind Professor Kurzweil had been to cast aspersions on *My Michael.* I believe he even called Agnon especially to complain to him about Kurzweil's review. Your father was proud of you in his own way, even though of course he was too shy to tell you, and he may also have been afraid of making you big-headed."

In the last year of his life his shoulders slumped. He had grim fits of rage, when he would hurl rebukes and accusations at anyone around, and shut himself away in his study, slamming the door behind him. But after five or ten minutes he would come out and apologize for his outburst, blaming it on his poor health, his tiredness, his nerves, and sheepishly asking us to forgive him for saying things that were so unjust and unfair.

He often used the words "just and fair," just as he often said "definitely," "indeed," "undoubtedly," "decidedly," and "from several points of view."

At this time, when my father was unwell, Grandpa Alexander, in his nineties now, was still at the height of his physical blossoming and in full romantic bloom. As pink-faced as a baby, as full of sap as a young bridegroom, he would come and go all day erupting and exclaiming, "*Nu, shto!*" or "Such *paskudniaks!* Such scoundrels! *Zhuliks!* Crooks!" or "*Nu, davai,* forward march! *Khorosho!* Enough, already!" Women flocked to him. Frequently, even in the morning, he would sip a "teeny-weeny brandy," and at once his pink face turned as red as the dawn. If my father and grandfather stood in the garden talking, or paced up and down on the pavement in front of the house, arguing, at least by their body language Grandpa Alexander seemed much younger than his younger son. He was to outlive his older son David and his first grandson Daniel Klausner, who were killed by Germans in Vilna, by four decades, his wife by two, and his remaining son by seven years.

One day, on October 11, 1970, some four months after his sixtieth birthday, my father got up early as usual, long before the rest of the household, shaved, splashed on some toilet water, wetted his hair before brushing it back, ate a roll and butter, drank two glasses of tea, read the newspaper, sighed a few times, glanced at the diary that always lay open on his desk so that he could cross things out when he had done them, put on a jacket and tie, made himself a little shopping list, and drove down the street to Denmark Square, where Beit Hakerem Road meets Herzl Avenue, to buy some items of stationery from the little basement shop where he used to purchase whatever he needed for his desk. He parked and locked the car, went down the half-dozen steps, got in line and even gave up his place politely to an elderly woman, bought everything on his list, joked with the woman who owned the shop about the fact that the word "clip" can be both a noun and a verb, said something to her about the negligence of the city council, paid, counted his change, picked up his bag of shopping, thanked the shopkeeper with a smile, asked her not to forget to pass on his greetings to her dear husband, wished her a good and successful day, greeted two strangers who were in line behind him, turned and walked to the door, and dropped dead of a heart attack. He left his body to science, and I inherited his desk. These pages are being written on it, not tearfully, because my father was fundamentally opposed to tears, particularly in men.

This is what I found written in his desk diary: "*Stationery: 1. Writing pad. 2. Spiral-bound notebook. 3. Envelopes. 4. Paper clips. 5. Ask about cardboard folders.*" All these items, including the folders, were in the shopping bag that his fingers were still clutching. So when I reached my father's home in Jerusalem, after an hour or an hour and a half, I picked up my father's pencil and crossed off the list, just as Father always used to cross things off as soon as he had done them.

57

WHEN I LEFT home and went to live in the kibbutz, at the age of fifteen, I wrote down some resolutions that I set for myself as a test that I absolutely must not fail. If I was really to start a brand-new life, I must start by getting a tan within a fortnight so that I looked just like one of them; I must stop daydreaming once and for all; I must change my last name; I must take two or three cold showers every day; I must absolutely force myself to give up doing that filthy stuff at nights; I must not write any more poems; I must stop chattering; and I must not tell stories: I must appear in my new home as a silent man.

Then I tore up the list. For the first four or five days I actually managed not to do the filthy stuff and not to chatter. When I was asked a question like, Will one blanket be enough? or Do you mind sitting in the corner of the classroom near the window?, I replied with a movement of the head, without any sound. To the questions Was I interested in politics? and Would I consider joining a newspaper-reading circle? I answered *Ahem*. If I was asked about my previous life in Jerusalem, I answered in fewer than ten words, which I held back for a few seconds on purpose, as though I was deep in thought: let them know that I'm a reserved, secretive kind of man, with an inner life. I even succeeded in the matter of the cold showers, although it took an act of heroism to force myself to strip naked in the boys' showers. It even looked as though for the first weeks I could manage to stop writing.

But not reading.

Every day after work and school the kibbutz children went to their parents' homes, while the outside boarders relaxed in the clubroom or played basketball. In the evenings there were various activities—dancing, for instance, or sing-alongs—which I avoided so as not to appear ridiculous. When everyone else had disappeared, I would lie down half naked on the grass in front of our dormitory sunbathing and reading till it was dark. (I was very careful to avoid lying on my bed in the empty room, because there my filthy mind lay in wait for me, swarming with Scheherazade-like fantasies.)

Once or twice a week toward evening I would check the progress of my tan in the mirror before putting on my shirt, then pluck up my courage and go to the veterans' block to drink a glass of fruit juice and eat a slice of cake with my kibbutz "parents" Hanka and Oizer Huldai. This pair of teachers, both originally from Lodz, in Poland, presided year after year over the cultural and educational life of the kibbutz. Hanka, who taught in the primary school, was a buxom, energetic woman, always as taut as a spring, and surrounded by a powerful aura of dedication and cigarette smoke. She shouldered the whole burden of organizing the Jewish festivals, weddings, anniversaries, putting on productions and shaping the local tradition of rustic proletarian life. This tradition, as Hanka envisaged it, was supposed to blend the flavor of the Song of Songs with the olives-and-carobs Hebraic taste of the new biblical tillers of the soil, Hasidic melodies from Eastern Europe with the rough and ready ways of

Polish peasants and other children of nature who drew their purity of mind and mystical joie de vivre straight from the Knut Hamsun-like *Growth of the Soil* under their bare feet.

As for Oizer Huldai, the director of the "continuation classes" or secondary school, he was a hard, wiry man whose Jewish wrinkles were plowed with suffering and ironic sagacity. Occasionally a mischievous sparkle of anarchic playfulness flickered for an instant among these tortured lines. He was lean and angular, short of stature but with devastating steely eyes and a hypnotic presence. He had the gift of the gab and a radioactive sarcasm. He could emanate a warmth of affection that melted anyone who was exposed to it to the point of total submission, but he was also capable of volcanic fits of rage that could put the fear of doomsday into those around him.

Oizer combined the intellectual acumen of a Lithuanian Talmud scholar with a dithyrambic Hasidic ecstasy that could make him suddenly screw up his eyes and burst forth in a rapturous song straining to break free from the trammels of the corporeal world. In a different time or place he might have become a revered Hasidic *rebbe,* a charismatic wonder-worker surrounded by a packed court of entranced admirers. He could have gone a long way if he had chosen to be a politician, a Tribune of the Plebs, leaving behind him a foaming wake of visceral admiration in some and no less visceral hatred in others. But Oizer Huldai had chosen to live as a kibbutz schoolmaster. He was a hard man of uncompromising principles who enjoyed a fight and could be domineering and even tyrannical. He taught, with an equal degree of detailed proficiency and almost erotic zeal, like a wandering preacher of the shtetl, Bible, biology, Baroque music, Renaissance art, rabbinic thought, principles of socialist ideology, ornithology, taxonomy, the recorder, and subjects like "the historic Napoleon and his representation in nineteenth-century European literature and art."

My heart pounded as I entered the one-and-a-half-room bungalow with a little front porch in the northern block at the edge of the veterans' quarters, opposite the alley of cypresses. The walls were adorned with reproductions of pictures by Modigliani and Paul Klee and a precise, almost Japanese, drawing of almond blossoms. Between two plain armchairs a small coffee table bore a tall vase that almost always contained not flowers but a tasteful arrangement of sprigs. The bright, rustic-style curtains were hand-embroidered in a faintly orientalizing pattern, reminiscent of the modified and adapted orientalism of the Hebraic folk songs written by German-Jewish composers seeking to incorporate the captivating Arab or biblical spirit of the Middle East.

Oizer, if he was not pacing briskly up and down the path in front of his house with his hands behind his back and his jutting chin slicing the air in front of him, would be sitting in his corner, smoking, humming to himself, and reading. Or inspecting some flowering plant through his magnifying glass while leafing through his botanical handbook. Hanka, meanwhile, would be striding vigorously around the room with a military gait, straightening a mat, emptying and rinsing an ashtray, her lips pursed, adjusting the bedspread, or cutting ornamental shapes out of colored paper. Dolly would welcome me with a couple of barks before Oizer startled her with a thunderous rebuke: "Shame on you, Dolly! Look who you're barking at! Look who you're daring to raise your voice at!" Or sometimes: "Really! Dolly! I'm shocked! I'm truly shocked at you! How could you?! How come your voice didn't tremble?! You're only letting yourself down with this shameful performance!"

The dog, at the sound of these torrents of prophetic rage, shrank like a deflated balloon, looked around desperately for somewhere to hide her shame, and ended up crawling under the bed.

Hanka Huldai beamed at me and addressed an invisible audience: "Look! Just look who's here! Cup of coffee? Cake? Or some fruit?" No sooner had these options left her lips than, as if a magic wand had been waved, the coffee, cake, and fruit landed on the table. Meekly but with a warm glow inside I politely drank the coffee, ate some fruit, in moderation, and chatted with Hanka and Oizer for a quarter of an hour about such pressing matters as the death penalty, whether human nature was truly good from birth and only corrupted by society, or whether our instincts were innately wicked and only education could improve them to some degree and in certain conditions. The words "decadence," "refinement," "character," "values," and "improvement" often filled that refined room with its white bookshelves, so different from the shelves in my parents' home in Jerusalem, because here the books were divided up by pictures, figurines, a collection of fossils, collages of pressed wildflowers, well-tended potted plants, and in one corner a gramophone with masses of records.

Sometimes the conversation about refinement, corruption, values, liberation, and oppression was accompanied by the mournful sound of a violin or the quiet bleating of a recorder: curly-headed Shai would be standing there playing, his back to us. Or Ron would be whispering to his violin, skinny Ronny who was always called "the little one" by his mother, and whom it was better not to try to talk to, even how-are-you-what's-new, because he was always entrenched in his smiling shyness and only rarely treated you to a short sentence like "Fine" or a longer sentence like "No problem." Almost like the dog Dolly who hid under the bed until her master's rage had subsided.*

Sometimes I found all three Huldai boys, Oizer, Shai, and Ronny, sitting on the grass or on the steps of the front porch, like a klezmer group from the shtetl, stirring the evening air with long-drawn-out, haunting notes on the recorder that gave me a pleasant sense of longing tinged with a pang of sadness for my worthlessness, my otherness, for the fact that no suntan in the world could make me really one of them, I would always be just a beggar at their table, an outsider, a restless little runt from Jerusalem, if not simply a wretched impostor. (I endowed Azaria Gitlin in my book *A Perfect Peace* with some of this feeling.)

At sunset I took my book to Herzl House, the cultural center at the edge of the kibbutz. There was a newspaper room here where on any evening you could find a few of the older bachelors of the kibbutz, gnawing their way through the daily papers and the weeklies, engaging each other in fierce political debates that reminded me a little of the arguments in Kerem Avraham, with Staszek Rudnicki, Mr. Abramski, Mr. Krochmal, Mr. Bar-Yizhar, and Mr. Lemberg. (The "older bachelors of the kibbutz" when I arrived were in their early to mid-forties.)

Behind the newspaper room there was another, almost deserted, room called the study room, which was sometimes used for committee meetings or for various group activities but was mostly unoccupied. In a glass-fronted cabinet stood row upon dreary row of tired, dusty copies

*Ron Huldai has been mayor of Tel Aviv since 1998.

of *Young Worker, Working Woman's Monthly, Field, The Clock,* and *Davar Yearbook.*

This is where I went every evening to read my book until nearly midnight, until my eyelids were stuck together. And this is also where I took up writing again, when no one was looking, feeling ashamed of myself, feeling base and worthless, full of self-loathing: surely I hadn't left Jerusalem for the kibbutz to write poems and stories but to be reborn, to turn my back on the piles of words, to be suntanned to the bone and become an agricultural worker, a tiller of the soil.

But it soon dawned on me in Hulda that even the most agricultural of agricultural workers here read books at night and discussed them all day long. While they picked olives, they debated furiously about Tolstoy, Plekhanov, and Bakunin, about permanent revolution versus revolution in one country, about Gustav Landauer's social democracy and the eternal tension between the values of equality and freedom and between both these and the quest for the brotherhood of man. While they sorted eggs in the hen house, they argued about how to revive the old Jewish holidays for celebration in a rural setting. While they pruned the rows of vines, they disagreed about modern art.

Some of them even wrote modest articles, notwithstanding their dedication to agriculture and their total devotion to manual labor. They wrote mostly about the same topics they debated with each other all day long, but in the pieces they published every fortnight in the local newsletter they occasionally allowed themselves to wax lyrical between one crushing argument and an even more crushing counterargument.

Just as at home.

I had tried to turn my back once and for all on the world of scholarship and debate from which I had come, and I had jumped out of the frying pan into the fire, or "as when a man flees from a lion and meets a bear." Admittedly, here the debaters were more suntanned than those who sat around Uncle Joseph and Aunt Zippora's table, they wore cloth caps, workaday garb, and heavy boots, and instead of bombastic Hebrew with a Russian accent they spoke humorous Hebrew with a juicy flavor of Galician or Bessarabian Yiddish.

Sheftel the librarian, just like Mr. Marcus, the proprietor of the bookshop and lending library on Jonah Street, took pity on my unquenchable thirst for books. He allowed me to borrow as many books as I wanted, far in excess of the library rules that he himself had compiled and typed in eye-catching letters on the kibbutz typewriter and pinned up at various prominent points in his fiefdom, whose vague dusty smell of old glue and seaweed attracted me to it like a wasp to jam.

What did I not read in Hulda in those days? I devoured Kafka, Yigal Mossensohn, Camus, Tolstoy, Moshe Shamir, Chekhov, Natan Shaham, Brenner, Faulkner, Pablo Neruda, Hayyim Guri, Alterman, Amir Gilboa, Leah Goldberg, Shlonsky, O. Hillel, Yizhar, Turgenev, Thomas Mann, Jakob Wassermann, Hemingway, *I, Claudius,* all the volumes of Winston Churchill's *The Second World War,* Bernard Lewis on the Arabs and Islam, Isaac Deutscher on the Soviet Union, Pearl Buck, *The Nuremberg Trials, The Life of Trotsky,* Stefan Zweig, the history of Zionist settlement in the Land of Israel, the origins of the Norse saga, Mark Twain, Knut Hamsun, Greek mythology, *Memoirs of Hadrian,* and Uri Avneri. Everything. Apart from those books that Sheftel did not allow me to read, despite all my entreaties, *The Naked and the Dead,* for example (I think that even after I was married, Sheftel hesitated to let me read Norman Mailer and Henry Miller).

Arch of Triumph, a pacifist novel by Erich Maria Remarque set in the 1930s, opens with a description of a lonely woman leaning on the parapet of a bridge at nighttime, about to end her life by jumping into the river. At the last minute a strange man stops and speaks to her, seizes her arm, saves her life, and spends a torrid night with her. That was my fantasy: that was how I, too, would encounter love. She would be standing alone on a deserted bridge one stormy night, and I would turn up at the last moment to save her from herself, and slay the dragon—not a dragon of flesh and blood like the ones I used to slay by the dozen when I was little, but the inner dragon of despair.

I would slay this inner dragon for the woman I loved and receive my reward from her, and so the fantasy developed in directions that were too sweet and awesome for me to contemplate. It did not occur to me at the time that the desperate woman on the bridge was, again and again, my dead mother. With her despair. Her own dragon.

Or take Hemingway's *For Whom the Bell Tolls,* a book I read four or five times in those years, populated by femmes fatales and tough-looking men who concealed a poetic soul behind their rough exterior. I dreamed that one day I would be like them: a gruff, virile man with the body of a bullfighter and a face full of contempt and sorrow, perhaps a little like the photograph of Hemingway himself. And if I did not manage to be like them someday, at least I would learn to write about such men: courageous men who knew how to scoff and to loathe, or how to punch some bully on the chin if the need arose, who knew precisely the right thing to order in a bar, and what to say to a woman, a rival or a comrade in arms, how to use a gun and how to make love superbly. And also about noble women, vulnerable yet unattainable temptresses, enigmatic, mysterious women, who lavished their favors generously but only on selected men who knew how to mock and despise, drink whisky, punch hard, etc.

The films that were shown every Wednesday in the hall at Herzl House or on a white cloth set up on the lawn outside the dining hall gave firm evidence that the big wide world was peopled mainly by men and women out of the pages of Hemingway or Knut Hamsun. The same picture emerged from the stories told by the red-bereted soldiers of the kibbutz who came home on weekend leave straight from reprisal raids by the famed Unit 101, strong, silent men resplendent in their paratroopers' uniforms, armed with Uzis, "clad in workaday garb, shod in heavy boots, and wet with the dew of Hebrew youth."

I almost gave up in despair: surely to write like Remarque or Hemingway you had to get out of here into the real world, go to places where men were as virile as a fist and women as tender as the night, where bridges spanned wide rivers and the evenings sparkled with the lights of bars where real life really happened. No one who lacked experience of that world could get even half a temporary permit to write stories or novels. The place of a real writer was not here but out there, in the big wide world. Until I got out and lived in a real place, there was not a hope that I could find anything to write about.

A real place: Paris, Madrid, New York, Monte Carlo, the African deserts, or the Scandinavian forests. In a pinch one could write about a country town in Russia or even a Jewish shtetl in Galicia. But here, in the kibbutz, what was there? A hen house, a barn, children's houses, committees, duty rosters, the small supplies store. Tired men and women who got up early every morning for work, argued, showered, drank tea, read a little in bed, and fell asleep exhausted before ten o'clock. Even in

Kerem Avraham where I came from there did not seem to be anything worth writing about. What was there there, apart from dull people leading gray, tawdry lives? Rather like here in Hulda. I had even missed the War of Independence: I was born too late to get more than a few miserable crumbs, filling sandbags, collecting empty bottles, running with messages from the local Civil Defense post to the lookout post on the Slonimskys' roof and back.

True, in the kibbutz library I did discover two or three virile novelists who managed to write almost Hemingway-like stories about kibbutz life: Natan Shaham, Yigal Mossensohn, Moshe Shamir. But they belonged to the generation that had smuggled in immigrants and arms, blown up British headquarters, and repelled the Arab armies; their stories seemed to me swathed in mists of brandy and cigarettes and the smell of gunpowder. And they all lived in Tel Aviv, which was more or less connected to the real world, a city with cafés where young artists sat over a glass of liquor, a city with cabarets, scandals, theaters, and a bohemian life full of forbidden love and helpless passion. Not like Jerusalem or Hulda.

Who had ever seen brandy in Hulda? Who had ever heard of daring women or sublime love here?

If I wanted to write like those writers, I first had to get to London or Milan. But how? Simple farmers from kibbutzim did not suddenly go off to London or Milan to draw inspiration for creative writing. If I wanted to have a chance to get to Paris or Rome, I first had to be famous, I had to write a successful book like one of those writers. But before I could write the successful book, I first had to live in London or New York. A vicious circle.

It was Sherwood Anderson who got me out of the vicious circle and "freed my writing hand." I shall always be grateful to him.

In September 1959 the Popular Library of Am Oved Publishing House brought out a Hebrew translation of Anderson's *Winesburg, Ohio* by Aharon Amir. Before I read this book, I did not know that Winesburg existed and I had never heard of Ohio. Or I may have remembered it vaguely from *Tom Sawyer* and *Huckleberry Finn*. Then this modest book appeared and excited me to the bone: for nearly a whole summer night until half past three in the morning I walked the paths of the kibbutz like a drunken man, talking to myself, trembling like a lovesick swain, singing and skipping, sobbing with awestruck joy and ecstasy: eureka!

At half past three in the morning I put on my work clothes and boots, ran to the tractor shed from which we set out for a field called Mansura to weed the cotton, snatched a hoe from the pile, and till noon I charged along the rows of cotton plants, racing ahead of the others as though I had sprouted wings, dizzy with happiness, running and hoeing and bellowing, running and hoeing and lecturing myself and the hills and the breeze, hoeing and making vows, running, excited and tearful.

The whole of *Winesburg, Ohio* was a string of stories and episodes that grew out of each other and were connected to each other, particularly because they all took place in a single, poor, godforsaken provincial town. It was filled with small-time people: an old carpenter, an absent-minded young man, some hotel owner, and a servant girl. The stories were also connected to each other because the characters slipped from story to story: what had been central characters in one story reappeared as secondary, background characters in another.

The stories in *Winesburg, Ohio* all revolved around trivial, everyday happenings, based on snatches of local gossip or on unfulfilled dreams. An old carpenter and an old writer discuss the raising of some bed, while a dreamy young man by the name of George Willard who works as a cub reporter on the local rag overhears their conversation and thinks his own thoughts. And there is an eccentric old man named Biddlebaum, nicknamed Wing Biddlebaum. And a tall dark-haired woman who for some reason marries a man called Doctor Reefy, but dies a year later. Then there is Abner Groff, the town baker, and Doctor Parcival, a large man with a drooping mouth covered by a yellow mustache, who always wears a dirty white vest out of the pockets of which protrudes a number of black cigars known as stogies, and other similar characters, types who until that night I had supposed had no place in literature, unless it was as background characters who afforded readers at most half a minute of mockery mixed with pity. And here, in *Winesburg, Ohio*, events and people that I was certain were far beneath the dignity of literature, below its acceptability threshold, occupied center stage. There was nothing daring about Sherwood Anderson's women, they were not mysterious temptresses. And his men were not strong, silent types swathed in cigarette smoke and manly grief.

So Sherwood Anderson's stories brought back what I had put behind me when I left Jerusalem, or rather the ground that my feet had trodden all through my childhood and that I had never bothered to bend down and touch. The tawdriness of my parents' life. The faint smell of flour-and-water paste and pickled herring that always wafted around the Krochmals, the couple who mended broken toys and dolls. Teacher Zelda's dingy brown apartment with its peeling veneer cabinet. Mr. Zarchi the writer with a heart complaint, and his wife, who suffered from perpetual migraines. Zerta Abramski's sooty kitchen, and the two birds that Staszek and Mala Rudnicki kept in a cage, the old bald one and the other one made out of a pinecone. And Teacher Isabella Nahlieli's houseful of cats, and her husband Getsel, the open-mouthed cashier in the cooperative shop. And Stakh, Grandma Shlomit's mournful old dog with the melancholy button eyes that they used to stuff full of mothballs and beat cruelly to get rid of the dust, until one day they didn't want him anymore and they wrapped him in old newspaper and threw him in the garbage.

I understood where I had come from: from a dreary tangle of sadness and pretense, of longing, absurdity, inferiority and provincial pomposity, sentimental education and anachronistic ideals, repressed traumas, resignation, and helplessness. Helplessness of the acerbic, domestic variety, where small-time liars pretended to be dangerous terrorists and heroic freedom fighters, where unhappy bookbinders invented formulas for universal salvation, where dentists whispered confidentially to all their neighbors about their protracted personal correspondence with Stalin, where piano teachers, kindergarten teachers, and housewives tossed and turned tearfully at night from stifled yearning for an emotion-laden artistic life, where compulsive writers wrote endless disgruntled letters to the editor of *Davar*, where elderly bakers saw Maimonides and the Baal Shem Tov in their dreams, where nervy, self-righteous trade-union hacks kept an apparatchik's eye on the rest of the local residents, where cashiers at the cinema or the cooperative shop composed poems and pamphlets at night.

Here too, in Kibbutz Hulda, there lived a cowman who was an expert on the anarchist movement in Russia, a teacher who was once put in eighty-fourth place on the list of Labor candidates for the elections to the Second Knesset, and a good-looking needlewoman who was fond of classical music and spent her evenings drawing the landscape of her native village in Bessarabia as she remembered it from before the village was destroyed. There was also an aging bachelor who enjoyed sitting on a bench on his own in the cool of the evening staring at little girls, a truck driver with a pleasant baritone voice who secretly dreamed of being an opera singer, a pair of fiery ideologues who had heaped scorn and contempt on each other, verbally and in print, for the past twenty-five years, a woman who had been the prettiest girl in her class back in Poland and had even appeared once in a silent film, but now sat on a rough stool behind the food store every day in a stained apron, fat, red-faced, and uncared-for, peeling huge piles of vegetables and occasionally wiping her face with her apron—a tear, perspiration, or both.

Winesburg, Ohio taught me what the world according to Chekhov was like even before I encountered Chekhov himself: no longer the world of Dostoevsky, Kafka, or Knut Hamsun, or that of Hemingway or Yigal Mossensohn. No more mysterious women on bridges or men with their collars turned up in smoky bars.

This modest book hit me like a Copernican revolution in reverse. Whereas Copernicus showed that our world is not the center of the universe but just one planet among others in the solar system, Sherwood Anderson opened my eyes to write about what was around me. Thanks to him I suddenly realized that the written world does not depend on Milan or London but always revolves around the hand that is writing, wherever it happens to be writing: where you are is the center of the universe.*

And so I chose myself a corner table in the deserted study room, and here every evening I opened my brown school exercise book on which was

---

*Years later I managed to repay a few pence of my debt. In America the wonderful Sherwood Anderson, friend and contemporary of William Faulkner, was almost forgotten; only in a handful of English departments were his stories still twitching with life. Then one day I received a letter from his publishers (Norton), who were reissuing a collection of his stories, titled *Death in the Woods and Other Stories*, and had heard that I was an admirer: would I kindly write a couple of lines of praise for the back cover of the book? I felt like a humble fiddle player in a restaurant who is suddenly asked if he would let his name be used to promote the music of Bach.

printed "utility" and also "forty pages." Next to it I laid out a ballpoint pen called Globus, a pencil with a rubber tip, printed with the name of the trade-union retail outlets, and a beige plastic cup of tap water.

And this was the center of the universe.

In the newspaper room, on the other side of the thin wall, Moishe Kalker, Alyoshka, and Alec are having a furious argument about Moshe Dayan's speech, which has "thrown a stone through the window of the fifth floor" in the Trade Union Building, where the Central Committee meets. Three men, none of them good-looking or young anymore, arguing among themselves in the singsong tones of yeshiva students. Alec, a vigorous, energetic man, always tries to play the part of the good sport who likes plain talking. His wife, Zushka, is not well, but he mostly spends his evenings with the single men. He is vainly attempting to interpose a sentence between Alyoshka and Moishe Kalker: "Just a moment, you've both got it wrong," or: "Give me just a minute to tell you something that will resolve your dispute."

Alyoshka and Moishe Kalker are both bachelors, and they have opposing views about almost everything, despite which they are hardly ever apart in the evening: they always eat together in the dining hall, take a stroll together afterward, and go to the newspaper room together. Alyoshka, who is as shy as a little boy, is a modest, good-natured man with a smiling round face, but his puzzled eyes are always downcast as though his life itself is something shameful. But when he is arguing, he sometimes heats up and starts flashing sparks, and his eyes almost start out of their sockets. Then his gentle childlike face looks not so much angry as panicky and offended, as though it is his own views that humiliate him.

Moishe Kalker, the electrician, on the other hand, is a thin, wry, sardonic man, and when he is arguing, he screws up his face and gives you an almost salacious wink, he smiles at you with a mischievous, self-satisfied air and winks again with Mephistophelian glee, as if he finally discovered what he has been searching for all these years, the whereabouts of some quagmire that you have managed to hide from the world but that you cannot conceal from those eyes of his, which pierce your disguises and take pleasure in the very swamp they have uncovered inside you: everyone thinks of you as such a reasonable, respectable man, such a positive figure, but both of us know the unsavory truth, even though most of the time you manage to hide it under seventy-seven veils. I can see through everything, chum, including your vile nature, everything is exposed to my gaze and I take nothing but pleasure in it.

Alec gently tries to quell the argument between Alyoshka and Moishe Kalker, but the two opponents gang up on him and both shout at him, because in their view he has not even begun to grasp what the argument is about.

Alyoshka says:

"Excuse me, Alec, but you're simply not praying from the same prayer book as us."

Moishe Kalker says:

"Alec, when everyone else is eating borscht, you're singing the national anthem; when everyone else is fasting for Tisha Be-Av, you're celebrating Purim."

Alec, offended, gets up to go, but the two bachelors, as usual, insist on accompanying him to his door while continuing to debate, and he, as usual, invites them in. Why not, Zushka will be delighted, and we'll drink some tea, but they refuse politely. They always refuse. For years now he has been inviting them both to tea in his home after the newspaper room, Come inside, come in for a while, we'll drink a glass of tea, why not, Zushka will be delighted, but year after year they always refuse his invitation politely. Until one day—

Here, that is how I will write stories.

And because it is night outside and jackals are howling hungrily very close to the perimeter fence, I will put them in the story too. Why not. Let them weep under the windows. And the night watchman who lost his son on a reprisal raid, too. And the gossipy widow who is called the Black Widow behind her back. And the barking dogs and the movement of the cypress trees that are trembling slightly in the breeze in the dark, which makes me think of them as a row of people praying in an undertone.

58

AND THERE WAS a kindergarten or primary school teacher in Hulda, whom I shall call Orna, a hired teacher in her mid-thirties who lived in the end room in one of the old blocks. Every Thursday she left to be with her husband, returning early on Sunday morning. One evening she invited me and a couple of girls in my class to her room, to talk about a book of poems by Natan Alterman, *Stars Outside,* and to listen to Mendelssohn's violin concerto and the Schubert octet. The gramophone stood on a wicker stool in a corner of her room, which also contained a bed, a table, two chairs, an electric coffeepot, a clothes cupboard covered by a flowery curtain, and a shell case that served as a vase and sprouted an arrangement of purple thistles.

Orna had decorated the walls of her room with two reproductions of Gauguin paintings, of plump, sleepy, half-naked Tahitian women, and some pencil drawings of her own that she had framed herself. Perhaps under the influence of Gauguin she had also drawn full-bodied nude women, in lying or reclining positions. All the women, Gauguin's and Orna's, looked sated and slack, as though they had just been pleasured. Yet their inviting poses suggested that they were willing to give plenty more pleasure to anyone who had not had enough yet.

On the bookshelf at the head of Orna's bed I found the *Rubaiyyat* of Omar Khayyam, Camus's *The Plague, Peer Gynt,* Hemingway, Kafka, poems by Alterman, Rahel, Shlonsky, Leah Goldberg, Hayyim Guri, Natan Yonatan and Zerubbabel Gilead, S. Yizhar's short stories, Yigal Mossensohn's *The Way of a Man,* Amir Gilboa's *Early Morning Poems,* O. Hillel's *Noonday Land,* and two books by Rabindranath Tagore. (A few weeks later I bought her his *Fireflies* out of my pocket money, and on the flyleaf I inscribed a soulful dedication that included the word "moved.")

Orna had green eyes, a slender neck, a caressing, melodic voice, small hands and delicate fingers, but her breasts were full and firm and her thighs were strong. Her normally serious, calm face changed the moment she smiled: she had a captivating, almost suggestive smile, as though she could see into the secret recesses of your mind but forgave you. Her armpits were shaved, but unevenly, as though she had shaded one of them with her drawing pencil. When she was standing, she generally placed most of her weight on her left leg, so that she unconsciously arched her right thigh. She liked to air her views about art and inspiration, and she found me a devoted listener.

A few days later I summoned up the courage to arm myself with Walt Whitman's *Leaves of Grass* in Halkin's translation (which I had told her about on the first evening) and knocked on her door in the evening—

alone this time. It was just the way I had run around to Teacher Zelda's flat in Zephaniah Street ten years earlier. Orna was wearing a long dress buttoned down the front with a row of big buttons. The dress was cream-colored, but the electric light, filtered through an orange raffia shade, gave it a reddish hue. When she stood between me and the lamp, the outline of her thighs and her underpants showed through the cloth of her dress. This time she had Grieg's *Peer Gynt* on the gramophone. She sat down next to me on the bed with its Middle Eastern bedspread and explained to me the feelings evoked by each of the movements. As for me, I read to her from *Leaves of Grass* and launched into a conjecture about the influence of Walt Whitman on the poetry of O. Hillel. Orna peeled me tangerines, poured me cold water from an earthenware jug with a muslin cover, placed her hand on my knee to indicate that I should stop talking for a moment, and read me a morbid poem by Uri Zvi Greenberg, not from the collection *Streets of the River,* which my father liked to recite from, but from a slim volume that was unfamiliar to me, with the strange title *Anacreon at the Pole of Sadness.* Then she asked me to tell her a little about myself, and I didn't know what, so I said all sorts of muddled things about the idea of beauty, until Orna placed her hand on the back of my neck and said, That's enough now, shall we sit in silence for a bit? At half past ten I got up, said good-night, and went for a walk under the starlight among the sheds and chicken batteries, full of happiness because Orna had invited me to come back, some evening, the day after tomorrow, even tomorrow.

Within a week or two, word had gone around the kibbutz and I was becoming known as "Orna's new bull calf." She had a number of suitors, or conversational partners, in the kibbutz, but not one of them was barely sixteen and not one of them could recite poems by Natan Alterman and Leah Goldberg by heart like me. Occasionally one of them would be lurking in the dark among the eucalyptus trees in front of her house, waiting for me to leave. Jealously I would hang around by the hedge, and I managed to see him go into the room where she had just made thick Arab coffee for me and called me "unusual," and let me smoke a cigarette with her even though I was still only a little chatterbox from class eleven. I stood there for a quarter of an hour or so, a shadowy figure in the shadows, until they turned the light out.

Once, that autumn, I went to Orna's room at eight o'clock, but she was not there. Because the dim orange light of her lamp poured out through the drawn curtains, and because her door was not locked, I went in and lay down on the rug to wait for her. I waited for a long time, until the voices of men and women on the porches died down to be replaced by night sounds, the howling of jackals, the barking of dogs, the lowing of cows in the distance, the chuk-chuk sound of the sprinklers and choruses of frogs and crickets. Two moths were struggling between the bulb and the orange-red lampshade. The thistles in the shell-case vase cast a kind of crushed shadow on the floor tiles and the rug. The Gauguin women on the walls and Orna's own nude pencil sketches suddenly gave me a vague idea of what her body would look like naked in the shower or on this bed at night after I left, not alone, maybe with Yoav or Mendi, even though she had a husband somewhere who was a regular army officer.

Without getting up from the rug, I raised the curtain in front of her clothes cupboard and I saw white and colored underwear and an almost transparent peach nightgown. As I lay on my back on the rug, my fingers groped to touch this peach of hers and my other hand had to reach out for the mound in my trousers, and my eyes closed and I knew I ought to stop I must stop but not right away just a little more. Finally, right on the edge, I did stop and without taking my fingers off the peach or my hand off the mound in my trousers I opened my eyes and saw that Orna had come back without my noticing and was standing watching me at the edge of the rug, with most of her weight on her left leg so that her right hip was slightly raised and one hand rested on this hip while the other lightly stroked her shoulder under her untied hair. So she stood and looked at me with a warm, mischievous smile on her lips and a laugh in her green eyes as if to say, I know, I know that you'd like to drop dead on the spot, I know that you would be less startled if there was a burglar standing here pointing a submachine gun at you, I know that because of me you're as miserable as can be, but why should you be miserable? Look at me, I'm not at all shocked, so you should stop being miserable.

I was so terrified and helpless that I closed my eyes and pretended to be asleep, so that Orna might imagine that nothing had happened, or that, if it had, it was just in a dream, in which case I was indeed guilty and disgusting, but much less than if I'd done it while I was awake.

Orna said: I've interrupted you. She wasn't laughing when she said it, but she went on to say, I'm sorry, and then she did a complicated kind of dance with her hips and said cheerfully that no, actually she was not exactly sorry, she'd enjoyed watching me, because my face had looked pained and lit up at the same time. Then she did not say anything else, she started to unbutton her dress, from the top button to the waist, and she stood in front of me so I could watch and carry on. But how could I? I closed my eyes hard and then I blinked and then I peeped at her and her happy smile begged me not to be afraid, what's wrong, it's all right, and her firm breasts also seemed to beg me. And then she got down on her knees on the rug to my right and lifted my hand off the mound in my trousers and put her own hand there instead, and then she opened and released and a trail of hard sparks like a thick rain of meteorites ran the whole length of my body, and I closed my eyes again but not before I saw her lift up and stoop, and then she lay on top of me and bent over and took my hands and guided them, there and there, and her lips touched my forehead and they touched my closed eyes, and then she reached down and inserted all of me, and instantly several soft rolls of thunder passed through me followed at once by piercing lightning, and because the hardboard partition was so thin she had to press her hand over my mouth hard and when she thought it was over and took her fingers away to let me breathe, she had to put them back again quickly because it wasn't. And after that she laughed and stroked me like a little boy and she kissed me again on my forehead and wrapped my head in her hair and I with tears in my eyes started to give her shy kisses of gratitude on her face her hair the back of her hand, and I wanted to say something but she didn't let me and covered my mouth again with her hand until I gave up.

After an hour or two she woke me and my body asked her for more, and I was full of shame and embarrassment, but she did not spare me, she whispered to me as though she was smiling, Come, take, and she whispered, Look what a little savage, and her legs were yellowy brown and there was a faint almost invisible golden down on her thighs, and after stifling my spurting cries again with her hand she pulled me to my feet and helped me button up my clothes and poured me some cold water from her earthenware jug with its white muslin cover, and stroked

499

my head and pressed it to her breast and kissed me one last time on the tip of my nose and sent me out into the chill of the thick silence of three o'clock on an autumn morning. But when I came back the next day to say I was sorry, or to pray for a repetition of the miracle, she said: Look at him, he's as white as chalk. What's come over you, here, have a glass of water. And she sat me down on a chair and said something like: Look, there's no harm done, but from now on I want everything to be the way it was before yesterday, OK?

It was hard for me to do what she wanted, and Orna must have felt it too, and so our poetry reading evenings accompanied by strains of Schubert, Grieg, or Brahms on the gramophone faded, and after a couple more times they stopped, and her smile settled on me only from a distance when we passed each other, a smile radiating joy, pride, and affection, not like a benefactor smiling at someone she has given something to, but more like an artist looking at a painting she has made, and even though she has moved on to other paintings, she is still satisfied with her work, proud to be reminded of it and happy to look at it again, from a distance.

And since then I have felt good in the company of women. Like my Grandpa Alexander. And even though over the years I have learned one or two things and I have occasionally gotten my fingers burned, I still have the feeling—just as that evening in Orna's room—that women possess the keys of delight. The expression "she granted him her favors" seems right, seems to hit the mark better than others. Women's favors arouse in me not only desire and wonderment but also a childlike gratitude and a wish to bow down in reverence: I am not worthy of all these marvels; I would be grateful for a single drop, let alone this wide ocean. And always I feel like a beggar at the gate: only a woman has the power to choose whether or not to bestow.

There may also be a vague jealousy of female sexuality: a woman is infinitely richer, gentler, more subtle, like the difference between a fiddle and a drum. Or there may be an echo of a memory from the very beginning of my life: a breast as against a knife. As soon as I came into the world, there was a woman waiting for me, and although I had caused her terrible pain, she repaid me with gentleness, and gave me her breast.

The male sex, on the other hand, was already lying in wait clutching the circumcision knife.

Orna was in her mid-thirties, more than twice my age that night. She scattered a whole river of purple, crimson, and blue and a mass of pearls before a little swine who did not know what to do with them except grab and swallow without chewing, so much I almost choked. A few months later she left her job in the kibbutz. I did not know where she went. Years later I heard that she had divorced and remarried, and for some time she had a regular column in some women's magazine. Not long ago, in America, after a lecture and before the reception, out of a crush of people asking questions and arguing, Orna suddenly shone out at me, green-eyed, lit up, just a little bit older than she was when I was a teen-ager, in a light-colored dress with buttons, her eyes sparkling with her knowing, seductive, compassionate smile, the smile from that night, and as though under a magic spell I stopped in the middle of a sentence, forced my way toward her through the throng, pushing everyone out of my way, even the blank-faced old woman that Orna was pushing in a wheelchair, and I seized her, hugged her, said her name twice, and kissed her warmly on the lips. She gently disengaged herself, and without switch-ing off that smile, which spoke of favors and which made me blush like a teenager, she pointed to the wheelchair and said in English: That's Orna. I'm her daughter. Sadly, my mother can no longer speak. She hardly recognizes people.

59

A WEEK OR so before her death my mother suddenly got much better. A new sleeping pill prescribed by a new doctor worked miracles overnight. She took two pills in the evening, fell asleep fully dressed at half past seven on my bed, which had become her bed, and slept for almost twenty-four hours, until five o'clock the following afternoon, when she got up, took a shower, drank some tea, and must have taken another pill or two, because she fell asleep again at half past seven and slept through till the morning, and when my father got up, shaved, and squeezed two glasses of orange juice and warmed them to room temperature, Mother also got up, put on a housecoat and apron, combed her hair, and made us both a real breakfast, as she used to before she was ill, fried eggs done on both sides, salad, pots of yogurt, and slices of bread that she could cut much finer than Father's "planks of wood," as she affectionately called them.

So there we sat once more at seven o'clock in the morning on the three wicker stools at the kitchen table with its flower-patterned oilcloth, and Mother told us a story, about a rich furrier who had lived in her hometown, Rovno, an urbane Jew who was visited by buyers from as far away as Paris and Rome because of the rare silver fox furs he had that sparkled like frost on a moonlit night.

One fine day this furrier forswore meat and became a vegetarian. He put the whole business, with all its branches, into the hands of his father-in-law and partner. Some time later he built himself a little hut in the forest and went to live there, because he was sorry for all the thousands of foxes that his trappers had killed on his behalf. Eventually the man vanished and was never seen again. And, she said, when my sisters and I wanted to frighten each other, we used to lie on the floor in the dark and take turns telling how the formerly rich furrier now roamed naked through the forest, possibly ill with rabies, uttering bloodcurdling fox howls in the undergrowth, and if anyone was unfortunate enough to encounter the fox-man in the forest, his hair turned instantly white with terror.

My father, who intensely disliked this kind of story, made a face and said:

"I'm sorry, what is that supposed to be? An allegory? A superstition? Some kind of *bubbe-meiseh*?" But he was so pleased to see Mother looking so much better that he added with a dismissive wave of his hand:

"Never mind."

Mother hurried us along so my father would not be late for work and I would not be late for school. At the door, as my father was putting his galoshes on over his shoes and I was getting into my boots, I suddenly let out a long, bloodcurdling howl, which made him jump and shiver with fear, and when he recovered himself, he was just about to hit me when Mother interposed herself between us, pressed me to her breast, and calmed us both down, saying, "That was all because of me. I'm sorry." That was the last time she hugged me.

We left home at about half past seven, Father and I, not saying a word because he was still angry with me over the rabid fox howl. At the front gate he turned left toward Terra Sancta Building and I turned right toward Tachkemoni School.

When I got home from school, I found Mother dressed up in her light skirt with two rows of buttons and her navy jumper. She looked pretty and girlish. Her face looked well, as though all the months of illness had vanished overnight. She told me to put my school satchel down and keep my coat on, she put her coat on too, she had a surprise for me:

"We're not going to have lunch at home today. I've decided to take the two men in my life out to a restaurant for lunch. But your father doesn't know anything about it yet. Shall we surprise him? Let's go for a walk in town, and then we'll go to Terra Sancta Building and drag him out of there by force, like a blinking moth out of a heap of book dust, and then we'll all go and eat somewhere that I'm not even going to tell you, so that you'll have some suspense too."

I didn't recognize my mother. Her voice was not her usual voice, it was solemn and loud, as though she were speaking a part in a school play; it was full of light and warmth when she said, "Let's go for a walk," but it shook a little at the words "blinking moth" and "book dust"; for an instant it made me feel a vague fear, which gave way at once to happiness at the surprise, at Mother's cheerfulness, at the joy of her return to us.

My parents hardly ever ate out, although we often met up with their friends in cafés on Jaffa Road or King George Street.

Once, in 1950 or 1951, when the three of us were staying with the aunts in Tel Aviv, on the last day, literally just before we left for Jerusalem, Father uncharacteristically declared himself to be "Baron Rothschild for the day" and invited everybody, my mother's two sisters with their respective husbands and only sons, out to lunch at Hamozeg Restaurant on Ben Yehuda Street, at the corner of Sholem Aleichem Street. A table was laid for the nine of us. Father sat at the head, between his two sisters-in-law, and seated us in such a way that neither sister sat next to her husband and none of us children sat between his parents: as though he had made up his mind to shuffle all the cards. Uncle Tzvi and Uncle Buma were slightly suspicious, as they could not understand what he was up to, and firmly refused to join him in a glass of beer, as they were not used to drinking. They chose not to speak, and left the floor to my father, who apparently felt that the most urgent and exciting topic must be the Dead Sea Scrolls that had been found in the Judaean desert. So he embarked on a detailed lecture that lasted right through the soup and the main course about the significance of the scrolls that had been found in some caves near Qumran and the possibility that more and more priceless hidden treasures were waiting to be discovered among the ravines in the desert. Eventually Mother, who was sitting between Uncle Tzvi and Uncle Buma, remarked softly:

"Perhaps that's enough for now, Arieh?"

Father understood and left off, and for the rest of the meal the conversation broke up into separate conversations. My older cousin Yigal asked if he could take my younger cousin Ephraim to the nearby beach. After a few more minutes I also decided I had had enough of the company of the grown-ups and left Hamozeg Restaurant to look for the beach.

But who could have imagined that Mother would suddenly decide to take us out for lunch? We had become so accustomed to seeing her sitting day and night staring at the window and not moving. Only a few days earlier I had given up my bedroom for her and run away from her silence to sleep with Father in the double sofa bed. She looked so beautiful and elegant in her navy jersey and light skirt, in her nylon stockings with a seam at the back and her high-heeled shoes, that strange men turned around to look at her. She carried her raincoat over one arm, and linked the other arm in mine as we walked along:

"You'll be my cavalier today."

And as though she had adopted Father's normal role as well, she added:

"A cavalier is a knight: *cheval* is a horse in French, and *chevalier* is a horseman or knight."

Then she said:

"There are lots of women who are attracted to tyrannical men. Like moths to a flame. And there are some women who do not need a hero or even a stormy lover but a friend. Just remember that when you grow up. Steer clear of the tyrant lovers, and try to locate the ones who are looking for a man as a friend, not because they are feeling empty themselves but because they enjoy making you full too. And remember that friendship between a woman and a man is something much more precious and rare than love: love is actually something quite gross and even clumsy compared to friendship. Friendship includes a measure of sensitivity, attentiveness, generosity, and a finely tuned sense of moderation."

"Good," I said, because I wanted her to stop talking about things that had nothing to do with me and talk about something else instead. We hadn't talked for weeks, and it was a pity to waste this walking time that was just hers and mine. As we approached the city center, she slipped her arm through mine again, gave a little laugh, and asked suddenly:

"What would you say to a little brother? Or sister?"

And without waiting for a reply, she added with a sort of jocular sadness, or rather a sadness wrapped in a smile that I could not see but that I heard in her voice as she spoke:

"One day when you get married and have a family of your own, I very much hope you won't take me and your father as an example of what married life ought to be."

I am not just re-creating these words from memory, as I did a dozen lines earlier with her words about love and friendship, because I remember this plea not to take my parents' marriage as an example exactly as it was said to me, word for word. And I remember her smiling voice precisely, too. We were on King George Street, my mother and I, walking arm in arm past the building called Talitha Kumi on our way to Terra Sancta Building to take Father away from his work. The time was one-thirty P.M. A cold wind mixed with sharp drops of rain was blowing from the west. It was strong enough to make passersby close their umbrellas so they would not blow inside out. We did not even attempt to open ours. Arm in arm, Mother and I walked in the rain, past Talitha Kumi and the Frumin Building, which was the temporary home of the Knesset, and then we passed the Hamaalot Building. It was at the beginning of the first week of January 1952. Five or four days before her death.

And as the rain grew heavier, Mother said, with an amused tone to her voice:

"Shall we go to a café for a bit? Our Father won't run away."

We sat for half an hour or so in a German Jewish café at the entrance to Rehavia, in JNF Street, opposite the Jewish Agency Building, where the prime minister's office was also located at the time. Till the rain stopped. Meanwhile, Mother took a little powder compact and a comb from her handbag and repaired the damage to her hair and face. I felt a mixture of emotions: pride at her looks, joy that she was better, responsibility to guard and protect her from some shadow whose existence I could only guess at. In fact I did not guess, I only half sensed a slight strange uneasiness in my skin. The way a child sometimes grasps without really grasping things that are beyond his understanding, senses them and is alarmed without knowing why:

"Are you all right, Mother?"

She ordered a strong black coffee for herself and for me a milky coffee, even though I was never allowed coffee-is-not-for-children, and a chocolate ice cream, even though we all knew perfectly well that ice cream gives you a sore throat, especially on a cold winter day. And before lunch to boot. My sense of responsibility forced me to eat only two or three spoonfuls and to ask my mother if she didn't feel cold sitting here. If she didn't feel tired. Or dizzy. After all she'd only just recovered from an illness. And be careful, Mummy, when you go to the toilet, it's dark and there are two steps. Pride, earnestness, and apprehension filled my heart. As though as long as the two of us were sitting here in Café Rosh-Rehavia, her role was to be a helpless girl who needed a generous friend, and I was her cavalier. Or perhaps her father:

"Are you all right, Mother?"

When we got to Terra Sancta Building, where several departments of the Hebrew University were relocated after the road to the campus on Mount Scopus was blocked in the War of Independence, we asked for the newspaper department and went up the stairs to the second floor. (It was on a winter's day like this that Hannah in *My Michael* slipped on these very stairs, and might have twisted her ankle, and the student Michael Gonen caught her by the elbow and said he liked the word "ankle." Mother and I may well have walked past Michael and Hannah without noticing them. Thirteen years separated the winter's day when I was in Terra Sancta Building with my mother from the winter's day when I began to write *My Michael*.)

When we entered the newspaper department, we saw facing us the director, gentle, kindly Dr. Pfeffermann, who looked up from the pile of papers on his desk, smiled, and beckoned us with both his hands to come in. We saw Father too, from behind. For a long moment we did not recognize him, because he was wearing a gray librarian's coat to protect his clothes from the dust. He was standing on a small stepladder, with his back to us and all his attention concentrated on the big box files he was taking down from a high shelf, leafing through and returning to the shelf, before taking down another and another file, because apparently he could not find what he was looking for.

All this time, kind Dr. Pfeffermann did not make a sound, but sat comfortably in the chair behind his big desk, his smile growing broader and broader in an amused sort of way, and two or three other people who worked in the department stopped working and smirked as they looked at us and at Father's back without saying anything, as though they were sharing in Dr. Pfeffermann's little game and watching with amused curiosity to see when the man would finally notice his visitors, who were standing in the doorway patiently watching his back, the pretty woman's hand resting on the little boy's shoulder.

From where he was standing on the top step of the ladder Father turned to his head of department and said, "Excuse me, Dr. Pfeffermann, I believe there is something—," and suddenly he noticed the director's broad smile—and he may have been alarmed because he could not understand what was making him smile—and Dr. Pfeffermann's eyes guided Father's bespectacled gaze from the desk to the doorway. When he caught sight of us, I believe his face went white. He returned the large box file he was holding with both hands to its place on the top shelf and carefully climbed down the ladder, looked around, and saw that all the other members of staff were smiling, and as though he had no choice, he remembered to smile too, and said to us, "What a surprise! What a great surprise!" and in a quieter voice he asked if everything was all right, if anything had happened, heaven forbid.

His face was as strained and anxious as that of a child who in the middle of a kissing game at a party with his classmates looks up and notices his parents standing sternly in the doorway, and who knows how long they have been standing there quietly watching or what they have seen.

First of all he tried to shoo us outside very gently, with both hands, into the corridor, and looking back he said to the whole department and particularly to Dr. Pfeffermann: "Excuse me for a few minutes?"

But a minute later he changed his mind, stopped edging us out, and pulled us back inside, into the director's office, and started to introduce us, then he remembered and said: "Dr. Pfeffermann, you already know my wife and son." And then he turned us around and formally introduced us to the rest of the staff of the newspaper department with the words: "I'd like you to meet my wife, Fania, and my son Amos. A schoolboy. Twelve and a half years old."

When we were all outside in the corridor, Father asked anxiously, and a little reproachfully:

"What has happened? Are my parents all right? And your parents? Is everyone all right?"

Mother calmed him down. But the issue of the restaurant made him apprehensive: after all, it was not anyone's birthday today. He hesitated, started to say something, changed his mind, and after a moment he said:

"Certainly. Certainly. Why not. We'll go and celebrate your recovery, Fania, or at any rate the distinct and sudden amelioration in your condition. Yes. We must definitely celebrate."

His face as he spoke, however, was anxious rather than festive.

But then my father suddenly cheered up, and fired with enthusiasm he put his arms around both our shoulders, got permission from Dr. Pfeffermann to leave work a little early, said good-bye to his colleagues, took off his gray dust coat, and treated us to a thorough tour of several departments of the library, the basement, the rare manuscripts section, he even showed us the new photocopying machine and explained how it worked, and he introduced us proudly to everyone

we met, as excited as a teenager introducing his famous parents to the staff of his school.

The restaurant was a pleasant, almost empty place tucked away in a narrow side street between Ben Yehuda Street and Shammai or Hillel Street. The rain started again the moment we arrived, which Father took as a good sign, as though it had been waiting for us to get to the restaurant. As though heaven were smiling on us today.

He corrected himself immediately:

"I mean, that is what I would say if I believed in signs, or if I believed that heaven cares at all about us. But heaven is indifferent. Apart from homo sapiens, the whole universe is indifferent. Most people are indifferent too, if it comes to that. I believe indifference is the most salient feature of all reality."

He corrected himself again:

"And anyway, how could I say that heaven was smiling on us when the sky is so dark and lowering and it's raining cats and dogs?"

Mother said:

"No, you two order first because it's my treat today. And I'll be very pleased if you choose the most expensive dishes on the menu."

But the menu was a modest one, in keeping with those years of shortages and austerity. Father and I ordered vegetable soup and chicken rissoles with mashed potato. I conspiratorially refrained from telling Father on the way to Terra Sancta I'd been allowed to taste coffee for the very first time. And to have a chocolate ice cream before my lunch, even though it was winter.

Mother stared at the menu for a long time, then placed it face down on the table, and it was only after Father reminded her again that she finally ordered a bowl of plain boiled rice. Father apologized amiably to the waitress and explained vaguely that Mother was not entirely recovered. While Father and I tucked into our food with gusto, Mother pecked at her rice for a little as though she were forcing herself, then stopped and ordered a cup of strong black coffee.

"Are you all right, Mother?"

The waitress returned with a cup of coffee for my mother and a glass of tea for my father, and she placed in front of me a bowl of quivering yellow jelly. At once Father impatiently took his wallet out of his inside jacket pocket. But Mother insisted on her rights: Put it right back, please. Today you are both my guests. And Father obeyed, not before cracking some forced joke about her inheriting an oil well apparently, which explained her newfound wealth and her extravagance. We waited for the rain to let up. My father and I were sitting facing the kitchen, and Mother's face opposite us was looking between our shoulders at the stubborn rain through the window that gave onto the street. What we spoke about I can't remember, but presumably Father chased away any silence. He may have talked to us about the Christian Church's relations with the Jewish people, or treated us to a survey of the history of the fierce dispute that broke out in the middle of the eighteenth century between Rabbi Jacob Emden and the adherents of Shabbetai Zvi, particularly Rabbi Jonathan Eybeschütz, who was suspected of Sabbataean leanings.

The only other customers in the restaurant that rainy lunchtime were two elderly ladies who were talking in very refined German in low, well-mannered voices. They looked alike, with steely gray hair and birdlike features accentuated by prominent Adam's apples. The elder of the two looked over eighty, and at second glance I supposed that she must be the other one's mother. And I decided that the mother and daughter were both widows, and that they lived together because they had no one else left in the whole wide world. In my mind I dubbed them Mrs. Gertrude and Mrs. Magda, and I tried to imagine their tiny, scrupulously clean apartment, perhaps somewhere in this part of town, roughly opposite the Eden Hotel.

Suddenly one of them, Mrs. Magda, the younger of the two, raised her voice and hurled a single German word at the old woman opposite. She pronounced it with venomous, piercing rage, like a vulture pouncing on its prey, and then she threw her cup against the wall.

In the deeply etched lines on the cheeks of the older woman, whom I had named Gertrude, tears began to run. She wept soundlessly and without screwing up her face. She wept with a straight face. The waitress bent down and silently picked up the pieces of the cup. When she had finished, she disappeared. Not a word was spoken after the shout. The two women went on sitting opposite each other without uttering a sound. They were both very thin, and they both had curly gray hair that started a long way up their foreheads, like a man's receding hairline. The older widow was still weeping silent tears, with no contortion of her face; they drained down to her pointed chin, where they dripped onto her breast like stalactites in a cave. She made no attempt to control her weeping or to dry her tears. Even though her daughter, with a cruel expression on her face, silently held out a neatly ironed white handkerchief. If indeed it was her daughter. She did not withdraw her hand, which lay extended on the table in front of her with the neatly ironed handkerchief on top of it. The whole image was frozen for a long time, as though mother and daughter were just an old, fading sepia photograph in some dusty album. Suddenly I asked:

"Are you all right, Mother?"

That was because my mother, ignoring the rules of etiquette, had turned her chair slightly and was staring fixedly at the two women. At that moment it struck me that my mother's face had turned very pale again, the way it was all the time she was ill. After a little while she said she was very sorry, she was feeling a little tired and wanted to go home and lie down a little. Father nodded, got up, asked the waitress where the nearest phone booth was, and went off to call a taxi. As we left the restaurant, Mother had to lean on Father's arm and shoulder; I held the door open for them, warned them about the step, and opened the door of the taxi for them. When we had got Mother into the backseat, Father went back into the restaurant to settle the bill. She sat up very straight in the taxi, and her brown eyes were wide open. Too wide.

That evening the new doctor was sent for, and when he had left, Father sent for the old one as well. There was no disagreement between them: both doctors prescribed complete rest. Consequently Father put Mother to bed in my bed, which had become her bed, took her a glass of warm milk and honey, and begged her to take a few sips with her new sleeping pills. He asked how many lights she wanted him to leave on. A quarter of an hour later I was sent to peep through the crack in the door, and I saw that she was asleep. She slept till next morning, when she woke up early again and got up to help Father and me with the various morning chores. She made us fried eggs again while I set the table and Father chopped various vegetables very fine for a salad. When it was time for us to go, Father to Terra Sancta Building and me to Tachkemoni School, Mother suddenly decided to go out too, and to walk me to school, because her good friend Lilenka, Lilia Bar-Samkha, lived near Tachkemoni.

Later we discovered that Lilenka had not been at home, so she had gone to see another friend, Fania Weissmann, who had also been a fellow pupil at the Tarbuth gymnasium in Rovno. From Fania Weissmann's she had walked just before midday to the Egged Central Bus Station halfway down Jaffa Road and boarded a bus bound for Tel Aviv, to see her sisters, or perhaps she intended to change buses in Tel Aviv and go on to Haifa and Kiriat Motskin, to her parents' hut. But when my mother got to the Central Bus Station in Tel Aviv, she apparently changed her mind: she had a black coffee in a café and returned to Jerusalem late in the afternoon.

When she got home, she complained of feeling very tired. She took another two or three of the new sleeping pills. Or perhaps she tried going back to the old ones. But that night she could not get to sleep, the migraine came back, and she sat up fully dressed by the window. At two o'clock in the morning my mother decided to do some ironing. She put the light on in my room, which had become her room, set up the ironing board, filled a bottle with water to sprinkle on the clothes, and ironed for several hours, until dawn broke. When she ran out of clothes, she took the bed linen out of the cupboard and ironed it all over again. When she had finished that, she even ironed the bedspread from my bed, but she was so tired or weak that she burned it: the smell of burning woke Father, who woke me too, and the two of us were astonished to see that my mother had ironed every sock, handkerchief, napkin, and tablecloth in the place. We rushed to put out the burning bedspread in the bathroom, and then we sat Mother down in her chair and got down on our knees to remove her shoes: my father took off one, and I took off the other. Then Father asked me to leave the room for a few minutes and kindly close the door behind me. I closed the door, but this time I pressed myself against the door because I wanted to hear. They spoke to each other for half an hour in Russian. Then Father asked me to look after my mother for a few minutes, and he went to the pharmacist's and bought some medicine or syrup, and while he was there, he phoned Uncle Tsvi in his office at Tsahalon Hospital in Jaffa and he also phoned Uncle Buma at work at the Zamenhof clinic in Tel Aviv. After these calls Father and Mother agreed that she should go to Tel Aviv that very morning, Thursday, to stay with one of her sisters, to get some rest and a change of air and atmosphere. She could stay as long as she liked, till Sunday or even till Monday morning, because on Monday afternoon Lilia Bar-Samkha had managed to get her an appointment for a test at Hadassah Hospital in Heneviim Street, an appointment that without Aunt Lilenka's good connections we would have had to wait several months for.

And because Mother was feeling weak and complained of dizziness, Father insisted that this time she should not travel to Tel Aviv alone, but that he would go with her and take her all the way to Auntie Haya and Uncle Tsvi's, and he might even stay the night: if he took the first bus back to Jerusalem the next morning, Friday, he could manage to get to work for a few hours at least. He took no notice of Mother's protests, that there was no need for him to travel with her and miss a day's work, she was perfectly capable of taking the bus to Tel Aviv on her own and finding her sister's house. She wouldn't get lost.

But Father would not hear of it. He was gray and stubborn this time, and he absolutely insisted. I promised him that after school I would go straight to Grandma Shlomit and Grandpa Alexander's in Prague Lane, explain what had happened, and stay overnight with them till Father got back. Only don't be a nuisance to Grandma and Grandpa, help them nicely, clear the table after supper, and offer to take the rubbish out. And do all your homework: don't leave any of it for the weekend. He called me a clever son. He may even have called me young man. And from outside we were joined at that moment by the bird Elise, who trilled her morning snatch of Beethoven for us three or four times with clear, limpid joy: "Ti-da-di-da-di . . ." The bird sang with wonderment, awe, gratitude, exaltation, as though no night had ever ended before, as if this morning was the very first morning in the universe and its light was a wondrous light the like of which had never before burst forth and traversed the wide expanse of darkness.

60

I WAS ABOUT fifteen when I went to Hulda, two and a half years after my mother's death: a paleface among the suntanned, a skinny youth among well-built giants, a tireless chatterbox among the taciturn, a versifier among agricultural laborers. All my new classmates had a healthy mind in a healthy body, only I had a dreamy mind in an almost transparent body. Worse still: I was caught a couple of times sitting in out-of-the-way corners of the kibbutz trying to paint watercolors. Or hiding in the study room behind the newspaper room on the ground floor of Herzl House, scribbling away. A McCarthyite rumor soon went around that I was somehow connected to the Herut party, that I had grown up in a Revisionist family, and I was suspected of having obscure links with the hated demagogue Menachem Begin, the archenemy of the Labor Movement. In short: a twisted upbringing and irreparably screwed-up genes.

The fact that I had come to Hulda because I had rebelled against my father and his family did not help me. I was not given credit for being a renegade from Herut, or for my helpless laughter during Begin's speech at the Edison auditorium: the brave little boy from "The Emperor's New Clothes," of all people, was suspected here in Hulda of being in the pay of the crooked tailors.

In vain did I endeavor to excel in farm work and fail at school. In vain did I grill myself like a steak in my efforts to be as brown as the rest of them. In vain did I show myself in the Current Affairs Discussion Group to be the most socialist socialist in Hulda, if not in the entire working class. Nothing helped me: to them I was some kind of alien, and so my classmates harassed me pitilessly to make me give up my strange ways and become a normal person like them. Once they sent me off on the double to the barn without a flashlight in the middle of the night, to check and report back if any of the cows was in heat and required the urgent attention of the bull. Another time they put me down for toilet-polishing duty. And yet another time I was sent to the children's farm to sex the ducklings. Heaven forbid that I should ever forget where I had come from or have any misapprehensions about where I had landed.

As for me, I took it all with humility, because I knew that the process of getting Jerusalem out of my system rightly entailed suffering, the pangs of rebirth. I considered the practical jokes and the humiliation justified not because I was suffering from some inferiority complex but because I really was inferior. They, those solidly built boys scorched by dust and sun and those proud-walking girls, were the salt of the earth, the lords of creation. As handsome as demigods, as beautiful as the nights in Canaan.

All except for me.

No one was taken in by my suntan: they all knew perfectly well—I knew it myself—that even when my skin was finally tanned a deep brown, I would still be pale on the inside. Though I forced myself to learn how to lay irrigation hoses in the hayfields, drive a tractor, hit the target in the rifle range with the old Czech rifle, I had still not managed to change my spots: through all the camouflage nets I covered myself with you could still see that weak, soft-hearted, loquacious town boy, who fantasized and made up all sorts of strange stories that could never have happened and didn't interest anyone here.

Whereas they seemed to me glorious: those big boys who could score a goal from twenty yards with their left foot, wring a chicken's neck without batting an eyelid, break into the stores at night to pilfer provisions for a midnight feast, and those bold girls who could do a twenty-mile hike carrying a sixty-five-pound pack on their backs and still have enough energy left afterward to dance late into the night with their blue skirts whirling as though the force of gravity had been suspended in their honor, then sit in a circle with us till dawn and sing to us under the starry sky, sing heartrending songs in rounds and canons, sing leaning back to back, sing while radiating an innocent glow that swept you off your feet precisely because it was so innocent, so heavenly, as pure as the angelic choirs.

Yes, indeed: I knew my place. Don't get too big for your boots. Don't get ideas above your station. Don't stick your nose into what's meant for your betters. True, all people are born equal, that is the fundamental principle of kibbutz life, but the field of love belongs to the realm of nature, not to the Egalitarianism Committee. And the field of love belongs to mighty cedars, not to little weeds.

Still, even a cat may look at a king, as the proverb says. So I looked at them all day long, and in bed at night too, when my eyes were closed, I never stopped looking at them, those tousled beauties. And I especially looked at the girls. How I looked. I fixed my feverish eyes on them. Even in my sleep I turned my wistful calf's eyes on them helplessly. Not that I nursed any false hopes: I knew they were not meant for me. Those boys were magnificent stags, and I was a miserable worm. The girls were graceful gazelles, and I was a stray jackal howling behind the fence. And among them—the clapper in the bell—was Nily.

Every one of those girls was as radiant as the sun. Every single one. But Nily—she was always surrounded by a trembling circle of joy. Nily always sang as she walked, on the path, on the lawn, in the wood, between the flower beds, she sang to herself as she walked. And even when she walked without singing, she looked as though she were singing. What's the matter with her, I would ask myself sometimes from the depths of my tormented sixteen years, why is she always singing? What is so good about this world? How, "from such a cruel fate / from poverty and sorrow / from unknown yesterday / and visionless tomorrow," could one draw such joy? Hadn't she heard that "The mountains of Ephraim / have received a new young victim / . . . and just like you we'll offer / for the nation's sake our lives . . ."?

It was a wonder. It exasperated me but fascinated me: like a firefly.

Kibbutz Hulda was surrounded by deep darkness. Every night a black abyss started a couple of yards beyond the yellow circles of light from the lamps along the perimeter fence and continued to the ends of the night, to the distant stars in the sky. Beyond the barbed-wire fence lurked empty fields, deserted orchards, hills without a living soul, plantations abandoned to the night wind, ruins of Arab villages—not like today, when you can see closely packed blocks of lights all around. In the 1950s the night outside Hulda was still totally empty. And in this great emptiness infiltrators, fedayeen, crept through the heart of the night. And in this great emptiness there was the wood on the hill, the olive grove, fields of crops, among which drooling jackals roamed, whose lunatic, blood-curdling howls penetrated our sleep and froze our blood toward dawn.

Even inside the fenced and guarded compound of the kibbutz there was not much light at night. Here and there a weary lamp cast a faint puddle of light, and then thick darkness reigned until the next lamp. Muffled night watchmen did their rounds among the chicken houses and barns, and every half hour or hour the woman on watch duty in the babies' quarters put down her knitting and went on a round from the nursery to the children's houses and back.

We had to make a noise every evening so as not to fall prey to the emptiness and sadness. Every evening we got together and did something noisy, almost wild, until midnight or later, to prevent the darkness from creeping into our rooms and into our bones and snuffing out our souls. We sang, we shouted, we stuffed ourselves, we argued, we swore, we gossiped, we joked, all to drive away the darkness, the silence, and the howling of the jackals. In those days there was no television, no video, no stereo, no Internet or computer games, there weren't even discos and pubs, and there was no disco music; there was only a film at Herzl House or on the main lawn once a week, on Wednesdays.

Every evening we had to get together and try to create some light and fun for ourselves.

Among the older members of the kibbutz, whom we called the oldies even though most of them were barely forty, there were quite a few whose inner light had faded from too many duties, commitments, disappointments, meetings, committees, fruit-picking details, discussions, duty rosters, study days, and party activities, too much culturalism and the friction of daily routines. Quite a few of them were already extinguished. By half past nine or a quarter to ten the faint lights went out one after another in the windows of the little apartments in the veterans' quarters: tomorrow they had to get up at half past four again, to pick fruit, milk the cows, work in the fields or the communal kitchens. On those nights, light was a rare and precious commodity in Hulda.

And Nily was a firefly. More than a firefly: a generator, a whole powerhouse.

She exuded abundant joie de vivre. Her joy was unconfined and unrestrained, it had no rhyme or reason, no grounds or motive, nothing had to happen to make her overflow with jollity. Of course, I sometimes saw her momentarily sad, weeping openly when she thought rightly or wrongly that someone had insulted her, or shamelessly sobbing in a sad film, or crying over a poignant page in a novel. But her sadness was always firmly enclosed within brackets of powerful joy, like hot spring water that no snow or ice could cool because its heat flowed straight from the core of the earth.

It may well have come from her parents. Her mother Riva could hear music in her head even when there was no music around. And

Sheftel, the librarian, would sing as he walked around the kibbutz in his gray T-shirt, he would sing as he worked in the garden, sing as he carried heavy sacks on his back, and when he said to you, "It'll be OK," he always believed it was true, without a shadow of a doubt or reservation: Don't worry, it'll be OK, soon.

As a fifteen- or sixteen-year-old boarder at the kibbutz, I viewed the joy that radiated from Nily the way one looks at a full moon: distant, unattainable, but fascinating and delightful.

Of course, only from a distance. I was unworthy. Such radiant lights as these the likes of me were permitted only to look at. For the last two years of school and during my military service I had a girlfriend outside Hulda, while Nily had a shining string of princely suitors, and around this string she had a second circle of dizzy, bewitched followers, and then a third circle of meek, humble votaries, and a fourth circle of distant admirers, and the fifth and sixth circles included me, a little weed that was occasionally touched unawares by a single extravagant ray, which could not imagine what its passing touch had done.

When I was caught scribbling poems in the shabby back room of the culture building in Hulda, it was finally clear to everyone that no good would ever come of me. Nevertheless, to make the best of a bad job they decided to give me the task of composing appropriate verses for various occasions: festivities, family celebrations, weddings, and festivals, and when necessary, also funeral eulogies and lines for memorial booklets. As for my soulful poems, I managed to hide them (deep in the straw of an old mattress), but sometimes I could not restrain myself and I showed them to Nily.

Why Nily, of all people?

Perhaps I had a need to check which of my poems of darkness would crumble to nothing the moment they were exposed to the rays of the sun, and which if any would survive. To this day Nily is my first reader. When she finds something in a draft that is wrong she says: That just doesn't work. Cross it out. Sit down and write it again. Or: We've heard that before. You've already written it somewhere. No need to repeat yourself. But when she likes something, she looks up from the page and gives me a certain look, and the room gets bigger. And when something sad comes off, she says, that passage makes me cry. Or if it's something funny, she bursts into peals of laughter. After her, my daughters and my son read it: they all have sharp eyes and a good ear. After a while, a few friends will read what I have written, and then the readers, and after them come the literary experts, the scholars, the critics, and the firing squads. But by then I'm not there anymore.

In those years Nily went out with the lords of creation, and I did not set my sights high: if the princess, surrounded by a swarm of suitors, walked past a serf's cottage, at most he might look up at her for a moment, be dazzled, and bless his fortune. Hence the sensation in Hulda, and even in the surrounding villages, when it emerged one day that the sunlight had suddenly lit up the dark side of the moon. That day, in Hulda, the cows laid eggs, wine came out of the ewes' udders, and the eucalyptus trees flowed with milk and honey. Polar bears appeared from behind the sheep shed, the emperor of Japan was seen wandering beside the laundry reciting from the works of A. D. Gordon, the mountains dripped wine, and all the hills melted. The sun stood still for seventy-seven hours above the cypress trees and refused to set. And I went to the empty boys' showers, locked myself in, stood in front of the mirror and asked aloud, Mirror mirror on the wall, tell me, how did this happen? What have I done to deserve it?

61

MY MOTHER was thirty-eight when she died. At the age I am today, I could be her father.

After her funeral, my father and I stayed at home for several days. He did not go to work, and I did not go to school. The door of the apartment was open all day long. We received a constant flow of neighbors, acquaintances, and relations. Kind neighbors volunteered to make sure there were soft drinks for all the visitors, and coffee, cakes, and tea. From time to time I was invited to their homes for a while, for a hot meal. I politely sipped a spoonful of soup and downed half a rissole, then hurried back to Father. I did not want him to be there alone. Not that he was alone. From morning until ten or ten-thirty in the evening our apartment was packed with comforters. The neighbors rustled up some chairs and arranged them in a circle around the walls of the book room. Strange coats were piled on my parents' bed all day long.

Grandpa and Grandma were banished to the other room for most of the day, at Father's request, because he found their presence too much. Grandpa Alexander would suddenly burst into noisy Russian weeping, punctuated by hiccups, while Grandma Shlomit never stopped running back and forth between the visitors and the kitchen, wresting their cups and cake plates from them almost by force, washing them carefully with dish-washing liquid, rinsing them well, drying them, and putting them away in the cupboard. Any teaspoon that was not washed immediately after use seemed to my Grandma Shlomit to be a dangerous agent of the forces that had brought about the disaster.

So my grandfather and grandmother sat in the other room with those of the visitors who had finished sitting with Father and me and yet felt it proper to stay a little longer. Grandpa Alexander, who had loved his daughter-in-law and always dreaded her sadness, walked up and down the room nodding his head with a kind of furious irony and occasionally bursting into loud wails:

"Why? Oh why? So beautiful! So young! And so talented! So gifted! Why? Explain to me why?"

And he stood in a corner with his back to the room, sobbing aloud as though he were hiccuping, his shoulders trembling violently.

Grandma rebuked him:

"Zussia, stop that please. That's enough. Lonya and the child can't stand it when you behave like this. Stop it! Control yourself! Really! Learn a lesson from Lonya and the child, how to behave! Really!"

Grandpa obeyed her instantly, sat down, and buried his face in his hands. But a quarter of an hour later another helpless bellow would burst from his heart:

"So young! So beautiful! Like an angel! So young! So talented! Why?! Explain to me why?!"

My mother's friends came: Lilia Bar-Samkha, Ruchele Engel, Esterka Weiner, Fania Weissmann, and another woman or two, childhood friends from the Tarbuth gymnasium. They sipped tea and talked about their schooldays. They reminisced about my mother as a girl, about their charismatic headmaster, Issachar Reiss, whom all the girls had secretly been in love with, and his rather unsuccessful marriage. They talked about other teachers, too. Then Aunt Lilenka had second thoughts, and asked Father delicately if he minded them talking in this way, reminiscing, telling stories. Would he rather they talked about something else?

But my father, who sat all day long wearily, unshaven, in the chair where my mother had spent her sleepless nights, only nodded apathetically and motioned for them to continue.

Aunt Lilia, Dr. Lilia Bar-Samkha, insisted that she and I must have a heart-to-heart chat, although I tried to get out of it politely. Since the other room was occupied by Grandpa and Grandma and some other members of my father's family, and the kitchen was full of kind neighbors, and Grandma Shlomit was constantly coming and going to scrub every bowl and teaspoon, Aunt Lilia took me by the hand and led me to the bathroom, where she locked the door behind us. It felt strange and rather repellent to be in a locked bathroom with this woman. But Aunt Lilia beamed at me, sat down on the covered toilet seat, and sat me down facing her on the edge of the bath. She eyed me in silence for a minute or two, compassionately, with tears welling in her eyes, and then she started talking, not about my mother or the school in Rovno but about the great power of art and the connection between art and the inner life of the soul. What she was saying made me cringe.

Then, in a different voice, she talked to me about my new grown-up responsibility, to look after my father from now on, to bring some light into his dark life and give him a little satisfaction, for example, by doing especially well at school. Then she went on to talk about my feelings: she had to know what I had thought when I heard what had happened. What were my feelings at that moment? What were my feelings now? To help me, she started to enumerate various names of feelings, as though inviting me to make my choice, or cross out the ones that did not apply. Sadness? Fear? Anxiety? Longing? A little anger perhaps? Surprise? Guilt? Because you have probably heard or read that guilt feelings can sometimes arise in such cases? No? And what about a feeling of disbelief? Pain? Or a refusal to accept the new reality?

I said sorry nicely and got up to go. I was terrified for a moment that when she locked the door, she might have hidden the key in her pocket and I wouldn't be allowed to leave until I had answered all her questions one by one. But the key was still in the keyhole. As I left, I could still hear her concerned voice behind me:

"Perhaps it is still a little too soon for you to have this conversation. Just remember that the moment you decide you are ready for it, don't hesitate for a moment, come and see me, and we'll talk. I believe that Fania, your poor mother, very much wanted a deep bond to continue between you and me."

I fled.

Three or four well-known figures of the Herut party in Jerusalem were sitting with my father; they and their wives had met in a café beforehand and come together, like a small deputation, to offer us their condolences. They had previously decided to try to distract my father with political talk: at that time the Knesset was about to debate the reparations agreement that Prime Minister Ben-Gurion had signed with Chancellor Adenauer of West Germany, an agreement that the Herut party saw as a disgrace and an abomination, a slur on the memory of the victims of Nazism and an ineradicable blot on the conscience of the young state. Some of our comforters maintained the view that it was our duty to thwart this agreement at any cost, even if it meant bloodshed.

My father hardly participated in the conversation, he merely nodded a couple of times, but I was fired with the courage to say a few sentences to these Jerusalem grandees, as a way of washing away some of the distress I felt after the conversation in the bathroom: Aunt Lilia's words grated on me like chalk on a blackboard. For several years afterward my face used to twitch involuntarily whenever I remembered that conversation in the bathroom. To this day when I recall it, it feels like biting into rotten fruit.

Then the Herut leaders went to the other room to bring comfort to Grandpa Alexander with their indignation over the reparations agreement. I went with them because I wanted to go on taking part in the discussion of plans for the coup aimed at foiling the abominable agreement with our murderers and finally toppling Ben-Gurion's red regime. And there was another reason that I accompanied them: Aunt Lilia had arrived from the bathroom and was advising my father to take some excellent sedative pill that she had brought with her, it would make him feel much better. Father made a face and refused. For once he even forgot to thank her.

The Torens came, and the Lembergs and the Rosendorffs and the Bar-Yizhars, Getsel and Isabella Nahlieli from Children's Realm came, and other acquaintances and neighbors from Kerem Avraham, Uncle Dudek, the chief of police, came with his pleasant wife Tosia, Dr. Pfeffermann came with the staff of the newspaper department, and other librarians came from all the departments of the National Library. Staszek and Mala Rudnicki came, and various scholars and booksellers, and Mr. Joshua Czeczik, Father's publisher from Tel Aviv. Even Uncle Joseph, Professor Klausner, appeared one evening, very upset and emotional; he silently shed an old man's tear on Father's shoulder and murmured some formal words of condolence. Our acquaintances from the cafés came, and the Jerusalem writers, Yehuda Yaari, Shraga Kadari, Dov Kimche and Yitzhak Shenhar, and Professor and Mrs. Halkin, and Professor Bennet, the expert on Islamic history, and Professor Yitzhak (Fritz) Baer, the expert on the history of the Jews in Christian Spain. Three or four younger lecturers, rising stars in the firmament of the university, also came. Two of my teachers from Tachkemoni School came, and some of my classmates, and the Krochmals, Tosia and Gustav Krochmal, the broken toy and doll repairers, whose little shop had been renamed the Dolls' Hospital. Zerta and Yakov-David Abramski came: the one whose eldest son Yonatan had been killed at the end of the War of Independence by a Jordanian sniper. The sniper's bullet hit twelve-year-old Yoni in the forehead when he was playing in his yard that Saturday morning years ago, at the very moment his parents were sitting with us, sipping tea and eating cake. And the ambulance went down our street hooting on its way to pick him up and again a few minutes later as it drove past with its siren wailing on its way to the hospital, and when my mother heard the siren she said, We spend all our time making plans, yet there's someone out there in the dark laughing at us and all our plans. And Zerta Abramski said, That's right, life is like that, and yet people will always go on making plans because otherwise despair would take over. It was ten minutes later that a neighbor came and gently called the Abramskis over and told them less than the truth, and they were in such a hurry to run after him that Aunt Zerta left her handbag behind with her wallet and her papers inside. When we went to see them the next day to offer condolences, Father silently handed her the handbag after embracing her and Mr. Abramski. Now they tearfully embraced my father and me but they didn't bring us a handbag.

My father suppressed his tears. In any case, he never wept in my presence. He firmly believed that tears were fitting for women but not for men. He sat all day long in Mother's old chair, his face growing darker day by day since as a mark of mourning he did not shave, greeting his visitors with a nod and nodding to them again when they left. He barely spoke during those days, as though my mother's death had cured him of his habit of breaking any silence. Now he sat silently for days on end, letting others do the talking, about my mother, about books and book reviews, about the twists and turns of politics. I tried to sit opposite him: I hardly took my eyes off him all day long. And whenever I passed close to his chair, he patted me wearily once or twice on the arm or back. But we did not speak to each other.

My mother's parents and her sisters did not come to Jerusalem during the mourning period and the days that followed: they sat and mourned separately, in Auntie Haya's apartment in Tel Aviv, because they blamed my father for what had happened and couldn't bring themselves to see him. Even at the funeral, I was told, my father walked with his parents while my mother's sisters walked with their parents and not a word was exchanged between the two camps.

I was not present at my mother's funeral: Aunt Lilia, Leah Kalish-Bar-Kamcha, who was considered our expert on feelings in general and children's upbringing in particular, feared the burial might have an adverse effect on the child's psyche. And from then on the Mussmans never set foot in our home in Jerusalem, and Father, for his part, did not go and see them or make any contact, because he was very hurt by their suspicions. For years I was the go-between. During the first week I even carried oblique messages concerning my mother's personal effects, and a couple of times I conveyed the effects themselves. In the years that followed, the aunts used to interrogate me cautiously about daily life at home, about my father's and grandparents' health, about my father's new wife and even about our material circumstances, but they insisted on cutting my answers short with: I'm not interested in knowing. Or: That'll do; what we've already heard is more than enough.

My father, too, sometimes asked me for a hint or two about the aunts, their families or my grandparents in Kiriat Motskin, but two minutes after I began to reply, his face turned yellow with pain and he gestured to me to stop and not go into further details. When my Grandma Shlomit died, in 1958, my aunts and my grandparents on my mother's side asked me to convey their condolences to Grandpa Alexander, whom the Mussmans considered the only member of the Klausner family who had a really warm heart. And fifteen years later, when I told Grandpa Alexander about the death of my other grandfather, he wrung his hands and then covered his ears with his hands and raised his voice, more in anger than in sorrow, and said: "*Bozhe moi!* He was such a young man still! A simple man, but an interesting one! Deep! You now, tell them all that my heart weeps for him! Make sure you tell them with these very words: Alexander Klausner's heart weeps at the untimely death of dear Mr. Hertz Mussman!"

Even after the mourning period was over, when the apartment was finally empty and my father and I locked the door and were alone together, we hardly talked. Except about the most essential things. The kitchen door is jammed. There was no mail today. The bathroom's free but there's no toilet paper. We also avoided meeting each other's eyes, as though we were ashamed of something we had both done that it would have been better if we hadn't, and at the very least it would have been better if we could have been ashamed quietly without a partner who knew everything about you that you knew about him.

We never talked about my mother. Not a single word. Or about ourselves. Or about anything that had the least thing to do with emotions. We talked about the Cold War. We talked about the assassination of King Abdullah and the threat of a second round of fighting. My father explained to me the difference between a symbol, a parable, and an allegory, and the difference between a saga and a legend. He also gave me a clear and accurate account of the difference between liberalism and social democracy. And every morning, even on these gray, damp, misty January mornings, at first light there always came from the soggy bare branches outside the pitiful chirping of the frozen bird, Elise: "Ti-da-di-da-di—," but in the depth of this winter it did not repeat the song several times as it had done in the summer, but said what it had to say once, and fell silent. I have hardly ever spoken about my mother till now, till I came to write these pages. Not with my father, or my wife, or my children or with anybody else. After my father died, I hardly spoke about him either. As if I were a foundling.

During the first weeks after the disaster the house went to the dogs. Neither my father nor I cleared away the leftover food from the oilcloth-covered kitchen table, we did not touch the dishes that we submerged in the murky water in the sink, until there were no clean ones left and we had to fish out a couple of plates, forks, and knives, and rinse them under the faucet, and after we had used them, we put them back on the pile of dishes that was beginning to stink. The garbage can overflowed and smelled because neither of us wanted to empty it. We threw our clothes over the nearest chair, and if we needed a chair, we simply threw anything that was on it to the floor, which was thick with books and papers and fruit peel and dirty handkerchiefs and yellowing newspapers. Gray coils of dust drifted around the floors. Even when the toilet was getting blocked, neither of us lifted a finger. Piles of dirty laundry overflowed from the bathroom into the corridor, where it met a jumble of empty bottles, cardboard boxes, used envelopes, and wrapping paper. (This was more or less how I described Fima's apartment in *Fima*.)

And yet, in all the chaos, a deep mutual consideration prevailed in our silent home. My father finally gave up insisting on my bedtime and left me to decide when to turn my light out. As for me, when I came home from school to the empty, neglected apartment, I made myself something simple to eat: a hard-boiled egg, cheese, bread, vegetables, and some sardines or tuna from a can. And I made a couple of slices of bread with egg and tomato for my father too, even though he had generally had something to eat earlier in the canteen at Terra Sancta.

Despite the silence and the shame, Father and I were close at that time, as we had been the previous winter, a year and a month before, when Mother's condition took a turn for the worse and he and I were like a pair of stretcher bearers carrying an injured person up a steep slope.

This time we were carrying each other.

All through that winter we never opened a window. As though we were afraid to lose the special smell of the apartment. As though we were comfortable with each other's smells. Even when they got very thick and concentrated. Dark half moons appeared under Father's eyes like those my mother had when she couldn't sleep. I would wake up in the night in a panic and peep into his room to see if he was sitting up like her, staring sadly at the window. But my father did not sit at the window staring at the clouds or the moon. He bought himself a little Phillips wireless set with a green eye and put it by his bed, and he lay in the dark listening to everything. At midnight, when the Voice of Israel stopped broadcasting, to be replaced by a monotonous buzz, he reached out and tuned to the BBC World Service from London.

Late one afternoon Grandma Shlomit suddenly appeared, carrying two dishes of food she had cooked for us. The moment I opened the door she was appalled at what met her eyes and by the stench that assailed her nostrils. Almost without a word she turned tail and ran. But by seven o'clock next morning she was back, armed this time with two cleaning women and a whole arsenal of cleaning materials and disinfectants. She set up her tactical command HQ on a bench in the yard opposite the front door, from where she directed the mopping-up operations, which lasted for three days.

So the apartment was put to rights, and my father and I stopped neglecting the household chores. One of the cleaners was hired to come in twice a week. The apartment was thoroughly aired and cleaned, and a couple of months later we even decided to have it painted.

But ever since those weeks of chaos I have been subject to a compulsive desire for tidiness that makes the lives of those around me a misery. Any scrap of paper that is not in its right place, any unfolded newspaper or unwashed cup threatens my peace of mind, if not my sanity. To this day, like some kind of secret policeman or like Frankenstein's monster, or with something of my Grandma Shlomit's obsession with cleanliness and tidiness, I scour the house every few hours, ruthlessly banishing to the depths of Siberia any poor object that has the misfortune to find itself on a surface, or hiding away in some godforsaken drawer any letter or leaflet that someone has left on the table because he or she was called to the phone, and emptying out, rinsing, and putting facedown in the dishwasher a cup of coffee that one of my victims has left to cool down a bit, mercilessly clearing away keys, spectacles, notes, medicines, a piece of cake that someone has unwisely taken his eyes off for a moment: everything falls into the jaws of this greedy monster so that there will be some order at last in this topsy-turvy house. So that it doesn't so much as hint at the way my father and I lived at that time when we tacitly agreed that we should sit down among the ashes and scrape ourselves with a potsherd, just so she should know.

Then one day my father made a furious assault on Mother's drawers and her side of their closet: the only things that survived his wrath were a few items that her sisters and parents had requested as keepsakes, via me, and in fact on one of my trips to Tel Aviv I took them with me in a cardboard box tied up with a stout length of cord. All the rest—dresses, skirts, shoes, underwear, notebooks, stockings, head scarves, neckerchiefs, and even envelopes full of photographs from her childhood—he stuffed into waterproof sacks that he had brought from the National Library. I accompanied him like a puppy from room to room and watched his frenzy of activity; I neither helped nor hindered him. Soundlessly I watched my father furiously pull out the drawer of her bedside table and empty all the contents, cheap jewelry, notebooks, pill boxes, a book, a handkerchief, an eyeshade, and some loose change, into one of his sacks. I did not say a word. And my mother's powder compact and hairbrush and her toilet things and her toothbrush. Everything. I stood hushed and terrified, leaning on the doorpost and watching my father tear her blue dressing gown off the hook in the bathroom with a ripping sound and cram it into one of the sacks. Was this the way Christian neighbors stood and stared, aghast, not knowing their own hearts because of the conflicting emotions, as their Jewish neighbors were taken away by force and crammed into cattle trucks? Where he took the sacks, whether he gave it all away to the poor people in the transit camps or the victims of that winter's floods, he never told me. By evening not a trace of her was left. But a year later, when my father's new wife was settling in, a packet of six plain hairpins appeared that had somehow managed to survive hidden for a whole year in the narrow gap between the bedside table and the side of the closet. My father pursed his lips and threw this away too.

A few weeks after the cleaners came in and the apartment was purged, my father and I gradually went back to holding a sort of daily staff meeting in the kitchen each evening. I began, telling him briefly about my day at school. He told me about an interesting conversation he had had that day, standing between the bookshelves, with Professor Goitein or Doctor Rotenstreich. We exchanged views about the political situation, about Begin and Ben-Gurion or about General Neguib's military coup in Egypt. We hung up a card in the kitchen again and wrote down, in our handwriting that was no longer similar, what we had to buy at the grocer's or the greengrocer's, and that we both had to go to have our hair cut on Monday evening, or to buy a little present for Aunt Lilenka for her new diploma or for Grandma Shlomit, whose age was a closely guarded secret, for her birthday.

After a few more months my father resumed his habit of polishing his shoes till they shone when the electric light hit them, shaving at seven o'clock in the evening, putting on a starched shirt and a silk tie, dampening his hair before he brushed it back, splashing himself with aftershave, and going out "to chat with his friends" or "for a discussion about work."

I was left alone at home, to read, dream, write and rewrite. Or I would go out and roam the wadis, checking the state of the fences around the no-man's-land and minefields along the ceasefire line that divided Jerusalem between Israel and Jordan. As I walked in the dark, I hummed to myself, Ti-da-di-da-di. I no longer aspired "to die or to conquer the mountain." I wanted everything to stop. Or at least I wanted to leave home and leave Jerusalem for good and go and live in a kibbutz: to leave all the books and feelings behind me and live a simple village life, a life of brotherhood and manual labor.

62

MY MOTHER ended her life at her sister's apartment in Ben Yehuda Street, Tel Aviv, in the night between Saturday and Sunday, January 6, 1952. There was a hysterical debate going on in the country at the time about whether Israel should demand and accept reparations from Germany on account of property of Jews murdered during the Hitler period. Some people agreed with David Ben-Gurion that the murderers must not be allowed to inherit the looted Jewish property, and that the monetary value should definitely be repaid in full to Israel to help with the absorption of the survivors. Others, headed by the opposition leader Menachem Begin, declared with pain and anger that it was immoral and a desecration of the memory of those who had been killed that the victims' own state should sell easy absolution to the Germans in exchange for tainted lucre.

It rained heavily almost without a break all over Israel through that winter of 1951–52. The River Ayyalon, Wadi Musrara, burst its banks and flooded the Montefiore district of Tel Aviv and threatened to flood other districts as well. Heavy flooding did extensive damage to the transit camps with their tents and their corrugated iron or canvas huts, which were crowded with hundreds of thousands of Jewish refugees who had fled from Arab lands leaving everything behind them and refugees from Hitler from Eastern Europe and the Balkans. Some transit camps were cut off by the floods, and there was a risk of starvation and epidemic. The state of Israel was less than four years old, and a little over a million citizens lived in it; almost a third of them were penniless refugees. Because of the heavy cost of defense and the absorption of immigrants and because of an inflated bureaucracy and clumsy management, the coffers of the state were empty, and the education, health, and welfare services were on the verge of collapse. At the beginning of that week, David Horowitz, the director-general of the Treasury, had flown to America on an emergency mission to obtain short-term credit to the tune of ten million dollars in a matter of a day or two so as to stave off disaster. My father and I discussed all these subjects when he got back from Tel Aviv. He had taken my mother to Auntie Haya and Uncle Tsvi's on Thursday and spent the night there, and when he got back on Friday, he learned from Grandma Shlomit and Grandpa Alexander that I seemed to have caught a cold but had nevertheless insisted on getting up and going to school. Grandma suggested we stay and celebrate Sabbath with them: she thought we both looked as though we were starting some sort of virus. But we opted to go home. On the way home from their house in Prague Lane, Father saw fit to report to me earnestly, like one grown-up to another, that when they got to Auntie Haya's, my mother's state of mind had immediately improved: the four of them had gone out together on Thursday night to a little café on the corner of Dizengoff Street and Jabotinsky Street, a stone's throw from Haya and Tsvi's. They had intended to stay out for only a short while, but they had ended up sitting there till closing time, talking about people and books. Tsvi had recounted all sorts of interesting stories about hospital life, and Mother had looked well and joined in the conversation, and that night she had slept for several hours, though she had apparently woken up in the small hours of the morning and gone to sit in the kitchen so as not to disturb anyone. Early in the morning when my father had left to get back to Jerusalem in time to put in a few hours at work, my mother had promised that there was no need to worry about her, the worst was over, and she had asked him to take very good care of the child: when they had left for Tel Aviv the previous day, she had had the impression that he was coming down with a cold.

Father said:

"Your mother was quite right about the cold, so let's hope she was right about the worst being over, too."

I said:

"I've only got a little bit of homework left. When I've finished, would you have time to stick some of the new stamps in the album?"

On Saturday, it rained for most of the day. It rained and it rained. It didn't stop. My father and I spent a few hours poring over our stamp collection. Our heads sometimes touched. We compared each stamp with its picture in the big fat British catalogue, and Father found the right place for it in the album, either in a set we had already started or on a new page. On Saturday afternoon we both lay down and rested, he in his bed and I back in my room, in the bed that had become my mother's sick bed recently. After our rest we were invited to Grandpa and Grandma's again, to eat gefilte fish in a golden sauce surrounded with slices of boiled carrot, but since by now we both had severe colds and coughs and it was still pouring with rain outside, we decided that we would be better off staying at home. The sky was so overcast that we had to turn the lights on at four o'clock. Father sat at his desk and worked for a couple of hours on an article for which he had already extended the deadline twice, with his glasses slipping down his nose, bent over his books and little cards. While he worked, I lay on the rug at his feet reading a book. Later we played checkers: he beat me once, I won once, and the third time we drew. It is hard to say if he meant it to turn out like that or if it just happened. We had a light snack and drank some hot tea and we both took a couple of Palgin or APC tablets from Mother's collection of pills. To help us fight our colds. Then I went to bed, and we both got up at six o'clock, and at seven Tsippi the pharmacist's daughter came over to tell us that we'd just had a phone call from Tel Aviv and they would ring again in ten minutes, Mr. Klausner was to go to the pharmacy immediately, and her father had said to say it was rather urgent please.

Auntie Haya told me that on Friday Uncle Tsvi, who was the administrative director of Tsahalon Hospital, had called in a specialist from the hospital, who had volunteered to come over after work. The specialist examined my mother thoroughly, unhurriedly, pausing to chat with her and continuing his examination, and when he had finished, he had said that she was tired, tense, and a little run down. Apart from the insomnia he could not find anything specifically wrong with her. Often the psyche is the worst enemy of the body: it doesn't let the body live, it doesn't let it enjoy itself when it wants to or get the rest it is begging for. If only we could extract it the way we extract the tonsils or the appendix, we would all live healthy and contented lives till we were a thousand years old. He thought that there was not much point now in having the tests at the Hadassah Hospital in Jerusalem on Monday, but they couldn't do any harm. He recommended complete rest and avoidance of any excitement. It was particularly important, he said, that the patient should get out of the house for at least an hour or even two hours every day, she could even dress up warmly and take an umbrella and simply walk around town, looking at shop windows or at handsome young men, it didn't matter what, the crucial thing was to get some fresh air. He also wrote her a prescription for some new, very strong sleeping pills that were apparently even newer and stronger than the new pills that the new doctor in Jerusalem had prescribed. Uncle Tsvi hurried out to the duty pharmacist's in Bugrashov Street to buy the pills, because it was Friday afternoon and all the other pharmacists had already closed for Sabbath.

On Friday night Auntie Sonia and Uncle Buma had come over with a tin food container with a handle, soup for everyone and fruit compote for dessert. The three sisters had crowded into the little kitchen for an hour or so preparing dinner. Auntie Sonia had suggested that my mother should go and stay with her, in Wessely Street, to give Haya a break, but Auntie Haya wouldn't hear of it, and even told her younger sister off for this strange suggestion. Auntie Sonia was offended, but said nothing. At the Sabbath dinner table the atmosphere was a little dampened by Sonia's umbrage. My mother seems to have taken on my father's usual role and tried to keep the conversation going somehow. At the end of the evening she complained of feeling tired and apologized to Tsvi and Haya for not having the strength to help them clear away and wash up. She took the new tablets that the Tel Aviv specialist had prescribed, and to be on the safe side she also took some of the tablets that the Jerusalem specialist had given her. She fell into a deep sleep at ten o'clock but woke up a couple of hours later and made herself a strong cup of coffee in the kitchen, and spent the rest of the night sitting on a kitchen stool. Just before the War of Independence the room where my mother was staying had been let to the head of Haganah intelligence, Yigael Yadin, who later, when the state was established, became Major-General Yigael Yadin, deputy chief of staff and head of operations of the newly formed Israeli army, but he continued to rent that room. Consequently the kitchen where my mother sat up that night, and the previous night too, was a historic kitchen, because during the war several informal meetings were held there that crucially shaped the course of the conflict. There is no way of knowing whether my mother thought about this in the course of that night, between one strong coffee and the next, but if she did, it is doubtful that she found it of interest.

––––––––

On Saturday morning she told Haya and Tsvi that she had decided to go for a walk and look at handsome young men, as per the doctor's instructions. She borrowed an umbrella and a pair of lined rubber boots from her sister and went for a walk in the rain. There cannot have been many people in the streets of north Tel Aviv that wet and windy Saturday morning. That morning, January 5, 1952, the temperature in Tel Aviv was five or six degrees Celsius. My mother left her sister's apartment in 175 Ben Yehuda Street at eight or eight-thirty. She may have crossed Ben Yehuda Street and turned left, or northward, toward Nordau Boulevard. She hardly encountered any shop windows on her walk, apart from the unlit window of the Tnuva Dairy where a greenish poster was fixed to the inside of the glass with four strips of brown sticky paper, showing a plump village girl against a background of verdant meadows, and above her head, against the bright blue sky, a cheery legend declared: "Milk every morning and milk every night will give you a life of good health and delight." There were still many vacant lots, the remains of the sand dunes, between the buildings in Ben Yehuda Street that winter, full of dead thistles and squills densely covered with white snails as well as scrap iron and rain-soaked rubbish. My mother saw the rows of plastered buildings that already, three or four years after they were erected, showed signs of dilapidation: peeling paint, crumbling plaster turning green with mildew, iron railings rusting in the salt sea air, balconies closed in with hardboard and plywood as in a refugee camp, shop signs that had come off their hinges, trees that were dying in the gardens for want of loving care, run-down storage sheds between the buildings, made of reused planks, corrugated iron, and sheets of tarpaulin. Rows of garbage cans, some of which had been overturned by alley cats, the contents spilling out onto the gray concrete pavement. Washing lines stretched across the street from balcony to balcony. Here and there rain-soaked white and colored underwear whirled helplessly on the lines in the high wind. My mother was very tired that morning, and her head must have been heavy from lack of sleep, hunger, and all the black coffee and sleeping pills, so that she walked slowly like a sleepwalker. She may have left Ben Yehuda Street before she reached Nordau Boulevard and turned right into Belvedere Alley, which despite its name had no view but only low plastered buildings made of concrete blocks, with rusting iron railings, and this alley led her to Motskin Avenue, which was not an avenue at all but a short, wide, empty street, only half built and partly unpaved, and from Motskin Avenue her tired feet took her to Tahon Lane and on to Dizengoff Street, where it began to rain heavily, but she forgot about the umbrella that was hanging on her arm and walked on bareheaded in the rain, with her pretty handbag hanging from her shoulder, and she crossed Dizengoff Street and went wherever her feet carried her, perhaps to Zangwill Street and then on to Zangwill Alley, and now she was really lost, without the faintest idea how to get back to her sister's or why she had to get back, and she did not know why she had come out except to follow the instructions of the specialist who had told her to walk the streets of Tel Aviv to look at handsome young men. But there were no handsome young men this rainy Saturday morning, either in Zangwill Street or in Zangwill Alley, or in Sokolov Street from which she came to Basle Street, or in Basle Street or anywhere else. Perhaps she thought about the deep shady orchard behind her parents' house in Rovno, or about Ira Steletskaya, the engineer's wife from Rovno who burned herself to death in the abandoned hut belonging to Anton the coachman's son. Or about the Tarbuth gymnasium and the vistas of river and forest. Or the lanes of old Prague and her student days there, and someone about whom apparently my mother never told us, or her sisters, or her best friend, Lilenka. Occasionally someone ran past, in a hurry to get out of the rain. Occasionally a cat went by, and my mother called to it, trying to ask something, to exchange views, or feelings, to ask for some simple feline advice, but every cat she addressed fled from her in a panic as though even from a distance it could smell that she was doomed.

Around midday she returned to her sister's, where they were shocked at her appearance because she was frozen and soaked through and because she jokingly complained that there were no handsome young men in the streets of Tel Aviv: if only she had found some, she might have tried to seduce them, men always looked at her with desire in their eyes, but soon, very soon there would be nothing left to desire. Her sister Haya hurried to run her a hot bath, and my mother got in; she refused to taste a crumb of food because any food made her feel sick; she slept for a couple of hours, and in the late afternoon she dressed, put on the wet raincoat and the boots that were still damp and cold from her morning walk, and went out again as the doctor had ordered to search the streets of Tel Aviv for handsome young men. And this afternoon, because the rain had let up a bit, the streets were not so empty and my mother did not wander aimlessly, she found her way to the corner of Dizengoff Street and JNF Boulevard and from there she walked down Dizengoff Street past the junctions with Gordon Street and Frishman Street with her pretty black handbag hanging from her shoulder, looking at the beautiful shop windows and cafés and getting a glimpse of what Tel Aviv considered as Bohemian life, although to her it all looked tawdry and secondhand, like an imitation of an imitation of something she found pathetic and miserable. It all seemed to deserve and need compassion, but her compassion had run out. Toward evening she went home, refused to eat anything again, drank a cup of black coffee and then another, and sat down to look at some book that fell upside down at her feet when her eyes closed, and for some ten minutes or so Uncle Tsvi and Auntie Haya thought they heard light, irregular snoring. Then she woke up and said she needed to rest, that she had a feeling that the specialist had been quite right when he told her to walk around the town for several hours every day, and she had a feeling that tonight she would fall asleep early and would finally manage to sleep very deeply. By half past eight her sister had made her bed again with fresh sheets, and slid a hot-water bottle under the quilt because the nights were cold and the rain had just started up again and was beating against the shutters. My mother decided to sleep fully dressed, and to make quite sure that she didn't wake up again to spend an agonized night in the kitchen, she poured herself a glass of tea from the vacuum flask that her sister had left by her bedside, waited for it to cool down a little, and when she drank it, she took her sleeping pills. If I had been there with her in that room overlooking the backyard in Haya and Tsvi's apartment at that moment, at half past eight or a quarter to nine on that Saturday evening, I would certainly have tried my hardest to explain to her why she mustn't. And if I did not succeed, I would have done everything possible to stir her compassion, to make her take pity on her only child. I would have cried and I would have pleaded without any shame and I would have hugged her knees, I might even have pretended to faint or I might have hit and scratched myself till the blood flowed as I had seen her do in moments of despair. Or I would have attacked her like a murderer, I would have smashed a vase over her head without hesitation. Or hit her with the iron that stood on a shelf in a corner of the room. Or taken advantage of her weakness to lie on top of her and tie her hands behind her back, and taken away all those pills and tablets and sachets and solutions and potions and syrups of hers and destroyed the lot of them. But I was not allowed to be there. I was not even allowed to go to her funeral. My mother fell asleep, and this time she slept with no nightmares, she had no insomnia, in the early hours she threw up and fell asleep again, still fully dressed, and because Tsvi and Haya were beginning to suspect something, they sent for an ambulance a little before sunrise, and two stretcher bearers carried her carefully, so as not to disturb her sleep, and at the hospital she would not listen to them either, and although they tried various means to disturb her good sleep, she paid no attention to them, or to the specialist from whom she had heard that the psyche is the worst enemy of the body, and she did not wake up in the morning either, or even when the day grew brighter, and from the branches of the ficus tree in the garden of the hospital the bird Elise called to her in wonderment and called to her again and again in vain, and yet it went on trying over and over again, and it still tries sometimes.

Amos Oz is the author of numerous works of fiction and essay collections. He has received the Koret Jewish Book Award, the Prix Femina, the Israel Prize, and the Frankfurt Peace Prize, and his books have been translated into more than thirty languages. Amos Oz lives in Israel.

Nicholas de Lange is a professor at the University of Cambridge and writes on a variety of subjects. He has won many prizes for his translations.